Virtual Immersive and 3D Learning Spaces:
Emerging Technologies and Trends

Shalin Hai-Jew
Kansas State University, USA

INFORMATION SCIENCE REFERENCE

Hershey · New York

Director of Editorial Content:	Kristin Klinger
Director of Book Publications:	Julia Mosemann
Acquisitions Editor:	Lindsay Johnston
Development Editor:	Dave DeRicco
Publishing Assistant:	Casey Conapitski
Typesetter:	Casey Conapitski
Production Editor:	Jamie Snavely
Cover Design:	Lisa Tosheff

Published in the United States of America by
    Information Science Reference (an imprint of IGI Global)
    701 E. Chocolate Avenue
    Hershey PA 17033
    Tel: 717-533-8845
    Fax: 717-533-8661
    E-mail: cust@igi-global.com
    Web site: http://www.igi-global.com

Library of Congress Cataloging-in-Publication Data

Virtual Immersive and 3D Learning Spaces : Emerging Technologies and Trends / Shalin Hai-Jew, editor.   p. cm.
  Includes bibliographical references and index. Summary: "This book helps push the conceptual and applied boundaries of virtual immersive learning, offer how virtual immersive spaces may be exploited for effective learning in terms of the technologies, pedagogical strategies, and directions"--Provided by publisher. ISBN 978-1-61692-825-4 (hardcover) -- ISBN 978-1-61692-827-8 (ebook) 1. Education, Elementary--Computer network resources. 2. Education, Secondary--Computer network resources. 3. Fluid dynamics--Mathematical models. 4. Numerical calculations--Verification. 5. Computer managed instruction. I. Hai-Jew, Shalin. LB1044.87.V575 2010
  371.33'468--dc22

British Cataloguing in Publication Data
A Cataloguing in Publication record for this book is available from the British Library.

All work contributed to this book is new, previously-unpublished material. The views expressed in this book are those of the authors, but not necessarily of the publisher.

For R. Max

Editorial Advisory Board

Table of Contents

Preface xvi

Acknowledgment xx

Section 1
Virtual Immersive Spaces and their Popularization

Chapter 1
Assessing the Application of 3D Collaborative Interfaces within an Immersive
Virtual University 1

Gavin McArdle, University College Dublin, Ireland
Bianca Schön, University College Dublin, Ireland
Michela Bertolotto, University College Dublin, Ireland

Chapter 2
Virtual Worlds: Corporate Early Adopters Pave the Way 25

Catherine M. J. Lithgow, University of Maryland Baltimore County, USA
Judi L. Davidson Wolf, University of Maryland Baltimore County, USA
Zane L. Berge, University of Maryland Baltimore County, USA

Section 2
Immersive Learning Strategies

Chapter 3
Practice What You Preach: Experiences with Teaching Virtual World Concepts in a
Virutal World 45

Laura Benvenuti, Dutch Open University, The Netherlands
Gerrit C. Van Der Veer, Dutch Open University, The Netherlands

Chapter 4
Learning Assignments in Virtual Worlds: Theoretical Systematization and
Didactical Requirements 54
    Tanja Adamus, University Duisburg-Essen, Germany
    Nadine Ojstersek, University Duisburg-Essen, Germany
    Axel Nattland, University Duisburg-Essen, Germany
    Michael Kerres, University Duisberg-Essen, Germany

Chapter 5
Immersive Language Learning in Collaborative Virtual Environments: The Current Status
and Possible Trends 78
    Ya-Chun Shih, National Dong Hwa University, Taiwan

Chapter 6
Unpacking Strong vs. Weak Presence in Second Life Enactive Role Play 95
    Caroline M. L. Ho, Nanyang Technological University, Singapore

Section 3
The Design of 3D Immersive Spaces

Chapter 7
Collaborating to Learn: Designing and Building 3D Immersive Virtual Learning
Environments for Exploring STEM Concepts in Middle School 123
    Nita J. Matzen, Appalachian State University, USA
    William Edward Roberts, Appalachian State University, USA
    Penny Barker, Ashe County Schools, USA
    Julie Marklin, Davie County Schools, USA

Chapter 8
Scaffolding Discovery Learning in 3D Virtual Environments: Challenges and Considerations
for Instructional Design 138
    Mark J.W. Lee, Charles Sturt University, Australia
    Barney Dalgarno, Charles Sturt University, Australia

Chapter 9
Legal and Ethical Aspects of Teaching in Selected Social Virtual Worlds: A Review of
the Literature 170
    Rosemary S. Talab, Kansas State University, USA
    Hope R. Botterbusch, Kansas State University, USA

Chapter 10

JavaMOO Virtual Cells in Science Learning.. 194

    Bradley Vender, North Dakota State University, USA

    Otto Borchert, North Dakota State University, USA

    Ben Dischinger, North Dakota State University, USA

    Guy Hokanson, North Dakota State University, USA

    Phillip E. McClean, North Dakota State University, USA

    Brian M. Slator, North Dakota State University, USA

Chapter 11

Capitalizing on Immersive Persistence as an Emergent Design Concept (A Position Paper)............ 212

    Shalin Hai-Jew, Kansas State University, USA

Section 4
Technological Accessibility Functionalities

Chapter 12

A Computational Model of Non-Visual Spatial Learning 226

    Kanubhai K. Patel, Ahmedabad University, India

    Sanjay Kumar Vij, SVIT, India

Chapter 13

Signing Avatars 249

    Nicoletta Adamo-Villani, Purdue University, USA

    Kyle Hayward, Purdue University, USA

Section 5
Risks in the Immersive Learning

Chapter 14

Crouching Tangents, Hidden Danger: Assessing Development of Dangerous Misconceptions
within Serious Games for Healthcare Education 269

    Miguel A. Garcia-Ruiz, University of Colima, Mexico

    Jayshiro Tashiro, University of Ontario Institute of Technology, Canada

    Bill Kapralos, University of Ontario Institute of Technology, Canada

    Miguel Vargas Martin, University of Ontario Institute of Technology, Canada

Chapter 15

Mitigating Negative Learning in Immersive Spaces and Simulations............................. 307

    Shalin Hai-Jew, Kansas State University, USA

Appendix
Unintended Negative Learning with an Industrial Simulation 330
    Roger W. McHaney, Kansas State University, USA

Appendix
Negative Learning and its Mitigation in Army Simulations 333
    Brent A. Anders, Kansas State University, USA

Compilation of References 336

About the Contributors 374

Index 383

Detailed Table of Contents

Preface xvi

Acknowledgment xx

Section 1
Virtual Immersive Spaces and their Popularization

Chapter 1

Assessing the Application of 3D Collaborative Interfaces within an Immersive
Virtual University 1

    Gavin McArdle, University College Dublin, Ireland
    Bianca Schön, University College Dublin, Ireland
    Michela Bertolotto, University College Dublin, Ireland

This chapter describes an online environment called CLEV-R (Collaborative Learning Environments with Virtual Reality) which fosters collaboration and social interaction via specialised tools. This article describes two studies which were conducted using the CLEV-R interface. The first study assesses the usability of this paradigm for e-learning while the second determines which factors influence performance in the Virtual Reality environment in order to ensure that some students are not unfairly advantaged by this means of e-learning. The studies have shown that several factors, such as age and experience in Virtual Reality games influence a user's success in Virtual Reality environments. Furthermore, the study shows that students enjoy and benefit from the opportunity to interact with each other.

Chapter 2

Virtual Worlds: Corporate Early Adopters Pave the Way 25

    Catherine M. J. Lithgow, University of Maryland Baltimore County, USA
    Judi L. Davidson Wolf, University of Maryland Baltimore County, USA
    Zane L. Berge, University of Maryland Baltimore County, USA

Multi-user virtual environments (MUVEs), the most popular of which is Second Life™, have great potential to provide engaging, interactive content to today's students using both synchronous and asynchronous delivery. Educators, as well as several forward-thinking corporations and military organizations, have proven to be early adopters of MUVEs as a training delivery medium, paving the way to begin evaluating the medium for use in professional development. The use of MUVEs for education will definitely grow. Corporations considering venturing into this arena would do well to consider the lessons learned by the early adopters, paying particular attention to the barriers that need to be overcome for successful implementation.

Section 2
Immersive Learning Strategies

Chapter 3
Practice What You Preach: Experiences with Teaching Virtual World Concepts in a
Virutal World...45
Laura Benvenuti, Dutch Open University, The Netherlands
Gerrit C. Van Der Veer, Dutch Open University, The Netherlands

This chapter addresses the application of a Virtual World as a teaching and learning environment for a course on Virtual Worlds. Too often, new technologies are discussed without being applied. The authors discuss an example of how this innovative technologies can be tackled. They show that application of innovative tools is useful to all parties: students, lecturers and researchers, even if it raises new problems from which all can learn.

Chapter 4
Learning Assignments in Virtual Worlds: Theoretical Systematization and
Didactical Requirements...54
Tanja Adamus, University Duisburg-Essen, Germany
Nadine Ojstersek, University Duisburg-Essen, Germany
Axel Nattland, University Duisburg-Essen, Germany
Michael Kerres, University Duisberg-Essen, Germany

The chapter describes different possibilities for the design of learning assignments in virtual worlds with a special emphasis on Second Life™. For this purpose, it relates to didactical requirements to obtain criteria for constructing learning assignments for different contexts and conditions. A difference has to be made between distinct forms of simple and complex learning assignments, which have to be solved in the virtual worlds, but serve for the attainment of learning objectives either from the real or the virtual world. Furthermore, it is possible to reach learning objectives concerning the virtual world by means of the real world. It becomes obvious, that the bounds between virtual worlds and the real world are blurring. The decision, whether learning assignments should be edited in virtual worlds, depends on to what extent an additional benefit compared with other (technical) solutions, can emerge in these contexts. For these purposes a closer consideration of virtual worlds' specific features becomes relevant.

Chapter 5

Immersive Language Learning in Collaborative Virtual Environments: The Current Status
and Possible Trends.. 78

Ya-Chun Shih, National Dong Hwa University, Taiwan

This chapter explores the role of collaborative virtual environments (CVE) in the language learning immersion experience. Despite the lack of strong empirical evidence, CVE-assisted language learning has become an interesting point in recent research on technology-supported language learning. The current work reviews specific issues in the context of CVE assisted language learning: (a) current research, theory and practice; (b) virtual reality assisted language learning; and (c) the link between CVEs and Web 2.0.

Chapter 6

Unpacking Strong vs. Weak Presence in Second Life Enactive Role Play 95

Caroline M. L. Ho, Nanyang Technological University, Singapore

This chapter focuses on investigating participants' presence in Second Life™ among students in enactive role play. The interest in the study is on the nature of participant interaction and the construction of discourse moves which reflect the nature and extent of their presence (identified as 'strong' or 'weak') in the virtual world. The chapter examines the key concept of presence and its association with related concepts of engagement and identity against the sociocultural approach to learning and functional linguistic theory which provide the theoretical underpinnings and frame the research focus of this study. A review of related studies in the field follows after which background information on the context of the study is provided. The method of analysis is explained after which an analysis and a discussion of findings are presented. The chapter closes with highlighting the pertinent pedagogical implications of virtual enactive role play in 3D immersive spaces for learning.

Section 3
The Design of 3D Immersive Spaces

Chapter 7

Collaborating to Learn: Designing and Building 3D Immersive Virtual Learning
Environments for Exploring STEM Concepts in Middle School 123

Nita J. Matzen, Appalachian State University, USA
William Edward Roberts, Appalachian State University, USA
Penny Barker, Ashe County Schools, USA
Julie Marklin, Davie County Schools, USA

STEM and ICT Instructional Worlds: The 3D Experience (STEM-ICT 3D) is funded by the National Science Foundation ITEST program. The project proposes to translate the success of earlier projects and reaches toward a model of implementing the use of 3D virtual immersive environments that can be replicated with other middle schools over time. STEM-ICT 3D is intended to inspire middle school students to pursue studies and careers in science, technology, engineering, and mathematics (STEM), as well as prepare students with the skills necessary to succeed in STEM education and careers. This chapter presents an applied case study that describes the design of the project, examines the first phases of implementation, and explores the use of students as technical experts collaborating with teachers, the pedagogical experts, to build 3D virtual worlds for middle school instruction.

Chapter 8

Scaffolding Discovery Learning in 3D Virtual Environments: Challenges and Considerations
for Instructional Design 138

    Mark J.W. Lee, Charles Sturt University, Australia
    Barney Dalgarno, Charles Sturt University, Australia

This chapter examines the importance of and possibilities for providing learner support and scaffolding in 3D virtual learning environments designed to promote and encourage learner exploration and discovery. The chapter begins with an overview of the need for scaffolding in discovery learning, before discussing scaffolding in technology-mediated learning environments. A framework is presented for understanding the types of scaffolding that can be provided in such environments. Using a case study based on the design of a 3D Virtual Chemistry Laboratory, examples illustrating the way each category of scaffolding within the framework could be provided within a 3D virtual environment are presented. The chapter concludes with coverage of the key considerations in designing scaffolded 3D virtual environments, as well as some of the important issues in adapting the concepts of scaffolding from face-to-face to technology-mediated environments.

Chapter 9

Legal and Ethical Aspects of Teaching in Selected Social Virtual Worlds: A Review of
the Literature 170

    Rosemary S. Talab, Kansas State University, USA
    Hope R. Botterbusch, Kansas State University, USA

Topics discussed in this chapter include Generations Y and Z and their acceptance of virtual reality, the increase in the number of virtual worlds, gaming virtual worlds, and the social virtual worlds for educators selected for inclusion in this discussion. Open-source virtual world platform portability issues are discussed in connection with the acquisition, development, and control of virtual property. The line between "play spaces" and real life is discussed in terms of the application of the "magic circle" test to teaching in virtual worlds with a real-money based virtual currency system, as well as how faculty can reduce student legal and ethical problems. Virtual world law is examined in light of the terms of service (TOS) and end-user license agreements (EULAs), the concept of virtual property, community standards/behavioral guidelines, safety/privacy statements, intellectual property and copyright. Ethical aspects of teaching in virtual worlds include a definition and analysis of griefing/abuse, harassment, false identity, and ways that each world handles these problems. Research findings and legal and ethical teaching guidelines are presented for those teaching courses using virtual worlds, with special considerations for teaching in Second Life™. These topics are for informational purposes, only. Instructors should seek competent legal counsel.

Chapter 10

JavaMOO Virtual Cells in Science Learning 194

Bradley Vender, North Dakota State University, USA
Otto Borchert, North Dakota State University, USA
Ben Dischinger, North Dakota State University, USA
Guy Hokanson, North Dakota State University, USA
Phillip E. McClean, North Dakota State University, USA
Brian M. Slator, North Dakota State University, USA

One of the World Wide Web Instructional Committee (WWWIC) at North Dakota State University's (NDSU) long running projects is the Virtual Cell, a desktop immersive virtual environment developed for biology education. The focus of the content in the Virtual Cell is cellular biology, and the underlying focus of the content modules is the scientific method and analytical reasoning. However, the technical challenges encountered during the course of the project include designing deployable server architectures, designing robust simulations, and developing high quality animations without losing interactivity.

Chapter 11

Capitalizing on Immersive Persistence as an Emergent Design Concept (A Position Paper) 212

Shalin Hai-Jew, Kansas State University, USA

In their evolution, virtual worlds have become more persistent. Their three-dimensional (3D) objects are more easily ported and interoperable between 3D repositories and may eventually be portable between synthetic world systems. If trend-lines continue, these synthetic spaces will become more integrated into the fabric of virtual learning and research, community-building, socializing, and digital information archival. Their continuity-in-time adds fresh capabilities for learning (human actualization, long-term virtual collaborations), digital resource protection (digital artifact preservation, long-term and evolving simulations, virtual ecologies), human relationship management (customer relationship management and branding, digital governance), and information exchange and management (international exchanges, and immersive long-term 3D libraries and knowledge structures). However, this immersive persistence must be balanced against the needs of temporality, transience, and forgetting.

Section 4
Technological Accessibility Functionalities

Chapter 12

A Computational Model of Non-Visual Spatial Learning 226

Kanubhai K. Patel, Ahmedabad University, India
Sanjay Kumar Vij, SVIT, India

A computational model of non-visual spatial learning through virtual learning environment (VLE) is presented in this chapter. The inspiration has come from Landmark-Route-Survey (LRS) theory, the most accepted theory of spatial learning. An attempt has been made to combine the findings and methods from several disciplines including cognitive psychology, behavioral science and computer science (specifically virtual reality (VR) technology). The study of influencing factors on spatial learning and the potential of using cognitive maps in the modeling of spatial learning are described. Motivation to use VLE and its characteristics are also described briefly. Different types of locomotion interface to VLE with their constraints and benefits are discussed briefly. The authors believe that by incorporating perspectives from cognitive and experimental psychology to computer science, this chapter will appeal to a wide range of audience - particularly computer engineers concerned with assistive technologies; professionals interested in virtual environments, including computer engineers, architect, city-planner, cartographer, high-tech artists, and mobility trainer; and psychologists involved in the study of spatial cognition, cognitive behavior, and human-computer interfaces.

Chapter 13
Signing Avatars 249

Nicoletta Adamo-Villani, Purdue University, USA
Kyle Hayward, Purdue University, USA

The chapter focuses on signing avatars and their potential to improve deaf education. In Sections 1 and 2, the authors give an overview of what signing avatars are and the benefits of using animated characters for deaf education. In Section 3, they explain how signing avatars are created. In particular, in Subsection 3.1, they describe different types of 3D models and skeletal deformation systems, and in Subsection 3.2, they discuss a variety of methods used to animate manual and non-manual signs. In Section 4, the authors report the state-of-the-art in signing avatars' research and development, and they discuss existing limitations and future trends. Section 5 includes a case study on the production of the signing avatars for SMILE™ and Mathsigner™. Conclusive remarks are presented in Section 6.

Section 5
Risks in the Immersive Learning

Chapter 14
Crouching Tangents, Hidden Danger: Assessing Development of Dangerous Misconceptions within Serious Games for Healthcare Education 269

Miguel A. Garcia-Ruiz, University of Colima, Mexico
Jayshiro Tashiro, University of Ontario Institute of Technology, Canada
Bill Kapralos, University of Ontario Institute of Technology, Canada
Miguel Vargas Martin, University of Ontario Institute of Technology, Canada

In this chapter, the authors examine different types of serious games for healthcare education and pose some hard questions about what is and is not known know about their effectiveness. As part of their analysis, they explore general aspects of the use of educational simulations as teaching-learning-assessment tools, but try to tease out how to study the potential such tools might have for leading students toward developing misconceptions. Being powerful instruments with the potential of enhancing healthcare education in extraordinary ways, serious games and simulations have the possibility of improving students' learning and skills outcomes. Their contribution is an overview of current education technologies related to serious games and simulations with a perspective of potential development of misconceptions in the healthcare education community, with a special focus on millennial students. In addition, they provide insight on evidence-based learning and give a perspective of future trends

Chapter 15
Mitigating Negative Learning in Immersive Spaces and Simulations...307
    Shalin Hai-Jew, Kansas State University, USA

The growing popularization in the use of immersive virtual spaces and simulations has enhanced the ability to "model" various scenarios, decision-making contexts, and experiential learning for a variety of fields. With these subliminal semi-experiential affordances have also come some challenges. Foremost is the challenge of designing virtual experiential learning that does not result in "negative learning." Negative learning involves unintended messages which lead to learners with illogical or inaccurate perceptions about reality. Negative learning may be subtle; it may exist at an unconscious or subconscious level; it may be biasing even without learner awareness. This chapter addresses some of the risks of negative learning in immersive spaces and simulations and proposes some pedagogical design, facilitation, and learner empowerment strategies to address negative learning—to increase confidence and assurance in the immersions.

Appendix
Unintended Negative Learning with an Industrial Simulation 330
    Roger W. McHaney, Kansas State University, USA

Appendix
Negative Learning and its Mitigation in Army Simulations...333
    Brent A. Anders, Kansas State University, USA

Compilation of References 336

About the Contributors 374

Index..383

Preface

INTRODUCTION

Virtual immersive spaces have become popularized first with immersive and persistent gaming multiverses, which then evolved into persistent virtual worlds with differing quests and wider varieties of human-embodied avatars. The types of virtual spaces that humans could interact in and through became more complex and more evocatively real. They encompassed more complex automation in digital objects, artificial intelligence-driven humanoid robots, and in-world physics and environmental spaces.

These virtual spaces enabled rich, mediated learning over distances and time—but in immersive and experiential ways that were unprecedented. The research literature describes role-playing scenarios, with whole regions built up for particular historical or cultural enactments. Rich social gatherings—concerts, dances, parties—are held to bring together human-embodied avatars, which connect also as people out in the real world. Businesses held conventions, rolled out new product lines, offered trainings, and set up automated experiences in 3D synethetic worlds. Budding filmmakers created machinima experiences and showcased their films both in-world and out in the real. Artists created fantastical multisensory objects; dancers collaborated with other dancers for new original performances; architects built creative structures online, and many engaged in co-design and virtual collaborations in immersive spaces. Scientists designed mixed-scale experiences at the nano-level, or they created weather events online. Instructional designers built various simulations of machines, biological ecosystems, environments, and social experiences. These new virtual immersive affordances sparked the interest of those in higher education and corporations.

For readers, it may be a bit of a mystery how *Virtual Immersive and 3D Learning Spaces: Emerging Technologies and Trends* came into being. The initial vision for this text came with the popularization of virtual worlds, immersive collaborative spaces, and 3D simulations, in higher education. These spaces may provide rich experiential and interactive learning for the new generations of learners today. The question then is how these spaces may be exploited for effective learning in terms of the technologies, pedagogical strategies, and directions.

A SELECT TALENT POOL

Once this project was greenlighted, I learned that while the pool of potential talent on a global scale is theoretically wide. There are dozens of electronic mailing lists, hundreds of direct email contacts, organizations, publishers, and many Web-based venues through which to publicize this endeavor—including the formidable contacts of the publisher. Yet, from the many who could, there are an elite few who actually delivered the goods on time and with high quality. The authors here bring decades of expertise to the topic, and they were willing to do the heavy lifting of research, writing, revision, and polishing to get this text into your hands.

Academic work has always necessarily been global. There is the camaraderie of shared research and learning work to enhance a field and to move it forward in constructive ways. In this loosely-coupled community, we find plenty of mutual respect and cooperation, in an environment of friendly competition. From this global mix emerge diverse ideas and research approaches. New knowledge may be surfaced through a variety of means: reflection and introspection; qualitative, quantitative, and mixed methods research; and the application of domain-specific, cross-domain, and interdisciplinary explorations.

Some contributors to this book worked singly; others worked on local (and global) teams to evolve their research, analysis, and writing. Each has brought some fresh insights and experiences to virtual immersive learning.

Rewards in publishing are often indirect, without much in the way of financial incentives. Those pursuing tenure may add an extra line to their tenure reports, and professionals may add a snippet to their curriculum vitaes (CVs). Those pursuing grants may add a line about their publications to further polish their professional standings. The truth is that those who've contributed already have long track records of accomplishments and collaborative work. Their writing—which certainly have required many, many long hours of research, analysis, and writing work—have been included in no small measure because of their goodwill and their dedication to their respective fields.

THE BOOK'S ORGANIZATION

Virtual immersive spaces bring with them plenty of promise, of sensory information-rich learning experiences that will enable a much wider range of experiential learning and training—delivered to computer desktops, augmented reality spaces, digital installations, and mobile projective devices. The perceptual affordances of 3D immersions with sound, and the integration of haptics and olfactory interactions, suggest a much wider range of mediated learning than has been achievable in the past. The work of the authors of this text helps push the conceptual and applied boundaries of virtual immersive learning.

This book consists of five sections. Section 1, "Virtual Immersive Spaces and their Popularization," opens with Gavin McArdle, Bianca Schön, and Michela Bertolotto's chapter *Assessing the Application of 3D Collaborative Interfaces within an Immersive Virtual University*. This chapter describes two studies examining the Collaborative Learning Environments with Virtual Reality (CLEV-R) interface for usability and performance in this virtual reality environment. Chapter 2, *Virtual Worlds: Corporate Early Adopters Pave the Way* by Catherine M. J. Lithgow, Judi L. Davidson Wolf, and Zane L. Berge, discusses the affordances of multi-user virtual environments (MUVEs) for training—in a variety of corporate, military, and educational contexts.

Section 2, "Immersive Learning Strategies," focuses on factors that enhance achievable learning in 3D environments. Laura Benvenuti and Gerrit C. van der Veer's *Practice what you Preach: Experiences with Teaching Virtual World Concepts in a Virtual World* (Chapter 3) work focuses on the application of a virtual world (Asterix Village) used to effectively teach about virtual worlds and the lessons learned for students, lecturers and researchers. In Chapter 4, *Learning Assignments in Virtual Worlds: Theoretical Systematization and Didactical Requirements*, the authors Tanja Adamus, Nadine Ojstersek, Axel Nattland, and Michael Kerres analyze the types of learning assignments that may best be applied in virtual worlds based on both learning theory and practice. Ya-Chun Shih, in Chapter 5, *Immersive Language Learning in Collaborative Virtual Environments: The Current Status and Possible Trends*, describes the acquisition of foreign language learning in collaborative virtual environments, with rich strategies to enhance the learning experience. Caroline M. L. Ho asserts the importance of strong learner presence in enactive role plays for learning because of presence-based implications on learner engagement and identity. She shows how discourse behaviors may be analyzed to detect strong vs. weak presence in Chapter 6, *Unpacking Strong vs. Weak Presence in Second Life*.

Section 3, "The Design of 3D Immersive Spaces," examines the way immersive spaces may be constructed for learning. Nita J. Matzen, William Edward Roberts, Penny Barker, and Julie Marklin, in Chapter 7, *Collaborating to Learn: Designing and Building 3D Immersive Virtual Learning Environments for Exploring STEM Concepts in Middle School* highlights a remarkable project that enhances science, technology, engineering and math concepts for middle school learners; theirs is an ambitious and effective project that characterizes the design of challenging fun for learning. Mark J.W. Lee and Barney Dalgarno's *Scaffolding Discovery Learning in 3D Virtual Environments: Challenges and Considerations for Instructional Design* offers a solid model for conceptualizing the scaffolding of discovery learning in immersive spaces—both theoretically and in practice; these authors use their learning from the design of a 3D virtual chemistry laboratory to illuminate their findings. Next, in Chapter 9, *Legal and Ethical Aspects of Teaching in Selected Social Virtual Worlds: A Review of the Literature*, Rosemary S. Talab and Hope R. Botterbusch present fresh insights on the laws and ethics that underpin the design and uses of virtual spaces for learning; they include insights for K-12 through university learning. Otto Borchert, Ben Dischinger, Guy Hokanson, Philip E. McClean, Brian M. Slator, and Bradley Vender, in Chapter 10, *JavaMOO Virtual Cells in Science Learning*, offers an in-depth look at the design of a 3D science learning space about cells. Shalin Hai-Jew, in Chapter 11, *Capitalizing on Immersive Persistence as an Emergent Design Concept (A Position Paper)*, considers some ways to magnify the benefits of time continuance of virtual spaces in terms of learning, digital resource protection, human relationship management, and information exchange and management.

Section 4, "Technological Accessiblity Functionalities" showcases two chapters that enhance human usages of immersive spaces through accessibility affordances. In Chapter 12, Kanubhai K. Patel and Sanjay Kumar Vij's *A Computational Model of Non-Visual Spatial Learning* offers a refreshing and mutli-disciplinary approach to non-visual spatial learning through virtual learning environments, based on the Landmark-Route-Survey (LRS) theory. Nicoletta Adamo-Villani and Kyle Hayward, in *Signing Avatars*, showcase a powerful tool of communications through animated (facial and gestural) signing avatars to improve deaf education in immersive spaces.

Section 5, "Risks in the Immersive Learning," examines the importance of thorough design to avoid learner misconceptions. Miguel A. Garcia-Ruiz, Jayshiro Tashiro, Bill Kapralos, and Miguel Vargas Martin examine the phenomena of potential dangerous misconceptions with serious games in healthcare in Chapter 14: *Crouching Tangents, Hidden Danger: Assessing Development of Dangerous Misconceptions within Serious Games for Healthcare Education*. Shalin Hai-Jew, Roger McHaney, and Brent A. Anders discuss *Mitigating Negative Learning in Immersive Spaces and Simulations* in Chapter 15. This last chapter includes appendices focusing on simulations in business and military applications and the ways that misconceptions may be headed off.

Virtual Immersive and 3D Learning Spaces: Emerging Technologies and Trends evolved from some serendipity and a lot of hard work by many. I hope that these chapters open up a sense of possibilities for effective learning in virtual worlds and also point the way to new directions for the design and deployment of virtual space tools.

Shalin Hai-Jew
Kansas State University, USA

Acknowledgment

Thanks to the many authors of the chapters included in this text. Their dedication to craft and learners is admirable. The experience of collaborating with these talented authors, sight-unseen and across distances, is very much a sign-of-the-times and the nature of virtual work today. Interestingly enough, this still involved a fair amount of coordination and last-minute work and stretched deadlines. Their rigorous peer critiques for each other's works enhanced the book and each other's skill sets. All top-level professionals, these authors demonstrated their ability to deliver on their initial chapter proposals even though they maintain many other professional and personal commitments. A byproduct of every collaborative work involves increased professional relationships and honed skills, and I think that occurred with Virtual Immersive and 3D Learning Spaces: Emerging Technologies and Trends as well.

Thanks also to the Editorial Advisory Board that helped find potential writers for this work. The members are as follows:

Editorial Advisory Board Members
- Geraldine Clarebout, University of Leuven, Belgium
- Jan Elen, University of Leuven, Belgium
- Esmahi Larbi, Athabasca University, Canada
- Iris Totten, Kansas State University, USA
- Fuhua Lin, Athabasca University, Canada
- Edgar Weippl, Vienna University of Technology and Science, Austria

IGI Global has been a wonderful publisher with a strong team that helps make projects come together smoothly and professionally. I want to thank Christine Bufton and Dave DeRicco especially for their consistent and friendly hands-on help. I want to thank the many others who worked behind-the-scenes at this publisher to handle the many details necessary to create, evolve, market, and distribute this book to a global audience.

Shalin Hai-Jew
Kansas State University, USA

Section 1
Virtual Immersive Spaces and their Popularization

Chapter 1
Assessing the Application of 3D Collaborative Interfaces within an Immersive Virtual University

Gavin McArdle
University College Dublin, Ireland

Bianca Schön
University College Dublin, Ireland

Michela Bertolotto
University College Dublin, Ireland

ABSTRACT

The need to stimulate and engage students is of paramount importance within any learning scenario. Despite this, recent developments in online learning have failed to take this requirement into account. As a result e-learning courses which utilise traditional online learning management systems have a higher dropout rate than their classroom based counterparts. The attrition rate is attributed to boredom with the interfaces used to deliver learning material and also to the lack of opportunities to interact socially with others. Furthermore, being in a virtual environment imposes a whole new set of challenges onto users due to the distinct lack of stimuli provided, compared to the real world. Technological advances now permit the development of multi-user, networked, virtual reality environments which can address these issues. Such environments provide an immersive desktop 3D interface which is used to deliver learning material. Real-time communication and collaboration tools permit interaction between students and tutors. This chapter describes one such environment called CLEV-R (Collaborative Learning Environments with Virtual Reality) which fosters collaboration and social interaction via specialised tools. Although there are systems which offer similar functionality to CLEV-R, these have not been adequately evaluated. This chapter describes two studies which were conducted using the CLEV-R interface. The first study assesses the usability of this paradigm for e-learning while the second determines which factors influence performance in the Virtual Reality environment in order to ensure that some students are not

DOI: 10.4018/978-1-61692-825-4.ch001

unfairly advantaged by this means of e-learning. The studies have shown that several factors, such as age and experience in Virtual Reality games influence a user's success in Virtual Reality environments. Furthermore, the study shows that students enjoy and benefit from the opportunity to interact with each other.

INTRODUCTION

Recent years have seen an increase in the use of computers as a form of e-learning. The primary focus in this area has been on providing tools to deliver course material using web pages, while also providing techniques to manage both the material and users within such systems. These systems are often referred to as Learning Management Systems (LMSs) and predominantly support asynchronous interaction between their users. While the penetration of such approaches is vast and their popularity continues to grow, research indicates that courses which rely solely on these mainstream e-learning applications have a higher dropout rate than their face-to-face counterparts (Martinez, 2003). Studies indicate boredom, ennui and a lack of motivation are contributing factors to the high attrition rates within online courses (Serwatka, 2005). Research in this area is ongoing with techniques to resolve the problems of the lack stimulation and interaction being explored (Mowlds, Roche & Mangina, 2005; Sun & Cheng, 2007). One major concern with conventional e-

learning techniques is the absence of mechanisms for instant communication. This leads to a lack of timely interaction between learner and instructor, hinders social interaction among learners and is one of the major drawbacks of standard online learning techniques. Ultimately, it has been shown that this absence of interaction and social connection with peers, and the tutor, can lead to feelings of isolation and loneliness for students (Kamel et al., 2005). Similarly the traditional approach relies on text-based web-pages which involve students reading large passages of text which they may find boring and unappealing (Anaraki, 2004). Figure 1 highlights the main issue with conventional LMSs.

Collaborating with peers is an important element of learning in the real world (Kitchen & McDougall, 1998; Vass, 2002). It teaches students about cooperation and teamwork. The asynchronous communication techniques provided by mainstream e-learning applications are not entirely suitable for organising group projects and consequently such tasks are generally absent from e-learning courses. Social interaction and the sense of a social presence among students are also

Figure 1. Issues with existing e-learning techniques

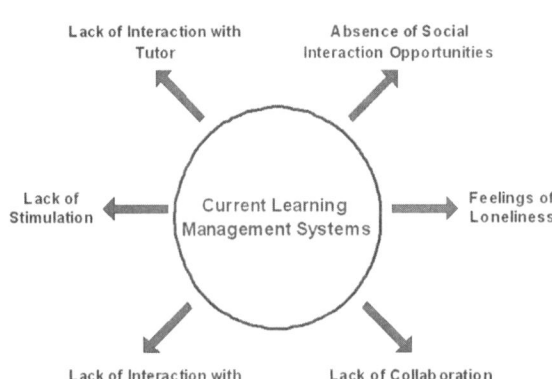

important (Laister & Kober, 2002). Students often build friendships with their classmates in the real world. This interaction with others plays a key role in the personal development of students and their formation of social skills. The asynchronous communication methods offered within traditional e-learning applications do not permit a natural flow of conversation which hinders social interaction among students. Consequently they may feel they do not have a social presence within the learning environment or experience a sense of a community, both of which can lead students to withdraw from their course of study prematurely (Serwatka, 2005).

Arguably, there are technologies available which can be combined and deployed successfully in the e-learning domain in order to address the issues discussed in this chapter. Increasingly the development of immersive 3D environments is seen as a possible approach to resolve these issues (Jones & Bronack, 2008; Wheeler 2009). For example, improvements in computing, such as increased internet connection speeds, permit more advanced technologies, including 3-Dimensional (3D) graphics and multimedia, to be utilised online. Researchers have already explored the use of immersive desktop 3D environments in a number of fields such as e-commerce (Chittaro & Ranon, 2002; Cordier, Seo & Magnenat-Thalmann, 2003) and data management (Cockburn & McKenzie, 2002) where they were shown to be successful. Some research on immersive 3D environments for use within e-learning has been also carried out (Bouras, Philopoulos & Tsiatsos, 2001; San Chee & Hooi, 2002; Bouras, Giannaka & Tsiatsos, 2003). Some research has been conducted in order to provide for example navigational aid in such environments in order to offer a better user experience (Darken & Peterson, 2000). However, a more in depth study of this paradigm is required to determine if it is usable and whether it is a means of e-learning which appeals to students. Furthermore, research in this area focuses on facilitating learning activities. The benefits of

such environments for social purposes still needs to be explored. The success of 3D environments in other domains motivates the examination of this paradigm to establish if it offers a suitable solution to the drawbacks of conventional LMSs. When combined with real-time communication methods, these technologies offer a powerful form of interaction and help overcome issues of solitude experienced by some e-learners (McInnerney & Roberts 2004). As highlighted in Figure 1, many of the shortcomings are rooted in the lack of instant communication tools and lack of stimuli, and so combining such features with a multi-user Virtual Reality (VR) environment offers a valid solution.

In order to determine the possibilities of these media within e-learning, this chapter describes the development of an e-learning platform called CLEV-R (Collaborative Learning environments with E-Learning). CLEV-R combines a collaborative desktop virtual reality learning environment with several real-time communication channels in order to facilitate learning and social interaction between students. The resulting system is then assessed on two levels. Firstly, the usability of the platform is gauged through a series of user trials; this is accompanied by a further user study that assesses factors that influence user performance in VR. This is an important facet of the evaluation as it helps to determine which factors could result in certain groups of students obtaining an unfair advantage when learning through VR and also highlights techniques to alleviate this problem. The results indicate that such systems are usable; however care must be taken to understand the user and offer suitable spatial support so that certain students are not disadvantaged by the VR paradigm.

RELATED WORK

Using multi-user 3D environments, CLEV-R engages and stimulates students on several levels. Novel communication tools augment the VR interface to offer facilities for real-time interaction between students, their peers and tutors. The goal of the system is to augment the tools provided by traditional LMSs in order to resolve the issues discussed in the previous section.

Several research studies also explore this area. Two such examples are EVE (Bouras, Giannaka & Tsiatsos, 2003) and INVITE (Bouras, Philopoulos & Tsiatsos, 2001). While these systems have some unique features and are targeted at diverse users, they both utilise 3D graphics to create a virtual onscreen environment in which students are immersed. Each user of these systems is represented on screen by an animated character. All other users, currently connected to the system can see this avatar. Learning content, including lecture notes and videos are displayed simultaneously in the 3D space of all users that are interacting with the system. Students can interact with each other using some synchronous communication techniques including text and voice chat, which permits collaboration between them.

Other systems such as C-Visions (Chee & Hooi, 2002) and Virtual European Schools (VES) (Bouras et al., 1999) focus on providing an environment for specific subjects. C-Visions uses VR to support science education. Interactive animations, experiments and hands-on tasks teach students about mass, velocity and acceleration. On the other hand, the VES project created a 3D environment with a number of themed rooms. Uniquely, book publishers provide the content for the themed rooms. Slideshows, animations and links to external sources of information, relevant to the specific theme or subject, are utilised.

When the systems above were evaluated in small user trials, the results indicated that they were popular with users. In particular any real-time communication methods were seen as a major advantage of the systems. The 3D paradigm itself was also rated highly by the test subjects who appreciated the interactivity which it offers. (Bouras & Tsiatsos 2006; Chee, 2001). No large scale evaluation was conducted to obtain a greater understanding of the usability of the VR environment for e-learning.

Second Life (Harkin, 2006) and Active Worlds (Hudson-Smith, 2002) are prime examples of online VR communities. In these systems, computer users have on screen personas and inhabit a virtual 3D environment. At present, researchers are examining techniques to utilise these systems within education. Kemp & Livingstone (2006) propose using Second Life as an interactive interface to access learning material currently maintained in a traditional text-based LMS. Doherty & Rothfarb (2006) have developed a science museum using Second Life. The interactive environment permits students to interact with historical objects and participate in online meetings and talks. Henderson et al. (2008) discuss Second China, which is another environment developed in Second Life. Second China educates students about Chinese culture and history. Users of the system can access information and participate in guided learning sessions while also collaborating with others. Dickey (2003) uses Active Worlds as a distance education tool within a university setting, while Riedl et al. (2001) describe an environment developed in Active Worlds, for teacher-training programmes. An evaluation carried out by Riedl et al. (2001) highlighted the awareness of others, which the on screen personas create, as a major benefit of such systems. The interaction with others, which was made possible through the shared virtual space, was also seen as an advantage of such systems.

The platforms discussed here address the needs of students by providing an interactive medium for accessing learning content. However, as shown in Table 1, they tackle the issues with existing LMSs to varying extents. One aspect which is lacking in many of these systems is the provision of dedicated tools for socialising online which has been shown to be important in face-to-face learning (Laister & Kober, 2002). In particular, the file sharing functionality, which is one of the key elements of social networking websites, is often absent from these systems.

While social facilities are provided in Second Life and Active Worlds, they are predominantly social environments which have been adapted for e-learning. Therefore they are not dedicated e-learning systems and instead use ad-hoc methods for delivering learning content. The quality of the learning tools thus depends on the creative abilities the course designer. In the system described in this chapter, CLEV-R, the need for social tools forms a major element of the design which is achieved through the addition of specialised tools for social interaction. While these facilities allow natural communication between students within the 3D environment, further dedicated functionality also permits students to share and discuss photos and videos. Many have the current systems have been evaluated using small scale or ad-hoc user trials. On the contrary, the system described in this chapter was evaluated using an in depth user trial with industry standardised usability questionnaires. Furthermore, in order to assess the factors which influence students' performance in such environments, a study to ascertain different performance levels among learners was also conducted. This is vital to ensure that no group of students obtains an unfair advantage caused by the medium in which learning material is presented.

CLEV-R SYSTEM DESCRIPTION

CLEV-R concentrates on providing collaborative tools, so students can work, learn, and socialise together. Mimicking a physical university setting, it consists of a central common area, a lecture room, meeting rooms, and social rooms. Multimedia techniques are used to display the learning content while text and audio allow users of CLEV-R to communicate with each other (Monahan, McArdle, & Bertolotto, 2008). The following paragraphs outline the most salient aspects of CLEV-R.

User Representation

In order to resolve one of the principle problems with existing LMSs which involves the lack of social presence and the feeling of isolation, CLEV-R endeavours to create a sense of community among learners and thus remove the sense of loneliness that is often experienced. This is achieved through multi-user support which permits multiple users to access the same virtual environment simultaneously. Within this framework, it is necessary for users to be aware of the presence of others. Therefore, within CLEV-R, each user is represented by a personal avatar. This 3D character is

Table 1. Comparison of features of current Immersive E-Learning Systems and CLEV-R

	VES	INVITE	EVE	Active Worlds	Second Life	CLEV-R
Multi-user	X	X	X	X	X	X
Avatars	X	X	X	X	X	X
Text Communication	X	X	X	X	X	X
Voice Communication		X	X			X
Web-cam Feeds						X
Tutor File Uploading		X	X	X	X	X
Student File Uploading		X	X			X
Defined Social Areas				X	X	X
Tutor-Led Activities	X	X	X	X	X	X
Student-Led Activities		X				X

the user's on-screen persona for the duration of a course. By allowing users to customise their avatar, each avatar unique and so users of the system can recognise others and hence feel a social presence in the learning environment.

Communication Tools

Collaboration is a key aspect of the design of CLEV-R, which means that communication technologies are imperative. As discussed above, the lack of real-time communication is a major drawback of traditional e-learning systems. In all learning scenarios, communication with peers and instructors is important which is well documented in the literature (Redfern et al., 2002; Laister & Kober, 2002). In particular, it has been shown that students learn from each other in an informal way. Such unstructured communication also helps remove feelings of isolation which may be experienced in single user learning environments. As such, a major aspect of CLEV-R is the provision of communication methods. These facilities are provided in a Graphical User Interface (GUI), as shown in Figure 2. Text and audio chat communication are supported. Users can send both public and private messages via text-chat and can broadcast audio streams into specific areas of the VR environment. Additionally, web-cams can be use to broadcast directly into the 3D environment which permits real-time, face-to-face conversations with others. The avatars in our system are equipped with gesture animations, which are a further form of communication. For example, avatars can raise their hand if they wish to ask a question and can also nod or shake their head to show their level of understanding or agreement.

Interactive Tools

In traditional web-based learning environments, content is mainly presented through various forms of text, primarily using the HTML format. This delivery method is neither motivating nor engaging for the student (Anaraki, 2004). To resolve this, CLEV-R provides multiple multimedia methods for presenting course content within a desktop 3D virtual reality learning environment. The system supports features such as PowerPoint slides, movies, audio, animations, and images. Rather than downloading these media files to the students' own PC, they can be experienced directly within the virtual environment in real-time simultaneously with other students. Many different services and facilities are available within the various virtual rooms of CLEV-R to support these file types. Each of the rooms is now discussed below.

Lecture Room

The *Lecture Room* is the virtual space where tutor-led synchronous learning occurs; it operates in a similar fashion to traditional classroom-based education. The room provides several features to enable a tutor to present learning content to several students simultaneously. An example of an online lecture can be seen in Figure 3. Lecture slides, such as PowerPoint files, can be displayed on a presentation board, which also supports image files. A media board is also provided, where the lecturer can upload both audio and video files. Where appropriate, the lecturer also has the option of streaming live Web-cam feeds into the *Lecture Room*. This can be used for demonstrating more practical aspects of a course or as a video conferencing tool for guest speakers.

Figure 2. CLEV-R graphical user interface

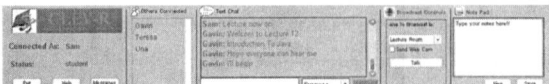

The tutor controls this presentation board and can advance through the slides at their own pace. Once the tutor changes the current slide, it is changed in the worlds of all connected students. In this way, students are always aware what learning content is currently displayed. The streaming audio facility can also be used to provide live commentary to accompany the presentation and answer any questions the students may have.

Meeting Rooms

Collaboration is of primary concern within the design of CLEV-R and so dedicated rooms to support student-to-student interaction are included. The *Meeting Rooms* provide specialised facilities for groups of students to meet and work together. The *Meeting Rooms* provide a similar set of tools found in the *Lecture Room*. For example, students can use audio and text messages to communicate their ideas. A presentation board, similar to that found in the *Lecture Room*, permits students to upload their own material for others to see. Each student can share slideshows, animations, and media clips. Live video can also be streamed into this room via a student's Webcam.

Social Rooms

As social interaction is a key component of CLEV-R, dedicated areas within the virtual university have been provided for this function. In these areas, students can mingle, interact and converse informally. While students can use these areas to discuss the course they are attending, they can also use them for social purposes. In a similar way to the *Meeting Rooms*, small numbers of students can gather together to share their experiences and stories as well as photos, pictures, and movies. A media board facilitates the sharing of files. In addition to the *Social Room*s, a centrally located lobby serves as an informal setting, where students can chat with others. Here users can talk about the course material or display their project work on special static presentation boards provided; others can then peruse these posters at their own pace.

Library

In addition to the synchronous learning which takes place in the *Lecture Room*, CLEV-R also provides asynchronous access to learning material through a library within the 3D environment. The *Library*, shown in Figure 4, contains a bookcase and a number of desks. Lecture notes, which have

Figure 3. CLEV-R 3D Interface showing a lecture taking place

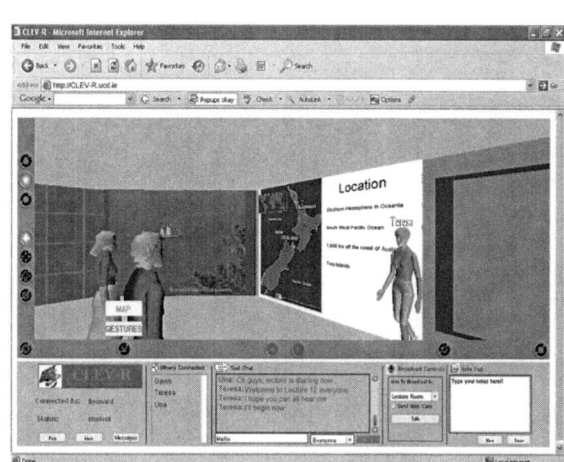

been uploaded by the tutor, automatically appear on the bookcase. Students can then display this material on a desk in the *Library* or download it to their own computer. Additionally, the bookcase in the *Library* also contains a number of links to external information sources such as online dictionaries and encyclopaedias.

EVALUATION

When adopting new technologies, it is important to carry out an evaluation to assess its benefits and to determine the effects this new technology will have on users. The evaluation of CLEV-R and its 3D virtual reality environment was carried out in two phases. Firstly in order to gauge users' opinions of the system and to test its functionality, a user trial was carried out. Secondly, recognising that this is a new paradigm for most, a study into the factors that influence performance in VR was also carried out. Detailed descriptions of these two studies are provided in the following sections.

Usability Study Setup

The first study, presented in this chapter, followed a previous user study which was carried out

when the prototype had reached a mature stage. Details of this study and its results can be found in McArdle & Bertolotto (2010). The purpose of the second trial was to gauge user opinions of the system and determine its usability. Usability testing involves studying the interface and its performance under real-world conditions and obtaining feedback from both the system and its users (Nielsen, 1993). With this in mind, a series of tasks was devised. The tasks established common scenarios which occur in learning situations. Participants in the user trial had to interact with CLEV-R, and the tools it provides, to complete the tasks. A total of 20 test-subjects took part in the user trial. The participants were representative of the target users of the system (university students), the profile of which can be seen in Table 2. All test-subjects stated that they had a good level of computer literacy while the majority had experience of using traditional e-learning systems. All test-subjects took on the role of students during the user trial, while a person familiar with the functionality acted as the lecturer.

Four tasks, indicative of typical scenarios within an e-learning system, were devised. Details of these tasks are detailed below.

Task 1. Social Interaction: The purpose of this task was to serve as a means of introducing

Figure 4. CLEV-R 3D interface showing the Library

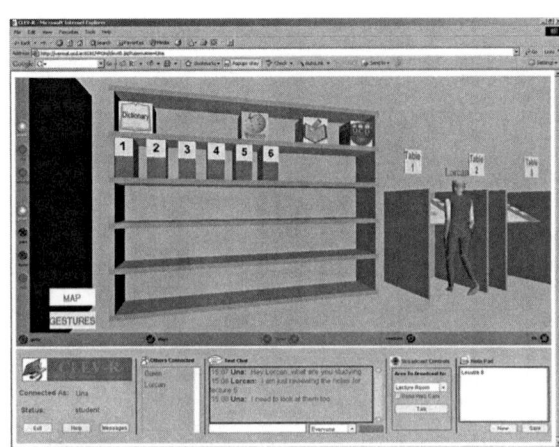

the participants to the CLEV-R interfaces and the modes of interaction which are available. The task consisted of an ice-breaker game, in which the test subjects needed to use the text and audio-chat facilities to converse with one another. The game, 'Who am I?', involved one participant taking on the identity of a famous person, the other participants then had to ask questions in order to identify the famous character. In this task, participants also needed to collaborate in order to choose a topic for a group project which they would present through the interfaces during the third task of the evaluation study.

Task 2. Learning: The second task consisted of the participants attending a synchronous lecture within CLEV-R. The lecture material concerned geography and the tutor provided facts, videos and music about a particular country. The participants were encouraged to ask questions and interact where appropriate. The tutor used voice chat and web-cam feeds during the class in order to demonstrate the facilities available.

Task 3. Collaboration: In order to assess the functionality of the *Meeting Rooms*, the participants were asked to work together to produce a group project. Users were required to upload a Microsoft PowerPoint file to the presentation board in one of the *Meeting Rooms* and use the audio communication facilities to talk about their part of the project.

Task 4. Social Interaction: The final task of the evaluation study was a free session. The purpose of this task was to permit participants to socialise and interact with each other. In particular,

the test subjects were encouraged to share different types of media with one another. This task gave the participants free reign with the system and permitted them to uncover any usability issues which might arise.

Evaluation Techniques

In order to obtain feedback from the test subjects, several standard usability questionnaires were administered during and after the user trial. These questionnaires were augmented with several questions which were specific to CLEV-R and its functionality. After each of the 4 tasks outlined above, the After Scenario Questionnaire (ASQ) (Lewis, 1991) was given to the test subjects. This questionnaire consists of 3 statements, shown in Table 3, which assess user satisfaction regarding the ease of completing the task, the time taken to complete the task and the support information available when completing the task. The satisfaction is measured on a 7-point Likert scale anchored at 1 by Strongly Agree and at 7 by Strongly Disagree. The results from these 3 questions can be condensed to give an overall rating of user satisfaction with the interface for completing a specific task. The ASQ was augmented with additional questions regarding the effectiveness of the features provided by the interfaces for each specific task.

Results and Discussion

There were 4 tasks in this usability study. A brief 6-item questionnaire was presented to participants after completing each task in the usability study. The questionnaires contained 3 items from the ASQ and 3 items, which were devised based on the current activity of the user. These 3 items were designed to give a clear understanding of the user's opinions of CLEV-R and its effectiveness.

Table 2. Profiles of the Evaluation Participants

	Number
Total Users	20
Males	15
Females	5
Average Age	26.27
Previous Experience of E-Learning	12

Table 3. The Three Questions of the After Scenario Questionnaire

The After Scenario Questionnaire (Lewis, 1991)
Overall, I am satisfied with the ease of completing the tasks in this scenario
Overall, I am satisfied with the amount of time it took to complete the tasks in this scenario
Overall, I am satisfied with the support information (online help, messages, documentation) when completing the task

Task 1. Social Interaction Tools

Task 1 involved participants interacting with each other, using the tools provided, to carry out the icebreaker game, 'Who am I?'. Firstly, the results relating to the 3 items on the questionnaire dealing with the effectiveness of the system to complete the task are presented and discussed. Figure 5 shows a graph detailing the questions and the findings. Lower ratings indicate a better the result. The majority of the subjects found the communication were tools effective for completing this task. This task was a social one and participants were asked to rate the effectiveness of the facilities for social interaction as well as rating the acceptability of the interaction as a means for socialising. All test-subjects felt the facilities provided during the task were sufficient to allow social interaction to take place. The average result returned for the statement regarding the acceptability of this as a form of socialising was 2.1, with favourable answers returned by the majority (90%) of test-subjects.

The results suggest this aspect of CLEV-R is an acceptable means of social interaction and the tools which support and facilitate it are more than sufficient.

The ASQ is an instrument used to assess overall satisfaction with completing a task or scenario. By condensing the results obtained from the questionnaire, it can be seen that on the 7-point Likert scale the average value returned for this task is 2.23. This is a positive result and indicates a high level of satisfaction among the test-subjects. This is further supported by the standard deviation value of 0.622 for this result. Looking at Figure 6, the results can be seen in more detail. In general, the responses are skewed towards the positive end of the axis. Satisfaction with the ease of completing the task was high. 90% of participants expressed agreement with the statement. When the graph is examined, it can be seen that 2 test-subjects declined to rate the statement about their satisfaction with the support information pro-

Figure 5. Results for user trial task 1

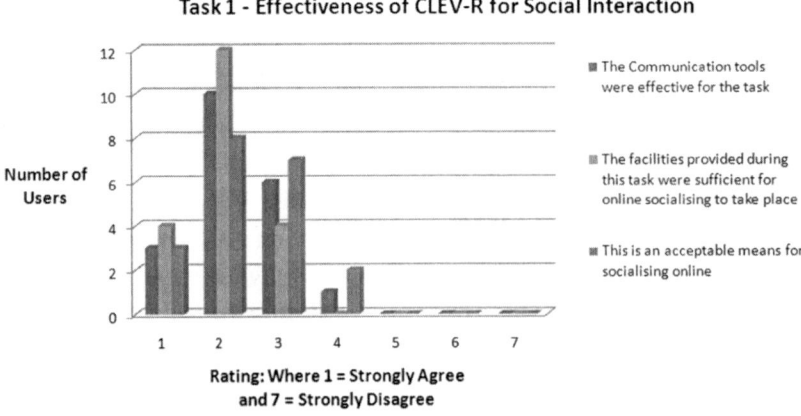

Figure 6. Results for user trial task 1

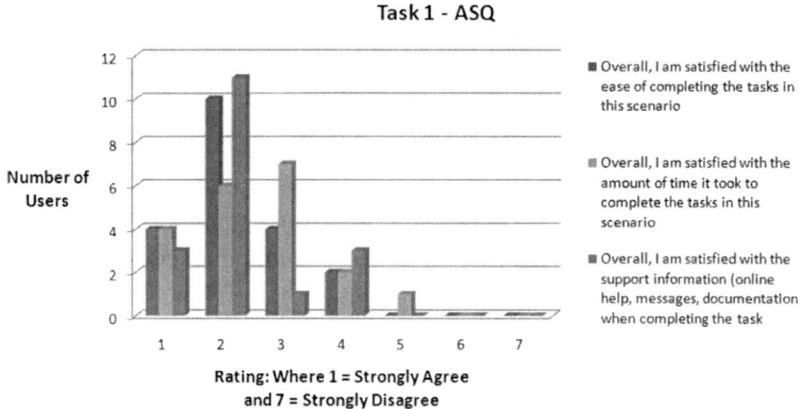

vided with the system. One possible explanation for this is that these participants did not see any support information. For example, help support is only provided when the user seeks it. The remaining 18 participants that did answer this question gave an average rating of 2.35. Although this result is not negative, it is perhaps one area that could be improved upon. It can be concluded that users are satisfied with the set of tools provided by CLEV-R to facilitate this form of social interaction and agree that the scenario they took part in is an acceptable means of socialising online.

Task 2. Learning Tools

The second task for this user study instructed participants to use the learning tools provided in CLEV-R to attend an online lecture. Although this was a learning task, feedback relating to the content of the learning material was not of interest, but rather feedback regarding the students' experience of interacting with CLEV-R was important. As in the previous task, a combination of the ASQ and 3 additional questions were administered after the task was completed. The results relating to the effectiveness of CLEV-R for learning are shown

Figure 7. Results for user trial task 2

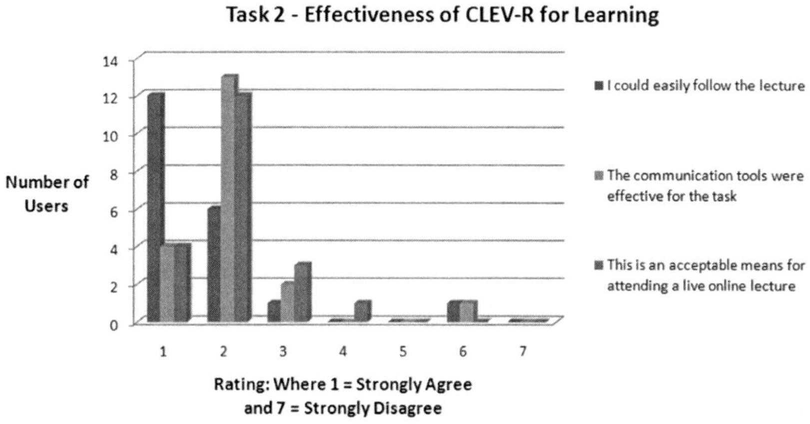

in the graph in Figure 7. 95% of the participants agreed that they could easily follow the lecture and stated it was an acceptable means for attending an online lecture. A negative response was seen from one test-subject in relation to communication tools and being able to follow the lecture. After examining individual questionnaires it was discovered this respondent had technical issues with their computer during this task.

The results pertaining to the ASQ elements of the questionnaire are shown on the graph in Figure 8. Combining the results from the ASQ shows the overall trend is one of satisfaction with an average rating of 2.02. However, the results, while skewed to the positive edge of the axes, are distributed across 4 of the scales. 90% of the participants agreed they were satisfied with the ease of completing the task. This suggests the tools provided in the *Lecture Room* of CLEV-R are easy to use. The majority of test-subjects did not see the amount of time taken to complete the task as an issue, as 95% agreed they were satisfied with the time it took. Examining the results for the third question on the questionnaire, it can be seen that a number of participants (in this case 4) failed to answer this question. The reasons for this are most likely that the subjects did not need to utilise the help files or they were unaware of their presence and so did not experience the sup-

porting material. Of those that did respond, 87.5% were positive towards the support information provided when completing the tasks, while the remainder were indifferent. Overall for this task it can be said that the satisfaction level towards CLEV-R in completing this task is high with an average rating of 2.02 (standard deviation: 0.82). Likewise, the tools provided by CLEV-R for completing this task were seen as easy to use.

Task 3. Collaboration Tools

The third task was a collaboration one in which the participants had to work together to share their knowledge by uploading relevant information to the presentation board in a designated *Meeting Room*. As with the previous 2 tasks the 6-item questionnaire was administered after the task had been completed. The 3 questions, which were added as a supplement to the standard ASQ, asked the respondents specifically about the tools for collaboration, the results of these questions are shown on the graph in Figure 9. Communication was seen as effective for this collaboration task for 90% of the participants. The average response relating to the effectiveness of the communication tools was 2.1. 95% (19) of the test-subjects agreed that the other facilities, such as those for uploading the Microsoft PowerPoint files, were suitable for this collaboration task. Similar results

Figure 8. Results for user trial task 2

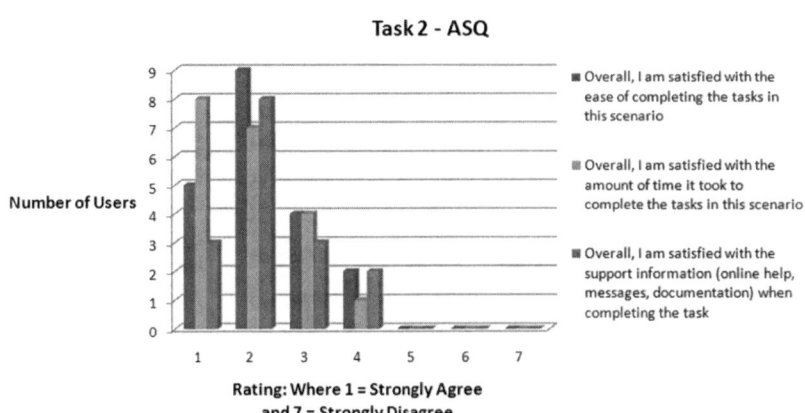

Figure 9. Results for user trial task 3

Task 3 - Effectiveness of CLEV-R for Collaboration

- The communication tools were effective for the collaboration task
- The facilities provided during this task were sufficient for online collaboration to take place
- This is an acceptable means for online collaboration

Rating: Where 1 = Strongly Agree and 7 = Strongly Disagree

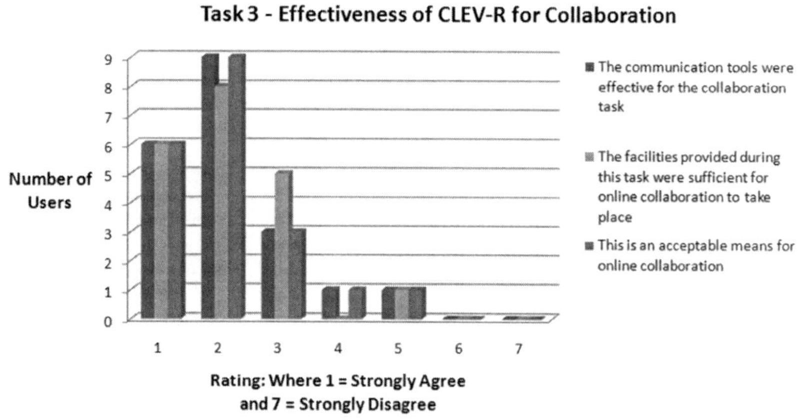

were returned for rating the task as an acceptable means of collaboration. The graph shows a correlation between the responses for effectiveness of communication and the rating of this task as an acceptable means of online collaboration. This suggests the quality of the communication tools directly impacts the users' perception of the acceptability of this as a form of interaction for collaboration and this supports the theory that audio (voice) communication is very important for collaboration. The negative responses seen in the graph were attributed to a single test-subject and further analysis of their questionnaire found

that they experienced technical problems with the prototype during this task.

The results for the ASQ elements of this questionnaire can be seen in Figure 10. The satisfaction with ease of completing the task was rated highly by 90% of participants with an average response value of 2.05 on the 7-point scale. This indicates the participants found this task particularly easy to complete. As seen in the previous 2 tasks, a proportion, in this case 40%, of test-subjects failed to rate their satisfaction with the support information for this task. The remainder, that did answer this question, overall agreed that

Figure 10. Results for user trial task 3

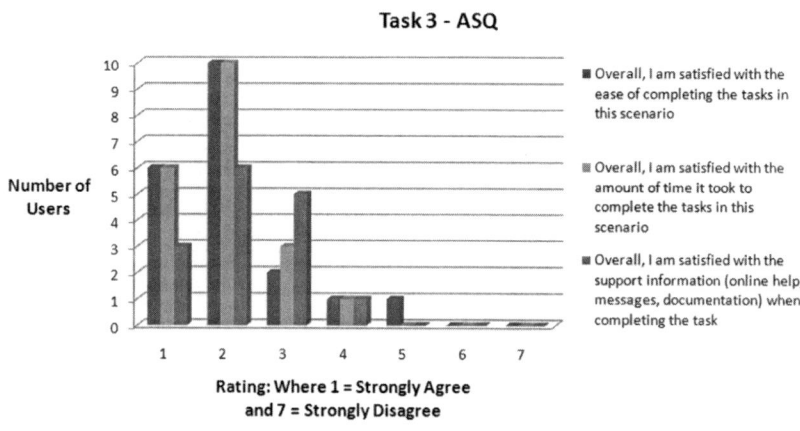

Task 3 - ASQ

- Overall, I am satisfied with the ease of completing the tasks in this scenario
- Overall, I am satisfied with the amount of time it took to complete the tasks in this scenario
- Overall, I am satisfied with the support information (online help, messages, documentation) when completing the task

Rating: Where 1 = Strongly Agree and 7 = Strongly Disagree

Figure 11. Results for user trial task 4

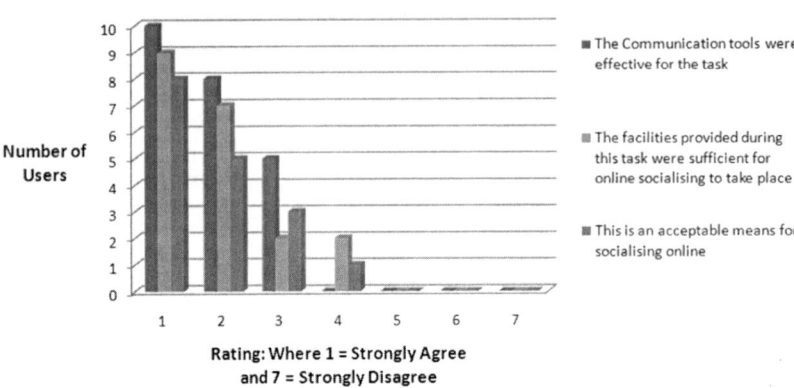

they were satisfied with the support information provided. After condensing the results of the ASQ, an overall satisfaction level of 2.03 (standard deviation: 0.776) is obtained. This is a favourable result and, when combined with the feedback relating to the questions regarding the effectiveness of the collaboration tools, indicates that CLEV-R and the tools it provides are useful and practical to support collaboration among students.

Task 4. Social Interaction Tools

The final scenario was a social one. The task involved the test-subjects using the various tools in the 3D environment to socialise with each

other. The aim of the task was to demonstrate the tools provided and how they can be used to build friendships online. The task involved sharing photos, videos and music. The 6-item questionnaire was administered immediately after the task was completed. The results, displayed in Figure 11, show a positive reaction to this task. All of test-subjects agreed that the communication tools were effective for the task. This task depended heavily on the communication facilities and the positive feedback, with an average score of 1.75, is a good endorsement that they are useful and valuable tools. The feedback regarding the other tools provided, such as the facilities for uploading

Figure 12. Results for user trial task 4

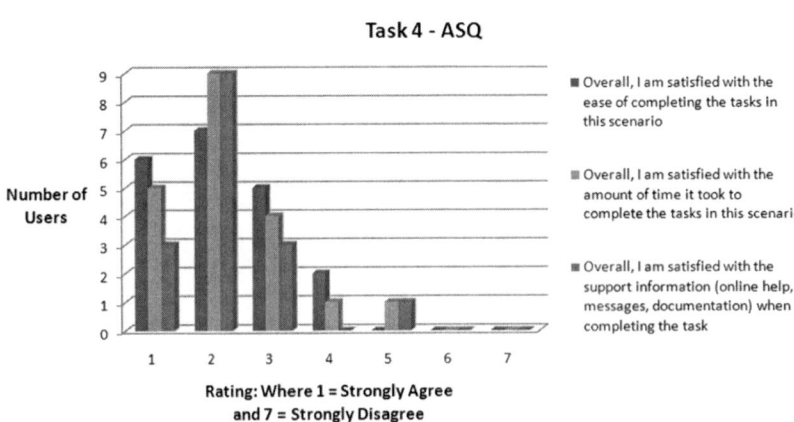

and sharing photos and videos, is also positive. 90% of respondents agreed that the facilities are sufficient for this type of socialising to take place. Further encouraging results were received for the statement regarding the acceptability of this type of scenario as a means for socialising online. The need for social interaction between students is very important and these results indicate CLEV-R succeeded in delivering an acceptable means for socialising online with 95% of test-subjects agreeing.

The results relating to the ASQ aspects of task 4 are shown in the graph in Figure 12. When the results are condensed, an overall satisfaction score of 2.15 is recorded. This indicates, that overall, the participants were satisfied with this social task. The ease of completing the task was rated positively by 90% of the test-subjects. Again, this indicates the tools required for this task have been designed in an intuitive way and the participants found them easy to use. While, the amount of time taken to complete the task was seen as satisfactory overall, 1 respondent did not agree. This result is surprising because this task had no set structure and the test subjects were free to do what they wanted, including finish the task when they felt it was appropriate. On the contrary, the other test-subjects engaged in this task and remained in the 3D environment for a longer period than anticipated. As in the previous ASQs a number of participants failed to respond to the statement regarding their satisfaction with the support information provided. The results suggest satisfaction among test-subjects towards this social task and indicate that the social tools, which have been

incorporated into CLEV-R, support social interaction between students.

Results for each of the 4 tasks have been presented in detail. A summary of the average satisfaction level of participants with CLEV-R following completion of each of the tasks is presented in Table 4. These results indicate a high level of satisfaction experienced by the participants during each task and with CLEV-R in general. This is supported by the relatively low standard deviation scores which indicate the responses returned by all the test-subjects were similar.

User Study

This section presents an additional user study which was conducted in order to assess influencing factors on performance in VR environments and to highlight that some students may have an unfair advantage due to the medium which is used to deliver learning content.

It is well known that e-learning courses are challenged by a higher dropout rate than their real world counterparts (Martinez, 2003). Boredom, ennui and lack of motivation (Serwatka, 2005) are suggested as reasons for this effect. This chapter argues that VR offers a means to resolve this issue. Consequently, associated effects of conducting learning in VR should be considered at the design stage of such environments. Relatively little research has thus far has investigated which factors influence performance in VR environments. Performance issues are particularly important in an e-learning environment where it is unfair to disadvantage students and as a result it is important

Table 4. ASQ Results for Each Task

Task #	Average	Standard Dev.
1	2.23	0.62
2	2.02	0.82
3	2.09	0.77
4	2.16	0.91

Table 5. Statistical Values

Variance	Mean	Median	Stand. Deviation	Skew	Stand. Error
0.21	0.63	0.55	0.46	0.77	0.1

to understand these factors and take them into account. Some research has identified gender as an influencing factor in VR, as it has been well reported that genders process spatial information differently. Dünser et al. (2006), for instance, investigated spatial ability in 3D navigational tasks for augmented reality and found that men perform significantly better than women. They attributed a general higher amount of experienced VR gamers within the male sample for the significant performance difference. Coluccia & Louse (2004), on the other hand, surveyed 14 studies examining gender differences in simulated environments. They concluded that gender differences are due to the characteristics of the task, rather than the task being in a virtual environment.

Although gender has been identified as one of the performance influencing factors in VR, research has yet to answer how this difference can be mitigated or at least how the effect can be reduced which is essential in an e-learning situation. Other factors, such as a possible connection between age or experience with VR gaming and performance are often assumed. However, performance influencing factors have yet to be properly investigated. This chapter presents results of a study that has been conducted to assess these factors. Understanding what really influences users in VR is crucial for improving participation and continued success in e-learning courses. The following factors have been investigated in this study:

- Gender
- Age
- Previous experience with VR gaming
- Sense of direction

Experimental Setup

The aim of this study is to investigate which of the previously listed factors affect performance during VR tasks. For this purpose the VR e-learning environment was employed in this study in order to conduct a trivial search task. Subjects were provided with a clue that was given to the users prior to commencing the task. It was expected that users would retrieve an object that was described in the clue (for example, a book in the library). Performance was evaluated with the use of the AMPERE algorithm (Schön, O'Hare, Duffy, Martin & Bradley, 2005), which delivers a performance value (pv) ranging from 0 (failed) to 1.0 (excellent) in normalised cases (otherwise the pv can go beyond 1.0).

Figure 13. Scatter plot gender comparison: PV

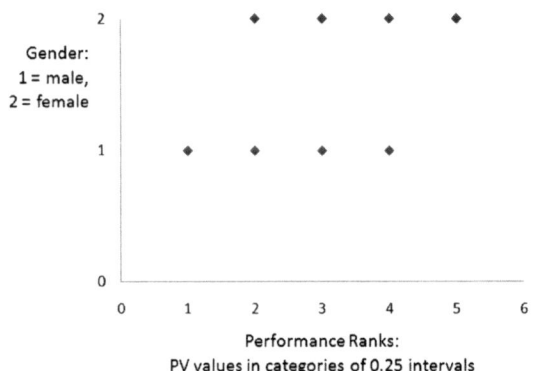

Evaluation Results and Discussion

This study was conducted with 20 subjects, 9 men and 11 women. The following statistical values describe this evaluation:

As illustrated in Table 5, this study's population did not follow a normal distribution. Consequently, non-parametric statistical methods are employed in the following paragraphs (Coolican, 2004, p.292).

Gender

Gender differences within spatial tasks have been well documented and have thus been anticipated to be reproducible within this study. Men achieved an average pv of 0.8, whereas women achieved an average pv of 0.42. Men's performance was therefore twice as good as women's performance. The Mann-Whitney U test (Coolican, 2004) confirmed that this is a significant difference with U=20 and the critical value at 23. Naturally, it can be followed that gender and performance are correlated within this study. Figure 13 illustrates the correlation diagram for gender and performance, where 1=female, 2=male and performance values are ranked in categories of 0.25 steps. The graph shows a linear pattern with zero slope that appears strong. This indicates correlation and the Spearman ρ test confirms this result with the correlation coefficient at ρ=0.57 and the critical value at 0.423.

This evaluation confirms that gender is a factor that influences performance in VR. Interestingly though, Coluccia and Louse (2004) evaluated 14 independent studies examining gender differences in VR. They concluded that gender differences occur as a result of the nature of the task rather than the task being conducted in VR. This a first indication that the gender gap could be significantly decreased and techniques, for example appropriate spatial help, might be instrumental in doing so thereby removing the advantage to male e-learners in VR environments would have over female e-learners.

Figure 14. Age distribution

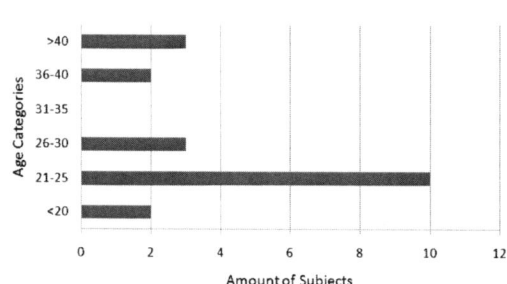

Age

Age is another factor that was expected to influence a user's performance in VR tasks. The general expectation is that younger subjects perform better in computerised environments and have also gained more experience using computers. This study grouped subjects into the following six age categories: ≤20, 21-25, 26-30, 31-35, 36-40 and >40. As the experiment was conducted within a university setting, it is not surprising that the age group of 21-25 year olds are represented strongest with 46%. 26-30 year olds formed the smallest group tested with a representation of just fewer than 3%. Figure 14 presents the age distribution within this study.

Figure 15. Distribution age to performance

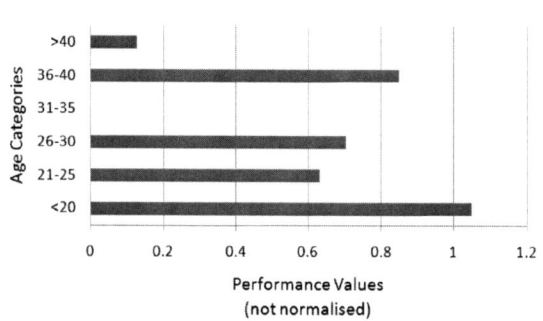

Figure 16. Scatter plot age and performance

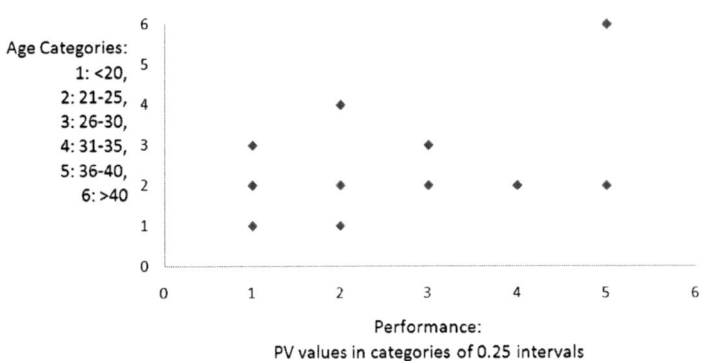

The figure shows the actual amount of people who participated in this study. We examined the results of this experiment towards a correlation between age and performance value (pv). Figure 15 presents the performance achieved according to age groups. This chart is not sufficiently representative though, as the age group of 31-35 year olds are not represented in this sample.

A scatter plot in Figure 16 illustrates the correlation between age and performance and shows zero slope and a linear pattern with several outliers. In order to test for a correlation between age and pv a Spearman ρ test is conducted, which delivered a correlation coefficient of $\rho=0.49$ and the critical value at 0.423. A correlation between age and pv could therefore be identified. Indeed, the scatter plot illustrates that younger candidates potentially perform better. It is generally anticipated that younger participants would perform better in VR tasks, as their exposure to computers and VR gaming has trained them to process digital information more rapidly. Care should be taken however not to generalise this effect by anticipating that older users underperform within

Figure 17. Experience with VR gaming

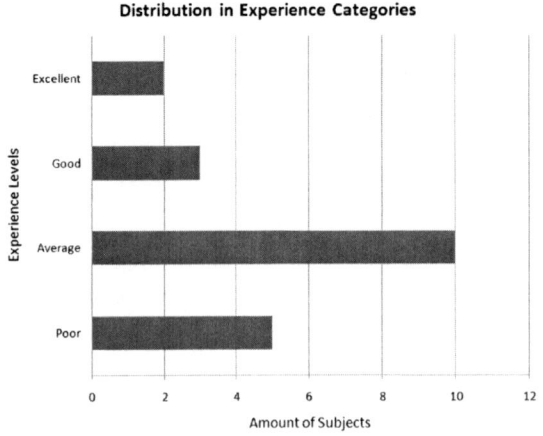

Figure 18. Correlation between VR gaming experience and performance

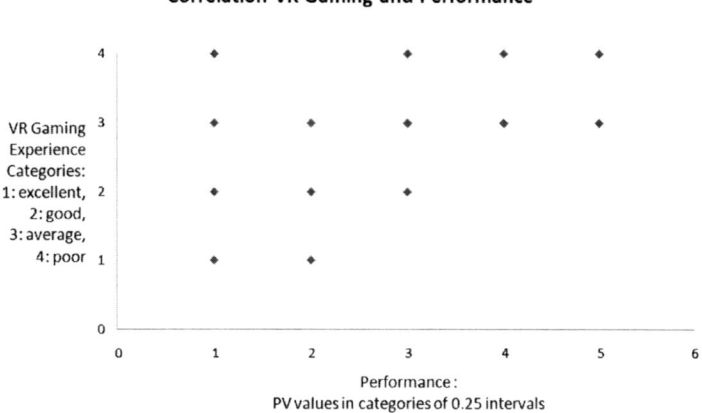

a VR e-learning environment because, as illustrated in Figure 16 this is not generally the case.

Gaming Experience

A recent study indicated that experience in VR gaming is a crucial factor in VR tasks (Burigat & Chittaro, 2007). Furthermore, experience is often perceived to be a main factor for achieving good performances regardless of the task. Therefore, it was desirable to include a variety of experience levels within this study. Naturally, it would be expected that users with good VR gaming experience would perform better in any VR task. It

is consequently of interest to test for this effect within this experiment.

Subjects were asked to rate their experience of computer games on a scale from poor to excellent. Out of a sample of 20 candidates half rated their level of VR gaming experience as average. However, a quarter of subjects rated their knowledge as poor. The distribution of expertise with VR games throughout the iterations is presented in Figure 17, which illustrates the amount of people who participated in each experiment.

Interestingly, self-ratings were distributed equally between men and women. Figure 18 illustrates the scatter plot for the gaming experience

Figure 19. Distribution of sense of direction

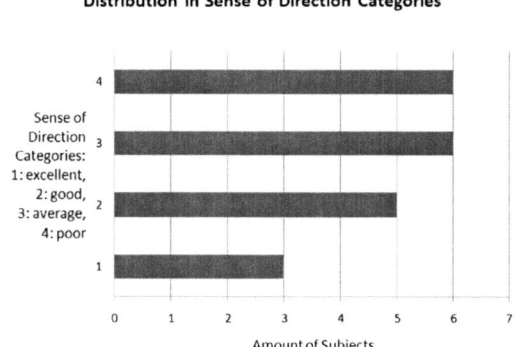

correlation. In order to compare gaming experience and performance values categories were introduced. Performance categories were incremented by 0.25 pv points, while experience as matched on a scale from excellent = 1 to poor = 4. Interestingly, the graph does not indicate any significant correlation. However, the Spearman ρ test indicates that there is a slight correlation with $\rho=0.478$ and the critical value at 0.423. Realistically however, this study could not identify a correlation between performance and experience, as the graph does not indicate a significant correlation and the statistical analysis barely indicates significance.

One explanation for this result may lie with the problems of self-evaluation. Many factors may influence an individual's self-rating. Lack of comparability or a different evaluation scale might be reasons. For future evaluations it would be beneficial to include a questionnaire that stabiles user experience in terms of usage frequency.

Sense of Direction

A further expectation relates to sense of direction and the expected performance within VR tasks, which are predominantly spatial in nature.

It would be natural to assume that subjects who rate their sense of direction as good or excellent would outperform subjects who rate their sense of direction as average or poor, as this particular evaluation was established as a search task.

Figure 19 displays the distribution of perceived sense of direction. Numbers denote the actual amount of people within this study. This study showed a relatively level distribution of ratings. The minority of subjects considered their sense of direction poor. Interestingly, twice as many men than women rate their sense of direction as excellent or good.

Figure 20 presents a scatter plot to illustrate if there is a correlation between the variables sense of direction and performance. As in the previous paragraph, performance values were categorised in intervals of 0.25 points. Sense of direction was categorised from 1=excellent to 4=poor. No pattern can be identified in this graph. The Spearman ρ test confirms that the two factors sense of direction and performance do not correlate, with $\rho=0.2$ and the critical value at 0.423. Similar to the previous test, further evaluations should include a separate test regarding the sense of direction. Female users appear more modest in their self-

Figure 20. Correlation between sense of direction and performance

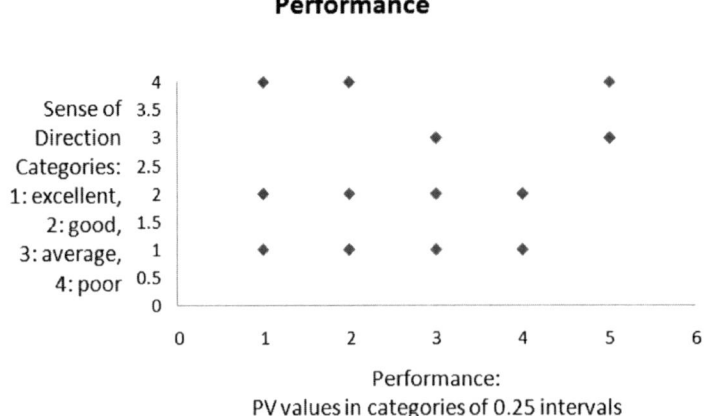

Correlation Sense of Direction and Performance

Performance:
PV values in categories of 0.25 intervals

evaluation, which might have distorted results in this study.

The experiment described in this section has highlighted the main issues to consider when designing a VR environment. These factors are particularly important in the e-learning domain where it is important that no students obtain an unfair advantage, due to the environment, over their peers. In the next section the results of this usability study and the previous user trial are discussed and used to provide guidelines for the design of e-learning environments which utilise VR.

CONCLUSION AND FUTURE WORK

Although the need to motivate and stimulate students is well known, such techniques have not been widely adopted and evaluated in the e-learning domain. This chapter has described and evaluated collaborative techniques which engage students with learning environments and promote a better learning experience for students. The approach relies on the use of a 3D VR environment which simulates a university setting. The platform is multi-user and students can use real-time communication tools to interact with each other. Learning material is delivered synchronously via live lectures. A user trial was conducted in order to gauge the opinions of users regarding this novel mode of e-learning. The results are positive and the test subjects involved in the trial could easily see the merits of the approach and felt it was a suitable technique for carrying out a series of tasks, common in an e-learning situation.

When using new modes of teaching, it is important that no student obtains an unfair advantage merely by the medium which is used to deliver material. To examine this, a user study was carried out to assess which factors influence performance in a VR situation. The user study outlined to which extent factors such as age, gender and gaming experience influence users' performances dur-

ing tasks in VR scenarios. Many of these factors are naturally assumed to influence performance. However, no prior significant studies into these effects have been conducted to date. Age, Gender, gaming experience proved to be significant factors to influence performance in VR. The perceived, sense of direction on the other hand, was not identified as a performance influencing factor. While factors such as age and gender are relatively simple to assess, fuzzy classifications such as the level of gaming experience and sense of direction are less trivial in their assessment. Within this study a self-evaluation questionnaire was employed. However, for future studies it would be beneficial to include a pre-test in order to evaluate these factors independently. The advantage of a pre-test as opposed to a self-evaluation is that users are assessed on a consistent and objective scale. Furthermore, some research has already been conducted in order to develop novel techniques that aim to minimise the effects of these factors (Schön & O'Hare, 2008) and indicates that more intuitive navigational support techniques, such as those offering subliminal stimuli, can be instrumental in creating a better user experience in VR.

While the focus of the research presented here has been on providing collaborative real-time support, the merits of asynchronous e-learning should not be overlooked. One of its benefits is the lack of time constraints which it places on students. While CLEV-R provides asynchronous access to lecture material via the *Library*, the synchronous lecture is where the majority of learning takes place. By offering both forms of e-learning, it is up to the student to decide which is most beneficial to them. Similarly, CLEV-R offers few opportunities for off-line, asynchronous communication such as message boards, emailing and forums. These can be easily incorporated into the design and form the focus of future studies to determine how they compare to the real-time communication which is currently offered in CLEV-R and ultimately improve the learning experience for students.

ACKNOWLEDGMENT

Research presented in this chapter was funded by a strategic Research Cluster grant (07/SRC/ I1168) by Science Foundation Ireland under the National Development Plan. The authors gratefully acknowledge this support.

REFERENCES

Anaraki, F. (2004). Developing an Effective and Efficient eLearning Platform. *International Journal of the Computer, the Internet and Management* *12*(2), 57–63.

Bouras, C., Fotakis, D., Kapoulas, V., Koubek, A., Mayer, H., & Rehatschek, H. (1999). Virtual European School-VES. In Proceedings *of the IEEE International Conference on Multimedia Computing and Systems* (pp.1055-1057), Florence, Italy, June 7 - 11, IEEE.

Bouras, C., Giannaka, E., & Tsiatsos, T. (2003). Virtual Collaboration Spaces: The EVE Community. In *Proceedings of the 2003 Symposium on Applications and the Internet* (pp. 48-55), Orlando, Florida, USA, January 27 - 31, IEEE.

Bouras, C., Philopoulos, A., & Tsiatsos, T. (2001). E-Learning through Distributed Virtual Environments. *Journal of Network and Computer Applications, 24*(3), 175–199. doi:10.1006/ jnca.2001.0131

Bouras, C., & Tsiatsos, T. (2006). Educational Virtual Environments: Design Rationale and Architecture. *Multimedia Tools and Applications, 29*(2), 153–173. doi:10.1007/s11042-006-0005-7

Burigat, S., & Chittaro, L. (2007). Navigation in 3D Virtual Environments: Effects of User Experience and Location-Pointing Navigation Aids. *International Journal of Human-Computer Studies, 65*(11), 945–958. doi:10.1016/j.ijhcs.2007.07.003

Chittaro, L., & Ranon, R. (2002). New Directions for the Design of Virtual Reality Interfaces to E-Commerce Sites. In *Proceedings of the 5th International Conference on Advanced Visual Interfaces* (pp.308-315), Trento, Italy, May 22 - 24, ACM Press.

Cockburn, A., & McKenzie, B. (2002). Evaluating the Effectiveness of Spatial Memory in 2D and 3D Physical and Virtual Environments. In *CHI '02: Proceedings of the SIGCHI Conference on Human Factors in Computing Systems* (pp.203-210), Minneapolis, Minnesota, USA, April 20 - 25, ACM Press.

Coluccia, E., & Louse, G. (2004). A UML-Based Software Engineering Methodology for Agent Factory. In *Proceedings of the 16th International Conference on Software Engineering and Knowledge Engineering*, Alberta, Canada.

Coolican, H. (2004). *Research Methods and Statistics in Psychology*. Hodder Arnold.

Cordier, F., Seo, H., & Magnenat-Thalmann, N. (2003). Made-To-Measure Technologies for an Online Clothing Store. *IEEE Computer Graphics and Applications, 23*(1), 38–48. doi:10.1109/ MCG.2003.1159612

Darken, R., & Peterson, B. (2000). *Handbook of Virtual Environment Technology, Stanney, K*. Spatial Orientation, Wayfinding and Representation.

Dickey, M. (2003). 3D Virtual Worlds: An Emerging Technology for Traditional and Distance Learning. In *Proceedings of the Ohio Learning Network; The Convergence of Learning and Technology-Windows on the Future*, Easton, Ohio, USA, March 3 - 4.

Doherty, P., & Rothfarb, R. (2006). Building an Interactive Science Museum in Second Life. In *Proceedings of the Second Life Education Workshop at the Second Life Community Convention* (pp. 19-24), San Francisco, California, USA, August 18 – 20.

Dünser, A., Steinbügel, K., Kaufmann, H., & Glück, J. (2006). Virtual and Augmented Reality as Spatial Ability Training Tools. In *Proceedings of the 7th ACM SIGCHI, Design Centred HCI*, (Vol. 158, pp. 125-132). ACM Press.

Harkin, J. (2006). Get a (Second) Life. *Financial Times*, Published: November 17 2006 .

Henderson, J., Fishwick, P., Fresh, E., & Futterknecht, F. (2008). An Immersive Learning Simulation Environment for Chinese Culture. In *Proceedings of Interservice/Industry Training, Simulation, and Education Conference (I/ITSEC)*, Orlando, Florida, USA, December 1 - 4.

Hudson-Smith, A. (2002). *30 Days in Active Worlds: Community, Design and Terrorism in a Virtual World. The Social Life of Avatars: Presence and Interaction in Shared Virtual Environments* (pp. 77–89). New York, New York, USA: Springer-Verlag.

Jones, J. G., & Bronack, S. C. (2008). *Rethinking Cognition, Representations, and Processes in 3D Online Social Learning Environments. Digital Literacy: Tools and Methodologies for Information Society* (pp. 176–217). Hershey, PA: IGI Global.

Kamel-Boulos, M. N., Taylor, A. D., & Breton, A. (2005). A Synchronous Communication Experiment within an Online Distance Learning Program: A Case Study. *Telemedicine Journal and e-Health*, *11*(5), 283–293.

Kemp, J., & Livingstone, D. (2006). Putting a Second Life Metaverse Skin on Learning Management Systems. In *Proceedings of the Second Life Education Workshop at the Second Life Community Convention* (pp.13-18), San Francisco, California, USA, August 18 – 20.

Kitchen, D., & McDougall, D. (1998). Collaborative Learning on the Internet. *Telemedicine Educational Technology Systems*, *27*(3), 245–258.

Laister, J., & Kober, S. (2002). Social Aspects of Collaborative Learning in Virtual Learning Environments. In *Proceedings of the Networked Learning Conference*, Sheffield, UK, March 26 - 28.

Lewis, J. (1991). Psychometric Evaluation of an After-Scenario Questionnaire for Computer Usability Studies: the ASQ. *ACM SIGCHI Bulletin*, *23*(1), 78–81. doi:10.1145/122672.122692

Martinez, M. (2003). High Attrition Rates in E-Learning: Challenges, Predictors, and Solutions. *The E-Learning Developers'. Journal*, *14*(1).

McArdle & Bertolotto. (2010). (in press). *Assessing the Application of 3D Collaborative Technologies within an E-Learning Environment, Interactive Learning Environments*. Boca Raton. FL:Taylor & Francis.

McInnerney, J., & Roberts, T. (2004). Online Learning: Social Interaction and the Creation of a Sense of Community. *Journal of Educational Technology & Society*, *7*(3), 73–81.

Monahan, T., McArdle, G., & Bertolotto, M. (2008). Virtual Reality for Collaborative E-Learning. [Elsevier Science.]. *Journal of Computers and Education*, *50*(4), 1339–1353. doi:10.1016/j.compedu.2006.12.008

Mowlds, F., Roche, B., & Mangina, E. (2005). ABITS: Learning More about Students through Intelligent Educational Software. *Campus-Wide Information Systems*, *22*(3), 131–139. doi:10.1108/10650740510606126

Nielsen, J. (1993). *Usability Engineering*. San Francisco: Morgan Kaufmann Publishers Inc. Redfern, S. & Naughton, N. (2002). Collaborative Virtual Environments to Support Communication and Community in Internet-Based Distance Education. *Journal of Information Technology Education*, *1*(3), 201–211.

Riedl, R., Barrett, T., Rowe, J., Smith, R., & Vinson, W. (2001). Sequence Independent Structure in Distance Learning. In *Proceedings of the Conference on Computers and Learning*, Coventry, UK, April 2 - 4.

San Chee, Y. (2001). Networked Virtual Environments for Collaborative Learning. *in Proceedings of ICCE/SchoolNet: the 9th International Conference on Computers in Education* (p. 311), Seoul, South Korea, November 11 - 14.

San Chee, Y., & Hooi, C. (2002). C-VISions: Socialized Learning through Collaborative, Virtual, Interactive Simulations. In *Proceedings of Computer Supported Collaborative Learning (CSCL)* (pp.687-696), Boulder, Colorado, USA, January 7 - 11.

Schön, B., & O'Hare, G. M. P. (2008). Navigational Support Methodologies for 3D Virtual Worlds. In *Proceedings of the 21ˢᵗ Annual Conference on Computer Animation and Social Agents (CASA 2008)*, Seoul. *Korea & World Affairs*, (September): 1–3.

Schön, B., O'Hare, G. M. P., Duffy, B., Martin, A., & Bradley, J. (2005). The AMPERE algorithm – Area-Based Masking with the PERformance Equation. *In Proceedings of FLAIRS 2005, AAAI*, Clearwater Beach, Florida, USA, May 15 - 17

Serwatka, J. A. (2005). Improving Retention in Distance Learning Classes. *International Journal of Instructional Technology and Distance Learning*, *2*(1), 59–64.

Sun, P., & Cheng, H. (2007). The Design of Instructional Multimedia in ELearning: A Media Richness Theory-based Approach. *Computers & Education*, *49*(3), 662–676. doi:10.1016/j.compedu.2005.11.016

Vass, E. (2002). *Friendship and Collaborative Creative Writing in the Primary Classroom. Journal of Computer Assisted Learning, 18(1).* New York: Blackwell Science.

Wheeler, M. (2009). Developing the Media Zoo in Second Life. *British Journal of Educational Technology, 40*(3). New York: Blackwell Publishing.

KEY TERMS AND DEFINITIONS

3D Environment: A virtual representation of a location in which users can interact with each other

Avatar: The onscreen persona which represents the user as they interact with the environment and other users

CLEV-R: Collaborative Learning Environments with Virtual Reality; this is the online learning system described in this chapter which uses virtual reality to provide an interactive environment in which users can collaborate.

Collaborate: To cooperate and work together on the same topic, can be done synchronously or asynchronously.

Immersive: An engaging experience in which the use feels they are part of the environment which they are experiencing.

Online Learning: Using the internet as a means of obtaining an education

Social Interaction: Using synchronous tools, such as voice chat and photo sharing to communicate with peers and fellow users of the system

Usability: Study: An evaluation method used to determine if the system being tested offers the functionality required by users

User: The individual who is interacting with the system. In the case of the system described here, that is generally a student or a teacher.

Virtual Reality: An onscreen representation of a real or imaginative environment in which the use can interact.

Chapter 2
Virtual Worlds:
Corporate Early Adopters Pave the Way

Catherine M. J. Lithgow
University of Maryland Baltimore County, USA

Judi L. Davidson Wolf
University of Maryland Baltimore County, USA

Zane L. Berge
University of Maryland Baltimore County, USA

ABSTRACT

Multi-user virtual environments (MUVEs), the most popular of which is Second Life, have great potential to provide engaging, interactive content to today's students using both synchronous and asynchronous delivery. Educators, as well as several forward-thinking corporations and military organizations, have proven to be early adopters of MUVEs as a training delivery medium, paving the way to begin evaluating the medium for use in professional development. The use of MUVEs for education will definitely grow. Corporations considering venturing into this arena would do well to consider the lessons learned by the early adopters, paying particular attention to the barriers that need to be overcome for successful implementation.

VIRTUAL WORLDS: CORPORATE EARLY ADOPTERS PAVE THE WAY

In the continuing quest for effective delivery methods for distance education, multi-user virtual environments (MUVEs), also known as virtual worlds (VWs), have become popular at the university and secondary school levels and, to some extent, in corporate training. While use is still varied, both in quantity and quality, early adopters—educators and several corporate learn-ing officers—provide ample evidence of the value of MUVEs as an instructional delivery medium. Although VWs are being used successfully for professional development and training, efforts to evaluate their effectiveness are still in early stages. Corporations that are considering venturing into MUVEs should consider the lessons learned by these early adopters, particularly in terms of the barriers that need to be overcome for successful implementation.

The evolution of multi-user virtual environments spans a long, logical, and progressive past. Although there are many in existence today, serv-

DOI: 10.4018/978-1-61692-825-4.ch002

ing a variety of age groups and demographics, the best known is probably *Second Life™* (SL). Launched in 2003 by Linden Lab Technologies, SL is a finite "grid" that currently accommodates millions of users around the world (WebProNews, 2009), although the number of "residents" logged in and actively using the service on a daily basis is estimated at closer to 60,000[1] (SL website, 2009).

Researchers suggest that the development of virtual worlds is based on a merging of gaming and social networking (Messinger, Stroulia & Lyons, 2008). Gaming began as interactive arcade games with tactical and strategic goals and has undergone a series of evolutionary changes. Early single-player, off-line games became multi-player, off-line games and then progressed to single- and multi-player networked games including those played via internet connectivity. The next step was unstructured games, which developed into those in which the player generates the content; the current stage features multiplayer online role-playing environments.

Evolving separately, social networking has increased in popularity as it meets a variety of social and networking goals manifested in products such as *Twitter, LinkedIN, Facebook, YouTube, My Space,* and *Skype.* These environments support members pursuing their own objectives of socializing and sharing information (Messinger, Stroulia & Lyons, 2008).

While SL is often thought of as a game it is, in fact, anything but. Kalning (2007) notes that typically games include both structured and unstructured goals as well as objectives for completion. Games have limits and theoretically, persistence and skill will allow the participant to win by reaching the outer limits of the established environment. However, in SL there is no inherent conflict or goals set by the programmer (Kalning, 2007). The goals and objectives are set by the users according to their individual needs. The only limit is one's imagination, since SL users create their own content and their own ever-changing objectives. Simultaneously, many "residents" are drawn to the environment by the opportunities for social networking and personalized goal achievement.

REAL LIFE USES FOR SECOND LIFE

Many organizations are seeking to establish a presence in virtual worlds. Although several initially envisioned SL as a commercial environment, that narrow vision only skims the surface. Educators have proven to be active, early adopters and have built a strong presence in SL, using the environment to conduct classes, collaborate with peers, and participate in conferences that they might otherwise be unable to attend. Several universities have established a presence using SL to conduct classes synchronously (Lagorio, 2007). Government agencies, including the military, as well as corporations, use it for teleconferencing, role-play, and simulation (New England Business Bulletin, 2009). Many of these organizations also use SL for recruitment (TMP, 2007).

The collaborative and active nature of a MUVE is being shown to offer creative possibilities for delivering learner-centered, engaging educational content with practical application and interaction at several levels:

- **Person-person.** Learners interact with other learners, instructors, or "the general public."
- **Person-object.** Learners interact with discrete objects or a particular environment.
- **Person-self.** Both instructors and learners find the MUVE setting engenders new roles and encourages self-reflection.

PERSON-PERSON INTERACTION

A MUVE is, by definition, a collaborative environment which provides engagement and a strong "sense of presence," fostering socialization among learners considered critical to success in distance education (Irwin & Berge, 2006). Minocha and Tingle (2008) provided a comprehensive list of socialization activities to help build community among learners, including tours, treasure hunts, and collaborative projects. Those new to the environment will need this kind of gentle, guided introduction, while more experienced students can become engaged more quickly (p. 220).

Strongly image-based, immersive environments foster "the death of distance" while creating "the power of presence" and a "sense of space" (Montoya, Massey, & Ketter, 2009) in a way that can be very powerful for learners. One educator stated,

What has attracted me to Second Life is what I've found lacking for quite some time in online classes—no sense of place and a strained sense of presence. . . . The sense of presence created by screens of text . . . [is] difficult for many students to hold onto. . . . The sense of community arises more quickly when we see images of others before us, behind us, to the sides and so on. . . . [As for sense of place, t]here's no "where" . . . with screens of text in Blackboard, Moodle or Angel. But there is a where in Second Life, an up, down, left, right, mountains, buildings, sky (SLED/Holt, 2009).

The synchronicity of the environment is another factor in building community and strengthening collaboration (Minocha & Tingle, 2008). Students may have difficulty connecting with each other in asynchronous learning and find it easier to collaborate with the more immediate feedback of a synchronous setting.

MUVEs provide exceptional training in the form of role-plays and simulations, even approximating apprenticeship-type experiences. In a "no-harm" practice environment, students interact to gain practical experience with soft skills such as language learning, decision-making, and leadership roles. A virtual world can portray a simulated environment that might require an "elaborate or expensive" set in the real world. It is fairly easy

to make a few changes to the "set" and produce a completely new environment:

Textures can be rapidly changed to completely alter the appearance of the space, allowing the same holodeck to be used as a set for many different role-plays. . . .[T]he appearance of a particular space can be altered around the group rather than the group being moved to another location. (Addison & O'Hare, 2008, p. 13)

In a military context, "live training exercises can be expensive, not to mention dangerous, to soldiers, as well as to the environment" (Stackpole, 2008).

Furthermore, "actors" in the role-play can be played by robots or scripts, reducing the need for large numbers of participants. In fact, "[s]tudents felt that role-play within the virtual setting was more likely to interest them and hold their attention as compared to face-to-face role play" (Gao, Noh,& Koehler, 2008 cited in Addison & O'Hare, p. 11). Such role-playing also allows the student to "gain authentic experience under the guidance of real world experts not available in a traditional campus setting" (Arreguin, 2007, p. 2).

A wide range of projects supports this notion, with some outstanding examples including the following:

- Students carry out an inspection of a food factory to determine if it meets regulatory requirements—a situation potentially dangerous in real life (Addison & O'Hare, 2000).
- Members of an emergency department team practice preparedness for multiple-victim disasters (trauma and nerve toxin exposure) (Heinrichs, Youngblood, Harter, & Dev, 2008).
- Trainees learn how to staff a Canadian border crossing, examining documentation and interviewing potential visitors into the country (Werner, 2008a/2008b).

- Students practice "assessing and remediating disability issues" in houses designed for this purpose (Gerald & Antonacci, 2009).
- A homeland security simulation "train[s] first responders to a dirty bomb or chemical weapons attack" (O'Brien, 2005).
- In an operating room simulation, nurse anesthetist students learn "complex medical procedures"; the students' actions are recorded and emailed to the instructor for assessment (Gerald & Antonacci, 2009).
- In a virtual early childhood education classroom, scripted "children" respond to teachers-in-training, or teachers-in-training role play the children and teacher, while an instructor observes and critiques (SLED/Freese, 2009).
- Soldiers operate on a virtual battlefield in an extremely realistic depiction of combat conditions, being trained for the "unconventional, unpredictable guerilla warfare the military didn't … envision in Iraq," as well as "learn[ing] cultural skills needed to operate in a hostile and foreign land" (O'Brien, 2005).

PERSON-OBJECT/ ENVIRONMENT INTERACTION

The 3D nature of virtual worlds allows learners to explore objects in ways that may be impossible in real life, transcending both distance and size (both macro and micro). For example, students can get inside a star in another galaxy, or a micron. The same is true for environments: in SL, students can transcend space and time, visiting recreated locations or time periods that are far away or no longer exist. The social interaction possible in these worlds also allows learners to experience and interact with real-world scenarios. For instance, SL's flourishing economy permits learners to examine business practices, marketing, and market trends.

For many students, simply inspecting and relating to objects or environments provides valuable learning experience. Others gain deeper understanding by creating content using programming, 3D rendering, scripting, and animation skills. The virtual world then also serves the function of displaying student work (Ryan, 2008).

SL also lends itself to blended learning, which is on the rise (Young, 2002). Blended learning is traditionally defined as "the combination of instruction from two historically separate models of teaching and learning: traditional [face-to-face] learning systems and distributed learning systems. . . [emphasizing] the central role of computer-based technologies" (Graham, 2006, p. 3). However, it can also be seen as a mélange of delivery methods supporting a combination of synchronous and asynchronous delivery. There are a number of examples of such asynchronous, or non-facilitated, training in SL:

- At the National Oceanic and Atmospheric Agency's island in SL, visitors can experience a virtual tsunami, observing tectonic plate movement under the ocean and the devastation that occurs to land-based structures.
- Visitors to Vassar University can sit in a virtual flying machine which provides a guided tour of the features of the island.
- The International Society for Technology in Education is one of many locations where users can follow a self-guided marked trail leading to "posters" providing directions for basic SL activities such as walking, using different camera views, and taking pictures.

Virtual worlds transcend the definition of blended learning by combining separate delivery models into one: they deliver both virtual "face-

Figure 1. Standing underwater at the NOAA tsunami simulation, read about and observe changes underwater

to-face" learning and asynchronous but interactive learning. Thus, we begin to see the potential for this technology as it evolves into what educators and trainers often demand: a "one-stop shop" for instruction.

PERSON-SELF INTERACTION

The mere idea of teaching this way can be difficult to envision; some educators see new technology as a threat to established ways of doing things (Haymes, 2008). The learning curve is steep, so that "[r]ather than feeling proficient in the teaching environment, instructors are often thrust into the learner role as they acquire new skills themselves" (Arreguin, 2007, p.8). Having accepted the challenge, educators and instructional designers may find that it is not easy to create content (Werner, 2008a) or even just to deliver content in a MUVE. Carr, Oliver, and Burn (2008) found the investment in instructor time was high, both for preparation

Figure 2. The virtual flying machine at Vassar University Island

and for delivery. Their training was labor intensive to run, requiring several instructors to be on hand; they characterized the experience as "intense and draining" (pp. 90-91).

Given the cost and effort of using a MUVE, the challenge may be to capitalize on its capabilities. Educators must take care that they "learn to use the benefits of virtual worlds to their best advantage and not merely recreate 'old ways' of teaching" (Arreguin, 2007, p. 11). A recent extensive discussion on the SLED list focused on the use of various tools to enhance pedagogy in SL. As is common with such debates, there were those at extreme ends of the argument. One group believed that instructors should *never* use lecture, Powerpoint slides, or other "transplanted Real Life" tools in SL. Or, to put it succinctly, "People can fly and you want them to look at slides" (SLED/Hunsinger, 2009). Others approached the issue from more of a design standpoint and argued that, as in any educational situation, the tool must be appropriate to the content, the delivery system, and the audience, and no tool should be ruled out. Partridge (SLED, 2009a) pointed out that using familiar tools can help people make the leap to teaching in SL. "Most teachers aren't ready for rapidly building 3D interactive landscapes and worlds."

Many newcomers to MUVEs find the learning curve—referred to as the "pain barrier" by Carr et al. (2008) —troublesome. Simple navigation tasks—moving around, getting from one location to another, or surveying the current location—can be frustrating. In addition, a principal means of communication, text chat, is not comfortable for everyone. "Some of the students struggled with following text discussions, and it became clear that participating in discussions in SL with confidence is an acquired skill, . . . We had not fully appreciated the problems associated with text-chat for beginners" (Carr et al., 2008, p. 90). A 2007 Pew study found that American use and understanding of technology is fairly shallow: only 8% of Americans are "deep users of

the participatory web" (Horrigan, 2007 cited in Haymes, 2008, p. 67).

For the technologically literate, part of the appeal of a MUVE is the challenge of building and scripting objects and environments. But for those who are not comfortable with technology, the learning curve is very steep and requires significant and often sustained training and effort. Kemp, Livingstone, and Bloomfield (2009) cite the New Media Consortium (2008) as noting that "Faculty and staff are usually unprepared to support students in these 3D spaces" and "building capacities sufficient to teach may take between 6 months and 12 months" (p. 551).

Interestingly, some educators are more eager than their students: "If I show SL to students who had been playing WOW [*World of* Warcraft] for example [and that is the majority of them] they hate it and laugh at it as old people's ridiculous attempt at being cool" (SLED/Tadros, 2009). However, constituents of younger generations may be very comfortable in this type of environment. "With the current generation of soldiers raised in an era of video games and the Internet, most are just as comfortable, if not more so, learning from a digital experience as they would be participating in real-world training scenarios" (Stackpole, 2008). Badger notes that the use of virtual worlds for training can be a recruiting advantage for companies, stating that "millenials want this technology" (2009, p. 4).

Clearly, in these vibrant learning environments, the characteristics of a simulation in a learning situation promote active learning and students are required to take an energetic role in directing and discovering their own learning content. As Antonacci and Modaress (2005) note, "you cannot be passive in a game or simulation"; "lurkers" will have to join in or take responsibility for failing to meet the goals and objectives.

In addition, an aspect of learning that is often neglected in both in-place and distance education classrooms is the opportunity for self-reflection and change. Having an alternate "self"—an avatar—in the learning space provides this opportunity.

I have dared to do MANY things in SL that would never have occurred to me in RL [real life]. Some involve trying new skills, some involve working alongside people that I never paid close enough attention to in my professional life, and some involve trying out behaviors that my RL mind says are MUCH too risky for someone of my years and reputation (SLED/Loon, 2009b).

Salmon (2009) echoes this thought, noting that having individuals engage in experiences outside their normal comfort zones can be a powerful learning tool. "If such an experience can be made purposeful and designed for learning, it seems to me that we have tools at our disposal ... the likes of which no educators have ever had before" (2009, p. 533).

BARRIERS TO CORPORATE ADOPTION OF SECOND LIFE

While the use of MUVEs is thriving in some quarters, there are still many barriers to full acceptance in the corporate training world. Chief among these is lack of management buy-in due to concerns that may not be well grounded in fact, such as the validity and cost of MUVEs.

There is considerable skepticism in the corporate world about allowing, much less encouraging, employees to "play games," and concern about verifying digital identities (Badger, 2008, p. 6). There is also apprehension that in the public areas, corporations are unable to protect their employees from exposure to unknown and undesirable factors. The fact that SL contains much "adult," even pornographic, content heightens the concern. The welcome islands are not well policed, giving newcomers a bad impression, and the potentially highly visible nature of inappropriate content,

coupled with occasional avatars who choose to act in very disruptive ways (known as "griefers"), are among the factors that lead many corporate executives to perceive a lack of seriousness or integrity (and therefore value) to activities in SL. Linden Lab is implementing changes that indicate the developers recognize that future revenue for SL will stem from legitimate business such as education, military, government, and corporate use. Gambling is one example of the type of undesirable content Linden Lab eliminated from SL in 2007. In 2009, Linden Lab launched an effort to isolate the adult content to a specific area of the grid, allowing educators and corporate entities to move about more freely in the virtual environment.

Corporations are interested in the bottom line, of course, and participation in a MUVE may require considerable investment. While casual use of SL is free and public space on a public server is available for purchase for a one-time cost of less than $2,000, such a venue does not bode well for workplace privacy. Additionally, a "fully customized, fully private virtual world with capacity for thousands of users" may run up to $1 million (*"What Does It Cost,"* 2008, p. 88). Although the spirit of collaboration prevails and many educators are willing to share their resources,[2] ultimately the creation of such items is costly and time-consuming, whether developed by an in-house team or purchased from vendors. In addition, supplying the appropriate technology for users is costly in and of itself. Hardware and software must both be high-end and in some cases customized. Thus, access to the required technology constitutes another common barrier.

Complicating the issue of cost is the unlikely notion that current training materials created for a different delivery method can be re-purposed for use in online format. Corporations must give careful consideration to the need for (and expense of) quality instructional design created by experienced individuals who have successfully designed and implemented other online training programs.

MANAGEMENT/EVALUATION OF USING SECOND LIFE

Since a virtual world is one alternative delivery method for distance education, many practices surrounding the management and evaluation of effectiveness in distance education—indeed, of effectiveness in any kind of education—have already been outlined and explored by experts and thus apply to this delivery medium. Moore and Kearsley (2005) suggest that management of a distance education initiative should include the following strategies: 1) strategic planning to define a mission; 2) goals and objectives; 3) prioritizing the goals; 4) continuous assessment including trends; and 5) noting emerging technological options that might increase efficiency when projecting future needs and determining how to meet them. As with any distance education initiative, the overall program mission must be driven by a strong commitment on the part of corporate management, at all levels, to ensure the program's potential for success.

Another key element to any successfully managed program is the need for entities to determine in advance how the chosen tool will provide the "best bang for the buck". To determine that, it is initially critical for each entity to define, relative to their own organizational mission and goals, what the bang is. If the bang is to reach a maximum number of people, SL may not be the answer. As of December 2008, *Facebook* had over 200,000,000 separate visitors worldwide, giving it the distinction of being one of the largest social networking sites in the United States. In contrast, SL reported just over 700,000 unique residents as of March 2009. Thus, it would seem counterintuitive to use SL for a "maximum coverage" marketing tactic. However, if the bang is to conduct synchronous meetings and conferences or provide a limited and targeted audience with the ability to collaborate on projects as a team, SL just might be the best option. Spend some time honestly outlining desired expectations before choosing the tool with which

to deliver it. A different tool may be more appropriate for the designated needs (joeeisner, 2009).

One caution, from Miner and Hofman (2009), is that it is important to focus on student success rather than on technology. To do that organizations must: 1) ensure the technology works before implementing it; 2) work with smaller courses and evaluate their effectiveness; 3) include interactivity; 4) require self-directed commitment with consequences if the student does not comply; and 5) review objectives carefully and ensure the chosen technology is the most appropriate delivery method. This was reflected recently by an educator who noted: "We are *way* too focused on asking 'How can SL enhance my teaching?' instead of asking first 'How can I teach better?'" (SLED/Loon, 2009a).

Companies that are just getting started exploring virtual worlds can learn from the best practices and standards that have been established by the early adopters of this technology. For example, a few forward-thinking corporations have demonstrated that it is advisable to regulate and standardize their employees' use of virtual worlds to maximize the corporate performance improvement goals. IBM's established rules of engagement set out expectations for frequency, type, and amount of interaction expected from users (IBM Virtual World Guidelines, n.d.). IBM provides advice on how to handle inappropriate behavior, appearance, digital personas (reputation), and proper usage of IBM resources "on the clock." Ultimately, IBM employees are considered responsible for conducting themselves in-world in much the same way they do in real life and are encouraged to use good judgment and follow IBM's values and Business Conduct Guidelines while in the public grid.

As for evaluating the success of a virtual world, most experts seem to agree that measuring the effectiveness of virtual worlds is challenging and represents a stumbling block for overall acceptance. Lockee, Moore and Burton (2002) suggest that management of student progress and evaluation are critical and that programs lacking a strong component of each are likely to fail. However, measuring the success of virtual worlds in distance education is still in its infancy. Evaluation of virtual worlds seems to generate mostly research focused on satisfaction, and particularly satisfaction levels comparing virtual worlds and other distance education delivery methods to "face-to-face" learning.

Massey, Montoya and O'Driscoll (2005) outline how important it is to align objectives with HPT (Human Performance Technology), which provides a logical evaluation framework for training initiatives. They suggest focusing on business issues and performance problems by linking the technology to performance outcomes. Although Massey and Montoya (Science Daily, 2008) have blazed the trail and developed a measurement tool called the PVP (Perceived Virtual Presence), to measure one's involvement or "perceived reality" within virtual worlds, currently experts seem to be unable to agree on any widely accepted measurement technique or tool. To date, the PVP is the newest and most promising tool available for researching the effectiveness of corporate training in a virtual world. Montoya and Massey (Science Daily, 2008) suggest that the more "real" the virtual experience is for employees, the more likely they are to find the community engaging and to collaborate, which leads to an enhanced virtual training experience and increased employee productivity.

PROFESSIONAL DEVELOPMENT IN SECOND LIFE

Individuals engage in professional development for many reasons: to achieve personal growth, to realize innovation through networking and collaboration, to maintain or enhance current skill levels, or to fulfill professional regulatory requirements. Mertens and Flowers (2004) highlight the fact that professional development contributes to employee retention and performance improvement. Depending on the organization, performance improvement can be manifested in different ways. In the educational realm, teachers who regularly engage in quality professional development are directly linked to an increase in student achievement (Mertens & Flowers, 2004). For the military, there is a major shift in the way in which troops prepare for war with the goal being the same for everyone: simply to survive (Vargas, 2006). In the corporate realm, innovation is linked to collaboration (Neal, 2006), innovation, and job performance, which are critical to business success.

Educators were early adopters of virtual worlds for professional development delivery, with such organizations as the International Society for Technology in Education (ISTE) quickly establishing a presence in SL. Training organizations such as the American Society for Training and Development (ASTD) also have active roles in SL. Conducting regular meetings, conferences, and training events, they seek to attract educators to the environment to provide networking opportunities for collaboration on both a national and an international level. Mertens and Flowers (2004) suggest that to be effective, teachers need to participate regularly in a variety of formal and informal professional development events. Formal events include workshops or classes, conferences, and visits to other schools. Informal events include collaboration with other teachers, lesson planning as a group, coaching peers, and reviewing students' work collaboratively. These professional development opportunities are important enough that they should already be in place for educators who teach in a face-to-face format. As an added benefit, teachers who experience the same events virtually, expand the pool of educators with whom they can interact.

Lighthouse Learning Island is one example of a community committed to the professional development of educators. Lighthouse, which is a collaborative effort of four school districts in Massachusetts, has purchased their own virtual island and is training their teachers how to use SL through professional development workshops in-world. The team's longer-term goal is to bring students into the SL Teen Grid (reserved for those under 18) and teach them the curriculum virtually (Schrock, n.d.). This collaborative tool will be an excellent case study regarding how much more effective the learning experience will be for everyone concerned if the teachers meet the students on their terms, using technology and online learning objectives that motivate the students to achieve and excel.

For the military also, well noted as being early adopters of virtual worlds for training and professional development, there are many opportunities to leverage the background of technology-savvy individuals. For example, today's soldiers are digital natives (Cabanero-Johnson & Berge, 2009) who are very comfortable with multi-tasking, social networking, and gaming tools. Soldiers who play games like *Full Spectrum Warrior*, *Call of Duty*, *Medal of Honor*, or *Halo 2*, are already experienced with first-person shooter games and immersive gaming experiences and will continue to achieve performance

improvement through training using digital simulations. In fact, they see using virtual worlds to accomplish military training as a natural and necessary progression (Vargas, 2006).

Additionally, for the military, an inevitable outcome of war is the undeniable need to provide for war veterans. Groups such as the Disabled American Veterans have established support groups in SL (Au, 2009). In addition, in an effort to respond to the presence of very real post-service adjustment challenges, military organizations are establishing a private world within SL to provide a "healing space" for veterans. This space is designed to meet a variety of accessibility challenges such as being geographically dispersed, perhaps physically disabled, and to circumvent the stigma associated with seeking mental health assistance. Morie (2009) notes that recent studies indicate soldiers take six months or more to report mental health issues post-deployment. The limited-access "healing space" in SL provides veterans access to a Complementary and Alternative Medicine area (meditation, breathing exercises, positive visualization, etc), a Resource area (links to outside services and additional information, guidance for

Figure 3. The lighthouse is a central focal point on Lighthouse Learning Island, which is divided into six areas: one for each of the four Massachusetts school districts, a sand box for development, and a common area for meetings and collaboration.

recommended therapies based on need, etc), and a Social Center for game-playing and group social gatherings. The most ringing endorsement of all for this application of SL is the fact that motivation for success stems from the desire to help vets. The technology is not the highlight, the results are.

For corporate use, virtual worlds expand the possibilities well beyond what corporate training was able to provide prior to the existence of VWs (New England Business Bulletin, 2009). Because private conversations and group conversations can occur simultaneously, communication is enhanced and matches the desired pace of both the individual participants and the group. Documents can be shared and collaboration is further encouraged to foster innovation and creativity. Additionally, Companies such as IBM are starting to provide case study statistics indicating that virtual meetings and conferences are being conducted at a significant savings over the same event held in the physical world (Virtual World News, 2009b). Virtual worlds are becoming increasingly integrated into the workplace and based on our research, we can only expect that trend to grow in the future.

THE GROWTH OF SECOND LIFE

A discussion about the future of emerging technologies should include a trend analysis. Tom Werner (2009), a Brandon Hall researcher, recently presented a graphical representation of an Acceptance Curve, the process by which new technological ideas are accepted into the mainstream.

Emerging technologies are generally subject to a curve of acceptance that begins with the introduction of the new technology, creative brainstorming by early adopters leading into inflated hype about what the product can do, the leveling off of the hype as the technology is adopted into the mainstream, evaluating and altering the adoptive techniques as needed, and finally the arrival of benchmarking and industry standards for the use of the technology.

According to Werner, SL and the use of virtual worlds in the workplace is just coming down from the hype bubble and entering into the early adoption phase (see Figure 4). Thus, some early adopters have moved further along in the curve and are developing and expanding virtual worlds with appropriate functions, while others have abandoned SL believing that they were victims of the hype and that the product did not deliver. Stevens and Pettey (2008) quote Gartner indicating "90 percent of corporate virtual world projects fail within 18 months" (p. 1). It is important to note that there are many possible explanations why a SL project may have failed. Focusing on the technology rather than on the users and the necessary content to make it a meaningful learning experience is one common error; another is the lack of a strategic plan outlining appropriate goals. Driven to match what competitors are doing, it is all too easy to implement a project without clear goals or objectives and a limited understanding of the composition and demands of virtual world communities and their residents.

The hype around digital virtuality over the past decade has been more about myth and less about cyberspace... Symptoms of virtualism include exaggerated expectations of anything described as 'virtual', and unrealistic expectations that digital technologies will solve social problems. (Shields, 2003)

Companies with interest in the field say that "virtual worlds [are] on the cusp of a major expansion" and are something to which people should be paying very close attention (Thomas, 2008, p. 1). Corporate experts have suggested that "virtual worlds provide a clean slate for organizational renewal, a transition from the rigid structures and boundaries of the industrial (physical) world to the flexibility and innovation of the knowledge (intangible) world" (Cross, O'Driscoll, & Trondsen, 2007, p. 1). These experts also suggest that SL, which is not the only virtual world in existence, may not be the proper fit for a particular organization; careful research is needed to choose the option which will adequately meet the corporation's needs.

SL remains the "virtual world of choice" for academia, particularly in the UK, where it is being used "in a very wide range of teaching and learning activities"[3] (Kirriemuir, 2009, p. 2). In fact, Kirriemuir (2009) notes that there has been a significant increase in SL use in the last two years. Factors contributing to this trend include that it has become "more academically acceptable" at the same time that improved technology makes it easier to access and funding has become easier to obtain. In May 2009, Texas State Technical College granted a certificate in digital media to the first-known student ever to graduate from an institution of higher learning based on classes taken entirely in a virtual environment (TSTC, 2009).

There are very good business reasons to explore and use more than one delivery platform simultaneously. Corporate use of public grid areas on SL servers are best used to provide outreach to a general audience, as in the case of NOAA noted earlier. People who might not otherwise know who NOAA is can now take a few self-directed minutes and gain insight into the mission and objectives of an organization they previously knew nothing about. Corporate use of public grids with private access on SL servers is traditionally used for employee training, collaboration between employees and perhaps even interfacing with clients and customers. Xerox provides an area in SL for their Research and Development team as does Intel who also provides advertising and market-testing of digital replicas of products. Closed grids not accessible to the general public are very much in vogue. Linden Lab is developing a proprietary stand-alone version of SL, which corporations can implement on their own corporate servers. This version is still being tested by several corporations, including IBM, who wish to reap the benefits of a virtual environment from behind their own firewall.

Another creative and cost effective use for a private grid is virtual prototype testing. Rather than building several physical prototypes representative of the product (at a cost) and making

Figure 4. The Adopter's Dilemma: the arrow indicates that SL is just entering the early adoption phase

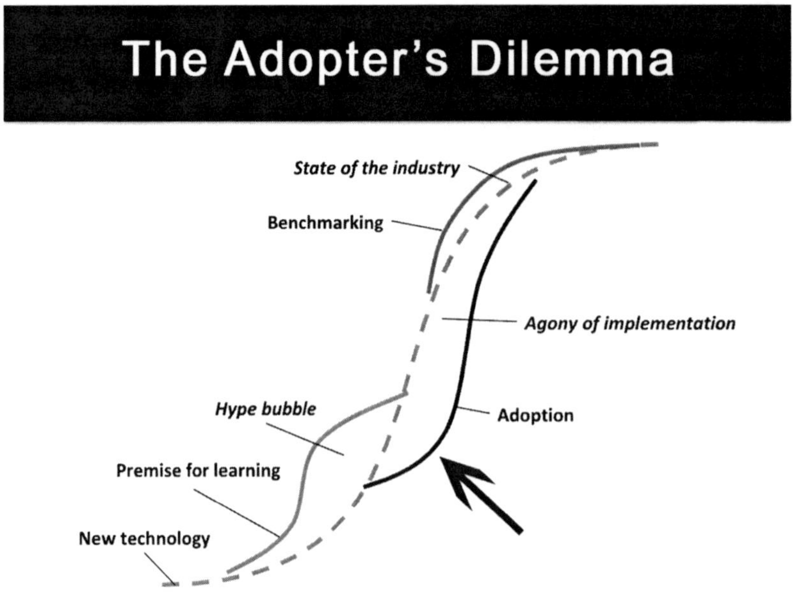

evolutionary changes along the way that require a rebuild of each version of the prototype, corporations can create a virtual prototype, allow it to evolve electronically, and then produce a better physical prototype later in the development cycle (Stackpole, 2008). Deere & Co. is using this process to develop a cotton picker that handles an increased volume of cotton without increasing horsepower.

Even SL is getting into the act: in May 2009, Case Western University announced a new venture as it became the first to "host a private, stand-alone version of SL behind its firewall" (Parry, 2009).

BEYOND SECOND LIFE

SL is, however, far from the only MUVE in town. Project Wonderland, developed by Sun Microsystems Laboratories in conjunction with the open-source community, is a completely extensible toolkit, based on Java, for creating collaborative 3D virtual worlds; it is "robust enough in terms of security, scalability, reliability, and functionality that organizations can rely on it as a place to conduct real business" (Project Wonderland, n.d.). Sun has used Project Wonderland to create MPK20, a virtual recreation of Sun's Menlo Park campus, which allows employees to "accomplish their real work, share documents, and meet with colleagues" in a virtual environment (MPK20, n.d.).

Another promising new technology is Caspian Learning's Serious Games authoring platform, Thinking Worlds, which provides a "drag and drop" capability to create simulations with custom assets, people, models, etc. "This thing was so easy to use, that in the UK tens of thousands of school children (8+) started using it virally to make their own games" (SLED/Partridge, 2009b).

IBM recently announced a new "3D conferencing product," Virtual Collaboration for Lotus Sametime. Universities as well as the aerospace and defense industries are pilot users (Virtual World News, 2009a). The U.S. military is using virtual worlds for training not only on the internet but also on a classified network known as SIPRnet (Wilson, 2008). In fact, O'Brien (2005) points out that "Many [virtual world design] contractors have so much work from the Army and the Marines, they have to turn new clients away". The Army is currently creating a new organization which will develop a simulation toolkit, scheduled for deployment between 2010 and 2015, that "allows end users to build and customized [sic] their own training scenarios without needing a contractor to do it for them" (Wilson, 2008, p. 5).

As mentioned earlier, closed grids on private servers are being examined with increasing interest because they can be built behind firewalls for greater privacy and security. In such cases, it becomes possible to utilize real names to facilitate identity verification, further enhancing security. Universities, for example, envision such systems as providing more control over which students are engaging in learning activities (and ensuring that only registered, paid students are doing so) (IBM, 2009). Case Western University, for example, intends to mix adults and children on its closed grid, something not easily possible in the commercial SL; with this tool, the campus Hispanic club will be able to provide mentors to Cleveland public-school students (Parry, 2009). On the other hand, corporations may shy away from SL in search of something more, well, corporate: a participant in a pilot using Forterra's Online Interactive Virtual Environment (OLIVE) noted that "A lot of what I've seen with SL feels very 'out there.' ... [OLIVE] was business-oriented and real for people" (Badger, 2008, p. 14).

THE FUTURE OF SL AND OTHER MUVES

That the popularity of MUVEs will continue to expand is clear; Gartner (2007, quoted in Salmon, 2009) predicted that "by the end of 2011, 80% of all active Internet users [will] have an avatar and

[will] be registered in one or more virtual worlds" (p. 528). What will those virtual worlds look like, and how will they provide more conducive spaces for learning? One trend is certainly the integration of the 3D features of virtual worlds with those of 2D applications; for example, document creation and collaboration, whether through traditional word processing software or social networking tools such as wikis and blogs.

In particular, educators, whether in academia, government, or corporate settings, are very interested in bringing the capabilities of 2D learning management systems (LMS) to bear on the 3D environment; SLOODLE is the most commonly cited application. Kemp (2009) notes that it provides features such as identity management, linking SL and Moodle for avatar registration; text chat support and integration; and archiving and retrieval of chat sessions. Other features include "blogging for reflection" (also known as taking notes) (Kemp, Livingstone, & Bloomfield, 2009, p. 553) and assessment tools such as quizzes and drop-boxes. Thinking Worlds, mentioned above, is designed with an integrated LMS and "even offers [a] SCORM compliant database" (SLED/ Partridge, 2009b).

Badger (2008) points out a number of significant lessons based on a pilot project on the use of MUVEs, conducted in collaboration with the Masie Center's Learning Consortium.[4] One of the most important lessons is the necessity of securing support from a corporation's IT department. Although eight companies were initially involved in the project, six dropped out, mostly because they could not get backing from their IT departments (Badger, 2008). Badger's recipe for success in establishing a corporate training venture in MUVEs contains the following ingredients:

- Define your use case
- Consider your team members and skills as they relate to the implementation
- Use the crawl-walk-run approach
- Get tutorials and training

- Keep an open mind in creating the prototype
- Pilot with affected users
- Conduct frequent post mortems (Badger, 2008, p. 18)

CONCLUSION

To truly understand the power and opportunities inherent in virtual worlds, most experts recommend that it is necessary to get into SL and experience it to determine if the virtual environment is a good fit for organizational strategies (Thomas, 2008). Adopting an emerging trend such as this without careful consideration of the many aspects outlined in this paper is done so "at [your] own peril" (Thomas, 2008). Follow the already tested and documented best practices and guidelines for distance education. Watch what others are doing and learn from their mistakes. Only then can a determination be made regarding a MUVE's appropriateness to meet the needs of an organization and the human capital that supports it.

REFERENCES

Addison, A., & O'Hare, L. (2008). How can massive multi-user virtual environments and virtual role play enhance traditional teaching practice? *Proceedings from Researching Learning in Virtual Environments International Conference (reLIVE 08)*, November 20-21. The Open University, UK. Retrieved from http://www.open.ac.uk/relive08/documents/ReLIVE08_conference_proceedings.pdf

Antonacci, D., & Modaress, N. (2005). Second Life: The educational possibilities of a massively multiplayer virtual world (MMVW). *Proceedings from EDUCAUSE Southwest Regional Conference*. February 16: Austin, Texas. Retrieved from http://net.educause.edu/ir/library/pdf/WRC0541.pdf

Arreguin, C. (2007). *Reports from the field:* Second Life *community convention 2007 education track summary.* New York: Global Kids, Inc. Retrieved from http://www.holymeatballs.org/pdfs/Virtual-WorldsforLearningRoadmap_012008.pdf

Au, W. J. (2009, March 23). *For Some Combat Veterans, Second Life Used For PTSD Therapy "Working when nothing else has"*, Ret. Lt. Col. Says. Message posted to http://nwn.blogs.com/nwn/2009/03/posttraumatic-stress.html

Badger, C. (2008). *Recipe for Success with Enterprise Virtual Worlds.* Retrieved from http://www.forterrainc.com/images/stories/pdf/recipe_for_success_10509.pdf

Cabanero-Johnson, C., & Berge, Z. (2009). Digital natives: back to the future of microworlds in a corporate learning organization. *The Learning Organization, 16*(4), 290–297. doi:10.1108/09696470910960383

Carr, D., Oliver, M., & Burn, A. (2008). Learning, teaching, and ambiguity in virtual worlds. *Proceedings from reLIVE 08: Proceedings of Researching Learning in Virtual Environments International Conference, 20-21 November 2008.* The Open University, UK. Retrieved from http://www.open.ac.uk/relive08/ documents/ReLIVE08_conference_proceedings.pdf

Cross, J., O'Driscoll, T., & Trondsen, E. (2007, March 22). Another life: Virtual worlds as tools for learning. *eLearn Magazine.* Retrieved from http://www.elearnmag.org/subpage.cfm?section=articles&article=44-1

Gao, F., Noh, J., & Koehler, M. (2008). *"Comparing Student Interactions in Second Life and Face-to-Face Role-playing Activities"*. In K. McFerrin et al. (Eds.), Proceedings of Society for Information Technology and Teacher Education International Conference pp. 2033-2035. Chesapeake, VA: AACE.

Gerald, S. & Antonacci, D. (2009). Virtual world learning spaces: developing a Second Life operating room simulation. *Educause Quarterly, 32*(1). Retrieved from http://www.educause.edu/EQ/EDUCAUSEQuarterlyMagazineVolum /VirtualWorldLearningSpacesDeve/163851

Graham, C. R. in Bonk, C. J. & Graham, C. R. (Eds.). (2006). Blended Learning Systems: Definition, Current Trends, and Future Directions. *Handbook of blended learning: Global Perspectives, local designs.* San Francisco, CA: Pfeiffer Publishing. Retrieved from http://www.publicationshare.com/graham_intro.pdf

Haymes, T. (2008). The three-e strategy for overcoming resistance to technological change. *Educause Quarterly.* Retrieved from http://net.educause.edu/ir/library/pdf/EQM08411.pdf

Heinrichs, L., Youngblood, P., Harter, P., & Dev, P. (2008). Simulation for team training and assessment: case studies of online training with virtual worlds. *World Journal of Surgery, 32*, 161–170. doi:10.1007/s00268-007-9354-2

Horrigan, J. B. (2007, May 7). *A typology of information and communication technology users.* Pew Internet & American Life Project. p. ii. Retrieved from http://www.pewinternet.org/~/media//Files/Reports/2007/PIP_ICT_Typology.pdf.pdf

IBM. (n.d.). *Virtual World Guidelines.* Retrieved from http://domino.research.ibm.com/comm/research_projects.nsf/pages/virtualworlds. IBM-VirtualWorldGuidelines.html

Irwin, C., & Berge, Z. (2006, March). Socialization in the online classroom. *e-Journal of Instructional Science and Technology, 9*(1). Retrieved from http://www.usq.edu.au/electpub/e-jist/docs/vol9_no1/papers/full_papers/irwin_berge.htm

joeeisner. (2009, May 13). *Bang for your online buck: Facebook vs. Second Life.* Message posted to https://forums.genesyslab.com/showthread.php?t=430

Kalning, K. (2007) *If Second Life isn't a game, what is it? MSNBC*. Retrieved from http://www.msnbc.msn.com/id/17538999/

Kemp, J., Livingstone, D., & Bloomfield, P. (2009, May). SLOODLE: Connecting VLE tools with emergent teaching practice in Second Life. [Retrieved from Academic Search Premiere Database.]. *British Journal of Educational Technology, 40*(3), 551–555. doi:10.1111/j.1467-8535.2009.00938.x

Kirriemuir, J. (2009). *Early summer 2009 Virtual World Watch snapshot of virtual world activity in UK HE and FE*. Eduserv.org.uk. Retrieved from http://virtualworldwatch.net/ wordpress/wp-content/uploads/2009/06/ snapshot-six.pdf

Lagorio, C. (2007, January 7) The Ultimate Distance Learning. *The New York Times*. Retrieved from http://www.nytimes.com/2007/01/07/education/edlife/07innovation.html

Locklee, B., Moore, M., & Burton, J. (2002). Measuring Success: Evaluation Strategies for Distance Education. *EDUCAUSE Quarterly, 1*, 20–26.

Massey, A. P., Montoya-Weiss, M. M., & O'Driscoll, T. M. (2005). Human Performance Technology and Knowledge Management: A Case Study. *Performance Improvement Quarterly, 18*(2), 37–55.

Mertens, S. B., & Flowers, N. (2004). Research summary: Professional development for teachers. *National Middle School Association*. Retrieved from http://www.nmsa.org/ Research/Research-Summaries/ Summary22/tabid/249/Default.aspx

Messinger, P., Stroulia, E., & Lyons, K. (2008). A Typology of Virtual Worlds: Historical Overview and Future Directions. *Journal of Virtual Worlds Research, 1*(1). Retrieved from http://journals.tdl.org/jvwr/article/view/291.

Miner, N., & Hofmann, J. (2009) It's [Not] The Technology Stupid. *American Society for Training and Development*. Retrieved from http://www.astd.org/lc/2009/0309_hofmann.html

Minocha, S., & Tingle, R. (2008). Socialisation and Collaborative Learning of Distance learners in 3-D Virtual Worlds. *Proceedings from Researching Learning in Virtual Environments International Conference (reLIVE 08)*, November 20-21. The Open University, UK. Retrieved from http://www.open.ac.uk/relive08/documents/ReLIVE08_conference_proceedings.pdf

Montoya, M., Massey, A., & Ketter, P. (moderator). (Recorded February 3, 2009). *Virtual Presence in Virtual Worlds. What it Means for Online Training* [webinar]. Retrieved from https://astdevents.webex.com/ec0605l/ event-center/recording/recordAction.do?siteurl= astdevents&theAction=archive

Moore, M. G., & Kearsley, G. (2005). *Distance Education: A Systems View* (2nd ed.). Belmont, CA: Wadsworth.

Morie, J. F. (2009, January 22). Re-Entry: Online virtual worlds as a healing space for veterans. *Proceedings of the Society for Photo-Instrumentation Engineers, 7238*,http://ict.usc.edu/files/publications/Morie-2009-2SPIE-FINAL.pdf.

MPK20. Sun's virtual workspace. Retrieved from http://research.sun.com/projects/mc/mpk20.html

Neal, L. (Interviewer) & Dublin, L. (Interviewee). Five Questions. . . for Lance Dublin. (2006). *eLearn Magazine* [Interview Transcript]. Retrieved from http://elearnmag.org/subpage.cfm?section= articles&article=41-1

New England Business Bulletin. (2009, May 22). *New Corporate training options include virtual worlds*. Retrieved from http://www.southcoasttoday.com /apps/pbcs.dll/article?AID=/ 20090522/NEBULLETIN/906010309

O'Brien, L. (2005). The game advances in ultrar-ealistic simulation let soldiers experience the war in Iraq—before they go. *SF Weekly.* Retrieved from http://www.forterrainc.com/index.php/resources/white-papers-a-articles/70-asymmetric-warfare

Parry, M. (2009). Case Western Reserve U. Debuts Private Version of Second Life. *The Chronicle of Higher Education.* Retrieved from http://chronicle.com/wiredcampus/ article/3758/case-western-debuts- private-version-of-second-life

Project Wonderland. Toolkit for Building 3D Virtual Worlds. Retrieved from http://developers.sun.com/learning/javaoneonline/2008/pdf/TS-6125.pdf

Ryan, M. (2008). 16 ways to use virtual worlds in your classroom: pedagogical applications of Second Life. *Proceedings from Researching Learning in Virtual Environments International Conference (reLIVE 08)*, November 20-21. The Open University, UK. Retrieved from http://www.open.ac.uk/relive08/documents/ ReLIVE08_conference_proceedings.pdf

Salmon, G. (2009, May). The future for (second) life and learning. *British Journal of Educational Technology*, *40*(3), 526–538. doi:10.1111/j.1467-8535.2009.00967.x

Schrock, K. (No Date). Message posted to http://www.hotchalk.com/mydesk/index. php/editorial/44-online-professional-development/86-second-life-interactive-professional-development-pt-1

Science Daily. (2008, October 31). *Researchers Find New Way of Measuring 'Reality' of Virtual Worlds.* Retrieved from http://www.sciencedaily.com/releases/2008/10/081029084038.htm

Second Life website. (2009). [Data illustrates current Economic Statistics (Raw Data Files)]. Retrieved from http://secondlife.com/statistics/economy-data.php

Shields, R. (2003). *The Virtual.* London: Routledge.

SLED. (Second Life Educators electronic mailing list), archived at http://tinyurl.com/y234ht

SLED/ Partridge, W. (2009b, April 6). Thinking worlds—immersive learning simulations via Shockwave.

SLED/Freese, W. (2009, March 13). Teaching Early Childhood Education.

SLED/Holt. D. (2009, February 23). Re: Playing Devil's Advocate: SL vs Virtual Worlds vs Better Learning: Second Life Educators electronic mailing list), archived at http://tinyurl.com/y234ht

SLED/Loon. R. (2009a, February 26). Re: Playing Devil's Advocate: SL vs Virtual Worlds vs Better Learning. Second Life Educators electronic mailing list), archived at http://tinyurl.com/y234ht

SLED/Loon. R. (2009b, March 17). *Re: the meandering thoughts of a girl who has gone to the dogs, darkside of the moon, and been a lion all before lunch. . . Second Life Educators electronic mailing list*), archived at http://tinyurl.com/y234ht

SLED/Partridge, W. (2009a, March 30). audiences in sl, was Re: Opinion—Text or voice?

SLED/Tadros. M. (2009, March 31). Re: Ouch – story from the UK Telegraph. Second Life Educators electronic mailing list), archived at http://tinyurl.com/y234ht

Stackpole, B. (2008, January 6). Military broadens use of virtual reality. *Design News.* Retrieved from http://www.designnews.com/article/ 7775-Military_ Broadens_Use_of_ Virtual_Reality.php

Stevens, H., & Pettey, C. (2008, May 15). Gartner Says 90 Per Cent of Corporate Virtual World Projects Fail Within 18 Months. *Gartner.* Retrieved from http://www.gartner.com/it/page.jsp?id=670507

Thomas, L. P. (2008). There's still a future for virtual worlds. *Media Bullseye*. Retrieved from http://mediabullseye.com/mb/2008/05/theres-still-a-future-for-virt.html

TSTC takes one small step for virtual worlds, one giant leap for virtual world education. (2009). *PRWeb*. Retrieved from http://www.prweb.com/releases/TSTC/virtual_education/prweb2419874.htm

Vargas, J. A. (2006, February 14). Virtual Reality Prepares Soldiers for Real War. *The Washington Post*. Retrieved from http://www.washingtonpost.com/wp-dyn/content/article /2006/02/13/AR2006021302437.html

Virtual World News. (2009b, February 27). *IBM Saves $320,000 With Second Life Meeting*. Retrieved from http://www.virtualworldsnews.com/2009/02/ibm -saves-320000-with- second-life-meeting.html

Virtual World News. (2009a, June 26). IBM Releases Virtual Collaboration for Lotus Sametime. Retrieved from http://www.virtualworldsnews.com/2009/06/ibm-releases-virtual-collaboration-for-lotus-sametime.html

WebProNews. (2009, March 16). Retrieved from http://www.webpronews.com/topnews /2009/03/16/second-life-still- alive-and-kicking

Werner, T. (2008a). *Travels with Tom*. Retrieved from http://www.slideshare.net/twerner/travels-with-tom-workplacerelated-places-in-second-life-presentation

Werner, T. (2008b, July 10). *Canadian border-guard training in Second Life*. Message posted to http://brandon-hall.com/tomwerner/?p=338

Werner, T. (2009, March 29). Using Second Life for workplace learning. *Brandon Hall Research Presentation*. Retrieved from http://www.slideshare.net/twerner/using- second-life-for- workplace-learning- 032509?type=powerpoint

What does it cost to use a virtual world learning environment? (2008, November). *T+D*, p. 88.

Wilson, C. (2008). Avatars, Virtual Reality Technology, and the U.S. Military: Emerging Policy Issues. *CRS Report for Congress*. Retrieved from http://fas.org/sgp/crs/natsec/RS22857.pdf

Worldwide Advertising, T. M. P., & Communications, L. L. C. (2007, February 12). TMP Worldwide Brings Recruitment To Second Life [Press Release]. Retrieved from http://www.tmp.com/articles/press_00004.html

Young, J. R. (2002, March 22). 'Hybrid' Teaching Seeks to End the Divide Between Traditional and Online Instruction. [Retrieved from Academic Search Premier Database.]. *The Chronicle of Higher Education*, 48(28), A33.

KEY TERMS AND DEFINITIONS

Avatar: A computer user's electronic representation of the self; the online persona of the individual user.

Blackboard: A web-based course management system.

Closed Grid: The architecture system within Second Life that is closed to the general public and only available to those with designated access.

Java: Developed by Sun Microsystems, Java is a computer language that extends the functionality of a typically static web browser to a variety of interactive functions.

Moodle/Angel: A free and open source Learning Management System.

MUVE: Multi-User Virtual Environments (another term for virtual worlds).

Open Grid: The architecture system within Second Life that is considered open to anyone who wishes to participate.

RL: Real Life

SCORM: Shared Content Object Reference Model is a technical model that distinguishes how online learning is designed and delivered.

Second Life: A virtual world create by Linden Lab in 2003.

SLED: The Second Life Educators list

SLOODLE: A free- plug-in for Second Life that combines and integrates the benefits of Moodle and Second Life. This product links avatar performance in Second Life to a learning management system allowing trackable performance goals and objectives.

Social Networking: The grouping of individuals into a collective unit for the purposes of socializing, developing relationships and sharing common interests

WOW (World of Warcraft): A very popular online multi-player role-playing game

ENDNOTES

[1] Stating how many *Second* Life users there are is not as easy as it may sound. Generally, readers will think of a "user" as a unique individual. In SL, many individuals have created more than one avatar. A "resident" is SL terminology for an avatar. Separately, while there are an average of 60,000 avatars in-world each day, it is easy to think that they may not be the same 60,000 avatars as were there the day before or the same that will be there tomorrow.

[2] Some recent examples of items offered to others on the SLED list include an Audio Content Delivery System; the use of land for testing and experimenting; a "simulated discussion group to help train group leaders and members" in which fake avatars respond based on scripts (SLED/Nor ris, 3/30/09); and various scripts and objects. Also, a number of locations for educators offer items such as free presentation tools, professional clothing, etc.

[3] The list includes Open University, Edinburgh, Coventry, Lancaster, Teesside, Southampton Solent, and Glasgow Caledonian (Kirriemuir, 2009).

[4] The MASIE Center, founded by Eliot Masie, is a "think-tank focused on how organizations can support learning and knowledge within the work force." The Learning Consortium is a "coalition of 240 Fortune 500 companies cooperating on the evolution of learning strategies" (Badger, 2008, p. 7).

Section 2
Immersive Learning Strategies

Chapter 3

Practice What You Preach:
Experiences with Teaching Virtual World Concepts in a Virtual World

Laura Benvenuti
Dutch Open University, The Netherlands

Gerrit C. van der Veer
Dutch Open University, The Netherlands

ABSTRACT

This chapter is not on the technology of Virtual Worlds. The authors discuss the application of a Virtual World as a teaching and learning environment for a course on Virtual Worlds. In their view, innovation and education should go hand in hand. Too often, new technologies are discussed without being applied. The authors argue that innovative technologies do belong in those classroom where their application is relevant to the topic. In thischapter, the authors discuss an example of how this issue can be tackled. They show that application of innovative tools is useful to all parties: students, lecturers and researchers, even if it raises new problems from which we all can learn.

INTRODUCTION

The Digital Communication curriculum of the Hogeschool Utrecht has, as one of its courses, a course on Virtual Worlds. As a strategic choice, the lecturers decided to rely on the same technology for the implementation of a learning and teaching environment.

New technologies in classroom offer opportunities for innovation. They also change the way students experience education. This can be challenging for educators who are confronted

with unexpected situations. But use also promotes understanding. Through an assignment in a virtual world the students would gain more familiarity with the technology. The lecturers would get better acquainted with de didactic possibilities of the medium.

In this paper we share our observations from practice. We focus on the educational possibilities of virtual worlds with no preset narrative by describing the Virtual Worlds course, which partially took place in an Active Worlds environment. We discuss the advantages of moving part of the action to a virtual setting, but also point at its limitations. We describe some problems that

DOI: 10.4018/978-1-61692-825-4.ch003

were raised by the medium and offer strategies to deal with them.

We show how to improve our understanding of new media and technology by combining education with research. In particular we measured the students' experienced "connectedness" and "learning" in the time span of the course.

A VIRTUAL VILLAGE AS A COMMUNITY OF LEARNERS

Virtual worlds with no preset narrative, such as Active Worlds or Second Life, are considered usable asset in education (Livingstone and Kemp 2006). The implementation of the learning environment in a virtual world is not necessarily successful.

The "Virtual Worlds" course of the Digital Communication curriculum of the Hogeschool Utrecht (University of Applied Science, Utrecht, the Netherlands) combines traditional instructional methods (classroom setting) with a collective practical assignment in an Active Worlds world. Starting with the spring of 2008, the students are asked to build an application, consisting of 3D-model of a house and its surroundings, and to place it in a common village situated in an Active Worlds environment. Figure 1, as well as Figure 4 and 5, show examples of students' work during the courses we analyzed.

The complementary approach of the Virtual Worlds course works very well: collaboration continues naturally in both worlds, virtual and real (Benvenuti et. al, 2008). The spring 2008 edition of the course was very successful. The relation between the courses subject and the applied technology was a powerful combination. Other success factors might be the choice for an immersive collaborative structure, or the village metaphor.

The question whether a virtual village is an appropriate tool to support a community of learners is not one-dimensional. Sense of community is a subjective concept. Some students consider participating in a community equivalent to sharing results with colleagues, others expect the results to be produced together.

The same applies to learning: the students who pass an exam frequently don't agree on what they have learned, nor on its significance. In 2008, we had investigated the students' opinion about the way the course was taught and about their own attitude. Though the answers were obviously positive – the students stated having found themselves involved and participating in the learning community - we noticed a large variety of opinions

Figure 1. the spring 2008 Asterix village: house of the bard and surroundings

on the usefulness and instructiveness of the collaboration in the virtual world.

With the introduction of the assignment in a common virtual world, the course's results had increased beyond the lecturers' expectations. In their opinion, this was due to the fact that the students had been able to learn from each other more than in the previous editions of the course. The students themselves seemed more cautious in sharing that conclusion.

In 2009, we had again the opportunity to perform measurements in the spring edition of the Virtual Worlds course. We decided to focus on the two issues mentioned above: experienced community membership and experienced learning.

MEASURING EXPERIENCED CONNECTEDNESS AND LEARNING

In our view, experience is not an isolated phenomenon, but a process in time, in which individuals interact with situations. During this process interpretation takes place: individual meaning is constructed. Therefore we consider experience a subjective and constructive phenomenon. Measuring experience should include assessment at three moments in time: the respondent's expectations before the experience, their assessment during the experience and afterwards (Vyas & van der Veer, 2006).

Vyas and van der Veer (2006) developed several strategies to assess the respondent's interpretation of the situation at different moments in time. Basically, they interview the respondents prior to the experience and afterwards. The assessment of the "living through" is done by observing the respondents who perform tasks while they talk aloud. This was not possible in a classroom setting, so we decided to assess the students' subjective impressions by conducting the same written survey at three moments in time.

A reliable tool for measuring subjective impressions is the Visual Analogue Scale. Visual

Analogue Scales or VAS scales are used in the medical world for subjective magnitude estimation, mainly for pain rating. They consist of straight lines of 10.0 cm long, whose limits carry verbal descriptions of the extremes of what is being evaluated. Because the interval between the limits does not carry any verbal label, the exact location of the value that respondents mark will not be remembered, so with repeated measurements it is impossible that respondents just repeat their previous scores. VAS scales are of value when looking at changes in time within individuals (Langley & Sheppeard, 1985).

The impressions we were interested in are the student's sense of belonging to a community and the extent to which student's learning goals are met. The Classroom Community Scale or CCS (Rovai, 2002) was a good starting point. The CCS is a psychometric scale, developed using factor analysis with 2 principal components: Connectedness and Learning. Connectedness indicates the perceived cohesion, spirit, trust and interdependence between members of the classroom community. Learning represents their feelings regarding interaction with each other as they pursue the construction of understanding. Learning also indicates the degree to which they share values and beliefs concerning the extent to which their educational goals and expectations are being satisfied.

Our variant of the Classroom Community Scale applied VAS-scales instead of Likert scales because this prohibits memory of previous scores when applied to repeated measures.

THE ASTERIX VILLAGE

The "Virtual Worlds"- course (3rd year in the curriculum) takes seven weeks. The course's goal is to teach students to think about virtual worlds in a conceptual way. The students should learn to establish when it is appropriate to make an application in a virtual world. Virtual worlds are powerful instruments, but developing a VR application can be very expensive. Sometimes a less demanding solution is better.

Half of the course is dedicated to theory, the other half is practical. Theory is assessed individually, with a written test. The course has two related practical assignments; in the laboratory the students work in pairs.

The course starts with an introduction to virtual worlds. Design concepts within virtual worlds are discussed. In this part, students develop a VR model of a house and its environment in 3D Studio Max. In order to stimulate relations between individual designs, the lecturers introduced a common theme. In 2008 and 2009 the common theme was "Asterix".

In the second part, theory focuses at the future of virtual worlds when artificial intelligence and photorealistic rendering increases. Students are also stimulated to find best practices. The focus switches to the second practical assignment which takes place in a shared Active Worlds context, the Asterix village. Active Worlds has no preset narrative; this triggers students to develop and implement interaction concepts individually as well as to develop these collaboratively for the entire village. The setting –a village– was chosen consciously, to obtain a common structure.

In the final weeks students reflect on the benefits of virtual worlds and of virtual worlds in cross-media concepts. At the end of the course students present their work in a plenary classroom meeting. Discussion and assessment of the practicum assignment also takes place in that meeting.

WHAT'S NEW, WHAT'S NEXT?

The spring 2008-edition of the Virtual Worlds-course was not the first one. The upper part of the course outline in Figure 2 also applies to previous editions, but those courses only had one practicum assignment: design and develop a new VR-concept. In 2008, the assignment in the shared virtual world was added. Nothing else changed. The teaching timetables remained unaltered. The class meets twice a week in the multimedia laboratory. Meetings last 2 hours. The first hour is dedicated to theory, during the rest of the time the students work on their assignments, in pairs. Students are – and always were - stimulated to ask questions to the lecturers and to ach other. Students are – and always were - stimulated to learn from each other.

Until the spring of 2008, students mainly exchanged information during laboratory time. If the lecturers were busy and a student had a well-defined question, it came naturally to ask other students. With the introduction of the assignment in the Active World world this pattern changed. Now students also "met" while working in the virtual world from home, in the evening or at night. As we can see in Figure 3, Active Worlds has a chat box. Communication comes easily. The

Figure 2. General course outline

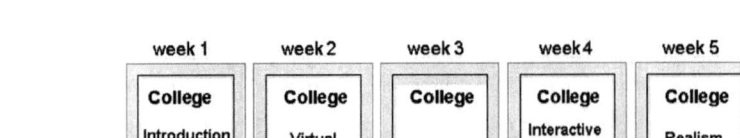

Figure 3. Active Worlds: the students' perspective with the chat box

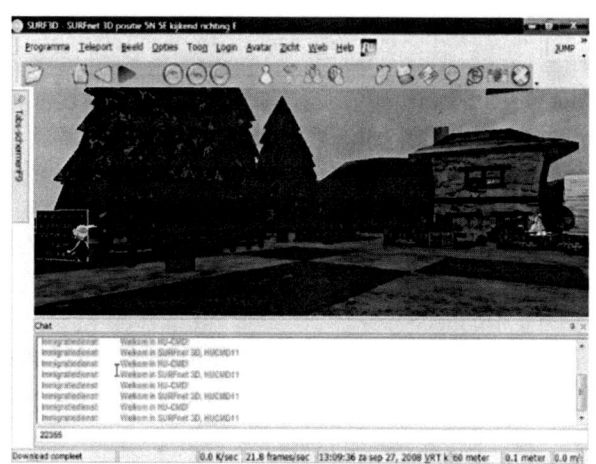

first improvement which came with Active Worlds lays in the increased possibilities for students to discuss issues while they are working, and to support each other on the spot without face to face contact.

This is a powerful feature. In the first edition of the Virtual Worlds-course in Active Worlds, implementing 3DS Max models into Active Worlds was challenging, since good tutorials had not been written yet. But the students succeeded to import their 3D-applications relatively fast by working as a group: one of them was very skilled in 3D developing and shared his knowledge generously. In the next editions of the course, the group had tutorials but lacked the experienced colleague. Technical problems seemed more difficult to overcome in that situation. In the spring of 2009, the lecturers added an extra meeting and invited an expert in 3DS Max and Active World to answer to the students' questions.

The second improvement concerns the possibility to follow each others' progresses. Before the introduction of the common virtual village, students only discussed each others' work thoroughly during the conclusive meeting. These discussions always concerned the final versions of the products. While working in Active Worlds, students can follow the process of creation of all products. Every prototype is published and is visible for everybody. This triggers a fertile competition between the students: everybody wants his application to excel.

Figure 4. The Spring 2008 Asterix village with the smoking chimneys

Software can be copied. The participants in the virtual village work in an open source environment: they can see and even copy parts of other students' work. This is very instructive and inspiring but also challenging. In 2008, one student had created animated smoke; a few days later most of the huts in the village had smoking chimneys (see Figure 4). This was disappointing for the student who had invested time in developing what he thought would be a unique feature. He felt robbed.

The lecturers wanted to encourage the students to share results, but they also wanted to grant the credits for interesting ideas to the right persons. An appropriate assessment policy had to be developed. 'Intellectual property" was discussed in classroom and a citation index was established. From that moment, copycat behaviour was not seen as "steeling" anymore but as a tribute to the conceiver of the particular feature.

The third improvement lies in the possibilities to share results, to learn and copy from each other.

Of course, the question was risen if it was appropriate to skip the traditional meetings and move the whole course to the virtual environment. The answer is negative. The traditional classroom setting offers opportunities to plenary discussion. This is difficulty to reproduce in a virtual environment, while it appears to be very useful. The problems concerning the intellectual property were discussed in classroom. Without the presence of all the students and their participation at the discussion it would not have been possible to come to a solution.

Presence is a cloudy concept in a virtual setting. Benvenuti et al (2008) discuss the case of a compulsory meeting in a virtual classroom, where the students had labelled their avatars with nicknames and made them misbehave. But even if the avatar is present and polite, it is difficult to tell if the student is.

Not everything turned out to be feasible. After the first edition, the lecturers had planned to store the "best practices" so that they could be re-used the next year. This way they wanted to establish a canon of interesting, inspiring applications made by students. At the same time, they wanted to prevent new groups to start with an empty 'world'. This turned out to be too ambitious. The best applications needed too much memory, therefore the system slowed down too much. This idea was frozen until technology will support it.

In order to overcome the "empty world" feeling, the lecturers instructed one group of students to provide for different strategies to induce the experience of being part of a village structure. They did so by implementing a palisade to demarcate the border, a map of the village to support navigation and several means of transport to encourage exploration. An impression of those solutions is given in Figure 5.

Figure 5. Strategies to delimit the action

PERCEIVED CONNECTEDNESS AND LEARNING

Our research goal was to investigate the students' experience on community membership and learning. First of all, we have to emphasize that conducting research in real-live educational setting is difficulty. We had the opportunity to witness two editions of the same course in two consecutive years, which is promising. In 2009 we collected data. But a course is not an experiment; there are many important variables we were not able to control, first of all, the composition of the group. But also the moment in time in the school's history, with the school starting a new program, and the lecturers' intermitted absence (because of illness and other personal circumstances) probably have had an impact on the way the course evolved.

Measuring experience included assessment of expectations prior to the experience, during the experience, and after the facts (Vyas, van der Veer, 2006). We measured the students' perception of belonging to a classroom community and their perception on accomplishing (subjective) learning goals. We used the questions of the Classroom Community Scale (Rovai, 2002), structured along the Visual Analogue Scales (VAS) to identify changes within individuals (Langley & Sheppeard, 1985). These questions consist of 2 domains: Connectedness (10 questions) and Learning (10 questions), that are scored on an analogue scale from 0-10. We had to delete one item of the learning questionnaire because it was poly- interpretable to our Dutch audience.

In 2009, 15 students followed the Virtual Worlds-course. The survey was filled in the first meeting (week 1), again in the meeting where the students gained access to Active Worlds (week 4) and finally in the conclusive plenary meeting (week 8). 5 students were absent in one of more of those meetings, so our findings concern the 10 students who filled all the surveys.

We calculated the initial change in connectedness and in learning by subtracting the scale scores of week 4 from week 1, and calculated the later change by subtracting those of week 8 from week 4 for each individual. We calculated the significance of the change scores by applying the student t-test against the 0-hypothesis of no change in the population.

We found that the sensed/perceived "connectedness" increased significantly (Student t-test, $p < 0.05$) in the first part of the course (between the start in week 1 and week 4, when students meet each other and start collaborating) as well as in the second part (from week 4 to week 8, when the collaboration is continued in the virtual world). The sensed/perceived "learning" only grew significantly in the beginning of the course (between week 1 and week 4) even though new experiences as well as new designed artifacts were in fact (objectively) evident from the students' behavior in Active Worlds.

We expected connectedness to increase after the common virtual world was introduced, despite of the fact that by then the students were acquainted to each other. But the lack of increase of the perceived learning puzzles us. It is possible that the setting triggers ambitions that are difficult to fulfill. The software might be easier to learn than to master, especially if none of the community members has real expertise in 3D-programming. This can be an interesting starting point for further investigations.

CONCLUSION

The application of the Active Worlds environment to the Virtual Worlds course was a very fruitful step, to the students, the lecturers and the researchers.

The students gained insight into the possibilities of virtual applications, even if their satisfaction on their own learning leveled off in the last weeks.

The lecturers discovered new features – and new problems - of virtual worlds. They developed educational strategies on how to optimize the use of a virtual world as an educational tool an how to cope with the problems it entails.

The researchers had the opportunity to test their hypotheses on the effect of the application of this new technology in education, and to formulate new research goals.

We summarize our findings.

Common assignments in a Virtual World lead to:

- Increased possibilities for students to support each other on the 'virtual' spot. This is traditionally an advantage of face2face meetings. Now, at any time (and from any location) students turned out to be able to discuss with their colleagues online.
- The possibility to follow each others' progress, which is inspiring and stimulating.
- The possibilities to share results, to learn and copy from each other in an 'open source' setting.
- A stronger sense of community. The perceived sense of connectedness, of belonging to a community, increases when the students collaborate in a virtual world as a group.

Traditional classroom meetings are still useful:

- To support plenary discussions.
- To capitalize the historical knowledge of classroom teaching. The lecturers intended to "reuse" the best practices by keeping them in the virtual village during the following editions of the course, to establish a canon of inspiring applications. Current technology does not (yet) support this option.

We found new questions for further discussion and research:

- Allow students to collaborate and even to copy from each other asks for a re-design of the assessment policy.
- Why does the perceived learning level?

Our recommendation is: practice what you preach in classroom and use the opportunities this combination offers to learn. Even if the topic of discussion is a moving target, indeed, precisely in that case it is important to rely on one's own experience to draw one's own conclusions.

AKNOWLEDGMENT

We thank the lecturers of the Virtual Worlds course, Bob Cruijsberg and Geeske Bakker, for having admitted us in their classroom. We also thank the students of both courses for their cooperation and their products.

REFERENCES

Benvenuti, L., Hennipman, E. J., Oppelaar, E. J., van der Veer, G. C., Cruijsberg, B., & Bakker, G. (2008). Experiencing Education with 3D Virtual Worlds. In Kinshuk, D. G. Sampson, J. M. Spector, P. Isaías, & D. Ifenthaler (Eds.), *Proceedings of the IADIS International Conference on Cognition and Exploratory Learning in the Digital Age* (pp. 295-300). IADIS: Freiburg, Germany.

Dede, C. (1995). The Evolution of Constructivist Learning Environments: Immersion in Distributed, Virtual Worlds. *Educational Technology, 35*(5), 46–52.

Dickey, M. D. (2005). Three-dimensional virtual worlds and distance learning: two case studies of Active Worlds as a medium for distance education. *British Journal of Educational Technology, 36*(3), 439. doi:10.1111/j.1467-8535.2005.00477.x

Eliëns, A., Feldberg, F., Konijn, E., & Compter, E. (2007). VU @ Second Life: Creating a (Virtual) Community of Learners. *EUROMEDIA 2007.* Delft, Netherlands.

Langley, G. B., & Sheppeard, H. (1985). The visual analogue scale: its use in pain measurement. *Rheumatology International*, *5*(4), 145–148. doi:10.1007/BF00541514

Livingstone, D. & J. Kemp (2006). Massively Multi-Learner: Recent Advances in 3D Social Environments. *Computing and Information Systems Journal* *10*(2).

Rovai, A. P. (2002). Developing an instrument to measure classroom community . *The Internet and Higher Education*, *5*, 197–211. doi:10.1016/S1096-7516(02)00102-1

VU University Amsterdam. (2007). *VU Second Life*. Retrieved May 28, 2008, from http://www.vu.nl/secondlife.

Vyas, D., & van der Veer, G. C. (2006). *Rich evaluations of entertainment experience: bridging the interpretational gap*. 13th European Conference on Cognitive Ergonomics, 2006, Switzerland. (pp. 137-144).

ADDITIONAL READING

Dewey, J. (1934). *Art as Experience*. New York: Perigree.

Garrett, J. J. (2002). *The elements of user experience: User-centred design for the Web*. Indianapolis: New Riders Publishers.

Hannafin, M.J., Land, S.M. (1997). The foundations and assumptions of technology enhanced student-centered learning environments. *Instructional Science*, (25), 167–202.

Hsi, S., & Soloway, E. (1998). *Learner-Centered Design: Addressing, Finally, The Unique Needs Of Learners*, CHI 98 (ACM Workshop)

Jafari, A., McGee, P., & Carmean, C., (2006). Managing courses, defining learning: What faculty, students, and administrators want. *EDUCAUSE Review*, *41*(4), 50–71. http://www.educause.edu/apps/er/erm06/erm0643.asp

Jonassen, D.H., Land, S.M. (2000) *Theoretical Foundations of Learning Environments*. Lawrence Erlbaum Associates

McCarthy, J., & Wright, P. (2004). *Technology as Experience*. Cambridge, MA: MIT Press.

Norman, D. (2004). *Emotional Design*. New York: Basic Books.

Vyas, D., & van der Veer, G. C. (2005). *Experience as Meaning: Creating, Communicating and Maintaining in Real-Spaces*. In the Interact-2005 workshop on Space, Place, Experience in HCI. Proceedings at, http://www.infosci.cornell.edu/place/16_DVyas2005.pdf

Woolfolk, A. (2004). *Educational Psychology* (9th ed.). Boston: Allyn and Bacon.

Chapter 4

Learning Assignments
in Virtual Worlds:
Theoretical Systematization and
Didactical Requirements

Tanja Adamus
University Duisburg-Essen, Germany

Nadine Ojstersek
University Duisburg-Essen, Germany

Axel Nattland
University Duisburg-Essen, Germany

Michael Kerres
University Duisburg-Essen, Germany

ABSTRACT

The chapter describes different possibilities for the design of learning assignments in virtual worlds with a special emphasis on Second Life. For this purpose, it relates to didactical requirements to obtain criteria for constructing learning assignments for different contexts and conditions. A difference has to be made between distinct forms of simple and complex learning assignments, which have to be solved in the virtual worlds, but serve for the attainment of learning objectives either from the real or the virtual world. Furthermore, it is possible to reach learning objectives concerning the virtual world by means of the real world. It becomes obvious, that the bounds between virtual worlds and the real world are blurring. The decision, whether learning assignments should be edited in virtual worlds, depends on to what extent an additional benefit compared with other (technical) solutions, can emerge in these contexts. For these purposes a closer consideration of virtual worlds' specific features becomes relevant.

DOI: 10.4018/978-1-61692-825-4.ch004

INTRODUCTION

The capabilities of virtual worlds for teaching and learning are of particular interest and can be explained by the associated hope for new potentials of e-learning. The focus is on the possibility for learners to create their own avatars, to explore the virtual worlds and the facilities to communicate and collaborate with others. This chapter will describe different types of learning assignments in virtual worlds with a special emphasis on Second Life and discuss the possibilities, which are offered here to design learning assignments taking advantage of the virtual world's full potential. Having illustrated the essential functions of learning assignments and the specific features of virtual worlds, we will subsequently explicate examples of simple and complex tasks. Finally, this article will demonstrate how the dividing line between real life and virtual worlds is blurring. By means of examples we will identify the prerequisites for the attainment of learning objectives either from the real world or virtual worlds via the adaptation of learning assignments.

BACKGROUND

In order to systemize the different possibilities and requirements for the design of learning assignments (e.g. appeal to the learners' emotions) in virtual worlds which ensure successful learning, their essential functions will be defined first. Afterwards, we will discuss the specific features of virtual worlds, which have to be considered for the design of learning assignments.

Functions and Didactical Requirements of Learning Assignments

A didactical preparation of the content does not suffice to ensure successful learning. Assignments encourage learners to examine learning contents, whereby learning processes are invoked. To what extent this attempt is successful depends on various factors as for example whether tasks should be solved alone or by working in groups, the type of assignment, the support or the feedback provided. Thus it is necessary to prepare a close matching with the contextual focus before designing a learning assignment. Previously, there are some fundamental questions which have to be considered as for example: What are the learning objectives? Do learners define their own objectives? What basic conditions (characteristics of the target group, external respectively institutional conditions) must be regarded? The answers to these questions are the basis for the design of learning assignments.

Learning assignments in media-supported learning environments have two main functions: to ensure and to activate learning processes (Petschenka, Ojstersek & Kerres, 2004). Referring to learning in virtual worlds, this claim implies that assignments have to be designed in a way, which requires more from the learner than just transiting a learning path superficially or clicking (interactive) objects randomly. Learning-/teaching processes are not automatically improved by the use of virtual worlds.

Learning processes can be encouraged by the use of virtual worlds, but to assure them is certainly a requirement for learning assignments. Instead of securing a learning process which already occurred, the main objective in this context is to inspire the actual learning processes by the use of adequate assignments. They invoke the learning processes themselves by stimulating the necessary cognitive operations as for example reflections on the learning objects as well as appealing to the learners´ emotions and motivations. This instance occurs particularly when learners recognize a reference to their living environment and if the assignment's relevance is directly recognizable for them.

Furthermore learning assignments can encourage social interactions among the learners, a fact which becomes very important in the case the learning process requires discussing an issue (for example if evolving and expressing opinions is required). Learning assignments can also contribute to the emergence of a representational outcome (for example the collaborative design of 3D-objects). In this case the learners achieve their objective by applied practice and the documentation of their learning processes.

Complexity of Learning Assignments

There are two different kinds of learning assignments: "simple types of tasks" and "complex types of tasks". The selected type of tasks should measure the stated learning objectives: Simple types of tasks (e.g. multiple-choice tasks, see next chapter) are used best for simple learning objectives (e.g. "cognitive domain/knowledge") as for example checking whether students have learned facts and routine procedures (e.g. quote prices from memory to a customer). Complex types of tasks (e.g. problem solving assignments, see next chapter) are best used for complex learning objectives as for example using a concept in a new situation or unprompted use of an abstraction (e.g. apply laws of statistics to evaluate the reliability of a written test.) (Bloom's Taxonomy of Learning Domains according to Bloom, 1956).

Considering automated learning assignments (as for example multiple-choice tasks), activation can be achieved by the use of a well designed construction of the questions, accompanied by an adequate complexity. However, a stronger activation can be attained by the use of more complex learning assignments (see the next chapter for a more detailed discussion of this aspect). Support and mutual encouragement among the learners can also contribute to the assurance of successful learning processes by the adaptation of complex learning assignments. Tasks learners can work on before they are taught the actual content can activate specific previous knowledge and on the other hand serve as an assistance to motivate

learners for the following contents since they recognize knowledge gaps (an example for such an assignment could be a quiz before the content is presented to them). Especially in the case of complex learning content it seems to be sensible to use embedded assignments and depict relations between each component of the content. This method is in particular expedient in the case that the understanding of learning content A is a prerequisite for the understanding of learning content B. Assignments which are presented after the exposure of learning contents can either offer the function of self-control or they can be used with the ambition to initiate processes of reflexion on the content discussed before (Petschenka, Ojstersek & Kerres, 2004).

Learning Theory

There are various possibilities for the design and adaption of learning assignments. Some of them will be exemplified with regard to different contexts and learning objectives in the following section of this article. Tests and feedback were regarded for a long period of time as the essential characteristics of learning programs: In the context of behaviorist theory a learning program without tests and feedback (enhancement) was unthinkable. Depending on the learners' answers they were presented further "fitting" learning contents (programmed instruction). This approach is to some extent still present in the domain of "artificial intelligence" until today. During the 1990s an opposing position appeared, when hypertext-applications offered the learners a much opener access to learning contents. By means of appropriate and intuitively associated contents the learners can opt for the contents on their own. This open form of assignments suits particularly learners with previous knowledge and high intrinsic motivation and can lead to a higher acceptance rather than the rigid form of narrowing the learning process by the use of predetermined learning paths, which otherwise proved to be successful when the learners are novices or extrinsically motivated (Kerres, 2001).

Even in the context of constructivist approaches assignments are of high importance. However in this case the requirements are even much higher especially concerning the assignments' complexity. The quality of a proposal for learning however does not depend on the chosen model of learning theories, nor on the question whether the medium itself enables self-directed learning processes or provides regulated learning paths. It rather depends on finding the accurate conceptual solution for the exactly specified requirements of a learning situation. The intention is to encourage learning activities which suit to certain learning objectives and types of knowledge. The simple replication of facts for instance has to be supported in a quite different way than the ability to formulate correct sentences in a foreign language. Depending on the type of knowledge there exist other and different requirements concerning the learning assignments. By integrating simple types of tasks in most cases the acquirement of declarative knowledge is supported (knowledge of facts, "knowing-that"), whereas complex tasks support the acquirement of procedural knowledge (practical knowledge, "knowing-how") (see the next chapter for a further discussion of this aspect).

Specific Features of Virtual Worlds

However not only the type of knowledge has to be considered for the design of learning assignments, but also the specific features of virtual worlds are of high importance in this context. In this article we consider virtual worlds as computer-based simulations of environments, which are intended to offer their users interaction via three-dimensional graphical representations (avatars). These virtual worlds allow multiple users to be online at the same time and each user has the possibility to manipulate elements of the virtual world. The communication is based on text chat or/and real-time voice communication is often also possible. Moreover, there are several variations in the technical terms used to describe these environments. Closed economic simulations are one example, which offer more security and performance and either built separate own worlds, or may be integrated into closed sections of already existing virtual worlds like Second Life (Gierke & Müller, 2008). However, due to their limited options, we will not observe them closer in this article.

In virtual worlds as for example Second Life (http://secondlife.com), which is currently the most popular and complex platform for avatar based interaction on the internet, users are producers and consumers at the same time. Virtual worlds are also persistent, unlimited and allow web-based synchronous communication and the interaction of multiple users. A virtual world does not feature the characteristics of a game, like for example a complex set of rules, a background story, a winning definition and a target (Gierke & Müller, 2008). Even if diverse game elements may be integrated, communication and interaction are still the core characteristics.

A virtual world like Second Life is based on very open design principles, which allow the user to generate objects, to program and to create an avatar. The scope for design depends on the own competencies. According to Schmidt (2006), due to the user generated content in virtual worlds, established patterns of thought have to be removed to free up creativity. Whether a complex scope for design is combined with a greater immersion and if immersion has a positive effect on teaching and learning processes, has not yet been clarified. The use of virtual worlds is often connected with the hope for stronger immersion, which is encouraged by the possibility of three-dimensionality and the representation of the learner as avatars. Additionally, a deeper feeling of social presence arises from the possibility of interaction between spatially near and physically displayed human beings. Virtual worlds can take this immersive potential into consideration, for example by motivating the user with tasks and avoiding the emergence of boredom. Rittmann (2008), by referring to the idea of flow-experience according to Csikszentmihalyi (2000), points out the requirement of balancing one's own abilities, needs and feedback. In agreement with Csikszentmihalyi (2000), Rittmann (2008) points out that the flow-experience is a mental state, which can be reached by a certain person, if new tasks have found the right balance between the person's abilities and the task's demand. Thus, the person performing the task is in the flow of action and reaction. A feeling of absent mindedness occurs by means of total concentration on the task. Virtual worlds, however, not only offer such chains of activities, but also provide the chance to discover landscapes and maintain social relationships.

The design of space becomes more important with the use of three-dimensionality. By taking the ego-perspective, events can be viewed through the eyes of an avatar and a 360-degree turn of the camera can be conducted. Thus, the user feels his/her presence in the virtual world and more than before gains the impression of "being there". The view from the ego perspective is not necessarily always more immersive. A more critical aspect is the ability to manipulate objects and people, the degree to which one can identify with the avatar and the user's feeling to be part of the world and to be able to move in it without perceiving the medial intermediation. Avatars allow getting a visual impression of one's counterpart. There exists the possibility to visualize physical presence and physical feelings (Rittmann, 2008). The communication partners or respectively their avatars are visible and audible if possible. A visual and auditive combination reinforces the perception of the interaction partner's presence (Götzenbrucker, 2001).

Regarding the question whether immersion is beneficial to the learning process, Gierke & Müller (2008) point out that a stronger emotional involvement with the learning content can be achieved by the use of avatars. The learner can assume the avatar's perspective and experience content from a personal point of view. The strong connection with the avatar's experiences and emotions has an intense impact on the learner.

It can be assumed that entering the virtual world is perceived consciously (Raschke, 2007). The level of immersion is strongly interwoven with the actual design of gameplay, avatar development and interaction. The flow experience in virtual worlds is supported by the world's design, gameplay elements and gratification systems. It reinforces itself by how quickly a person learns to control the avatar and how to adjust the interface, etc. to its individual preferences (Rittmann, 2008).

The requirements for the design of learning assignments are based on the presented theoretical systematization. We have already pointed out that the learning assignments have two functions: to ensure and to activate learning processes. Learning processes can be assured by the didactical design of learning assignments: adequate learning objectives and type of tasks stimulate an intensive examination of the learning contents. Further examples for didactical requirements for the design of learning assignments are triggering emotional and motivational processes or promoting social interaction.

Having emphasized the functions of learning assignments in general and the specific features of virtual worlds, we will continue discussing a range of simple and complex types of tasks with regard to their didactical design and application possibilities and illustrate them by the use of examples taken from the context of virtual worlds.

SPECIFICATIONS OF LEARNING ASSIGNMENTS IN VIRTUAL WORLDS

Designing assignments, the characteristics of virtual worlds (e.g. interactions between spatially near and physical depicted users' representatives, immersion, persistence, multiple users) must be considered. To assure learning processes assignments have to be developed that take advantage of the full potential of virtual 3D worlds. Here, the chance exists to implement creative concepts asking for activities on the learners' side. Assignments support and enhance distinct forms of collaboration as well as individual learning processes. Virtual worlds do not imply any objectives. The challenge in the design of group tasks can be defined as initiating the attainment of common intents. In this context, the current technical potentials and limitations will also be considered.

The individual composition of each user's avatar in conjunction with the aspect of 3-dimensionality and the impression of space enables new possibilities for the design of learning assignments. On the side of the learner, learning in virtual worlds does not only contain the hope of finding a copy of traditional teaching-/learning scenarios, but also of learning "differently" by immersing into a virtual world. The learners prefer activity, exploration and fun. Virtual worlds offer various possibilities to create a combination of contextual input and playful elements: Instead of building lecture halls and offering lectures, creative ideas can be translated which support the learner's activities, such as experiments (learners can try out possible solutions and their effects on the object involved), role-play games (managing a virtual company and production of games) and explorations (visits to other countries or conversion of historical and literary models) for example. Using the virtual world of Second Life as the basis for our examples, simple and complex types of learning assignments can be distinguished.

Simple Types of Tasks

This type of learning assignment plays a very important role concerning the examination of successful learning processes and the decisions for branching in learning paths. The correct answer to a certain task is the condition, which further contents are presented to the learner (compare our discussion concerning this aspect in the chapter

background). In virtual worlds for example, solving certain tasks could be the prerequisite for the entrance to a museum building or the use of a special interactive object. Such a restrictive proceeding can even be reinforced by restrictions concerning the time or a maximum number of attempts to solve the task. In virtual worlds such strategies only seem to make sense in a very limited way, because they stand in a complete contradiction to the core concept of virtual worlds as environments for free explorations. Alternatively, instead of an automatic branching, it would be possible to present suggestions for suitable ones. The learners can decide on their own which content or task they would like to engage in next. A possible way for the implementation of this approach could be the creation of learning paths, where the learner in the shape of its avatar walks along a given way. If he or she reaches an intersection he or she will be confronted with multiple-choice tasks dealing with content, which was presented to the learner in the form of posters or 3-D models along the way. Appropriate to his or her solutions there will be the offer to continue the way turning left or right. One way is for the repetition and deepening of the content already learned the other way conciliates knowledge which is based on the knowledge gathered before.

Among others, multiple-choice tasks can be described as simple types of tasks. They will be illustrated and exemplified in the following passage.

In multiple-choice tasks several possibilities for the answers to a certain question are offered as options. The learner has to find and choose the correct answer/s. This type of tasks is quite easy to generate, implement and evaluate. The difficulty can be explicitly increased, if there is not just one correct answer to identify, but several alternatives have to be named or the correct combination of answers has to be identified exactly (Kerres, 2001). The design of such tasks is not limited to alternative answers presented in the form of simple written texts. It is also possible that the learner has to localize a certain place on a graphic by clicking on it, has to bring a scroll bar in the correct position or has to allocate objects via drag & drop.

Example: Testis Tour (exemplary context: biology lesson at school)

In this tour the avatar is "miniaturized" and taken on a journey through the human body, in this case the testis. On this programmed learning path the production of sperms is illustrated. After the tour a multiple choice test is presented. Although the test itself must be described as a simple task, the advantages of virtual worlds are utilized to present and experience a microscopic object one could not explain and experience in this depth in real live.

Example: Intercultural Learning Space (exemplary context: key competence training)

The Society for Intercultural Education, Training and Research build up an intercultural learning space, where differences between cultures can be learned by visitors. For each culture a multiple choice test is presented in which the avatar has to find the right choices for different situations - mostly in communication settings. A game or competition is set up by a public ranking, displaying the score of each avatar, who has entered the task. Moreover the shared 3-dimensional space can actually enable intercultural communication, as one is aware of other avatars taking the tasks and thereby direct interaction becomes possible.

Critical voices claim that with regard to this (simple) type of tasks, there is only a low level of interactivity and also the way in which tasks are provided here, seduces learner to guess the answers. Schulmeister (1996) perceives them as a relapse to the times of "programmed education" and fears the loss of self-actuating learning processes. According to Petschenka, Ojstersek and Kerres (2004) the acceptability of this type of tasks depends on the concrete context of its implementation. A sound assignment of the tasks and adequate feedback can by all means offer the possibility for an intensive engagement with the learning content. However, in this way simply the acquisition of knowledge can be controlled. Yet, it is also possible by means of an elaborated construction of the tasks to train and test the utilization of skills.

Depending on a sound construction of the question, it is also possible to reach the desired level of activation by means of simple types of tasks.

The work on simple types of tasks is normally carried out in phases of self-directed learning and thus provides high demands on the competence to learn this way. By using more complex assignments, the level of activation and the added value of virtual worlds will increase (e.g. more possibilities for collaboration, complex learning objectives).

Complex Types of Tasks

Complex types of tasks require complex cognitive attainments. They can be provided in the form of texts or by the means of applying models. In simulations and management games complex problems display the initial point of a task (for example the start of an own business). Simulations can sup-

Figure 1. Ohio State Testis Tour: http://slurl.com/secondlife/OSU%20Medicine/73/93/302

Figure 2. SIETAR Intercultural Learning Space: http://slurl.com/secondlife/Bluepill/227/203/68

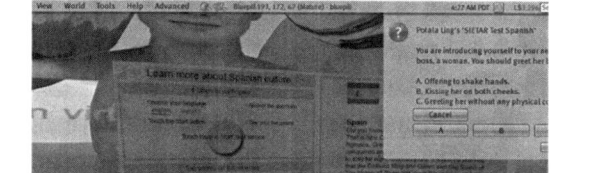

port the transfer of learning contents (Zimmer, 2004). The degree of success can be concluded from the particular system status or respectively by observing the direct consequences of the users' behavior (for example actual sales figures). Since the possibilities for error diagnosis and assistance in virtual worlds are limited, collaboration and support by tutors is necessary. Tasks which contain the graphical manipulation of objects on the screen can be realized easily in virtual worlds. Thus, it is possible to move, sort or rearrange elements (for example the single parts of a machine). In closed components of a simulation as for example in the simulation "Kitchen Fire" (see Figure 3), a direct analysis of the given answers follows the display of the consequences concerning the users' behavior during the simulation. If for example a user tries to pour a bucket of water on a burning chip pan, the fire and the smoke formation increase. Varying

the input parameters or the applied model leads to the achievement of a certain output.

Example: A school class deals with the topic of fire preventions, the students obtain the necessary previous knowledge in this context. Subsequently, the students enter the simulation "Kitchen Fire" in Second Life in small groups. Here they can experience in a three-dimensional environment via their avatars how the fire in the chip pan increases and what to do against it. The main objective is to apply the theoretical knowledge, the students gained at school, in the context of the simulation. After they entered the kitchen, the chip pan on the kitchen island starts to smoke and later it burns. The students have several possibilities for their actions. They can use different objects to stop the fire (for example use the fire blanket) or call the fire brigade first. At this juncture the adequateness of the chosen objects, as well as the sequence in which they are used, have

Figure 3. Kitchen Fire: Simulation: http://3.ly/euU (context: fire prevention)

an influence on the fire's intensity and dispersion. The students get an immediate feedback on their actions by the development of smoke, the particles of the flames, the animations of the flames, sounds, change of colors or objects and user interactions depending on their activities. Additionally, a teacher could also be present to support the students if necessary. By means of the representation of the students as avatars situated directly in the fire event, the spatial nearness to the other students and the possibility to observe their behavior in this situation, this type of assignment can contribute to the activation of the learning process, as on the one hand the students can reflect on the knowledge they gained before, and on the other hand they feel addressed in a strong emotional way by the fire situation. In this context a relation to the students' living environment is established, which makes the impact of the task immediately recognizable for the learners (compare our arguments concerning this aspect in the chapter "background"). Furthermore conducive, social interactions are encouraged and a discussion about the learning content is achieved, since the learners have to exchange their ideas, concerning which measure they want to carry out in which sequence. This simulation demonstrates that the technical possibilities and the effectiveness of Second Life are suitable for the implementation of demanding simulations.

According to Kerres (2001) the system's feedback should occur as detailed as possible and, in the ideal case, provide answers to the following questions: How will my answer be rated? What was the correct answer and why? What was wrong in my answer? How did this mistake occur? Particularly the last two questions are often not answered in a satisfying manner by the system alone. Considering for example Second Life as an environment for simulations – with regard to the example of marketing or starting a new business –, a new quality of feedback can be achieved: The learner does not only get the system's feedback but also an "authentic" reaction of

other users, as well as the possibility to exchange ideas with other learners and supporting-staff "directly on the spot". The integration of tutorial support can prove to be helpful with regard to the initiation of occasions to communicate and thus the encouragement of interpersonal discourses among the learner (Pätzold, 2007). According to Zimmer (2004) learners have to be activated (for example by means of learning assignments which encourage the communication among the learners). The emerging additional expenses on the side of the learners, as well as on the side of the lecturers are justified in this context, since it is not possible to provide adequate feedback only by the system. The following passage discusses two types of tasks exemplarily and illustrates them in the context of Second Life.

By the means of *application- and design-oriented tasks* it is feasible to transfer, what has been learned, to a new situation. A main function of learning assignments contains in the appliance of learning contents and the construction of a relation to a learner's own (professional) context, to secure the transfer of the learning contents. Furthermore, learners can be motivated to gather experiences beyond the mediated learning contents on their own and thus extend the acquired knowledge. Zimmer (2004) also alludes to the importance of application-oriented assignments.

For example the question, whether knowledge has to be applied (and not only to be recalled) or if it consists of procedures (and not only of declarative knowledge), which require practice, plays an important role (Kerres & de Witt, 2003). The learners can actively participate in the design and learning process by creating their own objects (individual or cooperative), manipulating interactive applications and by simulating models, which would be difficult to exercise or present under real conditions (for example testing a business idea or physical experiments). Although the technique is offering the requirements, the usage of the potential of interaction is essential. The more possibilities for interactions are offered, the stronger the feeling of being present in the virtual world occurs (Rittmann, 2008). The degree of co-designing in different virtual worlds varies a lot. The open design of Second Life for example is supported by modeling tools and interfaces to other 3D software, which allows the user to generate objects and to insert codes (Rittmann, 2008). Thus, it is possible that users work together on 3D computer models simultaneously and produce media and learning products themselves. On the one hand, virtual worlds offer the possibility to experiment without real risks (Hehl, 2008) and therefore allow interaction with objects, venues and people as well as the participation in events, which may be refused in the real world. On the other hand, the technical requirements for an extensive integration of text outside textchat and notecards are still missing. That is the reason, why the usage of virtual worlds is at the moment primarily suitable for practice-related learning assignments (Gierke & Müller, 2008).

In virtual worlds various avatars can be created, which may have any desired state (Götzenbrucker, 2001). The often occurring strong identification with the avatar induces immersion (Rittmann, 2008; Schmidt, 2006). Nevertheless, the adult user usually is able to distinguish between him/herself and the avatar (Rittmann, 2008). The advantage of the half anonymity of the internet compared to real contacts is that at first sight the strengths of a person are in the foreground and emotions are expressed more strongly, which creates quickly a verbal closeness. The design of the avatars can be considered as an identity encouraging offer and as an active involvement with oneself by changing into another role and thus trying out new possibilities (Raschke, 2007).

By means of *problem solving assignments* solutions can be depicted, which consider multitude perspectives and a distinct formulation of the objectives.

Communication is necessary when knowledge reaches a certain level of complexity. Then a deeper understanding of a theoretical framework is required or the knowledge consists of different competing concepts (Kerres & de Witt, 2003). The potential of Second Life lies in the various possibilities of communication and collaboration between teachers and learners and among learners respectively (e.g. role-plays, excursions). The development and maintenance of a community is of utmost significance (Gierke & Müller, 2008). The use of virtual worlds leads to the constitution of virtual groups and influences the structure and size of personal social networks in the real world. Through the specific communication modality (for example anonymity) relationships are expanded into various social groups and cultures. The development of social relationships mostly arises from the virtual world itself, because communication and collaboration processes are necessary to reach a certain goal (Hehl, 2008).

Hehl (2008) highlights the increasing degree of achieved digital interactivity through virtual worlds. This fact leads to a direct interactive cooperation among people, which may cause a feeling of togetherness and a flow-experience despite the distance. In virtual worlds the distance to face-to-face interaction in many relationships is rather small. Most of the time, group communication takes place when duplets and triplets form talking groups, in which avatars position themselves in "physical" closeness to the dialogue partner (Götzenbrucker, 2001). Through the reduced distance between learners the willingness to make contact is increased and an easier access to learning takes place due to the well-known classroom atmosphere. However, this may lead to traditional behavior (Gierke & Müller 2008). The challenge is to design learning assignments, which encourage communication and collaboration processes and support the spatial proximity of the avatars. In the following passage we will exemplify how voting tools can be used to fulfill these requirements.

Example: Voting tools to encourage communication

The following example describes a quick way to get an impression of the participants' mood during a course. Either they have to click on for example a pillar (Figure 4) or they have to stand on a certain field, (Figure 5) each of them will enlarge, depending on the number of votes they get. In our example the pillar-diagram tool asks the learners, how they judge the benefit of Second Life as a learning environment. The potential answers range from a high ("absolute positive" or "completely agree") to a low level ("absolute negative", "strongly disagree").

Tasks, which are not represented by the system, can be provided by a tutor, whereupon the learners have to frequent the adequate colored area to demonstrate what answer they chose. In the middle of the area a pie chart appears displaying the percentaged arrangement of the answers. Subsequently, the different opinions can be discussed by the learners (Figure 5). The MIT Information Space (Figure 6) can even display movement and text messages of avatars allowing tracking discussions and opinions over time. Thus it is possible to arrange a fast, visual perceptible voting.

The division into several smaller parts of tasks, which are based on each other, is more suitable than one substantial and complex learning assignment. Complexity only initiates a continuative comprehension, if the learning content is arranged with regard to a complex problem, so that the learner is able to understand the logical sense and does not feel overstrained. To avoid disorientation on the side of the learner, a certain form of instruction is also necessary with regard to complex and demanding learning material and assignments. Besides explaining the relation, the context and the function of the assignment, the patterns and criteria for the successful dispatch have to be announced (Frey & Frey-Eiling, 1992). A learning assignment must be designed in a way that at least 80% of all learners can pass it successfully (Petschenka, Ojstersek & Kerres, 2004).

Figure 4. Pillar-diagram tool at E-Learning 3D - University of Bielefeld: http://slurl.com/secondlife/European%20University/83/254/21

Figure 5. Voting tool E-Learning 3D – University of Bielefeld: http://slurl.com/secondlife/European%20 University/83/254/21

The connection to previous knowledge and the embedment in a realistic context can be implemented well in complex learning assignments. The following example illustrates this aspect with regard to a learning assignment concerning the virtual representation of the Cologne Cathedral in Second Life. This example also illustrates the importance of accounting for authentic contexts and cooperative learning processes in the design of assignments in virtual worlds. The example can be divided into three subtasks:

1) In the real world the learners are asked to articulate their previous knowledge about the cathedral.
2) Subsequently, the learners explore the virtual representation of the cathedral in Second Life with a specific task given to them. If it is possible, the tasks should be embedded in a realistic context.

3) A final presentation and discussion of the results can take place either in the real or virtual world.

Social Aspects Concerning the Adaptation of Assignments

The challenge in designing learning assignments consists of choosing a social form for the adaptation of the assignment, in such a way that a didactical additional benefit occurs. Instead of simply dividing subtasks on different learners, an essential goal should be to encourage communicative activities and an intensive exchange among the learners to perceive the other's positions, to respond to them, represent alternative positions, and take up the opinions of others and to merge them to an entire one. Single-, partner- and group-assignments can be distinguished.

On single-assignments the learners work self-directed. By means of designing single-assignments, individual interests, preconditions

Figure 6. MIT Information Space: http://slurl.com/secondlife/MIT/49/218/3

for learning and the individual rate of the learner can be considered, if necessary. On the contrary the opportunity for an exchange with other learners and therefore the dispute with other opinions and perspectives is missing. Thus single-assignments are above all suitable for activation processes and the intensive examination of learning contents, which do not mandatorily require an exchange with other learners, and for the individual control of learning processes (Petschenka, Ojstersek & Kerres, 2004).

For the adaptation of complex tasks however, cooperative treatments in the form of partner- or group-assignments are suitable to allow for different perspectives and reciprocal feedback. The adaptation of group-assignments requires a higher effort concerning coordination processes. Especially virtual worlds offer the possibility of cooperative learning over great distances, combined with an experience of spatial nearness by means of the learner's representation via avatars, an aspect which makes an exchange among learners possible. According to Pätzold (2007) collective commitments and social interactions occur especially by means of group-assignments and are not restricted to a professional discourse alone.

Scenario: The Viking Centre in Wonderful Denmark

The Viking Centre is the most entire Viking town in Second Life with lots of historically accurate buildings, items and information. Here, it

is also possible for lecturers as well as for learner to wear typical clothing and thus intensify the feeling of immersion.

Example for a learning assignment in this context (exemplary context: a history. lesson at school dealing with the topics of the Middle Ages or the Vikings):

You find yourself in the place of a Viking village. Your task is to discover the fundamental characteristics of the design of the Viking's tenement houses. For this task explore the village and one of the residential buildings on your own (single-assignment). In a next step you should bring together all conclusions of the group. Exchange the specific features, which attracted your attention, in the group and compare them with each other. Discuss possible reasons for the (different) construction methods.

The learners' answers to the assignments require feedback to provide them information concerning the adequateness of their suggested solutions. The question of the feedback's promptness, detailedness and its effectiveness on learning is discussed in a controversial way (for example in the research project on "assignment formulation and providing feedback" http://www.phil.uni-sb. de/~jakobs/wwwartikel/feedback/projekt.htm). We will not discuss this aspect any further in the context of this article. At this point we merely want to emphasize that different forms of feedback have to be distinguished: On the one hand feedback

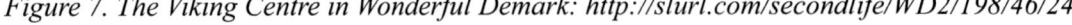

Figure 7. The Viking Centre in Wonderful Demark: http://slurl.com/secondlife/WD2/198/46/24

can be provided by the learner him- or herself (by comparing his or her answers to a sample solution) or an automated feedback informs the learners, whether their answers were correct or wrong. Furthermore feedback can be provided by other learners. This approach is reasonable in the case of complex learning assignments, whose answers cannot be classified explicitly as "right" or "wrong": for example in those cases, when contributions to discussions or estimations were intended as answers. Feedback provided by other learners can increase the feeling of personal responsibility; it fosters social learning processes and encourages the exchange of different perspectives. Very complex learning assignments on the contrary often require feedback and support by a tutor. It becomes obvious that a learning assignment depends on the learning contents and -objectives and therefore decisions have to be made whether and in which form communication should be aspired and facilitated (Petschenka, Ojstersek & Kerres, 2004).

Mixed Reality

Another challenge in the creation of assignments consists above all in considering the aspects of mixed reality, the merger of real life with the virtual worlds. The dividing line between real life and virtual worlds is blurring (Gierke & Müller 2008). A clear distinction is neither possible nor sensible. Based on contacts among people in a virtual world, friendships in real life can be extended. Thus meetings take place in the real world to intensify virtual contacts for example (Götzenbrucker, 2001). The point is not to offer education exclusively in virtual worlds or the real world, but to combine them (de Freitas, 2008, Gierke & Müller, 2008). The mistake of thinking that everything has to take place in one closed system has to be avoided (Gierke & Müller, 2008). The question must be raised, which skills can be attained in the virtual world and how these can be transferred into real life. Another question

to be raised is which skills are necessary at all to benefit from the full potential of virtual worlds (Raschke, 2007). For example, information from real life can be used to solve a virtual problem or emotions in the virtual world are experienced as real (Neuenhausen, 2004). Real world conducts of life are also present in virtual worlds (Raschke, 2007). The virtual reality is a place, where a person is thinking about the real world (Neuenhausen, 2004). In Second Life, for example the worlds are mixed up by purchases (Hehl, 2008), for example the purchase of virtual goods (Raschke, 2007) and virtual events, which are streamed to the real world or vice versa. Additionally, application programming interfaces allow getting into contact with the outside world (Gierke & Müller, 2008) (e.g. Sloodle). Thus specific control elements are offered to the user, like a repertoire of gestures typical for teaching, the possibility of saving chat protocols and to enter blog entries into Second Life via a chat line (Gierke & Müller, 2008). Erpenbeck & Sauter (2007) assume a regression regarding the development of skills, as immersion may create emotions and motivation, but the learner can also hide behind the identity of the own avatar or create a completely new identity, whereby no real social insecurities (dissonances) are created, which however are essential for the development of skills. Accordingly, as many real decision situations as possible should be initiated, for example by using role play games to create situations that are experienced as critical. Raschke (2007) points out the necessity, that users must have the competence to differentiate and reflect upon the different worlds. However, children aged up to approximately four years cannot see this difference. Additionally, some adults also lack this necessary competence.

Several examples for the design possibilities of learning assignments in Second Life were already described in the previous chapters. In a next step we will try to systemize them. With regard to the perspective of mixed reality three forms can be distinguished: Learning assignments can be integrated directly into the virtual world and support the achievement of learning objectives, which as regards content relate either to the virtual world (VW-VW) or respectively to real life (VW-RL) or the aim is the achievement of learning objectives in real life by means of assignments, which encourage activities in the virtual world (RL-VW) (Table 1).

Attaining Educational Objectives in Virtual Worlds By Means of Assignments in Virtual Worlds (VW-VW)

In the context of this scenario the main attention is drawn to particular educational objectives relating to topics emerging in a virtual world. Learners receive their assignments directly in a virtual world and are also expected to complete them in the virtual world.

Especially in the case of this variant a high level of immersion can be attained. The learning objective relates to the virtual world and the adaptation of the assignment takes place directly there, whereby an authentic context is created. A possible example for this scenario in Second Life is the assignment for a group of students to start a business in a shopping center in Second Life or to develop a marketing strategy. Having received feedback by their lecturer, the group starts their own business and implements the planned marketing activities, for example by distributing leaflets. Thus the learners receive an immediate feedback in the form of, among other, sales figures or the number of distributed leaflets as well as by

a potential correlation between them. Furthermore, the learners can provide feedback to each other, if necessary the lecturer can support the learners, and the inhabitants of Second Life provide direct feedback via direct communication or indirect by accepting or refusing leaflets.

Simple types of tasks, for example in the form of multiple choice tests, can be integrated easily in the virtual world, whereupon it is also possible to analyze the learners' answers directly there. These assignments serve as a way to control the success and to activate and motivate learners. As we already explained in the chapter "background", such assignment can - according to the tradition of tutorial systems - serve as prerequisites for the further adaptation of learning contents and therefore are predominantly suitable for cognitive learning objectives. Considering the impact of flexible knowledge for the stake in real problem situations with regard to successful learning processes, thus the examination of the appliance of the gained knowledge in real contexts, as well as a profound analysis of errors with an adequate feedback, is hardly possible. Actually, virtual worlds are contradictory to the principle of forcing learners to pass a certain test, which serves as the basis for getting access to further learning contents via branching in the learning paths, as it was the case with tutorial systems. Virtual worlds stand for exploration and openness. It should be considered to design such "learning paths" for novices in the virtual worlds, so that on the one hand they do not feel disorientated, but on the other hand they should also not be guided in a too restrictive way. Obvious MMORPGs (Massively Multiuser Online

Table 1. Mixed Reality: Variants of learning assignments

	Assignments - virtual world -	Assignments - real life -
Educational objectives - virtual world -	Attaining educational objectives in virtual worlds by means of assignments in virtual worlds (VW-VW)	Attaining educational objectives in virtual worlds by means of assignments in real life (VW-RL)
Educational objectives - real life -	Attaining educational objectives in real life by means of assignments in virtual worlds (RL-VW)	

Role Playing Games) function quite well according to this principle: The answer to a certain task is the prerequisite to unlock further areas, which can then be explored by the users. It can be assumed that this principle works so well, because the restricted areas in this context are so complex that the learner does not feel "restricted". Zimmer (2004) refers to the importance of possibilities for self-determined choices of recommended learning paths. Johnson, Levine & Smith (2009) point out the necessity that users "[...] have a need to control their environments, and they are used to easy access to the staggering amount of content and knowledge available at their fingertips" (p. 5). The potential of virtual worlds owes to active participation and interaction being in the center of the experience.

In contradiction to traditional learning programs, the term learning path can be taken literally in Second Life. Here, a learning path can be designed as a road, an avatar can walk along and stations are positioned along the way containing information, contents and tasks. Individual learning paths with branching can be realized and the depiction of the path is comprehensible for the learner. Figure 8 shows an example of a learning path in Second Life.

In the following section we will discuss how learning objectives and problems of the real life can be treated in the form of simple and complex assignments in virtual worlds.

Attaining Educational Objectives in Real Life By Means of Assignments in Virtual Worlds (RL-VW)

A virtual world such as Second Life is regarded and used as a tool to complete certain assignments in real life. At this juncture Second Life is frequented with the purpose of attaining a given educational objective. These scenarios can occur in the context of face-to-face instructions as well as within an e-learning setting.

Overcoming the divide between knowledge and appliance by working on complex learning assignments can be supported by the means of virtual worlds, for example as real life problems occur in the form of single-, partner- or group-assignments in virtual worlds.

For instance, a learning management system (LMS) is used for the distribution of contents and tasks. The students receive the assignment to acquaint themselves with the essential constituents of a biological cell. For this purpose they can refer to the material to be found in written form within the LMS and, on the other hand, visit (collectively) an accessible 3D-model in Second Life. Here they have the possibility to deepen their knowledge and to deal interactively with the 3D-model of

Figure 8. A learning path in Second Life - EnBW: http://slurl.com/secondlife/EnBW%20EnergyPark%20 WelcomeArea/218/25/33

Figure 9. The cell: http://slurl.com/secondlife/Genome/138/96/29

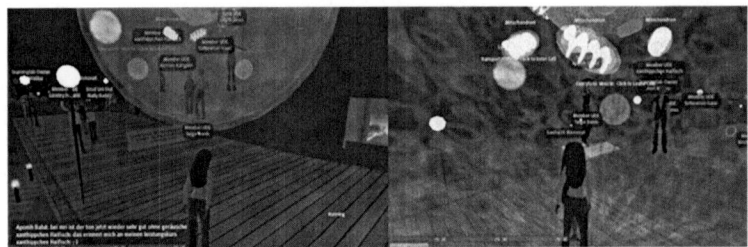

the biological cell. In this context the potential of the learners' representations in the form of avatars and the authentic 3D-environment of Second Life becomes obvious: The learners can submerge into the huge cell together and examine the several parts of the cell in more detail, gather information by clicking on certain objects and discuss their observations.

Example "Spanish class" (exemplary lesson: a Spanish course for beginners):

A learning unit was designed at the chair of educational media and knowledge management (University Duisburg-Essen) testing the potential of Second Life as a possible place to learn foreign languages. The unit bargains for a real life learning objective, but the learning assignment occurs in Second Life. The students are supported by tutors (Figure 10). They visit several Spanish locations and are confronted with application-oriented tasks. For example in the lecture hall they practice in advance, how to place an order in a restaurant and this knowledge is applied subsequently as the learners have to place an order in a coffee bar in a Spanish town. A tutor inherited the role of the waiter and could therefore provide immediate feedback.

Example citizenship test at the adult education centre Goslar (Figure 11):

Since the 1st of September 2008 everybody, who wants to obtain the German citizenship, has to prove that he or she knows enough about the German law, social order and living conditions. To prepare for this necessary citizenship test, the adult education centre Goslar offers possibilities to practice in Second Life. All questions are presented automatic in the form of a quiz. Since the three-dimensional environment is also a meeting point for communication, it makes sense to meet other persons simultaneously online to discuss the questions. The so-called knowledge camping for the test is available for free at every time.

After the presentation of several examples to illustrate how to design learning assignments, which can be worked on in virtual worlds, the

Figure 10. Unit "Spanish class in Second Life": http://slurl.com/secondlife/European%20University%20 II/88/218/25

following passages will exemplify how specific virtual world's learning objectives can be attained in real life.

Attaining Educational Objectives in Virtual Worlds By Means of Assignments in Real Life (VW-RL)

This scenario also focuses on particular educational objectives relating to topics emerging within the world of Second Life. However, assignments in this context are given to the learners in the scope of real life. The educational objective in this context might for example consist in the preparation of an exhibition, presenting innovating learning scenarios in Second Life. For the attainment of this objective a face-to-face workshop is offered to the learners to obtain knowledge concerning strategies for their research.

With regard to the above presented example of starting an own business in Second Life (VW-VW), the following strategy of implementation would be possible: The learning objective consists of gathering knowledge concerning Second Life specific marketing and sales strategies. By means of an on-campus course the students obtain the tasks to catch sight of the adequate technical literature and to analyze actual sales statistics.

Example "programming languages" (exemplarily context: a lesson in computer science/ a beginners' course for the programming languages "LSL" and "C"):

Second Life provides an own programming language called the Linden Scripting Language (LSL) which can be used to teach students the basic principles and structures of programming languages in general. Esteves et al. (2009) consider this a good way of introduction because LSL is not as complex as most other programming languages for example "C". A possible example for a concrete learning assignment could thus be to ask the students to discuss the differences between "C" and "LSL". In this way the educational objectives concerning Second Life (in this context the programming language "LSL") can be integrated into classroom instructions (face-to-face).

The crucial aspect in all three variants is the question concerning the adequateness of the relation between the efforts (development and adaptation of the assignments) and the output (attainable learning result), that is whether the high (technological and/ or organizational) efforts of the above described variants offer an additional benefit concerning the attainment of a learning objective in comparison with less costly solutions (for example learning platforms or books). Actu-

Figure 11. Citizenship test at the adult education centre Goslar: www.vhs-sl.de

ally Second Life already offers many possibilities with the usage of existing models and simulations as for example sights and museums. Nevertheless, a high effort remains linked to the technical framework requirements and the support of the learner concerning the exposure to the virtual world. In Second Life the main focus is still on the aspects of support in the technical and administrative area before and as well during the course.

FUTURE RESEARCH DIRECTIONS

Virtual worlds will gain more importance in the future, as well as all hybrid learning scenarios between virtual worlds and the real world (Hehl, 2008). Regarding the design of learning assignments, assignments have to be tested, which connect the real world with the virtual one. The relevance of three-dimensionality has to be focused on. Assumptions regarding the encouragement of social presence through avatars specifically raise the question of how the spatial-proximity information effect the communication and collaboration processes of learning environments and what kind of challenges for collaborative learning scenarios and the support of the learners are involved. Through the improvement of scalability to a greater number of users, the optimization of graphics and the improved possibilities of textual design, future development can correct the current weaknesses of virtual worlds regarding the design of learning assignments. However, rather than putting technical criteria into the foreground, it is more important to answer the question concerning which ambitions are related to the use of virtual worlds in the teaching/learning context and what kind of expectations the users have.

For pure declarative knowledge, presenting the learning content with subsequent multiple choice tasks can be sufficient in the case the student has appropriate previous knowledge. For demanding learning objectives, it is, however, necessary to have complex tasks. In recent years, this challenge

has been discussed with more and more urgency in educational contexts. A spontaneous transfer of learned knowledge into practice basically happens more rarely than it is often thought. This issue of how far one can promote the idea of overcoming the gap between knowledge and practice by using complex learning tasks (for example, solving complex problems together) – particularly by using virtual worlds - must be addressed more seriously in the future. Erpenbeck and Sauter (2007) begin, however, with the supposition that emotions and motivation can be produced by immersion, but the learner can 'hide' himself behind the identity of his or her avatar or can create whole new identities, which means that no real social uncertainty (dissonance) is generated. The real world is more and more merging with virtual worlds. From this merger it is expected that learners will be able to "transfer" the knowledge gained in the real world to the virtual world and vice versa. However, the latter is fundamental for the development of competencies. The question, whether transfers of knowledge and competencies from the virtual world into real life are actually successful, has yet to be clarified. In the area of game-based learning, we are already seeing the first efforts (Witting, 2007). One has to discover, how far the specific features of virtual worlds can make a contribution to the creation of complex learning tasks in a way that the learning process is stimulated and assured in the sense that they are linked as far as possible with real decision making situations. This can, for example, be initiated by carrying out role plays or situations that are experienced by the learners as being conflictual. One should therefore consider how, in particular, cooperative and practice-oriented methods can be implemented by using learning tasks and thus incorporate the specific features of virtual worlds. In this way, one should achieve additional benefit with respect to learning success compared with the use of other technology and simpler types of tasks.

Personal support and cooperative learning are easy to realize in virtual worlds and can be important for learning progress and the achievement of defined learning objectives. Tutorial support is important for the achievement of learning objectives, which require an interpersonal discourse. The challenge is to create and support learning tasks and activities that stimulate self-directed as well as cooperative learning. Attempts so far (Ojstersek & Kerres 2008) claim for further research and an answer to the question which specific demands the tutors are confronted with in virtual worlds and what competencies are required for the tutors, as well as for the learners.

CONCLUSION

As not only existing instructional design concepts and methods should be transferred to virtual worlds and their use should show a benefit, the ubiquitous virtual world offers various possibilities of self-directed learning and collaborative scenarios. Virtual worlds are not a necessary condition to pursue specific teaching contents, objectives or didactical methods. However, they can support and promote specific teaching and learning processes. An essential potential can be seen in the three-dimensionality and the possibilities of interaction, construction and collaboration with other users. The challenge is to initiate events, which encourage communication and collaboration processes and support the spatial proximity of the avatars. Virtual worlds gain the potential to be more immersive through the three-dimensionality and the representation of the learner by a virtual representative.

The possible potential of virtual worlds has to be taken into account by designing learning assignments. In this respect, one has to design learning tasks, which activate and secure learning processes in the sense that they stimulate an intensive examination of the learning contents and also trigger emotional and motivational processes, which promote social interaction amongst learners. This can happen with simple types of tasks, but,

primarily, complex task settings are required for the achievement of certain teaching objectives. Embedment in activity worlds or the use of simulations will facilitate the application of acquired knowledge in an authentic context. The feeling that the learner is directly in the location, where the activity is taking place, and the direct proximity of other avatars, implies that the learners can experience a stronger degree of social presence and immersion. This is particularly possible with the VW-VW learning task variation, because within these scenarios the relaying of the teaching content and the application of the knowledge takes place directly in the virtual world. Since, with this variation, the learning objective also originates from the virtual world, the gap between the acquisition of knowledge and application of it is small. With good task setting, however, the gap can also be bridged with both other variations. The examples in this chapter show that the virtual worlds and the real world intermingle and that various possibilities for self-directed and cooperative learning processes are available. But to a certain degree, there are still some technical limitations. The learner should indeed be given the opportunity of free exploration, but also if required, should be offered more restrictive learning options, such as, for example, self learning paths which offer the learner help with general orientation.

Constructing learning tasks, one should always take care that the effort expended in relation to the targeted learning result is appropriate. In this way, it is possible to generate additional benefit compared with other types of tasks, process variations or the use of other technologies.

REFERENCES

Bloom, B. S. (1956). *Taxonomy of Educational Objectives, Handbook I: The Cognitive Domain.* New York: David McKay Co Inc. Retrieved from: http://www.skagitwatershed.org/~donclark/hrd/bloom.html (02.12.2009)

Csikszentmihalyi, M. (2000). Das Flow-Erlebnis. Jenseits von Angst und Langeweile . In *Tun aufgehen. (The flow-experience. Beyond anxiety and boredom: merging into action.)*. Stuttgart: Klett.

de Freitas, S. (2008). *Serious Virtual Worlds. A scoping study*. Bristol: SGI.

Erpenbeck, J., & Sauter, W. (2007). *Kompetenzentwicklung im Netz. New Blended Learning mit Web 2.0. (Developing competence on the net. New Ways of Blended Learning with Web 2.0.)*. Köln: Wolters Kluwer.

Esteves, M., Fonseca, B., Morgado, L., & Martins, P. (2009). Using Second Life for Problem Based Learning in Computer Science Programming. *Journal of Virtual Worlds Research, 2*(1), 3–25.

Frey, K., & Frey-Eiling, A. (1992). *Allgemeine Didaktik. (General Didactics.)* Zürich, Switzerland: Verlag der Fachvereine an den schweizerischen Hochschulen und Techniken AG.

Gierke, C., & Müller, R. (2008). *Unternehmen in Second Life. Wie Sie Virtuelle Welten für Ihr reales Geschäft nutzen können. (Companies in Second Life. How to use virtual worlds for your real life business.)*. Offenbach, Germany: GABAL.

Götzenbrucker, G. (2001). *Soziale Netzwerke und Internet-Spielewelten. (Social networks and internet gaming worlds.)*. Wiesbaden, Germany: Westdeutscher Verlag.

Hehl, W. (2008). *Trends in der Informationstechnologie. Von der Nanotechnologie zu virtuellen Welten. (Trends in information technology. From nanotechnology to virtual worlds.)* Zürich. Switzerland: vdf.

Johnson, L., Levine, A., & Smith, R. (2009). *The 2009 Horizon Report*. Austin, Texas: The New Media Consortium.

Kerres, M. (2001). *Multimediale und telemediale Lernumgebungen. Konzeption und Entwicklung. (Multi- and telemedia based learning environments. Conception and Development.)*. München, Germany: Oldenbourg.

Kerres, M., & de Witt, C. (2003). A didactical framework for the design of blended learning arrangements. *Journal of Educational Media, 28*, 101–114.

Neuenhausen, B. (2004). *Bildung in der Digitale. Zur Bildungsrelevanz virtueller Welten. (Education in the digital. Concerning the relevance of virtual worlds for education.)*. Frankfurt am Main: Peter Lang.

Ojstersek, N., & Kerres, M. (2008). Lernen in Second Life betreuen. (Supervising learning in Second Life.) . In Hohenstein, A., & Wilbers, K. (Eds.), *Handbuch E-Learning (Handbook E-Learning) (Kap. 4.31, 25. Erg.-Lfg Juli 2008)*. Köln, Germany: Verlag Deutscher Wirtschaftsdienst.

Pätzold, H. (2007). E-Learning 3-D – welches Potenzial haben virtuelle 3-D-Umgebungen für das Lernen mit neuen Medien? (E-Learning 3-D – What is the potential of virtual 3-D-environments for learning with new media?) *Medienpädagogik*, Zeitschrift für Theorie und Praxis der Medienbildung (www.medienpaed.com/2007/paetzold0709.pdf)

Petschenka, A., Ojstersek, N., & Kerres, M. (2004). Lernaufgaben beim E-Learning. (Learning assignments for E-Learning.) . In Hohenstein, A., & Wilbers, K. (Eds.), *Handbuch E-Learning (Handbook E-Learning) (Kap. 4.19, 7. Erg.-Lfg. Januar 2004)*. Köln, Germany: Fachverlag Deutscher Wirtschaftsdienst.

Raschke, M. (2007). *Im Computerspiel bin ich der Held'. Wie virtuelle Welten die Identitätsentwicklung von Jugendlichen beeinflussen. („In computer games I am the hero". How virtual worlds contribute to the development of adolescents'identities.).* Hamburg, Germany: Diplomica Verlag.

Rittmann, T. (2008). *MMORPGs als virtuelle Welten. Immersion und Repräsentation. (MMORPGs as virtual worlds. Immersion and representation.).* Boizenburg, Germany: Werner Hülsbusch.

Schmidt, F. A. (2006). *Parallel Realitäten. (Parallel realities.).* Sulgen, Switzerland: Niggli.

Schulmeister (1996). *Grundlagen hypermedialer Lernsysteme. (Basic principles of hypermedial learning systems.)* München, Germany: Oldenbourg.

Witting, T. *(2007).* Wie Computerspiele uns beeinflussen. Transferprozesse beim Bildschirmspiel im Erleben der User. (How computer games influence us. Processes of transfer in the context of computer and video games in the users' experience.) *München, Germany: kopaed.*

Zimmer, G. (2004). Aufgabenorientierte Didaktik des E-Learning. (Task-oriented didactics in E-Learning.) . In Hohenstein, A., & Wilbers, K. (Eds.), *Handbuch E-Learning (Handbook E-Learning) (Kap. 4.15. 7. Erg.-Lfg. Januar 2004).* Köln, Germany: Fachverlag Deutscher Wirtschaftsdienst.

ADDITIONAL READING

Bell, D. (2009). Learning from Second Life. *British Journal of Educational Technology, 40*(3), 515–525. doi:10.1111/j.1467-8535.2009.00943.x

Boulos, M., Hetherington, L., & Wheeler, S. (2007). Second Life: an overview of the potential of 3-D virtual worlds in medical and health education. *Health Information and Libraries Journal, 24*(4), 233–245. doi:10.1111/j.1471-1842.2007.00733.x

Broadribb, S., & Carter; C. (2009). Using Second Life in human resource development. *British Journal of Educational Technology, 40*(3), 547–550. doi:10.1111/j.1467-8535.2009.00950.x

Cargill-Kipar, N. (2009). My dragonfly flies upside down! Using Second Life in multimedia design to teach students programming. *British Journal of Educational Technology, 40*(3), 539–542. doi:10.1111/j.1467-8535.2009.00940.x

Chang, V., Gütl, C., Kopeinik, S., & Williams, R. (2009). Evaluation of Collaborative Learning Settings in 3D Virtual Worlds. *International Journal of Emerging Technologies in Learning, 4,* pp. 6-17, Online: http://online-journals.org/i-jet/article/view/1112/1163 (24.11.2009).

Edirisingha, P., Nie, M., Pluciennik, M., & Young, R. (2009). Socialisation for learning at a distance in a 3-D multi-user virtual environment. *British Journal of Educational Technology, 40*(3), 458–479. doi:10.1111/j.1467-8535.2009.00962.x

Jennings, N., & Collins, C. (2007). Virtual or Virtually U: Educational Institutions in Second Life. *International Journal of Social Sciences, 2*(3), 180–186.

Kemp, J., Livingstone, D., & Bloomfield, P. (2009). SLOODLE: Connecting VLE tools with practice in Second Life. *British Journal of Educational Technology, 40*(3), 551–555. doi:10.1111/j.1467-8535.2009.00938.x

Lee, M. J. W. (2009). How Can 3d Virtual Worlds Be Used To Support Collaborative Learning? *Journal of e-Learning and Knowledge Society, 5* (1), pp. 149-158.

Lober, A. (Ed.). (2007). *Virtuelle Welten werden real. Second Life, World of Warcraft und Co: Faszination, Gefahren, Business. (Virtual worlds become reality. Second Life, World of Warcraft and co: Fascination, Perils, Business.)*. Hannover, Germany: Heise.

Müller, A., & Leidl, M. (2007). *Virtuelle (Lern-) Welten. Second Life in der Lehre (Virtual (learning) worlds. Using Second Life for teaching.)* Online: http://www.e-teaching.org/didaktik/gestaltung/vr/SL_lehre_langtext_071207_end.pdf (14.01.2008).

Oishi, L. (2007). Surfing Second Life: What does Second Life have to do with real-life learning. *Technology & Learning*, *27*(11), 54–64.

Oliver, M., & Carr, D. (2009). Learning in virtual worlds: Using communities of practice to explain how people learn from play. *British Journal of Educational Technology*, *40*(3), 444–457. doi:10.1111/j.1467-8535.2009.00948.x

Omale, N., Hung, W., Luetkehans, L., & Cooke-Plagwitz, J. (2009). Learning in 3-D multiuser virtual environments: Exploring the use of unique 3-D attributes for online problem-based learning. *British Journal of Educational Technology*, *40*(3), 480–495. doi:10.1111/j.1467-8535.2009.00941.x

Pätzold, H. (2008). Die dritte Dimension des Lernens – Versprechen und Wirklichkeit virtueller 3D-Umgebungen in Lernprozessen. (The third dimension of learning – Promises and reality of virtual 3D-environments in learning processes.) In U. Dittler, & M. Hoyer (Ed.), *Aufwachsen in virtuellen Medienwelten. Chancen und Gefahren digitaler Medien aus medienpsychologischer und medienpädagogischer Perspektive. (Growing up in virtual media worlds. Chances and perils of digital media from a mediapsychological and mediapedagogical perspective.)* München, Germany: kopaed, pp. 257–273.

Perez-Garcia, M. (2009). MUVEnation: A European peer-to-peer learning programme for teacher training in the use of MUVEs in education. *British Journal of Educational Technology*, *40*(3), 561–567. doi:10.1111/j.1467-8535.2009.00951.x

Pichler, M. (2007). Seminare in Second Life. (Seminars in Second Life.) . *Wirtschaft und Weiterbildung*, *10*, 48–54.

Salmon, G. (2009). The future for (second) life and learning. *British Journal of Educational Technology*, *40*(3), 526–538. doi:10.1111/j.1467-8535.2009.00967.x

Sanchez, J. (2007). *A Sociotechnical Analysis of Second Life in an Undergratuate English course.* Online: http://lisadawley.googlepages.com/edmedia07.Sl.Sociotech.pdf (07.01.2008).

Twining, P. (2009). Exploring the educational potential of virtual worlds – Some reflections from the SPP. *British Journal of Educational Technology*, *40*(3), 496–514. doi:10.1111/j.1467-8535.2009.00963.x

Warburton, S. (2009). Second Life in higher education: Assessing the potential for and the barriers to deploying virtual worlds in learning and teaching. *British Journal of Educational Technology*, *40*(3), 414–426. doi:10.1111/j.1467-8535.2009.00952.x

Yellowlees, P., & Cook, J. (2006). Education about Hallucinations using an Internet Virtual Reality System: A Qualitative Survey. *Academic Psychiatry*, *30*(6), 534–539. doi:10.1176/appi.ap.30.6.534

KEY TERMS AND DEFINITIONS

Virtual World: A three-dimensional computer-based simulation of a persisting environment which allows web-based synchronous communication and the interaction of multiple users.

Learning Assignment: A task designed to invoke learning processes. Its two main functions are ensuring and activating learning processes.

Simple Types of Tasks: Support the acquirement of declarative knowledge, which is the knowledge of facts, rules or figures. Multiple-choice tests can be examples for these tasks. In virtual worlds they are only sensible in a very limited way, because they are contradictory to the virtual worlds' core concept of free exploration.

Complex Types of Tasks: Support the acquirement of procedural knowledge, which is practical knowledge how to solve a certain tasks or problem. They require complex cognitive attainments. Simulations or management games are good examples for the successful integration of such tasks into virtual worlds.

Chapter 5

Immersive Language Learning in Collaborative Virtual Environments:
The Current Status and Possible Trends

Ya-Chun Shih
National Dong Hwa University, Taiwan

ABSTRACT

This chapter explores the role of collaborative virtual environments (CVE) in the language learning immersion experience. Despite the lack of strong empirical evidence, CVE assisted language learning has become an interesting point in recent research on technology-supported language learning. The current work reviews specific issues in the context of CVE assisted language learning: (a) current research, theory and practice; (b) virtual reality assisted language learning; (c) link between CVEs and Web 2.0.

OVERVIEW

Language is best learned and acquired in immersive environments where the learners experience significant target language and cultural immersion. Collaborative virtual environments (CVEs) facilitate the immersion experiences. The popular three-dimensional CVEs such as Second Life and Active Worlds enrich expression, communication and sophisticated interaction through incorporating different modalities, including written, spoken, avatar movement and gesture, objects, images and videos. The combination of different modalities in the virtual environments allows multimodal communication, and facilitates the language and cultural immersion.

The idea for this chapter originates from the Krashen's (1987, 1988) theory of second language acquisition, which has informed the author's belief that natural language acquisition occurs in context, in authentic communication, in immersion and never divorced from social activities. Previous studies (e.g., Warschauer, 1996) indicate that computer-mediated communication and interaction create favorable premises for a language learning environment. I also agree that, "People

DOI: 10.4018/978-1-61692-825-4.ch005

do not learn languages and then use them, but learning languages by using them" (as cited in CARLA, n.d., ¶ 4). This belief has brought a wide range of in-world events via computer-mediated communication in which language is used and language acquisition occurs into virtual worlds.

This chapter offers an overview of the issues involved in immersive language learning in CVEs and the status of CVE learning. The aspects of immersive experiences in language learning, such as negotiation of meaning, intercultural communication and understanding, as well as interactional strategies are available in the popular CVEs. This study reviews the research investigating the previous issues based on observation of language learners' interactions and the analysis of discourse occurring in CVEs to explore pedagogical possibilities. However, the systematic investigation, including development, testing, evaluation, and research of the related issues is still in its infancy despite many project teams' efforts to conduct it.

The chapter is also devoted to the discussion of the current studies and implications of the related research conducted in the VEC3D (3D Virtual English Classroom) system launched in 2003. The curriculum adheres to collaborative, interactive and immersive language learning. The study focuses on developing and implementing the computer-assisted language learning (CALL) tasks and, concurrently, exploring English as a Foreign Language (EFL) issues and implications: communicative competence, vocabulary acquisition, reading comprehension, verbal and nonverbal communication, cross-cultural understanding and awareness in the context of 3D CVEs.

The latter part of the chapter explores the possible future trends in incorporating Web 2.0 tools such as blogs and other social networking sites with virtual environments in the context of language learning. Experiences in incorporating these technologies into the language teaching and learning process are addressed to indicate research challenges and possibilities for future

interdisciplinary implementation and research in technology and language learning.

The chapter headings are: Current CVEs for Language Learning, Research Projects, Interactive and Immersive Language Learning and Acquisition in CVEs, Conceptual Framework of CVE Assisted Language Learning, Beyond CVEs: Incorporating Modalities in VEC3D, Connection between CVEs and Web 2.0 for Language Learning, Conclusion and Future Trends.

CURRENT CVES FOR LANGUAGE LEARNING

This chapter focuses on three-dimensional collaborative virtual environments (CVEs), also referred to as virtual worlds, multi-user virtual environments (MUVE), such as Second Life (Linden Research, Inc., n.d.), Active Worlds (Activeworlds, Inc., n.d.), Project Wonderland (Sun Microsystems, Inc., n.d.), and There (Makena Technologies, Inc., 2010). Tomek (2001) defines CVE as "a software environment that creates a configurable universe which emulates a number of serviceable aspects of physical reality, such as space, movable objects, navigation, and communication between (representations of) humans" (as cited in Schmeil & Eppler, 2008, p. 1). CVEs, in which people embodied as avatars gather, interact with others, embodied agents, virtual objects and environments, offer an ideal atmosphere for language learning.

3D CVEs allow users to experience and perceive information in a dynamic interactive way, have a "feeling of immersion, a perceptual and psychological sense of *being in the digital environment*" (McLellan, 1996; as cited in Schmeil & Eppler, 2008, p. 2) and good "for model building and problem solving" (Schmeil & Eppler, 2008, p. 3). According to the survey (Eduserv, 2008), the most popular educational 3D CVE that has been increasingly used in educational settings is Second Life, which incorporates interaction, immersion, collaboration, and communication. "Educational institutions are increasingly turning to Second Life (SimTeach, 2007) to provide an e-learning environment that is more interactive, immersive and communicative" (as cited in Vickers, 2007, Introduction section, ¶ 2).

Second Life in education facilitates fruitful collaboration team projects and produces effective results in different educational fields. Schmeil and Eppler (2008) indicate that Second Life enhances collaboration and knowledge managing. According to Second Life Education Wiki (SimTeach, 2008a), educational institutions use Second Life for many and various educational uses and projects. Based on Wiki consensus, SimTeach WiKi (SimTeach, 2008b) also lists the current top twenty educational spaces in Second Life.

Second Life in language learning is also blooming and promising. For example, the English Village (http://englishvillage.asia/) provided by Fire Centaur and LanguageLab (http://www.languagelab.com/en-gb/) offered by Languagelab. com allow learners to engage in virtual language classes, role-play in different scenes and interact with both native and non-native speakers. Active Worlds is another popular virtual platform for language education. The research projects, e.g., ViTAAL (Koenraad, 2007, 2008) and VEC3D 1.0 (Shih, 2003), were conducted in Active Worlds.

Many research teams and language institutions present and share ideas, works and papers at the SLanguages Conference (Consultants-E, n.d.), held annually in Second Life. The conference explores language education within 3D virtual worlds, a good place to search for publications relevant to this field and meet researchers and practitioners around the world. The following introduces several (international) projects presented at the SLanguages virtual conference and Indiana University's Quest Atlantis.

RESEARCH PROJECTS

The leading researcher, Ton Koenraad, in the field of 3D Virtual Reality Assisted Language Learning (VRALL), is involved in the ViTAAL Project (2007-2008) and the NIAFLAR (2009-2011) project. He builds websites named TELL (Technology Enhanced Language Learning) consultant (http://www.koenraad.info/tellconsult-2), and VRALL (http://www.koenraad.info/vrall-2) for those interested in VRALL to access the latest information about VRALL activities and publications.

The ViTAAL Project (Koenraad, 2007, 2008) uses 3D MUVEs for modern language education, conducted in voice-enabled, Active Worlds for language education, within a constructivist educational context. The project implements a learner-centered, task-based, role-play approach with thirteen to fourteen year-old French students as foreign language learners in secondary schools. This approach focuses on oral skills using various data collecting methods: pre-post questionnaires, video and in-world audio recording of class sections, instructor observation and so on. One of the pilot studies of the ViTAAL project, Language Village, shows positive findings in motivation and attitudes. The study concludes from student's post questionnaires and teacher observation that students develop positive attitudes towards learning, including "increased motivation, more time on task and less inhibition" (Koenraad, 2008, p. 2). The learners' self-report reveals that students learn more vocabulary words, and are more aware of grammatical rules and pronunciation during their conversation. Systematic investigation is currently being conducted with future findings expected from the research group.

The international NIAFLAR Project (Network Interaction in Foreign Language Acquisition and Research Project) (University of Utrecht, 2009) is funded by the European Union and coordinated by the University of Utrecht. The project is currently designed and implemented to develop, mainly foreign language learners' communicative competence and intercultural awareness in Dutch, Portuguese, Spanish and Russian. The project emphasizes the target language and cross-cultural learning through various interaction formats, authentic tasks and blended learning, such as blending two learning environments, a video web conferencing environment and 3D virtual environment, to fulfill the project aims.

Indiana University's Quest Atlantis uses a 3D MUVE or CVE, developed within the framework of Active Worlds, known for creating curricular tasks, called quests, to engage children aged nine to twelve in various themes, such as water quality and weather. Quest Atlantis produces "learning gains" among students in language arts, reading and writing studies (Warren, Stein, Dondlinger, & Barab, 2008; Warren, 2006), social and science studies. The Quest Atlantis website (http://atlantis. crlt.indiana.edu/) demonstrates quantitative measurements of learning gains in different research areas. The Anytown Language Arts Unit of Quest Atlantis was created to enhance reading and writing performance. Learners assume the role of a newspaper reporter investigating what happened to a town facing challenges such as graffiti and arson and finding solutions to the mysteries. Warren, Stein, Dondlinger and Barab (2008) describe the instructional design process and implement the Unit by comparing the same writing process of two fifth- grade classrooms, the traditional curriculum class and class experience with the Unit. They reported "a statistically increase in pre-post learning gains on the essay items for both classes, with the class using the Anytown Unit showing significantly more improvement ($F(1, 40)=4.32$, $p<.05$) than the class using the traditional curriculum" (Indiana University, n.d., Section: Language Arts/Writing Comparison Study, ¶ 2).

INTERACTIVE AND IMMERSIVE LANGUAGE LEARNING AND ACQUISITION IN CVES

Interaction, immersion and communication are critical components of language learning and acquisition. CVEs support these components in natural contexts as well as in instructional settings.

Krashen (1981) distinguishes between language acquisition in natural contexts and language learning in instructional settings. Krashen posits that second language acquisition "requires meaningful interaction [with other people] in the target language and natural communication in which speakers are concerned, not with the form of their utterances, but with the messages they are conveying and understanding" (Krashen, 1981, p. 5). Nevertheless, language learning arises from formal language instruction through guided interaction (Krashen, 1981; Capocchi Ribeiro, 2002) with instructors. In both natural and teaching situations, "the driving force is the interpersonal . . . desire to interact with the environment" (Capocchi Ribeiro, 2002, p. 4) CVEs provide such an interactive environment that uses language naturally, and in which language is learned under instruction. Second Life, for instance, provides numerous natural occasions for authentic communication and interaction and language lessons, such as grammar and vocabulary, offered by language institutes, such as Avatar Languages, relying on the virtual environment to allow both interaction and communication.

Research investigating language learning and acquisition through interaction and immersion in CVEs is still in its infancy. Ideal conditions for language learning and acquisition in CVEs might be developed on the basis of proven hypotheses and relevant theories about language learning and acquisition. Through reviewing "optimal language learning environments" (Egbert, Chao, & Hanson-Smith, 1999), sociocultural and interactionist perspective of language learning, and essential hypotheses and suggestions, identified by Chapelle (1998) for a multimedia CALL design process, the following discusses the possibility of enhancing language learning and acquisition via CVEs and curriculum design.

Egbert, Chao, and Hanson-Smith (1999) summarize the theoretical bases for the most favorable language learning environments in the fields of Second Language Acquisition (SLA), and English as a Second Language (ESL). The requirements of "optimal language learning environments" (pp. 3-7) as follows might fit well with the language teaching opportunities of CVEs, which strengthen important aspects of language learning.

Condition 1. Learners Have Opportunities to Interact and Negotiate Meaning ... Condition 2. Learners Interact in the Target Language with an Authentic Audience ... Condition 3. Learners Are Involved in Authentic Tasks ... Condition 4. Learners Are Exposed to and Encouraged to Produce Varied and Creative Language ... Condition 7. Learners Work in an Atmosphere with an Ideal Stress/Anxiety Level ... Condition 8. Learner Autonomy Is Supported (Egbert, Chao, & Hanson-Smith, 1999, p. 4)

Participants in CVEs interact in the target language with embodied avatars manipulated freely by real persons as real audience and interlocutors. As avatars, participants are masked for anonymity which helps reduce stress and anxiety. They are involved in authentic tasks and exposed to the target language, and culture-rich environments in which collaboration and social interaction are highly supported.

The sociocultural perspective (Vygotsky, 1962) and interactionist perspective of language learning (Long, 1983; Pica, 1996) hold that interaction is the key to language learning. Interacting in a social context facilitates language development. Peyton (1999) indicates that,

many scholars who have studied the development of cognitive abilities and independent judgment show clearly that interaction and negotiation are crucial for learning and language development.... certain types of interactions promote learning and language development more than other do (Peyton, 1999, p. 19)

Vygotsky's social development theory (1978) states that social interaction plays a significant role in developing cognition, which relies solely upon the zone of proximal development (ZPD). Persons involved in social interaction and peer collaboration, especially with mentor guidance, attain ZPD. Vygotsky's insights are applicable to CVEs that create a context for social behaviors and collaboration, and could be designed to bridge the gap between learner's current and potential skill level by problem solving, guided by experts. EFL learners may also benefit from the exposure to the target language and culture.

Reviewed and concluded by Luria in 1976, Vygotsky's social constructivist perspective indicates that there are no in-born cognitive and thinking capacities in human beings; instead, these capabilities develop from socio-cultural interaction. "That is, cognitive skills and patterns of thinking are not primarily determined by innate factors, but are the products of activities practiced in social institutions of the culture in which the individual grows up" (Ricardo, 2004, ¶5). From the constructivists' perspective, online learning allows learners to co-construct their personal meaningful knowledge in a virtual context. Ally (2004) mentions, "With online instruction, learners experience information first-hand, which gives them the opportunity to contextualize and personalize the information themselves" (p. 19). Online CVE is an ideal environment for facilitating learners to contextualize information to meet their own learning needs.

Vygotsky's views on ZPD, which lie in interaction, may be a similar concept to the interaction hypothesis (Long, 1983; Pica, 1985), which assumes that language acquisition occurs when people interact, and to Lave and Wenger's (1991) situated learning through legitimate peripheral participation, which proposes that learning occurs in meaningful and realistic contexts within a social environment. Linking the concept of language acquisition in CVEs with social learning, constructivism, language input, situated learning and related theories inform language learning practices in CVEs.

However, exposure to language in interactive environments does not necessary guarantee successful language acquisition. Comprehension (Krashen, 1980), negotiation (Long, 1983), and production (Swain, 1985; Schachter, 1983, 1984, 1986) are also crucial in language development. Negotiating meaning and modifying interaction in second language learning (e.g., Long, 1985; Pica, 1996; Pica, Holliday, Lewis, & Morgenthaler, 1989), promote language acquisition. Chapelle (1998) identifies seven essential hypotheses and corresponding suggestions below, for a multimedia CALL design process.

1. Making key linguistic characteristics salient
2. Offering modifications of linguistic input
3. Providing opportunities for comprehensible output
4. Providing opportunities for learners to notice their errors
5. Providing opportunities for learners to correct their linguistic output
6. Supporting modified interaction between the learner and the computer
7. Acting as a participant in L2 tasks

Chapelle (1998, pp. 23-25)

These points may still hold true for CALL design in CVEs. Immersion in CVEs incorporating with an appropriate CALL activity design may stimulate interaction, communication, increase language acquisition, and enhance language learning. The suggestions may possibly fit with the language learning and acquisition opportunities provided by CVEs for (language) learning mediated through interaction (Vygotsky, 1962, 1978; Pica, 1996), "comprehensible input" (Krashen,

1981), "comprehensible output" (Swain, 1985), and "negotiated meaning" (Long, 1996). Several studies (e.g., Peterson, 2006a; Toyoda & Harrison, 2002) are investigating in what ways the interaction and computer-mediated communication in CVEs, especially comprehensible input/output and negotiation of meaning, contributes to enhance language acquisition.

CONCEPTUAL FRAMEWORK OF CVE ASSISTED LANGUAGE LEARNING

Research relevant to virtual worlds assisted language learning is still in its infancy. "Language learning in Second Life is still fairly embryonic (which explains the paucity of research)" (Wikidot, 2007). Recent relevant research issues and preliminary findings provide researchers and practitioners a base to build upon for future studies. I construct a conceptual framework (see Figure 1) to illustrate, acknowledge and explore such issues from different perspectives. The terminology resides in the framework constructed according to the related literature review, pilot studies, and previous and current research of my studies. The current study does not intend this framework to be an exhaustive list, but it does cover some of the key existing, expanding and potential research in the area of 3D virtual world assisted language learning and work, specifically in the field of second or foreign language learning. Researchers (e.g., Koenraad, 2007, 2008; Peterson, 2008, 2005; Toyoda & Harrison, 2002; Campbell, 2003; Shih & Yang, 2008) seek to expand research opportunities for language teaching through 3D virtual reality.

Koenraad (2007, 2008) has undertaken the ViTAAL project, focusing on oral proficiency training, and the NIAFLAR project, emphasizing the development of communicative competence as well as intercultural awareness. (See project details and preliminary findings in the previous section: Research Projects.)

Mark Peterson's (2005, 2006a) publications promote using interactional strategies within the context of 3D CVE based on his research (2004, 2006b, 2008) in MOO (MUD, Object Oriented). In Peterson's (2006a), twenty-four subjects are intermediate level EFL learners who communicate via text-based chat and interact through their embodied avatars in Active Worlds. Through analyzing chat logs and interaction among them, Peterson found that communication strategies, interactional strategies and negotiation of meaning occur during interpersonal communication. He also indicates that more instances of negotiation occur when participants interact with decision-making tasks than with other tasks. Types of tasks along with other sociolinguistic, contextual and technical variables affect EFL participants' ways of managing interaction. Peterson concludes that "learner interaction is influenced by the complex interaction of a number of variables including task type, sociolinguistic factors, context of use and the mix of technical affordances provided by 'Active Worlds'" (Peterson, 2008, Abstract section).

Toyoda and Harrison's (2002) study constructed a Japanese-language Education Worldwide Electronic Learning Space (JEWELS) in Active Worlds, with a focus on negotiation of meaning, involving five participant undergraduates, advanced Japanese language learners. By applying discourse analysis to conversations between participants and native Japanese speakers, they provided convincing evidence that communication difficulties and negotiation of meaning occur in communication mediated by the text-based chat system of Active Worlds. They also classified negotiations in different categories such as "sudden topic change" as well as "intercultural communication gap" and suggested using and reviewing chat logs as materials for inter-language development. "Successfully negotiating communication problems is essential in order to take advantage of comprehensible input and modified output. Reviewing chat logs may facilitate improving students' inter-language" (2002, p. 95), indicated Toyoda and Harrison. The results of their study correspond to the essential hypotheses and suggestions (see p. 10), mentioned by Chapelle in 1998, for a multimedia CALL design process.

Campbell (2003) designed task-based learning events for English/Japanese language and

Figure 1. Conceptual framework within the context of 3D virtual world assisted language learning

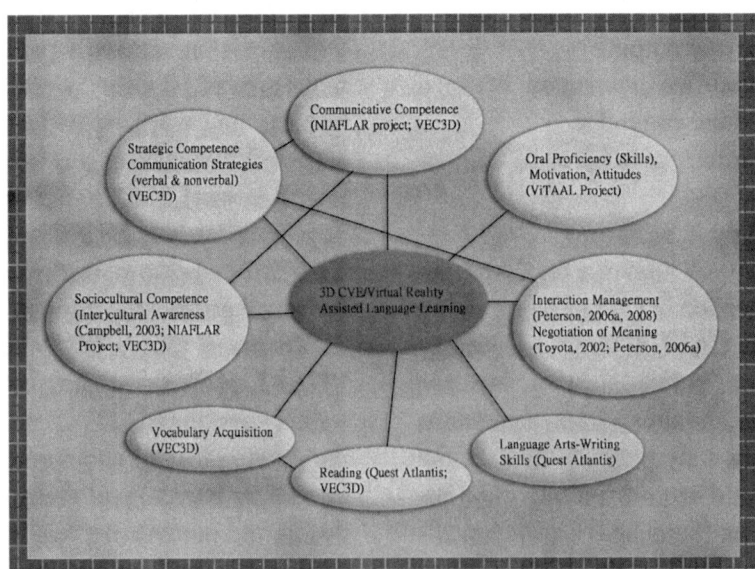

intercultural exchange to stimulate intercultural learning processes and tandem language learning. The paper describes the idea and implementation of integrating Active Worlds for synchronous discussion and co-creation of a 3D virtual environment with the Blackboard for asynchronous discussion. Within twelve weeks, twenty Japanese (English as a Foreign Language) and twenty British (Japanese as a Foreign Language) university level students engaged in activities, such as a virtual world field trip, co-construction in AW, a formal presentation and evaluation. Campbell's previous efforts contribute to fulfilling the following aims:

1. Fostering collaboration through positive interdependence and cooperative goal structures; 2. Encourage co-construction of knowledge through an interactive virtual environment; 3. Raise cultural awareness by working with foreign partners; 4. Increase language and computer skills; 5. Maintain student interest and motivation (Campbell, 2003, Discussion section)

The VEC3D project team, led by Dr. Ya-Chun Shih, investigated and reported on language learning and acquisition, communication, cultural and technical issues surrounding the use of 3D CVEs in English language learning. (See Figure 2 for screenshot of VEC3D website.) The VEC3D innovation starts with an inspired idea for integrating 3D virtual reality into the English classroom. The central research issues for the VEC3D project include reading comprehension, vocabulary acquisition, cultural awareness/understanding, and communicative competence, communication strategies, and (non)verbal communication, and linking areas of VRALL research.

The interdisciplinary research team of language educators and computer science experts includes initiatives to dissolve academic and practical boundaries between 3D virtual reality and language learning. The team endeavors to form a new method of teaching language in authentic contexts supplied by 3D virtual reality technol-ogy. The versions (1.0, 2.0, and 3.0) of VEC3D have been created and released to advance and satisfy future needs of technology solutions in this field. This work incorporates virtual worlds (VEC3D, Active Words, Second Life) as a new form of blended learning: namely, the VEC3D serves as an in-group interaction platform and the popular CVEs- Active Worlds and Second Life-enable VEC3D participants to virtually access the target language and community.

From 2003 to 2009, needs assessments and several pilot studies have been conducted in VEC3D 1.0, utilizing Active Worlds to develop college students' communicative competence and increase their motivation and engagement. Based on a needs assessment by college students, student virtual immersion experiences, needs and challenges occurring during their exploration in VEC3D 1.0 within the framework of Active Worlds are described. Shih (2003) concludes that "strategies for future 3D virtual ESL/EFL learning communities in college settings, and render virtual solutions for developing CALL materials for promising 3D virtual English classrooms" (p. 385).

In VEC3D 1.0 within the framework of Active Worlds, the research team is also exploring the possibilities of integrating 3D Virtual Reality into the elementary classroom to improve eleven to thirteen year-old pupils' reading comprehension, vocabulary acquisition, motivation and learning attitudes. One of the pilot studies, conducted in VEC3D 1.0, focuses on insights, curricula and ideas for incorporating Reader's Theater into CVE to enhance reading comprehension, motivation and attitudes.

A traditional Reader's Theater is created by the readers' imagination and is usually located in the classroom. Students as actors, take turns sitting or standing together to read through scripts, without memorizing and costumes, on a stage without props or scenery (Walker & Walker, 1990). Unlike a traditional Reader's Theater, which mainly relies on oral expression and gestures to build a "theatre of imagination" (Walker & Walker, 1990), the Reader's Theater in VEC3D allows students to read through scripts on a "virtual" stage while Reader's Theater is traditionally regarded as a "theatre of the imagination", in which students act out a story through oral reading and gestures.

The 3D Virtual Reality adds a visual dimension and context to Reader's Theater. By providing authentic audience embodied avatars controlled by participants and a voice-enabled virtual world context for reading aloud, performance and sharing stories, Reader's Theater in VEC3D 1.0 supplies struggling readers with the opportunity of acquiring vocabulary, becoming fluent in reading and improving reading comprehension. This study answers the question: How does integrating 3D Virtual Reality with Reader's Theater affect vocabulary acquisition, reading fluency and comprehension in the upper elementary grade classroom? The latest research (Shiau, 2009) demonstrates how curriculum integrated with 3D CVE and Reader's Theater contributes to elementary-school-age children's positive learning attitudes and reading comprehension.

Based on the belief that vocabulary acquisition occurs in context rather than out of context, another pilot study concentrates on an innovative way to incorporate Moodle (Modular Object-Oriented Dynamic Learning Environment) for asynchronous discussion and pre/post-event assessment with CVE in elementary school English teaching. The study explores new possibilities for enhancing vocabulary acquisition, especially word recognition and spelling, and improving upper graders' attitudes towards vocabulary acquisition using CVE in the elementary classroom. Preliminary findings show that vocabulary-learning tasks using CVE yield a high vocabulary retention rate and affect pupils' spelling over long time periods (Lin, 2009).

In sum, current and future studies of VEC3D need to investigate research questions, such as, In what ways does the interaction in CVEs, especially computer-mediated communication, enhance language learning and acquisition, specifically, negotiation of meaning, intercultural awareness, and strategic competence and (non)verbal communication?

Figure 2. Screenshot of VEC3D website

BEYOND CVES: INCORPORATING MODALITIES IN VEC3D

The technical support team also created VEC3D 2.0 and 3.0 (Figure 3) platforms (Shih, 2010) to increase research flexibility and feasibility. The team has investigated the possibility of providing integrated text and voice chat functions for VEC3D 2.0 and expanding communication from text or voice chat to multimodal communication, allowing natural conversations via verbal and nonverbal communication such as facial expression in VEC3D 3.0 (Shih, 2009, 2010).

The research team has conducted micro-ethnographic longitudinal case studies to explore how nonverbal communication can be used by EFL undergraduates to determine contributions of nonverbal features and to observe undergraduates' use of communication strategies and cross-cultural learning process in 3D CVEs. Interacting with a fluent native English speaking instructor in VEC3D 3.0, Second Life and Active Worlds, and other nonnative speakers provides EFL learners ample opportunity to gain cultural understanding and awareness. The points related to task implementation in VEC3D for cross-cultural understanding raised in Shih's (2009) journal paper, entitled "An innovative approach to task design and implementation in multimodal collaborative virtual environments" (see example for cross-cultural task in Figure 4 and Table 1).

The research team is also interested in exploring the impact of collaborative tasks in CVEs, enabling multimodal communication on an EFL learners' selection of communication strategies during the process of interlanguage. Curricula inspired by constructivist learning in virtual environments help learners acquire communication strategies. This study significantly explores the variation in the use of CSs in this innovative setting.

The research interests of the VEC3D group, to date, have focused on previous issues and exploring the possibility of integrating 3D virtual worlds and Web 2.0. These topics will constitute a part of VEC3D research work in the next few years.

CONNECTION BETWEEN CVES AND WEB 2.0 FOR LANGUAGE LEARNING

A language learning environment is currently needed that combines the best of both: 3D CVEs as the context for situated language learning and open social networking tools for collaborative

Figure 3. Screenshot of VEC3D 3.0

Table 1. Cross-cultural task: the trip to Banff

Mission 24 Cross-Cultural Role-Play	Task: **The Trip to Banff**	Duration: 90 minutes Location: VEC3D	Participants/Roles: Father (Teacher Jason), Son(s)/ Daughter(s)
Rules/Story Instruction/ Description	• You are planning and booking a family trip. 　　From: Vancouver Destination: Banff, Lake Louise, Alberta Budget: US$ 8000 　　Arrival: 08/04/2008 Departure: 08/14/2008 Adults: 1 Children: 3 • You will discover the protected wilderness surrounding Lake Louise, Banff (and Jasper) where you will explore spectacular natural mountain scenery and abundant wildlife in a protected National Park setting. (note: via YouTube) • Discuss with your family members, and plan communication strategies and language to use. (note: synchronous discussion in VEC3D 3.0) • Play out the scenario using the strategies and language you and the other members planned. (note: via VEC3D 3.0)		
Reference Materials	1. The Banff, Lake Louise Tourism Official Website http://www.banfflakelouise.com/ 2. Download Google Earth 4.2 http://earth.google.com/intl/en/download-earth.html#no_redirect 3. Google Map http://maps.google.com/ 4. Explore the Earth (Jason's home town/Vancouver/) on Google http://earth.google.com/ 5. Car Rental in Canada http://www.wheelsabroad.com/index_ca.php		

(Adapted from Shih, 2009, Table 3.)

language learning to form a community of practice or to facilitate e-tandem language learning. The NIAFLAR project, for instance, blends two environments: a video web conferencing environment and a 3D virtual environment. Campbell (2002) designed task-based events by integrating Active Worlds and the Blackboard, for pairs of Japanese and British students learning each others' languages.

The current trend draws interest and attention to linking or "mashing up" virtual worlds, such as CVEs, and Web 2.0 tools. Quest Atlantis blends

Figure 4. Website screenshot: Cross-cultural mission description webpage

3D CVEs constructed in Active Worlds and Web 2.0 such as weblogs for asynchronous discussion surrounding quest- or curriculum-related issues. Although the distinction between virtual worlds such as Second Life and the Web or Web 2.0 is blurred (Cashmore, 2006) or does exist, merging these two tools together is in the spotlight. The advantages and benefits of these social networking technologies open up innovative opportunities for integrating into language teaching. The popular CVE, Second Life serves as a new possibility for open social networking. Combining Second Life with blogs, for instance, has become a necessary language teaching technique since language learning is rooted in social interaction and collaboration. Language educators have recently shown interest in creating quests connecting immersive language learning into virtual worlds with media-rich Web 2.0 tools. SurReal Quest (Vickers, 2007), for instance, bridges real-life experiences and language learning, using Second Life and Web 2.0 tools such as blogs and podcast. The latest web development and combination allows learners to take an active role in collaboration, interaction, online community forming, resource sharing and language learning.

The connection idea originated from user needs. Teaching language entirely in virtual worlds without combining with other web tools seems somewhat barren of further information, new ideas, content, and discussion topics. The virtual world brings context to language learners, but by itself it is relatively insufficient for acquiring the target language, and cannot support prolonged engagement. Along with CVEs, Web 2.0 stimulates discussion, extends the conversation and provides more opportunities for collaboration and interaction in virtual worlds. Second Life, a CVE, "tends to add most value to language teaching when it is used in combination with other tools ... While the Web offers language learners a wealth of information" (Vickers, 2007, ¶ 24). Combining Web 2.0 and CVEs has facilitated the development of new forms of language learning

and acquisition. The connection also empowers users to contribute to develop content, expand social networking and co-construct knowledge in a dynamic and interactive way.

Connection is a must, but the challenge researchers face is how to make it work effectively and appropriately in educational settings. Web 2.0 tools allow "language teachers to integrate these tools very easily into the class setting. The potential of these tools is clear, but a greater body of research is required to inform the creation of guidelines to ensure these tools are integrated appropriately" (Wikidot, 2007). The research relevant to integrating Web 2.0 and virtual worlds is still in its infancy. However, blogs such as Avatar Languages Blog and discussions in CALL Sig, such as CALL Interest Section (CALL-IS), JALT (Japan Association of Language Teachers) CALL Special Interest Group (SIG) and CALICO Virtual Worlds Special Interest Group, are a rich source for insights into this brand-new teaching idea, effective language classroom practices, and future research. Currently, the VEC3D research team is designing tasks for merging CVEs and Web 2.0 (Shih, 2009, 2010).

CONCLUSION AND FUTURE TRENDS

This chapter is organized around the status and the future trends of 3D CVE assisted language learning. Within the framework of this research, research teams around the world still face the challenges of designing 3D VR applications for language learning and evaluating their effectiveness. A few research projects presented preliminary findings. Researchers also endeavor to bring hope to pedagogical research and investigation surrounding the integration of brand new technologies, such as 3D VR and Web 2.0 to support language learning and acquisition, specifically, cultural awareness such as the VEC3D project and SurReal Quest. The VEC3D team also creates platforms (VEC3D 2.0, 3.0) to ensure research feasibility and looks for the possibility of expanding voice chat in the virtual world and incorporating nonverbal communication such as body language with CVEs. Integrating virtual worlds and Web 2.0 is my current research interest. The territory of VRALL is expanding through integration, signaling it as a promising method for language learning, in research and in practice, in the future.

REFERENCES

Activeworlds, Inc. (n.d.). *Home page*. Retrieved January 24, 2010, from http://www.activeworlds.com/

Ally, M. (2004). Foundations of educational theory for online learning. In T. Anderson & F. Elloumi (Eds.), *Theory and practice of online learning* (pp. 3-31). Althabasca University: Canada. Retrieved January 24, 2010, from http://cde.athabascau.ca/online_book/pdf/TPOL_book.pdf

Avatar Languages. (n.d.). *Home page*. Retrieved January 24, 2010, from http://www.avatarlanguages.com/home.php

Avatar Languages Blog. (n.d.). *Dogme 2.0: What "Teaching 2.0" can learn from Dogme ELT*. Retrieved January 24, 2010, from http://www.avatarlanguages.com/blog/dogme-elt-web20-dogme20/

Campbell, A. P. (2003). *Foreign language exchange in a virtual World: An intercultural task-based learning event* [Electronic version], submitted as partial documentation for an M.Ed. in e-Learning at the University of Sheffield, U.K. Retrieved January 24, 2010, from http://e-poche.net/files/flevw.html

Capocchi Ribeiro, M. A. (2002). An interactionist perspective to second/foreign language learning and teaching. *Opinion Paper*. (ERIC Document Reproduction Service No. ED 469392).

CARLA (Center for Advanced Research on Language Acquisition). Content-Based Language Teaching with Technology. (n.d.). *Content-Based Second Language Instruction: What is it?* Retrieved January 24, 2010, from http://www.carla.umn.edu/cobaltt/CBI.html

Cashmore, P. (2006, May 30). *Second Life +Web 2.0= Virtual World Mashups*! Message posted to http://mashable.com/2006/05/30/second-life-web-20-virtual-world-mashups/

Chapelle, C. A. (1998). Multimedia CALL: Lessons to be learned from research on instructed SLA. *Language Learning & Technology*, *2*(1), 22–34.

Consultants-E. (n.d.). *SLanguages*. Retrieved January 24, 2010, from http://www.slanguages.net/home.php

Eduserv. (2008). *The Autumn 2008 Snapshot of UK Higher and Further Education Developments in Second Life*. Retrieved January 24, 2010, from http://www.eduserv.org.uk/foundation/sl/uksnapshot102008

Egbert, J., Chao, C. C., & Hanson-Smith, E. (1999). Computer-enhanced language learning environments: An overview . In Egbert, J., & Hanson-Smith, E. (Eds.), *CALL environments: Research, practice, and critical issues* (pp. 1–13). Alexandria, VA: TESOL.

Egbert, J., & Hanson-Smith, E. (Eds.). (1999). *CALL environments: Research, practice, and critical issues*. Alexandria, VA: TESOL.

Eppler, M. J., & Schmeil, A. (2009). Learning and knowledge sharing in virtual 3D environments: A classification of interaction patterns . In Bertagni, F., La Rosa, M., & Salvetti, F. (Eds.), *Learn how to learn*. Milan, Italy: FrancoAngeli.

Indiana University. (n.d.). *Quest Atlantis: Learning gains*. Retrieved January 24, 2010, from http://atlantis.crlt.indiana.edu/#66

Koenraad, A. L. M. (2007). *3D and language education.* White paper on the rationale for the ViTAAL project. Retrieved January 24, 2010, from http://www.koenraad.info/vrall-2/3d-and-language-education-1/view

Koenraad, A. L. M. (2008). How can 3D virtual worlds contribute to language education? Focus on the language village format. *Proceedings of the 3rd International WorldCALL Conference (WorldCALL 2008).* Retrieved October 30, 2009, from http://www.koenraad.info/vrall-2/how-can-3d-virtual-worlds-contribute-to-language-education/view

Krashen, S. (1980). The input hypothesis . In Alatis, J. (Ed.), *Current issues in bilingual education* (pp. 165–180). Washington, DC: Georgetown University.

Krashen, S. (1981). *Second language acquisition and second language learning.* Oxford, UK: Pergamon Press.

Krashen, S. (1987). *Principles and practice in second language acquisition.* New York: Prentice-Hall.

Krashen, S. (1988). *Second language acquisition and second language learning.* Upper Saddle River, NJ: Prentice-Hall International.

Lave, J., & Wenger, E. (1991). *Situated learning: Legitimate peripheral participation.* Cambridge, UK: Cambridge University Press.

Lemke, J. L. (1990). *Talking science: Language, learning and values.* Norwood: Ablex Publishing Company.

Lin, Y. C. (2009). *Research on vocabulary acquisition of upper elementary school students in a collaborative virtual environment.* Unpublished master's thesis, National Dong Hwa University, Hualien, Taiwan.

Linden Research Inc. (n.d.). *Second Life.* Retrieved January 24, 2010, from http://secondlife.com/

Long, M. (1983). Native speaker/non-native speakers conversation and the negotiation of comprehensible input. *Applied Linguistics, 4*(2), 126–141. doi:10.1093/applin/4.2.126

Long, M. (1985). Input and second language acquisition theory . In Gass, S., & Madden, C. (Eds.), *Input in second language acquisition* (pp. 177–393). Rowley, MA: Newbury House Publishers, Inc.

Long, M. (1996). The role of the linguistic environment in second language acquisition . In Ritchie, W., & Bhatia, T. (Eds.), *Handbook of second language acquisition* (pp. 413–468). San Diego, CA: Academic. doi:10.1016/B978-012589042-7/50015-3

Luria, A. R. (1976). *The cognitive development: Its cultural and social foundations.* Boston: Harvard University Press.

Makena Technologies, Inc. (2010). *There.* Retrieved January 24, 2010, from http://www.there.com/

McLellan, H. (1996). Virtual realities . In Jonassen, D. (Ed.), *Handbook of research for educational communications and technology.* New York: Macmillan.

O'Reilly, T. (2005). What is Web 2.0. *O'Reilly Network.* Retrieved January 24, 2010, http://oreilly.com/web2/archive/what-is-web-20.html

Peterson, M. (2004). MOO virtual worlds in CMC-based CALL: Defining an agenda for future research . In Jeong-Bae, S. (Ed.), *Computer-assisted language learning: Pedagogies and technologies* (pp. 39–59). Queensland, Australia: Asia-Pacific Association for Computer-Assisted Language Learning.

Peterson, M. (2005). Learner interaction in an avatar-based virtual environment: A preliminary study. *PacCALL Journal, 1*(1), 29–40.

Peterson, M. (2006a). Learner interaction management in an avatar and chat-based virtual world. *Computer Assisted Language Learning, 19*(1), 79–103. doi:10.1080/09588220600804087

Peterson, M. (2006b). Network-based computer assisted language learning (CALL): Emergent research issues . In Yoshitomi, A., Umino, T., & Negishi, M. (Eds.), *Readings in second language pedagogy and second language acquisition* (pp. 247–262). Amsterdam: John Benjamins.

Peterson, M. (2008). Non-native speaker interaction management strategies in a network-based virtual environment. *Journal of Interactive Learning Research, 19* (1), 91-117. Abstract retrieved October 30, 2009, from http://www.editlib.org/p/21889

Peyton, J. K. (1999). Theory and research: Interaction via computers . In Egbert, J., & Hanson-Smith, E. (Eds.), *CALL environments: Research, practice and critical issues* (pp. 17–26). Alexandria, VA: TESOL.

Pica, T. (1985). The selective impact of classroom instruction on second language acquisition. *Applied Linguistics, 6,* 214–222. doi:10.1093/applin/6.3.214

Pica, T. (1996). Second language learning through interaction: Multiple perspectives. *Working Papers in Educational Linguistics, 12,* 1-22.

Pica, T., Holliday, L., Lewis, N., & Morgenthaler, L. (1989). Comprehensible output as an outcome of linguistic demands on the learner. *Studies in Second Language Acquisition, 11*(1), 63–90. doi:10.1017/S027226310000783X

Quest Atlantis. (n.d.). *Learning gains.* Retrieved January 24, 2010, from http://atlantis.crlt.indiana.edu/#66 (Retrieved January 24, 2010)

Ricardo, S. (2004). Vygotsky & language acquisition. Retrieved January 24, 2010, from http://www.sk.com.br/sk-vygot.html

Schachter, J. (1983). Nutritional needs of language learners . In Clarke, M., & Handscombe, J. (Eds.), *On TESOL '82* (pp. 175–189). Washington, DC: TESOL.

Schachter, J. (1984). A universal input condition . In Rutherford, W. (Ed.), *Universals and second language acquisition* (pp. 167–183). Amsterdam: John Benjamins.

Schachter, J. (1986). Three approaches to the study of input. *Language Learning, 36,* 211–225. doi:10.1111/j.1467-1770.1986.tb00379.x

Schmeil, A., & Eppler, M. J. (2008). Collaboration patterns for knowledge sharing and integration in Second Life: A classification of virtual 3D group interaction scripts. *Proceedings I-KNOW 08,* Graz, Austria.

Schmeil, A., & Eppler, M. J. (2009). Knowledge sharing and collaborative learning in Second Life. *Journal of Universal Computer Science, 15*(3), 665–677.

Shiau, T. F. (2009). *Readers Theater in the virtual classroom: A case study of three sixth-grade readers.* Unpublished master's thesis, National Dong Hwa University, Hualien, Taiwan.

Shih, Y. C. (2003). 3D virtual immersion English learning experiences: College student views of their needs and challenges. *Proceedings of APA-MALL 2003 and ROCMELIA 2003* (pp. 385-394). Paper presented at The Seventh International Conference on Multimedia Language Education of ROCMELIA, National Chia Yi University, December 19-21.

Shih, Y. C. (2009). An innovative approach to task design and implementation in multimodal collaborative virtual environments. *The JALT CALL Journal, 5*(1), 61–73.

Shih, Y. C. (2010). *VEC3D Home page.* Retrieved January 24, 2010, from http://faculty.ndhu.edu.tw/~vec3d/

Shih, Y. C., & Yang, M. T. (2008). A collaborative virtual environment for situated language learning using VEC3D. [SSCI]. *Journal of Educational Technology & Society, 11*(1), 56–68.

SimTeach. (2007). *Institutions and organizations in SL*. Retrieved January 24, 2010, from http://www.simteach.com/wiki/index.php?title=Institutions_and_Organizations_in_SL

SimTeach. (2008a). *Second Life Education Wiki*. Retrieved January 24, 2010, from http://www.simteach.com/wiki/index.php?title=Second_Life_Education_Wiki

SimTeach. (2008b). *Top 20 Educational Locations in Second Life*. Retrieved January 24, 2010, from http://www.simteach.com/wiki/index.php?title=Top_20_Educational_Locations_in_Second_Life

Sun Microsystems, Inc. (n.d.). *Project Wonderland*. Retrieved January 24, 2010, from http://www.projectwonderland.com/

Swain, M. (1985). Communicative competence: Some roles of comprehensible input and comprehensible output in its development . In Gass, S., & Madden, C. (Eds.), *Input in second language acquisition* (pp. 235–256). New York: Newbury House.

Swain, M. (1995). Three functions of output in second language learning . In Cook, G., & Seidelhofer, B. (Eds.), *Principle and practice in applied Linguistics: Studies in honor of H.G. Widdowson* (pp. 125–144). Oxford, UK: Oxford University Press.

Swain, M., & Lapkin, S. (1995). Problems in output and the cognitive processes they generate: A step towards second language learning. *Applied Linguistics, 16*, 371–391. doi:10.1093/applin/16.3.371

Tarone, E., & Liu, G. Q. (1995). Situational context, variation, and second language acquisition theory . In Cook, G., & Seidelhofer, B. (Eds.), *Principle and practice in applied linguistics: Studies in Honor of H.G. Widdowson* (pp. 107–124). Oxford, UK: Oxford University Press.

Thornbury, S. (2000). A Dogma for EFL. *IATEFL Issues, 153*, 2. Retrieved January 24, 2010, from http://www.thornburyscott.com/assets/dogma.pdf

Thornbury, S. (2005). Dogme: *Dancing in the dark*? Folio, 9/2, 3-5. Retrieved January 24, 2010, from http://www.thornburyscott.com/assets/dancing%20in%20dark.pdf

Tomek, I. (2001). Knowledge management and collaborative virtual environments. *Journal of Universal Computer Science, 7*(6).

Toyoda, E., & Harrison, R. (2002). Categorization of text chat communication between learners and native speakers of Japanese. *Language Learning and Technology, 6*(1), 82-99. Retrieved January 24, 2010, from http://llt.msu.edu/vol6num1/pdf/toyoda.pdf

University of Utrecht. (2009). *NIFLAR Project Home Page*. Retrieved January 24, 2010, from http://cms.let.uu.nl/niflar

VEC3D. (2010). *Home page*. Retrieved January 24, 2010, from http://faculty.ndhu.edu.tw/~vec3d/

Vickers, H. (2007). *SurReal quests: Enriched purposeful language learning in Second Life*. Retrieved January 24, 2010, from http://www.avatarlanguages.com/articles/surrealquests1_en.php

Vygotsky, L. S. (1962). *Thought and language*. Cambridge, MA: The MIT Press. doi:10.1037/11193-000

Vygotsky, L. S. (1978). *Mind in society: The development of higher psychological processes*. Cambridge, MA: Harvard University Press.

Walker, H., & Walker, L. (1990). *Readers Theatre in the elementary classroom: A take part teacher's guide. North Vancouver, B.C.* Canada: Take Part Productions Ltd.

Warren, S. (2006). Researching a MUVE for teaching writing: The Anytown experience. In C. Crawford et al. (Eds.), *Proceedings of Society for Information Technology and Teacher Education International Conference 2006* (pp. 759-764). Chesapeake, VA: AACE.

Warren, S., Stein, R. A., Dondlinger, M. J., & Barab, S. A. (2008). A look inside a MUVE design process: Blending instructional design and game principles to target writing skills. *Journal of Educational Computing Research, 40* (3). Baywood Publishing Company.

Warschauer, M. (1996). *Computer-mediated collaborative learning: Theory and practice* (Research Note 17). Honolulu: University of Hawaii, Second Language Teaching Curriculum Center.

Wikidot. (2007). *Web 2.0/language learning: Second Life.* Retrieved January 24, 2010, from http://web20andlanguagelearning.wikidot.com/second-life

KEY TERMS AND DEFINITIONS

Computer Assisted Language Learning: CALL is the acronym for Computer Assisted Language Learning and is defined as (the study of) the use of computers in language learning and teaching. Computer technology in the language learning domain is a promising field in Information and Learning Technology, as well as in Language Instruction.

Collaborative Virtual Environment: CVE is the acronym for Collaborative Virtual Environment. CVEs, typically built in Virtual Reality Modeling Language (VRML), are created to support multi-user collaboration and interaction, regardless of the distance, and have currently been used in educational settings. Participants are embodied in avatars and use chat boxes and/or voice chat to communicate with others in CVEs.

Web 2.0: The term "Web 2.0" originates from "a brainstorming session between O'Reilly and MediaLive International" (O'Reilly, 2005). Web 2.0, including web applications, such as blogs, wikis, video-sharing Web sites, is used to foster collaboration, interaction, communication and information sharing on the World Wide Web.

Virtual Reality Assisted Language Learning: VRALL is the acronym for Virtual Reality Assisted Language Learning. A computer-generated three-dimensional environment, such as Second Life, is used to assist language learning. VRALL is the new frontier in CALL.

Chapter 6
Unpacking Strong vs. Weak Presence in Second Life Enactive Role Play

Caroline M. L. Ho
Nanyang Technological University, Singapore

ABSTRACT

This chapter focuses on investigating participants' presence in Second Life among students in enactive role play. The interest in the study is on the nature of participant interaction and construction of discourse moves which reflect the nature and extent of their presence (identified as 'strong' or 'weak') in the virtual world. The chapter examines the key concept of presence and its association with related concepts of engagement and identity against the sociocultural approach to learning and functional linguistic theory which provide the theoretical underpinnings and frame the research focus of this study. A review of related studies in the field follows after which background information on the context of the study is provided. The method of analysis is explained after which an analysis and a discussion of findings are presented. The chapter closes with highlighting the pertinent pedagogical implications of virtual enactive role play in 3D immersive spaces for learning.

INTRODUCTION

Virtual world environments are increasingly recognized as dynamic platforms for collaborative, participatory learning and co-construction of knowledge in various contexts for different purposes (Antonacci & Modress, 2008, Lee, 2009, Warburton, 2007). They provide new opportunities to enrich the educational experience through media-rich immersive learning (New Media Consortium, 2009; Wagner, 2008). Three-dimensional (3D) immersive spaces in virtual worlds actively engage participants in multi-party, interactive, digital simulations through digital personas or avatars created in a variety of ways-visually, aurally and interactively (Cruz-Neira, 1998). Interaction in immersive virtual environments has expanded the scope of what participants do in the real, physical world as participants have been noted to identify more strongly with avatars

DOI: 10.4018/978-1-61692-825-4.ch006

through learning to think, speak and act in role (Shaffer, 2006). Further, in directly being involved in actively creating content through their virtual experiences, this is acknowledged to facilitate social interactions closely related to those in reality (Gee, 2003). Ultimately, the vicarious experience arising from real time interaction in immersive learning spaces enables participants to better relate to complex issues which may be better dealt with than in reality (Shaffer, 2007). The growing interest shared among educators today in exploring the potential of virtual environments for supporting and enhancing teaching and learning (Good & Thackray, 2008; White, 2008) is not surprising. There are now around 5,000 educators who are active in virtual world environments, accounting for more than 300 institutions worldwide (Tamsyn, 2009).

The chapter draws on a larger research study (Ho, Rappa, Chee, 2009) of the Second Life (SL) immersive learning environment in the context of the subject General Paper (GP) offered at the pre-university level (Grade 12) in Singapore which emphasizes argumentation and critical thinking. The interest in the design experiment (Brown, 1992; Collins, 1992) is in providing students a creative opportunity to develop skills in purposeful dialogic interaction through enactive role play (Bruner, 1968, 1966; Varela, Thompson & Rosch, 1991) where they learn to critically think, construct arguments, and exchange viewpoints and perspectives in the process of virtual dialoguing with other participants.

Enactive role play in virtual worlds where participants assume and act out specific roles in various situations is acknowledged to enable students to acquire collective intelligence, skills of problem-solving, strategic thinking, interpreting contexts and imaginative play (Gee, 2004; Shaffer, 2007). This act of 'knowing by doing' (Bruner, 1968) emphasizes that 'embodied sensory and motor processes, perception and action are fundamentally inseparable in lived cognition' (Varela, Thompson & Rosch, 1991, p.172-173).

The advantages afforded by the multimodality in the 3D virtual space (Beach, Anson, Breuch, & Swiss, 2008; Beach & Doerr-Stevens, in press) facilitate a dynamic form of interactivity where students can visually identify and respond to other participants, and acquire collaborative argumentation skills (Beach & Doerr-Stevens, 2009). This underscores a sociocultural approach to learning (Vygotsky, 1986) which emphasizes that higher order functions and learning are embedded in active and engaged participant interaction.

Investigating the emerging technologies and trends through communication and interaction in virtual immersive environments and 3D learning spaces is an overarching theme in this volume. With this interest in view, this chapter specifically seeks to account for how participant presence is realized linguistically to varying degrees, and to identify specific discourse strategies adopted against the heteroglossic (Bakhtin, 1981) backdrop of voices of the 'other' within a specific immersive virtual learning environment. Attention is given to specific linguistic resources and strategies used by participants in their enactments to engage meaningfully with each other within the interactive, 3D, multi-party context of the virtual exchange.

THEORETICAL UNDERPINNINGS

Presence

The concept of presence carries different interpretations for various individuals in fulfilling diverse purposes in a range of contexts. It has been acknowledged that there are no formal definitions on presence (Stanney et. al., 1998) due to a lack of established and effective indicators to measure presence in the virtual world environments (Sadowski & Stanney, 2002). However, as a concept central to virtual worlds and immersive environments, it has a significant place in representing an individual's online behaviour in relation to other participants and to specific situations created, and in sharpening the focus, attention and motivation driving the multiparty interaction in the virtual context.

Presence is recognized to describe a user's sense of 'being there' when interacting with a mediated environment (Ijsselsteijn et al., 2000; Insko, 2003; Schubert, Friedmann & Regenbrecht, 1999). It has been alternatively defined as 'the subjective experience of being in one place or environment, even when one is physically situated in another' (Witmer & Singer, 1998). With regard to the virtual world, it is perceived as an experience that one has left the physical reality and is present in the virtual environment (Minsky, 1980). Indeed, presence in such an environment has been conceived as an existence in the virtual world where one is (Heeter, 1992; Sheridan, 1992; Steuer, 1992; Witmer & Singer, 1998) and the quality of experience in the virtual world (Gaggioli, Bassi & Delle Fave 2003).

It is to be noted that presence is unlike *immersion* and *involvement* per se although they are closely related. *Immersion* refers to the extent and nature of technology-provided sensory stimuli, and is often associated with the pervasiveness of visual, audio, olfactory, and tactile inputs (Schubert, Friedmann, & Regenbrecht, 1999) to the extent that users may begin to lose self- consciousness and their sense of time (Byrne, 1996) in the virtual world. *Involvement* requires a degree of attention and meaning from participants devoted to some set of stimuli (Witmer & Singer, 1998) with a focus, or the ability to 'concentrate on enjoyable activities and block out distraction' (in Schuemie et al, 2001, p.198). It involves engagement, that is, a 'sustained interest in participating in the world, especially at a social level (Pearce, 2006). Participants who are engaged are involved in a 'kind of substantial emotional investment' (Geertz, 1972/3, p. 432) where, particularly in gaming environments, this amounts to 'deep play' (Geertz, 1972/3) in their 'accessing or accumulating layers of meaning that have strategic value' (Carr in McMahan, 2003, p. 69).

Participants who display a characteristic presence project a distinct identity which, to Goffman (1956/1959/1973), parallels executing a 'performance' in the participants' 'project of the self' (Giddens,1991). What is reflected is the 'character who is the impression that is getting fabricated through the ongoing performance' (Giddens,1991). Gee (2003, p. 55) sees a fusion between participants and the personas they assume in a 'projective identity' in the virtual environment when they 'strongly identify with the character and thus have an immersive experience' (Jenkins at al, 2006,p.28). The digital persona or avatar in the virtual world is the player's entire self-representation in providing an online identity for the player. As an 'identity cue', it keys online behavior for the player (Yee & Bailenson, 2007) with the virtual characters becoming 'one's own project in the making' (Gee, 2003, p. 55). The identity is perceived in terms of 'being recognized as a certain "kind of person," ' in a given context (Gee, 2001, p.99) and is linked to roles. Roles, in turn, 'are linked to "ways of talk" of types of discourse' (Chee, 2007, p.10) which is what this paper is essentially interested in unpacking. The manner in terms of specific discourse moves and strategies adopted by participants in their virtual dialoguing with each other as they think in role and play out their assigned avatars is at the heart of this investigation.

In this study, presence involves executing influential discourse moves which are distinctive and explicit in impacting the nature and content of the virtual dialoguing. This chapter seeks to unpack presence in an immersive virtual world by examining, identifying and categorizing specific discourse moves and strategies which play a functional role in actively engaging participants, and are strategic in their use in directly evoking participants' response and action. The focus is on distinct moves generated by participants themselves in the enactments which are targeted at impacting and making a difference to the nature and content of real time virtual dialoguing.

The approach to the investigation in this study was predominantly language focused and informed by a few main traditions. It was underpinned by a sociocultural view of language as a cognitive and cultural tool used in dialogue to support the construction of shared knowledge (Kumpulainen & Wray, 2001; Mercer, 1995; Wells, 1999). Students are engaged in learning, thinking as knowing with relations fostered among people involved in 'activity in, with and arising from the socially and culturally structured world' (Lave,1991, p.67). The second influence derived from functional linguistic theory (Halliday, 1985) with a focus on the relationship between specific aspects of the context as in the roles assumed by participants in enactive virtual representation and the specific language use in the discourse moves and strategies adopted. The approach offered description of the way in which participants constructed their discourse moves in order to achieve different communicative goals and facilitated the tracking of participants in their virtual dialoguing across scenarios. Attention centred on specific discourse moves and salient features reflective of participants' establishing a presence in the virtual world and the degree of influence in engaging with other participants and in impacting viewpoints and perspectives.

LITERATURE REVIEW

Studies on Presence in Virtual Worlds

Available studies unpacked a range of methods for identifying characterizing features and precise measures for what constitutes presence. This was by no means a simple and straightforward venture, given that presence was acknowledged to comprise complex, multidimensional constructs which are composed of numerous factors (ljsselsteijn & Riva, 2003). Earlier investigation considered the extent and fidelity of sensory information, the mapping of actions and effects, content factors including characters, objects and events, as well as the characteristics and abilities of users (Ijsselsteijn et. al., 2000). Various other factors were identified to affect presence: control, sensory, distraction and realism factors (Witmer & Singer, 1998), and others comprising spatial presence, involvement, realness, immersion quality, drama, interface awareness, exploration and predictability (Schubert, Friedmann & Regenbrecht, 1999).

The concept of presence was researched from different dimensions to determine what distinguished it from traditional environments. Pearce's (2006) research with Uru refugees, as well as in other virtual play spaces, unpacked significant dimensions of presence, including Shared Fantasy/Consensual Hallucination, Seeing and Being Seen/The Avatar, Social Construction of Identity, Play Communities, citizenship/ownership. A multidisciplinary European project, Presenccia (2006), examined the phenomenon of presence from different angles, in particular, social presence in mixed reality. In the context of the project, a Persistent Virtual Community (PVC) provided a platform for entities of different degrees of virtuality to meet and interact. The environment allowed for both virtual and physical interaction by participants, and facilitated an installation that embodied an artificial intelligent entity that accommodated and learnt from its interaction with individuals.

Rowe, McQuiggan & Lester (2007, p.1) narrowed the focus to one of 'narrative presence', that is, 'the sense of being in or part of a story', where it is understood as 'an affective-cognitive construct that characterizes an audience's perceived relationship with a story' (p.2). It essentially involves 'feelings of participation, embodiment, or disembodied observation' in a narrative with participants reporting feelings of being transported into a story (Gerrig, 1993). In developing *Crystal Island,* a testbed of a narrative-centred learning environment for middle school students, Rowe, McQuiggan & Lester (2007) examined evaluative methods for subjective and objective assessment with design implications for interactive narrative-centred learning in the move towards implementing 'adaptive, effective pedagogy that is both motivating and meaningful' (Rowe, McQuiggan & Lester 2007, p. 1). In gaming environments, Chee and Lim's (2009) computer game, *Space Station Leonis*, showed how role playing could help to foster attitudes, values and beliefs desired of citizenship education. Carefully designed learning activities that provided students the opportunity to engage in dialectic interplay between role-playing in the game world and dialogic interaction outside of the game world (p.808) encouraged player empathies that derived from projecting player identities onto game characters (p.822).

Existing literature uncovered studies which have largely focused on identifying the characteristic features of and specific measures for what constitute presence. While there was substantial documentation of research for developing various methods for measuring presence and identifying factors or contributing causes affecting presence, it was also recognized that there may be little conclusive evidence regarding the relationship between presence and specific variables. A survey of research on presence in virtual reality indicated that while most theories and perspectives of presence devoted attention to specific roles played by the cognitive process and models of attention and virtual space, the link between emotional responses and virtual stimuli remained inconclusively proven (Schuemie et al, 2001). Further, rather than viewing the range of attributes representing presence as disparate features isolated and distinct from each other, we are reminded to see the various elements 'as a continuum' (McMahan, 2003, p.80) that each environment would realize differently, and where each dimension shares something in common with others. The search for meaningful investigations in the attempt to determine useful indices and specific criteria for coming to terms with this elusive concept continues even as educators seek to understand what contributes

to presence arising from environments, contexts, tasks or activities which could offer significant potential for enhancing students' immersive learning experiences.

Studies on Second Life in Language Education

Second Life, developed by Linden Lab. (Linden Research, Inc. 2008), is one of the most popular three dimensional, user-generated virtual world environments (Tamsyn, 2009). 'Residents' interacted with each other through personalized avatars, and used specially provided virtual and scripting tools to design objects or buildings in the virtual world. They could engage in a range of activities, individually and in groups, and create their own experiences and activities. SL has been used as a platform for students to participate in discussions by assuming the roles of the various avatars, which would be difficult to re-enact in reality (Brandsford & Gawel, 2006). Participation levels in SL more than 10 million users (Wagner, 2008). A 2008 SL survey conducted by the New Media Consortium (NMC) reported that more respondents were involved in an educational-related activity, from 54% in 2007 to 71% in 2008 with an increase in percentage of experienced SL educators from 30% in 2007 to 56% in 2008. The top most positive SL experiences gained comprised rich interactions through contact among individuals, network expansion (51%) and education, teaching and learning-related activities (24%).

Language-based SL projects have generated interest among learners in various parts of the world. The Kidz Connect (2009) project involved young people from different countries in collaborative performance and storytelling through the use of theatrical and digital technologies. Students were connected via media art, performance and collaborative creation in Teen SL, and live shows were created with others in distributed locations. They learnt about each other's culture in the process through music, dance, digital art and/or storytelling within the virtual environment. In 2006, the pilot project included young people from New York and Amsterdam and explored New York's Dutch heritage and the connection between historical and contemporary culture in New York and Amsterdam. In 2008, students at the Patel Conservatory in Tampa, Florida collaborated with students at the IVKO Montessori School in Amsterdam, Netherlands.

Other language-based projects provided opportunities for non-native English speakers to interact with native students and teachers of English. The English Village (2007), founded by Preibisch aka Fire Centaur in SL, is an immersive 3D simulation for language learners and teachers worldwide to create and collaborate as they explore the possibilities of teaching languages in SL through easy to use tools and features provided. A central feature of the English Village are holodecks offering a range of different scenes for role play that can be swapped at the click of a button. The Language Lab. (n.d.), by Edgware Marker aka David Kaskel, created immersive language learning opportunities in SL for learners to interact in a realistic environment with native-speaking teachers. The school's 120-acre island comprised a full city for student participation in various activities including role-play in realistically created settings as in hotels, nightclubs and offices or in scheduled classes which meet regularly. Social learning opportunities through game playing as in the football-field-sized Scrabble game, or socializing in the informal learning spaces were offered. Many of these available studies involved largely English as a Foreign Language (EFL) environments with a focus on building up basic language proficiency through increased contact between native and non-native speakers of the language.

Schools in Singapore are actively exploring the potential of virtual worlds to teach real life to students (*The Straits Times*, 2009). Lower secondary (Grade 7) students at a secondary school critique art pieces found in a gallery that exists only in Second Life and a pre-university college

is exploring the use of virtual worlds to teach Malay literature, with students (Grade 11) playing characters from the texts studied. Teachers have cited the plus points as the customisable nature of virtual platforms which offers 'tremendous flexibility in designing scenarios' and permitting 'actions not possible.. in real life, like putting a dog to sleep' (*The Straits Times*, 2009). Further, the interactive nature of such learning environments was encouraging generally passive and shy students to become more involved and to participate more often in class.

Unlike a number of existing language-based studies in SL which cater to primarily basic language proficiency needs of learners, this chapter seeks to harness the potential of 3D immersive environments in engaging pre-university students through enactive role play in a dynamic context to enhance their critical thinking and reasoning skills as they engage at a higher level to develop a distinct persona and voice of their own. This is in line with interest among researchers and to fill the existing gap in virtual world studies, particularly in this region.

RESEARCH FOCUS

This chapter seeks to address research concerns centering on identifying specific discourse moves and strategies which projected strength of presence, if any, in the virtual world. The degree or extent of participant presence which could be characterized as *strong* or *weak* is determined by unpacking participants' discourse moves as participants reacted and responded to each other's viewpoints and arguments raised in the virtual dialoguing. The explicit manner as to how participants dialogued with each other in real time in SL is of interest in this paper in determining the nature and extent to which participants exhibited control, influence and/or involvement in the enactments. The underlying pedagogical implications of enactive role play for developing participant presence in the virtual world and for promoting engaged real-time learning among students are further discussed.

INSTRUCTIONAL SETTING AND SUBJECTS

The GP, termed a 'Knowledge Skills' subject at Higher 1 (H1) level 'for broadening purposes' for tertiary level studies (Ministry of Education, 2004) in Singapore, requires students to 'draw on their knowledge from across disciplines as well as to show an awareness of current, global, and significant local or national issues' (Ho, 2006, p.3) in their argumentation. The emphasis is on the 'ability to convey a sustained and well thought–out argument' (Ho, 2006, p.3) through skills involving primarily logical and intellectual argument.

For the purpose of the study, a private island was acquired in SL for educational use by the researchers within the Teen Grid. The island was restricted to users who were under 18 years old and access was granted only to the researchers, teachers and student participants who voluntarily agreed and offered signed written consent to be involved in the study. The name of the island, '*You*Topia', conveyed to the participants that they could create an ideally perfect, secure and comfortable world where they could engage in decision-making and in carrying out activities which rested solely in their power and control.

The subjects were from an Arts class of final year, pre-university 17 to 18 year old students with average ability in the GP. This chapter focuses on a group of four male and female students drawn from the class of 23 students. The students were identified based on their participation in the virtual enactments across three scenarios. Selected students chosen for closer examination exemplified a range of indicators that showed varying degrees of presence compared to the rest of their peers. In order to maintain consistency across scenarios,

the students who enacted similar roles across the scenarios were focussed. This was to facilitate identification and comparison of discourse moves and strategies represented by the students in projecting a strong and/or weak presence.

Students were immersed in carefully constructed scenarios (Figure 1) for enactment and discussed issues that were related to euthanasia (Ho, in press). At the start of every scenario, students were provided information on the learning outcomes of the session and role cards with background input on their characters and situation. Each scenario depicted a problem or conflict which all parties involved aim to resolve. Roles were assigned to students in their groups. For this paper, the focus centred on the roles of doctor-Dr Martin Loh, pastor-Rev Matthew Chia, lawyer -Mr Mohd Faizal, parent of patient-Richard Wee and audience of TV chat show. Each enactment lasted for approximately seventy minutes.

This chapter examined developments in three scenarios. In scene one, the discussion centred on the definition of persistent vegetative state, the differences in the euthanasia laws and medical guidelines in America, the Netherlands and Singapore, with the aim of euthanising Amy, a lady who had brain damage for eight years. Scene two revolved around the issue of sanctity of life, with Kok Leong, Amy's husband, proposing to remove her feeding tube while Mr and Mrs Wee, Amy's parents, objecting and planning to make a video to show Amy had actions that reflected signs of life. Scene three centred on arguments for and against euthanizing Amy in a television studio for a live chat show with the guests, home and studio audience. Kok Leong, Mr and Mrs Wee were appealing for public support.

METHOD OF ANALYSIS

The logged transcripts of students' SL enactments were recorded in text format using a SL 'save' feature. Students' extracts of enactments were quoted verbatim in this chapter. A gloss was provided in brackets for non-standard representations of lexical items where relevant. The participant's first name was the student's chosen name (names changed to preserve student anonymity) followed by the second name, 'YouTopia', which was common to all participants, hence, *Jacky YouTopia*.

Discourse analysis is essentially the analysis of language in use and language in context with the context referring to the very shape, meaning and effects of the social world (Gee, 2005, Wetherell, Taylor & Yates, 2001). It emphasizes what individuals do when they communicate through a particular mode of discourse and shows how discourses are produced, reproduced and transformed through particular linguistic features. The focal point of interest in studying discourse revolves around meaning-making in a specific context. The framework for analysis was generated by the researchers using data from the logged transcripts of participants' virtual enactments. A discourse move, under current definition in prevailing studies, is regarded as 'a minimal free unit of discourse' that represents 'a coherent aspect of a subject of discussion' and 'calls for, or opens up the possibility of, a reaction (Hengeveld & Mackenzie, 2008). Each type of move has its own communicative intention and a perlocutionary effect (Genee &

DeVries, 2008). In this study, specific discourse moves were identified which played a role in influencing participants' virtual dialoguing. These included moves that elicited responses, probed for specifics, challenged viewpoints, opened up dissent, initiated new turns in topics, expanded arguments, clarified points and terminated the focus of discussion. The analysis of the transcripts was carried out manually by the researchers in identifying the various discourse moves in terms of their functional roles in the specific enactment. The systematic analysis in terms of the relationship between particular aspects of the context such as the functional roles of discourse moves adopted and the specific language features realized offers an explicit linguistic description of the way in which language in the virtual dialoguing is used to achieve different communicative purposes. Attention was given to the context of the particular enactment which realized the discourse move(s) adopted. The categorization of discourse moves was made independently by each researcher and then cross-checked with each other for consistency in classification. Frequency scores were tabulated for the various categories.

Figure 1. Screenshot of SL enactive role play

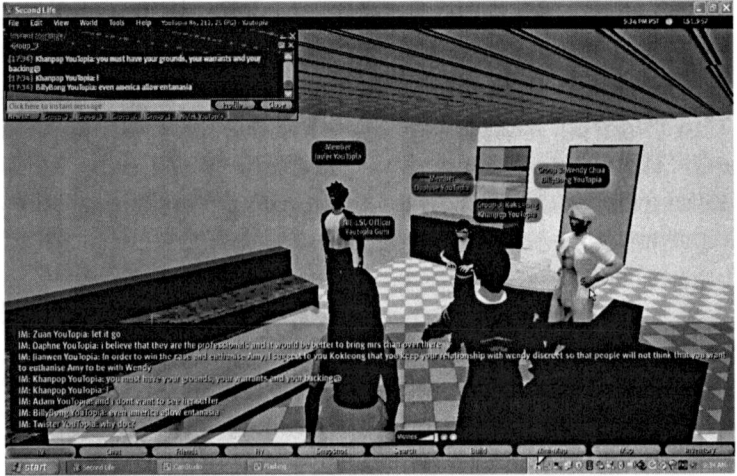

FINDINGS AND DISCUSSION

From the four participants, 155 discourse moves were recorded during the SL virtual enactments across the scenarios. Table 1 provides the breakdown of student participation in terms of the discourse moves adopted:

In terms of participation rate, students who exhibited a more active role in enactment were observed to contribute more entries overall (in the region of fifties as evident in Students A, B) compared to the fewer number of entries registered (in the region of twenties in Students C, D) by relatively less active students, despite the slight differences in frequency across students in specific individual moves. It is acknowledged that quantitative measures alone, while useful in a quick sieving out of participants in terms of enactment contribution rate, are to be supplemented by close qualitative text analysis of the transcripts which generated the specific discourse moves employed for a fuller picture of the nature, range and type of discourse moves and strategies adopted.

The following sections attempt to identify, classify and illustrate the various discourse moves and strategies employed by students in specific contexts.

A. Eliciting Responses

This move requested information from participants. The initiator was likely to pose a question based on an ongoing topic of discussion. Students who displayed a stronger presence were more active in adopting this move which registered the highest or second highest frequency of occurrence. They elicited participant response by explicitly setting their questions in context. The framing of questions involved building up the context of the

Table 1. Overall discourse moves adopted in students' enactive role play in Second Life

Discourse move Total no.:155	Student A Irene You-Topia Total No.: 54	Percentage of occurrence (%)	Student B Jacky YouTopia Total No.: 52	Percentage of occurrence (%)	Student C Will You-Topia Total No.: 22	Percentage of occurrence (%)	Student D Chris You Topia Total No.: 27	Percentage of occurrence (%)
Eliciting Responses	13	24.0	14	26.9	*2*	9.1	3	11.1
Probing for specifics	2	3.8	6	11.5	*3*	13.7	1	3.7
Challenging points	18	33.3	7	13.5	*5*	22.7	3	11.1
Opening up dissent	10	18.5	5	9.6	*3*	13.6	3	11.1
Initiating new turns in topic	3	5.5	8	15.4	*4*	18.2	6	22.3
Expanding arguments	5	9.2	2	3.9	*1*	4.5	5	18.5
Clarifying points	2	3.8	6	11.5	*4*	18.2	3	11.1
Terminating focus of topic	1	1.9	4	7.7	*0*	0	3	11.1

elicitation with a preface leading up to the actual request for information. There was attention to encouraging and inviting response ('In view of your insistent point, let me ask you a question, perhaps it may solve your problem') with a distinct point of focus as in:

```
Jacky YouTopia: In view of your
insistent point, let me ask you
a question, perhaps it may solve
your problem, if your daughter's
organs is damaged to an extent
that she could have a life ex-
pectancy of a average person
but everyday she lives is like
living in Hell, would you still
keep her alive?
```

The elicitations by such participants who exhibited control over the situation also carried specific addressees ('*Amy*, do you concur?') from whom response was targeted:

```
Jacky YouTopia: I would suggest
that the diet you should take
is by eating moderately and not
skip meals
Jacky YouTopia: Amy, do you con-
cur?
```

A direct interrogative structure: do+you+verb ('do you not know..', 'do you concur'), carrying a rhetorical force of its own. These participants came across as having a better grasp and control of the discussion compared to other participants.

By contrast, elicitations by students who did not display as strong a hold over discussions appeared shallow in the form of brief one-liners and entries with unspecified addressees that were terse and sparse:

```
Chris YouTopia: you all can get
church members to vote whether
```

```
to euthansise amy or not??
Chris YouTopia: why??
Will YouTopia: what do you
think? about euthanasia, about
the video, about amy
```

B. Probing for Specifics

This move sought details and specific information from participants. It was typically based on an inadequate response (from the initiator's point of view) given earlier in the dialoguing, as seen here where it was directed at a specific addressee:

```
Irene YouTopia: Dr Martin Loh,
you need to tell us more, why
you are so unsettled about it.
```

Dr Loh had been against euthanasia and was bent on upholding the sanctity of life. However, as a doctor, it was only professional of him to provide more information on the implications of euthanasia should Kok Leong (Amy's husband) decide to opt for this. He was now put in a position to explain his perspective of the situation.

Elicitations in this category carried an element of cajoling ('you need to tell us more') as in the above, and explicit prompts ('tell me your trouble and I may provide help') to invite specificity of information and detail as in the following:

```
Jacky YouTopia: tell me your
trouble and I may provide help
```

Students who were comparatively weaker in presence did not appear to adopt this probing move as frequently as other students. They did not exert that same level of control in delving into information specifics. In the following, it was interesting to note that the participant playing the role of a doctor (Chris) appeared to be cornered by the other participants, resulting in his being less in control and subject to the interrogation by the patient's father:

```
Desmond YouTopia: Dr martin
please answer my question
Zeeasta YouTopia: ok ok..
Chris YouTopia: what question?
Desmond YouTopia: have u seen
similar cases to amy's before?
Desmond YouTopia: how different
is she ?
Chris YouTopia: she can be re-
habilitated to swallow her
own food.....i have just said
that...
Desmond YouTopia: how so?
Desmond YouTopia: i don't under-
stand
```

The participant dominating the discussion (Desmond) was playing the role of the patient's father and seeking out specifics through his probing questions ('how different is she'?, 'how so'?) over his daughter's state.

C.   Challenging Points

This move occurred when a participant opposed earlier views presented. It featured among the top range of most frequently occurring moves in students with a stronger presence. It often demanded explanation or substantiation of the arguments raised in a pointed, direct fashion:

```
Irene YouTopia: who are you, to
judge her pain?
```

Kok Leong announced his decision to euthanize his wife on public television to put an end to her prolonged suffering in a vegetative state. An audience member (Irene) challenged his ability to understand the kind of pain Amy had been going through, especially when he had neither similar experiences nor expertise in the relevant field.

Participants with a stronger presence showed a markedly higher usage of adopting this challenging move. These participants typically framed their challenges explicitly and backed them up specifically in context. Clear explanation and reasoning for the challenge were also provided as in:

```
Jacky YouTopia: Seriously, there
is no value in having a un-
healthy diet and gaining a "per-
fect body", for what use is it
when you gain a "healthy body"
but loses your health?
```

An assertive force was evident in participants who went out of their way to challenge arguments put forth through pointed interrogative framing ('Who told you..'), the issuing of directives ('Show me proof'), and a definitive stance via modality expressing certainty 'will' ('I will not answer you..I will choose to answer the lady'):

```
Jacky YouTopia: On many occa-
sions, I have wished the con-
tent of the video true, but it
was till recently that I finally
render it untrue and a dream
Jacky YouTopia: Who told you I
am getting married with Wendy?
Jacky YouTopia: I did not
Jacky YouTopia: Show me proof
Jacky YouTopia: not empty talk
Jacky YouTopia: I will not an-
swer you now
Jacky YouTopia: I will choose to
answer the lady
```

By contrast, participants who were comparatively weaker in presence did not extend the challenge beyond statements of disagreement seen in brief propositions presented:

```
Chris YouTopia: hence.....we
strongly disagree amy to be eu-
```

```
thansise...
Will YouTopia: amy is a life....
it would be unfair for you to
end her life
```

There was neither a discernible building up of a challenge, drawing on information from the specific context, nor pointed questioning deliberately focused at targeted addressees.

D.   Opening Up Dissent

This move was evident when debate was initiated on contentious ideas and arguments. Participants with a stronger presence were assertive in opening up dissent which featured between third and fifth highest discourse moves employed. The move could be signaled explicitly by contrastive markers ('but') with participants following up their line of argument marked by if-conditionals ('if you end her life', 'if she still..', 'if she ever recover..') and the insistent qualifier 'still' ('if she still', 'there is still…') as a marker of enhancement:

```
Irene YouTopia: but the thing
is, if you end her life, she
cannot be revived anymore. she's
dead.
Joaquinn YouTopia: yes
Irene YouTopia: if she still has
the tube, there are chances of
survival
Joaquinn YouTopia: if she ever
recover, it is because that tube
is not removed
Shirlynn YouTopia: but what is
the use of keeping her "alive"
when she is not able to move or
eat
Joaquinn YouTopia: it depends on
individuals' perception
Irene YouTopia: there is still a
```

```
hope of her being alive
```

Participants appeared persistent on pursuing their line of argumentation with a questioning stance 'why do you want...quickly'), citing, as supporting evidence, the perspective from a medical personnel:

```
Irene YouTopia: why do you want
her dead so quickly
Irene YouTopia: she has improved
the doc says so
```

Realizations of participants' dissent carried the structure of a 'Yes-but' framing with an acknowledgement of a stance ('i know she is...', ' frankly speaking, i do not oppose...'), before countering it, explicitly signalled by the contrastive marker 'but' ('but it's been 8...', 'but based on my religion...'):

```
Irene YouTopia: i know she is my
daughter but it's been 8 WHOLE
YEARS and the pain is really un-
bearable and immense
Joaquinn YouTopia: as i said she
is not facing the same predica-
ment as my other patients but….
Irene YouTopia: frankly speak-
ing, i do not oppose passive
euthanasia...but based on my
religion...it is not right to do
that...
```

Participants who were relatively weaker did not offer extended expressions which opened up issues for further challenge other than to state them directly and, in fact, re-stating them as evident in the following entries by Will:

```
Will YouTopia: I feel that it is
wrong to pull out the tube...
Vanessa YouTopia: the doctors
```

```
told me that she had down syn-
drome
Vanessa YouTopia: so i aborted
her
Shin YouTopia: and u aborted it
right mrs wee?
Vanessa YouTopia: even though it
was against my religion
Will YouTopia: the only 'life
buoy' for her is the tube it-
self.
Shin YouTopia: good lord!! u
did???
Vanessa YouTopia: i'm so sorry -
cries / sniff / sob
Will YouTopia: 0_0
Shin YouTopia: -faints-
Shin YouTopia: (aside) lol
(laughs out loud)
Will YouTopia: from my Buddhist
point of view, we believe that
life is sacred as always and
nothing is more worthy than life
itself
```

No concrete justification for proposing a dissenting view was evident in the above except for a repeated call for not pulling out the tube which was regarded as a wrongful act. Even the Buddhist perspective referred to was not followed up with concrete justification for its rationale other than to reiterate the point over the sanctity of life.

E.   Initiating New Turns in Topic

This move was used in raising a new topic of discussion which offered a different focus from an earlier one. It was also evident in bringing up a topic earlier discussed which had ended abruptly or was neglected. It was evident in students who displayed both strong and weak presence with differing degrees in the extent to which the move influenced the nature of the discussion. For in-

stance, it played a role in impacting the depth of discussion as seen in what follows:

```
Jacky YouTopia (Mr Wee): Pastor,
can you help me understand and
evaluate my personal beliefs in
relation to the beliefs espoused
by the church?
```

Mr Richard Wee had prompted Dr Loh to share with the rest his medical evaluation of his daughter's condition. After hearing from him, he wanted to now hear views from Reverend Chia, seeking the Christian perspective on the issue of taking Amy's life. By considering both religious and medical perspectives, it would help him to craft his personal belief and, hence, make a more informed decision.

Students who initiated new turns were explicit in steering the ongoing discussion to a different topic of focus as evident in the discourse markers signalling the shift in attention: 'right now, I think we should talk about', 'which brings me to my next point' in a decisive and explicit manner:

```
Irene YouTopia: right now, i
think we should talk about amy
and euthanasia
Irene YouTopia: exactly
Irene YouTopia: which brings me
to my next point
Jacc YouTopia: i still suspect
his reasons.
Irene Sucexxy YouTopia: i want
to make a video of amy
```

By contrast, in the next, there was a sharp contrast in the limited scope of discussion from a comparatively weaker participant in strength (Chris):

```
Chris YouTopia: that simon cow-
ell say dat (that) girl very
```

```
fat...
Twister YouTopia: which girl?
Clarence YouTopia: so evil...
Desmond YouTopia: please use
standard english
Chris YouTopia: opps
Desmond YouTopia: come on
Zeeasta YouTopia: hey, that is
not fair. i used to be fat too
Desmond YouTopia: girls that
donot have the right image will
not win
Desmond YouTopia: no matter how
good they sound
Zeeasta YouTopia: oh really?
Chris YouTopia: i use to be very
fat too.
Chris YouTopia: i forget her
name already.
Twister YouTopia: i agree with
desmond
Desmond YouTopia: because it
will be almost impossible to
sell a lot of albums with the
image she had
Twister YouTopia: image is ev-
erything
Twister YouTopia: no looks no
talk
Zeeasta YouTopia: but got photo-
shop right?
Chris YouTopia: it's the sinfing
(singing) that is important.
Desmond YouTopia: image is ev-
erything especially in the media
circle
Twister YouTopia: so what?
Chris YouTopia: singing*
```

Fewer issues were prompted directly by the participant. The discussion revolved predominantly around a generally similar idea of image and perception as of the entertainment industry. In fact, it was the other participants who raised and developed the discussion around the emphasis on image in the media circle.

F. Expanding Arguments

This move was realized when a participant voluntarily expanded on his or her own ideas or arguments. There were slight differences in the frequency of occurrence of the move by both groups of students with individual variations in its use. The expansion of claims and propositions often extended to a contribution of more than a single point. Participants elaborated on their argument with a further explication of what was meant through a series of propositions building up on each other as evident in:

```
Jacky YouTopia: Richard, the
bible says that all man who be-
lieve in Him will have the power
to heal all diseases, though it
seems impossible in your case,
but at least that verse suggests
going against death.
```

The claim over the power of healing diseases from having faith was attributed to the Bible with the qualification that the present case of Richard's daughter, Amy, at hand 'seems impossible'. The participant then further argued not to support euthanasia since what Scripture suggested 'was going against death'.

Participants adopted a series of continuous moves over a stretch of discourse. These built up on each other in expanding the argument and extending the focus as in the following:

```
Irene YouTopia: people who end
their life so fast, definitely
have no determination
```

```
Irene YouTopia: pple (people)
with third stage cancer may get
cured, for all you know
Irene YouTopia: but you may
never know, the chances of sur-
viving.
Irene YouTopia: so doctors say
a patient has only 3,4 weeks to
survive
Irene YouTopia: but some pa-
tients end up staying alive for
years
```

Even with attempts at argument expansion, a participant who did not display as strong a presence offered points which nevertheless appeared scant and scattered with a limited discussion focus in terms of real issues. His points were not adequately expanded as in:

```
Chris YouTopia: she can be re-
habilitated to swallow her
own food.....i have just said
that...
Chris YouTopia: yes...
Chris YouTopia: i believe she
have a high chance of recovery.
Chris YouTopia: in the long run.
```

G. Clarifying Points

This move occurred when a participant sought elaboration on what appeared as contrary to earlier ideas or arguments raised and which contradicted each other.

Participants with a stronger presence went to great lengths to clarify their stand and arguments, making it clear to the other party their intentions, using explicit markers such as 'I was just trying to explain':

```
Jacob YouTopia: Yea, so I was
saying "perhaps", I was just
trying to explain that Simon was
```

```
making the girl to see the real-
ity
Jacob YouTopia: or the possibil-
ity
```

There was further acknowledgment of their contribution's apparent limitation before they articulated their position on an issue:

```
Jacky YouTopia: My words seem
rather contradicting and shows
signs of doubt in God
Jacky YouTopia: I certainly be-
lieve that Life is given by God
and should not be taken by any-
one
```

Although this clarifying move showed minimal quantitative differences between both groups of students, participants who were weaker in presence as in the next example, were seen to be trying to query other participant's questions rather than clarifying their own point:

```
Zeeasta YouTopia: doctor, YOU
ARE NOT ANSWERING OUR QUESTION!
Chris YouTopia: what question??
Chris YouTopia: what question??
```

H. Terminating focus of topics

This move signalled to other parties to stop discussing a current topic, given a lack of new development in the discussion. The objective was to terminate the discussion due to time constraint in class or to steer the discussion to another area. Students who were in control and decisive in bringing the discussion to a close exerted a greater presence in the enactment:

```
Irene YouTopia: You have been
going on and on about her suf-
fering.
```

```
Irene YouTopia: it's enough
```

The student enacting a TV chat show viewer earlier posed questions to Kok Leong. However, Kok Leong had been belabouring the point that Amy had been suffering-unable to eat, talk, feel. Here, this viewer strongly felt that it was time for him move on. She appeared less tolerant of others who kept bringing up the same points during discussion. She displayed an eagerness to have the TV chat show discussion move on to other areas of focus.

In the following, the student steered the ongoing discussion of whether Amy could be regarded as still alive ('only in the religious context') to a close:

```
Jacky YouTopia: I agree with
you, Richard, only in the reli-
gious context
Jacky YouTopia: Enjoy your chat
with the doctor, I have to medi-
tate now
Jacky YouTopia: Excuse me
```

A tongue-in-cheek boldness was discernible in the participant excusing himself from the ongoing dialogue: 'I have to meditate now'.

Evidently, students who displayed a strong presence took liberties with injecting humour and taking a mock jest at each other. This added to a spot of comic relief in the virtual dialoguing of what was admittedly a 'serious' discussion of issues. It was further interesting to note that in our data, this type of move was not significant (ranked second last in frequency) among students who were observed to have a relatively weaker presence compared to their peers.

- Tone of sarcasm and dramatization

This was evident when a message was sharpened by a deliberate sarcastic tone to provoke a reaction from others:

```
Jacky YouTopia: My dear, Amy,
the truth is sometimes mean, or
even meaner than Simon's words
Jacky YouTopia: I can then pity
you for seeing me as a foe in-
stead like a friend
Jacky YouTopia: Are you sure
that video is reliable
Jacky YouTopia: I am the one
which is always near to Amy
Jacky YouTopia: not my dear
father-in-law
Jacky YouTopia: Amy's brain dam-
age is caused by an accident
Jacky YouTopia: She had a car
accident while rushing to pick
up my dear father-in-law
Jacky YouTopia: you see, my
father-in-law, indirectly caused
her death
```

Jacob's entries were laced with witty, sarcastic remarks, particularly of his reiterated 'my dear father-in-law', and clever rebuttals reinforced by the overly attentive 'my dear Amy... I can then pity you..'. He was more 'in character' and involved with the assigned role which he played out admirably as Amy's husband in defence when attacked by his father-in-law. He cleverly tried to insinuate and show that Amy's death was, in fact, caused by his father-in-law who was trying to accuse him of murder.

A stark contrast to entries from such participants above, Chris, in the next extract, contributed entries which were not only devoid of similar sarcastic tones, but which were, to a large extent, descriptive and relied on the paralinguistic feature to signal 'shouting'. The entries were also marked by out-of-character banter which distracted his group members:

```
Chris YouTopia (shouts): start
exercising
Chris YouTopia (shouts):
com'on....yoyo...follow me
man....shake our bodies....
Chris YouTopia (shouts): ev-
eryone must eat 2 servings of
fruits and 2 servings of veg-
etables to stay healthy...u
know...u know...
Chris YouTopia shouts: i make
apple cookies or cabbage cookies
to stay healthy ah....
Chris YouTopia shouts: why
not...as most diaorreah....then
can help lose weight also...mu-
hahahax...
GuanHan YouTopia shouts: ok stop
shouting. its very disturbing
Chris YouTopia shouts: i open
sliming centre then you all come
ok...i give you all discount...1
session only $99.99....
Duhpaint YouTopia shouts: evry-
body ignore chris
```

Indeed, the disruptive behaviour by Chris led to his group mates ignoring him:'evrybody ignore chris'. In fact, Chris had shown, on many instances, that he was not taking the discussions seriously. Students with a weaker presence were observed to be comparatively less committed to the ongoing discussions.

OVERVIEW AND IMPLICATIONS

This study aimed to identify specific discourse moves and strategies in virtual enactments which explicitly reflected the nature and extent of the impact of students' interactive behavior in SL. In doing so, participants' discourse behavior was indicative of the level of strength of their presence in the immersive learning environment. The nature, frequency and manner whereby specific discourse moves were used to influence other participants, exert a targeted effect and impact the nature of the virtual dialoguing were of interest in this chapter.

There were discourse moves that showed quantitative differences in frequency of occurrence among students, with minor differences noted in specific individuals' adoption of particular moves. The discourse moves predominantly associated with students who displayed a relatively stronger presence comprised the following: eliciting response, probing for specifics, challenging points, opening up dissent and terminating focus of discussion. Although minimal differences were noted in the following- initiating new turns, expanding arguments and clarifying points - close text analysis facilitated the examination as to how these discourse moves were adopted and for what purpose in their respective contexts.

Table 2 is an overview of the criteria and corresponding linguistic realization for establishing strong and weak presence:

The criteria of distinguishing the strength of presence comprised explicit indicators ranging from initiative in making a discourse move, specificity in addressee, seeking out details and information, explicit and contextualized countering of perspectives, initiating disagreement, evidence of follow-up on stance taken, initiating topical change, elaborated argumentation, initiative in drawing closure to arguments, and heightened representation for emphasis and to provoke reaction. Specific linguistic features were identified (Table 2) which distinguished students in terms of their strength of virtual presence.

Students who displayed a relatively stronger presence generally exercised more control as well as dominance in the realization of moves in the virtual enactments. These included the moves of Eliciting response, Probing for specifics, and Challenging points made. Eliciting Response reflected the amount of dominance and influence that participants had over the discussion. The individuals' questioning showed evidence of control of the situation in the clarity of elicitations framed by an identifiable interrogative structure with a distinct force of its own. Further, the more influence the participant had, the greater the dominance and control in pushing the boundaries for discussion and probing for greater specificity in detail. The direct challenge posed in a pointed fashion to other participants to account for decisions made or claims proposed was also evident in such students. The stronger the participant presence, the more likely the participant would challenge others to a reply. Such students were further engaged in a skilful attack using sarcasm and dramatized role play through exaggerated behaviour mannerisms.

By contrast, students who were weaker in presence did not stand out in their enactments. Their contributions did not make a distinct difference to the virtual dialoguing. They lacked initiative in eliciting response and provoking a reaction from other participants. Their unelaborated propositions and sparse entries with unnamed addressees lacked depth with a limited scope of discussion. There was a noticeable detachment in such participants. They did not actively steer a discussion nor sustain a thread of argumentation through initiating rebuttal and following up on perspectives. They displayed a lack of commitment and staying power in pursuing a line of discussion to its fullest. Where there were attempts at expansion of arguments, these were superficial and incomplete. In fact, they appeared to be in less control of the dialoguing with a weak turn initiative and subsequent pick up. Indeed, they came across, at times, as being overpowered by participants who were more domineering in presence and insistent on an immediate and fuller response. Participants weaker in strength were also not instrumental in bringing an ongoing discussion to a close. There was a glaring omission in the use of sarcasm and other subtle means of provoking a response.

Little or no evidence of dramatized response to viewpoints raised was also noted in such students.

The pertinent pedagogical implications based on the virtual scenario-driven pedagogy of this study ranged from specifics pertaining to innovative scenario design and construction, maximizing interactivity through avatar management for active engagement, maximizing non-textual interactive functions, explicit teacher instruction and modelling, and teacher's role and involvement, among others. Enabling strategies as presented in the next section provide concrete steps for practitioners in the implementation. With greater understanding of what would be involved to evoke a stronger and sustaining presence in virtual enactments, the quality of real-time role play in such learning environments would be enhanced.

Enabling strategies in enactive role-play to develop participants' presence

- Learn to become comfortable and familiar with the workings of the virtual world environment yourself.
- Give students the scope to explore and experiment further on their own in the virtual world to develop greater affinity with the learning environment and each other within and beyond class time
- Develop participant ownership of the learning process through personalizing avatars
- Co-create scenarios between researchers and practitioners for participants to fully relate and identify
- Incorporate, adapt and fully utilize interactive functions in the virtual world to enhance interactivity
- Complement text-based interaction with non-textual features: verbal and gestural effects
- Design more complex and/or different scenarios for participants to employ a wider range of discourse strategies to enact their roles

Table 2. Criteria for determining strong versus weak presence in Second Life enactive role play

Criteria	Discourse move	Strong presence Linguistic features	Weak presence Linguistic features
Initiative in making a discourse move	Eliciting responses	Contextual preface	Brief one-liners
Specificity in addressee		Specific addressees Direct interrogative structure: do+pronoun+verb	Unspecified addressees
Seeking out details and information	Probing for specifics	Element of cajoling, explicit prompts Specific addressees (optional) Explicit prompts	Less frequent seeking out details and information
Explicit and contextualized countering of perspectives	Challenging points	Explicit framing of challenge Contextual preface Interrogative framing Directives Modality expressing certainty	Brief propositions
Initiating disagreement	Opening up dissent	Contrastive discourse markers Qualifiers Source of authority 'Yes-but' framing-acknowledgement of stance before contrasting perspective	
Evidence of follow-up on stance taken		Follow-up on stance	Lack of extended/followed up stance No concrete justification Restating assertions
Initiating topical change	Initiating new turns in topic	Explicit discourse markers signalling attention shift Further development of stance (sub-topical strands)	Prompting of fewer new issues
Elaborated argumentation	Expanding arguments Clarifying points	Elaboration of argument through series of propositions Alternative perspectives Explicit clarification of arguments Explicit discourse markers Acknowledgement of limitation of argument	Scanty points of argument Insufficient expansion Limited discussion focus Querying other arguments rather than clarifying their own points
Initiative in drawing closure to arguments	Terminating focus of topic	Steering discussion to a close Tongue-in-cheek humour, mock-jest	Not widely evident
Heightened representation for emphasis and to provoke reaction	Tone of sarcasm and dramatization	Sarcasm to provoke reaction Build up of questions Exaggerated orthographic representation for emphasis	Lack of sarcasm Descriptive Paralinguistic features

- Extend duration in class for students to be actively involved in virtual dialoguing to ensure focused attention and connectivity to their roles over a sustained period of time
- Enable participants to execute movement across the sets to other locations to engage in other tasks or activities
- Explicit instruction on specific discourse moves and strategies through instructors' modeling in enactive role play
- Explain use of specific linguistic features (Table 2) in various discourse moves for different purposes
- Sequence the introduction of new aspects one at a time and around each session. These could include planning, anticipating arguments, restructuring arguments, and examining contributions for structure and substantiation of points.
- Elicit feedback from learners on difficulties encountered and discuss implications in relation to specific contexts for particular purposes
- Discuss criteria (Table 2) for evaluating participant presence and apply these to students' contributions
- Compare and contrast strategies used by participants displaying strong and weak presence
- Show students how to evaluate discourse moves and strengthen participant presence by adopting, modifying or adapting specific strategies
- Monitor, track and reward instances where students exhibit strong presence as a result of strategic devices used in the dialoguing.

There is wide interest in capitalizing on immersive learning through simulations and online virtual events as represented in the studies captured in this volume. While this chapter has centred on SL virtual enactments involving a small group of students from one class in a specific learning context, there is room for further investigation

in following up on more students in different scenarios to investigate other discourse moves and strategies, if any, which may play a role in participants displaying a presence and projecting a distinct stance and voice of their own. Participant behaviour in SL at different grade levels and across other disciplines in acquiring particular skills set is another worthy area for further investigation. The scenarios in this study based on character roles such as doctor, parent of patient, pastor, patient's husband, TV host of chat show, chat show audience were noted to involve primarily text-based interaction with characters over a limited period of time. There is room for engaging participants with further interactive functions in the virtual world and more complex and/or different scenarios to resolve the creative tensions, conflicts or complications, and to stimulate active decision-making and problem-solving among participants. Studies such as these would ultimately lead to greater insights which contribute to a more comprehensive and informed framework and/or taxonomy of discourse moves and strategies of participant behaviour and interaction in 3D learning spaces. These would facilitate understanding of the impact of this technology platform on learning in various forms and for diverse purposes.

CONCLUSION

With the growing interest among scholars in immersive 3D learning spaces for teaching and learning, this chapter offered a study of teenage students' interactive behaviour in SL based on enactive role play drawing on the theme of euthanasia. The focus in this pre-university learning context was to develop critical thinking and reasoning skills. The systematic approach adopted for unpacking participants' specific discourse moves and strategies that reflected the strength of their presence in the virtual world highlighted a range of interactional moves which indicated the degree to which participants exhibited control, influence and/or involvement in the enactments. How participants explicitly initiated, provoked, challenged, probed, and/or steered the direction and nature of the real-time virtual dialoguing was at the heart of the investigation. The interest was in examining the dynamics involved in order to determine the extent, influence and reach of participants' engagement with each other in the SL immersive environment. Specific criteria which distinguished participants' level of presence included taking the initiative (be it response elicitation, information probing, disagreement, topical change and closure), addressee specificity, contextualized and elaborated argumentation, argument follow-up and heightened representation to activate response. Awareness of these and the appropriate linguistic resources for meaningful and impactful dialogic real-time exchange with other participants would ultimately enhance the overall learning process in 3D immersive virtual environments and enable learners to project, with confidence, conviction and commitment, an identifiable strong presence in the virtual world. The study has reiterated the need for carefully designed and innovatively structured learning opportunities supported by explicit instruction of appropriate linguistic resources required to allow participants to explore, strategize and learn to exert control or influence as they engage in immersive virtual spaces. Innovative scenario design and creative avatar conceptualization have a critical role to play as the greater the opportunity to imaginatively construct a virtual world, the more a sense of presence will be strengthened (Jacobson, 1999). Indeed, virtual persons, as with other virtual entities, are acknowledged to be the product of the mind or imagination (Jacquet-Chiffelle, 2009). For real-time enactments and their impact to be felt in dynamic, rich, digital learning environments, this requires the collaborative effort of all involved- academic researchers, instructional designers, classroom practitioners and learners.

ACKNOWLEDGMENT

The work reported in this paper is funded by a research grant, R59801118, from the Learning Sciences Laboratory, National Institute of Education, Nanyang Technological University, Singapore. The author is grateful to Amilyn Ong, Daniel Yip and Tan Li Wee for their contribution. The cooperation of all students involved in this study is deeply appreciated. The Ministry of Education, Singapore is acknowledged for the Lenovo Innovation Award (Merit) to the school for recognizing innovative ICT-mediated pedagogy.

REFERENCES

Antonacci, D. M., & Modress, N. (2008). Envisioning the educational possibilities of user-created virtual worlds. *AACE Journal*, *16*(2), 115–126.

Bakhtin, M. M. (1981). *The dialogic imagination* (Emerson, C., & Holquist, M., Trans.). Austin, TX: University of Texas Press.

Beach, R., Anson, C., Breuch, L., & Swiss, T. (2008). *Teaching writing using blogs, wikis, and other digital tools*. Norwood, MA: Christopher-Gordon.

Beach, R., & Doerr-Stevens, C. (2009). Learning argument practices through online role-play: Toward a rhetoric of significance and transformation. *Journal of adolescent and adult literacy*, March, *52* (6).

Beach, R., & Doerr-Stevens, C. (in press). Learning to engage in dialogic argument through participation in online role-play . In Kadjer, S., & Young, C. (Eds.), *Technology and English education*. Greenwich, CT: Information Age Press.

Brandsford, J., & Gawel, D. (2006). Thoughts on Second Life and learning. *Proceedings of the First Second Life Education Workshop, San Francisco, California.*

Brown, A. L. (1992). Design experiments: Theoretical and methodological challenges in creating complex interventions in classroom settings. *Journal of the Learning Sciences, 2*(2), 141–178. doi:10.1207/s15327809jls0202_2

Bruner, J. (1966). *Toward a theory of instruction.* Cambridge, MA: Belknap Press of Harvard University Press.

Bruner, J. (1968). *Processes of cognitive growth: Infancy.* Worcester, MA: Clark University Press.

Byrne, M. (1996). *Water on tap: the use of virtual reality as an educational tool.* Unpublished doctoral dissertation, University of Washington, Seattle.

Carr, D. (2005). The rules of the game, the burden of narrative: Enter the matrix . In Gillis, S. (Ed.), *The matrix trilogy: Cyberpunk reloaded* (pp. 1–10). London: Wallflower Press.

Chee, Y.S. (2007). Embodiment, embeddedness and experience: Game-based learning and the construction of identity. *Research and practice in technology enhanced learning, 2* (1), 3-30.

Chee, Y. S., & Lim, K. Y. T. (2009). Development, identity and game-based learning. In R.E. Ferdig (Ed.), *Handbook of research on effective electronic gaming in education* (pp. 808-825). Hershey, PA: Information Science Reference, IGI Global.

Cobb, P. (2001). Supporting the environment of learning and teaching in social and institutional context . In Carver, S., & Klahr, D. (Eds.), *Cognition and instruction: 25 years of progress* (pp. 455–478). Mahwah, NJ: Lawrence Erlbaum Associates, Inc.

Collins, A. (1992). Toward a design science of education . In Scanlon, E., & O' Shea, T. (Eds.), *New directions in educational technology* (pp. 15–22). New York: Springer-Verlag.

Cruz-Neira, C. (1998). Making virtual reality useful: Immersive interactive applications.? *J. Future Generation Computer Systems, 14,* 147–156. doi:10.1016/S0167-739X(98)00017-X

English Village. (2007). English Village. Retrieved January 2, 2008, from http://slurl.com/secondlife/English+Village/207/193/101/

Gaggioli, A., Bassi, M., & Delle Fave, A. (2003). Quality of experience in virtual environments . In Riva, G., Davide, F., & Ijsselsteijn, W. A. (Eds.), *Being There: Concepts, Effects and Measurements of User Presence in Synthetic Environments* (pp. 121–135). Amsterdam: IOS Press.

Gee, J. P. (2001). Identity as an analytic lens for research in education . In Secada, W. G. (Ed.), *Review of research in education, 25* (pp. 99–125). AERA.

Gee, J. P. (2003). *What video games can teach us about literacy and learning.* New York: Palgrave-Macmillan.

Gee, J. P. (2004). *Situated language in learning: A critique of traditional schooling.* New York: Routledge.

Gee, J. P. (2005). *Introduction to discourse analysis: Theory and Method.* Oxon: Routledge.

Gee, J. P. (2009). Games, learning, and 21st century survival skills. *Journal of virtual worlds research, 2*(1), 3-9, Pedagogy, Education and Innovation in 3-D Virtual Worlds. Geertz, C. (1972/3). Deep Play: Notes on the Balinese Cockfight. *The Interpretation of Cultures* (pp. 412-53). New York: Basic Books.

Genee, I., & De Vries, L. (2008, 3-6 September). Toward a typology of functions for the discourse move. Paper presented at 13th International Conference on Functional Grammar, University of Westminster, London.

Giddens, A. (1991). *Modernity and self-identity: Self and society in the late modern age.* Cambridge: Polity Press.

Goffman, E. (1956/1959/1973). *The presentation of self in everyday life.* Garden City, New York: Doubleday.

Good, J., & Thackray, L. (2008, Sept 9–11). Spanning the boundaries. Poster presentation at *ALT-C 2008 conference introduction and abstracts* (pp. 140–141), 15th International Conference of the Association for Learning Technology. The University of Leeds, UK.

Halliday, M. A. K. (1985). *An introduction to functional grammar.* London: Edward Arnold.

Heeter, C. (1992). Being there: The subjective experience of presence. *Presence (Cambridge, Mass.), 1*(2), 262–271.

Hengeveld, K., & Mackenzie, J. L. (2008). *Functional discourse grammar. A typologically-based theory of language structure.* Oxford, UK: Oxford University Press. doi:10.1093/acprof:oso/9780199278107.001.0001

Ho, M. L. C. (2006). Introduction . In Ho, C., Teo, P., & Tay, M. Y. (Eds.), *Teaching the General Paper: Strategies that work* (pp. 1–4). Singapore: Pearson Longman.

Ho, M.L.C. (in press). Dealing with life and death issues: Engaging students through scenario-driven pedagogy. *Journal of the Imagination in English Language Teaching, 9.*

Ho, M. L. C., Rappa, N. A., & Chee, Y. S. (2009). Designing and implementing virtual enactive role-play and structured argumentation: Promises and pitfalls. *Computer Assisted Language Learning, 22*(4), 323–350.

(•••).. . *Human Communication Research, 33,* 271–290. doi:10.1111/j.1468-2958.2007.00299.x

Ijsselsteijn, W., & Riva, G. (2003). Being there: The experience of presence in mediated environments . In Riva, G., Davide, F., & Ijsselsteijn, W. A. (Eds.), *Being There: Concepts, effects and measurements of user presence in synthetic environments* (pp. 3–16). Amsterdam: IOS Press.

Ijsselsteijn, W. A., de Ridder, H., Freeman, J., & Avons, S. E. (2000). Presence: Concept, determinants and measurements. *Proceedings of the Society for Photo-Instrumentation Engineers, 3959,* 520–529.

Insko, B. E. (2003). Measuring presence: Subjective, behavioral and physiological methods. In G. Riva, F. Davide, & W. A. Ijsselsteijn (Eds.), *Being There: Concepts, effects and measurements of user presence in synthetic environments* (109-119). Amsterdam: IOS Press.

Jacobson, D. (1999). On theorizing presence. Retrieved on 2 May, 2009, from http://www.brandeis.edu/pubs/jove/HTML/V6/presence.HTML

Jacquet-Chiffelle, D-O. (2009). Virtual persons and identities. The future of identity in the Information Society (FIDIS) Summit event - Challenges and Opportunities.

Jenkins, H., Clinton, K., Purushotma, R., Robinson, A. J., & Weigel, M. (2006). *Confronting the challenges of participatory culture: Media education for the 21ˢᵗ century.* Illinois, US: MacArthur Foundation.

Kidz Connect. (2009). Retrieved August 1, 2009, from http://www.kidzconnect.org/

Kumpulainen, K., & Wray, D. (2001). *Classroom interaction and social learning*. London: Routledge.

Languagelab.com. llc. (n.d.). LanguageLab. Retrieved June 2, 2009, from http://www.languagelab.com/en/

Lave, J. (1991). Situating learning in communities of practice . In Resnick, L. B., Levine, J. M., & Teasley, S. D. (Eds.), *Perspectives on socially shared cognition* (pp. 63–82). Washington, DC: American Psychological Association. doi:10.1037/10096-003

Lee, M. (2009). How can 3D virtual worlds be used to support collaborative learning? An analysis of cases from the literature. *Journal of e-Learning and Knowledge Society, 5*(1), 149 – 158.

Linden Research, Inc. (2008). *Second Life*. Retrieved January 2, 2006, from http://secondlife.com/

McMahan, A. (2003). Immersion, engagement and presence: A method for analyzing 3D video games . In Wolf, M. J. P., & Perron, B. (Eds.), *The video game theory reader* (pp. 67–86). New York: Routledge.

Mercer, N. (1995). *The guided construction of knowledge: Talk amongst teachers and learners*. Clevedon: Multilingual Matters.

Millrood, R. P. (2002). Discourse for teaching purposes. In Research Methodology: Discourse in Teaching A Foreign Language. Tambov: Tambov State University Press.

Ministry of Education. (2004). *Framework for the new 2006 "A" Level curriculum*. Retrieved April 11, 2005, from http://www.moe.gov.sg/corporate/preu_01.htm

Minsky, M. (1980). Telepresence. *Omni*, June, 45-52.

New Media Consortium. (2008). *2008 NMC Educators in Second Life Survey*. Retrieved 2 May, 2009, from http://www.nmc.org/publications

New Media Consortium. (2009). *Immersive learning initiative*. Retrieved 2 January, 2009, from http://www.nmc.org/initiatives/immersive-learning

Pearce, C. (2006, 25-27 October). *Seeing and Being Seen: Presence & Play in Online Virtual Worlds. Position Paper presented for Online, Offline & The Concept of Presence When Games and VR Collide, USC Institute for Creative Technologies*. Retrieved 12 April, 2009, from http://www.lcc.gatech.edu/~cpearce3/PearcePubs/PearcePosition.pdf

Presenccia (2006). Presence: Research encompassing sensory enhancement,neuroscience, cerebral-computer interfaces and applications. *European Sixth Framework Program, Future and Emerging Technologies*. Retrieved on 1 May 2009 from http://www.presenccia.org/

Rowe, J., McQuiggan, S., & Lester, J. (2007). Narrative presence in intelligent learning environments. *Working Notes of the 2007 AAAI Symposium on Intelligent Narrative Technologies* (pp.126-133). Washington, DC.

Sadowski, W., & Stanney, K. (2002). Measuring and Managing Presence in Virtual Environments . In Stanney, K. (Ed.), *Handbook of virtual world environments technology* (pp. 791–806). Mahwah, New Jersey: Lawrence Erlbaum Associates.

Schubert, T., Friedmann, F., & Regenbrecht, H. (1999). Embodied presence in virtual environments . In Paton, R., & Neilson, I. (Eds.), *Visual representations and interpretations* (pp. 269–278). London: Springer.

Schuemie, M., van der Straaten, P., Krijn, M., & van der Mast, C. (2001).Research on presence in virtual reality: A survey. *Cyber psychology and behavior, 4* (2). Retrieved June 2, 2007, from http://graphics.tudelft.nl/~vrphobia/surveypub.pdf.

Shaffer, D. W. (2006). Epistemic frames for epistemic games. *Computers & Education, 46,* 223–224. doi:10.1016/j.compedu.2005.11.003

Shaffer, D. W. (2007). *How computer games help children learn.* New York: Palgrave Macmillan Ltd.

Sheridan, T. (1992). Musings on telepresence and virtual presence. *Presence (Cambridge, Mass.), 1*(1), 120–125.

Stanney, K. M., Salvendy, G., Deisigner, J., DiZio, P., Ellis, S., & Ellison, E. (1998). Aftereffects and sense of presence in virtual environments: Formulation of a research and development agenda. Report sponsored by the Life Sciences Division at NASA Headquarters. *International Journal of Human-Computer Interaction, 10*(2), 135–187. doi:10.1207/s15327590ijhc1002_3

Steuer, J. (1992). Defining virtual reality: Dimensions determining telepresence. *The Journal of Communication, 42*(2), 73–93. doi:10.1111/j.1460-2466.1992.tb00812.x

Tamsyn, B. (2009, January 27). Educators reach out to more students through the virtual world. *The Globe and Mail.* Retrieved February 1, 2009, from http://www.theglobeandmail.com/life/article655208.ece

The Straits Times. (2009). Virtual worlds used to teach real life to kids. 21 May.

Varela, F., Thompson, E., & Rosch, E. (1991). *The embodied mind: Cognitive science and human experience.* Cambridge, MA: MIT Press.

Vygotsky, L. (1986). *Thought and language.* Cambridge, MA: The MIT Press.

Wagner, C. (2008). Learning experience with virtual worlds. *Journal of Information Systems Education,* October. Retrieved March 3, 2009, from http://www.highbeam.com/doc/1P3-1563618861.html

Warburton, S. (2007). *Virtual spaces, second lives: what are the potential educational benefits of MUVEs?* Retrieved December 19, 2008, from http://www.slideshare.net/stevenw/virtualspaces-second-lives-what-are-the-potential-educational-benefits-of-muves-presentation

Wells, G. (1999). *Dialogic inquiry: Towards a sociocultural practice and theory of education.* Cambridge: Cambridge University Press. doi:10.1017/CBO9780511605895

Wetherell, M. Taylor, S. & Yates, S. (2001). *Discourse theory and practice.* London: Sage.

White, D. (2008, September 9–11). From swords to hairstyles; bridging the divide between massively multilayer game design and Second Life. Paper presented at *ALT-C 2008 Conference Introduction and Abstracts* (pp. 16–17), 15th International Conference of the Association for Learning Technology, The University of Leeds, UK.

Witmer, B., & Singer, M. (1998). Measuring presence in virtual environments: A presence questionnaire. *Presence (Cambridge, Mass.), 7*(3), 225–240. doi:10.1162/105474698565686

Yee, N. & Bailenson, J.N. (2007). The Proteus effect: Self transformations in virtual reality.

ADDITIONAL READING

Au, W. J. (2008). *The making of Second Life: Notes from the new world.* New York: HarperCollins.

Buckingham, D. (2005). *The media literacy of children and young people: A review of the literature*. London: Centre for the study of children, youth and media, Institute of Education, University of London. Retrieved September 12, 2006, from http://www.ofcom.org.uk/advice/media_literacy/medlitpub/medlitpubrss/ml_children.pdf

Carr, D. (2008). Learning and virtual worlds. In N. Selwyn (Ed.), *Education 2.0? Designing the web for teaching and learning: a commentary by the Technology Enhanced Learning phase of The Teaching And Learning Research Programme* (pp. 13–17). London: Institute of Education and TRLP-TEL. Retrieved December 19, 2008, from http://www.tlrp.org/tel/files/2008/11/tel_comm_final.pdf

Heiphetz, A., & Woodill, G. (2009). *Training and collaboration with virtual worlds*. Australia: McGraw-Hill.

Ho, M. L. C. (In press). Engagement in the Second Life virtual world with students. In Taiwo, R. (Ed.), *Handbook of Research on Discourse behaviour and digital communication: Language structures and social interaction*. Hershey, PA: IGI Global.

Ho, M. L. C., & Ong, M. H. A. (2009). Towards evaluative meaning-making through enactive role play: The case of pre-tertiary students in Second Life. *Journal of Applied Linguistics, 4*(2), 171–194. doi:10.1558/japl.v4i2.171

International Journal of Virtual and Personal Learning Environments (IJVPLE). An official publication of the Information Resources Management Association, New in 2010.

Journal of computer-mediated communication, 3 (2), 1997. Special issue on Designing a sense of presence in virtual environments. Retrieved June 1, 2007, from http://jcmc.indiana.edu/vol3/issue2/

Journal of virtual worlds research, 2 (1): Pedagogy, education and innovation in 3D virtual worlds. Retrieved July 2, 2009, from http://journals.tdl.org/jvwr/article/view/623/468 and http://jvwresearch.org

Kirriemuir, J. (2008). *A spring 2008 'snapshot' of UK higher and further education developments in Second Life*. Eduserve Foundation. Retrieved December 19, 2008, from http://www.scribd.com/doc/7063700/A-Spring-2008-snapshot-of-UK-Higher-and-Further-Education-Developments-in-Second-Life

Lombard, M., & Ditton, T. (1997). At the heart of it all: The concept of presence. *Journal of computer mediated communication, 3*(2). Retrieved December 1, 2006, from http://jcmc.indiana.edu/vol3/issue2/lombard.html

Lyman, P. with Billings, A., Ellinger, S., Finn, M. & Perkel, D. (2005). *Literature review digital-mediated experiences and youth informal learning*. San Francisco: Exploratorium. Retrieved December 1, 2005, from http://www.exploratorium.edu/research/digitalkids/Lyman_DigitalKids.pdf

New Media Consortium. (2007). *The Horizon Report.* Austin, TX, NMC. Retrieved December 10, 2007, from http://www.nmc.org/pdf/2007_Horizon_Report.pdf

Rufer-Bach, K. (2009). *The Second Life grid: The official guide to communication, collaboration, and community engagement*. Indianapolis, Indiana: John Wiley and Sons Ltd.

Rymaszewski, M., Wagner, J. A., Ondrejka, C., Platel, R., van Gorden, S., & Cézanne, J. (2008). *Second Life: The Official Guide* (2nd ed.). John Wiley and Sons Ltd.

Singer, M. J., & Witmer, B. G. (1997). Presence: Where are we now? In Smith, M., Salvendy, G., & Koubek, R. (Eds.), *Design of computing systems: Social and ergonomic considerations* (pp. 885–888). Amsterdam: Elsevier Science Publishers.

SLanguages. (2009). *SLanguages 2009:The Conference for Language Education in Virtual Worlds*. Retrieved July 1, 2009, from http://www.slanguages.net/

Taiwo, R. (Ed.). (In press). *Handbook of research on discourse behaviour and digital communication: Language structures and social interaction*. Hershey, PA: IGI Global.

The MacArthur Foundation. (2006).*The John D. and Catherine T. MacArthur Foundation Series on Digital Media and Learning*. MIT Press. Retrieved 2 January, 2007, from http://www.mitpressjournals.org/loi/dmal?cookieSet=1

Virtual Worlds Research Consortium. Retrieved July 1, 2009, from http://vwrc.org

Wartella, E., O'Keefe, B., & Scantlin, R. (2000). Children and interactive media: A compendium of current research and directions for the future. New York:Markle Foundation. Retrieved January 2, 2005, from http://www.markle.org/downloadable_assets/cimcompendium.pdf

Weber, A., Rufer-Bach, K., & Platel, R. (2007). *Creating your world: The official guide to advanced content creation for Second Life*. John Wiley and Sons Ltd.

KEY TERMS AND DEFINITIONS

Enactive Role Play: Embodied approach to learning which involves doing something concrete instead of thinking in the abstract in the process of meaning-making.

Presence: Executing influential discourse moves which actively engage participants and are strategic in directly evoking participants' response and action, and impacting the nature and content of virtual dialoguing

Second Life: Internet-based, immersive, three-dimensional, virtual environment developed by Linden Lab, US.

Virtual World: Computer-mediated, simulated, three-dimensional environment that presents the user(s) with a rich, visual experience and real-time communication with other users.

Section 3
The Design of 3D Immersive Spaces

Chapter 7
Collaborating to Learn:
Designing and Building 3D Immersive Virtual Learning Environments for Exploring STEM Concepts in Middle School

Nita J. Matzen
Appalachian State University, USA

William Edward Roberts
Appalachian State University, USA

Penny Barker
Ashe County Schools, USA

Julie Marklin
Davie County Schools, USA

ABSTRACT

STEM and ICT Instructional Worlds: The 3D Experience (STEM-ICT 3D) is funded by the National Science Foundation ITEST program. The project proposes to translate the success of earlier projects and reaches toward a model of implementing the use of 3D virtual immersive environments that can be replicated with other middle schools over time. STEM-ICT 3D is intended to inspire middle school students to pursue studies and careers in science, technology, engineering, and mathematics (STEM), as well as prepare students with the skills necessary to succeed in STEM education and careers. This chapter presents an applied case study that describes the design of the project, examines the first phases of implementation, and explores the use of students as technical experts collaborating with teachers, the pedagogical experts, to build 3D virtual worlds for middle school instruction.

DOI: 10.4018/978-1-61692-825-4.ch007

INTRODUCTION

How can K-12 teachers successfully implement the use of 3D immersive virtual environments into instruction? What affect will this environment have on student learning as well as change the way that students learn science, technology, engineering, and mathematics (STEM) material? Online environments have become more complex due to higher bandwidth availability and new technology including the evolution of social networking sites such as My Space and Facebook, massive multiplayer online role-playing games (MMORPGs) such as the World of Warcraft, and virtual worlds such as Second Life. Despite evidence that today's K-12 students are actively engaged in the use of virtual environments, typically in a non-school leisure environment, there has been little effort to explore the role such settings can play in teaching, learning and collaboration. *STEM and ICT Instructional Worlds: The 3D Experience* (STEM-ICT 3D) is a National Science Foundation Innovative Technology Experiences for Students and Teachers (ITEST) strategies project that seeks to address this need.

STEM-ICT 3D is an initiative of the Carolinas Virtual World Consortium composed of Appalachian State University and Clemson University in partnership with Davie and Catawba County Schools in North Carolina, and Oconee and Pickens County Schools in South Carolina, the Appalachian State University Mathematics and Science Education Center (MSEC), North Carolina Department of Environment and Natural Resources (NCDENR), and Teleplace, Inc. The project is intended to inspire middle school students to pursue studies and careers in science, technology, engineering, and mathematics (STEM) – particularly information and communication technology (ICT) fields - as well as prepare students with the skills necessary to succeed in STEM education and careers. *STEM-ICT 3D* incorporates a series of activities that provide an engaging, safe environment for middle school students and teachers to explore STEM concepts through a unique approach where students, serving as the technical experts, collaborate with their teachers to develop an inquiry-based learning project for use in a 3D immersive virtual environment.

The objective of this chapter is to present an applied case study that describes the design of *STEM-ICT 3D*, examines the implementation, and explores the use of students as technical experts collaborating with teachers, the pedagogical experts, to build 3D virtual worlds for middle school instruction. The background of the project including the literature and research that contributed to the conceptualization of the program will be covered first, followed by a description of the student and student/teacher workshops. An overview of the Presence Pedagogy framework presented to the teachers for consideration in their instructional development will be discussed and a description of the 3D virtual worlds that were created will be provided. Finally, a discussion of student and teacher perceptions of the workshops, and successes, will point to future research and next steps for the project and broadening its impact.

BACKGROUND OF THE *STEM-ICT 3D* PROJECT

Faculty in the Leadership and Educational Studies department at Appalachian State University in Boone, North Carolina (USA) developed the AETZone more than eight years ago. A recipient of the *2006 Campus Technology Innovators: Virtual and Immersive Learning* award, the AETZone provides a protected 3D virtual environment for graduate programs of study including instructional technology, library science, school administration, and higher education. The interdisciplinary design of this virtual world for graduate education allows faculty to create and pilot best practices for online learning environments. For those who are interested, a more detailed description of the AETZone 3D virtual immersive learning environment is provided in other literature (Bronack, Riedl, & Tashner, 2006).

Although the concept of using virtual worlds in K-12 may seem radical or unproven, it is not entirely new. Several programs such as *Quest Atlantis* (Indiana University), *River City* (Harvard University) and *SciCentr* (Cornell Theory Center) have been in use for more than a decade. The research from these programs suggests that students exhibit gains in engagement, efficacy, and achievement (Barab, S., Thomas, M., Dodge, T., Carteaux, R., & Tuzun, H., 2005; Educause, 2006; Ketelhut, D. J., Dede, C., Clarke, J., & Nelson, B., 2006). Similarly, Kim (2006) suggested a statistically significant effect of 3D virtual environments on both achievement in and attitude toward science. The psychological processes active in immersive virtual reality, as noted by Winn (1993), are very similar to those used when people construct knowledge around interaction with objects and events in the real world. As such, the 3D context builds on learners' real-world knowledge by providing a visual metaphor of the course content. This provides both a familiar and engaging *place* for learning (Dickey, 2005). Furthermore, virtual environments enable the formation of learning communities to increase members' understandings or knowledge base in specific areas. Multi-user, three-dimensional, online learning environments exhibit the potential for numerous educational benefits, such as engaged immersion, situated learning, multi-modal communications, breakdown of socio-cultural barriers, bridging the digital divide, problem solving, and the ability to create empathy and understanding for complex systems (Jones, 2004). Chittaro and Ranon (2007) suggest that the ability to provide experiences which may not be available in real life, the resources to analyze phenomena from different points of view in order to gain deeper understanding, and the capability to work with virtual companions distributed over different geographical locations are other advantages to the use of virtual environments for education.

Utilizing this research and applying their experience in 3D immersive virtual environments, the faculty at Appalachian State University in cooperation with educators at South Davie Middle School in North Carolina conducted a pilot study in the spring of 2008. Funded by a Reich College of Education Successful Applications of Learning Technologies (SALT) grant, the *Digital Natives Best Practices Project* engaged 116 sixth grade students in a collaborative process of locating and identifying information on explorers and exploration and, using the building tools of a 3D virtual world, constructing a representation to communicate the information. Findings from the pilot study suggested a significant shift from individualized to peer-based/peer-assisted learning with technology during the course of the project (Sanders, et al, 2008). The teachers in the project also noted that they had to "step back" as the students quickly became the technical experts; allowing the students to then teach the teachers to become technical experts themselves. This shift aligns with necessary 21st Century skills and models a method for motivating students through more hands-on, peer-to-peer learning, as well as engendering student ownership of learning processes.

With a mission of bringing "the resources of multiple entities to bear on innovative design, scalable development, and meaningful research toward the most effective use of social and immersive technologies in learning environments," the Carolina Virtual Worlds Consortium (CVWC) is uniquely situated to develop immersive virtual world strategies and turn proof-of-concept prototypes into viable, scalable models that engage and inspire students. Relying on the literature and preliminary findings from the *Digital Natives Best Practices Project,* faculty from two CVWC universities, Appalachian State University and Clemson University conceptualized *STEM and ICT Instructional Worlds: The 3D Experience* to translate the success of the pilot project and reach out toward a model that can be replicated over time in other middle schools.

THE *STEM-ICT 3D* PROJECT

Project Description

The intent of the *STEM-ICT 3D* project is to motivate and provide the skills necessary for diverse, under-represented, middle grade students including minorities; students at risk or economically disadvantaged; and other student groups that are often ignored for these types of opportunities to pursue studies and careers in STEM disciplines, particularly ICT. The project incorporates a series of activities for under-represented middle school students and teachers in North and South Carolina to explore STEM concepts. Sixth grade teachers nominate rising 7th grade students to attend face-to-face workshops in the summer. During the first week of summer workshops, the students learn 3D virtual world modeling and design using Google Sketch-up and Teleplace. That same week, teachers work online in Teleplace to meet each other and become familiar with the 3D immersive virtual environment. Seventh grade teachers then join their future students the second week of the summer workshops. An innovative approach, based on results from the *Digital Natives Best Practices* project, is to have the students take on the role of the technical experts while the teachers focus on learning the pedagogy for using 3D virtual worlds. The students teach the teachers how to build in Teleplace and then the teachers and students collaboratively develop an inquiry-based learning project for use in a 3D immersive virtual environment. The summer workshops occur simultaneously on the campuses of Appalachian State and Clemson University with students and teachers using the virtual environment to work across state lines. During the summer of 2009, Appalachian State University hosted participants from Davie and Catawba counties in NC, while Clemson University hosted participants from Oconee and Pickens counties in SC. Students and teachers from Ashe County, NC will be added to the Appalachian State University group in the summer of 2010.

After the summer workshops, students and teachers return to their respective schools and implement their projects during the academic year. The *STEM-ICT 3D* program includes face-to-face and online follow-up sessions to further encourage the development of a community of practice where teachers engage colleagues in ongoing relationships on using *STEM-ICT 3D* in the classroom, and students and teachers act as mentors to others in the ongoing development and use of 3D virtual worlds. The formal follow-up sessions occur both face-to-face and online during the school year and include mini-sessions addressing content, pedagogical, or technical needs as well as time for sharing and collection of evaluation data. University faculty and other experts are active participants in the community and provide assistance as needed. The 3D modeler/programmer, the project manager, and graduate assistants also support the technical aspect of implementation.

Summer Workshops

The planning processes used in the project have taken full advantage of the Teleplace 3D immersive world. Most planning meetings, for example, have been held in the 3D environment. All documents are also readily accessible in the virtual world. The sense of presence and co-presence made possible through the use of a 3D virtual environment enabled the creation of a collaborative planning and development community. In beginning the workshop curriculum development process, team members from all aspects of the project, including experts in STEM related fields, participated in a series of meetings, some of which were held face-to-face, but the majority conducted in online workspaces. From the input and suggestions based on the project goals, objectives, and expected outcomes, the instructional team determined the content more specifically. Several factors were taken into consideration when creating the lesson plan framework for the summer workshops. The students had to be equipped with the knowledge and skills necessary to take on the role of technical experts, and the teachers needed some understanding of the pedagogical possibilities with 3D immersive environments. These two groups of participants were to be teamed together in developing virtual world technology applications that would promote continuous STEM learning and interest. To be successful, the workshops had to improve student engagement, communication, and collaboration, and ultimately form a community of learners that could think critically and develop solutions to real-world problems.

The two summer instructors, both of whom are current middle school educators with expertise and experience teaching middle school students and in using 3D virtual worlds, took the lead on creating the lesson plans for the student workshop. As they developed the lesson plans, they recognized that they were required to look past the traditional classroom instruction they were accustomed to and consider what instruction could look like in a 3D immersive virtual world. They also had to look at implementing science, technology, engineering, and math components into the lessons. Unlike the learning communities they were familiar with developing in the classroom, the virtual communities they were creating for the workshops were broader including both students and teachers. To gain an understanding of a community of learners, the participants had to first understand the importance and relevance of a community. Lessons had to encourage interaction among students, among teachers, and between students and teachers.

The workshop instructors determined that a variety of activities would need to be implemented in order for middle school students to remain engaged in the learning process. Lessons were created so that students would learn the necessary software application programs including Google Sketch-Up, Google Earth, and Teleplace.

In addition to these lesson plans, the instructors developed team building activities that were intended to improve student relations with others and create a sense of belonging. They also incorporated guidelines, policies, and expectations that would emphasize responsibility on the part of all participants. Field trips that were designed to develop an understanding and appreciation of STEM related careers were integrated into the daily activities for both weeks of workshops. Furthermore, activities were incorporated in the virtual world to encourage communication and collaboration across the two state sites. An outline of the activities and the objectives for the first week of face-to-face workshops conducted only with students are displayed in Figure 1.

A team of faculty with expertise in 3D pedagogy, adult learning, and professional development, lead the development of the teacher learning activities in collaboration with the workshop instructors. This faculty has described a 3D immersive virtual world pedagogical approach known as Presence Pedagogy (P2), which is grounded in the Reich College of Education conceptual framework (Reich College of Education - Appalachian State University, 2005). The conceptual framework, based on social constructivism (Vygotsky, 1978), is the foundation of the AET-Zone and guides teaching and learning in the virtual environment. The five primary beliefs expressed in the conceptual framework include the following:

- Learning occurs through participation in a Community of Practice;
- Knowledge is socially constructed and learning is social in nature in a Community of Practice;
- Learners proceed through stages of development from Novice to Expert under the guidance of more experienced and knowledgeable mentors and among like-minded peers in the Community of Practice;

- An identifiable knowledge base that is both general in nature and also specific to specialties emerges from focused activity within the Community of Practice;
- All professional educators develop a set of Dispositions reflecting attitudes, beliefs, and values common to the Community of Practice.

Jonassen (2006) suggests that technologies can be used to keep students active, constructive, collaborative, intentional, complex, contextual, conversational, and reflective. All of these are necessary components for developing a community of practice which allows participants to share their common interests, deepen their knowledge and expertise, identify needs, and solve problems by interacting in an ongoing basis (Wenger, McDermott, & Snyder, 2002). Unlike typical web-based learning management systems, 3D immersive environments allow participants to be aware of being someplace (presence) with someone (co-presence). Due in part to this sense of presence and co-presence, both planned and serendipitous interactions can occur. P2 incorporates this notion of presence and co-presence such that collaboration, reflective learning, and student engagement are cultivated enabling development of an online community of practice whereby students can "be-come members of a broader community of practice in which everyone in the community is a potential instructor, peer, expert, and novice—all of whom learn with and from one another" (Bronack, S., Sanders, R. Cheney, A., Riedl, R., Tashner, J. & Matzen, N., 2008, p. 59).

Asynchronous as well as synchronous activities were developed for *STEM-ICT 3D* teacher participants during a week of online work prior to the face-to-face student/teacher workshop. During these activities teachers became familiar with the Teleplace environment, read and participated in discussions about P2, and began identifying potential lessons to adapt for a 3D world. The following week, the teachers attended a week-long face-to-face workshop with their future students. Since research suggests that teachers initially use technology the way that they have been taught (Matzen & Edmunds, 2007), on the first day of the student/teacher workshops, teachers participated in "Virus World"- a lesson that was adapted for use with 7th grade students and that models P2. In the activity, participants learn more of the tools of Teleplace as they introduce themselves and exchange "viruses". After the initial introductory phase of the activity, the participants collaboratively graph the data they have collected, conduct research, and create a product to communicate their understanding of

Figure 1. STEM-ICT 3D week 1 summer workshop for students

Week 1 Student Workshop		
Day/Activity		**Learning objective(s)**
Day 1	Introductions/Rules and policies. Learn Teleplace – choose avatar color, photo, badge. Learn how to bring documents and web pages into Teleplace. Divide into groups to create social suites. Customize Suites. Collaboration discussion. Sharing time. Show demonstration world – Lego World	1) Students will learn the basics of Teleplace including choosing an avatar, moving in the space, adding/editing documents, images, web pages. 2) Students will learn advanced features of Teleplace including topic cards and inventory. 3) Students will be introduced to the field of engineering.
Day 2	Introduction to Google Sketch-Up - the digital warehouse, basic manipulation tools, and basic export tools. Students brainstorm and storyboard ideas for Utopia World.	1) Students will learn how to use Google-Sketch-Up including the digital warehouse, basic manipulation tools, and basic export tools. 2) Students will learn a process for planning a 3D virtual space.
Days 3-5	Students create Utopias. Students provide tours of virtual worlds to teachers	Students will collaboratively build a 3D virtual space

how viruses are spread. During the morning of the second day of the student/teacher workshops, a Clemson University engineering faculty member conducted an across site, virtual team building session titled "How to Think Like an Engineer" where students and teachers carry out observations of an everyday object and then brainstorm ideas on how to improve that object. In the afternoon of the second day, the students taught their teacher how to build in the Teleplace environment using Google Sketch-up. The students and teachers then worked together to create the 3D world that the teacher can use instructionally the following school year during the remaining 3 days of the student/teacher workshops, as well as participate in a STEM related field trip. Figure 4 outlines the activities and objectives of the week 2 student/teacher workshops.

Worlds Created

The worlds created for the student workshop consisted of six suite groups and six utopias. The suites supported four students, 2 from each site. The suites were intended to be a social environment where each student had her/his own wall that could be used to provide personal information and other items of interest. The students worked on their suite group rooms in between learning Google Sketch-up, and working in their utopia world groups. This gave the students the opportunity to practice in their own worlds learning how to import and export objects in and out of Teleplace using Google Sketch-up. The utopia spaces were based on themes that related to STEM careers. The choice of utopia themes included the following: Wild Kingdom, Build a City, Clean Green World, Invent It, Inner Space, Outer Space, Underwater Adventure, Geo-mania, and Mysterious Mystery. From this list of themes the students selected their top three choices for the utopia they wanted to work on and build. The nine utopias were narrowed to 6 based on student choices, while ensuring a balanced grouping of 4 students across sites. To encourage cross site

collaboration, the suite groups consisted of different students than were assigned to the utopia groups. The students worked on their worlds for a full week in preparation for the following week, when they were joined by their teachers.

One of the purposes of the second week of workshops was for students to teach their teachers how to model in the virtual world and how best to import and export objects into the virtual spaces to be used to teach the STEM topics in the upcoming academic year. Some of the most outstanding worlds that were created by the teachers and their expert student modelers included the following: The Zoo with African and Asian Habitats, Series of Unfortunate Events, Oconee-Pickens Speedway, and The Courthouse.

The Zoo with African and Asian Habitats is one of the most innovative spaces. Because of the openness, the forum is reminiscent of a game preserve that can be found in different countries. Upon entering the world, you are met by a large elephant with a sign pointing you to the African portal for math and science, and to the Asian portal for language arts and social studies. This forum took a lot of thought, planning, and imagination to create a realistic environment incorporating STEM topics across multiple curricular areas.

Oconee-Pickens Speedway virtual space is a world based on a NASCAR theme. Here the students learn how to list the steps in the design process; paraphrase the design process; sketch a race car on paper that demonstrates an understanding of aerodynamics and mass; examine, compare, and contrast sketches using the same principles of aerodynamics and mass; evaluate the sketch done on paper and make any necessary modifications. Lastly to design, develop, and construct a 3D model of a race car using Google Sketch-up based on the student's findings. From this lesson the students develop an understanding of the engineering design process which includes the ability to identify problems, gather and analyze data, model and test a solution, and refine the model. The students then share their ideas with the class.

The virtual world Series of Unfortunate Events focuses on topics related to severe weather. The students learn how hurricanes form and view pictures of damage caused by these dangerous storms. The students work collaboratively to investigate a storm of their choice and report to the class the consequences of this storm. Finally, the students create a disaster plan for a hurricane and present their disaster plan to the class.

The Courthouse is a virtual space that is used to present the various perspectives of controversial STEM topics. As students move through the courthouse they read and explore animal rights issues from the point of view of the animals, business, consumers, and activists. Students then have to decide how they stand on the issue and be able to support their stance. An extension of the activity will have students researching and creating additional courtrooms for other controversial STEM topics.

Student and Teacher Perceptions

STEM-ICT 3D proposes an innovative strategy for implementing the use of 3D immersive virtual environments into middle grades education. In the model, students assume the role of technical experts as they teach their future teachers how to use Google Sketch-up to build a 3D space. Workshop instructors also work with the students to develop the communication skills necessary to be leaders in the school as they assist other students in using the 3D environments during instruction. Because this approach is unique, the formative evaluation of the project is important to ensure success. During the summer workshops, surveys were administered every day to obtain feedback from the students and teachers. Modifications were made in the delivery of the workshops if deemed necessary after daily review of the survey results. An end of workshop survey was also administered the afternoon of the final day. The responses on the survey for the day the students taught the teachers,

Figure 2. STEM-ICT 3D week 2 summer workshop for students and teachers

Week 2 Student & Teacher Workshop		
Day/Activity		**Learning objective(s)**
Day 1	Teachers participate in Virus World, a model activity Teachers share topics with their students Teachers and students begin planning their worlds. Students locate objects for their teacher's world - work collaboratively across states.	Students will be able to work with teachers and other students to plan a virtual world to be used for instruction.
		1) Teachers will participate in a 3D immersive virtual world activity that can be used in the classroom with students. 2) Teachers will gain a greater understanding of the pedagogical strategies that can be used for teaching in 3D immersive virtual environments. 3) Teachers will be able to plan for instruction using a 3D immersive virtual world.
Day 2	Bio-engineering road show/team building in virtual world Students teach teachers Google Sketch Up	1) Students will gain an understanding of engineering as a career. 2) Student will be able to show teachers how to use Google Sketch-up.
		1) Teachers will gain an understanding of engineering as a career. 2) Teachers will gain a greater understanding of pedagogical strategies that can be used for teaching in 3D immersive virtual environments. 3) Teachers will learn Google Sketch-up
Days 3-5	Collaborative building of worlds Critical friends and sharing of worlds	Students will work with other students and teachers to develop a 3D virtual space to be used for instruction in the school/classroom.
		Teachers will work with students and other teachers to develop a 3D virtual space to be used for instruction in the school/classroom.

Figure 3. The zoo

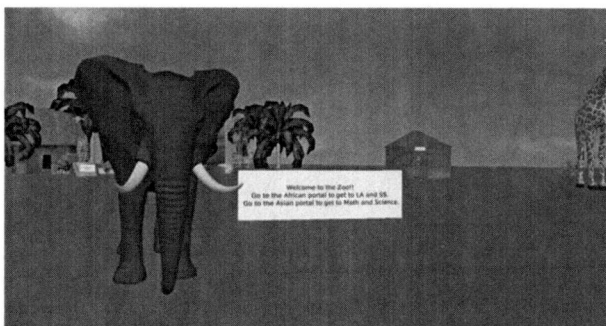

as well as the end of workshop surveys present participant perceptions of the summer workshop experience and this strategy.

The daily student survey contained two open-ended questions. One of the questions asked on the survey was "what were the key things you learned today?" Of the 23 students that recorded an answer to the question, 18 of the responses related to teaching the teachers. One student made the connection between the skills they learned and her/his being able to teach the teacher when s/he wrote "that we need to apply what we learn to help the teachers." Several students recorded a positive observation about their teacher such as "teachers are easy learners."An interesting statement noted by one student was, "That it is hard to teach teacher thing if they don't listen." Three students made comments about collaboration, communication, and leadership. One student suggested, "That you have to think logically and communicate with one another to get things done." The second open-ended question on the survey asked "what was the most useful part of this workshop? Why?" Responses were somewhat similar to the previous question with 10 students writing about teaching the teachers. One student, for example, stated, "Teaching the teachers how to use Google Sketch-Up because it really pays off for all the things that we learned last week." Some statements made by students about teaching reflect student perceptions of providing assistance such as "Being able to learn...all of it so I can help my teachers in middle school" or "teaching the teachers because we need to help them." Four students made comments related to learning communication and collaboration such as, "It teaches us communication and other ways to think about things."

Figure 4. Oconee-Pickens Speedway

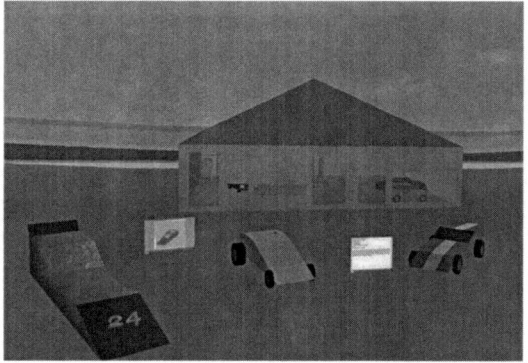

Figure 5. A series of unfortunate events

The daily teacher survey also included similar open-ended questions. Twenty-two of 24 teachers recorded that they learned Google Sketch-up in response to the question, "What were the key things you learned today?" The two remaining teachers mentioned learning about engineering. The other open-ended questions asked, "What was the most useful part of this staff development? Why?" Of the 23 respondents, 20 noted learning about Google Sketch-up and virtual worlds. Five teachers mentioned working with and learning from their student. For example, one teacher responded, "Having my student explain to me how to use the Google Sketch-Up. It was helpful to me to see how much of the program that she already knew." Another teacher commented, "The most useful part was being taught by the students because of their enthusiasm."

Both students and teachers completed a survey at the end of the workshop. Some of the questions used the Likert scale of "a huge amount," "a lot," "a little," hardly anything." Ninety-six percent of the 24 student reported they learned "a huge amount" or "a lot" about being able to work with other students to build a 3D virtual space, being able to work with teachers to build a 3D virtual space, and collaboratively building a 3D virtual space. Of the 22 teacher respondents, 77% reported that they learned "a lot" or "a huge amount" about being able to work with students to build a 3D virtual space to be used for instruction in the school/classroom; 23% reported they learned "a little." In response to being able to work with other teachers to build a 3D virtual space to be used for instruction in the school/classroom, 95% of the teachers recorded that they learned "a huge amount" or "a lot" and 5% reported "a little." Eighty-six percent of the

Figure 6. The courthouse

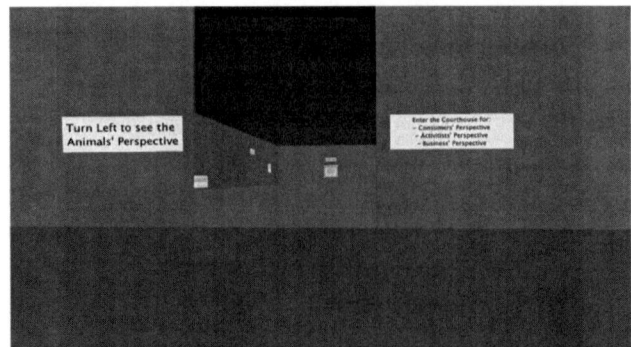

teachers reported gaining a greater understanding of the pedagogical strategies that can be used for teaching in 3D immersive virtual environments, including Presence Pedagogy (P2) "a huge amount" or "a lot" and 14% reported "a little." In the open-ended question, "Overall, what was the best thing you learned from the workshops?" 14 teacher responses related to learning how to implement virtual worlds in the classroom to engage students in learning. One teacher stated, "I learned how to take curriculum and put it into a virtual learning environment to help capture my students' attention. I believe they will be more engaged in the lesson." While another mentioned, "How I will implement a 3D environment in my classroom. I have learned how I can use my student's technological abilities to help make them excited about different science topics and possibly even get them to begin thinking of various locations where they can use these abilities." Eight of the open-ended responses from teachers were related specifically to learning the software, and 4 comments mentioned collaboration.

FUTURE DIRECTIONS

Teachers were also asked in the end of workshop survey how we could make the workshop better next year. Eight comments suggested that teachers needed more time to work with Teleplace prior to attending the face-to-face workshop. Based on this suggestion, the project planning team has decided to begin the program for year 2 participants earlier. This will provide more time for teachers to learn Teleplace as well as acquire a better understanding of P2 since there will be additional opportunities distributed over more time for teachers to be actively involved in model lessons.

Seven of the teacher responses to how we could make the workshop better related to selection of students. Since each school district determined their process for student selection, there was great variation in the commitment levels of the students, thus some students were more able to help the teachers than others. Therefore, during the first follow-up session, teachers were asked to generate lists of the characteristics for students who they thought would be most successful in the program. The lists were compiled and a rubric was created. After validation, the list of characteristics was shared with the teachers helping to select students for the second year of the project. Students are also going to be asked to sign a commitment form when enrolling in the program.

The responses to the surveys indicate the workshops were successful in helping all participants learn to use Google Sketch-up to build in Teleplace, a 3D virtual world. Although some students had a higher level of commitment to acquiring the skills to be able to teach their teachers, all students were able to teach their teachers the basics of Google Sketch-up. The next phase of the project involves teachers implementing the virtual world lessons in their schools while using their students as technical assistants to work with their classmates.

Initial tests at the schools during teacher follow-up sessions demonstrated that there may be issues with the amount of bandwidth required to run the program. These issues may require teachers to reconsider their lessons and their worlds. Many of the worlds that were developed were very realistic and detailed, using a lot of bandwidth, and taking a significant amount of time to load. At the same time the tasks associated with these spaces could be accomplished, as well with less detail. Although this can be explained and reiterated to teachers, they sometimes do not understand the concept until they actually see how slowly their world loads in the school setting.

One of the values of using a 3D space is the capability to communicate and collaborate with other people across a distance. Most teachers' initial lessons were designed to be used by an entire class and failed to take advantage of the potential to work with classrooms outside the school. Although several activities were modeled that placed participants in groups across sites, the one week workshop with the teachers was not sufficient to develop the level of comfort necessary for teachers to attempt such a task with a classroom of 30 students. To take full advantage of the sense of presence and co-presence enabled by 3D immersive virtual environments is going to require teachers to think outside of their traditional paradigms. The formal planned follow-up sessions as well as just-in-time implementation assistance are intended to help teachers overcome these hurdles as well as develop a community of practice where they work with and assist each other in developing a better understanding of teaching in 3D worlds.

CONCLUSION

The *STEM-ICT 3D* project proposes to explore an innovative model for disseminating the use of 3D immersive virtual environments in middle school. Through a progression of activities, rising 7th grade students become technical experts in using Google Sketch-up and building 3D spaces in Teleplace. The students then teach their future teachers these skills and collaborate to develop an inquiry-based learning project for instructional use during the academic school year. Teachers involved in the project learn about pedagogy for 3D immersive virtual environments. This novel approach engages students and teachers in a collaborative community where they can shift roles between novice, mentor, and expert as they learn. The *STEM-ICT 3D* project is still in the early stages of implementation. The students successfully taught their teachers how to build a 3D virtual world and most teachers have been able to work with their student to create a 3D immersive virtual environment to be used instructionally. The next phase of the project involves teachers actually using the space for instruction. As with any innovation, there are numerous issues to be resolved such as technical problems and other initiatives competing for teacher's time. Each phase of the *STEM-ICT 3D* project brings with it new insight and understanding about the roles that 3D immersive virtual environments can have on teaching, learning, and collaboration.

Stem and ICT Instructional Worlds: The 3D Experience (STEM-ICT 3D) is supported by the National Science Foundation Information Technology Experiences for Students and Teachers (ITEST) Program (Grant #0833552). Any opinions, findings, conclusions or recommendations expressed in this material are those of the author(s) and do not necessarily reflect the views of the National Science Foundation.

REFERENCES

Barab, S., Thomas, M., Dodge, T., Carteaux, R., & Tuzun, H. (2005). Making learning fun: Quest Atlantis: A game without guns. *Educational Technology Research and Development*, 1(53), 86–107. doi:10.1007/BF02504859

Bronack, S., Riedl, R., & Tashner, J. (2006). *Learning in the Zone: A social constructivist framework for distance education in a 3D virtual world. Interactive Learning Environments*, 14(3), 219–232. doi:10.1080/10494820600909157

Bronack, S., & Sanders, R. Cheney, A., Riedl, R., Tashner, J. & Matzen, N. (2008). Presence pedagogy: Teaching and learning in a 3D immersive world. *International Journal of Teaching and Learning in Higher Education*. Retrieved September 1, 2009 from http://www.isetl.org/ijtlhe/pdf/IJTLHE453.pdf

Chittaro, L., & Ranon, R. (2007). Web3D technologies in learning, education and training: Motivations, issues, opportunities. *Computers & Education*, (49): 3–18. doi:10.1016/j.compedu.2005.06.002

Dickey, M. D. (2005). Three-dimensional virtual worlds and distance learning: Two case studies of Active Worlds as a medium for distance education. *British Journal of Educational Technology*, *3*(36), 439–451. doi:10.1111/j.1467-8535.2005.00477.x

Educause (2006). *SciFair: Game worlds for learning.* Retrieved September 23, 2009, from http://www.educause.edu/ir/library/pdf/ELI5010.pdf

Jonassen, D. H. (1997). *INSYS 527: Designing constructivist learning environments.* Retrieved September 21, 2009 from http://www.coe.missouri.edu/~jonassen/INSYS527.html

Jones, J. G. (2004). 3D on-line distributed learning environments: An old concept with a new twist. In R. Ferdig & C. Crawford (Eds.), *Proceedings of the Society for Information Technology and Teacher Education International Conference.* (507-512). Atlanta, GA.

Ketelhut, D. J., Dede, C., Clarke, J., & Nelson, B. (2006). *A multi-user virtual environment for building higher order inquiry skills in science.* Paper presented at the American Educational Research Association, San Francisco, CA.

Kim, P. (2006). Effects of 3D virtual reality of plate tectonics on fifth grade students' achievement and attitude toward science. *Interactive Learning Environments*, *1*(14), 25–34. doi:10.1080/10494820600697687

Matzen, N., & Edmunds, J. (2007). Technology as a catalyst for change: The role of professional development. *Journal of Research on Technology in Education*, *4*(39), 417–430.

Reich College of Education – Appalachian State University. (2005). *Conceptual Framework.* Retrieved.

Sanders, R., Bronack, S., Riedl, R., Cheney, A., Matzen, N., Rhyne, S., et al. (2008, March). *The digital native best practice design project.* Presentation at the Teaching and Learning with Technology Conference, Raleigh, NC.

September 9, 2009, from http://ced.appstate.edu/about/conceptualframework.aspx

Vygotsky, L. S. (1978). *Mind in society: The development of higher psychological processes.* Cambridge, MA: Harvard University Press.

Wenger, E., McDermott, R., & Snyder, W. M. (2002). *Cultivating communities of practice: A guide to managing knowledge.* Boston: Harvard Business School Press.

Winn, W. (1993). *A conceptual basis for educational applications of virtual reality.* Human Interface Technology Laboratory, University of Washington. Retrieved September 21, 2009, from http://www.hitl.washington.edu/publications/r-93-9/

ADDITIONAL READING

Bronack, S., Cheney, A., Riedl, R., & Tashner, J. (2008). Designing virtual worlds to facilitate communication: Issues, considerations, and lessons learned. *Technical Communication*, *55*(3), 1–9.

Cheney, A., Riedl, R., Sanders, R., & Tashner, J. (in press). The new company water cooler: Use of 3D virtual immersive worlds to promote networking and professional learning in organizations . In Ritke-Jones, W. (Ed.), *Handbook of Research on Virtual Environments for Corporate Education: Employee Learning and Solutions.* Hershey, PA: IGI Global.

Cheney, A., Sanders, R., Matzen, N., Bronack, S., Riedl, R., & Tashner, J. (in press). A virtual world for collaboration: The AET Zone . In Mikropoulos, T. A., Pantelidis, V. S., & Chen, C. J. (Eds.), *Virtual Reality in Education*. Athens, Greece: Klidarithmos Books.

Cheney, A., Sanders, R., Matzen, N., & Tashner, J. (2009). Instructional design and pedagogical issues with Web 2.0 tools . In Kidd, T. T., & Chen, I. (Eds.), *Wired for Learning: An Educator's Guide to Web 2.0*. Charlotte, NC: Information Age Publishing.

Dede, C., & Honan, J. (2005). Scaling up success: A synthesis of themes and insights . In *Dede, C. Honan*.

2009 from http://www.co-i-l.com/coil/knowledge-garden/cop/lss.shtml

Garrison, D., Anderson, T., & Archer, W. (2001). Critical thinking, cognitive presence, and computer conferencing in distance education. *American Journal of Distance Education*, *15*(1), 7–23. doi:10.1080/08923640109527071

Gilman, R., Tashner, J., Riedl, R., Bronack, S., Cheney, A., & Sanders, R. (2008). Teaching IT through learning communities in a 3D immersive world – the evolution of online instruction . In Negash, S., Whitman, M., Woszczynski, A., Hoganson, K., & Mattord, H. (Eds.), *Distance Learning for Real-Time and Asynchronous Information Technology Education*. Hershey, PA: IGI Global.

Improvement (pp. 227-239). San Francisco: Jossey-Bass.

J., & Peters, L. (Eds.), *Scaling Up Success: Lessons from Technology-Based Educational*

Jonassen, D., Peck, K., & Wilson, B. (1999). *Learning with technology: A constructivist perspective*. Columbus, OH: Prentice Hall.

Lee, J., Carter-Wells, J., Glaeser, B., Ivers, K., & Street, C. (2006). Facilitating the development of a learning community in an online graduate program. *The Quarterly Review of Distance Education*, *7*(1), 13–33.

Ligorio, M. B., & Van Veen, K. (2006). Constructing a successful crossnational virtual learning environment in primary and secondary education. *AACE Journal*, *14*(2), 103–128.

Liu, X., Magjuka, R. J., Bonk, C., & Lee, S. (2007). Does sense of community matter? An examination of participants' perceptions of building learning communities in online courses. *The Quarterly Review of Distance Education*, *8*(1), 9–24.

Lock, J. V. (2002). Laying the groundwork for the development of learning communities within online courses. *The Quarterly Review of Distance Education*, *3*(4), 395–408.

Meyer, K. A. (2004). Evaluating online discussions: Four different frames of analysis. *Journal of Asynchronous Learning Networks*, *8*(2), 101–114.

Omale, N., Hung, W., Luetkehans, L., & Cooke-Plagwitz, J. (2009). Learning in 3-D multiuser virtual environments: Exploring the use of unique 3-D attributes for online problem-based learning. *British Journal of Educational Technology*, *40*(3), 480–495. doi:10.1111/j.1467-8535.2009.00941.x

Sanders, R. & McKeown. (2008). Promoting reflection through action learning in a 3D virtual world. *International Journal of Social Sciences*, *2*(1), 50–55.

Thompson, R., & Zeuli, J. (1999). The frame and tapestry: Standards-based reform and professional development . In Darling-Hammond, L., & Sykes, G. (Eds.), *Teaching as the learning profession: Handbook of policy and practice* (pp. 341–375). San Francisco, CA: Jossey-Bass.

Wenger, E. (1998, June). *Communities of practice: Learning as a social system*. Retrieved October 26,

KEY TERMS AND DEFINITIONS

AETZone: Appalachian Educational Technology Zone; 3D immersive virtual environment used for several graduate school programs at Appalachian State University.

Community of Practice: a group of people who share a common interest or profession.

Inquiry-Based Learning Project: series of activities in a classroom that engage students in actively asking questions and seeking answers. The teacher in an inquiry-based learning project is typically in a more facilitative role.

ITEST: Information Technology Experiences for Students and Teachers; a grant program of the National Science Foundation.

NSF: National Science Foundation

Pedagogy: approaches, practices, and strategies for teaching. A person's pedagogy is influenced by his/her philosophy of how people learn.

Presence Pedagogy: a teaching framework for 3D virtual worlds.

Social Constructivism: a theory of learning that emphasizes the need for interaction to enable meaning making and learning.

STEM: Science, Technology, Engineering, and Mathematics.

Teleplace: 3D virtual immersive world platform

Chapter 8

Scaffolding Discovery Learning in 3D Virtual Environments:
Challenges and Considerations for Instructional Design

Mark J. W. Lee
Charles Sturt University, Australia

Barney Dalgarno
Charles Sturt University, Australia

ABSTRACT

This chapter examines the importance of and possibilities for providing learner support and scaffolding in 3D virtual learning environments designed to promote and encourage learner exploration and discovery. The chapter begins with an overview of the need for scaffolding in discovery learning, before discussing scaffolding in technology-mediated learning environments. A framework is presented for understanding the types of scaffolding that can be provided in such environments. Using a case study based on the design of a 3D Virtual Chemistry Laboratory, examples illustrating the way each category of scaffolding within the framework could be provided within a 3D virtual environment are presented. The chapter concludes with coverage of the key considerations in designing scaffolded 3D virtual environments, as well as some of the important issues in adapting the concepts of scaffolding from face-to-face to technology-mediated environments.

INTRODUCTION

Proponents of immersive and three-dimensional (3D) virtual learning spaces have argued for designs based on a discovery learning paradigm, either explicitly (e.g. Chen, Toh, & Wan, 2003; Blanchard & Frasson, 2006; Bronack, Sanders, Cheney, Riedl, Tashner, & Matzen, 2008) or im- plicitly (e.g. Sanders & McKeown, 2007; Berge, 2008; Johnson & Levine, 2008; McKay, van Schie, & Headley, 2008). Discovery learning may be viewed as having its roots in the writings of authors such as Piaget (1973), who suggested that learners who are cognitively active will have learning advantages over learners who are cognitively passive, and Dewey (1938/1997), who stressed the need for learners to learn through concrete experience.

DOI: 10.4018/978-1-61692-825-4.ch008

It is Bruner (1961, 1962/1979), however, who is perhaps most widely regarded as the originator of discovery learning. Bruner claimed that discovery learning is an effective way of encouraging the learner to organize, assimilate, and integrate newly acquired knowledge in a cognitively active manner, as well as encouraging the learner to maintain a perspective on the purpose and significance of his/her learning, including developing an appreciation for the contexts and situations to which the knowledge may be applied.

Mayer (2004), however, cites compelling research evidence gathered over three decades that attests to the inefficiencies inherent in 'pure discovery learning,' and advocates the use of guided discovery strategies incorporating cognitive activities aligned to the intended curricular outcomes, along with the provision of appropriate instructional support. In an education landscape where we are witnessing the advent of new and nascent 'Web 2.0' and 'Web 3.0' technologies that shift the locus of control and place the power of information and content creation and manipulation firmly in the hands of the "people formerly known as the audience" (Rosen, 2006, para. 1), a number of other authors have also highlighted the tensions that exist between autonomous, learner-directed approaches to technology-mediated learning and the need to design and provide suitable supports to guide and assist learners in line with self-regulated learning theory (Hai-Jew, 2008; McLoughlin & Lee, 2010).

Wood, Bruner, and Ross' (1976) concept of scaffolding is particularly important in this context, as is the related and arguably underpinning concept of the zone of proximal development (ZPD) (Vygotsky, 1978). These ideas not only direct our attention to the importance of learning supports, but also stress that the instructional process must incorporate a level of responsiveness to the individual needs and state of conceptual understanding achieved by learners (McLoughlin, 2002; Azevedo, Moos, Greene, Winters, & Cromley, 2008). A wealth of research has been conducted leading to the formulation of theoretically and empirically grounded design principles, guidelines, and models for scaffolding learning in traditional or face-to-face settings (see, for example, Palincsar, 1986; Bliss, Askew, & Macrae, 1996; Hogan & Pressley, 1997; Sanders & Welk, 2005); more recently, a growing body of literature has emerged concerning the use of scaffolding in technology-mediated learning environments (McLoughlin, 1999; Winnips, 2001; McLoughlin, 2002; Brush & Saye, 2001; Davis & Miyake, 2004; Sharma & Hannafin, 2007; Jacobson & Azevedo, 2008). A key question, then, is how to apply these ideas from conventional instructional design to the design of 3D virtual learning environments (VLEs), including the new wave of 3D virtual worlds and multi-player online games whose purported educational uses and benefits are garnering much attention and excitement in all sectors of the education and training industry.

A commonly discussed and recurring issue in the literature on scaffolding is the need for and importance of fading, which involves gradually reducing and eventually removing scaffolds as the learner's capabilities increase. A number of authors (e.g. Guzdial, 1994; Collins, Brown, & Newman, 1989; Lepper, Drake, & O'Donnell-Johnson, 1997; Stone, 1998) assert that fading is a defining characteristic of scaffolding that differentiates it from other forms of learner support. Although there are some opponents of this view (e.g. Sherin, Reiser, & Edelson, 2004), the idea is quite well accepted at least within the context of face-to-face learning. In online and computer-based learning environments, however, a number of difficulties and problems with providing fading become apparent. For example, in a face-to-face classroom, a skilled teacher can use his/her observations of aspects of the learner's spoken discourse, intonation of voice, body language, and actual performance on tasks to determine when and how to fade support. In online environments a skilled facilitator may be able to make judgments about a learner's needs from their online actions and comments and gradually fade the support provided in a similar way. The automation of faded support within discovery learning environments is more problematic, however, because such adaptive behaviors are very challenging to implement in software without the use of sophisticated artificial intelligence (AI) techniques.

This chapter discusses the challenge of designing 3D VLEs that allow the learner to immerse him/herself within the virtual environment and undertake authentic, open-ended learning tasks, while simultaneously avoiding or minimizing the problems encountered in pure or unscaffolded discovery learning. It is our view that the high degree of representational fidelity provided by immersive learning environments can lead to authentic discovery learning experiences that can be highly motivating and engaging, but that this does not in any way reduce the pedagogical problems associated with a lack of support or scaffolding. We advocate the provision of support and scaffolding through system elements and through collaborative tools, in such a way as to maintain immersion and engagement and minimize interference to learners as they perform tasks. Key issues such as cognitive load considerations and whether or how to implement fading of scaffolds in 3D VLEs are also highlighted and addressed. Examples that build on and extend an existing environment, a 3D Virtual Chemistry Laboratory designed by one of the authors, are used to help explain and illustrate the ideas put forward.

DISCOVERY LEARNING AND SCAFFOLDING

Discovery learning is an umbrella term used to describe a variety of instructional design models and learning approaches that strive to encourage learners to learn through discovery. According to van Joolingen (1999), in discovery learning,

learners construct their own knowledge by experimenting with a domain, and inferring rules from the results of these experiments. The basic idea... is that because learners can design their own experiments in the domain and infer the rules of the domain themselves they are actually constructing their knowledge. ... [As a result] of these constructive activities, it is assumed they will understand the domain at a higher level than when the necessary information is just presented by a teacher or an expository learning environment. (p. 385)

Similarly, Ormrod (1995) defines discovery learning as "an approach to instruction through which students interact with their environment—by exploring and manipulating objects, wrestling with questions and controversies, or performing experiments" (p. 442). Problem-based learning, inquiry-based learning, exploratory learning, and learning through simulations can all be deemed kinds or instances of discovery learning. Another closely related concept is experiential learning (Kolb, 1984), which is based on the idea that experience provides a basis for observation and reflection by allowing the learner to make illuminating discoveries and develop a superior cognitive understanding as compared to listening to a teacher or reading from a textbook.

Notwithstanding the benefits and appeal of discovery learning, consistent with Mayer's (2004) aforementioned contention, Kirschner, Sweller, and Clark (2006) criticize and highlight the shortcomings of unguided and minimally guided approaches to instruction, in light of research on human cognitive architecture, expert–novice differences, and cognitive load. They believe that instructional guidance should only be reduced or removed when learners have amassed sufficiently high levels of prior knowledge to allow 'internal' guidance. Similarly, Hai-Jew (2008) claims that fully autodidactic or 'self discovery learning' may give rise to risks of poor decision-making, the acceptance of untested ideas and assumptions by learners, the drawing of inaccurate conclusions, and naïve mental modeling. Roblyer, Edwards, and Havriluk (1997, p. 68) echo this view, maintaining that discovery learning is "most successful when students have prerequisite knowledge and undergo some structured experiences." Guided discovery (Leutner, 1993) combines discovery learning with principles from cognitivist instructional design theory, in an attempt to achieve a balance between learner-driven discovery and open-ended exploration on one hand, and teacher/expert-supplied guidance and structure on the other. Evidence suggests that guided discovery increases the likelihood of deep learning occurring, when compared to didactic, transmissive modes of teaching (de Jong & van Joolingen, 1998). Spencer and Jordan (1999) list four key features of guided discovery learning (p. 1282):

- A context and frame for student learning through the provision of learning outcomes
- Learners have responsibility for exploration of content necessary for understanding through self-directed learning
- Study guides are used to facilitate and guide self-directed learning
- Understanding is reinforced through application in problem-oriented, task-based, and work-related experiences.

Guided discovery bears many similarities with and features heavily in a number of learning theories and pedagogical frameworks, such as Laurillard's (1993, 2002) conversational framework, which is based on the premise that students should be assisted, through conversation and other supports, to reconcile their views and observations of the world with the abstract, academic conceptualizations that they are required to learn as part of formal study. Within the conversational framework, learners and teachers negotiate mutual understandings by articulating and sharing their conceptions with one another. The teacher adapts the dialogue and objectives according to the learn-

ers' discourse and actions, while the learners adapt their actions based on feedback received from the teacher, reflecting on their experiences and modifying their conceptions in the process. This interactive process is both teacher- and learner-driven, as learners are not left to their own devices and simply expected to 'sink or swim,' nor does it rely on one-way transmission of information from teacher to learner. The goal is to create and foster an information-rich environment in which the student has control in discovering knowledge, albeit with the help of extra guidance functions that provide support and feedback for subsequent learning (Phillips, 1998).

Both guided discovery and Laurillard's conversational framework emphasize the need for scaffolding, a term commonly used in the constructivist literature to portray a process in which an expert such as a teacher provides support to a novice (learner) in accomplishing a task or attaining a goal (Wood et al., 1976). Scaffolding involves systematically providing the learner with supportive aids in the form of tools, strategies, and guides targeted to his/her ZPD (the gap between the learner's current or actual development level and his/her emerging or potential level), to assist him/her in progressing to the next potential level of development (Dabbagh, 2003). This is often accomplished by limiting the initial complexity of the assigned task, then gradually introducing complexity as learner competence increases. The expert typically slowly removes or 'fades' the support provided to the learner as he/she acquires the knowledge, skills, and confidence required to handle the task independently (Collins et al., 1989; Young, 1993; Lepper et al., 1997). In this way, the use of scaffolding within authentic tasks can help to avoid the problems of pure discovery learning, mitigating the risk of novice learners becoming "overwhelmed by the complexities of the field" (Sandberg & Wielinga, 1992, p. 136). Lepper et al. (1997) highlight three significant aspects of a scaffolding interaction: (i) It supports learners in the achievement of tasks beyond their unassisted capacity; (ii) when the support structure is removed, learners continue to function competently on their own; and (iii) removing the support structure does not reduce learning or functioning—instead, learners continue to function at the elevated plane reached via scaffolding.

SCAFFOLDING IN TECHNOLOGY-MEDIATED LEARNING ENVIRONMENTS

There have been a number of attempts made by various researchers to classify and taxonomize the types or applications of scaffolding that may be used in technology-mediated learning environments (see for instance, Winnips & McLoughlin, 2000, 2001; McLoughlin, 2002; Jang & Lim, 2008). According to Winnips and McLoughlin (2000), for example, applications of scaffolding can be categorized according to who regulates the scaffolding (e.g. the teacher, the software, peers, the learner him/herself), the technology used, the pedagogy used, or the intended learning outcome. McLoughlin (2002) outlines nine categories of learner supports/scaffolds, and proposes ten di-

mensions that she believes should be considered in the design of such supports.

For the purposes of the present chapter, the framework we have chosen to employ to structure our discussion on scaffolding in 3D VLEs (Table 1) is based around two dimensions: firstly, the type of knowledge development intended to be supported, and secondly, the way in which the scaffolding is provided, that is, the overarching pedagogical technique used. The *knowledge* dimension of our discussion framework consists of three categories—procedural, conceptual, and metacognitive—and the *pedagogical* dimension consists also of three categories—instruction, coaching, and the provision of supporting or enabling tools.

The categories in our first dimension, the knowledge dimension, draw on the definitions of knowledge types provided by Krathwohl (2002) in his overview of the revised version of Bloom's (1956) Taxonomy proposed by Anderson and Krathwohl (2001). Each of our categories here also appears in McLoughlin's (2002) aforementioned framework. In addition, they are in agreement with the categories of scaffolding in electronic performance support systems (EPSS)

Table 1. Dimensions of scaffolding in technology-mediated learning environments

Knowledge dimension	Pedagogical dimension		
	Instruction	Coaching	Tools
Procedural	*Example:* Presentation of a recommended sequence of steps to carry out an overall learning task, as part of an orientation or briefing preceding the task	*Example:* Advice about how to navigate through a part of the environment (i.e. when the learner has become stuck)	*Example:* Provision of a tool that allows the learner to bookmark a page or location for later viewing
Conceptual	*Example:* A video lecture on a particular theoretical concept in the learning domain	*Example:* Alternative explanation of a concept, delivered in response to the learner's unsuccessful attempt to carry out a task	*Example:* Provision of a visualization tool to aid the learner's understanding of concepts within the learning domain
Metacognitive	*Example:* Suggestion of a number of possible learning tasks that the learner could undertake to further develop or reinforce his/her understanding	*Example:* Rhetorical or leading questions in the form of prompts asked of the learner to help him/her solve a problem	*Example:* Provision of a concept-mapping tool that helps the learner to articulate and reflect on their current understanding of an aspect of the learning domain

identified by Cagiltay (2006), with the exception of Cagiltay's 'strategic' or 'intrinsic' scaffolding, which involves guiding learners as they approach learning tasks by emphasizing alternative pathways and courses of action that might prove helpful. We consider this type of scaffolding to be subsumed into the metacognitive knowledge category (see below).

The following is an outline of each of the three categories that we have used to classify applications of scaffolding according to the knowledge to be learned:

- *Procedural scaffolding:* An important element of constructivist learning theory is the idea that learners should be given the opportunity to carry out realistic tasks, with assistance of scaffolding provided to enable them to complete the larger task without needing to learn all of the subsidiary or sub-tasks involved (Bruner, 1986). Ideally, as a by-product of such procedural scaffolding, the learner will learn how to complete the sub-tasks so that eventually they will be able to carry out the larger task unassisted. This type of scaffolding corresponds to Krathwohl's (2002) procedural knowledge category, which he considers to be knowledge of "how to do something" (p. 214). This comprises knowledge of subject-specific skills and algorithms and knowledge of subject-specific techniques and methods, in addition to knowledge of the criteria to use to determine when to use the appropriate skills, algorithms, techniques, and methods.

Applied to technology-mediated learning environments, procedural scaffolding focuses on suggesting various ways to leverage the available resources and tools within the environment to achieve a desired result or outcome (Linton, 2000, cited in Cagiltay, 2006; McLoughlin, 2002). Hannafin, Land, and Oliver (1999) list a number of specific examples of this type of scaffolding, stating that it is "frequently provided to clarify how to return to a desired location, how to flag or bookmark locations or resources for subsequent review, or how to deploy given tools" (p. 133). Other forms of procedural scaffolding include advice or guidance on how to tackle an overall task, the offering of 'just-in-time' support in the form of cues or reminders during a task performance, and the provision of tools to reduce the complexity of a procedure or automate some of the more routine aspects of it.

- *Conceptual scaffolding:* Conceptual knowledge, according to Krathwohl (2002), entails an understanding of how basic factual elements are interlinked to form a larger pattern or structure. Conceptual knowledge includes: knowledge of classifications and categories, knowledge of principles and generalizations, and knowledge of theories, models, and structures (Krathwohl). Conceptual scaffolding therefore involves the provision of support to assist the learner in assimilating or constructing internal representations of these knowledge structures within the subject or problem domain at hand, or in the words of Hannafin et al. (1999), it is "designed to help learners reason through complex or fuzzy problems, as well as for concepts where known misconceptions are prevalent" (p. 132).
- *Metacognitive scaffolding:* Metacognitive knowledge is knowledge about cognition in general as well as awareness of and knowledge about one's own cognitive abilities and processes (Krathwohl, 2002). Metacognition is a key element of self-directed and self-regulated learning (Biggs, 1987; Zimmerman & Schunk, 1989; Simons, 1992; Boekaerts, 1995; Winne, 1995; Boekaerts, Pintrich, & Zeidner,

2000), and therefore has especially important implications for the design of learning tasks and environments that seek to afford a high level of learner autonomy and control. Metacognitive scaffolding is support for the learner as he/she manages and monitors his/her own learning, including but not limited to setting of learning goals, formulation and selection of cognitive strategies, self-regulation and management of learning processes, and engagement in reflection. Hai-Jew (2008) advocates giving learners agency and choice in selecting and customizing the supports provided to them, however because novice learners often lack the requisite knowledge and skills to do this effectively on their own, Pea (2004) suggests the need for 'metascaffolding' to assist them in making appropriate decisions in this regard.

In addition to procedural, cognitive, and metacognitive knowledge, Krathwohl (2002) identifies a fourth knowledge category, factual knowledge, which we consider to be less relevant to the present discussion on scaffolded discovery learning. This is because it is arguable that the learning of factual knowledge through discovery learning methods does not really require scaffolding in the way that the learning of procedural, conceptual, and metacognitive knowledge do. Although scaffolds may be implemented that point or direct learners to materials or resources aimed at developing their basic factual knowledge, we argue that suggesting resources in this way is a means of supporting the learner in regulating his/her own learning strategy, and as such it is more appropriately classed as a form of metacognitive scaffolding.

The second dimension of our scaffolding framework, the pedagogical dimension, categorizes the ways in which scaffolding can be provided in technology-mediated learning environments:

- *Instruction* is the provision of support for the learner through lectures, demonstra-

tions, or the modeling of ideal or 'expert' behaviors. It normally occurs prior to the commencement of a learning task or activity (front-loaded instruction), although instances of back-loaded instruction exist, for example in the form of summaries or reminders about key points following the completion of an activity. This category is linked to and comparable with Saye and Brush's (2002) depiction of 'hard' scaffolding, where 'hard' scaffolds are those that are largely fixed, static, and non-negotiable, in contrast to 'soft' scaffolds, which are dynamic, customized, and negotiable according to the needs and progress of individual learners. Although not explicitly named as a category in McLoughlin's (2002) framework, the notion of instruction is inferred in the descriptions of a number of categories she proposes, including 'orientation: communication of expectation,' where learners are given a (static) description of what they should aim to achieve, and 'expert regulation,' in which an expert shows examples and models/demonstrates the desired learning outcomes.

- *Coaching* is the provision of support for the learner during learning tasks. This support is normally reactive in that it is delivered to address identified misconceptions or gaps in the learner's knowledge or understanding. It is also adaptive in that each learner is provided with coaching that is individualized to suit his/her specific needs as distinct from those of other learners and changed as needed over the course of a particular task. Coaching is also featured in McLoughlin's (2002) framework; it can be provided by experts or by peers (Hai-Jew, 2008; Lai & Law, 2006), and may be carried out before, during, and after the learning activity. This category may be considered equivalent or similar to Saye and Brush's (2002) 'soft' scaffolding. A similar and overlapping concept is that of mentoring, which is generally regarded as a broader term that encompasses a range of functions, including but not limited to "coaching, moderating, tutoring, guiding, advising, supporting, signposting, safeguarding, facilitating and assisting" (Harris, 2008, p. 2; see also Goodyear, 2006). Though sometimes used interchangeably with 'coaching,' 'mentoring' seems to often be used in relation to one's overall academic/intellectual or professional development, such as in the context of a job role or profession (see, for example, Bierema & Merriam, 2002; Ensher, Heun, & Blanchard, 2003; Goodyear, 2006).

- A third way in which scaffolding can be achieved is through the *provision of tools*. (It should be noted that 'tools' here refers to both discrete software objects or functions within the virtual environment as well as features/attributes of the overall environment itself.) Such tools enable the learner to undertake given tasks or support the performance of those tasks by making certain aspects of the tasks easier. They include tools that help with the procedural tasks, tools that help with understanding concepts, and tools that help the learner to undertake metacognitive functions. Metacognitive scaffolding, for example, can be provided by supplying a cognitive tool (Jonassen, 1994) such as an electronic notepad or mind-mapping/concept-mapping tool that learners are encouraged to use to record their thinking and articulate their mental models (see also McLoughlin, 2002). In McLoughlin's description of her 'task support' category, she alludes to the provision of "heuristics or resources that enable task engagement and activity" (p. 153). This implies the use of supporting procedural tools.

The three techniques making up the pedagogical dimension within this framework can each be used to achieve each of the three types of knowledge development, resulting in nine different types of scaffolding. Table 1 illustrates this by providing an example of a way in which each of these nine types of scaffolding could be used within a technology-mediated learning environment.

SCAFFOLDED LEARNING IN 3D VIRTUAL ENVIRONMENTS

Bares, Zettlemoyer, and Lester (1998) discuss the design and use of "habitable 3D learning environments" (p. 76), in which learners control and direct avatars through virtual worlds and engage in role-based problem solving. They propose a framework for habitable 3D learning environments that they call SAIL (Situated Avatar-Based Immersive Learning). According to Bares et al.,

SAIL environments are intended to foster exploratory freedom... by allowing learners to explore the virtual world at will. Increased freedom leads to the design challenge of assisting learners to cope with this flexibility by modeling their problem-solving activities and offering guidance. Ideally operating in a guided discovery mode, the environments should enable learners to pursue paths in a curiosity-driven fashion while at the same time providing support. (p. 81)

How, then, can appropriate scaffolds be created to support guided discovery learning in 3D virtual environments? In the subsections that follow, we discuss various possibilities for providing scaffolding in 3D VLEs, as well as highlighting a number of important issues and considerations.

Scaffolding through Enhanced Navigation, Manipulation, and Visualization

One way of providing scaffolding within a 3D VLE is to allow learners to have greater navigational control than they would have in the real world, or more generally, empower them to perform 'magic' tasks and actions that are not possible in the real world. On a simple level, this might include the ability to manipulate system parameters, such as the speed at which time passes. Romano and Brna (2000) describe a 3D collaborative learning environment for firefighter training, which provides a number of what they term 'super-powers,' including the ability to switch to the point of view of another user within the environment as well as the ability to modify the speed of the simulation. In the simulated radioactivity laboratory described by Crosier, Cobb, and Wilson (2000), learners can carry out tasks and measure the results at the laboratory level and then zoom in and visualize what is happening at the atomic level.

Virtual Big Beef Creek (Campbell, Collins, Hadaway, Hedley, & Stoermer, 2002) is a 3D VLE that recreates a marine and coastal environment for the teaching of Ocean Science, in which learners can assume the roles of scientists to collect and analyze geo-scientific data, or alternatively, take on characters representing creatures that inhabit the environment. Depending on the type of creature assumed, the characters are variously able to walk over land, swim underwater, or fly across the sky. In this way, the learners are able to explore firsthand the abilities and limitations of the various animals, while simultaneously acquiring knowledge about the flora, fauna, ecosystem, and ocean environment at large.

Scaffolding Through the Use of Intelligent Agents

Scaffolding may in some cases take the form of an intelligent agent with a visual representation within the environment, acting as a guide to the learner. 3D environments provide the opportunity for a greater sense of realism in the use of such agents and a closer integration with the task at hand. This may lead to more effective task support by eliminating the need to switch between attending to the agent and attending to the task. Sims (2007) recommends the use of lifelike, interactive digital characters or 'virtual humans' to serve as mentors and role-playing actors. Ieronutti and Chittaro (2007) have devised a technology framework for developing such 'virtual humans' capable of supplying informal coaching and formal instruction. They present two case studies to illustrate how their architecture can be integrated into web-based 3D VLEs. In the first case, a virtual human served as a guide to explain the history of different buildings and their architectural differences, in a virtual reconstruction of a cultural heritage site. In the second case, the same virtual human was re-used in a computer science museum, providing information on the technical workings of different hardware devices dating back to the 1970s.

The *Virtual Singapura* project (Jacobson, Kim, Lee, Lim, & Low, 2008) uses a 3D multi-user virtual environment (MUVE) set in a historical context in 19th-century Singapore, to aid in the development of secondary students' scientific knowledge and inquiry skills. The synthetic characters in the MUVE are augmented with advanced agent technologies to adaptively provide informational and conceptual scaffolding, with the hope of helping students cognitively attend to conceptual dimensions of knowledge. For example, the agents are programmed to 'remember' if a student's avatar has visited a particular location before, and if they have explored certain resources in that location (such as pictures). Informational prompts and responses to students' queries are dynamically tailored according to this information.

Overall, the traditional problems in providing adaptive and dynamic ('soft') scaffolding in technology-mediated learning environments (see, for example, Azevedo et al., 2008) may be less significant in 3D VLEs. This is because whereas interpreting learners' cognitive scaffolding needs by analyzing their behaviors within text-based or hypermedia learning environments and/or deconstructing their answers to text-based questions (e.g. through the use of natural language processing) may be difficult to implement in software, making sense of their actions in a 3D environment may not be as problematic. Nevertheless, although there have been considerable advances in AI and expert systems technology over the years, the efficacy of such systems in providing adaptive support still pales in comparison to that which is possible through human–human interaction.

Productivity and Learning Support Tools and the Use of Fading

Another type of scaffolding in 3D VLEs involves the provision of support tools to help the learner undertake learning tasks. In some cases the tools may be developed specifically for this purpose, such as the lesson-planning tool described by Wild and Kirkpatrick (1996). Alternatively, general-purpose software, such as a language translator, spell checker, thesaurus, calculator, or spreadsheet program, can fill a similar role. There is scope for specifically 3D support tools such as a 3D graphing tool, which can be used to support the learner in carrying out authentic tasks that require the visualization of 3D data. Additionally, 3D VLEs allow for the realistic embedding of such tools within the environment (see the next subsection).

A point of contention here is whether the provision of certain tools that are never faded really constitutes scaffolding (Pea, 2004). Sherin et al. (2004) challenge the assumption in the original Wood et al. (1976) article that fading is a required component of the definition of scaffolding, arguing that "in the case of technological artifacts, there is less of an opportunity for interactive tuning of scaffolding" (p. 403). This is reflective of many educational technology researchers' conceptions of scaffolding in computer-based and online learning environments, which often involve the

provision of support without fading, possibly due to the difficulty of algorithmically implementing such techniques to allow software to assume these functions with little or no (human) tutor intervention (Puntambekar & Hubscher, 2005; Azevedo et al., 2008). The alternative is often to provide learner control over the degree of scaffolding or the types of scaffolding used, as suggested by Hai-Jew (2008). However, in doing so, it is crucial to acknowledge, as Pea (2004) has argued, that many learners with limited background knowledge of the learning domain may have difficulty regulating their own learning effectively.

Pea (2004) contrasts tools that are used to offer what he calls 'scaffolds-with-fading' with those that become part of a distributed intelligence and are not faded, instead providing continuing and ongoing support to learners to enable them to perform tasks ('scaffolds-for-performance'). The former type is suitable in cases where the scaffolding exists to support the internalizing of a specific task/process as one of the intended learning outcomes or objectives. In such cases it is necessary for purposeful fading to occur so that the learner is ultimately able to perform the task independently and autonomously. On the other hand, in situations where the learner will have regular access to the scaffolding supports when carrying out an activity, fading may not be appropriate. A calculator, for instance, may be used to scaffold learner performances by automating arithmetic operations and thus reducing cognitive load. However, calculator use has become a fixed and routine component of mathematics activity (Sherin et al., 2004); fading of this tool may not be necessary and in fact may be counterproductive in terms of developing the learner's ability to engage in complex and advanced forms of reasoning and problem-solving.

Our assertion, then, is that the provision of fading is not a necessary condition for a particular support technique to be classified as scaffolding. We believe that to restrict the definition in this way would force us to rule out the possibility of applying the powerful and useful scaffolding metaphor to many environments and applications. In particular, it would exclude Saye and Brush's (2002) 'hard' scaffolds, which are similar to our instructional scaffolds, and would also exclude many examples within our 'tools' category.

Design Considerations in Combining 3D VLEs with Instructional Resources

Sweller, van Merriënboer, and Paas (1998) discuss the importance of reducing the cognitive load in presenting instructional information, by minimizing the demands on working memory. One effect discussed by them is termed the 'split attention effect,' which occurs when the learner has to refer to two or more distinct information representations, such as a picture and a separate caption, resulting in an increased cognitive load. Sweller et al.'s research suggests that if the various sources of information can instead be integrated the demands on working memory can be reduced and consequently the cognitive load is reduced. The integration of graphical and textual information, possibly supported by audio, within a 3D environment is consistent with these ideas (Chen & Wan, 2008); an alternative to embedding instructional resources within a 3D VLE is to provide the resources with a conventional web-based or hypermedia interface, but with embedded 3D games, simulations, or microworlds within the resources.

Chen, Toh, and Wan (2004) have developed a body of theory on the design of 3D VLEs, drawing heavily on the work of Mayer, Sweller, and others. Systems and applications using their design typically consist of 3D resources embedded within a conventional web-based or hypermedia interface, to allow exploration of conceptual ideas or virtual places or the practicing of skills at relevant points within the learning environment. For example, Chen and Toh (2005; Chen, Toh, & Wan, 2003; Chen, 2006) describe a driver education resource containing interactive 3D simulations of driving scenarios, embedded within a tutorial web site.

The interface provided through such resources includes conventional multimedia instructional resources, supplemented by 3D VLEs displayed within a window on the page in a similar way to which video material would normally be provided in such resources.

We believe that embedding the 3D VLE itself within the resources sacrifices one of the key benefits of 3D VLEs, that is, the ability to immerse and engage learners in experiential and contextual learning through rich, authentic learning tasks (see Dalgarno & Lee, 2010). In our view, the provision of instructional resources in a realistic way *within* the environment can provide a similar level of structured/supported learning without sacrificing realism and authenticity. For example, Dede, Salzman, Loftin, and Ash's (1997) *Newton World*, an immersive environment for learning Newtonian physics, includes an embedded 'scoreboard' showing numerical and graphical representations of mass, velocity, momentum, and elasticity of objects within the environment. Multisensory cues are used to direct learners' attention to important variables. The embedding of supporting tools/resources as objects in the virtual environment can also be seen in many more recent applications using 3D immersive virtual world platforms such as Activeworlds and Second Life. Another example can be seen in the case of the River City MUVE (Harvard University, 2007; Dede, Clarke, Ketelhut, Nelson, & Bowman, 2005; Galas & Ketelhut, 2006), a 3D VLE based on the Activeworlds platform that was designed to teach scientific inquiry and 21st-century skills to middle school students through interactive simulation and game play, in addition to helping them learn core curriculum content aligned with U.S. national science standards. Learners travel back in time to visit River City, a 19th-century town plagued by illness and health problems, and work in small research teams to apply modern-day skills and technology to uncover the causes of these problems through scientific exploration, investigation, and experimentation. To assist their endeavors, the learners obtain support and information from a variety of tools and digital artifacts that are endogenous and authentic to the virtual world scenario and fantasy (described in detail in Dieterle, 2009), ranging from virtual 'library books' located in the River City library (including an online dictionary and a textbook on scientific research methods), to 'bug-catchers' scattered throughout the city that allow learners to determine the mosquito density of different geographic areas over time. An 'environmental health meter' that travels with the learner's avatar as a HUD provides dynamic readings on the general environmental health of an area, and learners are able to interview 'residents' of River City to find out clues as to why people are falling ill.

A DESIGN CASE STUDY: THE VIRTUAL CHEMISTRY LABORATORY

In order to contextualize and explore the challenges involved in the design of 3D scaffolded discovery learning environments, and to illustrate some of the solutions to these challenges that we would advocate, this section discusses a specific design scenario involving an existing Virtual Chemistry Laboratory environment (see Dalgarno, Bennett, & Harper, 2004; Dalgarno, Bishop, Adlong, & Bedgood, 2009), and the extension of that environment to encompass a broader range of learning outcomes than the environment was originally intended to address. We argue that the design that unfolds in this section would allow the learner to immerse him/herself within the virtual environment and to undertake authentic, open-ended learning tasks, but would not suffer from the well-documented problems of pure, unscaffolded discovery learning. Throughout this design case study we have tried to consistently argue for the provision of support and scaffolding through system elements and collaborative tools in ways that minimize interference to learners as they perform tasks.

The Virtual Chemistry Laboratory is based on the needs of undergraduate university chemistry students. The learning outcomes that need to be achieved by these students, and which a virtual laboratory might ideally help to address, can be classified into the following broad areas:

1. Familiarity with the laboratory environment
2. Procedural skills in undertaking experiments
3. Understanding of basic chemistry concepts (e.g. atoms, molecules, and the periodic table; chemical bonding; properties of molecules, elements, and compounds; reactions and equilibrium; solids, liquids, and gases; acids and bases; state changes and energy exchanges)
4. Skills in manipulating and solving chemical equations
5. Skills in analyzing quantitative data acquired from experiments
6. The ability to understand and use chemistry terminology
7. The ability to work effectively with others in undertaking experiments and analyzing results.

The existing version of the Virtual Chemistry Laboratory consists of a 3D model of the Charles Sturt University undergraduate chemistry laboratory, along with the main items of furniture and equipment and many of the items of apparatus used in experiments. The user can freely explore the laboratory and as part of this exploration, drawers and cupboards can be opened and shut, items of apparatus collected and carried to a workbench, and those items of apparatus connected together and manipulated as they would be as part of an experiment. The current version provides the learner with the opportunity to familiarize him/herself with the laboratory space and procedures, that is, addressing outcomes 1 and 2 from the above list.

It is arguable that the remaining outcomes could be achieved with the addition of simulated experiments and collaborative tools. For example, the inclusion of virtual experiments within the environment could potentially help to address outcomes 3, 4, and 5 by allowing the learner to 'discover' chemical properties and develop skills through trial and error as they carry out their own laboratory experiments. The current version of the environment is single user and so does not allow collaborative tasks or communication; the implementation of a multi-user capability with visible avatars and communication tools could potentially help to achieve outcome 7 and possibly outcome 6 by allowing learners to work together on tasks and discuss the associated chemistry terminology.

As argued by Mayer (2004), however, there would be a number of important limitations of such a pure discovery learning environment, the most fundamental being that learners need guidance to ensure that they actually encounter the intended learning material through their exploration. Table 2 provides some examples to illustrate the ways in which an enhanced version of the Virtual Chemistry Laboratory with the inclusion of virtual experiments and collaborative capability might address the above learning outcomes, as well as

sketching out the limitations of the resource if these enhancements were made without the addition of purposefully designed support or scaffolding. In the next section we provide design examples illustrating how these limitations could potentially be addressed through the inclusion of scaffolding.

Enhancing the Virtual Chemistry Laboratory with the Inclusion of Scaffolding

Using the scaffolding framework discussed earlier in the chapter and illustrated in Table 1, this section describes the ways in which some of the limitations of a pure discovery version of the Virtual Chemistry Laboratory identified in Table 2 could be addressed through the inclusion of scaffolding. Specifically, examples are provided of how each of the nine types of scaffolding identified in the framework could be provided in the Virtual Laboratory environment.

Overall Design Considerations for Incorporating Scaffolding

As discussed above, one of the key elements of the design approach that we are advocating is the

Figure 1. The existing Virtual Chemistry Laboratory environment

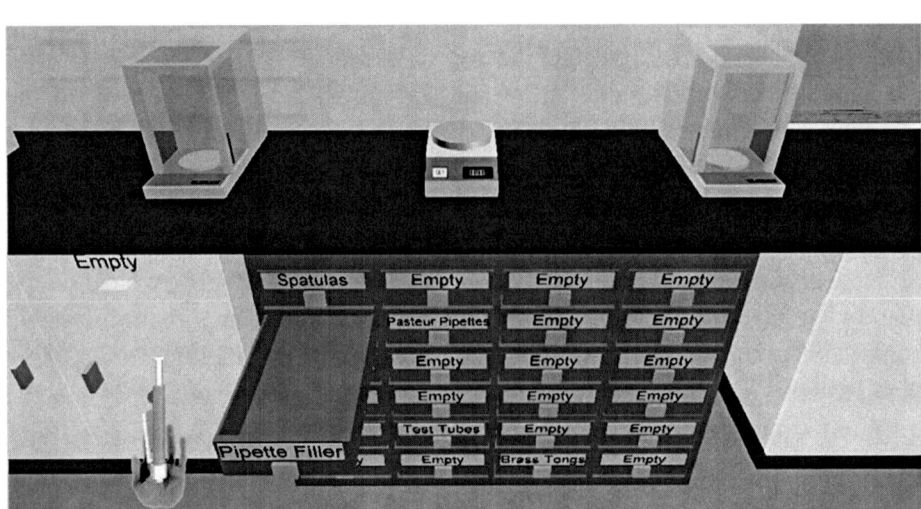

Table 2. Potential limitations of an enhanced Virtual Chemistry Laboratory, with virtual experiments and collaborative tools but no support or scaffolding

Chemistry learning outcome	How potentially addressed	Key limitations
1. Familiarity with the laboratory environment	The learner could develop familiarity with the environment by exploring and clicking on objects to see their labels and descriptions.	Without any task support many learners may become bored before they have explored the entire laboratory or alternatively may focus on obscure features or objects/equipment rather than the relevant items likely to be used in their own study.
2. Procedural skills in undertaking experiments	The learner could experiment with assembling and manipulating items of apparatus (for example, clamping a burette to a stand, attaching a pipette filler to a pipette, or attaching a Bunsen burner to a gas tap).	Without any support many learners are not likely to know which items connect to which other items and what the purpose of items of apparatus might be.
3. Understanding of basic chemistry concepts	Experiments focused on the various concepts may allow the learner to develop his/her understanding of each of the concepts.	It is unlikely that novice learners undertaking chemistry experiments in a pure discovery environment will 'discover' chemistry concepts on their own. The connection of the results of experiments to the chemical properties illustrated requires substantial instructional support.
4. Skills in manipulating and solving chemical equations	Some support might be provided by other learners (peers) through collaboration tools, but this will be very much dependent on who is online at the time and whether they have the required background knowledge.	This outcome is not likely to be addressed through a pure discovery environment.
5. Skills in analyzing quantitative data acquired from experiments	Again, some support could be provided through peer-to-peer methods using collaboration tools as discussed above.	Like the previous learning outcome, this outcome is not really likely to be addressed through a pure discovery environment.
6. The ability to understand and use chemistry terminology	The inclusion of signs and labels within the environment could allow some terminology to be learned in a pure discovery environment (especially terminology associated with equipment and apparatus). The ability to communicate and engage in discourse with one another may allow learners to gain practice in using this terminology.	It would be difficult to provide a way for learners to master the more complex and abstract terminology associated with chemistry concepts in a pure discovery environment.
7. The ability to work effectively with others in undertaking experiments and analyzing results	This could be addressed through the ability to work jointly and together with other learners on experiments within the virtual environment.	Effective collaboration is likely to depend on the provision of task support to ensure that peers/groups/teams of learners work constructively on an appropriate experiment.

inclusion of support and scaffolding in such a way as to maximize the degree to which the learner feels immersed in the virtual environment. This differentiates our approach from the approach proposed by researchers like Chen et al. (2004), whose environments tend to consist of traditional multimedia learning resources with small windows embedding virtual environments. Our proposed approach is to provide instructional support *within* rather than *beside* the environment. To some extent

liberties do need to be taken in doing this, that is by including some 'unreal' elements within the environment, but wherever possible we have tried to suggest ways of providing support that do not negatively impact on the degree of realism. This design principle is most relevant in the design of the mechanisms through which instructional and coaching scaffolds are provided.

The following are the key alternatives possible:

- The inclusion of personified intelligent agents that appear as avatars similar to other users present within the environment, and which provide instructional guidance in a similar way to which a teacher or tutor might provide guidance in a face-to-face environment (see Figure 2, in which the personified tutoring agent is demonstrating the procedure for an experiment).

- Embedding of a virtual Personal Digital Assistant (PDA) that is 'carried' by the learner and always visible at the bottom of the screen as a heads-up display (HUD) (see Figure 3). Such a virtual device could have the capability of showing text, diagrams, photos, animations, and videos and playing audio, and could provide an interface for communication with tutors and other learners through text, audio, or video. System-initiated support could be provided through the same interface as communication with other users (e.g. the system could send a virtual short message service (SMS) message to the learner suggesting a learning task or providing a link to an instructional video). Options could be provided to hide or partially hide the device so that it does not occupy screen area when not needed. Information from the virtual PDA might also be able to be ported out of the 3D VLE by 'syncing' the PDA with the local computer.

- The inclusion of an area of the screen for instructional support outside of the virtual environment window (see Figure 4).

In a similar way, scaffolding tools can be either tightly integrated as objects within the environment (e.g. the virtual PDA described above could also provide an interface to generic tools such as a text editor, a calculator, or a concept-mapping tool), or they can be provided within a separate window alongside the virtual environment. If such tools are provided within a separate instructional window they may nevertheless allow interaction with the environment, that is, by having manipulation or selection of options within the tools cause changes within the virtual environment window. For example, the existing version of the Virtual Chemistry Laboratory has an external apparatus menu to help the learner locate items of apparatus (see Figure 4). When the learner selects an item from this menu he/she is transported with an animated movement to the location of that item of apparatus within the environment. Such an interface can arguably allow learners to retain

Figure 2. Illustration of the way personified agents could be integrated into the virtual laboratory environment to provide instructional support

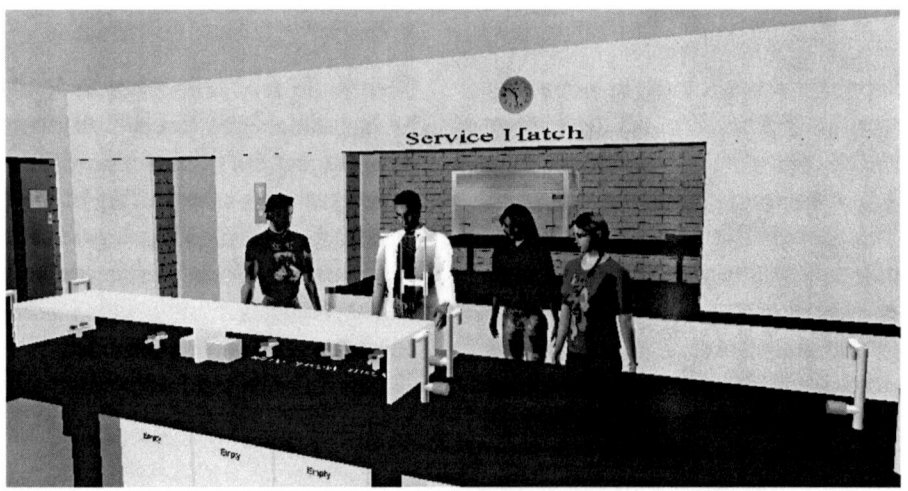

their sense of immersion within the environment even though the tool is provided outside of the environment window. If, however, the scaffolding tools provide functionality independent of the virtual environment, such as a standalone calculator, this may reinforce the notion that the learner is viewing an environment embedded within an instructional resource in a similar way to which he/she would view an embedded video.

For the purposes of this design case study we have proposed the use of a virtual smartphone or PDA within the environment. This device might, for example, look and feel like an iPhone (or similar), and in addition to acting as a HUD, provide for communication with instructors/tutors and other learners, viewing or listening of video or audio material, and the use of tools for navigation, calculation, and measurement. This idea was originally inspired by early (2D) multimedia resources such as *Exploring the Nardoo* (Interactive Multimedia Learning Laboratory, 1996; emlab, n. d.), in which learners, as ecologists working for a virtual research unit, 'carry' around a PDA that they use to access textual information, radio and archival television footage, and images of plants and animals, as well as to record information while they explore the virtual environment for later presentation as a multimedia report.

The following sections describe examples of the way that each of the nine type of scaffolding discussed earlier could be implemented in a 3D Virtual Chemistry Laboratory using this design approach.

Procedural Instruction

Procedural instruction is instruction about the steps involved in a particular procedure, which might be an overall task to be undertaken such as a titration experiment, or a subsidiary task such as operating a burette. As mentioned in the previous subsection, instruction like this could be provided through a personified agent appearing as an avatar within the Virtual Chemistry Laboratory environment, or as text, audio, or video material displayed on the virtual PDA. If carried out as a demonstration by a personified agent it would be possible for a group of learners to observe the demonstration from different positions within the virtual environment. A third way in which introductory instruction could be provided would be as a video displayed on a virtual video monitor or projection screen within the environment.

Using video displayed on a screen within the VLE or a scripted demonstration by a personified agent would be most appropriate if the environment was to be used in a synchronous fashion, with

Figure 3. Illustration of a possible design of an embedded virtual PDA within the virtual laboratory environment

all learners commencing the same task at the same time. Alternatively, the advantage of providing the instructional material on the virtual PDA would be that it would be more personal, and learners would be able to commence the task at any time with the ability to re-read, watch, or listen to the material again during the performance of the task without the overhead of needing to navigate to the location of the screen and/or change their view position and direction.

Procedural Coaching

Procedural coaching is similar to procedural instruction except that it is provided in response to some action (or lack thereof) performed by the learner, perhaps illustrating deficiencies or gaps in knowledge of a specific procedure. The simplest form of such coaching would be demonstrations of procedures provided as an option when the system determines that the learner is attempting a particular procedure. For example, if the learner was carrying out some sort of analysis of results of an experiment they could be offered a demonstra-

tion of the procedure for doing this. More complex to implement is coaching provided only when a particular procedural error has been detected. For example, if a learner placed a 50mL beaker under a burette containing 250mL of a solution, coaching may be provided (either through a text message or by a personified agent) indicating that "this beaker looks a little small—you may want to use a bigger one."

Rather than being completely dynamic, procedural coaching could consist of a scripted animation performed by an agent, a pre-recorded audio-visual presentation, or a series of text messages displayed on the virtual PDA, in a similar way to procedural instruction. The provision of such pre-created or scripted support could be implemented using a set of relatively simple rules or triggers, specifying which animations, videos, recorded audio, or text messages to activate in response to which learner actions.

An important issue to consider in the implementation of system-generated coaching of this kind is the fact that some learners will be less receptive to such coaching than others. Consequently, it may

Figure 4. Illustration of the way the existing version of the Virtual Chemistry Laboratory provides menus external to the environment window as a way of supporting navigation within the environment and a window external to the environment for providing instructional support and displaying information

be more appropriate to offer learners coaching when it is deduced that they are facing difficulty or are otherwise in need of support, but to let them make the final decision about whether the suggested video or animation is played. Such an offer of support could be delivered, for example, as a text message displayed on the virtual mobile device. If this approach was used it would not be quite so important to detect erroneous tasks undertaken by the learner. Rather, the system could just 'guess' at the task being attempted by the learner, and make available a list of suitable coaching sequences without waiting until the learner has shown a misconception or made a visible mistake with their current task. Providing the offer of support as a text message that can be quickly viewed and ignored with minimal interruption avoids the possible annoyance of more intrusive offers of support, such as those provided by the well-known 'Wizard' character in earlier versions of Microsoft Word.

Procedural Tools

A unique aspect of 3D VLEs is the way in which they can allow the learner to undertake tasks that provide for more effective learning than would occur through carrying out the equivalent tasks in the real world (Dalgarno & Lee, 2010). A key aspect of this is the provision of procedural tools that enable aspects of the task to be carried out more efficiently and effectively, so that the learner can focus his/her attention on the main task rather than on the individual challenges involved in carrying out the subsidiary tasks that may detract from the targeted learning objectives or outcomes. Examples include general-purpose tools such as graphing tools, calculation tools, or spell checkers, which could each be provided on the mobile device described earlier. More specific to the Virtual Chemistry Laboratory would be tools for instantly heating a solution to a particular temperature or adding a specific quantity of liquid to a beaker.

These latter two are examples of tools for which it would be appropriate to fade the scaffolds once the learner was able to successfully complete the larger task with scaffolding. Such fading would ensure that learners are able to heat a solution using a virtual Bunsen burner or measure a quantity of liquid using a pipette filler. This would be appropriate because the ability to operate these items of apparatus would be part of the expected learning outcomes. In contrast, there may be cases in which the procedural tasks are important only as a way of obtaining a conceptual understanding of some aspect of the learning domain. For example, a tool could be provided to allow the instant collection of the items of apparatus required for an experiment, to save the learner time. If a knowledge of the location of items of apparatus within the laboratory was not considered an important learning outcome, such a tool might never need to be faded because there would be no benefit for the learner in eventually being able to carry out the task without the support of this tool.

Conceptual Instruction

Conceptual instruction is instruction to help the learner understand the concepts involved in a task that they are either about to undertake or have just undertaken. For example, a titration experiment could be demonstrated, and the chemistry behind the color change that occurs when a particular concentration of the solution being added is reached could be explained. Alternatively, a molecular animation could be shown illustrating the way the bonds between particular molecules change when the solution is heated.

As with procedural instruction, this type of instruction could be provided as scripted animations carried out by a personified agent, or as video, audio, or text material displayed on the virtual PDA or on a display screen within the virtual laboratory.

Conceptual Coaching

Conceptual coaching differs from conceptual instruction in that it occurs as a result of an action carried out by the learner suggesting he/she is in need of assistance or guidance in relation to a conceptual aspect of his/her current task. If conceptual coaching is to be provided by the system (as distinct from a real tutor present within the environment, for example), then complex inferences about the learners' cognitive learning processes are required. That is, unlike procedural coaching, which may be provided by the system in response an unsuccessful attempt at a procedure by the learner, system-provided conceptual coaching requires the software to make assumptions about the cognitive aspects of the current task and about possible misconceptions indicated by the learners' behaviors or actions. For example, a learner may be asked to calculate the molarity of a solution by undertaking calculations using data collected in a titration experiment. Errors in the calculation procedure that illustrate particular misconceptions could result in system-generated messages being displayed on the virtual PDA identifying the errors made and explaining the concepts behind the task.

Although this dynamic generation of coaching interventions is complex and difficult to implement programmatically in any learning environment, it may be that 3D VLEs provide advantages in deducing the learner's current cognitive needs over other, technology-mediated learning environments that provide only menus, hyperlinks, and/or text input to interact with the learner. In other words, it may be that it is easier to make judgments or inferences about learners' cognition from their actions within a 3D world or space than from their selection of options or hyperlinks or by processing their text responses.

Conceptual Tools

Conceptual tools are tools within the environment that help the learner to understand the concepts involved in a task they are undertaking or in an aspect of the environment they are exploring. These tools can, for example, be visualization tools that allow the learner to observe aspects of the environment that are not normally visible to the naked eye. They can also be interactive components of the virtual environment that the learner can use to 'magically' carry out a task to help them to understand a particular concept.

For example, in the Virtual Chemistry Laboratory, a tool that allows the learner to zoom in to view a chemical reaction at the molecular level can be very helpful in understanding the chemistry concepts involved in an experiment. Additionally, a tool could be provided to examine molecules within this molecular view, and report, for example, the atomic elements making up the molecule, their position within the periodic table of the elements, valency, and so on.

Some tools that make certain procedures quicker or more efficient could also be considered conceptual tools because they actually scaffold the concepts to be encountered through the task. For example, a tool that dynamically calculates and displays the ratio of one solution to another during a titration may help the learner to understand the chemistry involved more effectively than using the traditional approach of manually calculating the ratios themselves at the completion of the experiment. A decision would need to be made about whether to eventually fade this support and require the learner to undertake the calculations themselves without the use of the tool. In making this decision it would be important to consider whether the ability to undertake the calculation was an important learning outcome of the task, or whether understanding the chemistry involved was sufficient.

Metacognitive Instruction

Metacognitive instruction may consist of instruction about the 'big picture' or high-level tasks that the learner should undertake within the environment in order to optimize or enhance his/her learning. Mayer (2004) highlights the absence of this initial orientation as one of the key reasons for the failure of pure discovery learning. Dalgarno, Bennett, and Harper (2010) also provide clear evidence for the learning benefits within a 3D VLE of tasks carefully and constructively aligned with the desired learning outcomes, as compared with tasks that are entirely open-ended and exploratory, implying the need for introductory metacognitive instruction.

An additional element of such introductory instruction could be the suggestion of self-regulatory and reflective strategies. As an example, in the Virtual Chemistry Laboratory, learners could be encouraged to keep a log of their reflections on the conceptual aspects of the chemistry experiment, or could be given some open-ended focus questions to answer during the task. Again, having the environment begin with a personified agent providing an introduction or a video shown on the virtual PDA would be possible ways of providing this instruction.

Metacognitive Coaching

Metacognitive coaching is coaching to encourage and facilitate metacognitive tasks such as goal setting, formulation and selection of cognitive strategies, self-regulation and management of learning processes, and reflection. For example, at a particular point in an experiment within the Virtual Chemistry Laboratory a learner could be asked, through the use of open-ended questions or prompts, to articulate what he/she has discovered so far about the nature of the substances involved in the reaction. Providing such opportunities for articulation may be beneficial because it not only highlights and draws the learner's attention to specific concepts in the context of the task being performed, but also promotes deep learning by encouraging the learner to be aware of and con-

sciously reflect on his/her evolving understanding of those concepts.

Like conceptual coaching, the provision of metacognitive coaching by the system is not straightforward, and this is largely due to the requirement to deduce the cognitive needs of the learner at a particular point in time. Again, an alternative is to provide a list of metacognitive support options potentially relevant to the current task, and have the learner choose the support that he/she needs, as and when he/she needs it.

Metacognitive Tools

Metacognitive tools are tools aimed at helping the learner to undertake metacognitive tasks such as goal setting, self-regulation, and reflection. In the Virtual Chemistry Laboratory, a tool could be provided allowing the learner to externalize his/her own personal representation of the chemistry concepts being explored through the larger task, for example using text or possibly a combination of text, shapes/graphics, and connecting lines (i.e. a concept-mapping tool). Another possibility would be a tool that allows the learner to construct a plan for undertaking an experiment, and to progressively mark/check off the steps or sub-tasks once each is completed, as a means of helping the learner to monitor his/her own progress through the larger task.

Such tools would ideally be provided through the virtual PDA within the environment rather than through a separate window outside of the environment so as to help learners to maintain their sense of presence within the environment and their engagement with the tasks at hand.

Implementation Issues

In considering the technical aspects of the implementation of the scaffolding elements described in the preceding subsections, there are three key challenges that need to be addressed. These are: the challenges in monitoring the learner's performance in order to make inferences about their cognitive needs; the problem of dynamically generating the required support either as textual messages or as actions of personified agents; and the technical issues in implementing a virtual PDA that is tightly integrated with other components of the virtual environment and the user interface.

As discussed above, the monitoring of learners' physical actions in order to make inferences about their performance on procedural tasks is less problematic than doing so in order to make inferences about their performance on cognitive tasks and thus about their understanding of concepts. One approach is to use techniques from intelligent tutoring system (ITS) design, that is, the inclusion of an expert or domain model, a student model, and an instructional model, and to apply rule-based techniques similar to those used in expert systems to identify the instructional support needed at a particular point in time (see Mills & Dalgarno, 2007 for a discussion). The provision of support once the learner's needs have been identified is somewhat less challenging because to a large extent this support can be pre-recorded (e.g. as video, animation or sequences of text) or scripted (e.g. as actions of a personified tutoring agent). The dynamic fading of support poses an additional implementation challenge. Again, the use of ITS learner modeling techniques could be helpful here, but clearly substantial research is needed to explore the feasibility of effectively implementing such techniques within immersive virtual environments.

The technical issues involved in the implementation of a virtual PDA are somewhat dependent on the virtual environment development platform used. The application programming interfaces (APIs) of many 3D game engines include specific features for providing HUDs, and many games contain user interfaces that make use of this. Similarly, the Virtual Reality Modeling Language (VRML) and its successor, X3D, have APIs available that make the implementation of such displays

feasible (the hand icon within the existing Virtual Chemistry Laboratory, seen in Figures 1 and 4, was implemented using this technique). Collaborative Virtual Environment (CVE) platforms such as Second Life also provide very powerful APIs allowing for the implementation of such tools.

DISCUSSION

There is clear agreement in the research community about, and strong empirical support for, the value of scaffolding when a discovery learning approach is used. Research on the use of scaffolding in technology-mediated/computer-facilitated learning environments has encountered a number of design issues that are unique to such environments, that is, which do not exist in face-to-face learning environments. This chapter has also identified some additional issues arising in the design and implementation of scaffolding and support in 3D VLEs.

One issue that has emerged in the wider literature on scaffolding in technology-mediated learning environments is the degree to which fading is an essential element of scaffolding. Clearly, effective fading is more difficult to accomplish in technology-mediated environments because it requires an ability to monitor the learner's progress, to dynamically identify the degree of scaffolding required, and to gradually remove the scaffolding as the learner progresses through his/her ZPD. While this does not provide a sufficient argument on its own for not including fading as a requirement within the definition of scaffolding, we have made the case that there are a number of types of task support that fit well with the metaphor of scaffolding but for which fading is neither essential nor in some cases desirable. For example, we have illustrated that in certain situations tools can reduce the complexity of procedural tasks, and in doing so can allow for a greater cognitive focus on the conceptual aspects of the task. We have argued that where the procedural aspects of these tasks are not part of the desired learning, it may never be necessary to fade the support, but that these support tools are nonetheless examples of scaffolding.

An important design issue that emerges in the provision of system-provided scaffolding, and also in the system-initiated fading of such scaffolding, is the degree to which it is desirable for system as distinct from learner control over the scaffolding provided. In face-to-face settings there is a continual balance between learner-initiated support (i.e. requests for help) and instructor-initiated coaching. A similar balance would be desirable within technology-mediated learning environments, however having the system undertake the complex process of monitoring the learners' learning processes and anticipating their learning needs is problematic. Although some researchers have attempted to create software that adapts and adjusts to the needs and progress of the learner, including the use of fading, such systems and technologies are still relatively primitive when compared to human intelligence—a human expert/tutor's abilities to deliver timely and calibrated support based on ongoing diagnosis of the learner's level of understanding is still far superior. The alternative is to allow learners to request guidance or make use of support tools as they see fit, and not have the system attempt to anticipate their learning needs. The possible problem with this approach is that some learners, especially those inexperienced in the particular learning domain, do not necessarily make appropriate self-regulatory decisions. This issue is a significant, ongoing one for research into the provision of scaffolding in technology-mediated learning environments in general and 3D VLEs in particular. In the meantime, a middle position where the system makes available coaching interventions and suggests the use of scaffolding tools, but where the learner has the option of ignoring such suggestions, is probably the ideal compromise. Configurable parameters specifying the degree to which support should be provided or suggested could also be helpful (e.g. "make all possible support available," "suggest support

only when I am clearly on the wrong track," or "never suggest support").

In our design case study we have advocated the provision of scaffolding and other instructional support within 3D VLEs in such a way as to maximize the degree to which the learner is immersed in discovery learning tasks. In particular, we are in favor of the provision of instructional support within the environment rather than alongside it. There are, however, both arguments for and against the alternative of embedding 3D resources within multimedia or hypermedia learning resources (*a la* Chen and colleagues, as cited earlier). A major advantage of this approach, for example, is the potential for cost savings, since conventional, 2D web interfaces are typically much less expensive and time consuming to develop than 3D environments. Such approaches may be appropriate in cases where is it has been determined that only certain aspects of the learning experience stand to gain from being presented in 3D, such as the facilitation of certain activities or the illustration of certain concepts. In some learning scenarios, the features and intricacies of a 3D environment may even prove to be a distraction, and therefore detract or discourage learners from attending to the key conceptual tasks and learning objectives at hand (Jacobson et al., 2008). The need to navigate and manipulate objects in 3D may also impose an additional cognitive load on the learner (Dalgarno & Harper, 2004; Christou & Bulthoff, 1999). These areas point to the need for further research.

When the 3D VLE is implemented using a multi-user platform such as Second Life (that is, when the environment is a CVE), an alternative to system-provided scaffolding is the provision of scaffolding by tutors or peers who are themselves also present within the environment and visible as avatars. This approach has not been a central focus of the present chapter, but it is acknowledged that when such support is feasible (i.e. when peers and tutors can always be expected to use the environment synchronously and/or find mutually suitable times to interact with one another within the environment), many of the problems of system-provided coaching and fading of support can be minimized or avoided altogether. An ideal environment may in fact be one in which a range of system-provided instruction, coaching, and support tools are available and these are supplemented by scaffolding provided by appropriate experts present within the environment.

CONCLUSION AND FUTURE DIRECTIONS

This chapter has identified a series of pedagogical and instructional design issues and suggested some specific design approaches in the provision of scaffolding for discovery learning in 3D virtual learning environments. Many of the design approaches are untested or have been used in a very limited range of learning contexts and virtual environment exemplars to date. Clearly there is a need for the development of environments incorporating the suggested approaches, along with research studies that attempt to validate or test the degree to which the anticipated learning benefits arising from those approaches can be and are achieved.

There are a number of areas in which empirical research is particularly needed. Firstly, research is needed to ascertain which type(s) of scaffolds are most appropriate and effective for different types of learning objectives and situations in 3D VLEs. Secondly, further work is needed to determine whether there are instances in which the use of scaffolding may be detrimental or counter-productive to the learning process and/or objectives at hand. There is also a need for comparative studies of the learning processes and outcomes in applications where the virtual environment is embedded within the instructional resources, and conversely, those where the instructional resources are embedded within the virtual environment. Important aspects of such studies would be an exploration of the cognitive load differences between the two types of resources, and an exploration of the differences

in intrinsic motivation or engagement between the two.

Yet another key area where research is needed is the value and importance of system-generated support and system-initiated fading in 3D VLEs, and the degree to which learner self-regulation through the choice of task supports used can be equally effective. Pea's (2004) aforementioned argument that this is to some extent dependent on how familiar the learner is with the learning domain would be a pertinent factor to consider in such research.

ACKNOWLEDGMENT

The authors would like to acknowledge the contributions of Andrew Rigney, Andrew Wilkinson, and Andrew Wrigley to the development of the existing Virtual Chemistry Laboratory, as well as the contributions of Andrea Bishop and Dan Bedgood to the design of the chemistry support within the environment. The design and development of the Virtual Chemistry Laboratory was supported by a Charles Sturt University Small Grant and by a Charles Sturt University Scholarship in Teaching Grant.

REFERENCES

Anderson, L. W., & Krathwohl, D. R. (Eds.). (2001). *A taxonomy for learning, teaching, and assessing: A revision of Bloom's Taxonomy of Educational Objectives*. New York: Longman.

Azevedo, R., Moos, D. C., Greene, J. A., Winters, F. I., & Cromley, J. G. (2008). Why is externally-facilitated regulated learning more effective than self-regulated learning with hypermedia? *Educational Technology Research and Development*, *56*(1), 45–72. doi:10.1007/s11423-007-9067-0

Bares, W. H., Zettlemoyer, L. S., & Lester, J. C. (1998). Habitable 3D learning environments for situated learning. In B. P. Goettl, H. M. Halff, C. L. Redfield, & V. J. Shute (Eds.), *Proceedings of the Fourth International Conference on Intelligent Tutoring Systems: Vol. 1452 Lecture Notes in Computer Science* (pp. 76-85). Berlin: Springer-Verlag.

Berge, Z. L. (2008). Multi-user virtual environments for education and training: A critical review of Second Life. *Educational Technology, 48*(3), 27–31.

Bierema, L. L., & Merriam, S. B. (2002). E-mentoring: Using computer mediated communication to enhance the mentoring process. *Innovative Higher Education, 26*(3), 211–227. doi:10.1023/A:1017921023103

Biggs, J. (1987). *Student approaches to learning and studying*. Hawthorne, Australia: ACER.

Blanchard, E., & Frasson, C. (2006). *Easy creation of game-like virtual learning environments*. Paper presented at the Workshop on Teaching with Robots, Agents, and NLP, held in conjunction with the Eighth International Conference on Intelligent Tutoring Systems (ITS 2006), Jhongli, Taiwan, June 26-30. Retrieved July 30, 2009, from http://facweb.cs.depaul.edu/elulis/Blanchard.pdf

Bliss, J., Askew, M., & Macrae, S. (1996). Effective teaching and learning: Scaffolding revisited. *Oxford Review of Education, 22*(1), 37–61. doi:10.1080/0305498960220103

Bloom, B. S. (Ed.). (1956). *Taxonomy of educational objectives: The classification of educational goals. Handbook 1: Cognitive domain*. New York: David McKay.

Boekaerts, M. (1995). Self-regulated learning: Bridging the gap between metacognitive and metamotivation theories. *Educational Psychologist, 30*(4), 195–200. doi:10.1207/s15326985ep3004_4

Boekaerts, M., Pintrich, P. R., & Zeidner, M. (Eds.). (2000). *Handbook of self-regulation*. London: Academic.

Bronack, S., Sanders, R., Cheney, A., Riedl, R., Tashner, J., & Matzen, N. (2008). Presence Pedagogy: Teaching and learning in a 3D virtual immersive world. *International Journal of Teaching and Learning in Higher Education, 20*(1), 59-69. Retrieved December 11, 2008, from http://www.isetl.org/ijtlhe/articleView.cfm?id=453

Bruner, J. S. (1961). The act of discovery. *Harvard Educational Review, 31*(1), 21–32.

Bruner, J. S. (1962/1979). *On knowing: Essays for the left hand*. Cambridge, MA: Belknap.

Bruner, J. S. (1986). *Actual minds, possible worlds*. Cambridge, MA: Harvard University Press.

Brush, T., & Saye, J. W. (2001). The use of embedded scaffolds with hypermedia-supported student-centered learning. *Journal of Educational Multimedia and Hypermedia, 10*(4), 333–356.

Cagiltay, K. (2006). Scaffolding strategies in electronic performance support systems: Types and challenges. *Innovations in Education and Teaching International, 43*(1), 93–103. doi:10.1080/14703290500467673

Campbell, B., Collins, P., Hadaway, H., Hedley, N., & Stoermer, M. (2002). Web3D in ocean science learning environments: Virtual Big Beef Creek. In *Proceedings of the Seventh International Conference on 3D Web Technology (Web3D 2002)* (pp. 85-91). New York: Association for Computing Machinery.

Chen, C. J. (2006). The design, development and evaluation of a virtual reality based learning environment. *Australasian Journal of Educational Technology, 22*(1), 39-63. Retrieved November 18, 2008, from http://www.ascilite.org.au/ajet/ajet22/chen.html

Chen, C. J., & Toh, S. C. (2005). A feasible instructional development model for virtual reality (VR)-based learning environments: Its efficacy in the novice car driver instruction of Malaysia. *Educational Technology Research and Development, 53*(1), 111–123. doi:10.1007/BF02504861

Chen, C. J., Toh, S. C., & Wan, M. F. (2003). Virtual reality: A potential technology for providing novel perspective to novice driver education in Malaysia. In N. Ansari, F. Deek, C.-Y. Lin, & H. Yu (Eds.), *Proceedings of the International Conference on Information Technology: Research and Education (ITRE 2003)* (pp. 184-188). Piscataway, NJ: Institute of Electrical and Electronics Engineers.

Chen, C. J., Toh, S. C., & Wan, M. F. (2004). The theoretical framework for designing desktop virtual reality-based learning environments. *Journal of Interactive Learning Research, 15*(2), 147–167.

Chen, C. J., & Wan, M. F. (2008). Guiding exploration through three-dimensional virtual environments: A cognitive load reduction approach. *Journal of Interactive Learning Research, 19*(4), 579–596.

Christou, C. G., & Bulthoff, H. H. (1999). View dependence in scene recognition after active learning. *Memory & Cognition, 27*(6), 996–1007.

Collins, A., Brown, J. S., & Newman, S. E. (1989). Cognitive apprenticeship: Teaching the craft of reading, writing, and mathematics . In Resnick, L. B. (Ed.), *Knowing, learning, and instruction: Essays in honor of Robert Glaser* (pp. 453–494). Hillsdale, NJ: Lawrence Erlbaum.

Crosier, J. K., Cobb, S. V. G., & Wilson, J. R. (2000). Experimental comparison of virtual reality with traditional teaching methods for teaching radioactivity. *Education and Information Technologies, 5*(4), 329–343. doi:10.1023/A:1012009725532

Dabbagh, N. (2003). Scaffolding: An important teacher competency in online learning. *Tech-Trends, 47*(2), 39–44. doi:10.1007/BF02763424

Dalgarno, B., Bennett, S., & Harper, B. (2004). *The design, development and formative evaluation of a 3D virtual chemistry laboratory*. Paper presented at the International Conference on Computers in Education (ICCE 2004), Melbourne, Australia, November 30 - December 3.

Dalgarno, B., Bennett, S., & Harper, B. (2010). The importance of active exploration, optical flow, and task alignment for spatial learning in desktop 3D environments. *Human-Computer Interaction, 25*(1), 25–66. doi:10.1080/07370020903586670

Dalgarno, B., Bishop, A. G., Adlong, W., & Bedgood, D. R. Jr. (2009). Effectiveness of a virtual laboratory as a preparatory resource for distance education chemistry students. *Computers & Education, 53*(3), 853–865. doi:10.1016/j.compedu.2009.05.005

Dalgarno, B., & Harper, B. (2004). User control and task authenticity for spatial learning in 3D environments. *Australasian Journal of Educational Technology, 20*(1), 1-17. Retrieved April 4, 2007, from http://www.ascilite.org.au/ajet/ajet20/dalgarno.html

Dalgarno, B., & Lee, M. J. W. (2010). What are the learning affordances of 3-D virtual environments? *British Journal of Educational Technology, 40*(6), 10–32. doi:10.1111/j.1467-8535.2009.01038.x

Davis, E. A., & Miyake, N. (2004). Scaffolding [Special issue]. *Journal of the Learning Sciences, 13*(3).

de Jong, T., & van Joolingen, W. R. (1998). Scientific discovery learning with computer simulations of conceptual domains. *Review of Educational Research, 68*(2), 179–201.

Dede, C., Clarke, J., Ketelhut, D. J., Nelson, B., & Bowman, C. (2005). *Fostering motivation, learning, and transfer in multi-user virtual environments*. Paper presented at the Annual Meeting of the American Educational Research Association Conference, Montréal, Canada, April 11-15.

Dede, C., Salzman, M., Loftin, R. B., & Ash, K. (1997). *Using virtual reality technology to convey abstract scientific concepts. Learning the sciences of the 21st century: Research, design, and implementing advanced technology learning environments*. Hillsdale, NJ: Lawrence Erlbaum.

Dewey, J. (1997). *Experience and education.* New York: Simon and Schuster. (Original work published 1938)

Dieterle, E. (2009). Neomillennial learning styles and River City. *Children. Youth and Environments, 19*(1), 246–279.

emlab. (n. d.). *Exploring the Nardoo.* Retrieved January 22, 2010, from http://emlab.uow.edu.au/products/nardoo.html

Ensher, E. A., Heun, C., & Blanchard, A. (2003). Online mentoring and computer-mediated communication: New directions in research. *Journal of Vocational Behavior, 63*(2), 264–288. doi:10.1016/S0001-8791(03)00044-7

Galas, C., & Ketelhut, D. J. (2006). River City, the MUVE. *Learning and Leading with Technology, 33*(7), 31–32.

Goodyear, M. (2006). Mentoring: A learning collaboration. *EDUCAUSE Quarterly, 29*(4), 51-53. Retrieved December 3, 2007, from http://net.educause.edu/ir/library/pdf/eqm0647.pdf

Guzdial, M. (1994). Software-realized scaffolding to facilitate programming for science learning. *Interactive Learning Environments, 4*(1), 1–44. doi:10.1080/1049482940040101

Hai-Jew, S. (2008). Scaffolding discovery learning spaces. *MERLOT Journal of Online Learning and Teaching, 4*(4), 533-548. Retrieved May 8, 2009, from http://jolt.merlot.org/vol4no4/hai-jew_1208.pdf

Hannafin, M. J., Land, S., & Oliver, K. (1999). Open learning environments: Foundations, methods, and models . In Reigeluth, C. M. (Ed.), *Instructional design theories and models: A new paradigm of instructional theory (Vol. 2,* pp. 115–140). London: Lawrence Erlbaum.

Harris, J. (2008). eMentoring—the future of online learner support. *International Journal of Excellence in e-Learning, 1*(2), 1-8.

Harvard University. (2007). *The River City Project.* Retrieved October 19, 2008, from http://muve.gse.harvard.edu/rivercityproject/

Hogan, K., & Pressley, M. (Eds.). (1997). *Scaffolding student learning: Instructional approaches and issues*. Cambridge, MA: Brookline.

Ieronutti, L., & Chittaro, L. (2007). Employing virtual humans for education and training in X3D/VRML worlds. *Computers & Education, 49*(1), 93–109. doi:10.1016/j.compedu.2005.06.007

Interactive Multimedia Learning Laboratory. (1996). *Exploring the Nardoo* [CD-ROM]. Developed by the Interactive Multimedia Learning Laboratory, Faculty of Education, University of Wollongong in collaboration with the New South Wales Department of Land and Water Conservation. Wollongong, Australia: Interactive Multimedia Pty Ltd.

Jacobson, M. J., & Azevedo, R. (Eds.). (2008). Scaffolded learning with hypermedia [Special issue]. *Educational Technology Research and Development, 56*(1). doi:10.1007/s11423-007-9066-1

Jacobson, M. J., Kim, B., Lee, J., Lim, S. H., & Low, S. H. (2008). An intelligent agent augmented multi-user virtual environment for learning science inquiry: Preliminary research findings. Paper presented at the 2008 Annual Meeting of the American Education Research Association (AERA), New York, March 24-28.

Jang, S., & Lim, W. C. (2008). The effects of scaffolding types on the problem solving phase. In J. Luca & E. Weippl (Eds.), *Proceedings of World Conference on Educational Multimedia, Hypermedia, and Telecommunications 2008* (pp. 2402-2406). Chesapeake, VA: Association for the Advancement of Computers in Education.

Johnson, L. F., & Levine, A. H. (2008). Virtual worlds: Inherently immersive, highly social learning spaces. *Theory into Practice, 47*(2), 161–170. doi:10.1080/00405840801992397

Jonassen, D. H. (1994). *Technology as cognitive tools: Learners as designers*. Retrieved June 3, 2005, from http://itech1.coe.uga.edu/itforum/paper1/paper1.html

Kirschner, P. A., Sweller, J., & Clark, R. E. (2006). Why minimal guidance during instruction does not work: An analysis of the failure of constructivist, discovery, problem-based, experiential, and inquiry-based teaching. *Educational Psychologist, 41*(2), 75–86. doi:10.1207/s15326985ep4102_1

Kolb, D. A. (1984). *Experiential learning: Experience as the source of learning and development*. Upper Saddle River, NJ: Prentice Hall.

Krathwohl, D. R. (2002). A revision of Bloom's Taxonomy: An overview. *Theory into Practice, 41*(4), 212–218. doi:10.1207/s15430421tip4104_2

Lai, M., & Law, N. (2006). Peer scaffolding of knowledge building through collaborative groups with differential learning experiences. *Journal of Educational Computing Research, 35*(2), 123–144. doi:10.2190/GW42-575W-Q301-1765

Laurillard, D. (1993). *Rethinking university teaching: A framework for the effective use of educational technology*. London: Routledge.

Laurillard, D. (2002). *Rethinking university teaching: A conversational framework for the effective use of learning technologies* (2nd ed.). London: RoutledgeFalmer. doi:10.4324/9780203304846

Lepper, M. R., Drake, M. F., & O'Donnell-Johnson, T. (1997). Scaffolding techniques of expert human tutors. In Hogan, K., & Pressley, M. (Eds.), *Scaffolding student learning: Instructional approaches and issues* (pp. 108–144). Cambridge, MA: Brookline.

Leutner, D. (1993). Guided discovery learning with computer-based simulation games: Effects of adaptive and non-adaptive instructional support. *Learning and Instruction, 3*(2), 113–132. doi:10.1016/0959-4752(93)90011-N

Mayer, R. E. (2004). Should there be a three-strikes rule against pure discovery learning? The case for guided methods of instruction. *The American Psychologist, 59*(1), 14–19. doi:10.1037/0003-066X.59.1.14

McKay, S. M., van Schie, J., & Headley, S. (2008). Embarking on an educational journey in Second Life. In K. McFerrin, R. Weber, R. Carlsen, & D. A. Willis (Eds.), *Proceedings of the Society for Information Technology and Teacher Education International Conference 2008* (pp. 1762-1766). Chesapeake, VA: Association for the Advancement of Computers in Education.

McLoughlin, C. (1999). Scaffolding: Applications to learning in technology supported environments. In B. Collis & R. Oliver (Eds.), *Proceedings of World Conference on Educational Multimedia, Hypermedia, and Telecommunications 1999* (pp. 1827-1832). Charlottesville, VA: Association for the Advancement of Computers in Education.

McLoughlin, C. (2002). Learner support in distance and networked learning environments: Ten dimensions for successful design. *Distance Education, 23*(2), 149–162. doi:10.1080/0158791022000009178

McLoughlin, C., & Lee, M. J. W. (2010). Personalised and self-regulated learning in the Web 2.0 era: International exemplars of innovative pedagogy using social software. *Australasian Journal of Educational Technology, 26*(1), 28-43. Retrieved August 26, 2010, from http://www.ascilite.org.au/ajet/ajet26/mcloughlin.pdf

Mills, C., & Dalgarno, B. (2007). A conceptual model for game-based intelligent tutoring systems. In R. Atkinson & C. McBeath (Eds.), *ICT: Providing choices for learners and learning. Proceedings of the 24th ASCILITE Conference* (pp. 692-702). Singapore: Nanyang Technological University. Retrieved January 19, 2010, from http://www.ascilite.org.au/conferences/singapore07/procs/mills.pdf

Ormrod, J. E. (1995). *Educational psychology: Principles and applications*. Upper Saddle River, NJ: Prentice Hall.

Palincsar, A. S. (1986). The role of dialogue in providing scaffolded instruction. *Educational Psychologist, 21*(1/2), 73–98. doi:10.1207/s15326985ep2101&2_5

Pea, R. D. (2004). The social and technological dimensions of scaffolding and related theoretical concepts for learning, education, and human activity. *Journal of the Learning Sciences, 13*(3), 423–451. doi:10.1207/s15327809jls1303_6

Phillips, R. (1998). Models of learning appropriate to educational applications of information technology. In B. Black & N. Stanley (Eds.), *Teaching and learning in changing times. Proceedings of the Seventh Annual Teaching Learning Forum* (pp. 264-268). Perth: The University of Western Australia. Retrieved December 19, 2009, from http://lsn.curtin.edu.au/tlf/tlf1998/phillips.html

Piaget, J. (1973). *To understand is to invent: The future of education*. New York: Grossman.

Pilling-Cormick, J., & Garrison, D. R. (2007). Self-directed and self-regulated learning: Conceptual links. *Canadian Journal of University Continuing Education, 33*(2), 13–33.

Puntambekar, S., & Hubscher, R. (2005). Tools for scaffolding students in a complex learning environment: What have we gained and what have we missed? *Educational Psychologist, 40*(1), 1–12. doi:10.1207/s15326985ep4001_1

Roblyer, M. D., Edwards, J., & Havriluk, M. A. (1997). *Integrating educational technology into teaching*. Upper Saddle River, NJ: Merrill.

Romano, D. M., & Brna, P. (2000). ACTIVE World: Manipulating time and point of view to promote a sense of presence in a collaborative virtual environment for training in emergency situations. In *Proceedings of the Third International Workshop on Presence (PRESENCE 2000)*. Delft, The Netherlands: Delft University of Technology. Retrieved August 23, 2008, from http://www.temple.edu/ispr/prev_conferences/proceedings/98-99-2000/2000/Romano%20and%20Brna.pdf

Rosen, J. (2006, June 27). The people formerly known as the audience. *PressThink* [web log]. Retrieved October 10, 2007, from http://journalism.nyu.edu/pubzone/weblogs/pressthink/2006/06/27/ppl_frmr.html

Sandberg, J., & Wielinga, B. (1992). Situated cognition: A paradigm shift? *Journal of Artificial Intelligence in Education, 3*(2), 129–138.

Sanders, D., & Welk, D. S. (2005). Strategies to scaffold faculty facilitator learning: Applying Vygotsky's Zone of Proximal Development. *Nurse Educator, 30*(5), 203–207. doi:10.1097/00006223-200509000-00007

Sanders, R. L., & McKeown, L. (2007). Promoting reflection through action learning in a 3D virtual world. *International Journal of Social Science, 2*(1), 50-55. Retrieved November 8, 2009, from http://www.waset.ac.nz/journals/ijss/v2/v2-1-8.pdf

Saye, J. W., & Brush, T. (2002). Scaffolding critical reasoning about history and social issues in multimedia-supported learning environments. *Educational Technology Research and Development, 50*(3), 77–96. doi:10.1007/BF02505026

Sharma, P., & Hannafin, M. J. (2007). Scaffolding in technology-enhanced learning environments. *Interactive Learning Environments, 15*(1), 27–46. doi:10.1080/10494820600996972

Sherin, B., Reiser, B. J., & Edelson, D. (2004). Scaffolding analysis: Extending the scaffolding metaphor to learning artifacts. *Journal of the Learning Sciences, 13*(3), 387–421. doi:10.1207/s15327809jls1303_5

Simons, P. R.-J. (1992). Constructive learning: The role of the learner . In Duffy, T. M., Lowyck, J., Jonassen, D. H., & Welsh, T. M. (Eds.), *Designing environments for constructive learning* (pp. 291–313). Berlin: Springer-Verlag.

Sims, E. M. (2007). Reusable, lifelike virtual humans for mentoring and role-playing. *Computers & Education, 49*(1), 75–92. doi:10.1016/j.compedu.2005.06.006

Spencer, J. A., & Jordan, R. K. (1999). Learner centred approaches in medical education. *BMJ (Clinical Research Ed.), 318*(7193), 1280–1283.

Stone, C. A. (1998). The metaphor of scaffolding: Its utility for the field of learning disabilities. *Journal of Learning Disabilities, 31*(4), 344–364. doi:10.1177/002221949803100404

Sweller, J., van Merriënboer, J. J. G., & Paas, F. G. W. C. (1998). Cognitive architecture and instructional design. *Educational Psychology Review, 10*(3), 251–296. doi:10.1023/A:1022193728205

van Joolingen, W. R. (1999). Cognitive tools for discovery learning. *International Journal of Artificial Intelligence in Education, 10*(3/4), 385–397.

Vygotsky, L. S. (1978). *Mind and society: The development of higher mental processes.* Cambridge, MA: Harvard University Press.

Wild, M., & Kirkpatrick, D. (1996). Multimedia as cognitive tools: Students working with a performance support system. In C. McBeath & R. Atkinson (Eds.), *The learning superhighway: New world? New worries? Proceedings of the Third International Interactive Multimedia Symposium* (pp. 412-417). Perth: Promaco Conventions. Retrieved December 19, 2008, from http://www.ascilite.org.au/aset-archives/confs/iims/1996/ry/wild.html

Winne, P. H. (1995). Inherent details in self-regulated learning. *Educational Psychologist, 30*(4), 173–187. doi:10.1207/s15326985ep3004_2

Winnips, J. C. (2001). *Scaffolding-by-design: A model for WWW-based learner support.* Unpublished doctoral dissertation, University of Twente, Enschede, The Netherlands.

Winnips, K., & McLoughlin, C. (2000). Applications and categorization of software-based scaffolding. In J. Bourdeau & R. Heller (Eds.), *Proceedings of World Conference on Educational Multimedia, Hypermedia, and Telecommunications 2000* (pp. 1798-1799). Charlottesville, VA: Association for the Advancement of Computers in Education.

Winnips, K., & Mcloughlin, C. (2001). Six WWW based learner supports you can build. In C. Montgomerie & J. Viteli (Eds.), *Proceedings of World Conference on Educational Multimedia, Hypermedia, and Telecommunications 2001* (pp. 2062-2067). Charlottesville, VA: Association for the Advancement of Computers in Education.

Wood, D., Bruner, J. S., & Ross, G. (1976). The role of tutoring in problem solving. *Journal of Child Psychology and Psychiatry, and Allied Disciplines*, *17*(2), 89–100. doi:10.1111/j.1469-7610.1976.tb00381.x

Young, M. F. (1993). Instructional design for situated learning. *Educational Technology Research and Development*, *41*(1), 43–58. doi:10.1007/BF02297091

Zimmerman, B. J., & Schunk, D. H. (Eds.). (1989). *Self-regulated learning and academic achievement: Theory, research, and practice*. New York: Springer-Verlag.

KEY TERMS AND DEFINITIONS

3D VLE: Three-Dimensional Virtual Learning Environment. In the last decade, the term 'VLE' has come to be used interchangeably with the term 'learning management system' (LMS) in reference to an integrated suite of software tools designed to manage academic or training courses, commercial examples of which are Blackboard and WebCT. However, in this chapter, a VLE refers more specifically to a computer-simulated environment or artificial space in which learning activities are undertaken. In a typical 3D VLE, learners, through their avatars, can experience, manipulate, and interact with virtual objects and places in three dimensions. The objects and places are either modeled according to the real world or instead depict fantasy worlds. In a collaborative or multi-user 3D VLE, communication and interaction between users is possible. *See also* avatar.

API: Application Programming Interface. An interface provided by a software program to enable programmers of other software to write code to interact with the program and use its services, without needing to understand its internal workings or implementation details.

Authentic Learning: Learning that encourages learners to engage in real-world problems and projects that have relevance beyond the walls of the classroom. *See also* contextual learning.

Avatar: In a 3D virtual environment, a visual representation of a user's real or surrogate identity and appearance. Through his/her avatar, a user consciously or unconsciously creates a virtual portrayal of him/herself (or of an alternative self) within the environment, and in doing so builds an online identity that is projected to others. Users are typically able to control their avatars' actions in real time, in addition to modifying their characteristics and appearance.

Cognitive Load: A term that refers to the demands or 'load' placed on an individual's working memory during instruction or while undertaking a learning task. Cognitive Load Theory (Sweller et al., 1998) emphasizes the limited capacity of a learner's working memory, and provides guidelines aimed at optimizing his/her intellectual performance, for example through the minimization of extraneous cognitive load (i.e. cognitive load that can be attributed to the design of instructional materials). *See also* split attention effect.

Collaborative Learning: An umbrella term for a variety of teaching and learning approaches that involve joint intellectual effort by students or students and teachers. Learners typically engage in a common task in which each individual depends on and is accountable to each other, or work together in searching for understanding, meaning, or problem solutions.

Contextual Learning: Learning that is closely tied to or embedded in a social and/or physical context. This term is similar to and often used interchangeably with 'situated learning.' *See also* authentic learning.

CVE: Collaborative Virtual Environment. A computer-simulated environment or space in which people can meet to interact and collaborate with one another. 3D multi-player games and multi-user 3D VLEs are examples of CVEs. *See also* 3D VLE, MUVE.

Discovery Learning: A general term that emphasizes active learning through exploration, experimentation, and discovery. The use of 'pure' discovery learning approaches devoid of instructional scaffolding and support has been heavily criticized; several forms or variants of discovery learning have emerged that feature different types and/or levels of scaffolding and support. *See also* guided discovery, scaffolding, experiential learning; inquiry-based learning, problem-based learning.

Experiential Learning: The process of making meaning from direct experience, or learning through reflection on doing, as opposed to learning by rote or through didactic/transmissive teaching methods. The idea of experiential learning was inspired by the Aristotle and popularized by Kolb, drawing on the Constructivist theories of Dewey and Piaget. *See also* discovery learning; problem-based learning.

Expert System: In artificial intelligence, a software system that simulates the judgment and actions/behavior of a human expert to provide answers to problems and/or clarify uncertainties that arise within a problem domain. Such a system typically incorporates a knowledge base containing accumulated or 'learned' experience, along with a set of rules for applying the knowledge to particular situations. Commonly seen examples are expert systems that play chess and those that attempt to perform medical diagnoses.

Fading: The gradual removal of supportive assistance (i.e. scaffolds) as learners develop greater levels of competence and confidence and become better equipped to cope with the full complexity of the learning context. *See also* scaffolding.

Guided Discovery: An instructional approach that combines constructivist principles,

most notably those from discovery learning, with principles from cognitivist instructional design theory. It represents an attempt to achieve a balance between active, learner-driven exploration and discovery and the provision of adequate and appropriate levels of instructional guidance and support. *See also* guided discovery.

HUD: Heads-Up Display. An element of a desktop computing application's graphical user interface (GUI) that facilitates the presentation of information to the user in way that minimizes the distraction from the primary task for which the information is needed. The term is a corruption of 'head-up display', which was coined in the field of military and aviation technology to reflect the desire to enable users to view information with their heads 'up' and eyes looking forward, as opposed to looking down at instruments or a keyboard.

Intelligent Agent: In Artificial Intelligence: an autonomous software-based entity that perceives or senses its environment and acts upon that environment with the aim of achieving specific goals. Intelligent agents vary in complexity, and often need to learn and use knowledge in order to achieve their goals. In some applications (e.g. virtual worlds and games), an intelligent agent may be personified through a visual representation and/or the use of artificial speech.

ITS: Intelligent Tutoring System. A computer-based system that provides customized instruction and/or feedback to students during a learning task, without the need for human intervention. Although ITS's may employ a range of technologies, they are typically artificial intelligence systems, more specifically expert systems that simulate the behaviour, actions, and decision-making processes of human tutors. *See also* intelligent agent, expert system.

Inquiry-Based Learning: A term used to describe a range of instructional strategies based on premises that are centered around the need for learners to ask questions, then actively seek out answers to those questions. It is commonly used in the teaching of science. The teacher takes on the role of a 'facilitator,' who supports learners rather than simply giving them the answers, encouraging them to take responsibility for their learning through active exploration, discovery, and refl:ection. *See also* discovery learning, problem-based learning.

MUVE: Multi-User Virtual Environment, also called a virtual world. In the late 1980s and early to mid-1990s, the term was used to refer to multi-user networked/online computer-simulated environments or artificial spaces, which encompassed a variety of text-based and graphical MUDs (multi-user dungeons), MOOs (MUDs, object-oriented), and multi-player games. In recent years the term has come to be used to describe three-dimensional, Internet-based, massively multi-user simulated worlds such as Second Life, in which users, through their avatars, can experience, manipulate, and interact with virtual objects and places that are either modelled according to the real world or depict fantasy worlds. Communication between users may occur via text, static graphical icons (e.g. 'emoticons'), visual gestures and 'facial' expressions, sound (including human or synthetic voice), and occasionally, may take more sophisticated forms such as touch, voice commands, and balance senses. *See also* 3D VLE, CVE.

Problem-Based Learning: A form of authentic, inquiry-based learning in which students learn by working collaboratively in groups to solve problems, and reflecting on their experiences. The problems are typically challenging and open-ended. They mirror problems in the real world in that they are often ill structured and do not result in neat, convergent outcomes. *See also* authentic learning, experiential learning, inquiry-based learning.

Scaffolding: An instructional technique involving the provision of supportive assistance or guidance to learners, particularly when they are first introduced to new concepts and skills, with the aim of limiting the complexities of the learning context. *See also* ZPD, fading.

Self-Directed Learning: An approach to learning that views learners as being principally responsible for managing and monitoring their own learning process, including establishing goals, locating resources, devising strategies and evaluating outcomes. *See also* self-regulated learning.

Self-Regulated Learning: A similar concept to self-directed learning (SDL), but unlike SDL, whose originators focused on the sociological and pedagogical aspects of learning, self-regulated learning (SRL) emerged primarily from the field of psychology (Pilling-Cormick & Garrison, 2007). In SRL, the emphasis has thus traditionally been on cognitive and metacognitive concepts and functions. In the last decade, motivational and management processes have also been incorporated into SRL research and theory. *See also* self-directed learning.

Split Attention Effect: According to Cognitive Load Theory (Sweller et al., 1998), the split attention effect occurs when a learner must attend to multiple sources of information simultaneously, forcing him or her to divide attention between tasks. Few, if any, humans are capable of dealing efficiently with cognitive tasks requiring split attention, due to the limited capacity of their working memory. *See also* Cognitive Load.

VRML: A text-based file format for representing 3D computer graphics in the form of scenes and objects, intended especially for use on World Wide Web. It has been superseded by X3D. *See also* X3D.

X3D: An open standards Extensible Markup Language (XML)-based file format for representing 3D computer graphics in the form of scenes and objects. It is the successor of VRML. *See also* VRML.

ZPD: Zone of Proximal Development. A Vygotskyan concept that refers to the gap between a learner's current knowledge and ability level (i.e. what he or she can perform without assistance) and his/her emerging or potential knowledge and ability level (i.e. what he or she can be challenged to accomplish with assistance in the form of scaffolding). *See also* scaffolding.

Chapter 9
Legal and Ethical Aspects of Teaching in Selected Social Virtual Worlds:
A Review of the Literature

R. S. Talab
Kansas State University, USA

Hope R. Botterbusch
Kansas State University, USA

ABSTRACT

Topics discussed in this chapter include Generations Y and Z and their acceptance of virtual reality, the increase in the number of virtual worlds, gaming virtual worlds, and the social virtual worlds for educators selected for inclusion in this discussion. Open source virtual world platform portability issues are discussed in connection with the acquisition, development, and control of virtual property. The line between "play spaces" and real life is discussed in terms of the application of the "magic circle" test to teaching in virtual worlds with a real-money based virtual currency system, as well as how faculty can reduce student legal and ethical problems. Virtual world law is examined in light of the terms of service (TOS) and end-user license agreements (EULAs), the concept of virtual property, community standards/behavioral guidelines, safety/privacy statements, intellectual property and copyright. Ethical aspects of teaching in virtual worlds include a definition and analysis of griefing/abuse, harassment, false identity, and ways that each world handles these problems. Whyville, SmallWorlds, and Second Life are examined in terms of legal and ethical aspects Research findings and legal and ethical teaching guidelines are presented for those teaching courses using virtual worlds, with special considerations for teaching in Second Life. These topics are for informational purposes, only. Instructors should seek competent legal counsel.

DOI: 10.4018/978-1-61692-825-4.ch009

THE NETWORKED "IGENERATION" AND VIRTUAL WORLDS

The term "Generation Y" is used to describe those born between 1980-1994 who have grown up using Information Communication Technology (McCrindle, 2006), and "digital natives" is a term describing the recent generations whose development is characterized by immersion in digital media and communications technology (Prensky, 2001, Palfrey & Gasser, 2008). "Generation Z" youth, or the "iGeneration" (Rosen, 2010), are networked and connected. The "i" stands for everything being individualized and customized for them. They were born after the mid-90's and are connected as a group. They take the internet for granted, and accept social networking and collaboration as norms. This group requires new pedagogical approaches that employ technology as routinely as they do. One of these technologies is virtual worlds. "The virtual world is utterly real to millions of young people and... it will prove an immensely powerful influence on every aspect of life and work." (Employee Factor, 2009).

Shen and Eder (2009) found through their research that, if used appropriately for the course and task, "virtual worlds have the potential to provide a rich, engaging, collaborative, and enjoyable learning environment for students." Constructivism (Talab & Botterbusch, 2009), constructionism (Dreher, Reiners, Dreher, & Dreher, 2009), learner-centered teaching and action learning (Wagner & Ip, 2009) pedagogies are well suited to teaching and exploring in virtual worlds.

Increase in Virtual Worlds

According to KZero, a United Kingdom-based consulting company, there were 175 virtual worlds in 2010, either in existence or in beta version (Keegan, 2010). Virtual worlds are being explored for military, civilian, and government inter-agency initiatives, such as by the Information Resource Management College of the National Defense University, which created the Federal Consortium for Virtual Worlds to work among and within federal agencies in 2007 ("Growth Forecasts", 2009b). "Virtual worlds" is an inclusive term, and there are various definitions, beginning with Biocca & Levy's first extensive book on virtual reality in 1995. Terms include immersive virtual environments (Blascovich, Loomis, Beall, Swinth, Hoyt, & Bailenson, 2002; Harris, Bailenson, Nielsen & Yee, 2009), synthetic worlds (Castranova, 2005) and virtual worlds (Arakj & Lang, 2008; Duranske, 2008; Virtual Worlds Review, 2009). Duranske (2009) states that the most common elements are visual computer-based simulation environments that are designed for users to interact with each other through avatars (digital (graphical) representations of people), and allow communication between users through various means.

Virtual worlds are volatile. Not all of them are designed for long-term use, and some do not get enough user support to be able to continue to function. Disney's Virtual Magic Kingdom had 15,000 players that chatted daily from ages 8-14. When it was closed in 2008, it was the subject of a user campaign to save it, and television and newspaper stories ("Thousands Protest", 2008). Eleven thousand people signed a petition to get Disney to reconsider its closing. When it was closed members had no personal information on those with whom they chatted, so these relationships were lost.

Virtual World Types

Virtual worlds vary by type, purpose, use, and age group ("Artesia Whitepaper", 2008). There are special interestworlds, such as Kaneva (entertainment), and vSide (music). Other worlds include branded or toys/games worlds, which are based on commercially sold toys and games, such as for Barbie Girls and Webkinz. Mirror worlds have the ability to revisit events and places from the past, and include Wazzamba and Amazing Worlds. Amazing Worlds, a mirror wold, uses 3D maps to promote tourism, were also not included in this review. (KZero, 2010).

Role-playing worlds usually have goals, levels, and points. Some have a system of monetary exchange, such as Entropia Universe, which has virtual items and currency that have to be gained through play and have value for players. As Sid Miers explained about Civilization, "….the things that you're learning about are history, different technologies, how government works, the importance of exploration, and things that are historical" (Meier, 2007, p. 4). Civilization does not have a currency system.

The largest massively multiplayer online role-playing games, or MMORPGs, has the user play a specific character as a main feature of the game, such as World Of Warcraft (WOW). Civilization IV, originally developed in 1972, has had many updates, as well as sequels. It has won two awards and is considered to be one of the most popular strategy-based games ever made. It has no intellectual property or economy.

Blizzard, owner of World of Warcraft, the most popular gaming virtual world, generated $704 million in profits on revenues of $1.3 billion in 2008, according to regulatory filings. Massively multiplayer online real-life/rogue-like games may or may not specifically disallow Real Money Trade (RMT) in the Terms of Service (TOS), such as World of Warcraft. However, "Even where RMT is prohibited by contract, however, thriving black markets exist "(Duranske, 2008 p. 4). Many game developers, such as Blizzard Entertainment oppose and often prohibit the practice as it is believed that monetary values make these games a form of gambling, though items in WOW (gold, swords, etc.) do have real monetary value and are traded on online auction sites. However, in most games, MMORPG users do not own any property; rather, their only property interests exist in what they carry (Law in the virtual world, p. 169). Gaming worlds, while interesting from a learning standpoint, it do not fit the criteria for inclusion in this discussion.

Virtual world platforms allow users to host virtual worlds of their own, such as Active Worlds, OpenSim, Multiverse, and Metaplace. They are mainly open source to allow for independent creation and retention of these virtual worlds by creators. One of these worlds is the Croquet Consortium, which was developed for collaboration and research. OLIVE is a proprietary effort to develop virtual worlds for customers in finance, education, healthcare, etc. OpenSim has only a few worlds on its platform that allow access, and the number of educators in this virtual world is low, as well. Worlds not included in this review were toys and games, roleplay, fantasy, quest, and mirror worlds. Other social virtual worlds are either private, or were rarely used by educators.

Social virtual worlds that will be discussed for those 16 and up, are social or general interest worlds, such as Second Life, Active Worlds,, and OpenSim. All of these are worlds in which there is nothing to conquer or win. There is no goal, no points, and no story to tell, except the user's own story. They are based on the concept of a virtual community (Chenin, 2006). Virtual worlds for youth, such as SmallWorlds (13 and over), and Whyville (middle school and those under 18) are the fastest-growing and largest segment of the virtual world market, with over 200 18-and-under live or developing worlds in 2009 (Engage Digital Media, 2009).

OpenSimulator (OpenSim)

OpenSim is a popular open source virtual world platform. This means that the source code for developing an open source virtual world platform is shared, thereby allowing the development costs to drop and allowing for portability of things that are built in that world to another one. For this reason, Open Source is important to instructors and institutions, since creating islands can be very expensive. . Incorrect statement. Old information - not correct now. All incorrect now.

OpenSim, reported growth of over 13% (June 2010). OpenSim has two modes, Standalone and Grid. Standalone essentially hosts the entire virtual experience on one server which limits the number of users; whereas, the grid option spreads the number of simulations across a number of different machines (Daly, 2010).

In another article OpenSim growth rate was cited at 177%, with projections that it would overtake Second Life in early 2011. This prediction was made after comparing the 29% increase in OpenSim regions between September and December 2009 with the 6% growth in Second Life resident-owned land in 2009. The OpenSim grid claimed 7,246 regions in December 2009, up from 5,613 in September. In contrast, Second Life's 6% annual growth rate included 23,900 regions at the end of 2009. (Korolov, 2010).

The OpenSim platform enables applications to run successfully, with a number of servers being used to host a number of processes. Standard web sites, whether using static or dynamic pages, simply do not require the memory or processing power of 3D applications, so this common framework, managed by a not-for-profit organization, offers the opportunity for many to at least dip their toes in the world of 3D. It can reasonably be concluded that this latest rise in figures can be translated to mean that virtual worlds across a whole range of areas on the OpenSim framework are increasing, not only in their number of users, but potentially the richness of the experience within them.

The extension to OpenSim is the "hypergrid", which was invented in 2009. The hypergrid enables avatars to teleport between virtual worlds within the hypergrid, and has addressed a valid criticism of virtual worlds, that the user was essentially locked solely into the experience within the preferred world. For example, in the OSGrid an avatar can teleport to ReactionGrid and back again with a click of their "virtual heels", by pressing the teleport home button. Virtual goods acquired in other OpenSim grids can often be transported back to the home grid through the avatar's inventory.

More control and backups in the OpenSim platform are more appealing to virtual and owners, noting that OpenSim region owners can save backups of their entire region on their local servers. If they want to shut down a region, or keep historical records of how a region evolves, they can do this and restore the region later. But this sort of backup-on-demand function will be difficult for Linden Lab to match. The SL system on which the SL in-world economy is based, and on-demand region backups and rollbacks create significant problems enforcing the "no-copy" content that can reside in either an avatar's inventory or in-world in SL. This issue is seen in the case of Eros, LCC. vs. Doe. Plaintiff Eros, LLC, a maker and seller of virtual adult-themed objects within the Second Life platform, sued defendants and alleged that they had made and sold unauthorized copies of plaintiff's virtual products within Second Life using plaintiff's trademark (Reuters, 2007).

Educators in post-secondary institutions and K-12 schools looking for lower costs, better controls and no age restrictions might consider switching from Second Life to its open source alternative, the OpenSim virtual world server platform. The OpenSim server software can be used to power an entire public grid or a small private, behind-the-firewall installation, and can be run on an institution's own server or hosted with third-party providers. In addition, anything created in Second Life can be easily transported to the OpenSim grids through back-up inventory programs and OAR files. OAR files can be created using the "save oar [filename]" command from the region console and can be loaded using the "load OAR [filename]" command. ReactionGrid is the top OpenSim hosting company for educators today. ReactionGrid also offers one-click install packages for behind-the-firewall installations, as well as remote management of self-hosted grids. A-la-carte support is $85 an hour and clients can get a lower rate if they sign up for support packages. Since OpenSim runs on an institution's own servers, or on external servers run by an institution's hosting company, an organization has full control over how OpenSim is configured. In addition, the open source nature of the software means that schools and colleges can plug in additional code at will, including replacement physics engines, commerce modules, and enterprise integration tools to connect with student and staff directories and learning management platforms (Hu, 2010).

It is for these reasons that many educators and their institutions are moving to the OpenSim platforms. And, there is no need to be concerned that OpenSim platforms do not have an economic base. The OSGrid has the G and V commerce system, and InWorldz has the Lz commerce system. Pay Pal and credit cards are used to establish accounts. Buying and selling of virtual goods and land are active in these OpenSim grids, often at a much lower cost than in Second Life. However, content creators must be aware that it's easy to steal objects and textures in the OpenSim platforms, as copybots are used there and are not usually regulated, as of this writing. These OpenSim grids are also social virtual worlds with most of the networking capabilities of Second Life. The one limitation is that voice is disabled in many of these OpenSim grids, but that is being beta tested at this writing.

Selected Social Virtual Worlds and Criteria for Discussion

Few of these virtual worlds are stable and every one is different. What further sets apart certain virtual worlds for legal and ethical analysis are these two factors: 1) "persistence of user-created content", a feature of most popular virtual worlds, and for which Second Life allows users to retain certain intellectual property rights, and 2) a designed economic system of some sort, called "real money trade" (RMT). RMT for virtual worlds was estimated to account for $2.1 billion worldwide in 2007 (Lehtiniemi, 2007).

According to Engage Digital Media (2009) "…the majority of virtual worlds monetize their user-base with a combination of revenue streams, mixing subscriptions, advertising, and virtual goods sales. Out of those, micro-transactions and subscriptions are the most popular, with 59 and 57 worlds using them respectively" (u.d.).

Whether in Linden dollars for Whyville Pearls, SmallWorlds Gold,, Second Life Linden dollars, or other currency systems, this discussion will focus on these selected virtual worlds, which have persistent user-created content and an economic system. They also have the largest current user bases, with Second Life far outpacing the others. Each of the aforementioned virtual worlds takes Paypal or credit cards for transactions. All users have the ability to create to some extent, with the tools available, though Second Life is the only virtual world in which users intellectual property rights in creations are protected. In this regard, Second Life is alone in this level of control (Duranske, 2008).

Age ranges vary with these worlds. Whyville is for those under 18, with most between 9-14. Second Life is currently for those 18 and over, although plans are intended to include those 16 and above by the end of 2010.. SmallWorlds is for those from 13-17. Those found to be under 13 are banned, although they can find ways to get in to Second Life In all cases, one can not be sure that the avatar is the sex or the age that is listed in an avatar's profile, though these requirements are clearly stated on all Terms of Service, End-User Licensing Agreements, Privacy for Safety Statements, depending on the world.

Whyville

Whyville is for" tweens" and teens (9-17)) (Whyville Demographics, 2010), particularly girls, with most under 18 and a user-base of about five million (Wikipedia, 2009). Avatars have only a round, undefined face until they purchase a "portrait" body, in which only the head and shoulders are visible. First launched in 1999, Whyville states that it has had 700,000 visitors in 2009, so far (Whyville Demographics, 2009). There are places to shop, play, and chat. It has extensive controls (blocking, vaporization and 911), as well as guides and buses to take children to destinations.

Figure 1. Whyville South Beach chat area

In order to be able to earn a "chat license" for one of the four places to chat in Whyville, the "newbie" has to take a test with 7 questions on divulging phone numbers, on blocking and vaporizing "annoying or mean chat" and member harassment.

It is acceptable in Whyville to share one's age, sex and location, as long as details are not given. If someone asks a street address/location or Facebook information or e-mail, password, profiles and links, then the user is asked to call 911. "City workers" are adults in Whyville that monitor the chat rooms and other places, such as the Getty Museum or other educational and recreations places. If someone says he/she is a City Worker and doesn't have a "beanie"(a type of hat), then this also warrants a 911 report.

Whyville uses both "pearls", which can be purchased using Paypal, or "clams". five hundred Pearls are $5 USD. Allowances can be set up for regular deposits for keeping one's head, face parts at "Grandmas" or Akbar's Face Mall, clothing and accessories, as well as for purchasing furnishings, etc.

Clams can only be earned by completing various learning missions, such as Getty ArtSets at the silver bronze or Gold levels.

Since Whyville collects information from children under the age of thirteen, it is required to comply with Federal Trade Commission (FTC) Children's Online Privacy Protection Act (COPPA), which was enacted in 2000. "Violators of COPPA are subject to FTC law enforcement action, including civil penalties of $11,000 per vio-

Figure 2. Whyville Welcome Lounge

Figure 3. Grandma's

lation. The FTC currently has a number of non-public investigations underway." (FTC, 2009).

Whyvilleeans participate in curriculum activities, such as Science and social activities. It is important to note that recent research found that after students who performed science activities in order to receive "pay" for their work reached the top level of pay for having completed all activities, interest waned (Feldon & Kafai, 2008). More research needs to be done to determine the impact of specific conditions on incentives.

SmallWorlds

SmallWorlds is a 3D virtual world for middle schoolers and older, though users tend to be high teens to adult ("Bubbles Mofobian", 2009) launched in New Zealand in 2007. It has nearly two million users (Wikipedia, 2009). Membership is free, as are basic body parts and clothing. Members can purchase clothing, face, and body parts that are special with Gold. Gold is $4.95 per 2000. Members can also get a VIP membership for $7.95 USD a month that entitles them

Figure 4. Whyville Getty ArtSets

to discounts, special merchandise, and Gold. It has many places to chat shop, and play, such as Game Planet, the SmallWorlds Emporium, etc. It is a social achievement world, in that it has citizen levels that one earns by going on missions, working in shops, or helping others. SmallWorlds integrates YouTube, Flickr, SoundCloud, iMeem and other social media and web-based services.

There are many missions in this world, such as UFO hunting, Art Appreciation, etc., and they are organized by type: artist, explorer, gamer, and social status. For example, finding and making friends, too smart for scammers, Ovarian Cancer, Musical Chair Emotes are some of the many missions. The missions are searchable, with active and completed missions listed. By taking part in them, the member earns a higher citizen level and SmallWorlds Gold, which is used to purchase and decorate a room, purchase clothing and play items, electronics, etc. The levels go from "1" (no citizenship points), to "Citizen" (acquired through helping and/or missions) up to "Grand Duke/ Duchess".

Each time a citizen comes to the SmallWorlds website, the member is presented with the "Small-Worlds Chronicle", which provides information on activities, such as having one's picture taken with Santa at Christmas, shopping tips, items that can be purchased for one's room or to wear, or weekly horoscopes, current available jobs, such as in "Burger Chef", new Helper opportunities in and new missions. One applies to be a Helper and upon acceptance Helpers have work hours and are identified with a "+" in a circle over their heads and a cape. "Scamming" is common enough in SmallWorlds that both the "Chronicle" and a mission are devoted to it. Each member has a toolbar with people, places, missions, my profile (passport), inventory of "stuff", mail, and sharing with others options.

SmallWorlds items can be purchased and it has an economy that includes tokens, which are "achievement currency", which are earned by doing and creating things, as well as winning things. Gold can be purchased, but tokens can't be exchanged for gold. It has a "staying safe" section that discusses false identities and abuse, which can be handled by blocking the offending avatar (SmallWorlds, 2009). Property can't be "stolen" in SmallWorlds, though it can it be exchanged with other avatars. SmallWorlds has Terms of Use, Privacy, and Safety statements. Users can create their own custom avatar, decorate their rooms, own pets, and socialize with others online by playing games, watching videos, or listening to music.

Figure 5. SmallWorlds

Figure 6. SmallWorlds Helper

SmallWorlds has virtual currency that can be used to purchase various items, such as monthly collectibles, new clothing, and furniture to personalize their rooms (Mack, 2009). Flickr images can be used as posters in the virtual bedroom, and YouTube clips can be seen on the 3D living room television (Nicole, 2008). Other applications, like Grafiti, which have become popular on networks, like Facebook and Bebo, are also present in SmallWorlds.

SmallWorlds offers a "VIP membership" option that allow members to be able access exclusive items, wearables, and spaces. They can be bought with either SmallWorlds Gold or with real money. Avatars are customizable. Members can submit missions and earn citizenship points or gold. They can also submit items for avatars to wear and use,

such as face parts, electronics, etc. Though the degree of creativity allowed in SmallWorlds is limited, there is fraudulent behavior. The SmallWorlds website explains various "scams", such as "muling", "fraudulent chargebacks" and selling items for real money. "Muling" is creating multiple accounts to earn and transfer tokens and/or gold by repeatedly completing the basic missions and tasks and then transferring tokens, gold, and items to original main account(s)" ("SmallWorlds Help Tips", 2009, Para. 5). A "fraudulent chargeback" occurs when someone purchases goods, gets them, and then makes a false complaint with the credit card company that these goods were not received. Selling items for real money occurs when someone tells another to put money into a Paypal account and then the seller will "gift" an item to the pur-

Figure 7. SmallWorlds Game Planet

chaser. However, the seller does not gift the item and the money is lost. SmallWorlds states that it does not have the responsibility to compensate people when this happens. It is supposed to be reported and is punishable by banning (account loss) for both the seller and purchaser. There are many scams in SmallWorlds, such as charging to enter a space or shop that is free.

Second Life

Second Life, the most popular social virtual world, was launched in 2003 Avatars are customizable and life-like or fantastical. Genitalia are usually purchased for an additional cost, but are also found at free marketplaces within Second Life. The number of a peek concurrent content users was over 88,000 and users transacted the equivalent of more than one billion US dollars with each other while spending more than one billion hours in Second Life in the third quarter of 2009 (Linden Lab, 2009), rivaling the incomes of small countries (Media Age 2007). With over nine hundred universities, schools, museums, schools and educational institutions world wide in SL, (Second Life Blogs, 2009) and total membership at roughly 7 million, SL is a powerful platform for teaching and learning (Tennesen, 2009).

Second Life is composed of many islands, both private and public. As of December 2009, there were a total of 23,900 resident-owned regions in Second Life (Second Life Blog, 2010). Each island serves a specific purpose, such as education (for example, Vassar College recreated the Sistine Chapel on its campus in SL), with PG, adult, and mature rated areas.

Avatars can walk, fly, and teleport from one island to another and communicate through public and private text chats, IMs, and public voice chat. Anshe Chung (Ailin Graef in real life) became the first millionaire by selling virtual real estate in Second Life in 2006 (Hof, 2007). Many Fortune 500 companies have established presences in Second Life, such as IBM and Microsoft (Mennecke, et al. 2007). Second Life is currently unique in the degree of intellectual property ownership that is accorded its avatar citizens (Duranske, 2008).

Aside from ownership issues of the virtual land or "sim" and the objects or "prims" located thereon, like real life, the higher the degree of freedom that a user (avatar) has in a virtual world, the more interesting and useful the world becomes and also the more challenges that arise in it. Worlds without these characteristics do not have sufficient user options available as to warrant any substantive legal and ethical analysis for teaching purposes.

The Second Life Main Grid was originally designed for those 18 and up. However, as of

Figure 8. The Association for Educational Communications and Technology (AECT) Second Life Educator's Conference Display

Figure 9. Vassar College Sistene Chapel Created by Stan Frangible

December 31, 2010, the Main Grid will be open to those 16 and up (Second Life Blog, 2010). Second Life is determining how best to incorporate those under 16 into the Main Grid at this time. This proposed lowering of the minimum age, will have ethical and legal considerations that are yet to be explored.

CHAPTER TOPICS

Topics discussed in this chapter about selected social virtual worlds include the concept of the "magic circle" as applied to virtual worlds, virtual property, such as terms of service (TOS) and end-user license agreements (EULAs), com-

munity standards, safety, and privacy statements and intellectual property and copyright. Ethical aspects include griefing/abuse, harassment, and false identity. Finally, guidelines for instructors who wish to use virtual worlds in their teaching include student release statements (See Appendix 1) and topics to be address before venturing into virtual worlds. The authors offer analysis of these topics for informational purposes, only, and direct faculty, teachers, and others to competent legal counsel for further discussion.

The "Magic Circle" Test

This term refers to a concept first articulated in his 1938 work, later translated into English in

Figure 10. K-State Virtual Learning/Second Life Graduation Party

1955, *Homo Ludens (Man the player)*. This test is a "dividing line between play spaces and reality" (Duranske, 2008). The "Magic Circle" proposed by Huizinga (1955) was later elaborated upon by Castranova (2005). It has evolved into the "Magic Circle Test". This test basically means that when a user undertakes an activity in a virtual world and does understand or should reasonably understand that the activity has real world implications, then the activity is subject to real world law (Duranske, 2009). The degree to which a virtual world fosters business and creative enterprises that offer goods and services in exchange for virtual currency that can be exchanged for real money determines the degree to which a space moves from "play" to "real life". The practical result of this test is that the older the members are that are involved, coupled with a higher degree of creativity, commerce, and a virtual currency tied to the value of real money in U.S. dollars, the more apt users will be to be unwitting recipients of illegal and unethical behavior.

Instructors should be aware of this "sliding scale" continuum from little creative freedom/ little commerce to high creative freedom/high commerce and prepare students accordingly for exploration in these worlds. For example, Whyville has a high degree of play, with little that can be bought or sold within it, and high controls for internet predators. SmallWorlds has a lower degree of play, since members have a higher degree of creative freedom, commerce is available and encouraged for various items, an older user group, and while it has "helpers", the more items are available for sale. Second Life has the highest degree of creative freedom, the highest degree of intellectual property control, the highest degree of commerce, and a virtual currency that fluctuates according to the value of the US dollar. Second Life exists at the farthest end of the play/real life continuum. It also has had the most legal and ethical difficulties.

Nowhere is this better illustrated than in the medium of exchange. Second Life, unlike in some other virtual worlds, "objects are indistinguish-able from real world property interests", since they can be purchased with Linden dollars and converted into currency (Lastowka & Hunter, 2004). Nota Bene, for example, operates a virtual notary business in SL that supports in-world commerce. SmallWorlds has two forms of currency – SmallWorlds gold, which is earned through service or through purchasing with real money. In Whyville, there are both "pearls", which are purchased with real money, and "clams", which are earned through service activities and enterprise. In the examples given, real money is exchanged for goods and services, so these social worlds are not strictly "play spaces", and each has a place on the continuum.

Reasonable expectations for what the instructor and student can expect, in terms of class and virtual community interactions, is the same, legally, in each world-Terms of Service (TOS), and end-user license agreements (EULA's), which apply to both virtual world providers, as well. This places the TOS as a factor in legal disputes between users and between users and providers, but not the determinative one. For example, if an angry partner destroys the inventory of a store as the result of a dispute, then, absent a real-world contract that ties the partners together legally and provides for destruction and repayment (absent in this instance), then the partner has no recourse, both in Second Life and real life.

A dispute occurred recently in Second Life with Wetherby's Couture Store that illustrates these issues. Second Life, like all the other social virtual worlds discussed in this section, are under no legal obligation to replace or help to replace the destroyed inventory. In the case of Wetherby's, Linden Labs found as much inventory as it could still existent on the servers and gave it all back to the owner. Customers donated Linden dollars, clothing, and petitioned Linden Lab to remedy the situation. Wetherby's has over 20,000 loyal customers who were outraged at the destruction of their beloved Wetherby's store, and with the large exchange of Linden dollars these patrons generate, Linden Lab responded.

The high degree of creativity that exists in Second Life is virtually the same as in real life, including the hazards. It is important, therefore, for the instructor to review the law as it applies to TOS and EULA, become familiar with each world's application of them, review the remedies available in a dispute in each world, and require students to be aware of their legal rights in order to better avoid difficulties with other members and the provider.

Terms of Service (TOS), End-User License Agreements

All virtual worlds have (TOS) or Terms of Use (TOU). Virtual world providers require each user to agree to one or both of these documents in order to gain access to the virtual world. In some cases, it is each time (Duranske 2008). Some have additional End-User License Agreements (EULAs). These documents stand as law in virtual worlds, though only a court case is determinative (Lastowka & Hunter, 2004; Fairfield, 2005).

These agreements generally include contract terms, dispute resolution, limitations of the liability of the provider and warranty information. They are subject to a fair amount of scrutiny, and in one notable case, *Marc Bragg v. Linden Research Inc. and Philip Rosedale*, there were elements in the agreement that were unenforceable, since the terms were found to be "unconscionable". In this case, the court found the agreement to be oppressive, since the bargaining was in favor of the provider and it had hidden terms that amounted to a "contract of adhesion", thus making the agreement subject to review and alteration by the court.

Should a school district or university seek to enter into an agreement, *Bragg* set the precedent for examining the terms of the TOS in order to be more fair to the user. If the terms of arbitration or the TOS can be found to be in favor of the provider, then they can be disputed. The *Bragg* terms had to do with forced arbitration in a state favorable to the provider and difficult for the user to afford,

the seizure of $8,000 of inventory in Bragg's account, and false advertising. Due to the *Bragg* case, settled in 2008, Linden Labs changed its TOS to allow binding non-appearance–based arbitration for claims less than $10,000. The circumstances of each case vary. However, the TOS can not cause undue hardship to the user and be enforceable. Additionally, other virtual world providers have been changing their TOS to alter the requirement for binding arbitration. Each provider required the prevailing law of the state or country in which the company was registered to be the forum for arbitration or court cases, but due to *Bragg*, this is disputable. Terms of Service items include user rights and seizure and forfeiture of membership, avatar and any virtual property.

What institutions should take away from the Terms of Service is 1) a careful review of what rights the user has to virtual property, particularly when the investment is sizable to that institution. Property forfeiture, loss through catastrophe, and virtual property ownership are issues of importance. This cost does not include the purchase of items for building or hours used in constructing buildings and other objects on the island or "sim".

End-user license agreements (EULAs) are considered to be contracts, along with TOS. Additional assent may or may not be required by the provider in the form of a EULA (as in any software application installed on a computer) for this purpose. These vary considerably from provider to provider (Duranske, 2008). They can include intellectual property rights, privacy, account transfer, account termination, and purchase and cashing-out of whatever currency is used, and under what terms this can be done. All providers discuss the results of a user's account being terminated.

Virtual Property

Virtual property rights in most of the popular worlds are delineated in the End-user license agreements (EULA's). "More mainstream articles have been written about intellectual property (IP) in virtual worlds than any other topic in virtual law" (Duranske, 2008, p. 139). This is particularly so of Second Life, due to its stance as the first virtual world to allow users to retain certain property rights (Horowitz, 2007). Horowitz called Second Life a "property-promoting" virtual world, versus certain other worlds considered to be "property-averse", such as World of Warcraft (WOW). However, a large market for virtual products has emerged on eBay and other online auction sites for various items related to these virtual worlds (t-shirts, books, etc.). Additionally, there are also online auction sales for WOW virtual property, such as a "foam sword rack loot card", usable in WOW, costing $80 USD. Most virtual world EULAs prohibit the trade of virtual products and deny any property claims users might wish to assert against operators. As a practical matter legal disputes between users and operators over virtual property in such worlds turns on these agreements. Virtual property exists to the greatest extent in Second Life, as well as theft of intellectual property (Lastowka, 2008). Texture theft also exists (SecondLifeUpdate.com, 2009). Textures are graphical images that make a door look like it is made of oak or steel, make a dress look like silk, or make fences look like wood, (See Figure 11). These are necessary to make virtual worlds look realistic or fantastic. Textures can be made or purchased, and this is of some concern, since textures can be bought and sold. If these are stolen and re-used without permission, then this is theft. One commentator noted that it was easy to do, did not require too much effort in order to execute, and was difficult to prevent (SecondLifeInsider. com, 2006).

Some of the content generated by users is illegal in virtual worlds. When users have the ability to upload content/virtual property, then they sometimes upload content that is pornographic or that violates copyright, trademark, and patent laws, such as stolen jewelry designs, clothing, cars, electronics, etc. "The greater the degree to which virtual worlds rely on user-generated content, the larger these problems loom and the greater the resources that must be spent responding to complaints" (Lastowka, 2008, p. 912). There is a procedure in Second Life for reporting such theft. Linden Labs accuracy in reporting transactions is controversial (Laffer, 2008), so it is difficult to ascertain the level of commerce or income of those working in Second Life or other virtual worlds. However, the term "buyer beware" is as true in virtual worlds as it is in real life, so shopping in virtual worlds should be restricted to shops and businesses that are reliable. Additionally, businesses change quickly, so what one day may be a shop selling textures may be something else the next.

Community Standards/Safety/ Internet Safety Guidelines

All virtual worlds have some form of standards that are enforced as part of the TOS or EULA, or in addition to them, that a user agrees to upon joining. These have to do with appropriate behavior, harassment, abuse, illegal behavior, such as sexual solicitation, pornography, false identities and those who are either under the age for membership, such as in Second Life, wherein one must be 18 or over for the adult grid, under 18 and over 13 for the Teen Grid, and over 13 for SmallWorlds. Whyville states, "If a child enters a birth date indicating that he/she is under 13, we require a parent's email address which we use ONCE to notify the parent that his/her child has registered at our site. This email address is not collected in our records." All virtual worlds that are intended for those under 18, and even for those who are supposed to be over 18 in Second Life, have warnings about not trusting the age or sex of that users state about their avatars. Unless the user knows the avatar's owner/user personally, it is very difficult to tell.

Second Life has "profiles", which can be clicked on to know more about the avatar and its owner. This profile allows members to make more informed judgments about the avatar/owner veracity. If a conversation makes the user uncomfortable for any reason, the user can always, mute an avatar, teleport immediately to another location or simply log off." This is good advice for all virtual worlds. Second Life provides the ability to eliminate communication with other avatars with a touch of a mute feature, and provides "radars" scripts to be able to detect the presence of other avatars within chat distance and long distance.

Second Life does not allow public avatar nudity, since avatars have life-like skins that can include genitalia. All other social worlds discussed in this chapter do not allow avatars to be nude. SmallWorlds, and Whyville only allow appropriate attire choices. Second Life has attire that runs the gamut from fully clothed, to that which stretches the Community Standards in public spaces. In private spaces, those owned by residents that can't be accessed except by invitation or membership, avatars may dress or undress, as they choose. Second Life, in 2009, added the designation of adult content, in addition to Mature and PG content, to help users choose appropriate vendors and regions.

Intellectual Property and Copyright

Virtual property has "exploded" since 1999 (Duranske, 2008) to the point that virtual reality evidence has been discussed by attorneys in court actions since 1996 (Joseph, 1996). Intellectual property varies a great deal among social virtual worlds. In SmallWorlds and Whyville there is little, certainly as compared to Second Life, along with the lack of intellectual property theft. The only world discussed in this review that has intellectual property issues is Second Life, which are extensive (Barfield, 2006; Quarmby, 2009; Talab & Botterbusch, 2009).

Most providers have a mechanism for reporting intellectual property theft that follows the provisions of the Digital Millennium Copyright Act (1998) and Second Life has such a mechanism, although policing so many violations seems to be difficult to monitor (Quarmby, 2009). Providers must comply with Section 512 of the DMCA in order to be protected against copyright infringement claims. Music provided by radio stations, disc jockeys, coffee houses, are often done without licenses, art is copied and distributed illegally, and movies are illegally distributed and watched throughout many virtual worlds.

A search of Second Life provides many shops that sell Gucci, Louis Vuitton, etc., as well as electronics and other products that are viola-

Figure 11. Some K-State Class Project: Student Textures

tions of trademark infringements. While some shopkeepers capitalize on the Gucci name, for example, but have clothing that does not resemble actual Gucci clothing or sunglasses, virtual "trade dress" has long been a problem (Bell, 1997). While a trademark is the Coca Cola symbol, the Coke bottle, itself, is an example of trade dress, since it is distinctive. An item may not be a true Harry Potter product, but it may copy the "look and feel" of it and therefore be a violation. There are regions in Second Life that are dedicated to Star Trek, are "inspired" by Harry Potter story settings, etc. Some of them are private and some are public.

The "copybot" is a controversial issue in Second Life. It was the pressure of the merchants in Second Life who thought that they were having their virtual property stolen, who asked for a ban on it. The developers of the products wanted to keep it so they could make quick copies of their own creations. However, copybots have been allowed to exist because the developers' needs far outweighed the merchants, as long as they do not violate the copyright law. Also, in order to preserve the intellectual property rights of the creator of items in Second Life, one needs to be able to understand how to set permissions for items sold in Second Life. They can be set to copy, modify, and transfer. So, if a developer doesn't understand these rights and sets the permissions wrong, then if someone steals it, the developer may have no grounds to sue.

Teaching In Virtual Worlds

When teaching in social virtual worlds, for any age group, quality teaching demands that the instructor explore and know the virtual world well before taking students into it. Each world requires many hours in it in order to be able to accurately and safely instruct students in its uses and possibilities

Teaching in virtual worlds requires planning. Second Life, SmallWorlds and Whyville are open 24/7.. Instructors should become familiar with the Terms of Service (TOS), behavioral guidelines/ community standards/internet safety guidelines and end-user license agreements of each world in order to know the potentials and pitfalls for each one. They should also look through the "Frequently Asked Questions" and any teacher/ instructor information to learn more about bringing classes in, as well as the educator Second Life blogs and wikis.

Once the instructor is able to navigate and do the same assignments that will be asked of students, then the next step is to instruct students in proper internet and virtual worlds use. See what

Figure 12. Hogwarts Lil Hogsmeade

help or monitoring is done in each world. If taking middle-school students into SmallWorlds or elementary students into Whyville, one should find out what help or options are available to handle "griefing", harassment or abuse.

Each virtual world has its own culture, behavioral norms, age group(s), and safety protections. Whyville has "City Management". In SmallWorlds there are "Moderators" for public places and "Helpers" for general help. One goes to the "help desk" and rings the bell for one of them. However, a helper doesn't always answer immediately, particularly at odd hours of the day. An e-mail to the provider may be wise when first taking students into these worlds. The providers in these worlds are knowledgeable and helpful.

For example, it is important to know that certain purchased avatar face parts/heads/clothing/hair are not permanent in Whyville. They cost varying amounts and last 92 days at the longest. Then they must be renewed or changed. The incentives to have face parts, clothing and electronics are strong, since the avatar issued at entry doesn't resemble a human. One can't chat in Whyville until a safety test has been taken, and some of the correct answers for it, at the time of this writing, may be a surprise. There are places to build, customizable avatars (which are changed in "spas'), forums, activities, and clubs. In the Main Grid section of Second Life, "newbies" (new players) are "griefed" or harassed at Help Island, so having a safe place to learn avatar controls and the "basics" of Second Life is necessary, as well having a list of safe, educational places to go. Since those under 16 may be allowed into the Main Grid in 2011, Second Life policies may change, as well. For educators, should this happen, high school students would then be able to be participate and attendant legal and ethical protections would need to be in place for this to occur.

The International Society for Technology in Education (ISTE) Island is a very good place to "rez" (appear in a virtual world), since it has a section on basic Second Life skills, resources,

and a group of educators to meet on a regular basis. A "home" can be set on Second Life URL (SLURL) that can be teleported to in case of abuse or finding oneself in an uncomfortable situation. Most often this is a residence or a Second Life classroom, but it can also be an educational area of a professional association, such as ISTE Island or the Association for Educational Communications and Technology's CAVE Island.

False identities are an issue in all virtual worlds. Adults can sign up for all of these pre-18 virtual worlds without detection as adults, either legally (the question is not asked) or illegally, answering as though the adult is a minor (under 18). One can't take an avatar's answers as truthful in these worlds, so monitoring and student education on appropriate behaviors are necessary.

While there is some information that indicates that student release forms have legal limitations in a court of law, it is still a good precautionary measure to have students sign a release form when virtual worlds are introduced to students. This is particularly true of those under 13, due to COPPA. Even though the virtual world mentioned (Whyville) and others, are reasonably safe due to adult monitors, monitors are not always available to help students to make wise decisions, so teachers should be aware of what students are doing in assignments in these virtual worlds. They are still various negative aspects to any virtual world.

Special Considerations: Teaching in Second Life

The New Media Consortium (NMC, 2007) conducted a survey in spring 2007 to capture insights about the work of 209 individual educators regarding their use of Second Life in education and research. According to this survey, the most positive experiences that they had were from the "rich interactions, meeting new people, expanding networks, generosity of community" (45%). Their worst experiences were with "technical issues/using SL" (62%) and "griefing/abuse (33%).

The next year, 2008, NMC conducted another survey of 358 individuals and found these changes in the subjects' response to SL. Once again, the "rich interactions" ranked highest at 51%. However, "griefing/abused/perceived violence" rose to the most negative experience in SL, with "technical issues/using SL" coming in second at 24%. Both years, the Second Life Educator listserv SLED remained the most important resource for educators.

The results of these surveys are consistent with research findings on teaching in Second Life. Three case studies found results similar to the two NMC surveys. Hollander & Thomas (2009) used, Schiller (2009) used a learner-centered teaching model, and Talab & Botterbusch (2009) used a constructivist/constructionist model. All studied the use of Second Life in teaching using learner-centered teaching. All three reported similar reasons for using this virtual world. "Rather than just showing a slide of a neighborhood in Amsterdam to make a point, Second Life allows us to, as a class, walk the streets of the neighborhood and experience a social, communal, and virtual fieldtrip" (Hollander, p. 110). Students experienced harassment and vandalism on several occasions in all three studies. The pedagogical model was based on gaming (Gee, 2003), using SL as an environment to accomplish learning. In Hollander & Thomas' study (2009), all four goals of the urban planning course were enhanced in Second Life, due to being able to construct "more authentic experiences" by allowing students to create 3-D models of buildings they were able to integration skills and knowledge in a safe and inexpensive virtual environment, increase teamwork and problem solving skills.

He suggested the use of a closed or exclusive island or site in SL where only authorized personnel can be allowed.

The Schiller study (2009) was conducted on an MBA course to complete business-related activities based on learner-centered teaching and Second Life was used for this purpose (Weimer, 2002). Schiller found Second Life to be "a highly immersive and interactive environment that facilitates active learning through individual and team activities" (p. 371). Schiller also discussed the technical issues that are of such importance in helping students to learn in SL.

.... Instructors should be aware of the potential harm and unexpected incidents that students might encounter in Second Life....it contains some level of sexuality, adult content, disturbance, and misbehavior. (p.371

In the Talab & Botterbusch case study (2009) of graduate students learning about virtual learning and teaching in Second Life, the findings included overall positive experiences in Second life largely due to the many field trips that they took and the project-based in-world assignments. Students saw the benefit in taking the fullest advantages of the many regions that there are in SL" (p. 233). Depending on the degree to which students ventured into SL, those students with skills and who ventured more freely in Second Life had similar experiences to instructor and faculty/staff experts with "griefing", lewd behavior (one student was approached by a prostitute), and false identities (one avatar being interviewed by a student flew away when asked about gender), though male and female avatars were treated differently. Copyright violations occurred often, as well (p.236).

Some universities and schools require signed releases from the parent and/or the student, depending on the student's age, with information on activities that will be done and potential issues that could arise. If those under 18 are to be allowed into virtual worlds, then K-12 schools will need to require parental permissions for student work in SL. Schools can also restricting students to their own regions or "sims". In this way, harassment and "griefing" are reduced, as well as other potential legal and ethical issues. If

SL is to be used to its fullest extent, then there will be good experiences and bad, but there are so many educational opportunities in SL and in virtual worlds. |

Mitigating Student and Teacher Liability and Danger

University attorneys, in print, have been silent on the use of virtual worlds in higher education. To date, only one article by a university attorney, on Second Life, has been written, with a cautionary approach. Melissa Blevins, an attorney in Des Moines, had this admonition:" If you're requiring participation, holding classes in Second Life, you and/or your institution also may be accepting liability for virtual events that happen there" (Bugeja, 2008, C1). Additionally, Bugeja found that "few campus lawyers were willing to go on the record with other suggestions or warnings because legal standards in this area have not yet been fully determined " (2008a, C1). Yet, university academics have been the quickest to utilize them (Young, 2008). As one academic observed, "Few college/university presidents or CIOs are currently prioritizing the exploration of virtual worlds, but it seems safe to predict that within the next three to five years, a higher education institution without a virtual worlds presence will be like an institution without a web presence today" (Collins, 2008).

Some Guidelines for Teaching and Learning in Virtual Worlds

As a result of these experiences with the subjects in the study, Botterbusch, in Talab & Botterbusch (2009) developed some SL teaching guidelines, which have been expanded to include more legal and ethical issues guidelines:

1. Be clear about your purpose in using a virtual world for teaching. Ask yourself if what you want your students to learn can be achieved more easily and cheaply in some other format. Use SL, and other "building" virtual worlds (Active Worlds, BlueMars, etc.) for what the instructor has called "three-dimensional representations of difficult or expensive concepts". It's cheaper, easier, and faster than in real life, though it's best done on private land, due to theft and griefing issues.

2. Caution students that, just as in video and computer games, virtual worlds can also become addictive. Tell them to limit their time spent to two-hour intervals. Emphasize that the real world and its people are more important than anyone or anything in a virtual world.

3. Students should sign a release form that they understand that there are both positive and negative aspects of virtual worlds. This release should hold the university harmless in the event of loss of virtual property through nefarious means or student negligence. It should detail their responsibilities to read the TOS, EULA, and community standards for each world, as well as take appropriate training suggested by that world in this regard.

4. Teach students about the Community Standards or behavioral guidelines of the virtual world, as well as and other legal and ethical issues, before leaving the virtual classroom.

5. Create exercises with students in which they must problem solve about difficult situations, such as being harassed, captured (in SL), or griefed, so that they know what their options are in handling these situations.

6. Teach students how to teleport home or to a safe place should unpleasantness occur.

7. Take students on virtual field trips before sending them out on their own.

8. Caution about creating or buying textures and objects that are copyrighted and trade-

marked. Gucci, Louis Vuitton, Nike, and the like are copyrighted, trademarked or both.

9. Teach students to read avatar profiles in Second Life and any other worlds that use them, prior to offering friendship to others. This can eliminate potentially unsavory characters; although not in all cases.

10. While music can be uploaded to most social virtual worlds, only 10 seconds of a work can be legally uploaded,. Music must be licensed to be streamed legally in virtual worlds.

11. Griefing and abuse are commonplace in Second Life, and occur in other social virtual worlds, as well, though to a lesser extent. If the instructor sends students into SL to search or explore, students must be aware of solicitation for prostitution, lewd behavior (nudity and pornographic pictures), "griefing" (for example, disturbing work in a sandbox), and being careful of role-playing sims (nude Roman baths, etc.), or avatars in role-playing mode.

12. Teach students how to determine who is probably safe to talk to and who is potentially a risk by staying in PG areas (Second Life), talking to others in areas where there are helpers (Whyville and SmallWorlds) and becoming aware of potential scams in each world.

CONCLUSION

This review of the literature about the legal and ethical issues of using virtual worlds for teaching and learning has provided an overview of selected virtual worlds by examining a few of the most popular versions used by educators. In order to utilize these amazing spaces, one must be as aware as possible of what to expect before attempting to explore and teach in each one.

Virtual worlds present many opportunities to experiment with ideas and concepts that can't be done in real life. They also offer worldwide social networking and educational and collaborative opportunities, which can foster a greater understanding and acceptance of cultural, religious and ideological differences. In all virtual worlds levels of interaction among users vary, skill levels are increased with time and practice, and expertise only comes with effort. Choose these worlds wisely for teaching, since each is unique. Just like life, the more potential there is, the more hazards there are, but what better way can there be for students to safely navigate these issues before trying them out in real life?

REFERENCES

Arakji, R., & Lang, K. (2008). Avatar business value analysis: A methods of the evaluation of business value creation in virtual commerce. *Journal of Electronic Commerce Research, 9*(3), 207–218.

Barfield, W. (2006). Intellectual property rights in virtual environments: Considering the rights of owners, programmers, and virtual avatars. *Akron Law Review, 39*, 649–700.

Bell, T. (1997). Virtual trade dress: A very real issue. *Maryland Law Review (Baltimore, Md.), 56*, 384–532.

Biocca, F., & Levy, M. (1995). *Communication in the age of virtual reality.* Philadelphia, PA: Lawrence Erlbaum Associates.

Blascovich, J., Loomis, J., Beall, A., Swinth, K., Hoyt, C., & Bailenson, J. (2002). Immersive virtual environment technology as a methodological tool for social psychology. *Psychological Inquiry, 13*(2), 103–124. doi:10.1207/S15327965PLI1302_01

Bugeja, M. (2008). Second thoughts about second Life. *The Chronicle of Higher Education, 54*(3), C1.

Castranova, E. (2005). *Synthetic worlds: The business and culture of online games.* Chicago: University Of Chicago Press.

Chenin, A. (2007). A practical look at virtual property. *St. John's Law Review, 80,* 1059–1090.

Collins, C. (2008). Looking to the future: Higher education in the metaverse. *EDUCAUSE Review.* Retrieved December 13th, 2009, from http://www.educause.edu/EDUCAUSE+Review/EDUCAUSEReviewMagazineVolume43/LookingtotheFutureHigherEducat/163164

Daly, C. (2010) Virtual worlds continue to make real-world gains. Retrieved on August 24, 2010 from http://technorati.com/technology/article/virtual-worlds-continue-to-make-real/

Dreher, C., Reiners, T., Dreher, N., & Dreher, H. (2009). Virtual worlds as a context suited for information systems education: Discussion of pedagogical experience and curriculum design with reference to Second Life. *Journal of Information Systems Education, 20*(2), 211-224. Retrieved November 7th, 2009, from ABI/INFORM Global. (Document ID: 1755224801).

Duranske, B. (2008). *Virtual law.* Chicago: ABA Books.

Employeefactor. (2009). *Generation z - The igeneration.* Retrieved August 23rd, 2010, from http://www.employeefactor.com/?p=275g

Engage Digital Media. (2009). *200+ youth-oriented worlds live or developing.* Retrieved November 9th, 2009, from http://www.virtualworldsmanagement.com/2009/youth-01-26-2009.html

Federal Trade Commission. (2009). *Web sites warned to comply with Children's Online Privacy Law.* Retrieved November 13th, 2009, from http://www2.ftc.gov/opa/2000/07/coppacompli.shtm

Feldon, D., & Kafai, Y. (2008). Mixed methods for mixed reality: Understanding users' avatar activities in virtual worlds. *Educational Technology, Research and Development,* 56(5/6), 575-593. Retrieved November 7, 2009, from Research Library. (Document ID: 1632036171).

Gee, J. (2007). *Good video games and good learning: Collected essays.* New York: Peter Lang Publishing.

Gee, J. (2007). *What video games have to teach us about learning and literacy.* (2003, Second Edition 2007).

Harris, H., Bailenson, J., Nielsen, A., & Yee, N. (2009). *Presence: Teleoperators & virtual environments.* Retrieved November 12, 2009, from http://vhil.stanford.edu/pubs/2009/harris-tracking.pdf

Hollander, J., & Thomas, D. (2009). *Journal of planning education and research 29*(1), 108-113. Retrieved November 9th, 2009, from http://jpe.sagepub.com/cgi/content/abstract/29/1/108

Hu, J. (2010) Educators save money switching to OpenSim. *Hypergrid Business.* Retrieved August 24, 2010, from http://hypergridbusiness.com/2010/04/educators-save-money-switching-to-opensims/

Huizinga, J. (1955). *Homo ludens; a study of the play element in culture.* Boston: Beacon Press.

Kane, Y. (2009). Online gaming-family edition. *Wall Street Journal Online Digital Network.* Retrieved on November 4th, 2009 from http://online.wsj.com/article/SB123802714524742875.html

Keegan, V. (2010). Virtual worlds: is this where real life is heading? The Observer. Retrieved August 24th, 2010, from http://www.guardian.co.uk/technology/2010/aug/22/discover-virtual-worlds-revolution

Kock, N. (2008). Collaboration and e-commerce in virtual worlds: The potential of Second Life and World of Warcraft. *International Journal of e-Collaboration, 4*(3), 1–13.

Korolov, M. (2010) OpenSim grows faster than Second Life. *Hypergrid Business*. Retrieved on August 24, 2010, from http://hypergridbusiness. com/2010/01/opensim-grows-faster-than-second -life/

KZero. (2010). *Radar chart: Toys/games, fantasy and mirror worlds*. Retrieved August 24th, 2010, from http://www.kzero.co.uk/blog/?cat=107

Lab, L. (2009). *1 billion hours, 1 billion dollars served: Second Life celebrates major milestones for virtual worlds*. Retrieved November 1st, 2009, from http://lindenlab.com/pressroom/re-leases/22_09_09

Laffer, B. (2008). *Second life money: The status of financial industries in Second Life*. Retrieved November 13th, 2009, from http://www.slentre. com/second-life-money-the-state-of-financial-industries-in-second-life/

Lehtiniemi, T. (2007). Measuring aggregate production in a virtual economy using log data. *Journal of Virtual Worlds Research, 2*(3), 3–21.

Mack, C. (n.d.). SmallWorlds grows bigger with hi5. *Inside social games; tracking innovation at the convergence of games and social platforms*. Retrieved November 12th, 2009, from http://www. insidesocialgames.com/2009/06/11/smallworlds-grows-bigger-with-hi5/

Matthews, V. (2008). Generation Z: New kids on the virtual block. *Personnel Today*. Retrieved November 12, 2009, from http://www.personnel-today.com/articles/2008/09/14/47303/generation-z-new-kids-on-the-virtual-block.html

Mofobian, B. (2009). Bubbles mofobian: A triumph of the human spirit. *Scene in smallworlds*. Retrieved from http://www.smallworlds.com/

New Media Consortium. (2007). *Spring 2007 survey of educators in Second Life*. Retrieved November 13th, 2009, from http://www.nmc.org/ pdf/2007-sl-survey-summary.pdf

New Media Consortium. (2008). *Spring 2008 survey of educators in Second Life*. Retrieved November 13th, 2009, from http://www.nmc.org/ pdf/2008-sl-survey-summary.pdf

Nicole, K. (2008). SmallWorlds has virtual Flickr posters, YouTube tv, and more. *Mashable; the social media guide*. Retrieved November 12th, 2009, from http://mashable.com/2008/05/21/ smallworld/

Palfrey, J., & Gasser, U. (2008). *Born digital*. Philadelphia, PA: Basic Books.

P.L. 105-304. (1998). *Digital Millennium Copyright Act*. Retrieved on November 12th, 2009, from http://www.copyright.gov/legislation/dmca.pdf

Prensky, M. (2001). *Digital game-based learning*. New York: McGraw-Hill.

Prensky, M. (2006). *Don't bother me mom – I'm learning: How computer and video games are preparing your children for twenty-first century success – and how you can help*. New York: Paragon House.

Privantu, R. (2007). *Tips on developing an MMO economy, part I. DevMaster.net*. Retrieved on November 11th, 2009, from http://www.devmaster. net/articles/mmo-economy/part1.php

Retrieved November 7, 2009, from ABI/INFORM Global. (Document ID: 1755224811).

Reuters, E. (2007). *Rival grids threaten Linden's monopoly on SL Technology*. Retrieved on August 24, 2010 from http://secondlife.reuters.com/ stories/2007/09/06/rival-grids-threaten-lindens-monopoly-on-sl-technology/

Rosen, L. (2010). *Rewired; understanding the igeneration and the way they learn*. New York: Palgrave Macmillan.

Schiller, S. (2009). Practicing learner-centered teaching: Pedagogical design and assessment of a Second Life project. *Journal of Information Systems Education, 20*(3), 369-381. Retrieved November 7, 2009, from ABI/INFORM Global. (Document ID: 1870617241).

Second Life Blogs. 2009 end of year Second Life economy wrap up (including Q4 economy in detail. Retrieved August 24th, 2010, from http://blogs.secondlife.com/community/features/blog/2010/01/19/2009-end-of-year-second-life-economy-wrap-up-including-q4-economy-in-detail

Secondlifegrid.net (2009) Retrieved on November 12th, 2009, from http://secondlifegrid.net/slfe/education-use-virtual-world

Shaffer, D., & Gee, J. (2006). *How computer games help children learn*. New York: Palgrave McMillan. doi:10.1057/9780230601994

Shen, J., & Eder, L. (2009). Intentions to use virtual worlds for education. *Journal of Information Systems Education, 20*(2), 225–233.

Sim, O. (2009). *Grid list*. Retrieved November 13th, 2009, from http://opensimulator.org/wiki/Grid_List

SmallWorlds. (2009). *Current known scams*. http://forum.smallworlds.com/showthread.php?t=1973

SmallWorlds. (2009). *Gold, tokens, and VIP memberships*. http://www.smallworlds.com/?target=/2009/08/05/help-and-support/

SmallWorlds. (2009). *Internet safety guidelines*. Retrieved November 13th, 2009, from http://www.smallworlds.com/?target=/newspaper/help-tips/

Talab, R., & Botterbusch, H. (2009). Ethical and legal issues in teaching and learning in second life in a graduate online course . In Russell, D. (Ed.), *Collaborative virtual learning environments; processes and interactions*. Hershey, PA: IGI Global.

Techcrunch. Retrieved November 7th, 2009, from http://www.techcrunch.com/2009/07/02/does-anybody-still-use-second-life-and-if-so-how-much-is-it-worth-today/

The Information Resource Management (IRM) College of the National Defense University. (2009). The federal consortium for virtual worlds. Retrieved November 8th, 2009, from http://www.youtube.com/watch?v=wKh8-QyL1Bs&feature=player_embedded

Thousands protest, sign petitions over closing of Disney online game. (2009). Retrieved November 12th, 2009, from http://www.clickorlando.com/technology/15881453/detail.html

Wagner, C., & Ip, R. (2009). Action learning with Second Life - a pilot study. *Journal of information systems education, 20*(2), 249-258. Retrieved November 7th, 2009, from ABI/INFORM Global. (Document ID: 1755224831).

Wauters, R. (2009). Does anybody still use Second Life? And if so, how much? TechCrunch. Retrieved August 25, 2010, from http://techcrunch.com/2009/07/02/does-anybody-still-use-second-life-and-if-so-how-much-is-it-worth-today/

Weimer, M. (2002). *Learner-centered teaching: Five key changes to practice*. San Francisco, CA: Jossey-Bass.

Whitepaper, A. (2008). *Introduction to virtual worlds*. Retrieved November 13th, 2009, from http://www.scribd.com/doc/5570819/Introduction-to-virtual-worlds

Wikipedia. (n.d.). *Whyville*. Retrieved December 12th, 2009, from http://en.wikipedia.org/wiki/whyville

APPENDIX 1

Memo of Understanding

Mature and Confidential Aspects

of the Virtual World, Second Life

KSU EDCI 786 - Spring 2009

Please complete, sign and return this document to your instructor on or before January 22, 2009.

1. I am aware that Second Life is like the Internet in general and has content that I may find offensive. _____ Yes _____ No

2. I am aware there are places in Second Life that are categorized as "mature". Although these may not necessarily contain materials that are offensive, I understand that if I am uncomfortable I am not required to visit these areas. _____ Yes _____ No

3. I understand that if I should find material or objects offensive to me, I may return to the K-State Classroom area and wait for the instructor to return. _____ Yes _____ No

4. I understand there may be people in Second Life who may use offensive language around me and I have the right to leave their presences, return to the K-State classroom and wait for the instructor to return. _____ Yes _____ No

5. I understand that taking photos of other avatars is considered an invasion of privacy and will not do so without permission granted from the agent behind the avatar. _____ Yes _____ No

6. I understand that avatars do not use their real name in Second Life, may hide their true identity and may want to remain anonymous. I, therefore, understand that I will not reveal an avatar's true identity or any information about them without their expressed permission. _____ Yes _____ No

7. I understand there are diverse populations residing in Second Life, and therefore, I will not discriminate or "grief" in any way, fellow residents. _____ Yes _____ No

8. I have read, understand and will abide by the Community Standards of Second Life as posted on the Second Life web site at http://secondlife.com/corporate/cs.php_____ Yes _____ No

Signature _____

Date _____

Chapter 10
JavaMOO Virtual Cells for Science Learning

Bradley Vender
North Dakota State University, USA

Otto Borchert
North Dakota State University, USA

Ben Dischinger
North Dakota State University, USA

Guy Hokanson
North Dakota State University, USA

Phillip E. McClean
North Dakota State University, USA

Brian M. Slator
North Dakota State University, USA

ABSTRACT

One of the World Wide Web Instructional Committee (WWWIC) at North Dakota State University's (NDSU) long running projects is the Virtual Cell, a desktop immersive virtual environment developed for biology education. The focus of the content in the Virtual Cell is cellular biology, and the underlying focus of the content modules is the scientific method and analytical reasoning. However, the technical challenges encountered during the course of the project include designing deployable server architectures, designing robust simulations, and developing high quality animations without losing interactivity.

DOI: 10.4018/978-1-61692-825-4.ch010

INTRODUCTION

The World Wide Web Instructional Committee (WWWIC) at North Dakota State University (NDSU) is engaged in research aimed at developing virtual environments to assist in the education and growth of students (Slator et al., 1999). Some of the key factors that lead to the success of these environments are a) the theory of role-based environments on which they are based, b) the use of graduate and undergraduate students in the development process, c) the use of the environments in actual classes, and d) the application of knowledge from one environment to the others.

An educational game should be both engaging and informative. Players should acquire concepts and skills because of playing the game, and this learning should transfer to contexts outside the game. The challenge then is to construct a game of sufficiently interesting complexity that is consistent with the subject it attempts to teach. When the player acts in the simulated environment, the environment must re-act in coherent and plausible ways. Without this consistency, the game will fail the ultimate test: students will not play it (Slator & Chaput, 1996).

Virtual role-playing environments can be a powerful mechanism of instruction, provided that they are constructed such that learning how to play and win the game contributes to a player's understanding of real-world concepts and procedures. WWWIC has developed environments to enhance student understanding of geology (Planet Oit), cellular biology (Virtual Cell), programming languages (ProgrammingLand), retailing (Dollar Bay), and history (Blackwood). These systems present a number of opportunities and challenges. Players are afforded a role-based, multi-user, 'learn-by-doing' experience, with software agents acting as both environmental effects and tutors, and the possibilities of multi-user cooperation and collaboration. The Virtual Cell environment, its particular challenges, and the solutions to these are presented.

THE VIRTUAL CELL

The Virtual Cell as implemented is a client server system where the server is responsible for the persistence of the shared environments, arbitrating state changes, and facilitating communication between players. The client is responsible for constructing the appropriate view of each shared environment and for providing the user interface elements appropriate to each environment and task. In order to display the environments, the primary role of the client is to load and display the scenes which are stored on the server and that compose that environment. As a result, the client's scene loading algorithm shapes how the client and server interact.

In the Virtual Cell, the basic element of the game is the *goal*. A goal represents either a single objective or a group of simple related objectives that the player is tasked to achieve, or a set of steps which the player is tasked with achieving. Also associated with each goal is a set of reference materials to explain various aspects of the activity that the player should be attempting to accomplish.

Goals are grouped together into a sequence to form a *module*, and the module is the format presented to players and instructors. At the midpoint of the project's current history, the Virtual Cell had three modules: (1) Organelle Identification, (2) Electron Transport Chain, and (3) Photosynthesis. The Organelle Identification module is used as an introduction to the game play and the acts of performing tests and comparing results. The Electron Transport Chain (ETC) module focuses on one part of the respiration process and traces the movement of hydrogen and electrons during the conversion of adenosine diphosphate (ADP) to adenosine triphosphate (ATP) in the mitochondria. The Photosynthesis module similarly focuses on the movement of hydrogen and electrons in one segment of the photosynthesis reaction in the chloroplast.

The Organelle Identification module is an introduction to the game and begins with the simple task of flying around the cell to collect assay results from each organelle. The two follow-up tasks for this module are simple diagnostic tasks in which the player is asked to verify a diagnosis by collecting further results and comparing the experimental or actual results to expected values.

The more elaborate Electron Transport Chain (ETC) module consists of a sequence of introductory tasks leading up to a more complicated diagnostic task. Much like a lab exercise, the introductory tasks in this module present the expected behavior of the individual components of the system and gradually combine the pieces together to help the player build up a model of how the system operates. The diagnostic task at the end of the module serves to test the expected understanding by presenting the player with a malfunctioning version of the system and asking the player to identify and replace the defective components to restore proper behavior.

The Photosynthesis module for the Virtual Cell in its current form differs from the ETC module by having a final task focused on process replication instead of diagnosis. In order to accomplish the goal, the player is asked to add the necessary photons and substrates to the system and induce a temporary imbalance in the hydrogen equilibrium, and as a side effect of the hydrogen imbalance being removed, the system will produce ATP from ADP. The crucial difference being that this photosynthesis activity requires the player to interact with the same system over a sequence of dependent steps, rather than the parallel independent steps used in the ETC.

As the player works through each module, a help and information system is available to supplement the interactive activities. In that system, the player can find descriptions of the system being studied and information about the structures and chemicals involved. For example, in the ETC module, as shown in figure two the player has access to overview diagrams such as the one on the left, the reference database shown in the middle, and an animated demonstration version of the system shown on the right.

One of the major goals of WWWIC research is to find ways to provide tutoring agents to communicate expert advice to students as they progress through the environment. These agents monitor the student and send advice as needed while being careful to never insist upon or block any course of action (Slator, 1999).

Figure 1. Various Scenes in the Virtual Cell

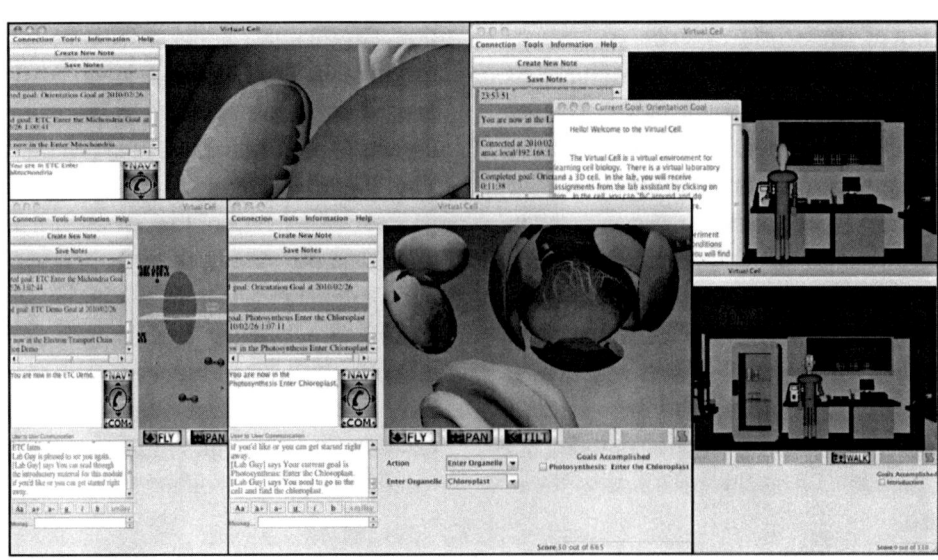

Feedback for the diagnostic activities is divided into four categories using the orthogonal characterizations of correctness and sufficiency of evidence. In other words, one response is given if the player's diagnosis is correct, but not enough evidence has been collected, as might happen if the player guessed. A different response is used if the diagnosis is incorrect despite having enough evidence, indicating that the player misunderstood the evidence collected or miscalculated.

In addition to the modules discussed, interactive simulations for transcription, translation and the lac operon have been developed but the narrative structure for those modules is still very primitive.

GUIDING PRINCIPLES

There were a number of design decisions in the development of the Virtual Cell. Those decisions were guided by a need to find an overall theme; the practicalities of deployment to the educational field; and other constraints that resulted from the technical decisions made during its design and implementation.

Theme

One of the difficulties in deciding on a theme and presentation for the Virtual Cell game was the difference in physical scale between the everyday world of the player and the biological processes under consideration. In homage to classic science fiction, the device of a miniaturized submarine was settled upon as the mechanism by which players would travel between the game regions and perform their investigations and activities.

Games developed by WWWIC have traditionally contained a back-story that helps to provide the player with an authentic motivation for their actions. In the Virtual Cell, that motivation is conveyed by a lab assistant and the background material for each module. This lab assistant, a figure referred to as the Lab Guy, serves as the primary taskmaster of the game.

The Constraints of Practicality

The Virtual Cell system is a client-server desktop immersive virtual environment. The environment was envisioned as a place where players could work through laboratory and other problems in biology in order to learn principles of biology and general science. Rather than target the greater complexities that were possible in a dedicated

Figure 2. Sample Additional Information Sources Available in the Game

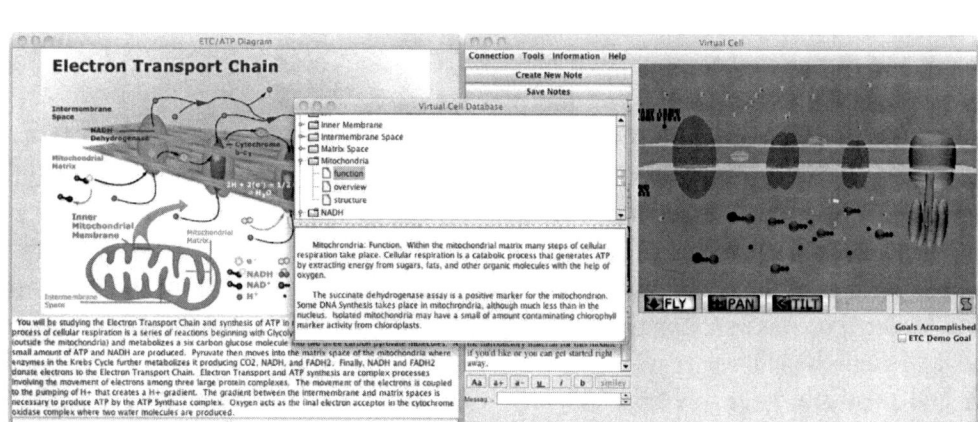

virtual reality environment, the project aimed for the desktop 3D environment. In order to maximize the usefulness and impact of the project, it was important that the software fit into the constraints of practicality. One of those constraints was, naturally, the limitation imposed by available funding, but there was a more important consideration. The most important constraint was that an educational environment for which no student or school district could be expected to afford the hardware costs can be considered practical. In other words, software requirements needed to remain low so the software would be usable in as many situations as possible.

Design

The Virtual Cell system is intended to provide a collection of virtual environments to its users. In order to be fully useful, these environments must be interactive and persistent. Additionally, these environments must be replicable in a controlled manner to prevent overcrowding without negating persistence. Naturally, the environments must also be shared among the users as appropriate. To support the educational goals of the project, a central storage was required in order to provide data persistence.

To be useful in educational settings, the system had to work on consumer-level or general computer cluster level hardware. At best, the desktop virtual environment could expected to be a window on the computer screen with a mouse and keyboard, and that any other input devices could only be pined for. One side effect of this restriction was that in addition to fitting into the educational setting, it was expected that it could also be experienced by a much larger audience: anyone who had access to a personal computer.

Educational settings of the region where and the era when this program was developed imposed an additional restrictions on the system—limited bandwidth and relatively large latencies. As a result, the communications protocols were biased towards low bandwidth and preferred reliable point-to-point communication to best effort broadcasts.

In order to support the mixed platforms common in educational environments, yet still try to minimize unnecessary development costs, Java was selected for the client program platform. Due to the security restrictions in unsigned Java applets, the network architecture is restricted to a strictly wheel and spoke client-server model.

VRML 2.0 was selected to display the 3D content of the environments. The primary factors in this decision were flexibility and animation support; open standards and portability; and the degree of support for dynamic content creation and animation. As an open standard, VRML viewers either existed or were under development for the various platforms expected in the educational environment. The animation and dynamic content support provided by the event model in VRML implied that one could build each user's view of the 3D environment using just VRML and that less effort would be required than for other graphics platforms.

Since there was a need for a central information store, a client-server model for the system was chosen. At the time that the project was starting, several different multi-user, text-based environment servers had been developed and were in use, and the most promising candidate was LambdaMOO.

THE ORIGINAL IMPLEMENTATION: LambdaMOO

The original implementation of Virtual Cell was created in the late 1990's by building a graphical user interface onto a MOO ("MUD, Object-Oriented", where MUD stands for "Multi-User Domain"). MUD's are typically text-based electronic meeting places where players build societies and fantasy environments, and interact with each other (Curtis, 1992). Technically, a MUD is a multi-user database and messaging system. The foundational components, though, support a basic spatial metaphor for navigating the database and communicating with other players. The root object classes of the database (in addition to the most generic root 'object' class) are 'player' (representing the user), 'container' (an object that can hold other objects), 'room' (an object that can hold players) and 'exits' (an object that lets players move from one room to another). A MUD supports the object management and inter-player messaging that is required for multi-player games, and also provides a programming language for customizing the MUD with new objects (such as vehicles), objects with independent behaviors (such as non-player characters in the game), and an environment with complex properties (for example, a simulated biological process).

At that time, the most flexible servers were LambdaMOO and LPMud. Both of these servers offered simple persistent, non-relational object databases featuring inheritance and command interpretation. These two servers were roughly equal in utility, but project members had more experience with the LambdaMOO server, and there existed a greater academic acceptance of LambdaMOO over the more game-associated LPMud family of servers. Thus, the LambdaMOO multi-user environment server was chosen to host the persistent environment and user data, to act as the central communication point for the environment, and to perform processing for any simulation associated with the environment.

In addition to the LambdaMOO server, an HTTP server was used to supply static assets, such as graphics and model information, to the client programs. It was decided at the time that in cases of dire resort, much of the information from that server could be distributed on physical media to fulfill low bandwidth requirements.

The primary goal when designing the scene loading algorithm for the Virtual Cell was to produce an incremental algorithm which would enable the server to know as little as possible about the state of any given client. An additional goal when the algorithm was being designed was the ability to support multiple object formats and mechanisms. In other words, if possible either a scene graph editing client or mirroring server should be able to use the same scene loading interface.

In order to implement the incremental loading algorithm, objects on the client-side are composed of three main components. The first component is the NodeStub and that component handles all of the common basic functionalities for an abject—being located in scene, being moved around in a scene, and so on. When the client receives the definition and parameters of an object from the server, the client constructs the local implementation object, a subclass of edu.nodak.ndsu.games.vcell.thing. Thing, and associates that local implementation with the NodeStub. The local implementation interprets the parameters for itself, requests the loading of the appropriate geometry files, and the creation of any necessary GUI elements.

It is quite common that when one object is loaded, the properties of that object will reference one or more objects that have not yet been loaded on the client. When this happens, the client creates a NodeStub for the unknown object, requests that object's representation asynchronously from the server, and arranges an optional notification for when that object's implementation is loaded.

In addition to this incremental loading scheme, the client also employs a simple scene pruning mechanism. The mechanism is simply that whenever the user, or an object recursively containing the user, has its location changed to an unknown object, the rest of the scene is discarded. As part of the scene pruning, the client notifies the server that the client is no longer interested in the pruned objects.

Throughout all of this incremental loading and pruning, the server is tasked only with supplying the appropriate object definitions and providing updates on the objects in which the client has expressed interest, with the provision that the client's interest begins with the definition request and ends with the previously mentioned object pruning. This both allows for a graphical client to use one scene loading algorithm while allowing a replication server to make use of the same loading mechanism, and avoids requiring any special accommodations for those clients in the server code.

The scene loading mechanism also serves as the mechanism by which the client's perspective of a scene is kept up to date. When the client requests the representation of an object, implicit in that request is a request to be informed of any state changes for that object. From that point until the client notifies the server that updates are no longer required, the server notifies the client of any changes.

As development of the system progressed, server side simulations of various processes were developed, and the various bits of record keeping necessary for a game such as player history logs and goals were implemented. The interactive simulations are where the bulk of the development time for the Virtual Cell has been spent.

Time passed and development continued on the content and the infrastructure to support that content. After developing initial versions of the first three game play modules, the very late 1990's and early 2000's saw testing of the software by biology students. As students tried to use the system, flaws in the system were discovered. The most significant flaw in the system was that the animations that were displayed for the simulations were of low quality. Student reports indicated that the animations felt slow and indicated that the various elements in the animations had a tendency to load slightly later than they should, which caused details to be missed.

When the system had been first designed, the goal of the system had been to provide a mechanism by which the client would display the various scenes contained on the server. An implicit decision had been made that as long as the client eventually caught up with the server's view of the world, then various minor discrepancies were acceptable. Unfortunately, those same various minor discrepancies, which had been acceptable earlier, were now accumulating and causing the poor animation quality. The question then became how the system could be improved so that the animation segments that the simulations were generating could be stitched together to produce a better quality animation.

A series of design elaborations were proposed and implemented to change how the scenes were loaded by the client. The first attempted improvement of the protocol was the implementation of caching and animations paths, and while this elaboration improved the visual quality of the animations, it did not change the fact that the animations were somewhat slow. The animations were slow because they were being generated from simple simulations running on the server at the same speed as the animations. Past a certain speed, if there were any delays in receiving or processing updates, the client would have to skip over parts of the animation in order to keep up with the server.

The first proposal to address the problem was to run the server simulation into the future instead of performing the simulation as the animation ran. Implementation of this proposal ran into several problems. The first problem is that this introduced time dependent property values on the server, and created two conflicting notions about the state of objects on the server. The second problem with this approach is that it introduced a conflict between interactivity and animation quality. The third problem is that the record keeping for the simulations became difficult to implement in the server's scripting language.

The second proposal to address the problem was to implement the simulations on the client. The client would perform the calculations to determine the animation segment for each step of the simulation, queue up each of those segments, and as the segments were played back, stitch them together and apply any necessary adjustments. This proposal was more successful than the original proposal for a variety of reasons: First, it turned out that no real adjustment of the animation segments was necessary. The two main factors in causing the original poor animation quality turned out to be variability in the arrival of the updates, and variability in the time required to process the updates. The main factor in the variability of processing time was the time required to initialize new scene elements, and frequently those delays would mean that an element was supposed to start moving about in the scene before it had been initialized. That delay could be addressed by the client by beginning the initialization of each scene element while the simulation was being calculated. Second, it was simply easier to keep track of the additional state information in Java on the client side than to track that additional state information on the server. Third, the client simply side steps the problem of conflicting object states since it only has to maintain its own view of the simulation elements.

Implementing the client-side simulations was not the end of the development work being done on the Virtual Cell system. As mentioned earlier, one of the difficulties encountered while trying to improve the animation quality was that there were several limitations in the server's scripting language. An alternative to LambdaMOO was being developed which appeared to address many of the limitations of that server and that new system will be described after describing the modules that have been developed to date.

VIRTUAL CELL SYSTEM COMPONENTS

The original Virtual Cell system consisted of little more than the LambdaMOO server which maintained the system's state, the individual client programs, and a web server to host static resource files. As a research project in addition to an educational software project, it was interesting to discover what additional system elements were necessary to support the development and use of the virtual environment. The two most important additional components which were needed by the system ended up being a well developed user registration system, and a mechanism for accessing the system state over the web.

Web Access to System State

One of the fundamental issues when developing on a centrally located, networked, persistent object store like the LambdaMOO server is that the default interaction with the state of an object is indirect, unlike development of a single user application where the files representing persistent object state would be directly accessible. As the World Wide Web became popular, various simple HTTP servers were implemented as part of the LambdaMOO object libraries and those servers provided another mechanism for exposing object state.

While developing the Virtual Cell system, one of our common desires was to have access to the live system information in a variety of ways. Whether the information is to be used for testing and debugging new modules in the system, for analyzing the performance of the system, or simply to keep track of students playing through the modules, there is almost always a desire for more access to the information in the system. With the development of the World Wide Web, one of the more convenient mechanisms for accessing that information was through a web browser.

The LambdaMOO server uses a byte-code interpreter with enforced cooperative task switching to execute the code associated with the objects in its object store. While this does not by itself preclude the implementation of a robust, high performance web server and associated computer-generated imagery (CGI) and dynamic page generation system, it does mean that any attempt at constructing such a system will be faced with a high probability of remaining a niche project not far removed from proof of concept levels.

LambdaMOO Virtual Cell's External Registration System

Naturally, any persistent system that moves past the initial development stage to the point where actual players are using the system ends up with a method for players to create new accounts and for the system administrators to maintain those accounts.

The LambdaMOO Virtual Cell system has two components to the server: The actual LambdaMOO server hosting the environment, and an Apache-MySQL-PHP login and registration front end which handles login, administration and other requirements of the learning management system. While this arrangement was serviceable for a centrally located service on the small scale, the additional components complicated various attempts at repurposing the server for local installation.

An additional unfortunate aspect of the system is that the learning management system duplicates player and account information present in the LambdaMOO object store. The duplication of information caused issues on a few occasions when the LambdaMOO object store and the external database contained conflicting registration information during server upgrades.

PROBLEMS WITH LambdaMOO

The LambdaMOO Virtual Cell was built on the standard LambdaMOO object library and extended the basic collection of objects to support working with 3D scenes rather than rooms, and developed a few mechanisms to specify animation and object manipulation within those scenes. While the animation system fulfilled the original requirements of facilitating simple, easy animations, problems began to arise when the requirements for the animation system became more sophisticated. Instead of displaying a scene with a dozen static elements and a few moving elements, scenes were being developed with several dozen moving elements which were being dynamically created in the middle of the animation.

Another limitation of the LambdaMOO version of the Virtual Cell system is processing speed. While LambdaMOO made it easy to quickly prototype and develop the Virtual Cell, that rapid prototyping and development was enabled by a somewhat antiquated byte code interpreter and command parser.

Rapid prototyping and development also contributed in a different manner to some of the limitations of the animation system. In order to avoid excessive server load for complex scenes, the client used a simple iterative algorithm to incrementally load scenes. The advantage of the incremental algorithm was that it allowed scene elements to be added and removed easily, but it became impractical to determine when any given scene was fully loaded. This difficulty was compounded by the rapid prototyping environment because quite frequently a scene would go through several incremental versions and the development paradigm of the time was to avoid having the server calculate and maintain information about the scene if possible.

JavaMOO

The Virtual Cell project was not the first WWWIC project to use the LambdaMOO server, and over the course of several projects, the group has become knowledgeable about the limitations of that server. The JavaMOO platform was developed by WWWIC in order to address several of the weaknesses of the LambdaMOO server.

The core deficiencies that JavaMOO was intended to address were: poor performance of the LambdaMOO interpreter; lack of debugging support; and lack of support for versioning systems. From the experience porting Dollar Bay from LambdaMOO to JavaMOO (Slator, 2006), we expected that the conversion would address these deficiencies.

Performance

Central to the LambdaMOO system is a database of objects. Each of the objects in the database can have properties and methods defined on them, and objects can inherit properties and methods from other objects in a Forth-like frame based manner. The body of a method contains code written in a C-like language also called LambdaMOO which uses dynamic types but which is compiled to byte code.

The object methods are executed in response to various events, and the most common event to trigger a method execution is the receipt of input from a connected user. The important features of method execution are: the methods are executed by a single interpreter; the interpreter uses co-operative multitasking to allow multiple tasks to operate simultaneously; the interpreter enforces the use of cooperative multitasking by limiting the amount of time any given task can operate before yielding; and the interpreter used for this purpose is specific to LambdaMOO.

The single threaded nature of the interpreter meant that the server failed to see performance improvements when operated on multi-core or multi-processor platforms. Further, because the interpreter was single threaded, the LambdaMOO language lacks any support for explicit synchronization between methods and the introduction of synchronization to the interpreter and language would be unavoidable if the interpreter were re-written to operate tasks in parallel threads. The introduction of truer parallelism would also have likely required significant changes to the commonly supplied LambdaMOO object libraries due to the change in the core task paradigm.

The fact that the interpreter in the LambdaMOO system is used only by the LambdaMOO system has as its consequence that the pool of contributors able to contribute to its improvement is very small. Because there is not a large community to support a separate language, and because those language changes would have been necessary to take advantage of modern hardware, the Java-MOO team made the difficult choice to convert to a different language that would have greater support, Java.

Debugging

While the LambdaMOO server performs reasonably well as a persistent object library, it is one of many development environments which lack sophisticated debugging tools. In fairness, the lack of debugging tools is a result of the design decisions that were common to all of the similar MUD servers. As a network based environment in which users can trigger arbitrary scripts in an environment without sophisticated developer clients, it was unreasonable for those systems to include breakpoints and similar debugging facilities. That is not to say that the system is completely without facilities, but those facilities end up limited to manual code instrumentation and automatic logging of exceptions.

The ability to use more fully featured development environments for the JavaMOO version of the Virtual Cell was therefore a very welcome change.

Versioning and Updates

Non-trivial software systems go through a sequence of versions, and eventually a point is reached where the system as it is deployed is not the most recent system as it has been developed. For LambdaMOO, there were two significant hurdles when attempting to perform updates to a deployed system: the absence of a clear separation between accumulated data and code in the object database; and the absence of well developed tool for automatically updating and transferring objects from one database to another. Naturally, one of the causes for this problem was simply the niche nature of the LambdaMOO system and its correspondingly small development pool, but unfortunately, that simply decreases the chances of directly paying for a solution and ameliorating the problem.

Moving from the LambdaMOO frame-based object model to a model like Java's object model in which the data and code for objects is cleanly separated simplifies updates for a variety of reasons. Most importantly, there are many readily available systems for version control of Java source code and for updating the classes supplied with a Java program. This means that changes in system logic which don't impact the structure of the objects in the database becomes a trivial problem for JavaMOO when for LambdaMOO systems it was often time consuming and error prone due to the lack of tools.

Of course, moving from one version of the system to another version of the system occasionally results in unavoidable changes to the structure of objects in the system. This is unavoidable but also a situation that is common enough among other systems that well established practices could be employed for JavaMOO.

THE NEW IMPLEMENTATION IN JavaMOO

The JavaMOO Virtual Cell system is a reimplementation of the original LambdaMOO based Virtual Cell system. To meet the goals of improved system performance, ease of maintenance, and increased stability, it was natural to redesign certain elements of the system to eliminate various limitations in the original system.

As noted before, JavaMOO and LambdaMOO use different programming languages, and as a result, the system had to be rewritten in Java. This necessity only served to reinforce the desire to redesign certain elements of the original system.

Changes to Modules and Goals

In the original implementation, the sequence of modules for the game, and the sequence of activities or goals for each module, was defined as a simple list. The activities and progress of a player as the player worked through each activity was stored in a history log for that player along with a list of which goals had been completed. This decision was made in the LambdaMOO implementation because of the unusually high cost of object creation in the LambdaMOO system. There were negative consequences that resulted from these choices. The first consequence was that it was difficult to determine which history events represented state information for a goal and which history events were used for generic activity tracking. The second consequence follows from the first and is that it became difficult to support the ability to repeat a module from a fresh start.

During the reimplementation of the goal and history system for the JavaMOO system, the opportunity was seized to restructure the system to support repetition of activities. Rather than attempting to store goal state information in the history system, the new system creates working copies of the master goal objects, and ensures that the state of the working copy accurately represents the player's current progress. This approach was feasible in the new system because of the reduced secondary costs associated with object creation in the JavaMOO system compared to the LambdaMOO system.

Client-Side Simulations

Naïve Finite State Simulations

In the LambdaMOO version of Virtual Cell, a series of eight simulations of various aspects of cellular respiration and photosynthesis were implemented on the server. The actors in these simulations can be divided into 'compounds' which represented the various substrates, ions and compounds in the system; 'item sources' which created the various compounds and acted as points for the compounds to collect; and 'pumps' which both moved the compounds between item sources and optionally transformed and combined the compounds into new compounds as they moved.

Network Lag as the Enemy of Visual Quality

During the course of a simulation, one of the common operation sequences was for a compound to be added to the scene and then moved to a different position in the scene before being transformed into a new compound. The client viewed this sequence of operations as the announcement of a new object in the scene, an announcement of the new object's definition, an announcement of the movement, and an announcement of the transformation. Because of natural delays in loading the newly introduced object and setting its geometry, and combined with an attempt for the client to not fall too far behind the server's version of the world, it was not unusual for an object's animation to begin before its geometry was fully loaded.

Re-implementation of the Simulations on the Client

Client-side implementation of the simulations has several advantages over the server side implementation. First, in the client-side implementation, the various compounds are implemented as purely client-side objects and as a result, the stability of the scenes is improved. Secondly, the simulations were adjusted to generate entire simulation sequences as a collection of animation steps instead of pausing between steps to allow the renderer to catch up. Thirdly, the client-side simulations proved to be more reliable than the server side simulations. A side effect of this change to the animation generation is that the animation steps could be paused, rewound, and watched again without needing to reset the simulation and step through it again.

Figure 3. Comparison of LambdaMOO and JavaMOO Server Organization

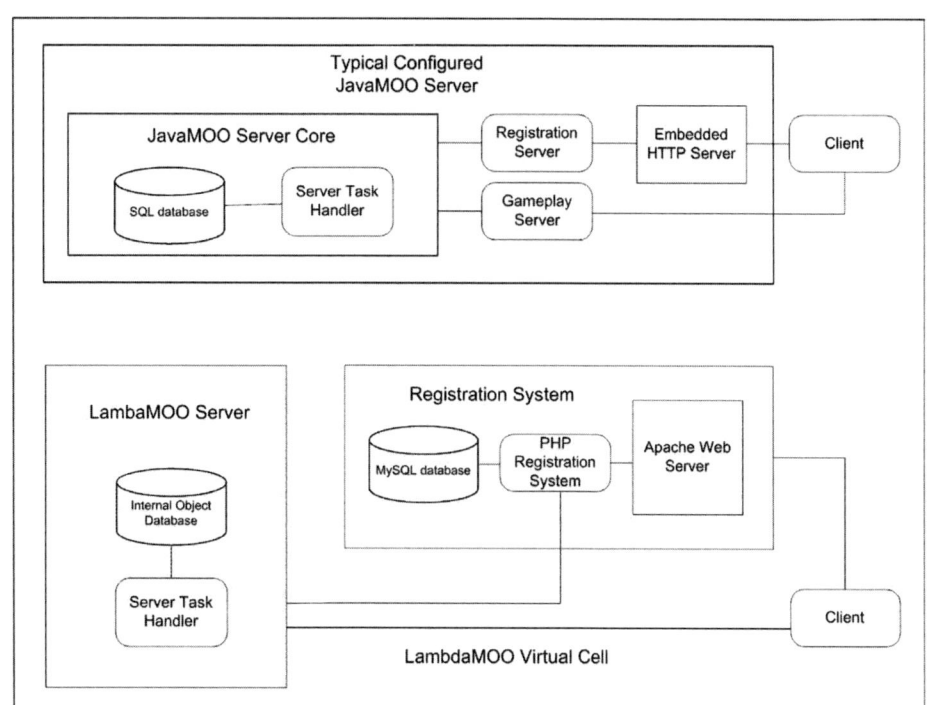

One complication of the client-side simulations is the need to place a significant amount of the simulation logic for each simulation in the client and then arrange for the client to notify the server as various steps are completed so that the state of the player's goals can be updated.

A second complication of the client-side simulations is that the state of the local simulations is not easily sharable between clients. In the current system, all of the simulations are restricted to single occupancy scenes. However, if it becomes desirable in the future to have multiple viewers of a simulation it will be necessary to implement additional logic to appoint one of the copies as the master copy and synchronize the states of the other simulations to the master copy through sharing of trigger events and synchronization of randomizer seeds.

Informing the Server about State Changes

The immediate and obvious hurdle when moving the simulations from the server to the client was the task of re-implementing the simulations in the client versions of the scene objects and providing additional infrastructure on the client to carry out the simulation loop and animation updates. A less obvious hurdle was that the goal state information still resided on the server, and so the client-side simulations would need additional instrumentation to ensure that the server would be notified when various events took place.

Flexibility vs. Complicated Scene Definitions

The first iteration of the LambdaMOO and Java-MOO Virtual Cell systems both featured a mixed object model where each persistent object in the system had a globally unique ID number. The ID was used to maintain the association between the persistent copy of the object resident on the server and the representation of that object on each of

the clients. In the first iteration, any interaction between objects in the system needed to be done by the server implementations of the objects.

In the second iteration of the system, it became expedient for the various client-side objects to communicate directly. The original purpose for this was the implementation of object definition collections, although the client-side simulation system also capitalized on this ability.

In the object definition cache scheme, it was conjectured that all of the temporary object definitions for a level could be loaded when the scene was first accessed in order to eliminate one source of delay in loading dynamically created object geometry. While the proposal to implement a definition cache object and objects that read their geometry definitions from those caches, this did necessitate adding a linking step to the scene loading algorithm.

Compared to the cache system, the client-side simulation system represented an entirely new level of work for the linking system. Instead of one object being linked in only one direction to some number of objects, the client-side simulations ended up requiring a large number of inter-object links.

Instance Factory

The various areas of the Virtual Cell game are defined by scene files, and each instantiation of a particular scene is referred to as an instance. The instance factory is responsible both for locating available existing instances when a player's activities involve traveling to a given scene and also creating new instances of a scene if none of the existing instances can accommodate the player.

LambdaMOO Version

The LambdaMOO version of Virtual Cell implements an instance factory which is either an elegant use of frames, or an atrocious hack, depending on whether it is viewed from the perspective of the implementer or the maintainer. As described earlier, LambdaMOO provides Forth-like frame based inheritance and this inheritance is used to create instances of a master scene by simply iterating over the scene and its elements creating child frames and performing a simple adjustment of the properties of those child frames to substitute references to the appropriate child frames for references to the parent frames.

In order to explain one of the problems with a long running LambdaMOO system, it is important to explain how LambdaMOO objects are referenced and recycled. At its most basic, the LambdaMOO system supports raw object creation and each newly created object will be ensured a unique integer identifier which will not be reused upon object deletion. However, the raw object creation and deletion is almost never used in practice because of the fear of identifier exhaustion. Instead, the standard object library takes advantage of the ability in LambdaMOO to change an object's inheritance and type to recycle objects that are no longer needed. Unfortunately, this leads to problems where an object can be created for use 'A', references to that object are passed around and stored in various places, and then the original object is recycled and recreated for use 'B' without invalidating the original references. This leads to an unfortunate bug where a process can find a reference to the object as it was used for 'A', see that the object appears to not have been recycled, and proceed to be apply good programming habits and recycle the object unknowingly for the second time.

This sort of double recycling became a concern in the development of the respiration and photosynthesis simulations. During the execution of each of those simulations, a comparably large number of temporary elements would be added to the scene, passed around between various complexes, removed from the scene and then recycled. Each element had to be tracked in the various lists associated with each complex, and periodically errors would cause a list to improperly retain elements

that were no longer present in the scene. Then, when the entire scene was reset, all of the lists of temporary objects would be cleaned out and all of the referenced temporary objects recycled, and that would lead intermittently to a crash in some other random scene when a temporary object unexpectedly became recycled while still in use.

JavaMOO Version

The instance factory in the JavaMOO version of the Virtual Cell differs from the LambdaMOO version in that the scene prototypes are stored in XML descriptions of the scene elements rather than cloneable objects. There were a few factors that contributed to this design change. The first was that the ability to construct scenes from external definitions provided a mechanism for authoring and changing scenes outside of the environment. The second was that replication of an existing scene in Java requires much more effort than scene replication in LambdaMOO. In addition, when the JavaMOO version of the system created a new version of the instance from the definition file, the assumption could be made that the scene definition was final and additional information about the scene could be computed to simplify the client-side object handling.

In both of these schemes, the central task consisted of gathering a collection of objects with interconnecting references stored in various data structures, extracting those objects into some intermediate format, and then reading that collection of objects into a new database while substituting references to the new objects in place of the old object. The standard LambdaMOO object database possessed a utility for this purpose, and a corresponding JavaMOO utility is simple enough to generate.

Webserver for JavaMOO Version

During the development of the JavaMOO server, it was discovered that it was completely trivial

207

to use the Apache Tomcat server in embedded mode with the JavaMOO server to expand on the equivalent functionality in the LambdaMOO HTTP servers. Most importantly, since the Apache Tomcat project had a much larger target audience, the Tomcat server provided a fully featured server being maintained and developed by other developers. In addition, as a fully featured Java-based web server, Tomcat provides support for Java Server Pages (JSP).

JavaMOO Virtual Cell's Integrated Registration System

One direct consequence of Tomcat's implementation of Java Server Pages is that the LambdaMOO Virtual Cell's external login and registration system was replaced by a much simpler JSP based login and registration system in the JavaMOO Virtual Cell. The most important consequence of this is that it eliminated the information duplication in the LambdaMOO Virtual Cell system, and it simplified deployment of the server as a single component.

OTHER IMPROVEMENTS OVER LambdaMOO

Fresh Starts vs. Lint Collections

The primary defect of the LambdaMOO system as a development environment is a tendency for the object database to collect junk and left over objects over the course of development. The integration of code from two divergent object databases frequently devolved into dumping the object definition on the one server to a text file, making manual corrections to that text file, and then uploading the modified object definitions to the new server. Frequently, additional unforeseen conflicts would then be discovered and additional time would be required to troubleshoot and patch the newly created object to make it compatible with the new host environment.

Data Types and Safety

The LambdaMOO and JavaMOO versions of Virtual Cell use different communication protocols between the client and the server to encode events. The directive and command systems for the LambdaMOO version of the system relied on the client and server agreeing on the meaning of the values in each position of the particular directives for functioning. For example, a given directive may be documented as having a specifically constructed list of values as its third argument, but only weak mechanisms were in place to enforce such a construction.

In contrast, the JavaMOO system relies on instances of the MOOEvent class for encoding both directives from the server to the client and requests from the client to the server. The system simply relies on the Java serialization mechanism to encode and decode the events.

Beyond the elimination of parameter mismatches, the change to sending and receiving objects also allows the system to avoid working around data type limitations. For example, in the LambdaMOO system, a table of property name and value pairs is typically represented as a list of those name and value pairs for various technical reasons. For JavaMOO, since both the sending and receiving party simply use the most convenient Java class or type for the data, such as a HashMap or Hashtable.

Improved Object Usage

The focus of LambdaMOO's object model was on supporting objects that would be used as a component in a scene or that would be subject to player interaction. Because of this focus, while LambdaMOO supports object oriented development and this support works well for several cases, the use of objects to record temporary information, or for general purpose data processing is not well supported. Missing features included both a notion of garbage collection and support for short object lifespans. This becomes especially problematic because LambdaMOO relies on the strategy of loading all objects into memory and expecting the operating system memory management to handle paging. JavaMOO addresses this by supporting two classes of objects. The first class of objects includes those objects that exist only during runtime operation and are not stored in the database. The second class contains the specific objects in the JavaMOO system that are stored and retrieved from the persistent object database. The two categories overlap slightly as non-persistent objects are serialized for storage when referenced by fields in persistent objects.

CHANGES IN DEPLOYMENT MODELS

The original deployment model for the Virtual Cell was simply not to have a deployment model for the server and instead operate the server from the lab room at NDSU. Users who wished to use the system were expected to visit the server's website, download and install the Cosmo Player plugin and then download and run the client program.

In the late 1990's and early 2000's, support by Cosmo Software became diminished as the company separated from its original parent company and went through a series of acquisitions that effectively ended support for the product. After searching for a more suitable renderer, the project transitioned to using Xj3D as a replacement for its VRML renderer. One positive effect of this transition was that the client program no longer required the use of a browser and could instead be used as an application.

In 2004, work began on a version of the Virtual Cell server that could be deployed in other locations. As one might expect, this effort experienced numerous issues caused by the change in system requirements including barriers caused by the licensing requirements for MySQL. The conclusion from initial trials was that it would be simpler to

install the server software on a minimal device such as a Mac Mini and distribute those configured devices than it would be to distribute installation software and instructions for the various portions of the server software.

As noted earlier, the JavaMOO Virtual Cell eliminates the need for external support software for the system. Because that external support software is the cause of most of the technical difficulties distributing the system, it would be much simpler to distribute the new server.

One unresolved issue involves the distribution of the client software in school clusters. Zero-configuration technologies are not perfect so there is typically a need to specify the server's address either during installation or when the client software runs for the first time. While this does not represent an impossible barrier, it does fall short of an ideal solution—the installation of the server software on a single machine in a computer cluster without requiring the installation of software on the rest of the machines in the cluster.

THE VIRTUAL CELL ANIMATIONS PROJECT

One of the sources of tension in the Virtual Cell project is the conflict between the production of a high quality animation of a process and the production of an interactive simulation of a process.

In the early stages of the project, illustrative animations of the processes were written in VRML using software like Cosmo Worlds and then an equivalent simulation was developed to operate on the server. As the project progressed, the project gained access to better animation software such as Autodesk (formerly Alias Wavefront) Maya.

The availability of this software to the group in 2003 was part of the impetus behind the attempts to increase the animation quality of the simulations in the system. While the Virtual Cell project has continued to work on producing interactive simulations, the Virtual Cell Animation Project has begun producing a series of non-interactive movie style videos that are being made available at http://vcell.ndsu.edu/animations/.

CONCLUSION

One might ask how big the Virtual Cell system is in terms of lines of code. There are approximately 30,000 lines of code in the standard LambdaMOO, LambdaMOOCore object database, and the source code for the LambdaMOO interpreter. The Virtual Cell LambdaMOO database contains approximately 35,000 lines of code in addition to the code present in the stock database. In comparison, the base JavaMOO system contains approximately 12,500 lines of code, and an additional approximately 11,000 lines of code were added for the Virtual Cell specific server side functions. The Virtual Cell client is an additional approximately 16,000 lines of code, but, unlike the server code, only a portion of the client code needed to be rewritten to support the new server and new animation system.

The grant that funded the conversion of the LambdaMOO Virtual Cell system to the Java-MOO system had three components relating to programming. The first component was the rewriting of the Virtual Cell object library for the JavaMOO system, the second component was the development of client-side animations for the two modules, and the third component was a software testing experiment intended to ensure that the LambdaMOO Virtual Cell and the JavaMOO Virtual Cell were equivalent systems. (El Ariss, 2010). As a result of the software conformance work, we are confident that the three primary game play modules in the JavaMOO Virtual Cell are functioning appropriately.

While the LambdaMOO server was useful in developing the Virtual Cell to initial prototype levels, as our experiences have shown, there are severe limitations to its use beyond the prototype

stages of a virtual environment. Switching over to a more modern multi-user server based on the JavaMOO system has improved the system performance, reliability, responsiveness and also reduced the complexity of server installation.

ACKNOWLEDGMENT

Part of the Virtual Cell project was supported by Grant Number R43RR024779 from the National Center for Research Resources. The content is solely the responsibility of the authors and does not necessarily represent the official views of the National Center for Research Resources or the National Institutes of Health (NIH).

The authors of this chapter would also like to acknowledge the work of the numerous students and professors who have worked on the project or participated in testing the software. Thanks to Omar El Ariss, Dr. Dianxiang Xu, and Santosh Dandey for their parts in the recent software testing project and the development of JavaMOO.

REFERENCES

Curtis, P. (1992). Mudding: Social Phenomena in Text-Based Virtual Realities. In *Proceedings of the Conference on Directions and Implications of Advanced Computing (sponsored by Computer Professionals for Social Responsibility)*. Berkeley,CA, April.

El Ariss, O., Xu, D., Dandey, S., Vender, B., Mcclean, P., & Slator, B. (2010). A Systematic Capture and Replay Strategy for Testing Complex GUI based Java Applications. In *Proceedings of the 7th International Conference on Information Technology: Next Generations*.

Slator, B. M. (1999) Intelligent Tutors in Virtual Worlds. In *Proceedings of the 8th International Conference on Intelligent Systems (ICIS-99)*. June 24-26. Denver, CO: 124-127.

Slator, B. M., & Chaput, H. (1996). Learning by Learning Roles: A Virtual Role-Playing Environment for Tutoring. In *Proceedings of the Third International Conference on Intelligent Tutoring Systems (ITS'96)*. Montréal: Springer-Verlag, June 12-14, (pp. 668-676). (Lecture Notes in Computer Science, edited by C. Frasson, G. Gauthier, A. Lesgold).

Slator, B. M., Chaput, H., Cosmano, R., Ben Dischinger, C. I., & Vender, B. (2006). A Multi-User Desktop Virtual Environment for Teaching Shop-Keeping to Children. *Virtual Reality Journal, 9*, pp. 49-56. Springer-Verlag. LambdaMOO version of Virtual Cell (thesis and/or other papers).

VRML. ISO 14772:1997. See also www.web3d.org/x3d/specifications.

KEY TERMS AND DEFINITIONS

Assay: A test or experiment to measure the biological or immunological activity or quality of a sample.

Cosmo Player: A popular VRML browser produced by the Cosmo Software division of SGI in the 1990's.

Electron Transport Chain (ETC): The structures and process associated with the synthesis of adenosine triphosphate (ATP) from adenosine diphosphate (ADP).

Lac Operon: The gene structure associated with transport and metabolism of lactose in Escherichia coli and other bacteria

LambdaMOO: A MUD developed by Pavel Curtis at Xerox Corporation.

LambdaMOOCore: The LambdaMOO core database. Sample or initial object library supplied with the LambdaMOO server.

LPMud: A MUD contemporary of LambdaMOO using a C like interpreted language and possessing less academic influence than LambdaMOO. Developed by Lars Pensjö.

MUD: Multi-User Dungeon (or sometime Dimension). A general term for text based multi-user environments.

Photosynthesis: The process of using sunlight to synthesis food.

VRML, VRML97, VRML 2.0, X3D: An open standards file format and run-time architecture to represent and communicate 3D scenes and objects currently maintained by the Web 3D Consortium.

Xj3D: Java-based open source library for rendering VRML 2.0 and X3D.

Chapter 11
Capitalizing on Immersive Persistence as an Emergent Design Concept (A Position Paper)

Shalin Hai-Jew
Kansas State University, USA

ABSTRACT

In their evolution, virtual worlds have become more persistent. Their three-dimensional (3D) objects are more easily ported and interoperable between 3D repositories and may eventually be portable between synthetic world systems. If trend-lines continue, these synthetic spaces will become more integrated into the fabric of virtual learning and research, community-building, socializing, and digital information archival. Their continuity-in-time adds fresh capabilities for learning (human actualization, long-term virtual collaborations), digital resource protection (digital artifact preservation, long-term and evolving simulations, virtual ecologies), human relationship management (customer relationship management and branding, digital governance), and information exchange and management (international exchanges, and immersive long-term 3D libraries and knowledge structures). However, this immersive persistence must be balanced against the needs of temporality, transience, and forgetting.

INTRODUCTION

Immersive 3D virtual worlds offer multisensory channels for multi-sensory experiential *being*, which may bypass the critical faculties of people and go right to their lived experience memories. The power of immersion is multiplied through live human-embodied avatar interactivity, which strengthens the experience even further.

DOI: 10.4018/978-1-61692-825-4.ch011

With interactivity, now we have the frontal lobes actively colluding in the project of believing; they are trying to solve some puzzle or talk to some character, which is not only interesting but also eats up still more of the resources that otherwise might go to the job of reminding every other structure in the brain that the whole thing is a construct. This job falls even further into the background due to a number of other features that games and only games have, such as sociality (more on that in a moment), and engagement of other senses, most especially touch ... Simply put, when a person is immersed in pleasurable game play, the mind has no motivation whatsoever to disbelieve any of the information it is receiving (Castronova, 2007, p. 29).

Adding persistence—the power of continuity—synthetic worlds now offer even more complex functions. With the lowering of the costs of re-acclimation, virtual worlds may strengthen virtual collaborative work and shared creativity. The shift has occurred from tele-immersion to tele-existence.

SYNTHETIC WORLDS NOW

Synthetic worlds and 3D spaces manifest commonly on screen-based media: desktop computers, immersive spaces, and mobile devices, with each manifestation more mobile. They may be accessed through augmented reality spaces, with multiple projector and speaker arrays creating 3D experiences, in fixed (and mobile) physical spaces. Mixed reality then builds on people's "pre-existing knowledge of the everyday" of "naïve physics," themselves, the environment, and other people (Jacob, Girouard, Hirschfield, Horn, Shaer, Solovey, & Zigelbaum, 2008, p. 201). These digital and physical installations—which mix digital analogues of material objects, totally imaginary digital objects, and real-world artifacts and spaces--may be especially effective in dealing with psychomotor, cognitive, affective, social, decision-making, and other skills. "Persuasive" 3D exer-games encourage motor and spatial activities to promote health and exercise and cardiovascular fitness (Nadler, 2008), as well as rehabilitation. There are digital experiences activated through location-sensitive mobile devices for more pervasive and available experiences (Walther, 2005).

Research and development (R&D) have enhanced the fidelity of transitions between the visual and auditory information. There's enhanced

localization of sound from 3D environments with "spatialized audio rendering" and place-based effects for immersive virtual environments (Naef, Staadt, & Gross, 2002). Physical classrooms have been set up with virtual environments that are navigable through "3D sound to enhance spatiality and immersion" (Moher, 2006, pp. 692 – 693). Aesthetic information may be sonified with socio-spatial and aesthetic information for multi-sensory communications; socio-spatial information is defined as "3D position, velocity, proximity to particular objects and boundaries) and social behaviour (i.e. the number of people, level of activity, clustering, timing of events)" (Beilharz, 2005, p. 12). The locative value of sound in 3D spaces supports those who are blind get a sense of locations of objects in such spaces (Sánchez & Sáenz, 2005). Fixed spaces may offer the consistency of "place presence" with "realistic context, natural engagement, (and) scaffolding" (Sutcliffe & Cault, 2004, as cited in Steed, 2009, p. 19).

There are virtual experiences enhanced by live digital data feeds, which capture information from the world. Innovations in this area include wearable computing and portable devices for interacting with virtual spaces. Cameras are used to read human gestures as inputs for less device-intensive and more human-natural ways to communicate—with 3D spatial gesture as interaction (Payne, Keir, Elgoyhen, McLundie, Naef, Horner, & Anderson, 2006). Human facial expressions and apparent emotions may also be captureable and put into play in interactions with artificial intelligence robots for more high fidelity interactions. There are ideas for nonverbal dictionaries to help read others' nonverbal body langauge via cameras or avatars, building on facial expression dictionaries (Ammar, Alimi, Neji, & Gouardères, 2004, n.p.). The move towards transparent interfaces lowers the awareness of the mediation of the virtual experience and the reality of the construct.

Haptic or touch channels have expanded for a fuller sense of reality and fidelity, to encourage more hands-on active learning, and support "more complex understandings" (Jones, Minogue, Tretter, Negishi, & Taylor, 2005, p. 112). The affordances of virtual immersiveness have broadened, with fewer constraints. Less of a reliance on screens and the use of real spaces for the "screened" imagery highlight this shift.

BEYOND PRIMITIVES: THE BACKGROUND

The persistence of virtuality may seem like an oxymoron. After all, virtuality is about transience, ephemeral experiences, and the adaptive flexibility that stems from the ability to create and project visions and sounds that coalesce into various experiences. Virtuality is ever-changing and full of surprises. The lower costs of server space and increasing carrying capacities of the Internet, some shared 3D and immersive space standards (such as those enabling interoperability and portability of 3D objects between some differing systems; the labeling of digital objects with persistent identifiers), shared understandings (of object granularity, of object functions, of descriptors), and growing interest by the mainsteam are leading to the immersive persistence of some virtual spaces.

A continuous virtual space or element does not imply *stasis*. The virtual spaces will change their look-and-feel and functions; digital objects will evolve and change. The human-embodied avatars will change. The expressiveness of the avatars will continue to evolve. The long-term momentum of communities of practice will intensify and subside (in a kind of punctuated equilibrium), and the stated and unstated goals of various groups will also evolve. "Hot groups" may spark and offer an intense creative run and fast burn out and team dissolution (Lipman-Blumen & Leavitt, 1999). Or there may be intermittent collaborative episodes. Persistent immersive spaces will still be highly transitory and flexible ones. To engage users, simulation spaces need to raise the hedonic

quality by raising curiosity; stimulating users; conveying "something positive about the user to other people"; evoking positive memories; being attractive, and offering desirable consequences (Burmester & Dufner, 2006, pp. 218 – 219). Building the hedonic quality of virtual spaces must encourage long-term interest to continually engage users. Immersive persistence though will allow for the protections of various types of 3D information and their "future-proofing" over time.

Interestingly enough, various players of games situated in immersive synthetic worlds have pushed for the recognition of the rights of avatars (Raph Koster) and pushed for fairer policies and governance (Castronova, 2007), more efficient technologies, economics infrastructures, digital property rights and enforcement, and virtual land zoning. Such users have advocated expanding the boundaries of a game to reify the virtual worlds.

Synthetic worlds have become more present and continous spaces. With this progress, these spaces have the potential to become a more stable part of virtual learning and research, community-building, socializing, and digital information archival. Their persistence makes virtuality more tangible and more aligned with real-world existence. Their continuity-in-time adds fresh capabilities for *learning and research* (human actualization, long-term virtual collaborations), *digital resource protection* (digital artifact preservation, long-term and evolving simulations, virtual ecologies), *human relationship management* (customer relationship management and branding, digital governance), and *information exchange and management* (international exchanges, and immersive long-term 3D libraries and knowledge structures).

However, this immersive persistence must be balanced against the needs of temporality, transience, forgetting, and obsolescence. This chapter addresses this necessary balance of persistence and obsolescence for immersive spaces. Forgetting is part of "human evolution" and is necessary for "healing" (Kohno, 2009, as cited in

DeWeerdt, 2009, p. 20); selective forgetting may aid fresh discoveries and new conceptualizations in a domain field.

Design Implications of Persistence: Conceptualizing immersive persistence has implications for the design of synthetic worlds; it has implications for the formulation of groups around shared long-term endeavors; it has implications for long-term 3D libraries and data structures.

Immersive Persistence

"Dreams feel real while we're in them. It's only when we wake up that we realize something was actually strange." -- Cobb, from Inception (2010)

Immersive persistence may be conceptualized in a multi-faceted way. At its most basic, the "immersive persistence" refers to the stability of the 3D virtual spaces over time for human use. To achieve persistence, though, various features must also be present. Table 1, "Immersive Factors and the Manifestation of Persistence," highlights how the immersive experience, 3D digital artifacts, human interactivity, the digital environment and ecology, simulation, and mixed physical elements may manifest in persistent time.

What is immersive persistence? "Immersive persistence" describes synthetic worlds, immersive environments, games, and 3D content repositories that last over time, often into projected perpetuity. Practically, this would enable the creation of digital contents to critical masses. They may create objects and practice inheritance over time—with newer generations receiving, using, and evolving the digital artifacts. Higher investments may be made to build simulations and immersive ecologies because these may be protected with longer time horizons; the work will

Table 1. Immersive Factors and the Manifestation of Persistence

Immersive Factor	Persistence
Immersive Experience	Persistence would suggest that the immersive experience would be selectively repeatable and reproducible. The underlying design of that experience would be editable and revisable. The experience itself should be recordable for replay and analysis.
3D Digital Artifacts	A persistent space would allow for the building, searching, finding, analysis, and uses of 3D digital artifacts, which are portable between digital systems and archival spaces. It should enable long-term preservationist endeavors.
Human Interactivity	Immersive persistence in terms of human interactivity would be wide-scale enabled, which means many around the world may participate simultaneously. This interactivity would be recordable and replayable. People's messages and contributions would be trackable.
Digital Environment and Ecology	An immersive environment and ecology that is persistent should be stable and accessible over time. It should offer full functionality. It should be flexible in interacting with other systems—and integrate information streams that go beyond 3D such as for audio or live information feeds from the real world. A persistent environment must evolve and adapt to changing human needs and to new technologies. This environment needs to be secure and free from hacks and other abuses of the shared and private spaces.
Simulation	Persistent simulations need to be accurate to the real-world object or system which is emulated. It must be replayable. It must be editable to incorporate new functions. It also should be assessable in terms of human use or performance within that simulation.
Mixed Physical	Mixed physical immersive spaces must be "smart" in the human interactions. These must be flexible and repurposable for new types of learning. These must be resilient. There should be little to no lag between the real and the digital. There must also be sufficient suspension of disbelief in the designed space but with sufficient differentiation for true analytical learning.

not be throwaway; rather, obsolescence may be staved off for a longer time span.

In interactive human-embodied spaces, this persistence would allow for the building of relationships, reputation management, and institutional memory—over time. Teams could co-develop in various developmental steps over much longer time horizons than the typical short-term project or brief learning event. They may "baseline" understandings and individual- and group- personalities and build on the strengths of this familiarity and built-trust; the members do not have to be re-socialized into the space, even though the turnover and churn of various participants will require constant adaptivity and shared leadership.

The different trajectories of those accessing a community of practice may vary. Wenger (1999) identifies five trajectories:

peripheral trajectories (which provide community access but never lead to full membership), inbound trajectories (which move from peripheral participation to identification with the community), insider trajectories (the ongoing renegotiation of identity within a community), boundary trajectories (involving participation in more than one community, which may lead to links being established or practices shared) and outbound trajectories (which involve leaving one identity behind in order to take up another) (as cited in Oliver & Carr, 2009, p. 448).

Projects may evolve with more complex, component parts—with greater task and sub-task differentation. Prior virtual experiences may be re-experienced at a later date—for entertainment, for sentimentality, for review and re-learning, and skills enhancement. Unpredictable large-scale effects may be possible, building to complexity. M. Mitchell (2009) defines a complex system as one in which

large networks of components with no central control and simple rules of operation give rise to complex collective behavior, sophisticated information processing, and adaptation via learning or evolution (p. 15).

Some virtual spaces are sunseted once human interest in the space wanes. Competitor spaces and entertainments may supplant current spaces. The life spans of virtual communities of practice end once the shared goals of the community no longer offer value to its various members (Wenger, 1998). A. Iriberri and G. Leroy (2009) conceptualize a virtual community model that moves from inception to creation to growth to maturity…and eventually to death when sustainability is no longer possible. Termination conditions could involve "if they were concerned about their identity being known, if contributions were unorganized, or if content was undersupplied" (Iriberri, 2005, as cited in Iriberri & Leroy, 2009, pp. 11:24 – 11:25). Other virtual communities fall into decline once a funding stream no longer supports the endeavor. The possibility of more persistent destination sites and resources as in the real world affords some powerful functionalities in terms of trust and also investments in immersions. Table 2, "Some Affordances of Immersive Persistence," illuminates some of the human benefits of immersive persistence.

Anticipated Barriers to Immersive Persistence

Virtual persistence has been achieved in some collections and some synthetic worlds (particularly gaming and social ones). These achievements have not occurred without much investment in technologies, costs, and participation by the larger publics.

Virtual worlds have existed since the early 1980s and have attracted some 300 million registered users (Hays, 2008, as cited in Warburton, 2009), but it's been several decades later that

Table 2. Some affordances of immersive persistence some affordances of immersive persistence

1. Learning and Research	Human actualization, long-term virtual collaborations, longitudinal information
2. Digital Resource Protection	Digital artifact preservation, long-term and evolving simulations, virtual ecologies
3. Human Relationship Management	Customer relationship management and branding, digital governance
4. Information Exchange and Management	International exchanges, immersive long-term 3D libraries and knowledge structures

these have become more widely integrated into professional training and higher education learning. For many, it's still unclear whether immersive learning will spark interest in the corporate sector (Harris, 2009, p. 43).

While some have observed hesitancy, others suggest a mass exodus to immersive spaces is likely within a generation. One economist suggests a "continuous migration" between the real and the virtual (Castronova, 2007) and suggests that people may prefer to stay in the virtual and emerge only to maintain their physical bodies. Many virtual world spaces have populations that exceed "five million inhabitants," and the rewards systems are important components of such spaces (Johnson & Levine, 2008, pp. 166 – 167).

Technology diffusion and public acceptance barriers have arisen based on cultural factors, which may also affect whether the uses of persistent immersive spaces broaden to larger publics. The lack of insitutional supports may limit participation. The high learning curve and time investment needed to get started in virtual worlds are also large barriers (Warburton, 2009). People's mental models of immersive spaces as transitory may also require some changes in expectations. A disjuncture has been observed between the learning that formal education recognizes and the types of learning in games (McFarlane, et al., 2002, p. 16, as cited in Oliver & Carr, 2009, p. 445); this barrier will also need to be overcome, with changes in both academia and game and simulation design.

With a third of leisure time for adults in 16 industrialized nations spent online (with the range at 30 – 40%) (Thomas, 2009, p. 575), the potentiality of online immersive engagements is likely. Highly connected students in the present age both through virtual worlds and augmenting Web 2.0 technologies (Harris & Rea, 2009) may define new generations of interactivity based on their own needs and mediated preferences. Bradshaw (2006) observes immersive multi-user virtual environments like *Second Life* as offering "endless possibilities for experimentations (e.g. experimentations in physical, social and cultural issues), and simulating an infinite array of social and physical situations for research and learning" (as cited in Wang & Braman, 2009, p. 236).

LEARNING AND RESEARCH

Learning and research are both about acquiring new knowledge, new to individual learners and new to the community of humans. Immersive spaces have been used to create rich "situated learning" opportunities with interactive discovery-learning and personal study environments, based on participant imagination and responses to engineered enviornments, and live human-embodied avatar interactions. Many common everyday educational interactions and practices use virtual learning environments (Jackson & Fagan, 2000).

Learners practice interview skills and bedside manner in medical simulations, for example. Or they practice foreign language skills. They work with machine simulations through interfaces that mimic real-world machines and systems. The design of simulations and modeling has offered a thin digital mirror to the real world, with immediate reflections of user actions, real-world topography, and physics (Smart, Cascio, & Paffendof, 2007). Learners practice medical screening and diagnosis; analysis, and complex decision-making. Real-time natural phenomena—from weather systems to artificial life forms (that interact and evolve) in ecologies—are depicted virtually. This mirror, which varies with different levels of fidelity, may be accessed singly or in groups.

Immersive spaces have been used for foreign language learning and practice; they have been used for immersing in different cultural milieu and historical periods; they are used as stages for digital acting via human-embodied avatars; they are used for simulations in human-hostile places—such as undersea environments, war zones, moonscapes, deep space, and other environments. Co-learners share storytelling (deHaan & Diamond, 2007); they role-play different personages in different scenarios.

Immersive learning is enhanced by the access to various 3D collections of spatialized information—less formal contents such as eportfolio work, amateur collections, and more formal curated collections of 3D digital objects (some born-digital and some collected as part of preservation efforts from the real world). Collections of audio, video, music, multimedia, simulations, and virtual ecologies are also distributed in immersive spaces. Live information channels are also fed into immersive environments—from media entities, content providers, and site sponsors.

The learning ranges from the informal to the formal. Informal learning stems from interest-based virtual groups that meet around shared domain-based interests and activities. Formal learning involves employer-sponsored meetings and trainings, as well as higher-education learning.

Human Actualization

When "cyberspace" first came to the fore in the late 1990s, a number of writers addressed the potential power of taking on different identities and roles through social experimentation (Turkle, 1998). With the greater development of human-embodied avatars and their ability to express humanity through more complex channels and the richness of human-to-human mediated interactions, this capability for human exploration has become more enriched. This has also become more international and global—with people forming relationships through their avatars interacting with others from different countries and cultural milieus and generations.

The concept of human actualization is a central one in human development. In Maslow's classic "hierarchy of needs," once people achieve physiological, safety, love / belonging and esteem needs, they may begin to build on their self-actualization—described as "morality, creativity, spontaneity, problem solving, lack of prejudice, and acceptance of facts" based on one interpretation of Maslow's pyramid (Simons, Irwin, & Drinnien, 1987, n.p.).

People may experiment with different expressions of the self in cyberspace (Turkle, 1998), and identity formation in virtual worlds (Junglas, Johnson, Steel, Abraham, & Loughlin, 2007). Immersive spaces may enhance human actualization with the presentation of various types of morality and with idealized societies co-created by people, with possible spillover into real governance and policy-making (Castronova, 2007). People may experiment with different points-of-view for multiple interpretations. They may reach across languages and cultures experientially. They may learn and build skills. They may build long-term relationships and "friending" virtually and in-the-real through virtual worlds.

Long-term Virtual Collaborations

Human interactivity in immersions involves active engagement with others in shared and complementary endeavors (Johnson, 2008). These spaces offer high connectivity through the synchronous and asynchronous expressions of self and the awarenesses of others. Immersive spaces strengthen social presence or the "salience" of the other persons in the interactions (Edirisingha, Nie, Pluciennik, & Young, 2009). Persistent immersive spaces provide rich functions: voice and text communications; avatar expressiveness; the ability to design and deploy 3D objects, including with limited scripted behaviors; image capture; record-keeping; and avatar-behavior surveillance and recording.

Work procedures may be built into these worlds, such as research processes, digital object building, and manufacturing design. Short-term collaborations have occurred around classes, conferences, events, presentations, art shows and openings, product roll-outs, historical simulations, concerts, and virtual plays. Longer-term collaborations may involve development work: co-created art, dance choreography, co-research, curating of a show, and learning endeavors (language practices, cultural immersions). These collaborations may be ad hoc ones, or they may be formal and planned. Long-term social networks may arise out of shared interests—like gaming or politics or technologies—with the collaborators interacting and sharing resources in virtual worlds as virtual work- and social- spaces. Immersive persistence may complement face-to-face and hybrid collaborations. Persistent spaces do not have to be stand-alone endeavors.

Longitudinal Information

Longitudinal information may be collected regarding the behaviors and communications of people in virtual spaces. Their individual and group trackability may offer more of a sense of reputation as well as "institutional memory" of a space—and the rich contributions by its various members. This extended information may augment personalization of services for the respective users and may surface ad hoc virtual communities to exploit for knowledge development (Alani, Dasmahapatra, O'Hara, & Shadbolt, 2003). Another powerful angle may be the use of aggregate interaction information to identify "hidden" patterns in human uses of a virtual space.

DIGITAL RESOURCE PROTECTION

Digital Artifact Preservation

The ability to archive 3D artifacts, object collections, environments, and human-embodied avatar identities is a critical aspect of virtual immersion. Research and new learning often occurs around collaborations around information, and the availability of 3D artifacts (such as preservationist endeavors around archaeological finds) may enhance the progress of a number of fields. Artifacts also need to be portable and transferable between various virtual worlds and 3D data repositories and websites, for greatest usability. While such contents may transfer easily, the metadata that follows each artifact is also important—in terms of the context of the image capture or creation, the ownership, the provenance, and other relevant details. Curator commentary on preservationist visuals would offer rich details, for example. Digital artifacts may also be used for object-based learning (Topp & Din, 2005).

Long-Term and Evolving Simulations

Simulations may be one-offs, created and scripted and then deployed. Simple laboratory experimentation is one example—to demonstrate different chemical interactions or to allow the simulated dissection of a digital frog or cat.

Or simulations may be evolving and co-created by the participants within the simulation. These may depict particular scenarios, time periods, power relationships, and emergency responses. Persistence may enhance the richness of sequential simulations that depict various phases of an event or which are complex and involve human decision-making and inputs (including live sensor data)—such as for environmental and ecological simulations.

Virtual Ecologies

Virtual ecologies and environments may also be preserved in time. Of particular note are those that build on biologically-inspired realities such as artificial life (a-life) forms existing in complex landscapes and interacting and co-evolving with other life forms.

HUMAN RELATIONSHIP MANAGEMENT

Customer Relationship Management and Branding

Many companies and organizations use immersive spaces for customer-relations management and branding / brand loyalty. They conduct product roll-outs online. They create AI-driven trade characters to interact with potential customers and customers. They create immersive games to show the family friendliness of the company. Many companies also use immersive spaces to deliver services, such as information exchange and intercommunications with customer service representatives.

Digital Governance

Various governments, particularly democratic ones, have an important duty to reach out to their citizens with information, services, and the solicitation of public feedback and commentary. Immersive spaces are used to share "citizen science" information about the weather and ocean health, for example. Other spaces are focused aroudn particular issues, policies, and proposed legislation. Some sites offer simulations of

epidemics as a warning and to change behaviors. Public officials and their representatives may hold press conferences online to highlight technology and other issues.

INFORMATION EXCHANGE AND MANAGEMENT

International Exchanges

Many of the challenges facing people today cannot be addressed in a unilateral way; rather, the coordinated actions of many around the world are needed to address issues of environmental protection, peaceful co-existence, collaborations around research, and public health. Collaborative projects between students of various fields—whether political science, business, art, military science, writing, and foreign language learning—have proliferated in virtual online spaces.

Immersive Long-term 3D Libraries Knowledge Structures

3D involves spatialized information. This involves geographic information, digital captures of real-world artifacts (like artworks and archaeological objects), fantasy creature modeling, and other types of visual information. Virtual machines may be archived with their internal scripted behaviors.

As more and more 3D visuals are collected, it will be more possible to build collections for different repositories. A 3D "green" environmental library to enhance people's choices and options for environmentally sound decision-making (Barack, 2009). Certainly, many of the creations of today will be archived in historical repositories of 3D artifacts of this age. Each new iteration of technology will add more information layers, closer fidelity of textures and aspects of the objects, and greater metadata richness.

More importantly, knowledge structures like ontologies and taxonomies may be created that show relationships between spatialized information.

FUTURE RESEARCH ANGLES AND USES OF IMMERSIVE PERSISTENCE

Plenty of research has been ongoing to align virtual immersive spaces with natural perceptions, behaviors, and interactions. Avatar gazes have been modified for more reality, and autonomic bodily functions have been coded into human-embodied and non-player-character avatars. In an attentional economy and with limits to human stamina in virtual spaces, 3D spaces may be partially immersive and may draw on a percentage of human cognitive, attentional channels. Much research on different learning applications of immersive applications would enhance the field, with user-based research both *in situ* and *in vitro*.

In the same way that a young man was induced to live isolated in his home and only interact with the world through the WWW for a year (as a marketing ploy), it's possible that individuals may be induced to live semi-virtually and continuously in a persistent virtual space for a period of extended time to study effects, modify virtual spaces, and enhance the value of long-term immersions. Long-term immersion in virtual games has not been particularly healthy or salutary, and reports of human addictions to virtual experiences, spaces, and avatars (Hai-Jew, 2009) have been raised in the research literature.

More research on how people handle differentiating the virtual and the real would enhance the field, to build on the neuroscience and human cognition research. Long-term immersive research projects may be explored to probe ways to promote leadership, enhance creativity, and strengthen immersive collaborations.

CONCLUSION

Immersive persistence really is a kind of pause in the head-long push for new and better forms of virtual 3D interactivity and gameplay and enagement; persistence will not be perpetuity necessarily. Persistence is a kind of short protected space for learning and work and sociability even as progress outpaces the pause. If virtual reality is a kind of individual consciousness (Steuer, 1992, as cited in deHaan & Diamond, 2007, p. 39) instead of any technology, then maybe immersive persistence is also something that involves human perception and conceptualization.

The realization of the persistence of these immersive technologies and resources may encourage content creators to allocate more time and creative resources to design, build, and script valuable digital contents.

This may enhance conceptualization of a longer term virtual life cycle—of human identities, with individuals trackable through different immersive environmental and the resulting longitudinal life tracks and the profiling of long-term behaviors (Andrejevic, 2007), which have been described for decades in various fictional and nonfictional writing.

The creation of persistence technologically is non-trivial given the many layers of dependencies that need to remain even as the "slow fires" of time burn at digital artifacts, authoring tools, and systems. Harnessing the power that comes with longer time horizons will require serious collaborative conceptualizations and shared hard work—to build "a forever kind of thing".

ACKNOWLEDGMENT

In the real, it takes something elusive and undefinable to be able to build persistence over time. For those who've made the long haul—Fidelius, Alan, Kristin, Emily, and Connie—thank you. For those along the path who've made a difference, I am grateful, too. For R. Max, always.

REFERENCES

Alani, H., Dasmahapatra, S., O'Hara, K., & Shadbolt, N. (2003). Intelligent information processing: Identifying communities of practice through ontology network analysis. *IEEE Intelligent Systems*, 18–25. doi:10.1109/MIS.2003.1193653

Ammar, M. B., Alimi, A. M., Neji, M., & Gouardères, G. (2004). Agent-based collaborative affective e-learning system. In *the proceedings of the First International Conference on Immersive Telecommunications* (n.p.). Bussolengo, Verona, Italy.

Andrejevic, M. (2007). *iSpy: Surveillance and Power in the Interactive Era.* Lawrence: University Press of Kansas.

Barack, L. (2009). Green libraries grow in SL: Eco-friendly Emerald City launches in Second Life. *School Library Journal*, *55*(1), 12–13.

Beilharz, K. (2005). *Gesture-controlled interaction with aesthetic information sonification. In the proceedings of the Second Australasian Conference on Interactive Entertainment* (pp. 11 – 18). Sydney, Australia. ACM.

Burmester, M., & Dufner, A. (2006). Designing the stimulation aspect of hedonic quality—An exploratory study . In Pivec, M. (Ed.), *Affective and Emotional Aspects of Human-Computer Interaction: Game-Based and Innovative Learning Approaches* (pp. 217–233). Amsterdam: Ios Press.

Castronova, E. (2007). *Exodus to the Virtual World: How Online Fun is Changing Reality.* New York: Palgrave Macmillan.

deHaan, J., & Diamond, J. (2007). The experience of telepresence with a foreign language video game and video. In *the proceedings of the Sandbox Symposium 2007* (pp. 39 – 46). San Diego, CA: Association of Computing Machinery.

DeWeerdt, S. (2009). A welcome disappearing act. *Columns: The University of Washington Alumni Magazine.* (pp. 20 – 21).

Edirisingha, P., Nie, M., Pluciennik, M., & Young, R. (2009). Socialisation for learning at a distance in a 3-D multi-user virtual environment. *British Journal of Educational Technology, 40(*3), 458 – 479. doi:10.1 111/j.1467-853 5.2009.00962.x

Hai-Jew, S. (2009). Exploring the immersive parasocial: Is it *you* or the thought of you? *Journal of Online Learning and Teaching, 5*(2). MERLOT.

Harris, A. L., & Rea, A. (2009). Web 2.0 and virtual world technologies: A growing impact on IS education. *Journal of Information Systems Education, 20*(2), 137 – 144. Retrieved Nov. 22, 2009, from http://www.jise.appstate.edu/Issues/20/V20N2P137-abs.pdf.

Harris, P. D. (2009). Immersive learning seeks a foothold. *Training & Development*, 40–45.

Iriberri, A. & Leroy, G. (2009). A life-cycle perspective on online community success. *ACM Computing Surveys, 41*(2), 11:1 – 11:29.

Jackson, R. L., & Fagan, E. (2000). Collaboration and learning within immersive virtual reality. In the *proceedings of the CVE 2000: The Third International Conference on Collaborative Virtual Environments* (pp. 83 – 92). San Francisco: Association of Computing Machinery.

Jacob, R. J. K., Girouard, A., Hirschfield, L. M., Horn, M. S., Shaer, O., Solovey, E. T., & Zigelbaum, J. (2008). Reality-based interaction: A framework for post-WIMP interfaces. *In the proceedings of the CHI 2008: ACM Special Interest Group in Computer Human Interface* (pp. 201 – 210). Florence, Italy.

Johnson, K. (2008). *Lost Cause, an interactive film project. MM '08: ACM Multimedia* (pp. 569–578). Vancouver, British Columbia, Canada: Association of Computing Machinery.

Johnson, L. F., & Levine, A. H. (2008). Virtual worlds: Inherently immersive, highly social learning spaces. *Theory into Practice, 47,* 166–167. .doi:10.1080/00405840801992397

Jones, M.G., Minogue, J., Tretter, T.R., Negishi, A., & Taylor, R. (2005). *Haptic augmentation of science instruction: Does touch matter?* Wiley InterScience. DOI 10.1002/sce.20086.

Junglas, I. A., Johnson, N. A., Steel, D. J., Abraham, D. C., & Loughlin, P. M. (2007). Identity formation, learning styles and trust in virtual worlds. *The DATA BASE for Advances in Informatin Systems, 38*(4), 90–96.

Lipman-Blumen, J., & Leavitt, H. J. (1999). *Hot groups: Seeding Them, Feeding Them, and Using Them to Ignite Your Organization.* Oxford, UK: Oxford University Press.

Mitchell, M. (2009). *Complexity: A Guided Tour* (p. 15). Oxford, UK: Oxford University Press.

Moher, T. (2006). Embedded phenomena: Supporting science learning with classroom-sized distributed simulations. In *the proceedings of CHI 2006: Conference on Human Factors in Computing Systems* (pp. 691 – 700). Quebec, Canada.

Nadler, D. (2008). Exergaming: Cardiovascular fitness in immersive virtual environments. *Learning & Leading with Technology. International Society for Technology in Education,* 28 – 29.

Naef, M., Staadt, O., & Gross, M. (2002). Spatialized audio rendering for immersive virtual environments. In *the proceedings of the VRST '02: Virtual Reality Software and Technology* (pp. 65 - 72). Hong Kong.

Oliver, M., & Carr, D. (2009). Learning in virtual worlds: Using communities of practice to explain how people learn from play. *British Journal of Educational Technology, 40*(3), 445–457. doi:10.1111/j.1467-8535.2009.00948.x

Payne, J., Keir, P., Elgoyhen, J., McLundie, M., Naef, M., Horner, M., & Anderson, P. (2008). Gameplay issues in the design of spatial 3D gestures for video games. In *the proceedings of CHI 2006: Special Interest Group in Computer Human Interface* (pp. 1217 – 1222). Montréal, Québec, Canada. Association of Computing Machinery.

Sánchez, J., & Sáenz, M. (2005). 3D sound interactive environments for problem solving. *ASSETS '05: The Seventh International ACM SIGACCESS Conference on Computers and Accessibility* (pp. 173 - 179). Baltimore, Maryland, USA.

Simons, J. A., Irwin, D. B., & Drinnien, B. A. (1987). Maslow's hierarchy of needs. *Psychology—The Search for Understanding.* New York: West Publishing Company. Retrieved Dec. 11, 2009, from http://honolulu.hawaii.edu/intranet/committees/FacDevCom/guidebk/teachtip/maslow.htm.

Steed, R. (2009). Instruction in cultural competency in a virtual 3D world. *Journal of Interactive Instruction Development, 21*(2), 19.

Thomas, M. (2009). A review of Edward Castronova's *Exodus to the virtual world. British Journal of Educational Technology, 40*(3), 575–577. doi:10.1111/j.1467-8535.2009.00969_3.x

Topp, R., & Din, H. W.-S. (2005). Modular small-scale media: Achieving community curation through rural Alaska. In *the proceedings of the International Conference on Computer Graphics and Interactive Techniques.* Los Angeles, California, USA. ACM.

Turkle, S. (1998). Identity in the age of the Internet: Living in the MUD. R. Holeton, Ed. *Composing Cyberspace: Identity, Community, and Knowledge in the Electronic Age.* Boston: McGraw Hill. 5 – 11.

Wagner, C. (2008). Learning experience with virtual worlds. *Journal of Information Systems Education, 19*(3), 263 – 266. Retrieved Nov. 22, 2009, from http://www.jise.appstate.edu/Issues/19/V19N3P263-abs.pdf.

Walther, B. K. (2005). Atomic actions—molecular experience: Theory of pervasive gaming. *ACM Computers in Entertainment, 3*(2), 1–13.

Wang, Y., & Braman, J. (2009). Extending the classroom through second life. *Journal of Information Systems Education: 20*(2), 235 – 247. Retrieved Nov. 22, 2009, from http://www.jise.appstate.edu/Issues/20/V20N2P235-abs.pdf.

Warburton, S. (2009). Second Life in higher education: Assessing the potential for and the barriers to deploying virtual worlds in learning and teaching. *British Journal of Educational Technology:* $0(3), 414 – 426. **doi:10.** 111I/j.1467-85 35.2009.009 52.x

Wenger, E. (1998). Communities of practice: Learning as a social system. *Systems Thinker, 9*(5), 1 - 10. Retrieved Dec. 8, 2009, from http://www.open.ac.uk/ldc08/sites/www.open.ac.uk.ldc08/files/Learningasasocialsystem.pdf.

KEY TERMS AND DEFINITIONS

Artificial Intelligence: The simulation of human intelligence via a machine

Avatar: A digital personification, a human embodiment

Immersion: Full-sensory experiential learning

Longitudinal: Length of time

Perpetual: Continuous, forever

Persistence: Continuity, long-term existence

Synthetic World: Artificial 3D immersive spaces that simulate real-world spaces

Virtual Reality: An analogue rendering of a part of the real world using 3D digital imagery, interactivity, human-embodied avatars, or other tools

Virtual World: Simulated online spaces where human-embodied avatars may interact in real time

Section 4
Technological Accessibility Functionalities

Chapter 12
A Computational Model of Non-Visual Spatial Learning

Kanubhai K. Patel
Ahmedabad University, India

Sanjay Kumar Vij
SVIT, India

ABSTRACT

A computational model of non-visual spatial learning through virtual learning environment (VLE) is presented in this chapter. The inspiration has come from Landmark-Route-Survey (LRS) theory (Siegel & White, 1975), the most accepted theory of spatial learning. An attempt has been made to combine the findings and methods from several disciplines including cognitive psychology, behavioral science and computer science (specifically virtual reality (VR) technology). The study of influencing factors on spatial learning and the potential of using cognitive maps in the modeling of spatial learning are described. Motivation to use VLE and its characteristics are also described briefly. Different types of locomotion interface to VLE with their constraints and benefits are discussed briefly. The authors believe that by incorporating perspectives from cognitive and experimental psychology to computer science, this chapter will appeal to a wide range of audience - particularly computer engineers concerned with assistive technologies; professionals interested in virtual environments, including computer engineers, architect, city-planner, cartographer, high-tech artists, and mobility trainer; and psychologists involved in the study of spatial cognition, cognitive behaviour, and human-computer interfaces.

INTRODUCTION

About 314 million people are visually impaired worldwide; 45 million of them are blind[1]. One out of every three blind people in the world lives in India - that comes to approximately 15 million.

The inability to travel independently around and interact with the wider world is one of the most significant handicaps that can be caused by visual impairment or blindness, second only to the inability to communicate through reading and writing. The difficulties in the mobility of visually impaired people in new or unfamiliar locations are caused by the fact that spatial information

DOI: 10.4018/978-1-61692-825-4.ch012

is not fully available to them as against it being available to sighted people. Visually impaired people are thus handicapped to gather this crucial information, which leads to great difficulties in generating efficient cognitive maps of spaces and, therefore, in navigating efficiently within new or unfamiliar spaces. Consequently, many blind people become passive, depending on others for assistance. More than 30% of the blind do not ambulate independently outdoors (Clark-Carter, D., Heyes, A., & Howarth, C., 1986; and Lahav, O., & Mioduser, D., 2003).

This constraint can be overcome by communicating spatial knowledge of the surroundings and thereby providing some means to generate cognitive mapping of spaces and of the possible paths for navigating through these spaces virtually, which are essential for the development of efficient orientation and mobility skills. It is obvious that reasonable number of repeated visits to the new space leads to formation of its cognitive map subconsciously. Thus, a good number of researchers focused on using technology to simulate visits to a new space for building cognitive maps. It need not be emphasized that the strength and efficiency of cognitive map building process is directly proportional to the closeness between the simulated and real-life environments. However, most of the simulated environments reported by earlier researchers don't fully represent reality. The challenge, therefore, is to enhance and enrich simulated environment so as to create a near real-life experience.

The fundamental goal of developing virtual learning environment for visually impaired people is to complement or replace sight by another modality. The visual information therefore needs to be simplified and transformed so as to allow its rendition through alternate sensory channels, usually auditory, haptic, or auditory-haptic. One of the methods to enhance and enrich simulated environment is to use virtual reality along with advanced technologies such as computer haptics, brain-computer interface (BCI), speech processing and sonification. Such technologies can be used to provide learning environment to visually impaired people to create cognitive maps of unfamiliar areas. We aim to present various research studies including ours for communicating spatial knowledge to visually impaired people and evaluating it through virtual learning environment (VLE), and thereby enhancing spatial behaviour in real environment. This chapter proposes taxonomy of spatial learning and addresses the potential of virtual learning environment as a tool for studying spatial behaviour of visually impaired people and thereby enhancing their capabilities to interact in a spatial environment in real life. It would be useful to understand as to how they learn and acquire basic spatial knowledge in terms of landmarks and configuration of spatial layout and also how navigation tasks are improvised. Understanding the use of such knowledge to externalize and measure virtually perceived cognitive maps is also important.

Following questions are addressed in this chapter:

- Does virtual learning environment (VLE) contribute to communicate the spatial knowledge and thereby the formation of a cognitive map of a novel space?
- Which are the major factors that influence the spatial knowledge communication to visually impaired people through VLE?
- Which are the factors that mediate for enhancement of the navigation performance of visually impaired people?
- Is learning via VLE more effective, accurate, interesting, and enjoyable than learning via conventional methods?
- How is the effectiveness of cognitive maps measured?
- Can we consider trajectory of subjects as cognitive map?
- Does the type of locomotion interface impinge on accuracy of spatial learning?

- Is navigating through treadmill-style locomotion interface less disruptive than navigating via conventional devices?

A computational model of non-visual spatial learning through virtual learning environment (VLE) is presented in this chapter. The inspiration has come from Landmark-Route-Survey (LRS) theory (Siegel & White, 1975), the most accepted theory of spatial learning. This NSL model is created by undertaking thorough literature review of the material existing in the area of spatial cognition and computer science. An attempt has been made to combine the findings and methods from several disciplines including cognitive psychology, behavioral science and computer science (specifically virtual reality (VR) technology). The study of influencing factors on spatial learning and the potential of using cognitive maps in the modeling of spatial learning are described. Motivation to use VLE and its characteristics are also described briefly. Different types of locomotion interface to VLE with their constraints and benefits are discussed briefly. We believe that by incorporating perspectives from cognitive and experimental psychology to computer science, this chapter will appeal to a wide range of audience - particularly computer engineers concerned with assistive technologies; professionals interested in virtual environments, including computer engineers, architect, city-planner, cartographer, high-tech artists, and mobility trainer; and psychologists involved in the study of spatial cognition, cognitive behaviour, and human-computer interfaces.

MODELING SPATIAL ENVIRONMENT

The topological component of map consists of a set of N place nodes and a set of links that connects pairs of places. Various objects like places, paths, obstacles etc. can be represent in topological map of an environment. They are linked by the various relations among them like places are along the paths, place is on left or right side of other place or path, etc. Before we explore this modeling technique, we should understand basic concepts of space and spatial cognition.

Space

Space (and time) is very elementary and ubiquitous for almost all human behaviour and reasoning (Freksa, 1997). Yet, it is difficult (or impossible) to find a single definition that covers all aspects of space. For example, while in mathematics the term space is frequently used to describe the dimensionality of sets or vectors (Bronstein & Semendjajew, 1979); this has little to no relevance in the context of human behaviour. However, since computers heavily rely on mathematical concepts, oftentimes spatial knowledge is stored in cartesian coordinates (e. g. in geographical information systems (GIS)). This somewhat contradicts the naive perception most people have of space as being the physical environment, in which we live and act. In psychology and other disciplines such as architecture, (everyday) space is often seen as being structured and hence being perceived differently according to its scale (see, for example, (Lynch, 1960). After initial approaches which introduced a binary portioning (e. g. Ittelson, 1973; Downs & Stea, 1977), the distinction between small- and large-scale spaces has been further refined (Freundschuh & Egenhofer, 1997).

Montello (Montello, 1993), for example, distinguishes four main categories of space as,

- Figural space
- Vista space
- Environmental space
- Geographical space

Figural space encompasses the space within the direct reach of a person, which is smaller than the body of the observer. Another term that is frequently used to describe this kind of space is table-top space (Ittelson, 1973). Vista space is the space that can be perceived visually from a single location without locomotion falls in this category. For example, the room a person is located in lies in vista space. If a portion of space cannot be perceived from a single location without the observer moving around, it can be classified as belonging to environmental space. A city is an example for an entity existing in this type of space. Montello defines geographical spaces as spaces that cannot be apprehended even with extensive knowledge but have to be reduced to figural or vista space in order to do so. This is the space of countries or continents. These different types of spaces are closely related to how humans encode and memorize spatial information such as constellations or routes.

Spatial Knowledge

When humans explore space they not only perceive it but they build up a mental representation of it (cf. (Tversky, 1993). Generally, we can distinguish three classes of spatial knowledge: landmark knowledge, route knowledge and survey knowledge (Werner et al., 1997). Landmarks are objects, which are embedded in the environment and which differ from other objects in their vicinity in one or more respects such as visual salience and/or conceptual salience (see, for example, Sorrows & Hirtle, 1999). Since they 'stand out' from their environment they are not only easy to remember but also easy to recognize. Therefore, they are highly relevant in a number of spatial processes such as object localization (Gapp, 1995) or wayfinding (Lynch, 1960; Raubal & Worboys, 1999). Landmark knowledge actually links specific landmarks to other knowledge. For example, by associating a turn instruction with a landmark at a decision point, a person can decide which path to follow in order to get to her target location. Route knowledge (also known as procedural knowledge) is most frequently gained from actively exploring the environment. (Alternatively, people can acquire route knowledge

indirectly, e. g. by listening to route instructions.) Route knowledge consists of a series of spatial actions such as turning or following a road, which together form a route from one location to another. Survey knowledge encodes information about the topology and/or spatial constellations in an area. People mainly acquire survey knowledge by extensively exploring a region of space, which enables them to establish multiple relationships between various locations within that area. Maps also represent survey knowledge, and hence, support the acquisition of survey knowledge. The main difference between survey knowledge and the two other categories lies in the way in which knowledge is organized: survey knowledge abstracts from single experiences and observations to form an integrated model. The amalgamation of spatial knowledge that is encoded in different ways forms the basis for human spatial reasoning, and is often defined as a cognitive map (Tolman, 1948) or cognitive collage (Tversky, 1993). It is important to highlight that these cognitive maps do not result from a homomorphic mapping of the real world to a representation, but that they are a conglomeration of possibly contradicting pieces of information. Nevertheless, they enable humans to efficiently store spatial information and to interact with space in a meaningful way most of the time.

Spatial Relation

Not only do humans act within space they also talk about it or refer to it verbally or by other means such as gestures. A frequent means to realize spatial references consists of spatial relations (Herrman & Grabowski, 1994). The region connection calculus (RCC) serves for qualitative spatial representation and reasoning. RCC abstractly describes regions (in Euclidian space or in a topological space) by their possible relations to each other. RCC8 consists of 8 basic relations (see Figure 1) that are possible between two regions:

- disconnected (DC)
- externally connected (EC)
- equal (EQ)
- partially overlapping (PO)
- tangential proper part (TPP)
- tangential proper part inverse (TPPi)
- non-tangential proper part (NTPP)
- non-tangential proper part inverse (NTPPi)

From these basic relations, combinations can be built. For example, proper part (PP) is the union of TPP and NTPP.

Other versions of the region connection calculus include RCC5 (with only five basic relations - the distinction whether two regions touch each other are ignored) and RCC23 (which allows reasoning about convexity).

Modeling Spatial Environment

The topological component of environment consists of a set of N place nodes and a set of links that connects pairs of places. We represent various objects like places, paths etc. in topological map of an environment. They are linked by the various relations among them like places are along the paths, place is on left or right side of other place or path, etc. The topographical layout, color-coded identifiers for objects, and force feedback correlation with objects can develop through man-machine interaction. The Spatial Layout Designer mainly helps to create layout of particular area or premises easily and without having any technical knowledge. It should provide a user friendly interface to quickly design and develop virtual environment of particular area or premises easily by placing objects (such as places and paths) of different sizes and shapes. Vector graphics technique of graphics drawing to draw objects is to be used. It has advantages compare to raster graphics technique.

Objects are provided in the toolbox under different categories viz. building, road, obstacle, gate, entrance, etc. Various attributes of objects such as size, location, direction and form of an object can be set or updated through property window. These objects may also have default attributes such as color, speech tag, label tag, movement, type and intensity of force feedback. Force feedback effect and audio label to these components can be set or updated. Different shapes of objects to be covered are square, rectangle, circle, line polygon, curve polygon, line, curve and oval etc. Different types of objects are mainly covering areas (places), passages/roads and boundaries. User can create templates for objects for future requirements also.

Following are the colors that may be used to encode some of the objects (see as an example Table 1).

Using Spatial Layout Designer, one can proportionately map the real world's objects to their size and their distance from other objects. Various

Figure 1. The RCC8 calculus can be used for reasoning about spatial configurations

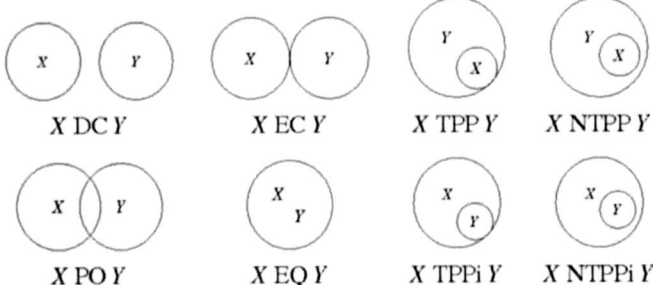

properties like position, shape, orientation, height, and size of objects can be set or updated through drag and drop also. Simple to complex environments can be created trivially. There should be relation between Macro and Micro level objects. It means user can create hierarchy of the objects. One object can have multiple parents. Layout can be stored in either in XML format, EMF or in database.

NON-VISUAL SPATIAL LEARNING RESEARCH BACKGROUND

In recent years, a plethora of assistive navigation technologies have been designed to enhance and maintain the independence of the community of blind and visually impaired. The available spatial learning aids for the visually impaired can be categorized into,

1. Passive aids
2. Active aids and
3. VR based aids.

Passive aids are providing the user with information before his/her arrival to the environment. For example, verbal description, tactile maps, strip maps, Braille maps, and physical models (Ungar, S., Blades, M., & Spencer, S., 1996; Rieser, J.J., 1989).

Active aids are providing the user with information while navigating, for example, Sonicguide (Warren, D. & Strelow, E., 1985), Talking Signs or embedded sensors in the environment (Crandall, W., Bentzen, B., Myers, L. & Mitchell, P., 1995), and Personal Guidance System, based on satellite communication (Golledge, R., Klatzky, R., & Loomis, J., 1996). The research results indicate a number of limitations in the use of passive and exclusive devices, for example, erroneous distance estimation, underestimation of spatial components and objects dimensions, low information density, or misunderstanding of symbolic codes used in the representations.

Virtual reality has been a popular paradigm in simulation-based training, game and entertainment industries (Burdea, G. & Coiffet, P., 2003). It has also been used for rehabilitation and learning environments for people with disabilities (e.g., physical, mental, and learning disabilities) (Standen, P. J., Brown, D. J. & Cromby, J. J., 2001; Schultheis, M. & Rizzo, A., 2001). Recent technological advances, particularly in haptic interface technology, enable blind individuals to expand their knowledge as a result of using artificially made reality through haptic and audio feedback. Research on the implementation of haptic technologies within virtual navigation environments has yielded reports on its potential for supporting rehabilitation training with sighted people (Giess, C., Evers, H. & Meinzer, H., 1998; Gorman, P., Lieser, J., Murray, W., Haluck, R. & Krummel, T., 1998), as well as with people who are blind (Jansson, G., Fanger, J., Konig, H., & Billberger, K., 1998; Colwell, C., Petrie, H., Kornbrot, D., Hardwick, A., & Furner, S., 1998).

Table 1. Predefined color code for various segments

Objects	Color
Building	Red
Road, Path	Black
Garden	Green
Entrance/Door	Yellow
Parking Area	Grey

This research can also be classified into navigational assistance for

1. Indoor environments (e.g. Sabelman et. al., 1994),
2. Outdoor environments (e.g. Strothotte et. al., 1996; Dodson, A.H., Moore, T. & Moon, G.V., 1999), and
3. A combination of both (e.g. Golledge, et. al., 1998; Helal, A.S., Moore, S.E. & Ramachandran, B., 2001).

In relation to outdoor environments, Petrie (Petrie, H., 1995) distinguishes between 'micro-navigation' technologies, which provide assistance through immediate environment, and 'macro-navigation' technologies, which provide assistance through the distant environment. For instance, ETAs (Electronic Travel Aids) such as obstacle avoidance systems (e.g. Laser Cane (Kay L., 1980) and ultrasonic obstacle avoiders (Bradyn, J.A., 1985) have been developed to assist visually impaired travelers for micro-navigation. Whereas, Global Positioning Systems (GPS) and Geographical Information System (GIS) have been used to assist visually impaired for macro-navigation. Examples include the MOBIC Travel Aid (Strothotte, et. al., 1996), Arkenstone system (Fruchterman, J., 1995) & Personal Guidance System (Golledge, et. al., 1998). Radio Frequency (RF) beacons have also been used to assist navigation for both micro and macro navigation (Kemmerling, M. & Schliepkorte, H., 1998).

Navigation through indoor environments, on the other hand, has been developed using similar systems. As GPS is ineffective inside buildings, most systems depend on relative positioning using sensors such as digital tags, active badge, accelerometers, temperature, photodiodes and beacons (Ertan, et. al., 1998; Golding, A. R. & Lesh, N., 1999; Long, et. al., 1996).

Human navigation and wayfinding consists of both sensing the immediate environment for obstacles and hazards, and navigating to remote destinations beyond the immediately perceptible environment (Loomis et. al., 2001). Navigation therefore involves updating one's orientation and position; a process involving position-based navigation, velocity-based navigation, and acceleration-based navigation (all of which are described by Loomis et al (Loomis et al., 2001). Visually impaired people are therefore at a huge disadvantage in unfamiliar routes, as they 'lack much of the information needed for planning detours around obstacles and hazards, and have little information about distant landmarks, heading and self-velocity'(Loomis et. al., 2001).

Cognitive mapping research focuses on how individuals acquire, learn, develop, think about and store data relating to the everyday geographic environment (e.g. encoding locations, attributes and landmark orientations to navigate) (Downs, R. M. & Stea, D., 1997). Jonsson (Jonsson, E., 2002) describes how maps can change for one particular area depending on the (i) time of day (i.e. day/night), (ii) season (e.g. summer vs. winter), and (iii) direction of travel (traveling the same route forward or back).

A number of theories (e.g. landmark-based learning strategies and route-based strategies) and mechanisms (e.g. images, dual coding, genetic coding, etc.) have been advanced to account for how knowledge is learned, stored, and structured. However, the unique strategies and mechanisms used by visually impaired people have not been given sufficient investigation in current research (Kitchin, R. M., Blades, M. & Golledge, R.G., 1997). Kitchen & Jacobson (Kitchen, R.M. & Jacobson, D., 1997) argue that cognitive mapping research could reveal 'what spatial information should be given to visually impaired pedestrians, in what form and at which particular locations'.

Different forms of visual impairment might also impact on cognitive map development. Someone experiencing a loss of central vision would perhaps find reading text (e.g. road signs) extremely difficult, whereas someone with only one half of their field of vision would possibly be more dependent on information within the side that was lost. The use of VE technology helped people who are blind in exploring an unknown novel room (Lahav & Mioduser, 2003). Research on the use of haptic devices by people who are blind for construction of cognitive maps includes (Lahav and Mioduser, 2003; Semwal & Evans-Kamp, 2000).

Motivation for VE Based Assistance

Some of the many general factors underlying the idea that VE technology is likely to be useful for training spatial behavior in the real world are summarized (by Darken et al, 1997) in the following paragraphs.

- Training in the real space may be inappropriate or impossible because of inaccessibility, cost, excessive danger, security requirements, etc.
- A single VE installation can be used for training individuals in a wide variety of tasks in a wide variety of spaces because it is software reconfigurable.
- When a VE system is used for training, it is possible to automatically and reliably (a) provide immediate feedback to the trainee and (b) record the trainee's actions for later analysis.
- VE training systems can be used to assess basic spatial abilities and skills and to upgrade these abilities and skills, as well as to train individuals to perform specific tasks in specific spaces.
- VE training systems can be modified adaptively in real time to optimize the training of specific individuals at specific stages of learning under the guidance of specific instructors.
- VE training systems can be used for training team behavior not only by providing common, shared environments in which real team members can interact, but also by providing virtual team members with whom an individual trainee can interact.
- VE training systems can be used to provide unreal situations especially designed to enhance training effectiveness.

An understanding of formation of cognitive maps by VIP for successful navigation and way-finding through non-visual virtual environment is required for designing computer-simulated (virtual) environment.

A COMPUTATIONAL MODEL OF NON-VISUAL SPATIAL LEARNING (NSL)

Although isolated solutions have been attempted, no integrated solution of spatial learning to visually impaired people (VIP) is available to the best of our knowledge. Yet no researcher has given a computation model to cover all the aspects of the non-visual spatial learning process. Our non-visual spatial learning (NSL) model provides abstraction of non-visual spatial learning by VIP. Special emphasis is placed on internalizing and externalizing cognitive maps and online assessment of perceived cognitive maps by users. Understanding how spatial learning tasks are constructed is useful in determining how best to improve performance. We should decompose the various tasks of spatial learning in a generic way. So that we might be able to determine where assistance is needed, or where training can occur.

To describe the computational model of the spatial learning, we divided whole process into following four phases (see Figure 2).

1. Constructivist Learning
2. Instruction modulator
3. Behavior monitoring
4. Assessment

The model works like this. In first phase, a constructivist learning experience is to be provided that emphasizes the active participation of users in spatial learning through virtual environment exploration. This is kind of learning-by-exploring approach of learning. Virtual environment exploration should be as familiar and natural as actually walking through the regions. In second phase, simulated agent explores the area and creates the knowledgebase to provide guidance and directs user by generation of the various kinds of instructions. Instruction modulator conforms the instructions and conveys to participants in various ways (speech, force feedback, and/or non-speech sound). Besides this assistance, participant can get contextual cues that help them to structure cognitive maps. Participant can interact with the various objects of virtual environment and structure cognitive map of an environment. In third phase, partial cognitive map build till now, it is evaluated in terms of participant's behavior, navigating style (i.e. normal walk or drunkard/random walk) and

participant's course with obstacles (where and when). Need based further instructions may be provided for any adjustment.

In the final phase, once the participant gets confident and memorizes the path and landmarks between source and destination, he is allowed to go for assessment. Participant's navigation performance, such as path traversed, time taken and number of steps taken to complete the task are recorded and evaluated. The participant's performance is evaluated in terms of statistical measures like bi-dimensional correlation coefficients (BCC), navigation time and number of steps taken to reach the destination place from source place. The sequence of objects falling on the traversed path and the positions where he seemed to have confusion (and hence took relatively longer time) are also recorded and conveyed to them. Performance feedback is to be given to participant.

Figure 2.Components of Non-visual Spatial Learning (NSL) Model

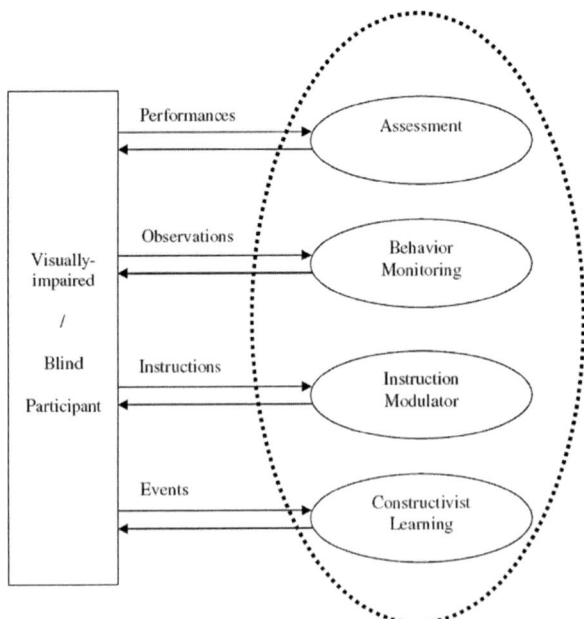

Constructivist Learning

A constructivist learning experience is to be provided that emphasizes the active participation of users in spatial learning through virtual environment exploration. The participant interacts with the various objects of an environment. Also virtual environment exploration should be as familiar and natural as actually walking through the regions portrayed on a traditional paper map.

A constructivist learning experience is to be provided that emphasizes the active participation of users in spatial learning through virtual environment exploration. This is kind of learning-by-exploring approach of learning. The participant interacts with the various objects of an environment. Participant can load layout of premise or area through interface easily. Participant can get the brief description of the layout in the beginning through text-to-speech conversion. Participant can choose starting location and destination through speech recognition guided selection. Participant can start session by pressing a particular key (for say F5). Session start date-time (that is also start break date-time for first break) is to be stored by system. Now participant can start navigation. The participant navigates or explores the virtual environment using a force feedback joystick, mouse or locomotion interface. Virtual environment exploration should be as familiar and natural as actually walking through the regions. Before starting training session, participant can configure a) foot step size, b) height and c) length of their foot. System maintains session starting and ending time. Participant can end the session by pressing a particular key.

In case of confusion or any difficulty, participant can take assistance from system. Participant can get information regarding orientation, whenever needed, through help key (for say F3). Participant can also get information (help) regarding Near-by (, near to near-by, or far) objects from his current location (i.e. knowing orientation) by pressing key (for say F4). Participant also gets options and direction available to move by pressing key (for say F8), number of steps taken and distance covered from origin or from particular location. Participant also gets information like distance remains to travel to reach the destinations. When participants takes these type of helps, system stores information regarding helps taken (i.e. When and Where – Current location). This information is used to find the confidence level of the participants. The System also generates audible and vibration alerts when the participant is approaching any obstacle.

Following are the some of the common operations need to be implemented that performed by participant:

- Load layout (as prepared by sighted)
  void loadLayout(layout_name);
- Select source and destination locations
  void selectSourceLocation(location_name);
  void selectDestinationLocation(location_name);
- Starting and ending session
  int startSession();
  void endSession(sessionNumber);
- Take break
  int takeBreak(); return next break number.
- Get orientation help
  String[] getOrientationHelp();
- Get present route help
  String getPresentRouteHelp();
- Taking assistance
  void askOptionToMove(presentPosition);

Following are the some of the common operations need to be implemented that performed by system:

- Transition / Acceleration
  void transition (stepNumber);
  void accelerate();

Instruction Modulator

This is kind of directed mode of navigation. The basic concept of directed mode of navigation is to augment the standard user interface in a virtual environment with a system that has knowledge about the content of the virtual world and lets users find objects and locations through assistance.

This is kind of directed mode of navigation. The basic concept of directed mode of navigation is to augment the standard user interface in a virtual environment with a system that has knowledge about the content of the virtual world and lets users find objects and locations through assistance.

The simulated agent explores the area and creates the knowledgebase to provide guidance and directs user by generation of the various kinds of instructions. Instructor modulator conforms the instructions and conveys to participants in various ways (speech, force feedback, and/or non-speech sound).

Following are the type of instructions generated by the Instructor modulator:

1. Directional Instructions
2. Obstacles avoidance Instructions
3. Orientation Instructions
4. Contextual Instructions
5. Temporal Instructions

In this mode of navigation, the Instruction modulator guides the blind participant through speech by describing surroundings, guiding directions, and giving early information of a turning, crossings, etc. Additionally, occurrences of various events (e.g. arrival of a junction, arrival of object(s) of interest, etc.) are signaled through vibration using consumer-grade devices. User can navigate the virtual environment either using flying-with-joystick or keyboard method or walking on locomotion interface. Current position in virtual environment is changed as user walks on the locomotion interface or takes steps through joystick or keyboard. They use the force feedback joystick, or mouse to control and move the current position indicator (referred to as cursor in this paper). System generates (non-speech) sound for each step taken by User.

Besides this assistance, participant can get contextual cues that help them to structure cognitive maps. Whenever the cursor is moved onto or near an object, its sound and force feedback features are activated. Thus a particular sound, which may also be a pre-recorded message, will be heard by the participant. As long as the cursor is on the object, the participant will feel the force feedback effect associated with this object. Participant can get contextual information continuously during navigation according to session's time like Morning, Afternoon, Evening, or Night. Contextual information is also according to different events of the place. For example for Railway station, contextual information is different for different events like at train arrival time, departure time and normal waiting time period. When participant is approaching or passing through class room (for school or college premises) he gets sound of teacher and students. When participant is passing through fountain or river, they heard the sound of flowing of water. Participant gets information about path surface (i.e. Sandy, Muddy, Concrete, Slippery, or Grass-root/loan etc.) through tactile effects. Participant can interact with the various objects of virtual environment and structure cognitive map of an environment.

Optimal Path Finding

As mentioned earlier various objects like places, paths etc. in topological map of an environment are linked by the various relations among them like places are along the paths, place is on left or right side of other place or path, etc. An algorithm is formulated for finding optimal path between two places in topology map based on Boundary Relation Heuristic (BRH). According to the BRH, boundary relations supply sub goals for the wayfinding algorithm.

Here first Route-to-route relation matrix and Route-to-place relation matrix are to be created based on boundary relation. We use two basic behavioral modes, wall following and object avoidance. In the wall following mode, the blind person tries to stay close to the wall, once it detected one. This is a more opportunistic strategy. As per this strategy, simulated agent finds the exact route with number of steps and directions to reach the destination. Object avoidance is implemented by turning away from objects upon contact, to avoid collision in the near future. Object avoidance is an exploratory strategy. Consider the following layout (Figure 3) which has eight places (P1, P2,…, P8) and three routes (R1, R2 and R3).

In our algorithm, search process to be guided by the BRH by providing sub goals and then the way in which sub goals can be further explored. This algorithm uses various wayfinding strategies of human being for these sub goals. As shown in fig. 5 to reach P8 (that is Computer lab) from P1 (that is entrance), system finds out the route R1->R2->R3 from route-to-route connectivity matrix.

Here R2 is on left side of R1, so we get the route along the P2 building for R1->R2. The heuristic estimates the cost to reach the goal node from the current node; the heuristic estimate is usually referred to as the h(n) value. It also keeps track of the cost needed to get to the current node from the start node, this cost is generally referred to as g(n). The total cost of a node, f(n), is the sum of the cost to reach the current node from the start node and the heuristic estimate.

The simulated agent moves to a successor node by choosing the most promising node (the one with the lowest f(n) value) from it's list of potential successor nodes (i.e. from the open list). An OpenList contains all the nodes that have been reached but haven't been visited and expanded yet and ClosedList contains all the nodes that have been visited and expanded, i.e. they have been removed from the open list and added to the closed list.

Figure 3. Optimal route by the simulated agent

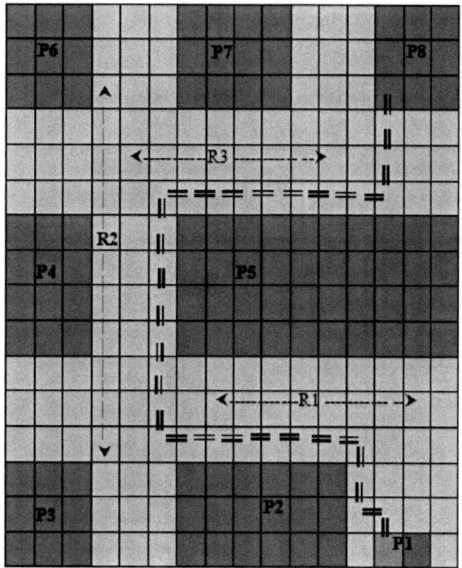

Behavior Monitoring

The system continuously monitors and records following type of participant's behaviors:

- Navigating style (normal /random walk)
- Mental state (confusion/fear/lost/excited/ confident)

During learning, the system continuously monitors and records participant's navigating style (i.e. normal walk or drunkard/random walk) and participant's course with obstacles (where and when). Participant can take break at any time during the session by pressing the Escape key. System stores break number, break start time and end time, and user's trajectories in the database. Once the system finds the participant confident and memorizes the path and landmarks between source and destination, it allows him to go for assessment. The system monitors the number of step taken and distance traveled by the participant for the each break and session. If these two values are reducing or coming near the expected values and if participant's navigation style is proper then system finds that the participant is confident and ready for performance test.

Assessment

In the assessment phase, participant navigates without system's help and trying to reach the destination. Participant gets only contextual information. The system records participant's navigation performance, such as path traversed, time taken and number of steps taken to complete this task. It also records the sequence of objects falling on the traversed path and the positions where he seemed to have confusion (and hence took relatively longer time). The System evaluates the participant's performance in terms of statistical measures like bi-dimensional correlation coefficients (BCC), navigation time and number of steps taken by participant to reach the destination place from source place and gives performance feedback to participant.

As mentioned earlier the simulated agent finds out the possible best path(s) between source place and destination using optimal path algorithm. The System compares optimal paths with participant's earlier recorded navigation path (during un-guided VE navigation). Navigation paths of the participant are evaluated quantitatively using bi-dimensional regression analysis developed by Tobler (Tobler, W., 1976). Bi-dimensional regression is applied to calculate the bi-dimensional correlation coef-

Figure 4. Route-to-route and Place-to-route connectivity matrices

Route-to-route connectivity matrix (reach-ability matrix)				Place-to-Route connectivity matrix			
Route	R1	R2	R3		R1	R2	R3
R1	-	1	∞	Route Place/			
R2	1	-	1	P1	1	∞	∞
R3	∞	1	-	P2	∞	1	∞
				P3	∞	1	∞
				P4	∞	1	∞
				P5	∞	1	∞
				P6	∞	1	∞
				P7	∞	∞	1
				P8	∞	∞	1

Table 2.

ALGORITHM	
1.	INPUT:: StartNode and GoalNode
2.	OpenList ← ⊘; ClosedList ← ⊘;
3.	Insert StartNode to OpenList;
4.	while OpenList is not empty
5.	Pick the node n which has the least f(n) value from OpenList; //make it the current node
6.	if isGoal(n) then
7.	Return (n);
8.	End if
9.	Find all successor nodes of n;
10.	For each successor node n' of n do
11.	g(n') = g(n) + the cost to get from n to n';
12.	find n' on OpenList;
13.	if (n' is on OpenList && has lower g(n')) then
14.	continue;
15.	End if
16.	If (n' is on ClosedList && has lower g(n')) then
17.	continue;
18.	End if
19.	Delete all occurrences of n' from OpenList and ClosedList;
20.	Parent(n') ← n;
21.	Find h(n'); //Use the heuristic to estimate the distance to the goal node
22.	Insert n' to OpenList;
23.	End for
24.	Insert n to ClosedList;
25.	End while

ficients. The value of BCC near to 1 indicates that participant's performance is satisfactory and cognitive maps are satisfactorily formed. If its value is one then the cognitive map is almost precise. The trainer may ask the participant to give a verbal description of the area and then performs orientation and mobility tasks in the real target space.

Quality Factors for Spatial Learning Techniques

There are few categories of virtual environment applications that are currently in use for productive, consistent work, but the requirements of these applications for spatial learning techniques cover a wide range. Further, there are many new applications of VEs being researched, which also may require spatial learning techniques with different characteristics. It is therefore impractical to evaluate spatial learning techniques directly within each new application. Instead, we propose a more general methodology, involving a mapping from spatial learning techniques to a set of quality factors. Quality factors are measurable characteristics of the performance of a technique. With this indirect mapping, application designers can specify desired levels of various quality factors, and then choose a technique which best fits those requirements. Our current list of quality factors for VE-based spatial learning techniques includes:

1. Speed of learning (time taken to develop cognitive map)
2. Navigation Efficiency (Distance traveled, number of steps taken and time taken to complete the task)
3. Accuracy (proximity to the desired target)
4. Spatial Awareness (the user's knowledge of his position and orientation within the environment during and after exploration)
5. Ease of Learning (the ability of a novice user to use the technique)
6. Ease of Use (the complexity or cognitive load of the technique from the user's point of view)
7. Information Gathering (the user's ability to actively obtain information from the environment during exploration)
8. Presence (the user's sense of immersion or 'being within' the environment due to navigation)
9. User Comfort (lack of simulator sickness, dizziness, or nausea)

This list may not be complete, but it is a good starting point for quantifying the effectiveness and performance of virtual spatial learning techniques. Some of the quality factors, such as speed, navigation Efficiency and accuracy, are simple to measure quantitatively. Others, however, are difficult to measure due to their inherent subjective nature. To quantify these factors, standard questionnaires for factors such as ease of use (e.g. Chin, Diehl, & Norman, 1988), presence (e.g. Slater, 1995), and simulator sickness (e.g. Kennedy et al., 1993) should be part of the experimental method.

Measuring Cognitive Load

A person has a limited amount of cognitive resources which they must allocate amount all mental tasks being concurrently performed. Cognitive load refers to the total amount of mental activity on working memory at an instance in time (Cooper, G., 2004). Short term memory is limited in the number of elements it can contain simultaneously (Chandler, P., & Sweller, J., 1999). If a design requires the user to hold too many items in short term memory, it will fail (Balogh, J., Michael C., & Giangola J., 2004). When a user's working memory is available to concentrate on the details of to-be-used information, usability is increased (Cooper, G., 2004).

There are many different methods of measuring a user's cognitive load, ranging from direct measurement of neuro-physiological response to post-event questions. While techniques measuring physical responses such as EEG and pulse rates are very accurate, they are also expensive and require special equipment and training. Following are the three methods which are easily applied within a simple usability test.

NASA TLX

The NASA TLX test was developed to measure the overall work load of equipment operation. "It can be used to assess workload in various human-machine environments such as aircraft cockpits; command, control, and communication (C3) workstations; supervisory and process control environments; simulations and laboratory tests". To assess the workload experienced while completing multiple tasks, six rating scales have been established: mental demand, physical demand, temporal demand, performance, effort, frustration. The user rates each of these on a Likert scale and then has 15 questions that pair up two scales and ask the user to select the one which is the most important contributor to workload for the task.

The concept of the NASA-TLX is to allow the user time to access the workload situation once the testing is complete. The subscales provide detailed information, not just one-answer questions. We must consider that it measures workload as an afterthought. NASA-TLX does not test the user while they are in the process of completing the task. The user is forced to rely on what they remember and provide and opinion based on memory. NASA TLX is designed for work loads which often had a higher physical component than computer mouse operations. On the other hand, for the information seeking activities which are the norm on web sites, the cognitive load a person experiences tends to be directly related to the work load.

An electronic version of the test can be downloaded at http://www.nrl.navy.mil/aic/ide/NASATLX.php.

Sternberg Memory Test

As originally designed, the Sternberg Memory Test was designed to measure how quickly people can search for and retrieve information from short-term memory. People were give a small set of number (1-6) to memorize and were then give a sequence of probe numbers. The subjects had to respond yes/no to whether the probe number was one of the numbers they had memorized. For example, you memorize 3 and 6. The probe number is 8, you say "no." The probe number is 6, you say "yes." The part of the website or system using high cognitive resources can be determined because the yes/no response will take longer. According to Sternberg, several theories of short-term memory can be tested by altering the number of items on the list. Sternberg found that as the theory set increased, reaction times increased, and whether the probe was or was not committed to memory, did not alter the reaction time (Cog Lab Wadsworth). While this test sounds very simple, the speed of response (saying yes/no) varies with the cognitive load. For high load situations, a user responds slower and if they are overloaded, there could be a substantial delay

or out-right forgetting of some of the numbers which were memorized (Miyake, Y., Yohei O., & Ernst P., 2004).

Tapping Test

Using tapping is a simple way of imposing a secondary load on the user. If the subject's concentration is focused at processing information other than tapping, it is hard for subjects to apply the concentration needed to execute the tapping task (Miyake, Y., Yohei O., & Ernst P., 2004). While seemingly a trivial task, it does require cognitive resources to continue to rhythmically tap either a finger or foot. This imposes the additional load which helps push the user into cognitive overload.

Simulator Sickness

The Simulator Sickness Questionnaire (SSQ) introduced by Kennedy et al. (Kennedy, R.S., Lane, N.E., Berbaum, K.S. & Lilienthal, M.G., 1993) can be used as a measure in the simulator sickness experiments. There is an ambiguity in the use of the term "simulator sickness". In informal usage, "simulator sickness" tends to refer to the generic experience of feeling sick as a result of exposure to computer-generated stimuli. However, it is frequently used in a more restricted sense, as including only the sickness caused by poor simulations. For instance, Pausch et al. (Pausch, R., Crea, T. & Conway, M., 1992) mention that "The term simulator sickness is typically used to refer to sickness caused by the incorrect aspects of the simulation, not sickness caused by a correct simulation of a nauseating experience, such as a turbulent airplane flight." Else where in the same special issue on simulator sickness, one may find "simulator sickness" used in the more generic sense. For instance, in the preceding article Biocca (Biocca, F., 1992) states that "Simulator sickness is the term that has been attached to a host of symptoms associated with visual and vestibular disturbances that resemble motion sickness." The generic usage of "simulator sickness" is implicit in the title of the special issue, "Spotlight On: Simulator Sickness" (covering all sickness symptoms induced by simulators).

To take another example of the generic usage, Kennedy et al.'s widely-used "Simulator Sickness Questionnaire" (Kennedy, R.S., Lane, N.E., Berbaum, K.S. & Lilienthal, M.G., 1993) records motion sickness symptoms. It appears that there are three ideas present for which only two terms are in wide-spread use. The best solution is to introduce a third term. The three ideas are:

1. The generic feeling of sickness resulting from exposure to a computer-generated space.
2. The component of "1" which is inherent to the stimulus itself, and which would be present even if the simulation were a perfect representation of the real world.
3. The component of "1" which results from an imperfect simulation, for instance due to lag, poor inter-ocular adjust, poor resolution, etc.

There is general agreement that "2" should be referred to as "motion sickness". The problem lies with "1" and "3". Both are important ideas, and the term "simulator sickness" tends to oscillate between them depending on the topic of discussion.

LOCOMOTION IN VIRTUAL WORLD

Virtual reality provides for creation of simulated objects and events with which people can interact. The definitions of virtual reality (VR), although wide and varied, include a common statement that VR creates the illusion of participation in a synthetic environment rather than going through external observation of such an environment (Earnshaw, R. A., Gigante, M. A., & Jones, H., 1993). Essentially, virtual reality allows users to interact with a computer-simulated environment. Users can interact with a virtual environment either

through the use of standard input devices such as a keyboard and mouse, or through multimodal devices such as a wired glove, the Polhemus boom arm, or else omni-directional treadmill. The locomotion interface is used to simulate walking from one location to another location. The device is needed to be of a limited size, allow a user to walk on it and provide a sensation as if he is walking on an unconstrained plane.

Generally, a locomotion interface should cancel the user's self motion in a place to allow the user to go to anywhere in a large virtual space on foot. For example, a treadmill can cancel the user's motion by moving its belt in the opposite direction. Its main advantage is that it does not require a user to wear any kind of devices as required in some other locomotion devices. However, it is difficult to control the belt speed in order to keep the user from falling off. Some treadmills can adjust the belt speed based on the user's motion. There are mainly two challenges in using the treadmills. The first one is the user's stability problem while the second is to sense and change the direction of walking. The belt in a passive treadmill is driven by the backward push generated while walking. This process effectively balances the user and keeps him from falling off.

The problem of changing the walking direction is addressed by Brooks (Brooks, F. P. Jr., 1986) and Hirose et al., (Hirose, M. & Yokoyama, K., 1997), who employed a handle to change the walking direction. Iwata (Iwata, H. & Yoshida, Y., 1997) developed a 2D infinite plate that can be driven in any direction and Darken et al., (Darken, R. P., Cockayne, W.R., & Carmein, D., 1997) proposed an Omni directional treadmill using mechanical belt. Noma (Noma, H. & Miyasato, T., 1998) used the treadmill which could turn on a platform to change the walking direction. Iwata (Iwata, H. & Fujji, T., 1996) used a different approach by developing a series of sliding interfaces. The user was required to wear special shoes and a low friction film was put in the middle of shoes. Since the user was supported by a harness or rounded handrail, the foot motion was canceled passively when the user walked. The method using active footpad could simulate various terrains without requiring the user to wear any kind of devices.

Type of Locomotion in Virtual World

It has often been suggested that the best locomotion mechanism for virtual worlds would be walking, and it is well known that the sense of distance or orientation while walking is much better than while riding in a vehicle. However, the proprioceptive feedback of walking is not provided in most virtual environments. Good number of devices has been developed over the last two decades to integrate locomotion interfaces with VR environments. We have categorized the most common VR locomotion approaches as follow:

- Treadmills-style interface (Darken, Cockayne & Carmein, 1997; Hollerbach, Xu, Christensen, & Jacobsen, 2000; Iwata, & Yoshida, 1999; De Luca, Mattone, & Giordano, 2007),
- pedaling devices (such as bicycles or unicycles) (Iwata and Fuji, 1996),
- walking-in-place devices (Sibert, Templeman, Page, Barron, McCune & Denbrook, 2004),
- the motion foot pad (Iwata, Yano, Fukushima, & Noma, 2005),
- actuated shoes (Iwata, Yano, & Tomioka, 2006),
- the string walker (Iwata, Yano, & Tomiyoshi, 2007), and
- Finger walking-in-place devices.

CONCLUSION AND FUTURE DIRECTIVES

Knowledge based systems help to enhance capacity of machine or computer system to behave intelligently, similar to human being in some aspects at least. Machine based training simulators are equivalent or better than human trainers in terms of efficiency and effectiveness. Our Non-visual spatial navigation (NSL) model provides computational framework for spatial knowledge representation, acquisition and assessment of the acquired spatial knowledge. This model is effective to promote the development and online evaluation of cognitive maps of users. We are encouraged by preliminary results from our prototype implementation, which suggest that such spatial learning techniques would help visually impaired and blind people to get effectively learned for independent navigation. This is an ongoing study and we feel that our system based on our NSL model will be progressively enriched to become increasingly effective for spatial learning by them.

REFERENCES

Balogh, J., Michael C., & Giangola J. (2004). *Voice User Interface Design: Minimizing Cognitive Load. Addison Wesley Professional* 2004.

Biocca, F. (1992). Will simulation sickness slow down the diffusion of virtual environment technology? *Presence (Cambridge, Mass.), 1*(3), 334–343.

Bradyn, J. A. (1985). A review of mobility aids and means of assessment. In Warren, D.H. & Strelow, E.R. (eds.), *Electronic spatial sensing for the blind.* Martinus Nijhoff, 13-27.

Bronstein, I. N., & Semendjajew, K. A. (1979). *Taschenbuch der Mathematik.* Verlag Harri Deutsch, Thun and Frankfurt am Main, reprint of the 20th edition.

Brooks, F. P., Jr. (1986). Walk Through-a Dynamic Graphics System for Simulating Virtual Buildings. *Proc. of 1986 Workshop on Interactive 3D Graphics*, (pp. 9-21).

Burdea, G., & Coiffet, P. (2003). *Virtual Reality Technology.* New York: John Wiley & Sons.

Chandler, P., & Sweller, J. (1999). Cognitive Load While Learning to Use a Computer Program. [University of New South Wales.]. *Applied Cognitive Psychology*, 1996.

Chin, J., Diehl, V., & Norman, K. (1988). Development of an Instrument Measuring User Satisfaction of the Human-Computer Interface. *Proceedings of CHI*, 213-218.

Clark-Carter, D., Heyes, A., & Howarth, C. (1986). The effect of non-visual preview upon the walking speed of visually impaired people. *Ergonomics*, *29*(12), 1575–1581. doi:10.1080/00140138608967270

Colwell, C., Petrie, H., Kornbrot, D., Hardwick, A., & Furner, S. (1998). Haptic virtual reality for blind computer users," in *Proceedings of the 3rd International ACM Conference on Assistive Technologies (ASSETS '98)*, (pp. 92–99), Marina del Rey, Calif, USA.

Cooper, G. (2004). *Research into Cognitive Load Theory and Instructional Design at UNSW*. University of New South Wales. <http://www.google.com/scholar?hl=en&lr=&q=cache:BP2u yE_8R1EJ:www.uog.edu/coe/ed451/tHEORY/LoadTheory1.pdf+research+into+cognitive+load+theory+and+instructional+design+at+unsw>.

Crandall, W., Bentzen, B., Myers, L., & Mitchell, P. (1995). *Transit accessibility improvement through talking signs remote infrared signage, a demonstration and evaluation, Tech*. San Francisco, Calif, USA: Rep., The Smith-Kettlewell Eye Research Institute, Rehabilitation Engineering Research Center.

Darken, R. P., Cockayne, W. R., & Carmein, D. (1997). The Omni-Directional Treadmill: A Locomotion Device for Virtual Worlds. *Proc. of UIST'97*,(pp. 213-221).

De Luca, A., Mattone, R., & Giordano, P. R. (2007). Acceleration-level control of the CyberCarpet. *2007 IEEE International Conference on Robotics and Automation*, Roma, I,(pp. 2330-2335).

Dodson, A. H., Moore, T., & Moon, G. V. (1999). A Navigation System for the Blind Pedestrian [Genoa, Italy.]. *GNSS*, *99*, 513–518.

Downs, R., & Stea, D. (1977). *Maps in Minds: Reflections on Cognitive Mapping*. New York: Harper and Row.

Downs, R. M., & Stea, D. (1997). Cognitive Maps and spatial behaviour: Process and Products. In R.M. Downs & D. Stea (Eds,), *Image and Environment* (pp. 8-26). Chicago: Aldine.

Earnshaw, R. A., Gigante, M. A., & Jones, H. (Eds.). (1993). *Virtual Reality Systems*. Academic Press, 1993.

Ertan, S., Lee, C., Willets, A., Tan, H., & Pentland, A. (1998). A Wearable Haptic Navigation Guidance System. *2nd International Symposium on Wearable Computer* (pp. 164-165). Pittsburgh, PA

Espinosa, M., & Ochaita, E. (1998). Using tactile maps to improve the practical spatial knowledge of adults who are blind. *Journal of Visual Impairment & Blindness*, *92*(5), 338–345.

Freksa, C. (1997). *Spatial and Temporal Structures in Cognitive Processes* (LNCS 1337, pp. 379–387).New York: Springer, Berlin, Heidelberg.

Freundschuh, S. M., & Egenhofer, M. J. (1997). Human conceptions of spaces: Implications for geographic information systems. *Transactions in GIS*, *2*(4), 361–375.

Fruchterman, J. (1995). Archenstone's orientation tools: Atlas Speaks and Strider. In Gill, J.M. & Petrie, H. (Eds.). *Orientation and Navigation Systems for Blind Persons*, Hatfield, UK. 1-2 February 1995. RNIB.

Gapp, K. P. (1995). An empirically validated model for computing spatial relations. In Wachsmuth, I., Rollinger, C.-R., & Brauer, W., editors, *KI-95: Advances in Artificial Intelligence. 19th Annual German Conference on Artificial Intelligence,*(pp. 245–256) New York: Springer.

Giess, C., Evers, H., & Meinzer, H. (1998). Haptic volume rendering in different scenarios of surgical planning, in *Proceedings of the 3rd Phantom Users Group Workshop (PUG '98)*, (pp. 19–22). Cambridge, MA: MIT.

Golding, A. R., & Lesh, N. (1999). Indoor navigation using a diverse set of cheap, wearable sensors. *Third International Symposium on Wearable computers*, San Francisco, CA, 29-36.

Golledge, R., Klatzky, R., & Loomis, J. (1996). Cognitive mapping and wayfinding by adults without vision . In Portugali, J. (Ed.), *The construction of cognitive maps* (pp. 215–246). The Netherlands: Kluwer. doi:10.1007/978-0-585-33485-1_10

Golledge, R. G., Klatzky, R. L., Loomis, J. M., Speigle, J., & Tietz, J. (1998). A geographical information system for a GPS based personal guidance system . *International Journal of Geographical Information Science*, 12(7), 727–749. doi:10.1080/136588198241635

Gorman, P., Lieser, J., Murray, W., Haluck, R., & Krummel, T. (1998). Assessment and validation of force feedback virtual reality based surgical simulator, in *Proceedings of the 3rd Phantom Users Group Workshop (PUG '98)*Cambridge, MA: MIT.

Helal, A. S., Moore, S. E., & Ramachandran, B. (2001). Drishti: An integrated Navigation System for Visually Impaired and Disabled. *5th International Symposium on Wearable Computers.* Zurich, Switzerland.

Herrman, T., & Grabowski, J. (1994). *Sprechen – Psychologie der Sprachproduktion.* Berlin, Heidelberg: Spektrum Akademischer Verlag.

Hirose, M., & Yokoyama, K. (1997). Synthesis and transmission of realistic sensation using virtual reality technology. *Transactions of the Society of Instrument and Control Engineers*, 33(7), 716–722.

Hollerbach, J. M., Xu, Y., Christensen, R., & Jacobsen, S. C. (2000). Design specifications for the second generation Sarcos Treadport locomotion interface. Haptics Symposium, *Proc. ASME Dynamic Systems and Control Division,* (DSC-Vol. 69-2,pp.1293-1298) Orlando, Nov. 5-10, 2000.

Ittelson, W. (1973). *Environment and Cognition. Environment perception and contemporary perceptual theory* (pp. 1–19). New York: Seminar Press.

Iwata, H., & Fujji, T. (1996). Virtual Preambulator: A Novel Interface Device for Locomotion in Virtual Environment. *Proc. of IEEE VRAIS'96,*(pp. 60-65).

Iwata, H., Yano, H., Fukushima, H., & Noma, H. (2005). CirculaFloor. *IEEE Computer Graphics and Applications*, 25(1), 64–67. doi:10.1109/MCG.2005.5

Iwata, H., Yano, H., & Tomioka, H. (2006). Powered Shoes, SIGGRAPH 2006 Conference DVD (2006).

Iwata, H., Yano, H., & Tomiyoshi, M. (2007). String walker. Paper presented at SIGGRAPH 2007.

Iwata, H., & Yoshida, Y. (1999). Path Reproduction Tests Using a Torus Treadmill. *Presence (Cambridge, Mass.)*, 8(6), 587–597. doi:10.1162/105474699566503

Jansson, G., Fanger, J., Konig, H., & Billberger, K. (1998). Visually impaired persons' use of the phantom for information about texture and 3D form of virtual objects, in *Proceedings of the 3rd Phantom Users Group Workshop.*Cambridge, MA: MIT.

Jonsson, E. (2002). *Inner Navigation: why we get lost and how we find our way* (pp. 27–126). New York: Scribner.

Kay, L. (1980). Air sonar with acoustical display of spatial information . In Busnel, R. G., & Fish, J. F. (Eds.), *Animal Sonar System* (pp. 769–816). New York: Plenum Press.

Kemmerling, M., & Schliepkorte, H. (1998). *An Orientation and Information System for Blind People based on RF-Speech-Beacons*. Helsinki: TIDE.

Kennedy, R. S., Lane, N. E., Berbaum, K. S., & Lilienthal, M. G. (1993). Simulator Sickness Questionnaire: An enhanced method for quantifying simulator sickness. *The International Journal of Aviation Psychology*, *3*(3), 203–220. doi:10.1207/s15327108ijap0303_3

Kitchin, R. M., Blades, M., & Golledge, R. G. (1997). Understanding spatial concepts at the geographic scale without the use of vision. *Progress in Human Geography*, *21*(2), 225–242. doi:10.1191/030913297668904166

Lahav, O. (2003). *Blind Persons' Cognitive Mapping of Unknown Spaces and acquisition of Orientation Skills, by Using Audio and Force-Feedback Virtual Environment*. Doctoral dissertation, Tel-Aviv University, Israel (Hebrew).

Lahav, O., & Mioduser, D. (2003). A blind person's cognitive mapping of new spaces using a haptic virtual environment. *Journal of Research in Special Educational Needs*, *3*(3), 172–177. doi:10.1111/1471-3802.00012

Long, S., Aust, D., Abowd, G. D., & Atkeson, C. (1996). Cyberguide: Prototyping Context-aware Mobile Applications. In *CHI '96 Conference Companion*, pp.293-294.

Loomis, J. M., Golledge, R. G., & Klatzky, R. L. (2001). GPS-Based Navigation System for the Visually Impaired . In Barfield, W., & Caudell, T. (Eds.), *Fundamentals of Wearable Computers and Augmented Reality* (pp. 429–446). Mahwah, NJ: Lawrence Erbaum Associates.

Lynch, K. (1960). *The Image of the City*. Cambridge, MA: MIT Press.

Miyake, Y., Yohei, O., & Ernst, P. (2004). Two Types of Anticipation in Synchronization Tapping. *Acta Neurobiol*, *64*, 415–426.

Montello, D. R. (1993). Scale and multiple phychologies of space . In Frank, A., & Campari, I. (Eds.), *Spatial Information Theory: A theoretical basis for GIS* (pp. 312–321). New York: Springer.

Noma, H., & Miyasato, T. (1998). Design for Locomotion Interface in a Large Scale Virtual Environment. *ATLAS: ATR Locomotion Interface for Active Self Motion ASME-DSC*, *64*, 111–118.

Pausch, R., Crea, T., & Conway, M. (1992). A Literature Survey for Virtual Environments: Military Flight Simulator Visual Systems and Simulator Sickness. *Presence (Cambridge, Mass.)*, *1*(3), 344–363.

Petrie, H. (1995). User requirements for a GPS-based travel aid for blind people . In Gill, J. M., & Petrie, H. (Eds.), *Orientation and Navigation Systems for Blind Persons* (pp. 1–2). UK: February. RNIB.

Raubal, M., & Worboys, M. (1999). A formal model for the process of wayfinding in built environments. In Freksa, C. & Mark, D. M.(Eds.), *Spatial Information Theory (Proceedings of COSIT 99). Springer, Berlin*, (pp. 381–399).New York: Springer.

Rieser, J. J. (1989). Access to knowledge of spatial structure at novel points of observation. *Journal of Experimental Psychology. Learning, Memory, and Cognition, 15*(6), 1157–1165. doi:10.1037/0278-7393.15.6.1157

Sabelman, E. E., Burgar, C. G., Curtis, G. E., Goodrich, G., Jaffe, D. L., Mckinley, J. L., et al. (1994). Personal navigation and wayfinding for individuals with a range of disabilities, Project report: Device development and evaluation. http://guide.stanford.edu/Publications/dev3.html.

Schultheis, M., & Rizzo, A. (2001). The application of virtual reality technology for rehabilitation. *Rehabilitation Psychology, 46*(3), 296–311. doi:10.1037/0090-5550.46.3.296

Semwal, S. K., & Evans-Kamp, D. L. (2000). *Virtual environments for visually impaired.* Paper presented at the 2nd International Conference on Virtual worlds, Paris, France.

Sibert, L., Templeman, J., Page, R., Barron, J., McCune, J., & Denbrook, P. (2004). *Initial Assessment of Human Performance Using the Gaiter Interaction Technique to Control Locomotion in Fully Immersive Virtual Environments. (Technical Report).* Washington, D.C: Naval Research Laboratory.

Siegel, A. W., & White, S. H. (1975). The development of spatial representations of large-scale environments. In Rees, H. W. (Ed.), *Advances in child development and behavior* (*Vol. 10*, pp. 9–55). New York: Academic Press.

Slater, M., Usoh, M., & Steed, A. (1995). Taking Steps: The Influence of a Walking Metaphor on Presence in Virtual Reality. *ACM Transactions on Computer-Human Interaction, 2*(3), 201–219. doi:10.1145/210079.210084

Sorrows, M. E., & Hirtle, S. C. (1999). The nature of landmarks in real and electronic spaces. In Freksa, C. & Mark, D. M.,(Eds.) *Spatial Information Theory (Proceedings of COSIT 99)*,(pp. 37–50), New York: Springer.

Standen, P. J., Brown, D. J., & Cromby, J. J. (2001). The effective use of virtual environments in the education and rehabilitation of students with intellectual disabilities. *British Journal of Educational Technology, 32*(3), 289–299. doi:10.1111/1467-8535.00199

Strothotte, T., Fritz, S., Michel, R., Raab, A., Petrie, H., Johnson, V., et al. (1996). Development of Dialogue Systems for the Mobility Aid for Blind People: Initial Design and Usability Testing. *ASSETS '96*, Vancouver, British Columbia, Canada, 139-144.

Tobler, W. (1976). The geometry of mental maps. In Golledge, R. G., & Rushton, G. (Eds.), *Spatial choice and spatial behavior* (pp. 69–82). Columbus, OH: Ohio State University Press.

Tolman, E. (1948). Cognitive maps in rats and men. *Psychological Review, 55*, 189–208. doi:10.1037/h0061626

Tversky, B. (1993). Cognitive Maps, Cognitive Collages, and Spatial Mental Models. In *Spatial Information Theory. A Theoretical Basis for GIS, COSIT'93*, (pp. 14–24).

Ungar, S., & Blades, M. M., & Spencer, S (1996). The construction of cognitive maps by children with visual impairments, In J. Portugali, (Ed) *The Construction of Cognitive Maps*, pp. 247–273, The Netherlands: Kluwer Academic Publishers.

Warren, D., & Strelow, E. (1985). *Electronic Spatial Sensing for the Blind.* Boston: Martinus Nijhoff.

Werner, S., Krieg-Bruckner, B., Mallot, H. A., Schweizer, K., & Freksa, C. (1997). Spatial cognition: The role of landmark, route, and survey knowledge in human and robot navigation . In Jarke, M. (Ed.), *Informatik '97 GI Jahrestagung* (pp. 41–50). New York: Springer.

KEY TERMS AND DEFINITIONS

Bi-dimensional Correlation Coefficients: Bi-dimensional regression is applied to calculate the bi-dimensional correlation coefficients.

Blindness: Legal blindness (which is actually a severe visual impairment) refers to a best-corrected central vision of 20/200 or worse in the better eye or a visual acuity of better than 20/200 but with a visual field no greater than 20° (e.g., side vision that is so reduced that it appears as if the person is looking through a tunnel).

Cognitive Load: A person has a limited amount of cognitive resources which they must allocate amount all mental tasks being concurrently performed. Cognitive load refers to the total amount of mental activity on working memory at an instance in time.

Constructivist Learning: Within the constructivist paradigm, the accent is on the learner rather than the teacher. It is the learner who interacts with his or her environment and thus gains an understanding of its features and characteristics. The learner constructs his own conceptualisations and finds his own solutions to problems, mastering autonomy and independence. According to constructivism, learning is the result of individual mental construction, whereby the learner learns by dint of matching new against given information and establishing meaningful connections, rather than by internalising mere factoids to be regurgitated later on.

Landmark-Route-Survey Theory: The longest standing model of large-scale space representation is the Landmark, Survey, Route (or LRS) model (Siegel and White 1975). LRS theory states that we first identify landmarks in an environment, add route knowledge between landmarks as we traverse the environment and finally add survey (or configurational) knowledge as we become familiar with the environment. Once survey knowledge has been added, we have the capability to propose novel, previously un-traversed paths between landmarks.

Locomotion Interface: Locomotion interface should cancel the user's self motion in a place to allow the user to go to anywhere in a large virtual space on foot.

Presence: Presence is a multi-dimensional concept that involves psychological processes.

Simulator Sickness: In informal usage, "simulator sickness" tends to refer to the generic experience of feeling sick as a result of exposure to computer-generated stimuli.

Virtual Environment: VE provides for creation of simulated objects and events with which people can interact. The definitions of VE, although wide and varied, include a common statement that VE creates the illusion of participation in a synthetic environment rather than going through external observation of such an environment.

ENDNOTE

[1]   Source: http://www.who.int/mediacentre/factsheets/fs282/en/ as access on 05-Sep-2009

Chapter 13
Signing Avatars

Nicoletta Adamo-Villani
Purdue University, USA

Kyle Hayward
Purdue University, USA

ABSTRACT

The chapter focuses on signing avatars and their potential to improve deaf education. In sections 1 and 2, the authors give an overview of what signing avatars are and the benefits of using animated characters for deaf education. In section 3, they explain how signing avatars are created. In particular, in subsection 3.1, they describe different types of 3D models and skeletal deformation systems, and in subsection 3.2 the authors discuss a variety of methods used to animate manual and non-manual signs. In section 4 they report the state of the art in signing avatars' research and development and we discuss existing limitations and future trends. Section 5 includes a case study on the production of the signing avatars for SMILE™ and Mathsigner™ Conclusive remarks are presented in section 6.

INTRODUCTION

Deaf education, especially in science, technology, engineering, and math (STEM), is a pressing national problem. Unfortunately, current and past statistics show that too many deaf students do not reach their potential. Despite years of trials with different teaching and communication methodologies, little progress has been made. Less than 10% of deaf children have both deaf parents fluent in ASL, so the overwhelming ma-

jority suffers from inadequate communication with one or both parents. Deaf individuals face barriers in school, workplace, and social venues which prevent them from having equal opportunity for success. The underlying cause that needs to be addressed is that deaf students are unable to access and interact with grade-level curriculum materials because of their historically low literacy levels. Less than 12% of deaf students at age 16 can read at a 4th grade reading level or higher (Hoffmeister 2000; Padden & Ramsey 2000; Prinz 2002; Strong & Prinz 1997, 2000). Other barriers to successful STEM education for the

DOI: 10.4018/978-1-61692-825-4.ch013

Deaf: (a) *Lack of adequate early interactive communication.* The challenge facing deaf children is not acquisition of speech, as many assume, but acquisition of language skills that underlie successful use of speech, signing, reading, and writing. Significantly, there is a strong correlation between ASL fluency and English literacy (Strong & Prinz 1997, 2000). English literacy improves as ASL skills improve and knowledge of ASL as a first language is beneficial because it taps normal capacities at appropriate developmental stages (Wilbur 2000). (b) *Inaccessibility to incidental learning,* i.e. exposure to media and other sources of information in which math/science concepts are present. Research literature refers to this as 'the limited input problem' (Johnson et al. 1989; Wilbur 2000).

Signing avatars have the potential to overcome all these barriers. A signing avatar is a three-dimensional (3D) animated character that can communicate in sign language, i.e. through hand gestures, facial expressions and upper body motions. Computer animated signing characters can teach young deaf children and their hearing parents how to sign and can make digital content completely accessible to deaf students who do not know how to read yet. They provide a low-cost and effective means for adding sign language translation to any type of media such as educational games and Virtual Learning Environments (VLE).

BENEFITS AND USES OF SIGNING AVATARS

Like videos of live signers, signing avatars allow for direct presentation of ASL in its dynamic visual form, eliminating the need for closed-captioned text, awkward representations of signs, or static sign images. Compared to video, animation technology has the following fundamental advantages.

(a) 3-D animation offers great control over the visualization of the signs; the point of view of the virtual camera that renders the signing character and the location of the character in relation to the background can be optimized to enhance clarity. (b) The speed of the signing motion can be adjusted to the ASL proficiency of the user, of great importance for children who are learning ASL. (c) Individual animated signs can be linked together smoothly to form sentences, without abrupt jumps or collisions as would happen when concatenating video clips. (d) 3D animation allows for user programmability; unlike videotapes and CD-ROMs of video clips for which programmability is very limited (clips can be composed but with great difficulty and discontinuous results). Programmability can be utilized for: generating infinite number of drills; unlimited text encoding; real time translation; limitless combinations of signs. For example, manual signs and facial expressions can be combined in any desired manner under program control. (e) Animations can be stored and transmitted remotely using only a small fraction of the storage and bandwidth costs of comparable video representations.

Moreover, some recent findings support the value of computer animation of ASL. The pioneering work in applying computer animation to ASL was carried out by Vcom3D (Vcom3D, 2007) Vcom3D products, now in use in over 30 school systems, have demonstrated the advantages of using three-dimensional animated characters that can communicate in ASL (and other variant sign languages) to provide multimedia access and increase English literacy for the Deaf. Data show improved reading comprehension as a result of using these products. In one evaluation, comprehension scores of young learners reading below grade level increased from 17% to 67%; in another evaluation, scores increased from 40% to 80% (Sims, 2000).

CONSTRUCTION OF A SIGNING AVATAR

Graphical Models

A signing avatar consists of a geometric skin and an articulated skeleton (see Figure 1). The skin is usually modeled as one or several polygon meshes while the skeleton is a hierarchical structure of joints connected by bones. To pose the character, the joints can be rotated using Forward or Inverse Kinematics (FK or IK). In order to move with the skeleton, the surfaces that make up the skin are either parented or attached (skinned) to the skeletal joints.

Signing avatars can be divided into two groups based on their geometrical characteristics: (1) segmented and (2) partially segmented or seamless. (1) The skin of a segmented avatar is a collection of rigid geometrical components (segments) organized in a hierarchical structure. Because the segments do not deform during motion, they are parented to the skeletal joints. In other words, each geometrical component rotates with the parent joint but does not change shape as a result of the rotation. Examples of segmented avatars are robots and artist mannequins.

(2) A partially segmented avatar consists of a series of rigid and non-rigid geometrical segments, whereas a seamless character consists of one continuous deformable mesh. Because both partially segmented and seamless avatars show organic deformations during motions, they are 'skinned' to the skeleton. Skinning is the process of attaching the character's 'skin' (represented by one or several 3D surfaces) to the skeleton. As a result of the skinning process, the skeleton acts as a deformation system in which the joints affect the position of the skin vertices. Every time a skeletal joint is rotated, the corresponding skin vertices are moved with the joint and therefore the skin changes shape. Two skinning methods are commonly used to rig characters: rigid and smooth. In rigid skinning a skin control vertex can be influenced by one joint only; in smooth skinning a skin control vertex can be influenced by several joints. The influence (or skin weight) that a joint has on a CV ranges from zero (0) (i.e. no influence) to one (1) (i.e. 100% influence) and can be edited to optimize the deformations. Figure 2 shows examples of segmented and seamless characters.

Figure 1. From the left: character skeleton; polygonal mesh (skin); skin with textures

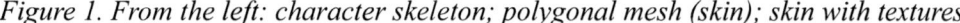

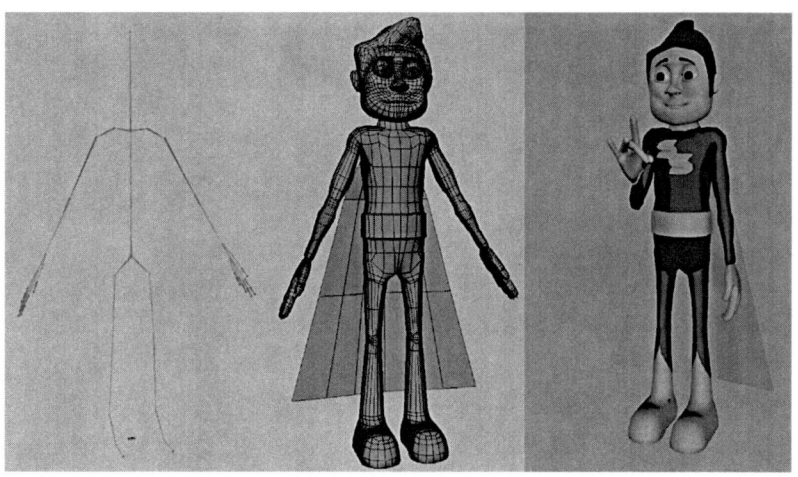

Animation

The ASL (American Sign Language) sign can be decomposed into 5 components: the handshape, the orientation of the hand, the position of the hand in relation to the body (which determines the pose of the signer's arm), the motion (within the sign, if dynamic, and across signs), and the non-manual components (i.e. facial articulations, head rotations, shoulder and torso motions). Three animation techniques can be used to animate these components: keyframe animation, motion-capture (mocap) animation, and synthetic animation generated on the fly.

In *keyframe animation*, the animator manually rotates the character skeletal joints in order to pose the avatar. Once the desired pose has been attained, the animator saves the joints' rotation values at a particular point in the timeframe; this process is called *setting a keyframe*. After the animator has defined all keyframes (which represent the main poses of the sign), the animation system interpolates the joints' rotation values between the keyframes, and thus generates the motion.

The quality of keyframed signing animations (i.e. their accuracy and fluidity) depends entirely on the skills of the animator and on the ability of the animation system to provide the animator with fine control over the timing, pacing and duration of the signing motions.

Motion capture animation, also referred to as performance animation or digital puppetry ". . . involves measuring an actor's (in our case a signer) position and orientation in physical space and recording that information in a computer-usable form".* (Dyer et al., 1995) In general the position or orientation of the actor is measured by a collection of input devices (optical markers or sensors) attached to the actor's body. Each input device has three degrees of freedom (DOF) and produces 3-D rotational or translational data which are channeled to the joints of a virtual character. In order to capture handshapes and finger motions two approaches can be used: direct-device and

Figure 2. From the left: seamless avatar showing organic deformations while signing "+"; segmented avatar showing rotations of rigid body segments while signing "6"

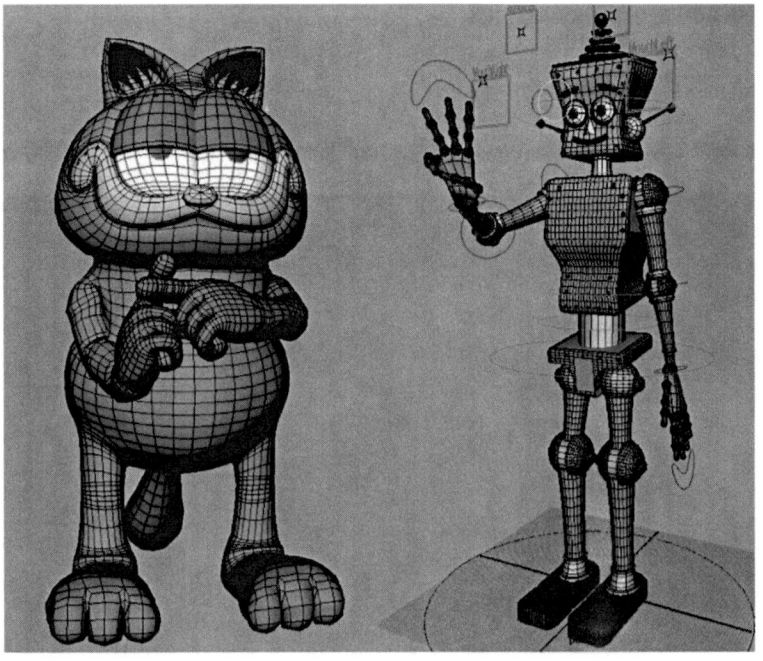

vision-based input. The direct-device approach uses a number of commercially available instrumented gloves and flexion sensors. Vision based approaches use one or more video cameras to capture images of the hands and interpret them to produce visual features that can be used to recognize gestures. As the signer moves, the body and hand input devices send data to the computer model. These data are used to control the movements of the virtual character in real time, and to generate the animation sequences.

The advantages of motion capture animation are speed – in general mocap animation is less time consuming than keyframe animation; and the ability to capture (and recreate), in a physically accurate manner, complex body movement and realistic physical interactions, such as secondary actions. The main problem with motion captured animation of sign language is that current approaches to hand gesture input are not able to capture the hand shapes and finger motions with sufficient accuracy. Generally, the captured hand motions require a substantial amount of editing (i.e. keyframing) in order to be acceptable. Therefore, it is often more effective to keyframe the hand poses and finger motions.

Synthetic animation is produced by translating high-level commands from an external application into character gestures and facial expressions, through a system of rules and states. Body and facial poses can be composed in real-time to form sequences of signs. The advantage of synthetic animation lies in the fact that sign sequences can be generated fast and by users who do not have expertise in animation. However, a significant limitation of fully synthetic animation of ASL is its inability to capture the nuances typically portrayed by skilled ASL users. While synthetic animation can approximate sentences produced by ASL signers, the individual hand shapes and rhythm of signing are often unnatural, and the facial expressions do not convey meanings as clearly as a live signer.

Facial Animation

Facial expressions are a fundamental component of ASL, in addition to being an essential contributing factor to the realism of the animated character. While it is possible to understand the meaning of an English sentence without seeing the facial expressions, this is not the case for signed communication. In ASL, facial articulations are key elements of grammar as they perform significant semantic, prosodic, pragmatic, and syntactic functions, in addition to social interaction and conversational regulation. For example, speakers of English tend to inflect their voices to indicate they are asking a question whereas ASL signers inflect their questions by using non-manual markers. When signing a question that can be answered with "yes or no" the signer raises her eyebrows and tilts her head slightly forward. When signing a question involving "who, what, when, where, how, why" the signer furrows her eyebrows while tilting the head back a bit.

Animating natural facial expressions is a challenging task because of the complexity of the human face, which consists of a large number of muscles (i.e. 40 bilaterally symmetrical muscles of facial expression and 4 muscles of mastication). These muscles pull the skin, temporarily distorting the shape of the eyes, brows, and lips, and the appearance of folds, furrows and bulges in different areas of the skin. Such muscle movements result in the production of rapid facial signals (facial expressions) which convey different types of messages such as emotions; emblems - symbolic communicators, culture-specific (e.g., the wink); manipulators - manipulative associated movements (e.g., lip-biting); and illustrators - movements that accompany and emphasize signing and speech (e.g., a raised brow) (Ekman and Friesen, 1978).

Two approaches are currently being used to model facial signals for real-time animation of sign language: (1) joint deformers and (2) morph targets.

Figure 3. From the left: Example of facial skeletal system with floating joints (red circles) bound to a polygonal mesh. Mesh with joints of the upper face (top), and facial deformations induced by rotating the upper face joints (bottom).

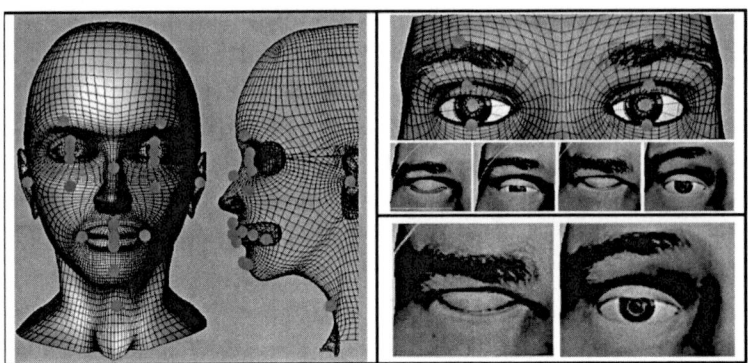

(1) The avatar's face can be set up for facial animation using a system of joints. Figure 3 (left) shows an example of a 43 - floating joint facial skeletal deformation system specifically designed for animation of ASL facial expressions. Each joint (or pair of joints) controls a facial articulator, such as Eyebrows, Upper Eyelids, Lower Eyelids, Eye gaze, Nose, Cheeks, Upper Lips, Lower Lips, Tongue, Teeth, Chin, etc. By translating and/or rotating the joints it is possible to induce specific facial deformations and movements. Transitions between successive facial configurations can then

be produced by setting keyframes for the positions of the joints. Figure 3 (right) shows an example of facial deformations induced by the translation and rotation of the joints of the upper face.

(2) Facial deformations can also be produced by defining keyshapes, i.e. morph targets. Using this approach, the animator begins by making several duplicates of the facial model to be animated; the original model is called the 'base' and the duplicates are called 'targets'. The animator then moves control points or polygon vertices on each target to produce different facial deforma-

Figure 4. From the left: character with 'base' face; 36 morph targets representing 36 different facial deformations

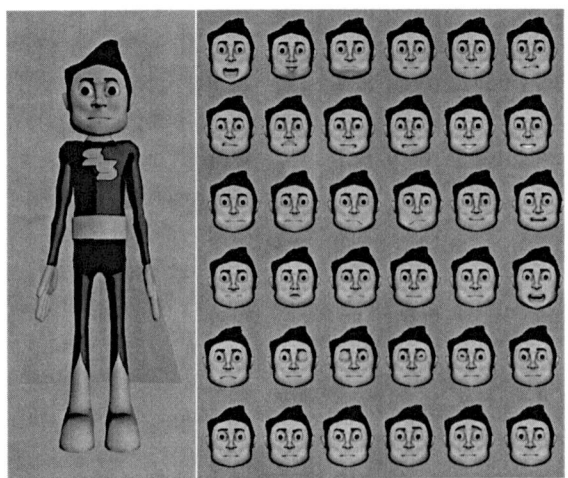

Figure 5. Facial expression (circle) produced with multiple-target morphing by combining 4 morph targets (squares)

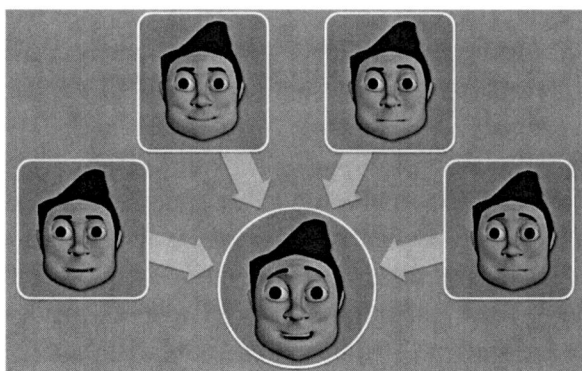

tions. Figure 4 shows the 36 morph targets used to animate the facial expressions of one of the Mathsigner avatars. Facial animation is produced by setting keyframes for the morph targets and interpolating between the base and the targets to create the intermediate keyshapes that come between them. Two morphing techniques can be used to animate facial signals: single-target and multiple-target morphing. Single-target morphing allows for blending between the base and one target at a time, whereas multiple-target morphing allows for blending between the base and several targets at the same time, thus allowing for more complex facial articulations. Figure 5 shows an example of asymmetrical facial articulation produced by combining 5 targets.

The amount of blending between base and target(s) is controlled by the morph target weight, which is a value that indicates how much a facial deformation contributes to an expression. A value of zero equates to no contribution, while a value of one equates to full contribution Figure 6 shows an example of morph target with different weights.

In 1999, the Moving Pictures Experts Group released MPEG-4 as an ISO standard (ISO, 1999) The MPEG-4 Facial Animation (FA) (Pakstas, 2009) standard defines a set of key facial parameters (Facial Animation Parameters or FAP) that provide a standardized format for facial animation. The interface defines two FAPs for visemes and expressions, and sixty-six lower level FAPS that correspond to specific locations on the face. FAP values correspond to translations of feature points in relation to the neutral face.

There has been a considerable amount of research in facial animation that use the facial animation standard of MPEG-4. iFACE (http://img.csit.

Figure 6. From left, base head; Smile morph target with weight =0 .5; Smile morph target with weight = 1.0

carleton.ca/iface) is a powerful environment that facilitates creating realistic facial animations that relate to defined personality traits. Users can create facial animations by modifying FAPs, and setting key frames. iFACE can also dynamically analyze a voice audio stream and create a facial animation by analyzing the pitch, inflection and other properties. Xface (http://xface.itc.it/), another application that is based on FAPs, allows users to not only create facial animations and expression, but also create their own morph targets, negating the need for an artist to create multiple morph targets inside a professional modeling package.

STATE-OF-THE-ART AND CURRENT LIMITATIONS

Three research groups in the US are currently engaged in research and development of signing avatars for improving deaf accessibility to educational content: Vcom3D (VCom 3D, 2007)) TERC (TERC, 2007), and Purdue University (Mathsigner, 2009; SMILE 2007).

Researchers and developers at Vcom 3D have been the first to reveal the potential of computer animation of sign language for improving deaf accessibility to digital content and environments. Two of their commercial products are designed specifically for adding sign language to media: Signing Avatar® and Sign Smith Studio®. SigningAvatar® software uses animated 3D characters to communicate in sign language with facial expressions; has a vocabulary of over 3500 English words / concepts, 24 facial configurations, and can fingerspell words not in the sign vocabulary. Sign Smith Studio® is an authoring tool that enables digital content developers to add 3D animated signing characters to their content.

In 2005, TERC collaborated with Vcom3D and staff from the National Technical Institute for the Deaf (NTID) on use of the SigningAvatar® accessibility software to sign the web activities and resources for two Kids Network units. Recently,

TERC has developed a Signing Science Dictionary (SSD), using the same software (Signing Science, 2007) SSD has been designed to support access to standards-based science content among elementary and middle-grade students who are deaf or hard of hearing and whose first language is sign.

Purdue University Animated Sign Language Research Group is focusing on research, development, and evaluation of innovative 3D animation-based interactive learning environments to improve K-4 math/science education for deaf children. The team is currently working on two projects: Mathsigner™ and SMILE™ (Adamo-Villani et al. 2005; Adamo-Villani and Wilbur, 2008). Mathsigner™ is a 3D animation ASL-based interactive software package that contains sets of standards-based learning activities designed to teach K-4 math concepts, signs, and corresponding English terminology to deaf children, their parents, and teachers. SMILE™ is an immersive learning game that employs a fantasy 3D virtual environment and bilingual avatars (English/ASL) to engage deaf and hearing students in math and science-based educational activities. SMILE and Mathsigner are described in detail in section 5.

In Europe, the main research on signing avatars has been done by Prof. John Glauert at the University of East Anglia, UK. Prof. Glauert led the ViSiCAST project (Bangham et al. 2000) whose goal was to provide deaf citizens with improved access to services and facilities through animated sign language. The specific objective of the ViSiCAST project was the realization of a natural text-to-sign language animated translation through the use of innovative avatar technology. The project is now being continued by eSIGN (eSIGN 2003).

Although the quality of 3D animation of ASL has improved significantly during the past decade, its effectiveness and wide-spread use is still precluded by two main limitations: low realism of the signing characters and low rendering quality, which reduces the legibility of the animated signs and the appeal of the virtual signer.

Low realism of existing signing characters. This is due primarily to non-natural motions across signs (i.e. movement epenthesis) and simplistic animation of facial expressions. Many signs include motion as a semantic component, and even when a sign is static, the signer must move from sign to sign during continuous discourse. Current algorithms synthesize these in-between movements by linear interpolation of joint angles, which yields a robotic, unnatural effect because it does not represent any variation in the tempo of the motion, or in its path. The lack of variation in motion timing and the use of straight lines as movement trajectories contradict two fundamental principles of animation, namely, the 'Slow-in and Slow-out' and the 'Arcs' principles (Johnston and Thomas, 1995). Failure to implement these principles in ASL animation has resulted in puppet-like animated characters unable to represent signing with life-like quality.

Unrealistic appearance is further accentuated by crude, simplistic animation of non-manual markers such as facial expressions. As mentioned previously, the non-manual components of ASL carry important semantic, prosodic, pragmatic, and syntactic information that may not be provided by the manual signing itself. Therefore, ineffective animation of such components not only detracts from the realism of the character, but it also directly reduces the clarity and accuracy of the concepts being signed. Existing animation of ASL has been unable to represent facial articulations with realism and accuracy for the following reasons:

- The animation of the signer's face is based on a limited set of pre-modeled facial expressions rather than on a set of individually modeled facial deformations that can be combined to represent any possible facial articulation. The result is animated signers that show mechanical repetition of identical and symmetrical, and therefore unrealistic, facial expressions. We note that facial expressions are never exactly identical and people's faces are never symmetrical.

- The signer's face lacks a holistic connection within itself. Existing ASL animation has focused almost exclusively on eyes, mouth and head motions and has completely ignored the primary facial connectors (i.e. cheeks, nose and ears). In order to achieve life-like quality, the character's face needs to be animated as a set of interconnected regions that affect each other, not as a collection of independent, disconnected parts. For instance, it is not possible to smile without rising up the cheeks, to sneer without wrinkling up the nose, or to open the mouth wide without lowering the ears slightly.

- The timing of the facial expressions and the transitions between them is controlled via linear interpolation only. While it is possible to adjust the overall speed, and therefore the duration of the facial articulations, it is not possible to control variations in acceleration and deceleration within and across facial signals. We note that fine control of facial deformations' timing is fundamental to effective animation of ASL. For instance, a signer can produce one of three types of blinks: startle reflex, involuntary periodic (e.g. wetting the eye), and voluntary. Each type of blink has different frequency and different timing. For example, periodic blinks, which have been shown to be markers of the end of intonational phrases in ASL, occur much more frequently, have a shorter duration, and are characterized by a fast, accelerating closing motion of the eyelid and a slower, decelerating opening motion. The situation is reversed for voluntary blinks which occur less frequently, last longer and show the opposite speed pattern for the eyelid motion (Wilbur, 1994).

Low rendering quality. The visual quality of ASL animation depends on the underlying rendering algorithm that takes digital representations of surface geometry, color, lights, and motions as input and computes the frames of the animation. The sophistication of rendering algorithms and the raw power of their hardware implementation has greatly advanced in recent years, yet present ASL animation systems employ rendering algorithms that are one or several steps behind the state of the art. Two problems stand out: lack of motion blur and simplistic local illumination models. A rendering algorithm without motion blur capability simply takes instantaneous snapshots of the scene. A rapidly moving object such as the hand of an ASL signer will be captured by consecutive animation frames at distant, non-overlapping positions, which leads to a truncated visual depiction of the motion that is cryptic to the viewer. Motion blur is needed to integrate intermediate hand positions enhancing the visual perception of trajectories during rapid signing (see Figure 7 left). Motion blur is an effect characteristic to all physical cameras including a video camera that recorded a signer or a human eye that observes a signer live.

The second rendering approximation with a particularly large negative effect in our context is the assumption that scene surfaces receive light only through direct exposure to light sources (see Figure 7 middle). Such a local illumination model ignores the light that reaches a surface indirectly, through one or several intermediate reflections off other scene surfaces. Images rendered under the local illumination assumption lack detail and do not convey shape well. The amount of indirect illumination is an important cue in shape perception: depressions, creases, and closed regions are darker, while convex exposed regions are brighter, which accentuates the three-dimensional appearance of the scene imaged. Figure 7, right, shows the hand rendered with ambient occlusion, i.e. taking into account indirect lighting.

The problem of low quality appearance of the signing characters is particularly severe if we consider that the emotional aspect plays a decisive role in learning for deaf students (Lang et al. 1993) Future research in Computer Animation of sign language must address the basic problem of representing the signs with clarity, realism and emotional appeal to learners. While it is technologically more accessible to produce puppet-like animations of signing characters, it is worthwhile to invest research effort to create emotionally engaging 3D signers (both human-like and fantasy) with fluid movements and natural facial expressions.

In the next section we describe the development of the signing avatars for SMILE™ and Mathsigner™ and we discuss the approach taken by the Purdue ASL research team in order to overcome some of these current limitations.

Figure 7. From the left: Frame of rapidly moving hand correctly rendered with motion blur. (Middle) hand shape rendered w/o and w/ ambient occlusion.

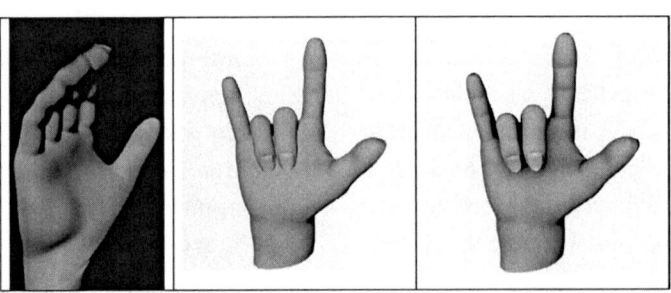

EXAMPLE OF APPLICATION: THE SIGNING AVATARS FOR MATHSIGNER™ AND SMILE™ - ADVANCING THE STATE OF THE ART IN ASL ANIMATION

Mathsigner and SMILE are two novel 3D animation-based approaches to deaf education. Mathsigner is an interactive software package that contains sets of activities designed to teach K-4 math concepts, signs, and corresponding English terminology to deaf children, their parents, and teachers. SMILE is an immersive Virtual Learning Environment (VLE) in which deaf and hearing children ages 5-10 learn STEM concepts and ASL terminology through user interaction with fantasy 3D characters that communicate in ASL and spoken English. Figure 8 shows screenshots of the two applications.

Both applications are being developed using cutting-edge interactive 3D animation technology that improves on existing 3D animation-based signing products. The innovative aspects of Mathsigner and SMILE signing avatars are discussed in the next sections.

Improved Character Skinning

Several skin deformation methods can be used to set up skeleton-based models for real-time animation. Linear blend skinning is one of the most widely used because it is both fast and straightforward to implement. However, it presents two limitations: it requires a full 4x3 matrix to represent position and rotation per bone, and suffers from the "candy wrapper" effect (i.e. twisting motion at joints causes pinching, or a loss of volume). Because in SMILE and Mathsigner we perform skinning on the graphics processing unit (GPU), which limits the amount of data that can be sent to it, linear blend skinning would have constrained the avatars to a limited set of joints (i.e. 80), and therefore to a limited number of degrees of freedom (DOF). In order to allow more joints and maintain the character volume during animation, the signers in SMILE and Mathsigner make use of dual-quaternion skinning (Kavan et al. 2007). This method only uses two quaternions to represent position and rotation per bone (allowing up to one hundred bones) and prevents loss of volume while only being slightly slower to calculate the skinning transformation than linear blend skinning. With this method the virtual signers are not only able to perform complex gestures and movements, but also to show realistic organic deformations during motion. Figure 9 shows the difference in deformation between the two skinning methods.

Figure 8. From the left: screenshot of the city of SmileVille (top) and signing avatar in SMILE bakery (bottom); screenshot of Mathsigner with avatar signing "butterfly"

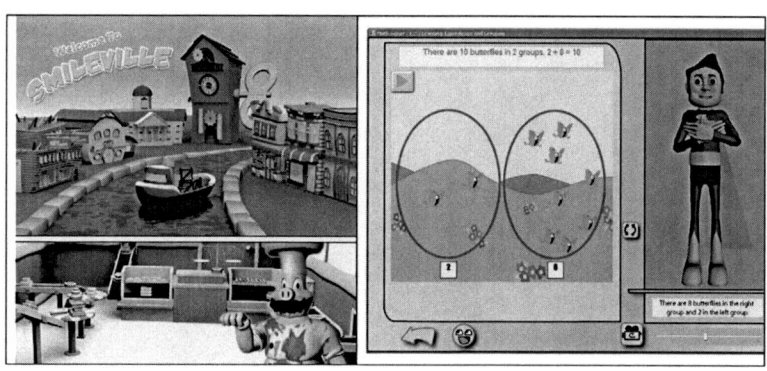

Improved Animation

Sign Animation. Each individual sign in SMILE and Matsigner was produced by a skilled animator/ASL signer using keyframe animation technique; all signs were reviewed for accuracy and realism (and subsequently refined) by two Deaf educators. The animated signs are stored in a database as individual clips accessed at run-time. The applications dynamically determine which signs are required for a particular ASL message, load the required signs into memory, and unload the signs that are no longer needed. Keeping a small subset of signs in memory at a time allows for a very large database of signs and therefore a large ASL vocabulary. Once the required signs are imported from the database, they are concatenated together in real-time with inter-sign transitions that are computed dynamically to produce smooth continuous signed sentences (The blending technique used in Mathsigner and SMILE is discussed in detail later in the section).

Facial Animation. Realistic facial articulations are achieved through vertex tweening using multiple target morphing. Vertex tweening is the process of blending from a single facial deformation (morph target) to another facial deformation. Morph targets are stored in a database and are loaded into the applications together with the avatar. Different facial deformations with varying weights are then combined in real-time to produce a facial expression. The strength of multiple-target morphing is that it allows for creating a large range of facial expressions that never look identical. The avatars in SMILE and Mathsigner are the only existing animated signers that make use of this powerful facial animation technique.

Facial expressions can also be imported from a database of pre-made facial articulations. The database consists of a collection of images visualizing the facial expressions and encoding the deformation weights that comprise the facial expression. Realistic facial animations are created by setting keyframes for each facial pose; keyframes are then interpolated at run-time using spline curves.

In order to maintain interactive rates on a variety of computer hardware, three methods of facial morphing can be used: hardware morphing, software morphing, and a hybrid approach that combines hardware and software morphing. Hardware facial morphing blends facial deformations entirely on the GPU. While this allows for high interactive rates, the drawback is that only a limited amount of facial deformations can be combined at one time to form a facial expression (when combined with skeletal animation a maximum of eight targets can be used). This results in simplified facial articulations that are not able to convey the subtle details of the human face. Software facial morphing is able to blend a virtually unlimited amount of facial deforma-

Figure 9. From the left: character skinned with dual quaternion skinning; character skinned with linear blend skinning. In both images, a rotation of 120 degrees has been applied to the character's waist joint.

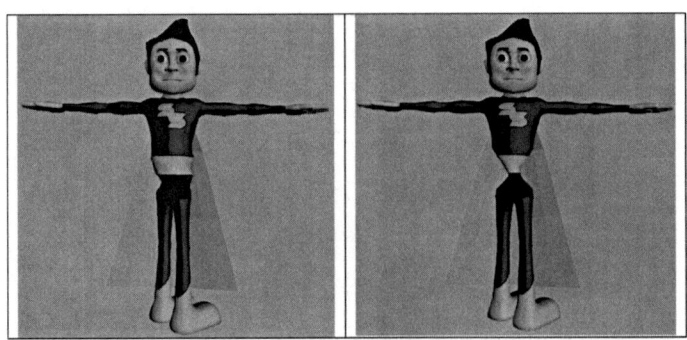

tions at a time on the CPU at a cost of speed (i.e. interactive rates are much lower; therefore transitions between consecutive facial expressions do not appear smooth). Hybrid morphing combines both methods to enable a virtually unlimited number of morph targets to be combined to form a complex facial articulation, while maintaining fast execution. With this method, the first eight morph targets are computed on the GPU while additional morph targets are computed on the CPU. The avatars in SMILE and Mathsigner use hybrid morphing because it allows for high visual quality and fast real-time performance.

Animation Blending. The quality of the blending motions between individual animation clips and keyframes drastically affects the realism of the sign animations. Simple linear interpolation-based blending can result in mechanical, non-fluid movements. In Mathsigner and SMILE, motions within and across signs are generated in real-time using spline-based interpolation, which allows for extending/reducing, pausing, and adjusting ease-in and ease-out variables to enhance the quality of the movements. Utilizing spline curves virtually eliminates visual recognition of keyframes and transitions between animations, thus the motion appears smooth and not jerky. Fluidity of motion is also achieved through the use of spherical linear interpolation, which is employed to blend between joint rotations. This type of interpolation ensures that angular velocity remains constant (and therefore smooth) between keyframes. In addition to these interpolation techniques, ease-in and ease-out variables are used to amplify or retard an animation time curve, i.e. to simulate natural acceleration and deceleration in hand movement. Finally, the animations can be stretched and paused for a user-defined quantity of time. Pausing, extending, and reducing animation significantly enhances the rhythm of the ASL discourse. Figure 10 shows an example of a spline-based animation curve with keyframes and timing controls.

The ASL Script Editor. There is no generally accepted system of "written ASL" and it is not possible to translate English into ASL word-by-word. Therefore, to write ASL signs and sentences, linguists and educators use glossing. In ASL gloss, every sign is written in CAPITAL LETTERS, i.e. PRO.1 LIKE APPLE. Gestures that are not signs are written in lower-case letters between quote marks, i.e. "go there". Proper names, technical concepts and other items with no obvious translation into ASL may be finger-spelled, which is glossed either as fs-MAGNET-IC or m-a-g-n-e-t-i-c. Upper body, head and facial articulations that are associated with syntactic constituents are shown above the signs with which they co-occur, with a line indicating the start and end of the articulation. For instance,

<u>wh-q</u> <u>wh-q</u>
YOUR NAME? or YOUR NAME WHAT?
'What is your name?'

where 'wh-q' indicates a facial articulation with lowered eyebrows (Weast 2008).

To speed up the generation of real-time sign animation sequences, Mathsigner and SMILE include a tool that understands ASL gloss: the ASL Script Editor. The ASL script editor enables a user with knowledge of ASL gloss, to simply type an ASL script including both ASL gloss and mathematical equations; the script is then automatically converted to the correct series of animations and facial expressions. The ASL script editor dynamically compiles an ASL script into an ASL syntax tree. Multiple passes are executed over the tree to generate the correct sequences of animation. First, the parser determines whether the script is of correct ASL gloss syntax. Once the script is determined to be of correct syntax, an animation selection pass iterates over the script to dynamically build an animation sequence. The compiler searches the database of existing signs and automatically generates the correct animation – signs not found in the database need to be created by the user. Once all signs have been retrieved from the database, the compiler searches

Figure 10. Interface used to control the timing of motion. The interface allows for extending and reducing keyframe spacing, and modifying the acceleration and deceleration of the animation time curve

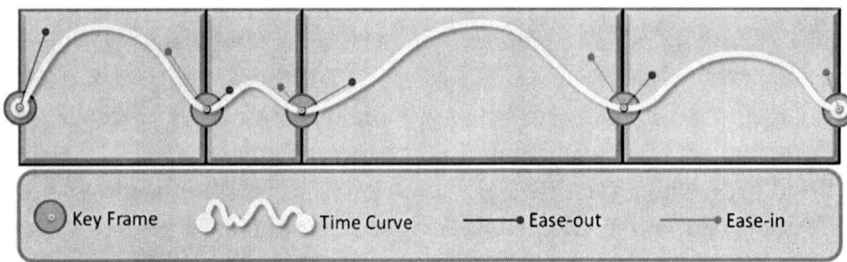

over the script for additional modifiers, which include spatial directions and temporal pauses. These modifiers are converted into additional animation layers that modify the sign to which they are attached. Facial expressions are also queried from the database and are inserted into user-defined segments in the script. The user is able to specify the duration of a facial expression and can also give a word range over which the expression will persist. Punctuation is also interpreted into relevant facial animations, such as question expression for question marks, inserting pauses in place of commas, etc. Once the animation is generated, the user is then able to modify time curves, clip length and insert pauses to adjust the rhythm of the ASL discourse. Figure 11 shows the process of generating a sign animation sequence using the ASL script editor.

Secondary Actions. One problem with current real-time animation of ASL is the lack of 'secondary actions'. Any movement of a living creature is composed of a primary action and secondary actions. For example, in a walk cycle the legs and hip movement is the primary action, all other motions such as swinging arms, bobbing head, flapping ears, etc. are secondary actions. In a signing sequence, the hands, arms and facial movements can be considered the primary actions, while torso, shoulder, head motions and involuntary facial signals (such as blinks) are secondary actions. Representing all these different types of interconnected motions is fundamental to the creation of 'a believable whole within any movement' (Clark, 2002). Failure to adhere to the principle of secondary actions results in disjointed, puppet-like characters; the motion does not appear to come from within but rather appears to be applied from an external source.

In SMILE and Mathsigner the signers' secondary actions are produced in real time with a technique known as layering. Animation layering is the process of combining multiple independent animations running in unison into a final, single animation. For example, a walking animation that only affects the legs is combined with a waving animation that affects the arm into a final walking and waving animation.

In animation of ASL, layering is particularly useful also because it can be used to animate descriptive classifiers, which are an important component of sign language. Classifiers modify a handshape in such a way as to include information about a referent's type, size, shape, movement, or extent. For example, when describing a cage, the box handshape is modified by (or layered onto) the jail hand shape to produce the sign for cage (see Figure 12).

Improved Rendering

Another aspect that bears heavily on the visual comprehension of signed animation is rendering quality. To this extent, Mathsigner and SMILE implement a number of techniques that improve

Figure 11. Visualization of the ASL syntax tree generated by the script compiler. Top right: example of ASL script including ASL sentence and facial expression persisting from the word "See" to the word "Bowl". Bottom: output animation sequence generated by the compiler.

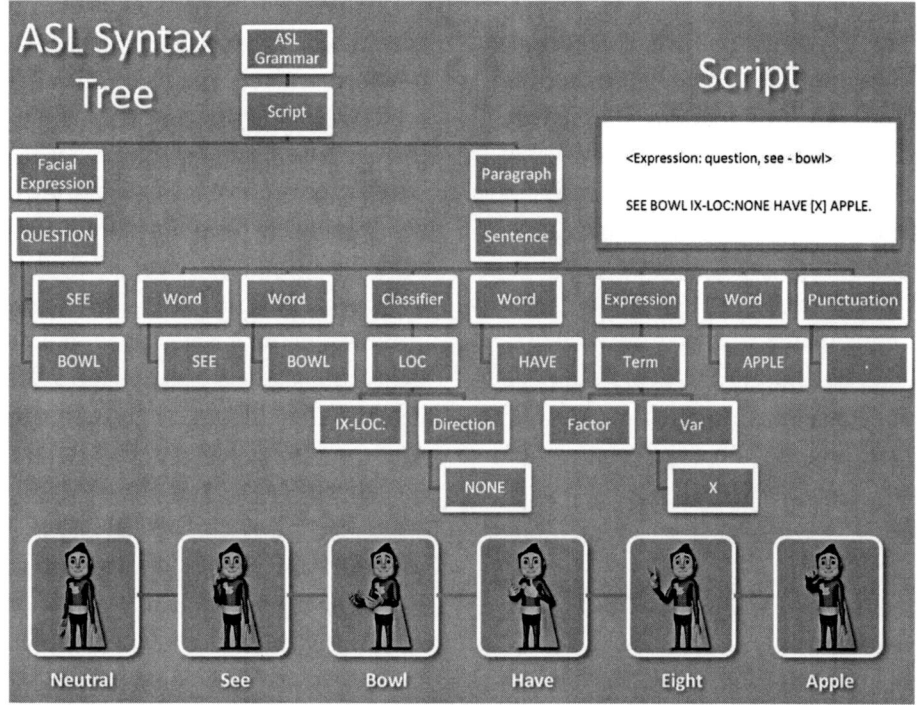

recognition and perception of the signs – such as ambient occlusion, motion blur, and depth-of-field. As mentioned previously, ambient occlusion adds realism to the character model by improving upon diffuse shading and taking into account how light reacts with surfaces in real life. For example, two extended fingers that touch each other are delimited by a visually salient dark line which is accurately conveyed by ambient occlusion. Motion blur is used to bring the user's focus to the hands of the character by simulating how human eyes react to fast moving objects. This effect improves the

Figure 12. Left: box handshape. Middle: 4 handshape modifier. Right: Box handshape modified by the 4 handshape to form the cage handshape.

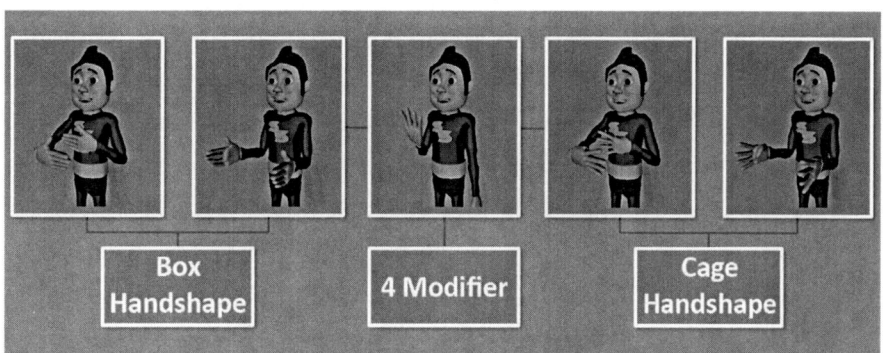

readability of the trajectory of fingers and hands during rapid signing motion by visualizing several intermediate positions in a single frame, the same way the human eye or a camera blends several positions of a rapidly moving object. Without motion blur, the visualization is discontinuous and the information conveyed by important intermediate positions is lost. Depth-of-field is used to bring focus to the signing character itself by blurring out of focus secondary objects. Depth of field can be seen in Figure 13. Lighting is another important aspect when presenting signed animation. Lighting rigs are constructed in a way that ensures uniform lighting over an entire avatar, minimize over shadowing, accurately represent skin and light interaction, and provide a presentation that enhances visual cognition.

DISCUSSION AND CONCLUSION

In the authors' opinion the great potential of signing avatars lies in their ability to drastically improve access to educational materials for deaf children, and therefore improve young deaf students' learning. We view learning as a process of domain-specific knowledge construction.

This view is grounded in research on human cognition and cognitive development (Gelman & Brenneman 2004) and the belief that children are active learners (Bruner 1996; Piaget 1955). For children to learn domain-specific conceptual structures and processes, they must actively interact with materials designed to help them acquire core ideas and ways of thinking. Currently, such activities are not deaf-accessible; thus, interaction and subsequent learning do not occur. Signing avatars can increase deaf students' interaction with materials and hence their domain-specific learning. Learning materials can be annotated with signed translations at language levels appropriate to deaf children's linguistic comprehension. Age-appropriate fantasy characters embedded in educational games and virtual learning environments can help teach concepts, ask questions, and provide feedback through the most natural communication channel for young deaf learners.

Unfortunately, the potential of signing avatars to improve deaf education has not been fully realized yet, primarily because of two limitations. Manual and non-manual animated signs are not sufficiently accurate and realistic - this problem has been discussed extensively throughout the chapter; current ASL animation efforts proceed

Figure 13. Scene rendered with Depth of Field (DoF). The character is in focus while the background is slightly blurred.

in isolation, which leads to duplication of technology development and content creation, lack of society-level evaluation of intervention effectiveness, and limited adoption of proposed solutions. Future research in ASL animation needs to address both problems. The authors are confident that as technology progresses, the quality of ASL animation will continue to improve. However, it will take the coordinated effort of many educators, students, deaf education researchers, and technology researchers in order for ASL animation to become widely accepted and used. In the authors' opinion, the accessibility barrier to digital educational content for deaf students could be overcome by creating a public domain, low learning-curve authoring system that will enable deaf educators to easily create signing avatars and embed them in educational environments as sign language interpreters. The system should be made available to all deaf members through an ASL online community where animated signs and deaf-accessible materials covering all subject matters and all educational levels, are created, shared, evaluated, and used by the Deaf, regardless of geographic distance.

REFERENCES

Adamo-Villani, N., Doublestein, J., & Martin, Z. (2005). Sign language for K-8 mathematics by 3D interactive animation. *Journal of Educational Technology Systems*, *33*(3), 243–259. doi:10.2190/KUB1-6M7X-NHY5-3BWG

Adamo-Villani, N., & Wilbur, R. (2008). Two Novel Technologies for Accessible Math and Science Education. *IEEE Multimedia – Special Issue on Accessibility*, October -December 2008, pp. 38-46.

Bangham, J. A. Cox, S.J., Elliott, R. Glauert, J.R.W. Marshall, I., (UEA) Rankov, S., Wells, M. (2000). An Overview of ViSiCAST. *IEE Seminar on Speech and language processing for disabled and elderly people*, London, April 2000.

Bruner, J. (1996). *The culture of education*. Cambridge: Harvard University Press.

Chamberlain, J. P. Morford, & R. I. Mayberry (eds.), *Language acquisition by eye*,(pp. 165-190). Mahwah, NJ: Lawrence Erlbaum Associates.

Clark, K. (2002). *Inspired 3D Character Animation*. Portland, OR: Premier Press.

Dyer, S., Martin, J., & Zulauf, J. (1995) *Motion Capture White Paper*.

Ekman, P., & Friesen, W. V. (1978). *Facial Action Coding System (Manual)*. Palo Alto, CA: Consulting Psychologists Press.

eSIGN at UEA (2003). Retrieved from http://www.visicast.cmp.uea.ac.uk/eSIGN/

Gelman, R., & Brenneman, K. (2004). Science learning pathways for young children. *Early Childhood Research Quarterly*, *19*, 150–158. doi:10.1016/j.ecresq.2004.01.009

Handley, B. (2000). *Another path: Homeschooling Deaf and Hard of Hearing Children*.Retrieved from http://www.pacinfo.com/~handley/index.html

Hoffmeister, R. (2000). A piece of the puzzle: ASL and reading comprehension in deaf children . In Chamberlain, C., Morford, J. P., & Mayberry, R. I. (Eds.), *Language acquisition by eye* (pp. 143–164). Mahwah, NJ: Lawrence Erlbaum Associates.

ISO/IEC JTC1/SC29/WG11. Overview of the MPEG-4 Standard. Available at: http://www.chiariglione.org/mpeg/standards/mpeg-4/mpeg-4.htm

Johnston, O. &Thomas, F. (1995). *The Illusion of Life: Disney Animation.* Disney Editions; Rev Sub edition (October 5, 1995).

Kavan, L., Collins, S., Zara, J., & O'Sullivan, C. (2007). Skinning with dual quaternions. *Proc. of the 2007 symposium on Interactive 3D graphics and games,* (pp. 39-46). Seattle, Washington.

Lang, H. G., McKee, B. G., & Conner, K. (1993). Characteristics of effective teachers: a descriptive study of the perceptions of faculty and deaf college students. *American Annals of the Deaf, 138*(3), 252–259.

Mathsigner (2009). Retrieved from http://idealab. tech.purdue.edu/Mathsigner/Home.html

Padden, C., & Ramsey, C. (2000). American Sign Language and reading ability. In C.

Pakstas, A. (2009). MPEG-4 Facial Animation: The Standard, Implementation and Applications. Adobe Digital Editions. Prinz, P. (2002). Cross-linguistic perspectives on sign language and literacy development . In Schulmeister, R., & Reinitzer, H. (Eds.), *Progress in sign language research: In honor of Siegmund Prillwitz* (pp. 221–233). Hamburg: Signum.

Piaget, J. (1955). *The construction of reality in the child (Trans. M. Cook).* Routledge and Kegan Paul.

Signing Science. (2007). Retrieved from http:// signsci.terc.edu/

Sims, E. (2000). *SigningAvatars. Final Report for SBIR Phase II Project, U.* S. Department of Education.

SMILE. (2007). Retrieved from http://www2. tech.purdue.edu/cgt/I3/SMILE/

Strong, M., & Prinz, P. (1997). A study of the relationship between ASL and English literacy. *Journal of Deaf Studies and Deaf Education, 2,* 37–46.

Strong, M., & Prinz, P. (2000). Is American Sign Language skill related to literacy? In Chamberlain, C., Morford, J., & Mayberry, R. (Eds.), *Language acquisition by eye* (pp. 131–141). Hillsdale, NJ: Lawrence Erlbaum Associates.

TERC. (2007). Retrieved from http://www.terc. edu/

Vcom3D (2007). Retrieved from http://www. vcom3d.com/

Weast, T. (2008) *Questions in American Sign Language: A quantitative analysis of raised and lowered eyebrows.* Doctoral dissertation, University of Texas, Arlington.

Wilbur, R. B. (1994). Eyeblinks and ASL phrase structure. *Sign Language Studies, 84,* 221–240.

Wilbur, R. B. (2000). The use of ASL to support the development of English and literacy. *Journal of Deaf Studies and Deaf Education, 5,* 81–104. doi:10.1093/deafed/5.1.81

KEY TERMS AND DEFINITIONS

3D Character: A 3D character is a graphical model consisting of a geometric skin and an articulated skeleton. The skin is usually modeled as one or several polygon meshes or spline patches; the skeleton is a hierarchical structure of joints connected by bones. 3D characters can be posed and animated by rotating the skeletal joints.

Animated Signing: A technology that uses 3D animated characters for displaying sign language.

Assistive Technology: Technology that is designed for, and used by people with disabilities in order to perform tasks that would be otherwise impossible (or very difficult) to carry out. Assistive technology includes mechanical devices, hardware, and software.

Computer Animation: Animation is defined as the illusion of life, movement. Computer Animation involves the production of a series of images (called frames) showing some kind of progressive change over time. If these images are played back one after the other fast enough (e.g. 24/30 frames per second - fps), they produce the illusion of continuous change or motion. In computer animation the frames can be created with a 2D vector/raster computer program (e.g. Adobe Illustrator, Photoshop), or with a 3D animation software (e.g. Autodesk Maya, Max). The frames are then combined together to form an animation sequence; the final sequence can be produced using a video production program (e.g. Adobe Premiere, After Effects)

Deaf Education: A field of study that deals with methods of teaching and learning designed specifically for deaf individuals.

Sign Language: A communication system consisting of hand gestures, facial expressions and body poses. This visual language is typically used by the Deaf.

User Interface: The way a person interacts with a computer, electronic device, or software.

Section 5
Risks in the Immersive Learning

Chapter 14

Crouching Tangents, Hidden Danger:
Assessing Development of Dangerous Misconceptions within Serious Games for Healthcare Education

Miguel A. Garcia-Ruiz
University of Colima, Mexico

Jayshiro Tashiro
University of Ontario Institute of Technology, Canada

Bill Kapralos
University of Ontario Institute of Technology, Canada

Miguel Vargas Martin
University of Ontario Institute of Technology, Canada

ABSTRACT

In this chapter, the authors examine different types of serious games for healthcare education and pose some hard questions about what they know and do not know about their effectiveness. As part of our analysis, the authors explore general aspects of the use of educational simulations as teaching-learning-assessment tools, but try to tease out how to study the potential such tools might have for leading students toward developing misconceptions. Being powerful instruments with the potential of enhancing healthcare education in extraordinary ways, serious games and simulations have the possibility of improving students' learning and skills outcomes. Their contribution is an overview of current education technologies related to serious games and simulations with a perspective of potential development of misconceptions in the healthcare education community, with a special focus on millennial students. In addition, the authors provide insight on evidence-based learning and give a perspective of future trends.

DOI: 10.4018/978-1-61692-825-4.ch014

INTRODUCTION

Our work in the health sciences identified a number of issues in the literature that raise concerns about possibilities of health sciences students developing misconceptions while working within certain types of instructional modalities. Some of these misconceptions could have deadly consequences as these students progress into positions of healthcare providers and become engaged in patient care. Misconceptions can be defined as students' mistaken thoughts, ideas, notions, an underdeveloped pattern recognition (Balkissoon, Blossfield, Salud, Ford, & Pugh, 2009), and can develop before, during, and after learning, leading to erroneous concepts in conceptual and performance competencies (Ozmen, 2004). A number of students' mistaken beliefs about the sciences are present in incoming student population, which affect students' performance in undergraduate and even graduate courses (Halloun & Hestenes, 1985; Ozmen, 2004). Literature describes a number of studies regarding students' misconceptions in the health sciences, including students' erroneous concepts, such as in respiratory physiology (Michael et al., 1999). Emerging computer simulations have been used to uncover and address serious health science students' misconceptions, such as erroneous preconceptions in clinical digital rectal examination (Balkisoon et al., 2009), a critical procedure used in the detection of colon cancer that needs to be properly learned and practiced.

In this chapter, we argue that serious games (video games whose main objective is educational in contrast to entertainment) and computer simulations appear to have a high potential for shifting the way content and skills are taught and possibly improving higher order reasoning. However, we also point out that evidence is lacking for a generalized theory of how and why to build serious games so that they "really work" to improve learning in predictable ways and so that they do not promote development of misconceptions. We feel there has been very little attention given to how misconceptions are developed. Certainly, there are some interesting and important contributions to research on misconceptions. As mentioned above, there have been studies of misconception development by medical students, undergraduates working in respiratory therapy, and a major review of misconceptions developed by students studying chemistry (Balkissoon et al., 2009; Michael et al., 1999; Ozmen, 2004). And, we note very interesting work by Barab and colleagues related to conceptual understanding and consequential engagement in virtual, immersive learning environments (Gresalfi, Barab, Siyahhan, & Christensen, 2009; Barab, Scott, Siyahhan, Goldstone, Ingram-Goble, Zuiker, & Warren, 2009; Hickey, Ingram-Goble, & Jameson, 2009). Even so, given the importance of misconception development in healthcare training, the paucity of research is surprising.

What Really Works in Education

Over a decade ago, Tashiro & Rowland (1997) published a challenge to educators and researchers, posing the confounded questions of: What really works in instructional approaches and materials, for whom, when, why, and with what outcomes? At the time, they were focusing on biological and environmental sciences domains, but they extended their work to look more broadly into a variety of disciplines. In particular, they began to focus on essential problems related to how undergraduate students learn and what types of instructional materials are likely to address seven questions, first posed as an integral set by the United States National Research Council (2000, 2001, 2005):

1. How do instructional materials enhance disposition to learn?
2. How do the materials provide multiple paths for learning?

3. How does an instructional package help students overcome limitations of prior knowledge?

4. When, how, and why do the educational materials provide practice and feedback?

5. Can the instructional materials help students develop an ability to transfer knowledge acquired by extending knowledge and skills beyond the contexts in which they were gained?

6. How will the instructional package incorporate the role of social context?

7. How and why will the instructional materials address cultural norms and student beliefs?

Analyses of instructional materials during the past decade reveal that few address all seven questions.

Interestingly, in the decade since the National Research Council (NRC) posed these questions, there has been increasing interest in use of gaming technologies and simulations as well as publication and use of a diverse array of electronic instructional materials. Certainly, recent syntheses by the Federation of American Scientists (2006) and the American Association for the Advancement of Science (AAAS) Invention and Impact Conference (2004) provided convincing evidence for exploring the use of educational technologies. In particular, advances in artificial intelligence algorithms as well as advances in gaming and simulations open important opportunities to build educational materials that might improve learning and skills development. Educational publishers are already re-organizing to support development of serious games for teaching and learning at all academic levels. Major conferences in education and gaming have been focusing a large percentage of their sessions on papers related to the use of serious games in science, technology, engineering, mathematics, and health sciences education. Yet, there are still few well-developed frameworks for evidence-based learning that might provide guidance for development of serious games and simulations that really work to improve educational outcomes.

During the past year, we synthesized a better understanding of what we do not know about "what really works" in educational simulations and serious games. In particular, our work in the health sciences raised some concerns about the possibility of health sciences students developing misconceptions that could have deadly consequences as these students made the school to work transition and assumed responsibilities for patient care. Consequently, we conducted a comprehensive literature review of educational simulations and serious games (Tashiro, 2009, Tashiro & Dunlap, 2007). This review revealed there are important gaps in our knowledge about effective use of educational simulations and serious games:

1. How does a simulation or serious game enhance disposition to engage in a learning process?

2. What are the relationships between the level of realism in a simulation or game and learning outcomes?

3. How do you define the threshold of experience within a game or simulation that leads to measurable learning outcomes?

4. What are the cognitive processes being developed during learning while working within a game or simulation?

5. In what knowledge domains is learning being retained and how stable is the retention?

6. What is the disposition to act on the knowledge gained during work within a simulation?

7. How well can the knowledge gained within a game or simulation be transferred?

8. What are the differences in learning that manifest as conceptual competencies and performance competencies?

The results of this literature review led us to conclude that many studies of simulations and serious games reporting improved learning and skills development had methodological flaws. Furthermore, the sample sizes were often small and limited attention was focused on the multitude of variables shaping learning, and how so many of these variables are confounded. In brief, we were left still fretting about "what really works" in the use of educational simulations and serious games. We also became more interested in the shifting technological savvy, but not necessarily literacy, of students entering undergraduate institutions. In addition, there appears to be differentials between students and faculty members with respect to adaptability to and usability of education simulation and serious gaming environments. As we continued to look at simulation and serious game environments, we could not escape the gnawing uncertainties about what is being learned in such environments, how learning progresses, and what opportunities there are for following tangents to the educational objectives that lead to inculcation of misconceptions, some of which could be quite dangerous in health-related disciplines. Of course, we have no illusions about more traditional methods and materials of education being free of potential for developing misconceptions. Even so, the tremendous emphasis on simulation and serious game usage in education ought to be tempered by the same kinds of standards for evidence-based practice used in healthcare, which led us to promote the idea of evidence-based learning.

We started our path towards evidence-based learning by re-examining what some have called the millennial students and also more critically examining educational publishers' roles in creating electronic educational materials as well as faculty members' roles in using such materials. We present some thoughts on these areas of student and faculty technological literacy, because they serve as a foundation for the rest of the chapter, which unfolds in four additional sections. Following this introduction, we explore types and impacts of emerging educational technologies. Building on such technologies, we go more deeply into an analysis of serious games and simulations in healthcare education, where misconceptions could have more immediate and deadly impacts during patient care planning and delivery. The next section provides a synthesis of how and why misconceptions could develop and how clinical judgment might be impaired. We then turn to an analysis of why we have had so little evidence-base learning in education and how evidence-based frameworks could sensibly be developed. In this context, we offer some thoughts on future trends and conclusions we have drawn from studying serious games and simulations developed for education.

Millennial Students

A great deal of discussion has surrounded the generation called the "millennials," also known as Gen Y and Generation Next. Strauss and Howe probably give the best summary description of the millennial generation in the course of four books (Strauss & Howe, 1991, 1997; Howe and Strauss, 1993, 2000; and references therein). Traditional teaching-and-learning environments are often quoted by the millennial generation as "boring" and not addressing the unique learning needs of this generation (Hanna, 2003 p. 44). According to Oblinger (2003), millennials exhibit distinct learning preferences. They prefer team work, experiential activities, structure and the use of technology. Millennials are very technologically literate and see technology as a necessity, both in life and in learning (Mangold, 2007). The fact that the millennial generation has always been digitally connected has led to a mindset unlike any that educators have ever seen. Understanding this mind set is an important aspect of educational planning and course development. This generation highly regards "doing rather than knowing," making interactive, experiential learning, a necessity for their educational success. They self-report that they do not appreciate or learn as much from passive learning which most often occurs in lecture style teaching. Instead, they want to be actively involved, preferring, expecting, and appreciating the use of technology in learning (Sinclair & Ferguson, 2009). However, the use of such technology has not been widely adopted to address the learning needs of today's students.

Virtual environments and video games offer students the opportunity to practice their skills and abilities within a safe learning environment, perhaps leading to a higher level of self-efficacy when faced with real life situations where such skills and knowledge are required (Mitchell & Savill-Smith, 2004). Virtual reality and videogame technologies have been noted as some of the most effective means of promoting interactivity and active involvement in learning (Cowen & Tesh, 2002). Gaming and interactive simulation environments support learner-centered education in which learners are able to actively work through problems while acquiring knowledge through practice. Students can engage with the problem, perform research, gather information, perform analysis and evaluate hypotheses through experimentation. Such environments may be more effective for engaging the current generation of students (Annetta et al., 2006).

With these experience-based, instructional methods, faculty can work as facilitators, attending more closely to the experience and subsequent knowledge acquisition. These experience-based methods: (1) incorporate more complex and diverse approaches to learning processes and outcomes; (2) allow for interactivity; (3) allow for cognitive as well as affective learning; and (4) perhaps most importantly, foster active learning (Ruben, 1999). The active learning inherent in games is believed to be a more effective method of obtaining and retaining information than traditional passive forms of learning (Sprengel, 1994).

Yet, we are still faced with the uncomfortable question of "what really works" to improve higher order thinking without instilling misconceptions. For example, even given the propensity of mil-

lennials (perhaps because of the propensity) to engage in new models of instructional environments, how do we know if misconceptions are developed. What are the potentials for embedded interactions to lead students on tangents in their development of cognitive schema? Such cognitive schema may have flaws in pattern recognition and so lead to misconceptions. Misconceptions can lead to incomplete understanding of complexity in many discipline areas and certainly to the possibility of adverse medical effects and possible death of patients when health sciences students become healthcare practitioners.

The Ethics of Building and Using New Educational Technologies

As our appreciation grew for millennial students' attributes and their preferences for teaching-learning environments (Pew Research Center, 2007), we turned to studies of publishers of electronic instructional materials at the undergraduate level. What were publishers producing for student consumption as educational materials? In addition, how were faculty members shaping publishers' development of electronic materials such as educational simulations and serious games? Furthermore, how are faculty selecting and then implementing instructional methods and materials based on simulations and serious games?

Educational materials are developed by publishers and educational methods utilizing these instructional materials are developed and implemented by faculty members. We examined the ethical issues of developing and using electronic educational materials designed for healthcare education at the undergraduate level. Our approach used an ethical framework called "the four principles with attention to scope" in order to examine the roles of publishers and faculty members in development and usage of electronic healthcare educational materials (Tashiro, 2009). In particular, we focused on the extent to which publishers and faculty achieve the four ethical principles of autonomy, benefi-cence, non-maleficence, and justice. The results of our study suggested that both publishers and faculty members do not achieve what is required by these four principles. However, the story is complicated by the confounding of publishers' and faculty members' roles in developing educational materials and then selecting these materials for students as well as implementing them in teaching, learning, and learning assessment environments. We concluded that an ethical analysis must be coupled to an evidence-based learning framework. From such coupling, we argued that it would be possible to define praxis frameworks for evidence-base learning that would delineate ethical strategies for developing, choosing, and using instructional materials.

Finally, faculty members select and implement the educational materials for their respective courses. It is possible that some electronic educational products actually could improve learning, but only if properly implemented in a course. What responsibility does a publisher have? What responsibility does a faculty member have in selecting and implementing a set of educational materials? Importantly, the diversity of electronic instructional materials is growing rapidly. Almost none of these materials have an evidence base for how and why they really work to improve learning. Thus, educational materials developers and faculty do not have a sound research foundation for estimating the potential of an educational instructional package for helping students learn. Furthermore, as a concomitant, developers and faculty have "virtually" no adequate measures of an instructional packages potential for inculcating misconceptions, some of which may be dangerous when applied by students in real-world settings.

We can obtain a sense of the complexities of understanding development of learning and misconceptions by first examining the diversity of educational technologies now being applied to teaching, learning, and assessment in education.

Chapter Overview

The objective of this chapter is to analyze the potential of serious games and computer simulations to improve learning in predictable ways, and so that they do not promote development of misconceptions in health science students. In this **Introduction** section, we have outlined some of our concerns about what we might know and do not know about "what really works" in educational simulations and serious games. We included reflections on millennial students' experience with videogames. This introduction section also briefly addressed ethical aspects of building and using new educational technologies.

In Section 2, **What is Possible: Emerging Educational Technologies** we, provide an overview of recent and novel educational technologies that use different human sensory modalities, such as haptics (related to the sense of touch), smell interfaces for learning, and augmented reality. In brief, we explore combining various human sensory channels to support learning. This section also poses a number of questions about how to build those emerging educational technologies to improve learning and skills development, leading ultimately to overcome students' misconceptions.

For Section 3, we explore **Serious Games and Simulations in Healthcare Education**. In this section we outline a general description of research and applications of serious games, the 3D social network called Second Life, and simulations in healthcare education. We examine how games and simulations could support development of skills training and learning in healthcare education.

Section 4, **Exploring Potential for Development of Misconceptions in Clinical Judgment**, offers a vision of the possibility of health sciences students developing misconceptions that could have deadly consequences if these students became healthcare providers and engaged in patient care.

We close the chapter with Section 5, **Evidence-based Learning and Future Trends**. In this last section we examine some of the literature that converges on the idea that there are educational benefits to electronic educational materials that use simulations and gaming technology. In addition, this section points out the important opportunity to build evidence-based frameworks for learning, based on serious gaming and simulations.

WHAT IS POSSIBLE: EMERGING EDUCATIONAL TECHNOLOGIES

Tactile Interfaces for Training

A number of tactile interfaces have been developed to help develop psychomotor skills, often with coupling of tactile manipulation to problem-solving or decision making while implementing a complex procedure. Although simplified somewhat, tactile interfaces are generally the integration of a haptic device with a suite of expert algorithms or knowledge systems that allow an end user to manipulate the haptic device and receive tactile and visual feedback on manipulation outcomes. An interesting evidence-based approach was taken by Reznek, Chantal, & Krummel (2002) in their study of a virtual reality intravenous insertion simulator. These researchers explored the construct and content validity of the experience of virtual IV insertion and also studied end users' perceptions of the simulator. This simulator allows the user to see the patient on a computer screen and through a haptic device allows one hand to apply traction to the skin of the virtual patient while using the other hand to insert the catheter. Tactile, visual, and auditory feedback is provided.

A diverse array of tactile interfaces are now being studied in surgery, diagnostic imaging, laboratory techniques, dentistry, and other domains in which tactile feedback and complex decision making must be coupled (as a starting point the reader might be interested in Akkary, Bell, Roberts, Dudrick, & Duffy, 2009; Desser, 2007; Souza, Sanches, & Zuffo, 2009). A growing literature is examining how and why such interfaces work to improve learning and development of skills that require physical manipulation coupled to complex reasoning.

Olfactory Interfaces for Training

Although visual, auditory, and tactile human sensory channels have been successfully researched in virtual reality settings for training, there is emerging research on the sense of smell. We used to joke that "scratch and sniff" smell cues for computing (or perhaps click and sniff), but smell has been used in virtual reality for training. Work also has progressed on the technical aspects related to how to incorporate odors in educational virtual reality (i.e. usability, storage and dissemination of odors). Washburn et al. (2003) have found that employing the sense of smell in virtual reality is an effective way of supporting learning and technical training, without compromising the cognitive load of students and trainees.

Most of the advances with respect to virtual reality systems that incorporate olfactory information have evolved in military training. According to Vlahos (2006), the U.S. military, based on research and development carried out by the University of Southern California and theme-park designers, have developed virtual reality simulators to train U.S. soldiers. In the simulation environment, researchers have integrated some artificially-created odors to enhance the ambience of a simulated war scenario. The soldiers don an electronic device around the neck where the scents are generated, and each odor is activated remotely through a wireless network, according to the events generated in the virtual reality simulation and from the soldiers. When soldiers shoot simulated weapons in the virtual environment, they perceive the smell of gun powder, generated by the electronic device they wear. Preliminary research on this application claimed that the use of smells enhanced mental immersion of the soldiers in a realistic war zone simulation, and smell may be key element that favours improved training outcomes.

Spencer (2006) reviewed a number of research projects about using artificially-generated odors used along with 3D medical simulators for teaching and training, since olfactory cues are key factors in medicine to make a correct patient diagnosis in some diseases. Spencer discussed the technical feasibility of using odors in virtual reality simulations for medical training, thanks to recent technological devices for smell production in a computer interface. There are a number of efficient ways to activate such smell production, both remotely over the Internet and in local networks. Spencer demonstrated that adding simulated odors to a virtual reality medical simulator is an effective way to complement diagnosis and enhance training skills in medicine students.

Augmented Reality Interfaces to Support Training

Sanne, Botden, & Jakimowicz (2009) examine different types of simulators, focusing on augmented reality simulators for training in laparoscopic surgery. While there are a variety of augmented reality interfaces being developed and used in education, these authors contrast a set of simulators that combine elements of real-world activities set within an augmented environment. They define the augmented simulators as integrated systems that use hybrid mannequin environments with haptic feedback and capable of engaging users in more physically realistic training that utilizes real instruments that the user manipulates in order to interact with real objects. An interesting facet of the work described by these authors is their comparison of different simulation systems with the intent to understand how such augmented environments can be constructed and used in ways that provide unbiased and objective assessment of end users' performance within the system. They also extended their analysis to discuss how such performance measurements could enhance training and be used as a complementary assessment tool to knowledge-based examinations.

Such approaches could allow the development of new types of combined assessment activities that would define benchmarks for certification in a particular skill area.

Sanne and colleagues (2009) point out that augmented reality interfaces or environments allow an end user to use the same instruments they would in a real-life situation. Depending on the design of the augmented reality interface, the simulator may add to the variety of virtual experiences (internal body views as seen through a laparoscope), learning resources (demonstration videos), and assessment subsystems (recording of the end users actions and choices). These types of augmented reality systems for laparoscopic surgery have been studied to evaluate construct validity, face validity, skills acquisition, and comparisons between augmented and virtual reality systems as teaching, learning, and assessment systems.

Augmented reality systems are emerging in other educational domains, such as learning a second language (Wagner & Baraconyi, 2003), and understanding 3D structural amino acids (Chen, 2006), among other learning areas. We believe strongly that a broad and diverse literature has pointed out factors shaping learning and these factors can help us understand how to build educational methods and materials to improve learning and skills development. We examined only three areas above, touch, smell, and combined facets of real-world and virtual world elements. What about the impacts of sound within a teaching-learning environment? How might sound impact development of skills and higher order reasoning (see Bishop & Cates, 2001, for a discussion of the benefits of sound with respect to learning)? What about the real-world hustle and flow of a rapidly changing situation in one place, such as care for a trauma patient just entering an emergency room? Can we imagine, build, and evaluate an environment that allows exploration of the complexity of temporal and spatial variability, such as a teaching-learning-assessment system that provides an experience of ecological research that takes the end user into the tributaries of a major river system at different times of the year. Furthermore, how do we authentically assess the construct and face validities of such a system, the reliabilities of different learning-skills assessment probes, the extension of knowledge gained to related problem areas, the retention and transfer of knowledge after exposure to the teaching-learning-assessment environment, and the costs in equipment, facilities, and instructor time to implement a system that might actually optimize learning and skills development for diverse end users.

In the next section, we turn to discussions of a general description of research and applications of serious games, the 3D social network called Second Life. We also examine simulations in healthcare education. This approach allows us to explore the use of multimodal human sensory channels through 3D graphics, sound, and haptics, supporting skills training and learning.

SERIOUS GAMES AND SIMULATIONS IN HEALTHCARE EDUCATION

Serious Games

In addition to games intended specifically for training of healthcare workers, there are a many games designed to educate healthy lifestyles and promote health-related behaviour changes. This includes promotion of healthy diet (Thompson et al., 2007, Baranowski et al., 2003), physical activity/fitness (Madsen et al., 2007, Tan et al, 2001, Unnithan et al., 2006), behavioural issues in asthma (McPherson et al., 2006), diabetes-related behaviour changes (Aoki et al., 2004, Brown et al., 1997), and educating paediatric cancer patients about cancer and its treatment (Kato and Beale, 2006). ImmuneAttack™ is freely available educational game developed by the American Federation of Scientists that introduces basic concepts of human immunology to middle school, high school, and entry-level college/university students. Students guide a *nanobot* through a 3D environment of blood vessels and connective tissue trying to save a sick patient by retraining her non-functional immune cells. Along the way, students learn about the biological processes that enable the body to detect and fight infections (see http://fas.org/immuneattack/download).

The term "serious games" has emerged to denote games with at least some intent for learning to take place. Although no particularly clear definition of the term is currently available, serious games usually refer to games that are used for training, advertising, simulation, or education and are designed to run on personal computers, video game consoles, or Web-based portals. Serious games can be designed to provide a high fidelity simulation of particular environments and situations that focus on high level skills that are required in the field. They present situations in a complex interactive narrative context coupled with interactive elements that are designed to engage the trainees. Goals and challenges require the trainees to solve specific problems that they may have never seen prior to engaging in the game, which may increase the fun or entertainment value to the player. In addition to promoting learning via interaction, there are various other benefits to serious games. More specifically, they allow users to experience situations that are difficult (even impossible) to achieve in reality due to a number of factors including cost, time, and safety concerns. In addition, serious games support the development of various skills, including analytical and spatial interpretation, strategic decision-making, recollection, psychomotor development, and visual selective attention skills (Mitchell & Savill-Smith, 2004). Further benefits of serious games include the potential for improved self-monitoring, problem recognition and solving, improved short- and long-term memory, increased social skills, and increased self-efficacy (Michael & Chen, 2006).

In contrast to traditional teaching environments in which an instructor controls the learning (e.g., teacher centered), serious games present a learner-centered approach to education in which the student as player controls the learning through interactivity. Such engagement may allow the student-player to learn via an active, critical learning approach (Stapleton, 2004). Game-based learning provides a methodology to integrate game design concepts with instructional design techniques to enhance the educational experience for students (Kiili, 2005). Video games provide students the opportunity to learn to appreciate the inter-relationship of complex behaviors, sign systems, and the formation of social groups (Lieberman, 1997). Games inherently support engagement and, if engagement is sustained, the play in the game may facilitate experiential learning by providing students with concrete experiences and active experimentation (Kolb, 1984; Squire, 2008). By designing the scenario appropriately, a problem-based learning approach can be realized (Savery & Duffy, 1995). Similar to a good game designer, an educator should provide trainees or learners with an environment that promotes learning through interaction (Stapleton, 2004). Very interesting reviews on games and learning have been provided by Aldrich (2004, 2005). Bogost (2007), Gee (2003, 2004, 2007), Juul (2005), and Gibson, Aldrich, & Prensky (2007), Selfe (2007), and Shaffer (2006), and Squire (2008).

In addition, key conclusions by the Federation of American Scientists (2006; also see American Association for the Advancement of Science, 2004) provided important insight into building educational games. In a 2005 summit, there was interesting convergence on eight conclusions reached by expert working groups:

1. It is clear that the modern workforces of technology-oriented countries require the skills that many video games require players to master.

2. Attributes of games could be useful in applications in learning (contextual bridging, increased time on task, improved motivation and goal orientation, personalization of learning, feedback, cues and partial solutions).

3. Games for education differ from games for entertainment.

4. Rigorous research is required to help translate the art and technologies of gaming into teaching, learning, and assessment systems.

5. Video game and educational materials industries are inhibited by high development costs and uncertain markets for educational innovations developed as learning games.

6. There are a variety of barriers that inhibit markets for educational games, including market fragmentation, faculty members' and parents' negative attitudes about video games, and lack of evidence for efficacy and evidence-based learning through gaming.

7. Educational institutions are slow to transform practices and organizational systems that take advantage of new technology, including gaming and simulations.

8. There is no serious evidence-based learning framework that currently exists for implementing large-scale evaluations of the outcomes of using educational games.

Previous Work

Game playing dates back several thousands of years to the start of civilization (Bartfay & Bartfay, 1994), and the benefits of games to learning, has been used as a teaching tool for centuries (Henry, 1997). However, despite recent emergence and increased application of serious games, and game-based learning in healthcare education and training, their use is still fairly limited (Corbett & Lee, 1992). With respect to nursing education, a variety of "traditional" (non-video) games have been used in the past (Cowen & Tesh, 2002). Lewis et al. (1989) described the use of crossword puzzles and bingo-type games in nursing curricula while Stern (1989) described the use of games based on popular board games and television game shows for nursing education. The results of such studies suggested Jeopardy!-type games are effective for learning new knowledge, reviewing information, and applying concepts. Cessario (1987) developed a board game designed to motivate students to learn conceptual nursing models. This game appeared to be motivational and enjoyable while reinforcing students' learning. Such "traditional" games were not specifically tailored to the various subdiscipline areas of nursing.

Another approach was taken by Tashiro and colleagues beginning in 1996 (Tashiro, 2001a, 2001b, 2003a-d, 2009). With funding from a series of National Science Foundation grants, funding from the National Institute of Nursing Research, and contractual work with major publishers of educational materials, Tashiro and colleagues developed a diverse array of educational games. He stimulated this work by challenging educators and researchers to answer the nested questions, "What really works in the educational games, for whom when, how, and with what outcomes (Sullins, Hernandez, Fuller, & Tashiro, 1995; Tashiro & Rowland, 1997). The very first simulation model was one of the first virtual hospital systems for education and was based on the game Myst, created within Adobe Director.™ The learning environment anticipated the kind of movement and interactions now possible in Second Life. These learning environments were built from an evidence-based framework. Interestingly, although student end users enjoyed the gaming quality, faculty did not.

Tashiro rebuilt the simulations as flash-based applications that could be executed from CD-ROM and were designed to meet faculty concerns while still appealing to students. This next generation of the virtual hospital system addressed the National Research Council's seven critical issues in developing improved learning outcomes, especially in areas of higher order thinking like clinical judgment and understanding what nurses "do" as they engage in the nursing process. Over 70 major simulation suites evolved from that first virtual

hospital system, including a series of different virtual hospitals, a virtual medical office, and a virtual patient encounter simulation for training emergency medical technicians and paramedics. These serious games allowed students to move around within a virtual setting and encounter patients with complex physiological and often psychosocial problems. Cases were developed by experts in a particular type of disease or injury state, reviewed by expert clinical panels, and developed into simulated scenarios of patient care. Patients had full medical and nursing records, usually with more than 50,000 data fields. These records were automatically updated within the simulations as time passed, just as they would in a real hospital. Later versions of the simulations followed students' choices and provided diagnostic feedback on students' clinical performance compared to choices that would be made by expert clinicians. As the simulations evolved, conditional logic systems were embedded into patient care so that as students' made choices their choices impacted patient outcomes, for better or worse. Together these simulations reach over 50,000 students each year (a small sample includes: Tashiro, Sullins, Long, and Kelly, 2001a; 2001b; 2003a-d; Mathers, 2006; Fulcher 2007a, 2007b, 2007c).

There are a number of virtual simulations/ serious games for healthcare training that cover community health nursing to some degree (emergency management and preparedness, and first responders in particular). More specifically, the Center for the Advancement of Distance Education (CADE) within the School of Public Health at the University of Illinois at Chicago has developed a public health simulation within Second Life that allows public health workers to test their skills in scenarios, such as bioterrorism attacks, smallpox outbreaks, and natural disasters. The focus of this simulation is not so much community health but rather first response preparedness. Players must assess the medical needs of "patients" and take appropriate action (e.g., send them to the proper station or dispense medicine if needed). The goal of the game is to maximize the number of patients handled per hour.

HumanSim™ is a software simulation platform that provides enhanced initial, refresher and sustained medical education and training developed by Virtual Heroes, Inc. (Pulley, 2007). The simulation employs the latest in gaming technology and was designed for use by a wide range of healthcare students and professionals including physicians, nurses, emergency medical personnel, first responders, as well as for use by educators and researchers. HumanSim allows users to practice scenarios in a safe environment where they do not have to fear the consequences of failure. The game addresses the treatment of patients when dealing with different events.

Pulse!! is an immersive virtual learning space (i.e., a serious game) for training healthcare professionals in clinical skills. Game development was funded by the United States Office of Naval Research and developed by BreakAwayGames and Texas A & M University - Corpus Christi. Pulse!! includes cutting-edge graphics to recreate a lifelike, environment where civilian and military heath care professionals practice clinical skills in order to better respond to injuries sustained during catastrophic incidents, such as combat or bioterrorism. Code Orange™ is another serious game developed by BreakAwayGames geared towards the training of first responders for emergency preparedness in the event of mass casualties. This game supports a multi-player environment. Players are part of a medical team and their task is to work together to save lives. Code Orange™ is based on the Hospital Emergency Incident Command System (HEICS) protocol (http://www.heics.com/).

Cowan et al. (2008) describe a serious game for critical care team training meant to foster interprofessional education. The game provides a pedagogical approach enabling healthcare practitioners to develop a clear understanding and appreciation of the roles, expertise, and unique contributions of other disciplines within teams of participating healthcare providers. In each scenario, a critically ill patient requires the immediate attention of a critical care rapid response team consisting of a number of healthcare professionals including nurses, doctors, and respiratory therapists. The goal of the trainees is to stabilize the patient through the collaboration of all response team members. The simulation supports an "online multi-player" environment allowing trainees to participate from remote locations. Heinrichs et al. (2008) developed three virtual worlds for team training and assessment in acute-care medicine: (1) emergency department (ED) teams to manage individual trauma cases; (2) pre-hospital and in-hospital disaster preparedness; and (3) ED and hospital staff to manage mass casualties after chemical, radiological, nuclear, or explosive disasters. Evaluations of these virtual worlds indicated that virtual emergency department simulations were able to provide "repeated practice opportunities in dispersed locations with uncommon, life-threatening trauma cases in a safe, reproducible, flexible setting" (Heinrichs et al., 2008, p. 161). Stytz et al. (1997) describe the Virtual Emergency Room (VER) project, a simulation system designed to enable emergency department personnel to practice emergency medical procedures and protocols. The simulation is built upon a distributed virtual environment architecture to enable real-time, multi-participant simulations allowing practitioners from a wide variety of expertise to work together remotely and ultimately to improve the readiness of emergency department staffs for a wide variety of trauma situations (Stytz, et al., 1997).

The interested reader is directed to a number of available resources including the Games For Health Project (http://www.gamesforhealth.org/) that sees the application of cutting edge games and game technologies to a range of public and private policy, leadership, and management issues. Games For Health also holds an annual conference where attendees from a variety of disciplines including medical professionals, and game developers to discuss and share information about games and game technologies and their application and impact on healthcare and policy.

A serious game utilizing behavioral simulation for acquisition of community health nursing skills safely was developed by Hogan et al. (2007), called mSTREET. It presents cost-effective experiential learning, learner-centered approach that addresses the learning needs of millennial students within a community health nursing curriculum. The serious game was built as a module upon the Modular Synthetic Research Evaluation and Extrapolation Tool (mSTREET) serious game platform. mSTREET is designed to deliver computerized virtual training and research environments in a variety of investigative and direct response settings. mSTREET provides a "base framework" for developing specific field modules that are specifically designed to emulate the functional and behavioural processes in various disciplines. Trainees and educators in the supported fields can use the software to easily construct "scenarios" that can be played out in real-time within the safe and controlled environment of a virtual 3D world. The community health nursing module consists of scenarios with specific learning objectives, feedback, and predictors of attainment of the learning outcomes related to community health nursing. A screenshot of one of those scenarios is shown in Figure 1.

Second Life

The previous subsections provide a sense of the breadth of serious games. However, we want to explore at least one serious game environment in some depth. We chose Second Life, a 3D social network that also has been used as a serious game. Second Life (SL) is as an interesting environment and one that is being increasingly used for healthcare education. We note at the start of this subsection that e-learning technologies are emerging at unprecedented rates. A number of areas have been studied thoroughly, including repositories of learning objects, ubiquitous learning environments, ranking systems based on user patterns of online bibliographic items, and automatic paper recommender systems (Ternier et al., 2009; Chang et al. 2009; Tang & Mc-Calla, 2009). Some scholar technologies based on bibliographic indexing have been advanced to available products by Elsevier and Springer (SciVal, 2009; AuthorMapper, 2009). We believe that the right combination of emerging e-learning technologies could potentially be integrated into a unified system, for example within SL. Such consolidation could result in an interesting and powerful suite of learning modules capable of capturing and measuring learning outcomes, as

Figure 1. Sample screenshot of the mSTREET community health nursing module, showing a nurse working in a neglected area of the community

well as being able to perform competency assessments in a number of disciplines.

A number of research institutions around the world have developed and tested networked collaborative virtual reality environments (CVREs) for education and training since the early nineties. Using a local network or the Internet, CVREs allow users from multiple remote locations to interact and collaboratively to work, learn, train, and perform other activities despite being thousands of miles apart (Benford et al., 2001). However, until recently, there were insufficient computational resources and network power or adequate coding-decoding algorithms (codecs) to carry out smooth communications and immersion of participants in CVREs. Consequently, a trade-off between speed and realism was typically made. These types of constraints have limited human modality interactions, except for those focused almost exclusively on the exchange of visual and auditory information (Gutierrez et al., 2004; Chan & Lau, 2004).

Developed by Linden Labs in 2003, SL is a social network in the form of virtual world where millions of Internet users have been registered, and presently contribute to SL by developing and uploading graphical objects (Second Life, 2009). Users of SL can communicate through their graphical avatars (virtual personifications) using gestures, text messages and their voice, employing voice over IP (VoIP) technology. In general, SL graphics and a number of its features can be personalized. For instance, users can modify their avatar's clothing/appearance, as well as trade and sell goods and services using SL's own "currency", referred to as "Linden Dollars". The ability to personalize the Second Life environment is considered by many to be compelling and fun. The SL virtual world contains virtual "islands" (also called "sims") that can be purchased for a fee directly from Linden Labs or from other third-part sellers, including other SL users. Once purchased, the user can opt for using his/her island for their desired purpose. We note that there are

two versions of SL, one is for adults and one is for users between 13 and 17 years of age, called Teen Second Life.

SL applications have been developed primarily for entertainment and socializing purposes, although some of its islands are increasingly being applied to education and training. Although the primary purpose of SL education and training applications is not necessarily "fun" and entertainment, this does not imply that such applications cannot be fun and entertaining and, in fact, fun and entertainment can play an integral role. For instance, in foreign language learning, fun and humor can lower the "Affective Barrier." By lowering the affective barrier to learning, student anxiety may decrease, along with other negative feelings towards a learning experience in a collaborative virtual world (Krashen, 1982, 1988). There exist a number of educational islands where courses are being taught, many owned by universities and private firms throughout the world. In addition, some educational institutions provide virtual facilities to students, such as virtual classrooms, laboratories, and libraries (Gollub, 2007). SL also boasts virtual museums that can be used in educational activities as well.

Consistent with Stephen Krashen's hypothesis (Krashen, 1982, 1988) about the affective filter and language learning, there are presently numerous educational institutions offering second language learning classes in Second Life, including the internationally recognized Instituto Cervantes of Spain. This institution also has developed a virtual library containing books in Spanish and Spanish memorabilia, and also a virtual expo hall (Cervantes Institute, 2009).

Literature reporting the use of SL for training in the IT industry has recently started appearing. For example, according to Gronstedt (2007), large IT companies such as IBM, Intel, and Dell, amongst others, are investing in the development of virtual islands, offering courses and technical training in SL to their employees. Still in its infancy, reported studies regarding SL applications and cognitive gains for general training are sparse. That being said, a number of the developers working on these SL training initiatives predict that the number of SL training applications will grow steadily, especially in countries with emerging economies such as Brazil, India, and China (Gronstedt, 2007).

Second Life and Health Training

Large government organizations have shown interest in SL for healthcare education. The United States National Library of Medicine has established a virtual hospital, a medical library, and a health and wellness center in SL's Health Info Island (Pellerin, 2007). In addition, the United States Centers for Disease Control and Prevention (CDC) developed an information center in SL (CDC, 2008). In this information center, virtual staff members explain CDC's goals and mission, providing introductory information about the CDC, and answering questions asked by its virtual visitors. The CDC virtual space currently includes displays of posters and video projections about CDC products, and includes external links to open relevant Web pages. CDC is planning to add a virtual laboratory in the near future, although its purpose has yet to be announced.

Lafsky (2009) reported a number of educational institutions that have been using SL for health training. The Imperial College in London, UK, developed a replica of an operating room (OR) in SL, where medical surgery students can learn and practice OR procedures before they are permitted to practice in a real OR. The Imperial College has also created a virtual respiratory ward, where students can interview avatar patients, guided by volunteers and professors, and make adequate diagnosis, and recommend treatments. Lafsky reports other anecdotal evidences of SL uses in health training. A heart murmur simulator with six virtual patients was created at San Jose State University in the U.S., with the objective of allowing students to listen to real cardiac sounds, perform cardiac auscultations, and identify a number of types of heart murmurs, (data are still

being collected and analyzed from 2,500 users who have participated in this training). In addition, a simulator for training nurses in SL was created in Tacoma, WA (United States), called MUVErs Medical Simulation. It contains a "bot" (an avatar patient who has a set script, is semi-autonomous, and can communicate with people), and that can experience chest pain symptoms. Nursing students have to learn to make quick decisions about this "patient" and know how to use equipment (such as a virtual defibrillator).

According to John Lester of the Education and Healthcare Market Developer at Linden Labs (Lafsky, 2009), one of the primary advantages of the simulated operating rooms in SL is their collaborative aspect. They bring together students, nurses, residents, doctors, and even real patients who collaborate in training drills, no matter where those persons are physically located, and to interact in real time through their avatars present in the simulated operating room. Lester also pointed out that another advantage is reduced costs, since it can be very expensive (sometimes in the order of millions of dollars) to build and equip a real training OR facility. In contrast, simulated ORs in SL can be developed for just a fraction of that cost. Another benefit of using collaborative virtual environments such as SL for training is the reduction of travel to and from their educational institutions by both students and instructors. Reduced travel results in reduced fuels costs and reduced carbon footprints may help shape "green" models for education (Theil, 2008).

The creators of SL announced in the Virtual Worlds London Conference held on October 2008 development of a stand-alone SL version (Linden, 2009), which can run on a local server and on a local area network (LAN). One of the benefits of the stand-alone SL version is that it can be custom-configured, and cannot have access to the Internet-run SL metaverse, thus improving confidentiality and privacy issues. Some medical schools have shown interest to acquire and use their own instance of SL for their courses, running in an intranet.

Potential pedagogical benefits of using SL for healthcare training include lowering student anxiety, increasing competencies in learning a new skill, promoting student cooperation and collaboration, learning how to deal with conflict resolutions, and enhancing student self-reflection and active learning (Jackson & Fagan, 2000; Winn, 1993). Further experimental studies are needed to confirm those benefits. Such research is still in an early stage, without clear conclusions about the medium and long-term training gains of SL.

Despite the potential benefits with respect to education and training SL offers, Hansen (2008) warns that there are many issues and questions that need to be answered about educational and skill gains related to health training in SL. The applications in health training are still in a relatively nascent state. Hansen found that a main issue related to use SL for training is how relevant training in SL is for teaching medical professionals, including how fast, and to what extent SL will be embraced by healthcare trainees and educators. We note that none of the reviewed articles on SL have directly addressed students' misconceptions.

Technical Issues on Second Life

In order to run smoothly, SL requires a considerable amount of computational resources, such as an efficient video graphics card, a large RAM memory, and a reliable Internet connection with large bandwidth, (from 1.544 to 6 Mbps). According to SL's web page (http://secondlife.com/support/system-requirements/?lang=en-US). SL needs a cable or DSL connection for accessing the Internet, and the latter Web page warns that "Second Life is not compatible with dial-up internet, satellite internet, and some wireless internet services." These requirements are strict, since we have collaboratively tested SL with very modest success in a local network connected to the Internet through fiber optics and with about 500 kbps at the time of testing. It was not possible to run SL with slower Internet connections or with

computers with 1 GB video RAM and less. It may be possible to improve access to Second Life by arranging a guaranteed Service Level Agreement (SLA) with the Internet service provider, or to increase the bandwidth connection, however these can be costly solutions.

Although the network requirements of SL to run efficiently specify a cable or DSL internet connection, evidence indicates that SL may run with IEEE 802.11g wireless networks for a small group of users accessing the wireless network at the same time. However, from our own observations, we recommend the use of SL over WiMAX (Worldwide Interoperability for Microwave Access) technology, already available in some cities throughout the world. WiMAX is a recently created wireless communication medium to provide up to 72 Mbit/s symmetric broadband speed, suitable for multimedia and other types of data, based on the broadband wireless access IEEE 802.16 standard (Kumar, 2008).

A major problem with collaborative VR environments such as SL is the lag and latency inherent with such environments particularly with a "slow" network connection. This latency can negatively affect VE visualization, sound transmission, and user communication in the shared virtual environment and lead to user frustration and in some cases, motion sickness (Fraser et al., 2000). In addition, increased latency will almost certainly hinder user performance, affecting completion of training objectives in VR applications. One of the main causes of slow collaborative virtual world access is network delay that is caused by: (1) the way VR information (in the form of packets) is delivered onto a local network or over the Internet; and (2) how that information is processed at each computer connected to that network (Gutwin et al., 2004). Network delay, or the period of time to update and display the shared virtual environment for all the users, also produces latency in collaborative virtual environments such as SL. This can negatively affect user interaction, ultimately leading to a reduction in the immersive capabilities of the virtual world (Burdea & Coiffet, 2003). There may be some work-around solutions, for example trying a third-party Second Life viewer (client) called Onrez (http://viewer.onrez.com/). Onrez runs somewhat faster than the viewer developed by Linden Labs. There are other third-party companies and research groups that have developed Second Life viewers, available from: http://wiki.secondlife.com/wiki/Alternate_viewers.

Technical Causes that Potentially Hinder Training in Second Life

As summarized in Table 1, there are a number of technical issues with SL that may hinder training. This table is not an exhaustive list of problems, but is meant to provide an overview of issues we have identified. Some of these issues can lead to student misconceptions, for instance, inaccurate representations of the 3D graphical models fail to provide the necessary detail required to perform a task accurately. Student engagement and interest in the simulation may also decline when players are faced with these types of technical problems. Simply put, we need more rigorous research on what really works within SL teaching, learning, assessment environments.

EXPLORING POTENTIAL FOR DEVELOPMENT OF MISCONCEPTIONS IN CLINICAL JUDGMENT

The earlier sections of this chapter introduced some of the emerging technologies and specific examples of serious games with an emphasis on healthcare and with a deeper exploration of Second Life as a likely model for serious games now emerging. We have argued that serious games and simulations appear to have a high potential for shifting the way content and skills are taught and possibly improving higher order reasoning. However, we also point out the evidence is lacking for a generalized theory of how and why to build serious games so that they "really work" to improve learning in predictable ways and so that they do not promote development of misconceptions.

As we mentioned in the Introduction, we have tried to clarify what we do not know about "what really works" in educational simulations and serious games. Certainly, in the health sciences we should be very concerned about the possibility of health sciences students developing misconceptions that could have deadly consequences if these students became healthcare providers and engaged in patient care. We argued earlier that there are

Table 1. Technical issues that may affect training in SL

Issue	Cause
Inaccurate graphical representations or sounds of models/simulations used for training	Poor graphics and auditory design.
Distracters in the training setting	Unnecessary virtual objects placed in the virtual educational setting, or persons flying or teleporting (they are common ways of avatar navigation) around the virtual training facility, as described in Wong (2006).
Network delays	High network latency.
Inadequate computer equipment to run the SL client	Low RAM memory, slow CPUs, inadequate graphics card, etc.

eight gaps in our knowledge about effective use of educational simulations and serious games:

1. How does a simulation or serious game enhance disposition to engage in a learning process?
2. What are the relationships between the level of realism in a simulation or game and learning outcomes?
3. How do you define the threshold of experience within a game or simulation that leads to measurable learning outcomes?
4. What are the cognitive processes being developed during learning while working within a game or simulation?
5. In what knowledge domains can we measure learning as being retained and how stable is the retention?
6. What is the disposition to act on the knowledge gained during work within a simulation?
7. How well can the knowledge gained within a game or simulation be transferred?
8. What are the differences in learning that manifest as conceptual competencies and performance competencies?

An important issue is that each serious game or simulation has its own idiosyncrasies in the construction of how and why the developers mimicked elements of the real world and the interactions that occur in the real world. At the very least, then, we need to contextualize "what really works" within the situated learning experience of each different type of serious game. Even when we break out studies by serious game type, we encounter a variety of problematic issues related to developing an evidence-based approach to learning:

- Many studies purporting improved learning and skills development had methodological flaws.

- A large number of studies are based on small sample sizes with little information on the power of the test.
- Many studies pay limited attention to the multitude of variables shaping learning, especially how so many of these variables are confounded.
- While research studies on educational experience and outcomes tend to focus on a group of student-users, we do not see enough attention paid to covariates that would provide a deeper understanding of effects of computer literacy, familiarity with gaming environments, age and gender differences in preferences for design of environments and navigational schema, and differentials in access to gaming environments as well as machine power and graphics in computers being used.
- There may be new types of differentials between student users and faculty members facilitating use of the serious games for education.

Our ongoing studies of simulation and serious game environments leave us with uncertainties about what is being learned in such environments, how learning progresses, and what opportunities there are for students to engage in and follow tangents to the educational objectives, and that may lead to development of misconceptions. Again, we emphatically note that more traditional methods and materials of education are certainly not free of the potential for students to develop misconceptions. However, we actually have an opportunity to shift education to a more evidence-based framework and to be more thoughtful about and critical of educational methods and materials as faculty members and students become increasingly interested in simulation and serious game usage in education.

We will explore these ideas more deeply by examining a hypothetical virtual world and asking some hard questions about the potential for the environments of that world to potentiate development of misconceptions, especially dangerous misconceptions. Prior to writing this chapter we conducted a series of Gedanken experiments (thought experiments that serve to illuminate a hypothesis or theory). The experiments were conducted on a virtual world that we have been building over the past few years. Earlier versions of these types of Gedanken experiments were described by Tashiro & Dunlap (2007) in their analysis of the impacts of realism on engagement within serious games. For convenience, we will call this virtual world E-LAN, a pun on élan, not to be confused with the Elan programming language, and simply an acronym for Electronic Learning and Networking. We have built and evaluated components of E-LAN. All of the functional specifications have been developed and run through our Gedanken experiments, which we use to imagine a large variety of use cases within E-LAN.

Imagine E-LAN as a virtual world in which the student-player must get to a hospital at a certain time in order to start a clinical rotation. We have built virtual hospitals for nursing students, so we will imagine this version of E-LAN as a serious game for nursing students. Also, for this version of E-LAN, we will create a single-player environment in which the student-player moves through the world in a first-person perspective, that is, looking through the "game character's eyes.". Along the way to the hospital, the student-players will encounter engaging characters and events that may help or hinder them from reaching the hospital on time – sort of like a Grant Theft Auto environment on the way to clinical rotation. They encounter avatars and can talk with these avatars through a voice-recognition system. However, they have to reach the clinical rotation on time, and can earn points by arriving early, but also accrue "difficult" encounters in the hospital if they arrive late. Getting to the hospital is more of a game but some problem solving and critical thinking is possible as student-players try to get to clinical rotation on time.

Once student-players arrive at the hospital, they select a unit and begin clinical rotation. The environment of the virtual hospital and selecting a unit for rotation provide a transition that also interjects a few moments of cognitive dissonance from the possibly wild ride of the gaming environment to get to the hospital. We will return to this idea of cognitive dissonance and shifts along a gradient from entertainment to edutainment, that is from the mostly entertaining elements of a serious game to the mostly educational elements of a serious game.

Within the virtual hospital unit, a preceptor avatar assigns the student-player to one or several patients and asks the student to begin planning and implementing care. The points earned for arriving early can be used by student-players to seek help from their avatar preceptors and clinical decision support systems as they encounter problems or difficult situations. Student-players encounter a variety of difficult situations, such as not being able to find medications, patients developing emergent problems related to their disease-injury state or to a psychosocial crisis, problems with patients' significant others, being interrupted by a preceptor of Nurse Supervisor who is rude or demanding or asking them to stop what they are doing and help with another patient. Problems for student-players who arrived late are built into the rules of the game, with difficult encounters more frequent for late arrivals.

When we designed E-LAN and began Gedanken experiments, we already had developed sets of virtual patients using clinical experts to create cases and expert clinical panels to review and revise cases. This process yielded detailed cases with hundreds of thousands of data for each patient case. These cases represent some of the most comprehensive patient case studies for simulations developed to date for healthcare education at the undergraduate level. We also had figured out virtual environments in which a student-player could engage in almost every aspect of patient care. We also learned how to layer monitoring middleware into the simulations so that we could record student-players' decisions and time spent in various activities. The monitoring data and learning assessments within the simulations allowed us to map student-players' learning and competency outcomes against expectations delineated by expert clinical panels.

Essentially, E-LAN emerged from our review and analysis of the major problems we encountered from building serious games and from our critique of a diverse array of serious games. We then developed solutions to the problems we identified. These problems and solutions, presented in simplified form below, were our attempt to design the virtual world E-LAN as an "ideal" immersive virtual world for education.

Evidence-based Learning Maps and Serious Game Development. There is a gradient that we suggest ranges from games that are totally for entertainment and educational intent is incidental, to games that are designed as educational materials and entertainment is incidental. As a serious game becomes more seriously educational in intent, the entertainment portions and the educational portions need to be planned out carefully. We suggest that the combination of the fun (or at least engagement) and education can be driven by what the US National Research Council (2000, 2001, 2005) described as learning maps. We argue that learning maps should be based on evidence and so then could provide a framework in which the complex interactions within a game are mapped from planned interactions that have evidence for being both engaging and improving some type of learning. Thus, for E-LAN, let us assume that we developed learning maps based on evidence-based clinical guidelines for planning and implementing care as well as on careful attention to what is most engaging within various gaming environments. We also will assume that these maps were reviewed by expert panels and revised according to their recommendations. Finally, the development process involved expert clinical panels and game developers who worked together to study how the learning maps could be expressed as an environment in the virtual world of E-LAN.

Embedded Learning Activities, Learning Resources and Scaffolding. Not unrelated to building a serious game from evidence-based learning maps, learning activities generally, would be embedded as gaming interactions around which were nested or made available in some way a variety of learning resources for use in learning. There also would be scaffolding available to provide ongoing support for the learning process. For E-LAN, let us imagine that the gaming environment was developed through a process of using the learning maps with expert clinical panels delineating clinical scenarios and, with help of gaming experts, the possible interactions within these scenarios. This process could result in serious game development following US National Research Council guidelines (2000, 2001) as well as recommendations from the Federation of American Scientists (2006). Such games would be more likely to enhance students' disposition to learn, provide multiple paths for learning, help students overcome limitations of prior knowledge, provide practice and feedback, help students develop an ability to transfer knowledge acquired by extending knowledge and skills beyond the contexts in which they were gained, incorporate the role of social context, and address cultural norms and student beliefs? In addition, careful structuring and usability testing of virtual teaching-learning-assessment environments could provide embedded learning activities and as-needed educational resources and scaffolding that could facilitate embedding clear learning goals, broad experiences and practice opportunities, continuous monitoring of progress with detailed diagnostic feedback, contextual bridging, personalized learning experiences, and innumerable opportunities for students to repeat the serious game without increasing faculty workload.

Such a process would necessarily involve close collaboration among expert clinicians, educators, and game developers. These collaborations would focus on the gaming facets of the serious game and the educational facets of the serious game as well as the coupling of these into an interesting and engaging environment, shaped by rigorous usability studies and tested with critical end users just as big-name video games are developed and evaluated prior to release. Imagine our panels of experts working together to select and sensibly embed learning resources and scaffolding within the virtual world of E-LAN, paying attention to the game and the education of the serious game. We actually followed this very same process for some of the virtual worlds the authors have built and studied.

Authentic Assessment. In order to know if learning has taken place, learning outcome or competency assessments also can be embedded in the serious game. When and where they occur depend on what type of learning the developer is hoping student-players will engage in and achieve. The concept of "authentic assessment" is important in the sense of developing assessments of what the developer really thinks the game can teach and what the student-players can actually learn, with such assessments having reliability as well as face and construct validity. Imagine that for E-LAN we have authentic assessment methods and instruments with sound reliability and validity. Furthermore, assume that we have been able to automate the assessments tied to encounters with embedded leaning activities and learning resources within the serious game environment of E-LAN. Finally, the system will be built so that an instructor can set the assessments so they map to different types of diagnostic feedback arrays (see below).

Diagnostic Feedback. In serious games, diagnostic feedback would be tied to learning resources and scaffolding and be mapped by the developer to provide sensible feedback on student-players' performance on assessments embedded in the game. When and how feedback is provided depends on educational intent. A simple example in healthcare is learning a pro-

cedure accomplished by completing a set of tasks in a particular sequence. One type of assessment would measure the student-player's understanding of each step, with feedback for that step to help the student-player understand the rationale for and performance of a discrete task. Such an assessment-feedback strategy helps students develop a deeper understanding of each task in a sequence of tasks, but would introduce a type of Bayesian bias if you also wanted to see if the student knew the sequence as well as understanding each step. Thus, assessing a student-player's understanding of a sequence might be set up in a way to provide diagnostic feedback based on an assessment that waited until a student completed what s/he thought was the proper sequence. For our virtual world E-LAN, we will assume we have a sophisticated diagnostic feedback system that easily can be set by a faculty member to provide assessment-feedback coupling for learning activities as individual, clusters, or sequences of tasks. This coupling would assess performance and provide feedback on students' knowledge of facts, concepts, procedures, and metacognitive processing (Anderson and Krathwohl, 2001).

Instructor Time. One interesting problem is the time a faculty member must take to learn a serious game and then effectively implement the game. If faculty members decide they take on an avatar in Second Life for example, then they are spending real time engaging with students in a virtual world. It is clear that close faculty mentoring (Quality Education for Minorities Network, 1992) and also careful debriefing may be very valuable to help students consolidate what they have learned while also providing remediation for errors in judgment or underdeveloped pattern recognition while working on a clinical problem. However, how many hours does a faculty member have to work in Second Life or provide such mentoring? Is there any other solution, for example, a knowledge or expert system, or perhaps even a system analogous to clinical decision support systems that could provide ongoing support for student-players in a serious game. For E-LAN, we assume that we have a very versatile expert system, linked to an avatar who can provide as-needed mentoring. We also would have a virtual computer-based knowledge and clinical decision support system that provides on-going cognitive support for student-players (modeled after the recommendations of the U. S. National Research Council, 2009).

Adaptive Learning. We have built and are testing an adaptive learning system that tracks student-players' choices in a serious game and then maps these to learning and competency outcomes to develop a deeper understanding the pathways of how students are learning, their efficiencies, their cognitive processing, and the knowledge and skills development. Imagine that E-LAN has this adaptive learning capacity.

Levels of Realism. We also have studied and now can create modular worlds that allow us to set switches on a gaming platform that can create different combinations of realism, including visual realism of the environment and objects in the environment – including avatars, auditory elements of the environment (such as the complex sounds on a particular type of hospital floor), fine motor activity in avatars, psychosocial attributes and language exchange between student-players and avatars, use of instrumentation, amongst others. Consequently, we can adjust the levels of realism and study the impact of realism on engagement within the serious game as well as study the impact of realism and engagement on realized learning and competency outcomes. In the future, E-LAN also could have levels of realism for sensory perception related to tactile, smell, and sonification elements within the virtual world.

Network Requirements and Adequate Computer Equipment. Some of the technical issues, as described for Second Life, are harder to control, but for E-LAN, let us suppose that we manage network, computer equipment, and other technical issues by setting up a cost-efficient workstation environment that can be easily controlled and is reliable under heavy student usage.

Thus, by solving various problems with current games, we have imagineered the virtual world E-LAN as a pretty interesting and engaging serious game with a variety of student-centred capacities and grounded in the theory and practice of evidence-based learning as well as evidence-based practice in healthcare. We then engaged in Gedanken or "thought" experiments in which we ran the iterations of use cases within E-LAN in order to study how our virtual world could potentiate development of misconceptions as student-players worked and played in the virtual world of this serious game.

At the start of use case iterations, we examined how cognitive and learning sciences inform instructional design in a serious game. Patel, Yoskowitz, Arocha, & Shortliffe (2009) point out that healthcare is general collaborative (or should be collaborative) in its processes of patient care. However, within care delivery settings cognition will be shaped by the situated encounters in that workplace, which are dynamic and strongly influenced by social contexts as well as by a diverse array of other elements in the setting such as technology, temporal and spatial heterogeneity in the patient's condition, changing shifts of providers caring for the same patient, and ongoing coordination of many different tasks and decisions as well as health information management (Patel et al., 2009). Effective action requires development of pattern recognition capabilities as providers move from novice to expert. Such pattern recognition capabilities are critical to clinical judgment and decision-making during planning and implementing care. Often, the decision making unfolds in a "heuristically-guided" sequence (Patel et al., 2009, p. 177). Yet, we need to know what happens if pattern recognition development is incomplete. For example, what is the probability that working in a serious game leads the student-user to tangential analyses and making decisions that are logical to the result of such analyses but that are flawed as pattern recognition?

Pushing more deeply into use case studies, we discovered a sense of the difficulty in finding the "crouching tangents, hidden dangers" in flawed pattern recognition. Our approach focused on the gaps in our knowledge about what serious games and simulations are capable of doing, for better or worse. Earlier we described eight knowledge gaps. We used the use cases to push E-LAN to its limits of "really working" in the context of these gaps. Below, we provide our findings.

How does a simulation or serious game enhance disposition to engage in a learning process? We could figure this out. There are various methods and measures that we can use to study how engaged a student-player will be and we can develop research designs to see how engagement is related to learning outcomes. E-LAN has that capacity built into the environment, although the vast majority of serious games do not examine complex relationships between engagement and learning. Earlier, we also mentioned the transition from the Grand Theft Auto type of environment to the hospital environment and our attempt to help students make a cognitive shift from the games of a serious game to the educational elements of a serious game. Since the E-LAN design would allow us to create a variety of transitional environments, we could work across the spectrum of mostly game to mostly education. In our Gedanken experiments, we identified a large number of combinations of game-education mixes, but these have not been discussed in the literature. For example, one combination would be to have a distinct shift that occurs after the "wild ride' to the hospital and begins to increase the inclusion of more and more educational elements related to nursing, but also allows breaks for student-players in the Nurses' Lounge to re-engage in games and perhaps accrue points towards advice or use of clinical-decision support tools. You can imagine the diversity of combinations that repeated use-case analyses would reveal and the differences

in individual preferences that might map out on different combinations. We felt that the research is not clear on what mix would optimize learning while preventing development of misconceptions.

What are the relationships between the level of realism in a simulation or game and learning outcomes? Again, we knew this was a problem with serious games and we built into E-LAN a way to modify realism levels and to study learning outcomes. In fact, we can even study engagement as a function of realism and the impact of engagement-realism coupling on learning outcomes. We previously had implemented a series of Gedanken experiments to study possible relationships between engagement, realism, and learning outcomes (Tashiro & Dunlap, 2007). This work led to the authors identifying key problems and building prototype learning environments designed around serious games in which realism could be easily modified. Thus, now we could build a system like E-LAN to allow shifts in level of realism at any level of the serious game. Such capacity opens the door for studying the complex relationships of student-players' preferences as well as their actual learning outcomes. However, the literature is still weak in detailed studies of how realism impacts learning and possible development of misconceptions.

How do you define the threshold of experience within a game or simulation that leads to measurable learning outcomes? Basically, you could define threshold through rigorous studies of the relationships between work within a serious game and performance on authentic assessments of learning outcomes. E-LAN was imagineered as an environment with coupled research and teaching-learning-assessment capacities. No serious games have this capacity yet, although the authors have built the prototype for such coupling. We know it can be done, and surprisingly economically. Even so, the threshold of experience that leads to stable knowledge retention as well as disposition to act on that knowledge has not been carefully studied for serious games. Furthermore, threshold is likely to be idiosyncratic to each individual and shaped by intrinsic and extrinsic motivational factors that in turn are likely to shape disposition to engage in what some call effortful cognitive endeavor (Cacioppo, Petty, Feinstein, & Jarvis, 1996). We would have to build additional subsystems into E-LAN to allow us to study these complexities in individually defining threshold for stable knowledge retention. Even if we did build such subsystems, we still would have to build additional subsystems to assess the types and frequency of misconceptions within the stable retained knowledge. Currently, data mining techniques are being applied to this approach.

What are the cognitive processes being developed during learning while working within a game or simulation? Here is where we began to stumble in our own work and to have concerns about serious games for healthcare. We realized that we had very little sound evidence for deciding what cognitive processes were being developed for the vast majority of educational materials, not just serious games and simulations. However, the great interest in serious games and their displacement of many "traditional" instructional methods and materials encouraged us to start asking in earnest, "What really works in serious games, for whom, why, how, and with what outcomes?" In fact, we started challenging all educators and educational researchers to "show us the data" that provided at least a basic foundation that a method-material combination in a teaching-learning-assessment strategy actually worked to improve learning and specifically higher order reasoning. Our abilities to follow and evaluate cognitive processes were made more difficult by the nonlinear opportunities available in serious games.

How did student-players move through the game, and what did they think and then do at each point or moment of choice in the game? Suppose there was a set of tasks that required implementation in a specific sequence. How would we follow the student-player through their exploration of these tasks and assess both their understanding

of the task as well as their understanding of the procedural knowledge inherent in the correct sequence of the tasks? Well, we would "test" them in some way. But the interesting feature of serious games is that a student-player could actually engage in many more combinations of activities than they would likely engage in by reading a textbook or watching a video about the tasks and sequence of tasks. Now, we imagineered E-LAN to be able to follow the choices made by students and map these to educational outcomes. However, we still would have a very difficult time trying to get much resolution on the actual cognitive processes of any individual student-player, let alone an overall picture of a class of 20, 50, or 130 students..

In what knowledge domains is learning being retained and how stable is the retention? Not unrelated to the above discussion of developing cognitive processes during learning, we looked at a broad research literature on cognition and learning to better understand how knowledge domains are created during cognitive processing and how stable such "knowledge" might be. Certainly, many faculty members agonize and express their disappointment in students' knowledge, especially students' "inherited" from a prerequisite course who did not have the prerequisite knowledge we had hoped they would have retained. As a simple example, one of the authors (Tashiro, a PhD in Biology) returned to school late in his career to become a nurse and was stunned that the majority of his classmates could not trace blood flow through the heart after two semesters of anatomy and physiology and one semester of pathophysiology. These nursing students had all passed courses perceived as rigorous and taught by well-respected faculty using traditional methods and materials.

We did not mention in the discussion about cognitive processing and knowledge formation that there are a variety of models of cognition (Patel et al., 2009) as well as a variety of models of cognitive taxonomies that try to represent the intersection of cognitive processes and formation of knowledge domains (e.g., Bloom's revised taxonomy; see Anderson & Krathwohl, 2001). Even our imagineered E-LAN would have difficulty assessing how cognitive processes result in knowledge domains developed as cognitive schema in our student-player. We would be overwhelmed by trying to assess the probability of the relative stability of the knowledge developed. We could, of course, measure the realized stability by assessing the student-player's retention of what was learned at the end of the gaming sessions and then through time examining the stability of the retained knowledge. However, through time a student is exposed to many new educational and life experiences. So, how do we tease out factors shaping knowledge gained and knowledge retained in the context of a particular situated learning experience?

What is the disposition to act on the knowledge gained during work within a simulation? To add to the complexity, imagine that the knowledge gained during serious game sessions was stable for a couple of months. We could then examine the disposition of student-player to act on the knowledge. For example, we could ask them to act within another level of the serious game or we could ask them to act on their knowledge in a real-world situation, such as a supervised clinical rotation. In the first case, following the student-player's decisions to act in the serious game could allow evaluation of conceptual competencies and might also allow evaluation of their propensity for performance competencies. In simple terms, the conceptual competencies are the student-player's understanding of the content and skills learned in the serious game, while the performance competencies are the student-player's planning, commitment to, and then implementation of actions based on their understanding of the content and skills learned in the serious game.

The student-player's disposition to act on their knowledge would be shaped by a host of factors, some intrinsic to the student (e.g., set of intrinsic motivational factors) and some extrinsic to the student (e.g., extrinsic motivational factors). These factors tend to unfold in fairly complex patterns, even in simple situations of real-world patient care. If a patient is going through a very difficult transition (e.g., trauma, rapid deterioration, emotional crisis coupled to physiological collapse) the emerging dynamics and interactions become enormously complex. The complexity impacts the intrinsic and extrinsic factors shaping disposition to act on knowledge. Even though we imagineered E-LAN to overcome many of the problems in serious games, we could not yet imagine the systems and subsystems of serious games that allowed us to authentically probe conceptual and performance competency development, especially during situations of rapidly changing physiological and psychosocial conditions for a patient and how these impact a healthcare provider.

How well can the knowledge gained within a game or simulation be transferred? As we continued Gedanken experiments to study the complexities of assessing dispositions to act on knowledge gained, we realized that we could not easily or accurately delineate the details of a student-player's knowledge of facts, concepts, procedural knowledge, and metacognitive capacities. An enormous array of learning and competency assessment instruments and our imagineered E-LAN were not sufficient to provide us with much more than the broad strokes of what knowledge had been gained while working within a serious game, what knowledge was acted on, and so what knowledge was transferred into action. Patel and colleagues (2009) raised some additional complications. Examining medical education, Patel's group identified four common types of medical curricula. Simplified here, the four types were: (1) conventional approach; (2) problem-based learning, (3) a physiological system-organ based approach, and (4) hybrid integrations of two or more of the other three approaches (see descriptions in Patel et al., 2009, pp. 188-189).

Patel's work led us into another type of Gedanken experiment. We began asking what would happen if different skin-rules combinations for a serious game led to different types of reasoning, and if so, what might be the results of such reasoning. Here, we are using the term "skin" to mean the sense of the fictional world created by graphics and sound, while for "rules" we mean the underlying programming that provides fictional interactions within the virtual setting. We realized right away as the Gedanken experiments were implemented that a very sophisticated virtual world might be valuable to partially test components of some of the theoretical frameworks that have been proposed for cognition (e.g., cognitive load theory, cognitive flexibility theory, adaptive character of thought theory, situated learning theory). Some of these theories cluster into more individualistic structured learning, such as adaptive character of thought and cognitive load theories, while others fit within the domain of what educators call constructivist learning theories such as cognitive flexibility theory and situated learning theory (Patel et al., 2009). We also realized that serious game developers have generally not mapped the skin and rules of their games to a particular theoretical framework or a synthesis of frameworks that had some empirical foundation.

As we examined different skin-rule combinations in E-LAN, we became increasingly concerned about how and why to study knowledge transfer without mapping such transfer from educational activities and assessment of such activities that were based in a particular cognitive theoretical and praxis framework. These types of Gedanken experiments revealed that we could not very easily trace misconceptions unless we had a better understanding of how to build learning-assessment maps for each theory of cognition and then follow knowledge and skill acquisition through time within a serious games as well as post-gaming experiences for a wide range of applications in real world settings. A simple example of a Gedanken iteration was a serious game in which an 18 year-old woman presents in the Emergency Department. She speaks English, and we try to

figure out what she is experiencing and what we should do. Note again, we were working with Nursing, so imagine a student-player working with a triage nurse in the Emergency Department (ED) of the virtual hospital. This iteration was based on an interesting paper by Welk (2002), which provided an example of training students to develop pattern recognition. We built a prototype in which an avatar walks into the ED. The avatar will engage with the first-person student-player through a voice recognition system that allows the student-player to ask questions in English, with English responses from the avatar. She is emitting a variety of non-verbal cues and, and the student can pose any query from a possible pool of 20 questions and respective responses by the avatar.

With some background knowledge, a student-player could figure out her condition should be considered as possibly an emerging myocardial infarction (MI). A common misconception is that this young avatar woman would be too young for an MI. We then ran other iterations in which the avatar spoke only Spanish or some English and some Spanish, trying to figure out how various student-players would react in terms of keying out the cardinal signs of an emerging MI. We discovered that slight variations in the skin-rules combinations dramatically increased our ability to trace misconception development.

What are the differences in learning that manifest as conceptual competencies and performance competencies? Building on the discussion above, as we looked more closely at different types of competencies that would be foundational for clinical judgment in Nursing, we returned to the research literature for medical education. Again, the medical education research literature is substantially more developed than that of Nursing or the allied health professions. Examining comparisons of conventional and problem-based approaches to medical curriculum development and instruction, Patel and colleagues argued that conventional curricula taught basic science as an independent suite of disciplines (usually in the first two years of medical school), but in contrast clinical contexts drive the organization and teaching of basic sciences in problem-based learning (with clinically meaningful problems introduced in the early courses of a curriculum).

The problem is that conventional curricula tend to inculcate a broadly applicable foundation of scientific knowledge, while problem-based learning creates more of a situated learning of clinical contexts in which scientific knowledge is integrated. This means that conventional curricula may teach science principles early but not within in meaningful clinical contexts while problem-based learning may inhibit knowledge transfer into practice across clinical applications if the knowledge gained in clinical contexts is too narrowly confined to a particular context (see more detailed arguments, Patel et al., 2009, p. 189).

Although the research literature provides a complex picture, there is some evidence that medical residents from conventionally trained programs were more likely to use heuristically-driven reasoning while residents from problem-based learning programs were more likely to use hypothesis-driven reasoning. Patel and colleagues (2009) argued that conventional curricula could lead to overconfidence in use of data-driven reasoning and these patterns of reasoning may become difficult to alter when errors or misconceptions are generated (e.g., when under-sampling of patient data occurs). Problem-based learning instruction, on the other hand, may not sufficiently help medical students develop the types of data-driven reasoning that are particularly efficient and accurate for routine problems and for problems in which the practitioner's knowledge is adequate (Patel et al., 2009, p. 189).

In terms of healthcare competencies within our E-LAN for Nursing, what conceptual and performance competencies could be assessed. Here, we are using conceptual competencies as a thorough understanding of a knowledge and/or skills domain. Often conceptual competencies are further elaborated as: (1) competencies in which

a person can describe how and why to use the knowledge or skill in different but appropriate contexts (generativity; Patel et al., 2009); and (2) competencies in which a person can describe how to use the knowledge or skill in situations that are unfamiliar (robustness; Patel et al., 2009). However, performance competencies are those competencies in which knowledge is acted on as an expression of a variety of behaviors and decisions or skills that are implemented in the real world or some very close simulation of the real world.

Serious games can be built so that opportunities to demonstrate competencies can be embedded and student-player's knowledge is demonstrated and their activities monitored to see if competencies were achieved. For serious games without haptic interfaces or augmented reality simulations, we could not embed and measure performance competencies involving psychomotor activities. We might be able to assess conceptual competencies and through longitudinal studies see how measures of conceptual competencies and disposition to act on knowledge and skills acquired might predict performance competencies. However, through many Gedanken iterations, we did not believe we could trace development of misconceptions without first starting with a stronger theoretical framework for cognition and building serious games like E-LAN around such frameworks.

Even though we simplified the review of Patel and colleagues (2009), the important point is that serious gaming is currently not being developed with these sorts of complexities in mind. Just as there is ongoing debate and controversy about the rationale for educational approaches in medicine, there should be an active and ongoing debate about how experiences within serious games are likely to shape knowledge and skill acquisition as well as transfer to clinical applications with real human beings. Importantly, even as there is still an underdeveloped evidence-base framework for medical education, there is an underdeveloped evidence-based framework for how knowledge is developed and transferred in serious games.

And, sadly, the educational practices of Nursing and allied health professionals have been less well studied than for medicine.

EVIDENCE-BASED LEARNING AND FUTURE TRENDS

Certainly, there is a very large and diverse literature that converges on the idea that there are educational benefits to electronic educational materials that use simulations and gaming technology. These benefits include: involving students in complex practice skills without risk, improved psychomotor skills, enhanced retention of knowledge as well as enhanced decision-making skills, interactive learning, opportunities for replay at a particular step in a sequela as well as repeated practice of a sequela, options for immediate feedback, and retention of knowledge related to procedures. Some of this literature was reviewed in the report on the recent Summit on Educational Games sponsored by the Federation of American Scientists Federation (2006). Additional literature reviews and syntheses have also been provided by Bogost (2007) and Gee (2007, 2004, 2003). Work in healthcare has been reviewed by Feingold, Calaluce, and Kallen (2004), while the United States National Research Council (2000, 2001, 2005) presented summaries of research covering topics in the areas of how people learn and the science and design of educational assessment.

These works extend a very large and diverse research literature from artificial intelligence, simulation, education, and psychology. Recent work on cognitive taxonomies (Anderson & Krathwohl, 2001) also holds promise for informing how and why to build electronic educational materials. While the evidence for the benefits of electronic educational materials is accumulating, the development and usage of such materials still lacks a sensible evidence-based approach to improving learning. Publishers and faculty members share responsibility in the lack of evidence-based

approaches to building and using electronic educational materials (Tashiro, 2009). Our analysis suggests there are important ethical issues that must be explored in the development and usage of electronic instructional materials. In particular, we argue it would be worthwhile to examine more closely the processes by which publishers decide to build educational materials for undergraduate healthcare students and how faculty members decide to use such materials. We hope this chapter provokes some deeper thinking and further ethical analyses of publishers' and faculty members' roles in developing and using electronic educational materials for undergraduate healthcare students. Indeed, we would like to see a broader approach that goes beyond undergraduate healthcare education into other disciplines and also reaches into other academic levels. We feel that an ethical analysis coupled to an evidence-based learning framework may lead to educational frameworks that define educational materials development frameworks and evidence-base learning praxis frameworks for developing, choosing, and using instructional materials.

The Federation of American Scientists (FAS) recommended a rigorous research program and also delineated ten specific game attributes for application in learning. These were derived from advances in cognitive and learning science (Federation of American Scientists, 2006; see pages 18-20) and FAS argued games should provide:

1. Clear learning goals.
2. Broad experiences and practice opportunities that continue to challenge the learner and reinforce expertise.
3. Continuous monitoring of progress and use of this information to diagnose performance and adjust instruction to a learner's level of mastery (see also research on adaptive learning and teaching).
4. Encouragement of inquiry and questions, and response with answers that is appropriate to learner and context.

5. Contextual bridging, which is closing the gap between what is to be learned and its usefulness to the learner.
6. Engagement leading to an increased time on task within a learning game environment.
7. Motivation and strong goal orientation.
8. Scaffolding in the form of cues, prompts, hints, and partial solutions to keep learners progressing through the activities in a learning game.
9. Personalization that allows tailoring of learning to the individual learner.
10. Infinite patience inherent in a game environment that literally does not tire of repetitive actions and so provides learners with innumerable opportunities to try an activity over and over.

We used these recommendations to conceptualize our partially built and completely imagineered E-LAN and also as pathways for Gedanken experiments to iteratively study a large number of use cases for working within E-LAN as a serious game. We came to the conclusion that four major problems in electronic educational materials, simulation, and serious design for undergraduate healthcare impede widespread development of educational games and simulations. Importantly, these problems point out the difficulty of developing electronic educational materials that can be used to develop evidence-based frameworks for learning in academic healthcare programs as well as in clinical settings. The four problems described below appear to inhibit development of electronic educational materials that meet the FAS and National Research Council recommendations (Tashiro & Dunlap, 2007):

1. Instructional designers seldom conduct the research necessary to demonstrate their products actually improve learning or skills. In healthcare, an empirically-driven approach becomes especially critical in the context of the Institute of Medicine's call for broadly based core competencies (AACN, 2003; Institute of Medicine, 2003). Similar deficiencies in research foundations for effectiveness exist throughout the educational games and simulations available at the K-12 and undergraduate levels.
2. With few exceptions, commercially available electronic educational materials have not been shown to improve what some call critical thinking (including the important higher levels of declarative, procedural, and metacognitive knowledge) of users while also improving disposition to engage in higher order thinking (Anderson & Krathwohl, 2001; Alessi & Trollip, 2001; Sadowski & Gülöz, 1996; see also papers by Cacioppo and colleagues, 1996). Such materials have remained elusive, despite many different types of simulations that are being evaluated, and principally because designers have not used empirical approaches to build disposition to improve critical thinking into educational materials.
3. Few commercially available electronic educational materials have been developed to mesh sensibly with the strategic needs of K-12 and undergraduate curricula or with professional development, continuing education, and training programs.
4. There are few commercially available products related to improving learning outcomes or skills competencies that are designed to become part of an evidence-based education framework as well as an evidence-based practice framework that improves students' and practitioners' learning-training outcomes.

These four basic problems are exacerbated by the complexity of studying the impact of realism and engagement on educational game and simulation design as well as the ultimate impact on student learning (Tashiro & Dunlap, 2007). However, the role of faculty members adds another layer of complexity to these four problems. The faculty members and other experts providing input to a publishers' business decision may not reflect the normative values of the majority of faculty in a discipline area. This is because most faculty members are not well grounded in the research related to what really works to improve education. On the other hand, while perhaps reflecting a larger percentage of faculty members in a content domain, advances in educational materials and methods are not likely to evolve from input of educators who are not well versed in educational research on methods and materials that really work. A publisher's strategic planners, subject matter experts and business algorithms may be based on success of sales and market exploitation rather than on whether or not a product actually improves educational outcomes. Why? Simply put, there are so few studies of product-outcomes coupling.

Another layer of complexity, and one of the oddities of undergraduate educational materials, is that faculty members are generally the purchasers of most instructional materials but students are the end users of the materials. That is, faculty members are the purchasers because they select materials, order them, and set the required usage in a course. Even though students actually pay for the materials, faculty members dictate the conditions of purchase. In discussions with both faculty and students, there was considerable dissonance in what each group felt they needed faculty to teach and students to learn. One of the most striking features of this dissonance was noted by the author during his case study of his classmates in a nursing program (Tashiro, 2009). Most students in his courses purchased large textbooks but very few actually read the textbook assignments the faculty member required for a course.

We are not discouraged by our findings that there may be innumerable crouching tangents-hidden dangers in serious games. The opportunity to build evidence-based frameworks for learning is very exciting and challenging. Even the failure of

our virtual world E-LAN to allow detailed tracking and prediction of misconceptions provided us with the chance to better understand the complexities of building serious games and understanding their likelihood of inculcating misconceptions. Certainly, we look forward to rebuilding E-LAN and taking another step towards shaping serious games within a framework of evidence-based learning.

ACKNOWLEDGMENT

All trademarks, trade names, service marks, and logos referenced in this chapter belong to their respective companies. Author Miguel A. Garcia-Ruiz acknowledges partial support from the National Council of Science and Technology (CONACYT) of Mexico, grants no. FOMIX Colima-2008-C01-83651 and 94140, and participated in the preparation of this chapter while he was a Visiting Professor at the Faculty of Business and IT, University of Ontario Institute of Technology, Oshawa, Canada. Author Jayshiro Tashiro acknowledges support of funding from the National Science Foundation (DUE CCLI-EMD 9950613) and the National Institute of Nursing Research (1R43 NR05102-01) for research contributing to portions of this chapter. Authors Miguel Vargas Martin and Jayshiro Tashiro acknowledge support from the Social Sciences and Humanities Research Council of Canada. Author Bill Kapralos acknowledges the financial support from the Social Sciences and Humanities Council of Canada in the form of an Image Text Sound and Technology grant, and the support of the Natural Sciences and Engineering Research Council of Canada in the form of a Discovery grant.

REFERENCES

AAAS. (2004). *Invention and Impact: Building Excellence in Undergraduate Science, Technology, Engineering and Mathematics (STEM) Education*. Washington, DC: American Association for the Advancement of Science.

AACN - American Association of Colleges of Nurses. (2003). *The Role of the Clinical Nurse Leader*. Washington, DC: American Association of Colleges of Nursing.

Akkary, P. L., Bell, E., Roberts, R. L., Dudrick, S. J., & Duffy, A. J. (2009). The role of haptic feedback in laparoscopic simulation training. *The Journal of Surgical Research*, *156*(2), 312–318. doi:10.1016/j.jss.2009.04.018

Aldrich, C. (2004). *Simulations and the future of learning*. San Francisco: Pfeiffer.

Aldrich, C. (2005). *Learning by doing*. San Francisco: Pfeiffer.

Alessi, S. M., & Trollip, S. R. (2001). *Multimedia for Learning: Methods and Development*. Boston: Allyn and Bacon.

American Association for the Advancement of Science. (2004). *Invention and Impact: Building Excellence in Science, Technology, Engineering and Mathematics (STEM) Education*. Washington, DC: American Association for the Advancement of Science.

Anderson, L., & Krathwohl, D. (2001). *A taxonomy for learning, teaching, and assessing*. New York: Longman.

Annetta, L., Murray, M., Laird, S., Bohr, S., & Park, J. (2006). Serious games: Incorporating video games in the classroom. *EDUCAUSE Quarterly Magazine*, *29*(3), 16–22.

Aoki, N., Ohta, S., & Masuda, H., Naito, Sawai, T., Nishida, K., Okada, T., Oishi, T.M. Iwasawa, Y., Toyomasu, K., Hira, K., & Fukui, T. (2004). Edutainment tools for initial education of type-1 diabetes mellitus: initial diabetes education with fun. *Studies in Health Technology and Informatics*, *107*(Part 2), 855–859.

AuthorMapper. (2009). *AuthorMapper*. Retrieved September 18, 2009, from http://qa.authormapper.cmgsites.com/

Balkissoon, R., Blossfield, K., Salud, L., Ford, D., & Pugh, C. (2009). Lost in translation: Unfolding medical students' misconceptions of how to perform a clinical digital rectal examination. *American Journal of Surgery*, *197*, 525–532. doi:10.1016/j.amjsurg.2008.11.025

Barab, S. A., Scott, B., Siyahhan, S., Goldstone, R., Ingram-Goble, A., Zuiker, S., & Warren, S. (2009). Transformational play as a curricular scaffold: Using videogames to support science education. *Journal of Science Education and Technology*, *18*, 305–320. doi:10.1007/s10956-009-9171-5

Baranowski, T., Baranowski, J., & Cullen, K. W. (2003). Squire's quest! Dietary outcome evaluation of a multimedia game. *American Journal of Preventive Medicine*, *24*(1), 52–61. doi:10.1016/S0749-3797(02)00570-6

Bartfay, W. J., & Bartfay, E. (1994). Promoting health in schools through a board game. *Western Journal of Nursing Research*, *16*(4), 438–446. doi:10.1177/019394599401600408

Benford, S., Greenhalgh, C., Rodden, T., & Pycock, J. (2001). Collaborative virtual environments. *Communications of the ACM*, *44*(7), 79–85. doi:10.1145/379300.379322

Bishop, M. J., & Cates, W. M. (2001). Theoretical foundations for sound's use in multimedia instruction to enhance learning. *Educational Technology Research and Development*, *49*(3), 5–22. doi:10.1007/BF02504912

Bogost, I. (2007). *Persuasive Games – the expressive power of videogames*. Cambridge, MA: MIT Press.

Brown, S. J., Lieberman, D. A., Germeny, B. A., Fan, Y. C., Wilson, D. M., & Pasta, D. J. (1997). Educational video game for juvenile diabetes: results of a controlled trial. *Medical Informatics, 22*(1), 77–89. doi:10.3109/14639239709089835

Burdea, G., & Coiffet, P. (2003). *Virtual reality technology* (2nd ed.). New York: John Wiley and Sons.

Cacioppo, J. T., Petty, R. E., Feinstein, J. A., & Jarvis, W. B. G. (1996). Dispositional differences in cognitive motivation: The life and times of individuals varying in need for cognition. *Psychological Bulletin, 19*(2), 197–253. doi:10.1037/0033-2909.119.2.197

CDC. (2008). *Virtual worlds – ehealth marketing*. Retrieved September 14, 2009 from http://www.cdc.gov/healthmarketing/ehm/virtual.html

Cervantes Institute. (2009). *Instituto Cervantes*. Retrieved September 22, 2009, from http://secondlife.cervantes.es/

Cessario, L. (1987). Utilization of board gaming for conceptual models of nursing. *The Journal of Nursing Education, 26*(4), 167–169.

Chan, K. K. P., & Lau, R. W. H. (2004). Distributed sound rendering for interactive virtual environments. *IEEE International Conference on Multimedia and Expo*, 1823-1826.

Chang, W.-C., Wang, T.-H., Lin, F. H., & Yang, H.-C. (2009). Game-based learning with ubiquitous technologies. *IEEE Internet Computing, 13*(4), 26–33. doi:10.1109/MIC.2009.81

Chen, Y. (2006). A study of comparing the use of augmented reality and physical models in chemistry education. In Proceedings of the 2006 ACM international Conference on Virtual Reality Continuum and Its Applications (Hong Kong, China) (VRCIA'06, pp. 369-372). New York: ACM.

Cowan, B., Shelley, M., Sabri, H., Kapralos, B., Hogue, A., Hogan, M., et al. (2008). Interprofessional care simulator for critical care education. *In Proceedings of the ACM FuturePlay 2008 International Conference on the Future of Game Design and Technology* (pp.260-261) Toronto, Ontario, Canada, November 3-5 2008.

Cowen, K. J., & Tesh, A. S. (2002). Effects of gaming on nursing students' knowledge of pediatric cardiovascular dysfunction. *The Journal of Nursing Education, 41*(11), 507–509.

Desser, T. (2007). Simulation-Based Training: The Next Revolution in Radiology Education? *Journal of the American College of Radiology, 4*(11), 816–824. doi:10.1016/j.jacr.2007.07.013

Federation of American Scientists. (2006). *Summit on Educational Games – Harnessing the power of video games for learning*. Washington, DC: Federation of American Scientists.

Feingold, C. E., Calaluce, M., & Kallen, M. A. (2004). Computerized patient model and simulated clinical experiences: Evaluation with baccalaureate nursing students. *The Journal of Nursing Education, 43*(4), 156–163.

Fraser, M., Glover, T., Vaghi, I., Benford, S., Greenhalgh, C., Hindmarsh, J., & Heath, C. (2000). Revealing the realities of collaborative virtual reality. *In Proceedings of the Third international Conference on Collaborative Virtual Environments* (San Francisco, California, United States) (pp.29-37). E. Churchill and M. Reddy, Eds. CVE '00. ACM, New York, NY.

Fulcher, G. (2007a). *Virtual Medical Office for Bonwit-West: Clinical Procedures for Medical Assistants* (6th ed.). Philadelphia: Elsevier-Saunders.

Fulcher, G. (2007b). *Virtual Medical Office for Young: Kinn's The Administrative Medical Assistant* (6th ed.). Philadelphia: Elsevier-Saunders.

Fulcher, G. (2007b). *Virtual Medical Office for Young and Proctor: Kinn's The Medical Assistant* (10th ed.). Philadelphia: Elsevier-Saunders.

Gee, J. P. (2003). *What video games have to teach us about learning and literacy?* New York: Palgrave MacMillan.

Gee, J. P. (2004). *Situated language and learning: A critique of traditional schooling.* London: Routledge.

Gee, J. P. (2007). *Good video games + good learning – Collected essays on video games, leaning, and literacy.* New York: Peter Lang.

Gibson, D., Aldrich, C., & Prensky, M. (2007). *Games and simulations in online learning.* Hershey, PA: Information Science Publishing.

Gollub, R. (2007). *Second life and education.* ACM Crossroads, 14.1. Retrieved September 12, 2009, from http://www.acm.org/crossroads/xrds14-1/secondlife.html

Gresalfi, M., Barab, S. A., Siyahhan, S., & Christensen, T. (2009). Virtual worlds, conceptual understanding, and me: Designing for consequential engagement. *Horizon, 17*(1), 21–34. doi:10.1108/10748120910936126

Gronstedt, A. (2007). Second Life produces real training results. *T + D Magazine,* August.

Gutierrez, M., Vexo, F., & Thalmann, D. (2004). The mobile animator: interactive character animation in collaborative virtual environment. *In Proceedings of Virtual Reality conference,* 125-284.

Gutwin, C., Benford, S., Dyck, J., Fraser, M., Vaghi, I., & Greenhalgh, C. (2004). Revealing delay in collaborative environments. *In Proceedings of the SIGCHI Conference on Human Factors in Computing Systems* (Vienna, Austria, April 24-29, 2004). CHI '04. ACM, New York, NY, 503-510.

Halloun, I. A., & Hestenes, D. (1985). The initial college state of college physics students. *American Journal of Physics, 53,* 1043–1055. doi:10.1119/1.14030

Hanna, D. E. (2003). *Building a leadership vision: Eleven strategic challenges for higher education. EDUCAUSE.* July/ August.

Hansen, M. M. (2008). Versatile, immersive, creative and dynamic virtual 3-D healthcare learning environments: A review of the literature. *Journal of Medical Internet Research, 10*(3). doi:10.2196/jmir.1051

Heinrichs, W. L., Youngblood, P., Harter, P. M., & Dev, P. (2008). Simulation for team training and assessment: Case studies of online training with virtual worlds. *World Journal of Surgery, 32,* 161–170. doi:10.1007/s00268-007-9354-2

Henry, J. M. (1997). Gaming: A teaching strategy to enhance adult learning. *Journal of Continuing Education in Nursing, 28*(5), 231–234.

Hickey, D., Ingram-Goble, A., & Jameson, E. (2009). Designing Assessments and Assessing Designs in Virtual Educational Environments. *Journal of Science Education and Technology, 18,* 187–208. doi:10.1007/s10956-008-9143-1

Hogan, M., Sabri, H., & Kapralos, B. (2007). Interactive community simulation environment for community health nursing. *In Proceedings of ACM FuturePlay 2007 International Conference on the Future of Game Design and Technology.* Toronto, Ontario, Canada, November 15-17.

Howe, N., & Strauss, W. (1993). *13th Gen – Abort, retry, ignore, fail?* New York: Vintage Books.

Howe, N., & Strauss, W. (2000). *Millennials Rising: The Next Generation. New York: Vintage Books Institute of Medicine (2003). Health professions education – A bridge to quality.* Washington, DC: National Academy Press.

Jackson, R. L., & Fagan, E. (2000). Collaboration and learning within immersive virtual reality . In *Proceedings of Collaborative Virtual Environments.* San Francisco: ACM.

Juul, J. (2005). *Half-Real: video games between real rules and fictional worlds.* Cambridge, MA: MIT Press.

Kato, P. M., & Beale, I. L. (2006). Factors affecting acceptability to young cancer patients of a psychoeducational video game about cancer. *Journal of Pediatric Oncology Nursing, 23,* 269–275. doi:10.1177/1043454206289780

Kiili, K. (2005). Digital game-based learning: Towards an experiential gaming model. *The Internet and Higher Education, 8*(1), 13–24. doi:10.1016/j.iheduc.2004.12.001

Kolb, D. (1984). *Experiential learning: experience as the source of learning and development.* Englewood Cliffs, NJ: Prentice-Hall.

Krashen, S. D. (1982). *Principles and practices in second language acquisition.* New York: Prentice-Hall, Prentice Hall International.

Krashen, S. D. (1988). *Second language acquisition and second language learning.* New York: Prentice-Hall.

Kumar, A. (2008). *Mobile broadcasting with WiMAX: Principles, technology, and applications.* Boston: Focal Press.

Lafsky, M. (2009). Can training in Second Life teach doctors to save real lives? *Discover Magazine.* July-August, 15.

Lewis, D. J., Saydak, S. J., Mierzwa, I. P., & Robinson, J. A. (1989). Gaming: A teaching strategy for adult learners. *Journal of Continuing Education in Nursing, 20*(2), 80–84.

Lieberman, D. (1997). Interactive video games for health promotion: Effects on knowledge, self-efficacy, social support and health. In Gold, R.L. & Manning, T. (eds.) *Health Promotion and Interactive Technology,* (103–120). Norwell, NJ: Lawrence Erlbaum Associates.

Linden, A. (2009). *Second life lives behind a firewall.* Retrieved October 26, 2009, from https://blogs.secondlife.com/community/workingin-world/blog/2009/04/01/second-life-lives-behind-a-firewall

Madsen, K.A., Yen, Wlasiuk, S.L., Newman, T.B., & Lustig, R. (2007). Feasibility of a dance videogame to promote weight loss among overweight children and adolescents. *Archives of Pediatrics & Adolescent Medicine, 161*(1), 105–107. doi:10.1001/archpedi.161.1.105-c

Mangold, K. (2007). Educating a new generation: Teaching baby boomer faculty about millennial students. *Nurse Educator, 32*(1), 21–23. doi:10.1097/00006223-200701000-00007

Mathers, D. (2006). *Virtual clinical Excursions – for Black and Hawks Medical-Surgical Nursing: Clinical Management for Positive Outcomes* (7th ed.). Philadelphia: Elsevier-Saunders.

McPherson, C., Glazebrook, C., Forster, D., James, C., & Smyth, A. (2006). A randomized, controlled trial of an interactive educational computer package for children with asthma. *Pediatrics, 117*(4), 1046–1054. doi:10.1542/peds.2005-0666

Michael, D., & Chen, S. (2006). *Serious games: Games that educate, train and inform.* Boston: Thomson Course Technology.

Michael, J. A., Richardson, D., Rovick, A., Modell, H., Bruce, D., & Horwitz, B. (1999). Undergraduate students' misconceptions about respiratory physiology. *Advances in Physiology Education, 22*(1), 127–135.

Misconception (2009). *The American Heritage Dictionary of the English Language*, Fourth Edition. Boston: Houghton Mifflin Company.

Mitchell, A., & Savill-Smith, C. (2004). *The use of computer and video games for learning: A review of the literature.* Retrieved January 13, 2010, from http://www.LSDA.org.uk.

National Research Council. (2000). *How people learn: Brain, mind, experience, and school.* Washington, DC: National Academy Press.

National Research Council. (2001). *Knowing what students know: The science and design of educational assessment.* Washington, DC: National Academy Press.

National Research Council. (2005). *How students learn: History, mathematics, and science in the classroom.* Washington, DC: National Academies Press.

National Research Council. (2009). *Computational Technology for Effective Care: Immediate Steps and Strategic Directions.* Washington, DC: National Academies Press.

Oblinger, D. (2003). *Boomers & Gen-Xers, Millennials: Understanding the "New Students".* *EDUCAUSE Review.* July/August.

Ozmen, H. (2004). Some student misconceptions in chemistry: A literature review of chemical bonding. *Journal of Science Education and Technology, 13*(2), 147–159. doi:10.1023/B:JOST.0000031255.92943.6d

Patel, V. L., Yoskowitz, N. A., Arocha, J. F., & Shortliffe, E. H. (2009). Cognitive and learning sciences in biomedical and health instructional design: A review with lessons for biomedical informatics educaiotn. *Journal of Biomedical Informatics, 42*, 176–197. doi:10.1016/j.jbi.2008.12.002

Pellerin, C. (2007). *U.S. Government presence grows in Second Life online world.* Retrieved September 14, 2009, from http://montevideo.usembassy.gov/usaweb/2007/07-234EN.shtml

Pew Research Center. (2007). *How Young People View Their Lives, Futures and Politics: A Portrait of Generation next.* Retrieved October 5, 2009, from http://people-press.org/report/300/a-portrait-of-generation-next

Pulley, J. (2007). Serious games. *Health IT, 2*(2).

Quality Education for Minorities Network. (1992). *Together we can make it work: A national agenda to provide quality education for minorities in mathematics, science, and engineering.* Washington, D.C.: QEM Network.

Reznek, M. A., Chantal, L. R., & Krummel, T. M. (2002). Evaluation of the Educational Effectiveness of a Virtual Reality Intravenous Insertion Simulator. *Academic Emergency Medicine, 9*(11), 1319–1325. doi:10.1111/j.1553-2712.2002.tb01594.x

Ruben, D. (1999). Simulations, games, and experience-based learning: The quest for a new paradigm for teaching and learning. *Health Education Research . Theory into Practice, 30*(4), 498–505.

Sadowski, C. J., & Gülöz, S. (1996). Elaborative Processing mediates the relationship between need for cognition and academic performance. *The Journal of Psychology, 130*(3), 303–307. doi:10.1080/00223980.1996.9915011

Sanne, M. B., Botden, I., & Jakimowicz, J. J. (2009). What is going on in augmented reality simulation in laparoscopic surgery? *Surgical Endoscopy*, *23*(8), 1693–1700. doi:10.1007/s00464-008-0144-1

Savery, J., & Duffy, T. (1995). Problem based learning: An instructional model and its constructivist framework. *Educational Technology*, *35*(5), 31–38.

SciVal. (2009). *Unlock the promise of your research*. Retrieved December 31, 2009, from http://www.scival.com/

Second Life. (2009). *Linden's Second Life*. Retrieved September 23, 2009, from http://www.secondlife.com

Selfe, C. L., & Hawisher, G. E. (2007). *Gaming lives in the twenty-first century – Literate connections. New Yor*. Palgrave Macmillan. doi:10.1057/9780230601765

Shaffer, D. W. (2006). *How computer games help children learn*. New York: Palgrave Macmillan. doi:10.1057/9780230601994

Sinclair, B., & Ferguson, K. (2009). Integrating simulated teaching/learning strategies in undergraduate nursing education. *Int J Nurs Educ Scholarsh.*, *6* (1), Article 7.

Souza, I. A., Sanches, C. Jr, & Zuffo, M. K. (2009). A virtual reality simulator for training of needle biopsy of thyroid gland nodules. *Studies in Health Technology and Informatics*, *142*, 352–357.

Spencer, B. S. (2006). Incorporating the Sense of Smell Into Patient and Haptic Surgical Simulators. *IEEE Transactions on Information Technology in Biomedicine*, *10*(1). doi:10.1109/TITB.2005.856851

Sprengel, D. (1994). Learning can be fun with gaming. *The Journal of Nursing Education*, *33*(4), 151–152.

Squire, K. D. (2008). *Videogame literacy: A literacy of expertise. Handbook of research on new literacies* (pp. 635–669). New York: Lawrence Erlbaum Associates.

Stapleton, A. (2004). Serious games: Serious opportunities. *In Proceedings of the 2004 Australian Game Developers Conference*, 1-6, Melbourne, Australia.

Stern, S. B. (1989). Creative teaching strategies. *Journal of Continuing Education in Nursing*, *33*(4), 151–152.

Strauss, W., & Howe, N. (1991). *Generations: The history of America's future*. New York: William Morrow and Company, Inc. 1.

Strauss, W., & Howe, N. (1997). *The Fourth turning: An American prophecy*. New York: Broadway Books.

Stytz, M. R., Garcia, B. W., Godsell-Stytz, G. M., & Banks, S. B. (1997). A distributed virtual environment prototype for emergency medical procedures training. *Studies in Health Technology and Informatics*, *39*, 473–485.

Sullins, E. S., Hernandez, D., Fuller, C., & Tashiro, J. S. (1995). Predicting who will major in a science discipline: Expectancy-value theory as part of an ecological model for studying academic communities. *Journal of Research in Science Teaching*, *32*(1), 99–119. doi:10.1002/tea.3660320109

Tan, B., Aziz, A. R., Chua, K., & The, K. C. (2001). Aerobic demands of the dance simulation game. *International Journal of Sports Medicine*, *23*(2), 125–129. doi:10.1055/s-2002-20132

Tang, T. Y., & McCalla, G. (2009). A multidimensional paper recommender: experiment and evaluations. *IEEE Internet Computing*, *13*(4), 34–41. doi:10.1109/MIC.2009.73

Tashiro, J. (2009). Ethical analysis of publisher and faculty roles in building and using electronic educational products. *Journal of Electronic Commerce in Organizations*, *7*(1), 1–17.

Tashiro, J., & Dunlap, D. (2007). *2007. ACM digital Library 978-1-59593-943-2/07/0011.* The Impact of Realism on Learning Engagement in Educational Games. In Proceedings of FuturePlay.

Tashiro, J., & Rowland, P. McD. (1997). What works: Empirical approaches to restructuring courses in biology and environmental sciences. In McNeal, A. & D'Avanzo, C. (Eds.) *Student-active science: Models of innovation in college science teaching,* 163-187. Orlando, Fl: Harcourt Brace and Company.

Tashiro, J. T., Sullins, E. S., & Long, G. (2003c). *Virtual clinical excursions for nursing care of infants and children.* St. Louis, MO: Mosby.

Tashiro, J. T., Sullins, E. S., & Long, G. (2003d). *Virtual clinical excursions for fundamental concepts and skills for nursing.* St. Louis, MO: Mosby.

Tashiro, J. T., Sullins, E. S., Long, G., & Kelly, M. (2001a). *Virtual clinical excursions in medical-surgical nursing: assessment and management of clinical problems.* St. Louis, MO: Mosby.

Tashiro, J. T., Sullins, E. S., Long, G., & Kelly, M. (2001b). *Virtual clinical excursions for fundamentals in nursing.* St. Louis, MO: Mosby.

Tashiro, J. T., Sullins, E. S., Long, G., & Kelly, M. (2003a). *Virtual clinical excursions medical-surgical nursing: clinical management for positive outcomes.* St. Louis, MO: Mosby.

Tashiro, J. T., Sullins, E. S., Long, G., & Kelly, M. (2003b). *Virtual clinical excursions for basic nursing: essentials for practice.* St. Louis, MO: Mosby.

Ternier, S., Verbert, K., Parra, G., Vandeputte, B., Klerkx, J., & Duval, E. (2009). The Ariadne infrastructure for managing and storing metadata. *IEEE Internet Computing*, *13*(4), 18–25. doi:10.1109/MIC.2009.90

Theil, S. (2008). Tune in tomorrow. *Newsweek*, August 18-25 issue.

Thompson, D., Baranowski, J., Cullen, K., & Baranowski, T. (2007). Development of a theory-based Internet program promoting maintenance of diet and physical activity change to 8 year old African American girls. *Computers & Education*, *48*(3), 446–459. doi:10.1016/j.compedu.2005.02.005

Unnithan, U. V., Houser, W., & Fernhall, B. (2006). Evaluation of the energy cost of playing a dance simulation video game in overweight and non-overweight children and adolescents. *International Journal of Sports Medicine*, *27*(10), 804–809. doi:10.1055/s-2005-872964

Vlahos, J. (2006). The smell of war. *Popular Science*, 8.

Wagner, D., & Barakonyi, I. (2003). Augmented reality Kanji learning. *In Proceedings of the 2nd IEEE/ACM international Symposium on Mixed and Augmented Reality* (October 07 - 10, 2003). Symposium on Mixed and Augmented Reality. IEEE Computer Society, Washington, DC, 335.

Washburn, D. A., Jones, L. M., Vijaya Satya, R., Bowers, C. A., & Cortes, A. (2003). Olfactory use in virtual environment training. *Modelling and Simulation (Anaheim)*, *2*(3), 19–25.

Welk, D. S. (2002). Designing clinical examples to promote pattern recognition: Nursing education-based research and practical applications. *The Journal of Nursing Education*, *41*(2), 53–60.

Winn, W. (1993). A Conceptual Basis for Educational Applications of Virtual Reality. *HITLab Tech Report R-93-9*. Seattle, WA: University of Washington, Human Interface Technology Laboratory.

Wong, G. (2006). *Educators explore 'Second Life' Online*. CNN online, Technology section. Retrieved September 14, 2009 from http://www.cnn.com/2006/TECH/11/13/second.life.university/

KEY TERMS AND DEFINITIONS

Collaborative Virtual Reality: A shared virtual world using a local network or the Internet as a communication medium, where its users interact to work, learn, train, and carry out other activities together.

Competency: The sum of knowledge, skills, and characteristics that allow a person to perform an action successfully and productively.

Computer Simulation: A computer program that attempts to simulate an abstract model of a particular system, which generally uses input variables.

Misconception: In the area of education, erroneous student's understanding or mistaken notion of a scientific or technological concept or phenomenon.

Network Latency: Network delay, consisting of how much time it takes for a data packet to get from one designated point to another in a computer network.

Second Life: A social network in the form of 3D virtual world shared by millions of registered users, using the Internet as a communication medium.

Serious Games: Video games that are used for training, advertising, simulation, or education, and are designed to run on personal computers or video game consoles.

Virtual Environment: A computer-generated 3D space, also called virtual world, where 3D graphical objects and sounds reside. Its user is represented in the virtual environment by an avatar (a graphical personification) and can interact with the virtual objects and its environment.

Virtual Reality: Computer technology capable of generating a three-dimensional space called virtual environment, which is highly user interactive, multimodal, and immersive.

Chapter 15
Mitigating Negative Learning in Immersive Spaces and Simulations

Shalin Hai-Jew
Kansas State University, USA

ABSTRACT

The growing popularization of immersive virtual spaces and simulations has enhanced the ability to "model" various environments, scenarios, decision-making contexts, and experiential learning for a variety of fields. With these subliminal semi-experiential affordances have also come some challenges. Foremost is the challenge of designing virtual experiential learning that does not result in "negative learning." Negative learning involves unintended messages which lead to learners with illogical or inaccurate perceptions about reality. Negative learning may be subtle; it may exist at an unconscious or subconscious level; it may be biasing even without learner awareness. This chapter addresses some of the risks of negative learning in immersive spaces and simulations and proposes some pedagogical design, facilitation, and learner empowerment strategies to address negative learning—to increase confidence and assurance in the immersions.

"This is to say that perceptions are not confined to stimuli, just as science is not limited to signals or available data; neither, of course, is confined to fact." -- R.L. Gregory

"You create the world of the dream. We bring the subject into that dream, and they fill it with their subconscious." -- Cobb, from Inception (2010)

DOI: 10.4018/978-1-61692-825-4.ch015

INTRODUCTION

Immersive spaces and simulations (also known as "goal-based scenarios" that enable problem-based learning) offer fresh ways to enhance e-learning. Persistent virtual worlds offer continuous learning in three dimensions (Mihal, Kirkley, Christenberry, & Vidali, 2003) and longitudinal academic research possibilities; various learning contexts may be evoked—for cross-cultural interactions, foreign language learning and practices, digital "wetlabs," co-design, and problem-solving. Designed simulations may be deployed on a variety of systems and in different learning contexts. Artificial life (a-life) evokes evolutionary and complex systems and the interrelationships between living creatures. Mobile environments that offer ubiquitous learning may allow "anytime, anywhere" immersions, with location-sensitive delivery of digital information to enhance the embodied experiences of learners. Augmented reality and ambient intelligence spaces combine physical spaces and "smart" manual objects and wearable computers for real-space immersions, where manual objects may offer "state dependent feedback during manual interactions" (LI, Patoglu, & O'Malley, 2009, p. 3:3). These experiences tap into the physical situatedness of the learning while drawing value from digital effects.

Simulations may offer large cost savings at less risk in situations where live, physical simulations would be prohibitively expensive and physically risky, such as in military and first-responder scenarios. These may also be scalable for large-scale (numbers of participants) and wide-scale (geographical dispersion) interactions. While these technologies have become more popular, there have not been sufficient discussions about how to maximize the learning. In what Dovey and Kennedy label "permanent upgrade culture," the perpetual technological innovation will not settle into stabilization, and the "polygons and mesh," math and light, will continue to embellish reality (Dovey & Kennedy, 2006, pp. 53 – 54).

Digital-based educational games (also termed "serious games" or "intelligent learning games") are another type of immersion with a focus on "hard fun" (Prensky, 2002, p. 5) vs. aimless play ("ludic" play). These games were built for particular educational goals (Burgos, Tattersall, & Koper, 2005). The concept here is that learners engage more deeply and for longer periods of learning when they're enjoying the game experience. Games involve defined and undefined rules of play based on its design, game theory, and the

particular learning domain's principles. The design of games relies on game studies—about what people learn, how they interact with each other and the game, and various types of strategies in competitive situations (often involving political science, economics, and military planning).

One commonality between virtual learning is the importance of the experiential element. Experiential learning involves the use of human perception (five senses), translated through human cognition, for the interpretation of these signals in a meaningful learning context. Kolb's experiential learning cycle (1994) is often evoked to describe this transformative experience. This cycle begins with a concrete experience. The learner then observes and reflects on the experience. The learner formulates abstract concepts and generalizations from that experience, and then he / she tests the implications of these concepts in new situations (Schönwald, Euler, Angehrn, & Seufert, 2006, p. 17).

Risks from the Environment, Other People, and the Self: However, there are concerns about whether immersions and simulations may lead to some unintended residual consequences. The "security" of a learning experience suggests that there is freedom from risk. Risks may come from the environment; they may come from other people; they may come from inside the self. Environmental risks in simulations may involve embedded inaccurate messages or experiences for learners; they may involve data compromises or user authentication problems. Risks from other people may come from "social engineering" ploys to capture privy information, locate people, create false relationships, or contravene intellectual property rights. Risks from the self may stem from informational asymmetries, misconceptions, insufficient learning, or inaccurate estimates of one's own abilities. A secure learning experience is one that is assured and accurate and which minimizes risks from the environment, others, and self. It delivers what it professes to deliver, and it does not leave learners with inaccuracies or misconceptions—that may skew their decision-making and actions in the real world and ultimately lead to hazards or losses.

Environmental Risks. Immersions and simulations embody inherent learning risks through indirection and nuance. The immersive learning is inductive and often subtle: learners accrue observations and experiences, consciously and subconsciously, in the virtual environment, and when a critical mass has been reached, they begin to draw conclusions about the learning context and domain. The use of underlying models behind multiverses and simulations mean that many assumptions of the model are not spelled out. Novice learners who do not have sufficient information about the field or about experiential learning from simulations and immersions may go through these learning experiences and not have their misconceptions directly addressed. The focus of simulations means that they will not evoke complete or fully complex systems. The asymmetrical nature of information (namely, that people always have incomplete or incorrect information) also means that designed virtual experiences will always be necessarily limited—by the amount of available information, the limits of technologies in conveying the concepts, and the human ability to perceive and attend to what is relevant. As an example, an artificial life scenario can barely simulate the real-world complexity of biological ecosystems, and they cannot mimic the complex discoveries that may occur over longitudinal (decades-long or generational) studies that bring into play complex organism interactions and minute toxic chemical effects. Another limit to experiential learning involves the tendency for people to tend to see what is familiar and probable but to not see the improbable (Gregory, 1980, p. 182). Using sensory data, learners interpolate or fill in gaps of knowledge; they extrapolate meaning from what they see as known information. Experiential learning may enhance interpretation of signals in typical situations, but they may be highly misleading in atypical ones; learners then need to test the validity of their perceptions and to be aware of systematic errors in their perceptions and interpretations.

Greater transparency in the creation of immersive spaces and simulations—in terms of underlying modeling—and a cultural shift to appreciate the artifice in both scenarios, would enhance possible learning and the application of simulations to real-world knowledge. The promotion of creativity or divergent thinking *from* the immersive spaces and simulation models may enhance greater real-world flexibility in dealing with emergencies or unexpected contingencies. "Original thinking" is required for complex and pressured work environments (Csikszentmihalyi, 1996, p. 93). Some real-world situations, particularly those involving far-transfer analysis and problem-solving, may require solutions that have not been taught (McDaniel & Schlager, 1990), and prior learning itself may be a hindrance to arriving at novel and applicable solutions. Scripted and unthinking responses to highly volatile situations may themselves be risk-causing. Another environment risk may include the misconception that "conceptualizing" something is tantamount to "actualizing" that reality—when hard work is critical to creative success (Gladwell, 2008).

Risks from Others. Learners who enter fantastical virtual environments may assume that the usual rules of the world do not apply in their relationships with each other. They may assume that telling a human-embodied avatar something private will have no potential repercussions. They may enter into a range of relationships and assume that the virtual will stay in the virtual. The mainline press has offered plenty of cautionary tales of false identities, fraudulent schemes, personal identity compromises, mass information losses, parasocial (imaginary) relationships, stalking, intellectual property theft, and other risks from people. Being aware of the limitations of the virtual environment and simulations will be important to offer more protections for those who've gone online to learn.

Risks from the Self. Learners may complete their immersive and simulation learning with dangerous misconceptions. They may mistake cause-and-effect relationships where none exist. They may misunderstand the nature of various entities or objects. They may emerge with unnoticed gaps in knowledge. They may revert to habituated mental models which are inaccurate and not break from inaccurate knowledge; they may fail to un-learn inaccuracies or re-learn correct information over the old. Their muscle memory or kinesthetic training may be inaccurate to real-world physics; logical experiences in immersive spaces may cause a person to be blind to counter-intuitive realities. Learning through experience may be "myopic," particularly in circumstances of ambiguity and complexity, according to researchers:

Experience is often a poor teacher, being typically quite meager relative to the complex and changing nature of the world in which learning is taking place (Levinthal & March, 1993, p. 96).

The risks to negative learning multiply as these ideas are brought out into the world and put into practice. The concept of the anti-pattern from software engineering may be applied here—as "something that looks like a good idea, but which backfires badly when applied" (Cockburn et al., 2004, as cited in Van Biljon, Kotzé, Renaud, McGee, & Seffah, 2004, p. 176) Real-world decision-making and analysis requires a deep knowledge of what doesn't work, why it doesn't work, why that bad solution may seem superficially or initially appealing, and what may be done instead. Anti-patterns are negative solutions used as way stations in the analysis, decision-making, troubleshooting, and problem-solving process.

In situations where the situational awareness has been compromised (poorly captured and / or analyzed), the live decision-making may be deeply errant and not based on real-time realities. Individuals may emerge from simulated experiences with mistaken ideas of their own self-efficacy;

they may emerge with ideas of their own outsized power and omniscience from risk-free virtual environments. Multi-scale environments may lead to perceptual misunderstandings beyond the awkwardness of immersive interactions (Zhang & Furnas, 2002). Perceptual learning itself may lead to misperceptions, of perceiving "stimuli when none are physically present" (Seitz, Nanez, Holloway, Koyama, & Watanabe, 2005, p. 9080), so the cost-benefits of perceptual learning must be balanced. Simultaneous mixes of skills—such as exploring and exploiting the scenario (McMahon, Scott, & Browne, 2005)—may be required instead of one or the other. The negative learning multiplies as people share inaccurate information, skills, and knowledge.

Learning designs enhance the intended knowledge and skill acquisition, and they mitigate negative learning. Optimally, these lead to true and fresh discoveries, not just a re-hashing of known information. Often, these learning design endeavors are piecemeal. For example, one strategy may be to use *realia* and photo-realistic imagery instead of virtual depictions for representations. Or the branching logic of a simulation is enhanced with wider degrees of freedom to capture potential reality. Stochastic or non-predictive models strive to consider random chance and to offer outcomes variances. The choice of what to represent in immersions and simulations should also clearly be considered. Some simulations are beyond the technologies, and there may well be insufficient information to model others.

Negative learning may lead to security compromises in the environment, in interactions with others, and with misconceptions and poor decision-making in the self. This chapter provides an overall strategy to minimize negative learning in immersive spaces and simulations based on the research literature and in some live pedagogical projects. Negative learning may lead to mistaken conceptualizations and false mental models that do not map to the real world. Internalized mental models need to be sufficiently matched against future problems and challenges. They may leave learners with inaccurate perceptions that make them vulnerable to social engineering exploits, information-hunting schemes, and privacy compromises. They may lead to poor perceptions and decision-making in the individual. This chapter's mitigations will consider the design of the immersions, pre-immersion priming and post-immersion debriefing strategies, and the empowerment of immersive learners. This will also explore contextualization, and add-on or augmentation learning, to enhance the validity of immersive spaces and simulations.

LITERATURE REVIEW

Immersions and simulations involve prodigious work employing the human imagination, cognition, emotions, and physical senses. They draw learners into different situations. The best designed immersions engage learners (Galarneau, 2005) and convey positive learning and mitigate for negative learning.

Positive learning is defined as "the change in any aspect of the uncertainty of an outcome occurring as a result of theory development, modeling, observation, or experiment" in terms of decision-making (Oppenheimer, O'Neill, & Webster, 2008, p. 158). These authors define negative learning as

a decrease or sustained divergence in the correspondence between the true outcome and the uncertainty characterization (or belief) over time. In the case of probabilistic characterizations, this will occur when the probability density near the true outcome decreases over time, or when the distance increases between the true outcome and the outcome considered most likely (Oppenheimer, O'Neill, & Webster, 2008, p. 158).

The power of this conceptualization relates to the concept of "true state" objective realities that are quantifiable, observable, and ultimately prac-

ticable. Learning from models may be high-risk if they lead to negative learning because mistaken policy decisions (for example) may take years to manifest in the real-world, and the resulting hazards in policies and actions may persist over time. The real world is full of paradoxes and apparent contradictions, and capturing and conveying that may be difficult.

The nature of the learning in immersive spaces and simulations often involves underlying models of systems—whether social, machine, biological, or other. These involve complex variables and rules that are not directly conveyed but that are learned through trial and error, discovery learning, experimentation, and inference (de Jong & van Joolingen, 1998); the making of mistakes in the systems and noticing nuanced differences in outputs or changes often lead to learning. Underlying organizational structures or schemas have to be discovered indirectly and over time. Learners extrapolate learning from the abstract (and nonrestrictive) scenarios and apply the new learning in a deep learning and far-transfer way to different situations (Albano, Iovane, Salerno, & Viglione, 2005). Knowledge may not be left inert but has to be made actionable.

A learner who can recite every bone in the human body cannot necessarily diagnose a problem with a given bone, nor know how to splint one if an accident occurred. Even if taken through a number of steps necessary in splinting a bone, it's unlikely by observing another person in the learning process Lave and Wenger refer to as 'legitimate peripheral participation'. There is a huge disconnect between knowing something in abstract and being able to make the knowledge actionable (Galarneau, 2005).

The contradictions between learners' mental models and the conceptual models represented by the immersive spaces and simulations optimally lead to cognitive dissonance; the contrast between internal models and external ones may show the incompleteness, illogical aspects, over general-izations, or invalidity (Nardi & Zarmer, 1991) of the novice mental models and lead to increased sophistication of understanding. The degrees and quality of interactions affect the learning, with a need for reflection spaces (Ahdell & Andresen, 2001) and dialogue (Levin, 2003) to enhance cognitive processing and retention. Interactivity may be reactive with little learner control, coact-ive with learner control for "sequence, pace and style," and proactive where learners may affect the "structure and content" (Rhodes & Azbell, 1985, as cited in Ahdell & Andresen, 2001, pp. 60 - 61).

Interactivity often occurs with objects, spaces, sequencing, communications with artificial intel-ligence robots (in humanoid avatar form), live human interactions with others, and creative engagements with building in the environments. Learners posit hypotheses about the immersive learning, test out their theories through inputs to the system, and the proper feedback informs them about the validity or invalidity of their hy-potheses. The feedback may also enhance their reflexive learning and self-discovery. Learners make informed choices based on both in-world and out-world inductive logic (arrived at through a collective body of observations and facts) and deductive logic (extrapolating proper behaviors from a set of logical principles and premises and identifying logical inconsistencies).

In persistent virtual spaces, the social experi-ences and mediated contacts through human-embodied avatars may be motivating and learning enriched. Interactivity, in all forms, needs to be meaningful to the learners to explore, test hy-potheses, and acquire new knowledge (Thomas, 2001). Simulations may involve human-embodied avatars who are role-playing particular characters or positions or interests in participatory simula-tions. They make decisions based on their role profiles, and the interactions that stem from that may involve learning values and personal and group empathies (Ip & Naidu, 2001). Participants monitor the results of their actions and reflect on

the relationship between their own decisions and the resulting consequences (Schönwald, Euler, Angehrn, & Seufert, 2006, p. 14). Research in human relationships with their avatars has found an identification process in the building of an avatar and its original styling; the vicarious experi-ences may lead to a sense of success and personal confirmation (Raab, 2003). At the extreme end, humans may overly identify with their avatars and the mediated pseudo-relationships via the "immersive parasocial" phenomenon (Hai-Jew, 2009). The risks of others may be enhanced in virtual spaces because of the interplay of real people with their avatar selves. For some, it may be easier to victimize others whom they never meet face-to-face. For others, it may be easier to extend "swift trust" in virtual environments which feel more ordered and safe.

Immersive learning is often situational and context-sensitive. In other words, a scenario is portrayed that involves a particular situation in time and space. One way to understand this is through Baecker, et al.'s "Metaphor Theory." Here, a source domain offers "tangible, concrete, (and) recognizable" facts; those fundamentals are mapped metaphorically to a target domain of "concepts (and) processes" (Wells & Fuerst, 2000, p. 1). A machine's functions may be metaphorically linked to a virtual interface which emulates some of the machine's behaviors. Some key aspects of a biological ecology may be mapped to a virtual artificial life scenario. A learning situation may be mapped to a mock artificial intelligence tutor-and-learner avatar scenario.

Risks from the Environment. All simula-tions involve the selection of information and the design of virtual mediated experiences. These experiences are all artificial contrivances, with low-to-medium fidelity, imprecise and equivocal outputs, and varying levels of verisimilitude in emulating the real. The spatial approximations are partial. The scales of size are mixed, and time itself is compressed and manipulated. Serendip-ity is often non-existent. And even with haptic (touch-based or tactile) devices, physical learning and muscle memory are approximations (shapes, textures, entities, relationships, movements, and ecologies) with low transfer into the real world. All simulations work in a context of unreality even though the endeavor is for realistic experiences (Bajcsy, Enciso, Kamberova, & Nocera, 1998). These involve a game conceit (Bartle, 2006) and a suspension of reality. There are illusions that there are "no direct real-life consequences of one's performance in the game" (Thiagarajan & Stolovitch, 1978, p. 11). Simulations are often used for "internalizing processes, understanding systems, decision-making, perspective-shifting, (and) team-building / cooperation" (Galarneau, 2004, p. 5). Different types of learning may be connected to simulations: directed learning, self-directed learning, and collaborative learning (Babich, Senk, & Mavrommatis, 2005, p. 2). Simulations often teach about something or how to do something (Kreiger, 2006). Some researchers suggest improved learner retention through simulations ("A comparison…").

A close-ended simulation may be used to represent an open-ended reality; it may prepare learners for "convergence" tests with specific right answers when reality is more of a divergence test with a much larger possible range of answers (Gladwell, 2008, pp. 86–89). Simpler simulations may support a sense of "make-believe mastery" and fulfill "power fantasies" but not encourage a person to continue learning in relevant ways (Koster, 2005, p. 134). The simulated pressures to force decisions in immersions may not manifest realistically in real spaces. Most simulations force short-term decision-making instead of promoting a more complex strategic long-term angle. Analogical connections all have a breakdown when the extended comparisons no longer apply, and that breakdown point needs to be clearly defined for effective learning (Mandrin & Preckel, 2009).

The simulated time compression in simulations that collapse time into smaller units may change time and pacing expectations. The game

(and simulation) cycles may belie the unrelenting continuous nature of "meat space" life. The iterative "do-over" aspects of simulated time may be misleading about real-world opportunities, which may be unrepeatable one-offs (a one-time-non-replayable chance). The constant introduction of new and rewarding interactions to increase participant "longevity" in an immersive game may lead to attention deficit in the real world where new experiences to do emerge formulaically; learners may have a hard time adjusting to real-world tedium. Intense attention focus may lead to "change blindness," which leaves many details in the larger environment unseen (Gallagher, 2009, p. 19). Selective attention may create alternative personal realities. Immersions may, however, allow learners to project into the future with predictive analytics and trend-lining, based on time-series data, and this may enhance their macro-perspectives.

The limited "range of possibility" choices in simulations may lead to either-or fallacies or false constraints in decision-making; a kind of "learned helplessness" may result in tighter degrees of freedom. The linear experiences of many educational games may create the sense of limited information flows, instead of the synchronous and multiple flows of live information. Extrapolations of information may be "infinitely daring" but also "dramatically wrong" (Gregory, 1980, p. 187). Sometimes, absences of data may be read as the "presence" of something; people bring more meaning to the "signal data" than the data may warrant.

High-end immersions are expensive to conceptualize, design, develop, and deploy (Withers, 2005). To build these with sufficient richness to head-off and address negative learning may reach a point of prohibitive expense. In that light, researchers advise caution in the use of virtual environments for training:

…since…intuitive training schemes in computationally mediated environments with visual and

auditory feedback may not result in positive transfer effects and can even lead to negative transfer [Kozak et al. 1993; Lintern 1991; Lintern and Roscoe 1980; Gamberini 2000]. Negative transfer effects are attributed mainly to limitations in the fidelity of the virtual task compared to the real task due to simplifications required for rendering. Negative transfer effects may also be attributed to the augmentation of task dynamics due to the presence of virtual guidance (Li, Patoglu, & O'Malley, 2009, p. 3:2)

To hedge against negative learning and "negative transfer", designers need to be aware of the learning human being: his / her sensory tools, cognition, affective nature, and memory and retention. It is important to note that learning happens on unconscious, subconscious, and conscious levels—and often in ways that involve free associations. Subtleties matter. It is critical to be aware of human manipulations in group situations—especially those that carry over into virtual spaces—such as herd behavior, contagion, stampeding, group-think and rushes to consensus, and the Abilene Paradox.

Risks from Others. The black-hat hacker culture suggests that there will always be attempts on breaking codes and systems, and knowing that manipulations may occur in immersive spaces and simulations may also suggest another frontier for protections against manipulations and negative learning through graffiti-ing, griefing, and other exploit-based twists. The literature has chronicled incidences of avatar-on-avatar violence, harassment, assault, and "offensive mischief" (Bugeja, 2007).

Risks from the Self. The bedazzlement from the shimmering online spaces may suspend cognitive bases for decisions and encourage more emotional, affective, and whimsy in choice-making; the synaesthesia may be alluring and ultimately misleading. For example, beauty may be conflated with efficiency, accuracy, or virtue. One researcher notes:

However, good graphics do not make a training simulation good; if the underlying representations of the real world processes that are being simulated are not valid, the simulation can actually cause negative learning (Might, Why do we build models and simulations?, Fact Sheet #3, n.d., n.p.)

SOME INTERVENTIONS

The knowledge of negative learning risks suggests a risk posture that involves the design of immersive learning, pre-immersion priming and post-immersion debriefing work, and the empowerment of learners as they engage in full-sensory 3D learning. The design then focuses on the actual technologies and contents; the pre-immersion priming and post-immersion debriefing focuses on the instructional design and facilitation pieces, and the strengthening of learners focuses on the learner aspect. These are the three core elements related to learning using the immersion spaces and simulations: the technologies, the facilitation, and the learners.

Positive learning depends on information quality, the developmental fit to learners, and the effects on learners. Table 1: "Positive Learning vs. Negative Learning in Immersive Spaces and Simulations" highlights important points in differentiating between positive and negative learning.

IMMERSIVE SPACE AND SIMULATION DESIGNS

At the heart of an effective immersive experience is the model underlying the immersion experience or the simulation. The pedagogical approach is the core competitive advantage in the design and development of games and simulations (Galarneau, 2005). Immersions and simulations tend to rely on information-heavy models to achieve representations of the real-world; predictive analytics; proscriptive decision-making supports, and theoretical / imaginary / speculative applications (Hai-Jew, 2008).

The strengths of a model involve a range of factors. The accuracy and comprehensiveness of the depicted information is critical—both at the user-experience level and for the back-up underlying structure (Might, What are the most common mistakes made when building a simulation?, Fact Sheet #6, n.d., n.p.). Information must be focused (de-noised), timely, and non-obsolete. Some models use information gathered qualitatively, without reliance on statistics or empirical methods.

Table 1. Positive learning vs. negative learning in immersive spaces and simulations

Positive Learning	Negative Learning
Information Quality	
On message, transparent, and explicitly defined	Off message, opaque, implicitly or explicitly defined
Intended	Unintended
Factual, accurate, informed	Non-factual, inaccurate, misinformed
Within paradigm in a domain field	Counter paradigm understandings in a domain field
Offers proper and sufficient feedback	Does not offer proper and sufficient feedback
Is modeled logically on timely, accurate, and sufficient information	Is not modeled logically on timely, accurate, or sufficient information
Is updatable and flexible	Is hard-to-update; is inflexible
Is delimited and does not over-extend beyond the known information	Is not delimited and over-extends beyond the known information; over-reaches
Addresses all the key parameters	Fails to address all the key parameters
Focuses on the relevant information	Focuses on irrelevant or peripheral information
Developmental Fit to Learners	
Supports the defined learning objectives	Does not support the defined learning objectives
Supports the proper developmental phase of the learner	Does not support the proper developmental phase of the learner
Conveys the proper affective learning	Does not convey the proper affective learning
Conveys the proper cognitive learning	Does not convey the proper cognitive learning
Effects on Learners	
Is consciously received	Is unconsciously, subconsciously, or consciously received
Results in learner clarity	Results in learner confusion
Enables carryover to different situations; far transfer learning	Does not enable carryover to different situations; no far transfer learning
Leads to earned learner self-efficacy	Does not lead to earned learner self-efficacy
Leads to learner meta-cognition	Does not lead to learner meta-cognition
Builds on learner cognition, neurophysiology, psychology, physiology, and other aspects	Does not build on learner cognition, neurophysiology, psychology, physiology, and other aspects
Promotes original and creative thinking	Promotes rigid or formulaic thinking

Others use quantitative information. Still others triangulate data from multiple sources.

Some simulations may have real-time value for situational awareness. Some may involve augmented virtuality with the embedding of real-time, time-varying, information-rich, multi-stream feedback to enhance the immersive experience: for example, there may be live webcams or live weather systems representations integrated into a desktop web-delivered simulation.

The model may be designed with low- to medium- to high-fidelity to the real-world. Some suggest that high realism leads to high learner engagement (Radcliff, 2005) while others suggest that increased fidelity could inhibit learners by overwhelming them with details (Alessi, 1988, as cited in Thomas & Milligan, 2004). There is a point of diminishing returns with information overflow (Weber & Fayed, 2008). Some suggest that the more abstract the learning concepts, the more abstract the simulation should be (Boehle, 2005).

Functional fidelity (defined as depicting realistic cause-and-effect relationships) may be most critical for cognitive processing; "dynamic fidelity" may be understood as promoting "instructional effectiveness" and improvements based on learner performance (Thomas & Milligan, 2004). All models need to align with the real world to represent it effectively and authentically.

Simulations need to have a powerful utility in terms of trend-lining and predictive analytics. Such systems often rely on years of information with numerous data points. They also have to capture all the main influences on a particular potential outcome. Even with such heavy computing processing and information, the predictive power of many simulations is approached with high caution and skepticism. The assumptions of the models must be logically sound, without inherent biases.

Models—whether immersions or simulations—must be expressible or communicable through their use of symbols, visual designs, metaphors, analogies, characters (non-playable characters and playable ones), sound, and environmental elements. The aesthetics should be conducive to the learning and not distracting. Digital models expressed in immersions and simulations must be updatable and flexible, so the information is timely and non-obsolete.

Technologically, models must be able to be used in conjunction with other simulations to reflect a complex environment (Withers, 2005). These have to be portable between platforms. Legally, these must be clean of any conflicts with intellectual property. Ideally, all simulations would be fully accessible. The models should be original and unique, especially given the often high costs of conceptualizing, designing, developing, and deploying simulations and immersions.

Simulations that are built on "meager" experiences such as "near-histories" (events that almost happened) and plausible hypothetical histories may be deeply instructive (March, Sproull, & Tamuz, 1991, p. 4). Hypothetical scenarios offer the value of rich interpretations from a range of areas of expertise, and these employ the imagination for richer learning.

PARTIAL IMMERSION / PARTIAL SIMULATION DESIGNS

In most fields, one may ask the subject matter experts (SMEs) where the novice mistakes occur. A research scientist may explain that novices do not know how to shake a test-tube to mix a solution effectively—not with a flipping motion but by tapping the vial. Or the scientist may note that experience in one lab may be so constricting that the individual learner is not aware of universals among labs globally in terms of color coding of measures. Novices may not understand real-world contingencies that may arise and how to handle those. They may assume that the foreign language used in the real world is a purist academic form instead of one full of dialects, slang, and cultural nuances. Understanding the gap between expert and novice approaches is one way to begin structuring a simulation—to capture the learning and to dissipate assumptions. Table 2, "Points of Difference between Novices and Subject Matter Experts," highlights some disparate areas of perception, awareness, and decision-making.

A Biosecurity Immersion with Embedded Decision-making. In one biosecurity simulation, those who work in US agriculture are asked to determine whether signs and symptoms of disease in a crop are indicative of the presence of a dangerous select agent (as defined by the USDA). This simulation was enhanced through the uses of photo-realistic images instead of visual depictions. The decision-making was kept simple and clear for easier applicability to the field and to

help decision-makings de-noise the environment for what was relevant.

The modules in the automated learning had a consistent look-and-feel for sufficient consistency. The information was de-noised for what was relevant to the learning and decision-making. There were also plenty of support aids to scaffold the learning—with word definitions, opt-in practice questions, and branching logic based on learner decision-making. Figure 1, "Using *Realia*, Consistency, and Scaffolding in an Automated Learning Biosecurity Project," shows some of the back-end screens that create learning supports.

Potential Negative Learning Risks: Negative learning risks in this biosecurity project could result in misconstruals of the scientific realities

Table 2. Points of difference between novices and subject matter experts

Points of Difference	Novices	Subject Matter Experts (SMEs)
Overview of the Domain Field, Perspective	Incomplete, naïve, simple, non-representative of reality, inconsistent, contradictory, illogical, and limited	Complete, informed, complex, representative of reality, consistent, logical, broad and comprehensive
Theoretical Underpinnings and Understandings	Incomplete, unclear about implications	Complete, aware about implications
Understandings of the Domain Field integrations and Contrasts with other Fields	Difficulty with cross-referencing and comparing	Aware of overlaps, complementarities, contrasts, and paradoxes
Analytical Skills (Defining Relevance, Having the "Eyes" to See)	Inability to achieve a macro perspective; difficulty critiquing the field	Ability to move between the macro and micro perspectives; analytical critiques of the field
Troubleshooting Skills, Ranges of Applied Strategies	Problem-solve ineffectively, without sufficient strategy or tactics, without the proper short-term and long-term views; may not be able to explain rationales for action	Problem-solves more effectively, while considering both short and long-term views; can explain rationales for action
Ability to Deal with Contingencies	Unable to respond effectively; responses may complicate the problem	May respond with varying levels of effectiveness; may be able to apply prior contingency training and foresight
Self-Confidence / Self Efficacy Levels	May lack a sense of self-efficacy to act	Has the self confidence and self-efficacy to act, based on past experiences, learning, training, and skill sets
Connections to Informational and Material Resources	May not be aware of the full range of available information; may not have the wherewithal to pursue relevant information	Has knowledge of the various available resources; maintains a consistent 360-degree environmental scan of relevant topics
Connections to Other Professionals and Practitioners	Has minimal connections with others; lacks a professional support community	Networks with a variety of professionals and others in the field; has a diverse and dispersed professional support community
Formal Credentialing	Lacks formal credentialing; may have initial learning or informal learning	Has formal credentialing but learns well beyond the confines of the official knowledge domain

behind plant diseases and their spread. It could result in learners using improper methods for capturing digital imagery about plant diseases and losing precious time for diagnosis. Another risk could be the improper packaging of plant parts and the unwitting dissemination of a pathogenic agent to other regions. The concept of the anti-pattern would be helpful here—what a sign and symptom are *not," and the steps *not* to take (even if they may seem intuitive and proper early on).

A Native American Gaming Learning Ecology. For a case study about Native American gaming, an original single case was broken up into three separate (stand-alone or mixable) cases in order to more thoroughly incorporate the research and facts. The three frames were socio-cultural, economic, and political. These focused on defined competencies of knowledge, attitudes, and skills.

This curricular build also involved the incorporation of rich applied assignments and role plays that would send learners out into the world to collect fresh information to enhance the real-time aspects of this issue and case. An instructor manual was also created to enhance the human-facilitation of the case studies. Learner aids included digital vocabulary flashcards, slideshows, interactive assignments and opt-in self-assessments, digital

visuals (timelines, tables, charts), and case analytics. The learning design (this part yet to be actualized because of the difficulty of getting access to Native tribal casinos) involved the development of multimedia like slideshows and videotaped interviews to enhance the learning. This curriculum development involved the integration of Native American voices and values in the development, for larger mainstream understandings. To localize the curriculum, learners were encouraged to use their local resources in terms of tribal casinos and to add to the body of knowledge with jigsaw-type research; this type of assignment encouraged open-ended learning and the sharing of learner-generated work and examples to enhance future learning. Figure 2, "A Triptych Screenshot of a Native American Gaming Case Study," captures some visuals defining the learning ecology.

Potential Negative Learning Risks: Potential negative learning in this Native American gaming project could be misunderstandings of this legal government-sanctioned phenomena and public outcries against Native gaming. Stereotypes of Native Americans may proliferate and lead to discriminatory or biased attitudes and actions.

A Series of Public Health Mystery Cases. In a public health mystery case study, the text described a "you" who works in a public health

Figure 1. Using Realia, consistency, and scaffolding in an automated learning Biosecurity project

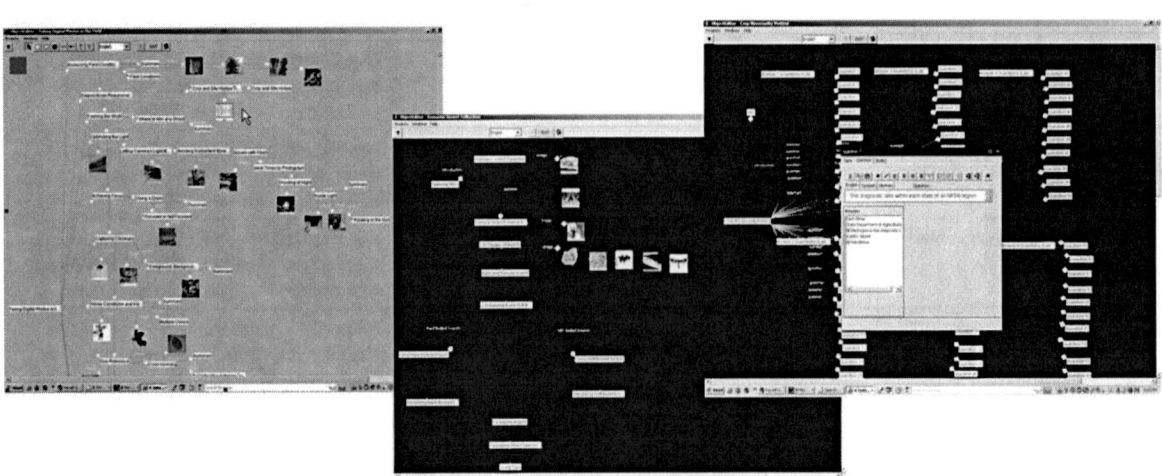

Figure 2. A Triptych screenshot of a Native American gaming case study

office part-time while going to school. The "you" is described in a neutral way to be as inclusive as possible. The case then moves through various information revelations and light decision-making. The "you" may tap into the expertise of various professionals in the field—an epidemiologist, a food safety expert, a dietitian, and others.

While the mystery case study used images that were distorted to show the fictionality of the case, the actual debriefing used real facts and real imagery. Learners were linked to valid and reliable public health sources beyond the fictional case. Figure 3, "Digital Storytelling in a Semi-Immersive Space with a Factual Debriefing at the End," shows how a fictional public health case study involves in-depth factual debriefing at the conclusion.

Potential Negative Learning Risks: Negative learning in the public health case studies could involve incorrect mental models of the various public health issues and inappropriate protective and preventive measures against transmissible diseases. Incorrect information may also lead to inaccurate information dissemination and poor uses of public health resources.

INHERITED IMMERSIONS

Sometimes, the immersive learning is inherited, which means little modding (modification) may be done to the original code. Off-the-shelf immersions may not be modifiable at all, depending on the company creating the simulation. Instructors may want to design pre-immersion priming and post-immersion debriefings to enhance the positive learning.

Figure 3. Digital storytelling in a semi-immersive space with a factual debriefing at the end

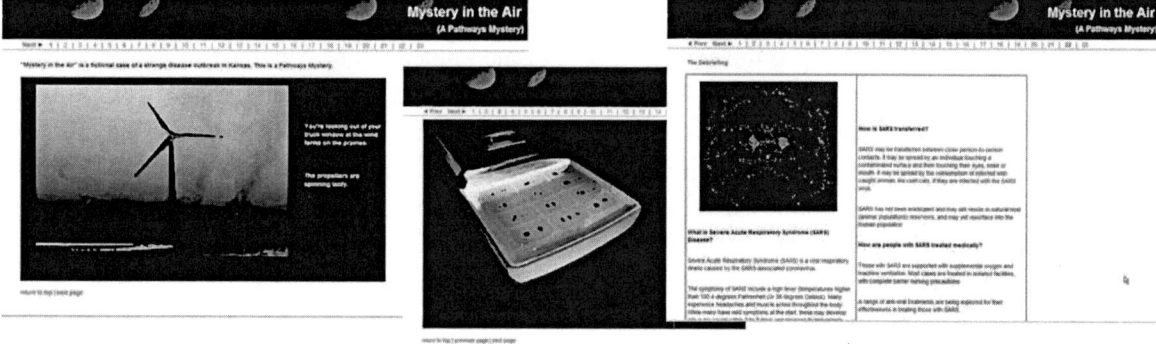

Pre-Immersion Priming

Priming learners may be visualized as calibrating the learners' imaginations and attentional focuses for the immersion. One important way is to surface learner assumptions and pre-conceptions. Raising these to the learner's awareness may help them form meta-cognitive insights (awareness of their own learning and thinking) as they move through the simulation.

Defining the Learning. Prior to the immersion, a facilitator may help set up the learning situation by providing a briefing about the learning. This should cover the learning objectives of the simulation. It should provide a clear task overview along with related details (Radcliff, 2005, p. 5).

Pre-Testing for a Baseline. This may involve a pre-test to set a baseline for program metrics.

Practicing the Tools. The actual simulation and the controls need to be introduced for familiarity. If there are uncommon tools—input devices, haptic / tactile devices, physical manipulables—these should also be introduced and used in low-value practice simulations before the actual learning-based one.

The Underlying Model and Schema. If relevant, the underlying model should also be introduced for transparent uses of the system albeit without "giving away" the experience. In the same way that "advance organizers" may offer schemas for those who approach a more complex reading, introducing models and schemas for an immersive simulation may lighten some of the cognitive load present in novice learners approaching new learning.

Some will purposefully leaving things unexplained for learner self discovery (Moher, 2009). There are times when strategic ambiguity may be necessary to enhance the learning experience: one example may be when interrupted disclosures are used in teaching case studies, where learners have incomplete information at various stages of the case analysis. The relevant aspects of the forthcoming experience need to be addressed to reinforce that learning. Delimitations of the simulation experience should be addressed.

Scaffolding the Learning. Various augmentations may be added to enhance the learning, whether it's the introduction of a virtual coach, priming virtual or physical or mixed-reality experiences, the uses of decision aids, learning aids, reflection aids (for example, think-aloud tools, digital journals, and digital doodle spaces), or some other tools. Such record-keeping may lead to enriched individual and group debriefings.

Simulations are said to not "inherently teach" but require instructional supports (Mihal, Kirkley, Christenberry, & Vidali, 2003): virtual artificial intelligence coaches and tutors, decision aids, scaffolding, and other types of augmentation. Human attention to various cues is selective and "irrational"; given this, highlighting salient learning may reduce errors (Kruschke, 2003, pp. 171 – 173).

Introducing the Larger Context. Facilitators should set up the immersion in a larger context by introducing learning aids, relevant information, and augmentations to the immersions. An immersive learning experience does not exist in isolation. The learners should be primed for the learning ahead. In the same way that simulations and immersions are situated cognition experiences, the actual immersive learning exists within a larger learning domain context.

Post-Immersion De-Briefing

Debriefings occur after the learner experiences of the immersion or simulation, or series of immersions and simulations. These reaffirm the intuitive knowledge gained during the simulation (Schönwald, Euler, Angehrn, & Seufert, 2006). Some suggest that the real learning with simulations only occurs after the simulation game with proper follow-on activities (Thiagarajan & Stolovitch, 1978).

Debriefings often involve a review of the learner and team performances. There may be playbacks and annotations of the performances captured by the immersive space or simulation (Thomas, 2001).

A facilitator may offer coaching based on the performances. There may also be application of a post-test for a pre-and-post metric.

There are different types of debriefings. "Plenary debriefings" involve facilitators leading participants through reflections and discussions to highlight particular learning goals. "Individual reflections" may help individuals reflect on their learning through questionnaires. Participants may form pairs and interview each other about their experiences and then share their findings with the group. Debriefings offer opportunities for strategic highlighting of special aspects of the learning and repetitions of the critical takeaways. Lists of questions may be applied for "small group debriefings" (Kriz & Nöbauer, 2002, as cited in Schönwald, Euler, Angehrn, & Seufert, 2006, p. 23).

Debriefings may tap into several models of change. The Lewinian approach focuses on un-freezing and dismantling people's extant mind sets, considering new facts, and then freezing into new mindsets (Gredler, 1992). The Piagetian model suggests that when learners encounter new information, they either assimilate it into their existing worldview, or they must make greater systemic mental changes to accommodate the new information that may not fit with the earlier worldview (Van Eck, 2007, p. 286).

Learners often benefit from direction about post-instructional skill and knowledge mainte-nance. A "continuous learning mechanism" may be applied to help learners master the requisite behaviors and skills (Radcliff, 2005, p. 5). Further explanations and analysis of the model may be offered in the debriefing.

Because of the inaccuracies in immersive design, in human perception and cognition, and in co-learners, individual learners and learning groups may benefit from an open-minded sense of caution. The debriefing may also emphasize maintaining a healthy skepticism testing—a counterfactual strategy in testing assumptions and old and new knowledge—in order to seek out disconfirming information and inconsistencies.

Evaluating the Efficacy of Immersive Simulations

A few models exist currently for the evaluation of simulations. One that has been used in the Kirk-patrick Evaluation Process (1998) that suggests that evaluation should be evaluated at four levels: Level 1 – Reaction; Level 2 – Learning; Level 3 – Behaviour, (and) Level 4 – Results" (Kreiger, 2006, p. 6). The Kenworthy model "Building a Standard Evaluation Framework" (for Simula-tions) focuses on a sliding scale range of numerous factors that describe the simulation including the amount of competitiveness, the amount of visual fidelity, the realism, the usage environment, the teacher role, the amount of learner control, the value of errors, and cultural sensitivity, among others (Kenworthy, 2006). Schönwald, Euler, Angehrn, and Seufert (2006) offer a rubric of learning outcomes form a simulation based on subject matter competencies, social competen-cies, and self competencies. Within each of these groupings, they list knowledge, attitudes, and skills (2006, pp. 19 - 20).

This chapter would argue that the underlying information and logics to the model, and the clarity of its expressiveness are critical factors to the as-sessment of an immersive space and a simulation. The designs of the scenario, the story, the art, and the characterizations are critical elements. User testing of the immersive learning, their receptive-ness to the simulations, their behaviors within it, and their takeaways in the debriefing should also be assessed. Common learner problems in discovery learning and conclusion-drawing in the designed simulations should be identified (de Jong & van Joolingen, 1998) and addressed. The amount of negative learning should be a factor in evaluating an immersive experience or simulation's efficacy.

Security-Aware Learners in Immersive Spaces and Simulations

Learners going through informal or formal learning in immersive spaces and simulations need to be aware of the risks of the environment, others, and their own weaknesses in learning.

New Media Literacy. Learning from immersions and simulations requires new media fluency and literacy. These virtual contexts are often culturally situated. They require complex visual and new media semantics. There are understandings linked to sound effects, digital symbology, avatar body language, and nuanced responses to the designed looks-and-feels. Mass media communications involve highly recognizable "stereotypes" of characters and spaces that communicate in-depth meanings in milliseconds because these tap into enculturated understandings and media message exposures.

A necessary skill set will be the understanding of the underlying models powering the simulation and game engines. These consist of the rules that define the various objects and their relationships; these consist of the physics engines underlying virtual worlds. Learners need to see through the transparency of the virtual experience, by engaging in thinking vs. scripted behavior. An immersive experience is only as valid as the underlying rules, and incorrect understandings there can be highly detrimental to the learning.

Simulations may offer various skews to human expectations. Learners approach various decision-points and forced-decision junctures with a sense that they've been empowered to make a decision, when real-life decision-points may involve asymmetrical access to information and potentially insufficient data points to decide. There may be excessive real-world noise in the real environment vs. the sterilized and designed immersions. Virtual spaces may suggest the solvability of entrenched and unsolvable problems; they may posit certitude where in the real world, there is uncertainty, unpredictability, and Gödel's

mathematical proof of unknowability. Games may reward cheating in a more ethics-free play environment (Koster, 2005, p. 112) with different implications in the real world. Simulated triggers lead up to irrevocable moments in a simulation which are communicated through transition scenes, when face-to-face lived realities may not be so clearly announced.

Knowing Others. Savvy learners in immersive spaces are aware of the many potential abuses of the learning spaces for various security risks. They are aware that the people they engage with may have mixed motives. They need to realize how little information they truly have about those that they're studying with. They should see how little authentication there is of others' integrity or characters or pasts. Going with the surface appearance of an avatar alone is a very superficial way to interact, and given that context, people need to approach their immersive learning with a healthy skepticism and caution.

Individuals who would pursue live identities in the real world may use social engineering techniques to elicit and capture personal information. They may cross-compare information from different databases, social networking sites, immersive spaces, and publicly available records to track and stalk individuals. Many may use emotions and feigned relationships to cause vulnerabilities. Individuals may work with each other to tag-team a target for information. Communications may be prone to "man-in-the-middle" attacks which may result in compromised information or changes to intercepted original messages. Learners need to know which ones are secure and insecure information channels. They need to understand how vulnerable communications on wireless networks and email systems (without digital certificates) may be. They must be sufficiently confident to take discussions off-list if there are any chances of sensitive information compromise.

Using a healthy skepticism in approaching other human-embodied avatars, with very ephemeral identities and challenges to authentication, will offer a stronger protective stance. For example, if learners are asked to interact with others in open immersive virtual worlds for learning, the "swift trust" that often is embodied in these interactions may have to be short-circuited for a greater range of safety. Those who may ask for private and personally identifiable information (PII) should be rebuffed, even if they appear to be authoritative or benign. Learners need to be wary of those who invite them to join groups without context, to donate virtual or real moneys for various political or social aims, or to meet in the real world.

The Self. Human perceptions in immersive spaces are directed by visuals, movement, sound effects, dialogue, and other designed experiences—to represent complicated realities. The virtual learning is paced as well by the introduction of new scenes, transitions, and action sequences—which may be partially (and sometimes fully) user controllable for accessibility. Because humans learn on levels of the unconscious, subconscious, and conscious, they need to be observant of the various informational inputs and the perceptions that are being formed. This requires a deeper level of metacognition (awareness of self-perception and learning) than many types of learning may require.

Human learners tend to be highly suggestible to nuance. They notice plenty of detail, some of which remains in their short-term memory for a short time, and some of which is rehearsed into their long-term memories. Their use of attentional resources determines what is remembered and what isn't. Information may be stored in their un-

conscious or subconscious without the awareness of their waking minds. Human decision-making tends towards higher risk-taking in so-called aroused or hot-state conditions, choices that they would not otherwise make in a cold-state condition (Ariely, 2008). People need to have their awareness raised to certain risks before many may actually be able to see that risk. Many will also not respond to warnings or cautionary tales. Figure 4, "Promoting Learner Awareness of Negative Learning in Immersive Learning Spaces," emphasizes the importance of informational nuances.

An initial skim of an immersive system may not necessarily give non-experts a sense of the underlying modeling or the limits of that model; it may not allow them to deconstruct the experience to understand the underlying, unconscious messaging and learning. Often, it takes in-depth experience with a system and even privy information to be able to draw out the design structures. Learner awareness of the artificiality of the learning situation may help them to source information more logically and less affectively or emotionally. After all, immersive spaces represent an amalgam of various influences: the designed semiotics, the sound design, the information visualization, the instructional design, the information architecting, the avatar body language and vocalizations, the designed interactivity, the immersive ecologies, the pseudo-game designs, the culturally-based modeling, and the rule-based machine underpinnings. The polysemic or many-meaninged nature of language, symbols, multi-

Figure 4. Promoting learner awareness of negative learning in immersive learning spaces

media communications, gestures (Roth, 2001), and imagery makes the communication of a clear message that much more difficult. Modern learners need to be aware of potential information gaps and the constraints of the systems and multimedia languages. These awarenesses support them to ask relevant questions of the learning. This awareness is even more critical with the integration of values (in "values sensitive design" and "value centered design") and social activism in game design (Flanagan & Nissenbaum, 2007), particularly if such aims are nuanced and un-declared. Game designers discuss the importance of avoiding propagandistic uses of games (Williams & Smith, 2007). They may "interrogate" both their simulated experiences and their own responses to them.

No socio-technical systems are foolproof, no matter how well designed or how many layers of security are designed into the system. If learners are aware of the security risks in immersive spaces—risks of identity usurpation, fraud, information compromises, privacy infringements, intellectual property losses—then there may be less of a chance of direct and experiential negative learning (of their own vulnerabilities in the system). Their greater alertness may enhance the security of the overall system, particularly if they are willing to speak up to notify their peers, their instructors, and the administrators—depending on where the risks are coming from (whether internal or external, for example). Their awareness of how porous the boundaries of virtual worlds are may help them be more cautious. In this realm, digital information is highly portable and may be easily misused and abused—with the users hidden behind layers of anonymity.

Future Considerations

Security risks in an immersive environment stem from that space, the other learners, and the self. Using a well rounded frame to understand risks in immersive learning and simulations will be impor-

tant to the field. This area of minimizing negative learning would benefit from research based on the unique immersion and simulations situations used in higher learning and in industry, which will likely reveal additional effective strategies. Ways to build immersions and simulations that are more transparent and supportive of increased learner agency and awareness of subliminal learning would be important to strengthen this type of learning. The underlying models designed into the foundation of a simulation need to consider both desirable learning patterns and undesirable anti-patterns, and the simulation experience needs to raise this to the level of cognitive awareness for learners. If learning is irreversible, then deeper understandings of the human learner and ways to help them un-learn and re-learn over mistaken concepts and practices would also enhance the work.

CONCLUSION

Negative learning is a risk in immersive spaces and simulations because of the complex communications streams. Negative learning may be minimized through proper model design (with user testing optimally from the design and prototyping stages), as well as pre-immersion priming and post-learning debriefings, and immersive learner awareness. This is an especial risk in high reliability organizations (HROs) and in learning for which human practitioners have little margin for error. Simulated depictions in immature and undeveloped domain fields may be more risky by prematurely offering unfounded mental models, preempting future research, or limiting future work. Even in mainstream education and training, negative learning can involve a serious loss of resources and time. Effective and efficient learning in immersive spaces and simulations require positive learning, and that may require heading-off all anticipatable negative learning and multi-directional learning risks.

ACKNOWLEDGMENT

Thanks to Dr. Roger W. McHaney and Brent A. Anders for their insightful sidebars. It is my pleasure to work with such talented and gracious colleagues as you. Thanks to R. Max.

REFERENCES

A comparison of simulation-based and conventional training methods. (n.d.) Experience Builders LLC. 1 – 6.

A Training Technology Evaluation Tool. Retrieved Oct. 28, 2009, from https://www.benning.army.mil/arifb/Research/Report%20Summary/2005/A%20Training%20Technology%20Evaluation%20Tool.htm.

Ahdell, R., & Andresen, G. (2001). *Games and simulations in workplace eLearning: How to align eLearning content with learner needs*. Master of Science Thesis, Norwegian University of Science and Technology. 1 - 158.

Albano, G., Iovane, G., Salerno, S., & Viglione, S. (n.d.) *Web based simulations for virtual scientific experiment: Methodology and tools*. 1st International EleGI Conference on Advanced Technology for Enhanced Learning. 1 – 9.

Ariely, D. (2008). *Predictably irrational: The hidden forces that shape our decisions*. New York: Harper Collins.

Babich, A., Senk, D., & Mavrommatis, K. (2005). *Combination of lab experiments and online simulations in master course* (pp. 1–7). Tainan, Taiwan: Exploring Innovation in Education and Research.

Bajcsy, R., Encisco, R., Kamberova, G., & Nocera, L. (1998). 3D reconstruction of environments for virtual collaboration. *Proceedings of the 4th IEEE Workshop on Application of Computer Vision. IEEE*. 160 – 167.

Bartle, R. A. (2006). Virtual Worldliness . In Balkin, J. M., & Noveck, B. S. (Eds.), *The State of Play: Law, Games and Virtual Worlds (34.)*. New York: New York University.

Boehle, S. (2005). Simulations: The next generation of e-learning. *Training (New York, N.Y.)*, 1–6.

Bugeja, M. J. (2007). Second thoughts about Second Life. The Chronicle of Higher Education. Retrieved Oct. 31, 2009, from http://chronicle.com/article/Second-Thoughts-About-Second/46636/

Burgos, D., Tattersall, C., & Koper, R. (2005). Repurposing *existing generic games and simulations for e-learning*. n.p.

Carr, D. (2005). Research into computer games and learning: A brief overview. Games and Simulations, *Interact. The Learning Technology Support Service, University of Bristol*(31), 22 – 23.

Castronova, E. (2005). The Right to Play . In Balkin, J. M., & Noveck, B. S. (Eds.), *The State of Play: Law, Games, and Virtual Worlds* (pp. 68–85). New York: New York University Press.

Castronova, E. (2005). *Synthetic Worlds*. Chicago: The University of Chicago Press.

Csikszentmihalyi, M. (1996). *Creativity: Flow and the Psychology of Discovery and Invention* (p. 93). New York: HarperCollins Publishers.

De Jong, T., & Van Joolingen, W. R. (1998). Scientific discovery learning with computer simulations of conceptual domains. Review of Educational Research: 68(2), 179–201. American Educational Research Association. Retrieved Dec. 28, 2009, from http://www.jstor.org/stable/1170753.

Dovey, J., & Kennedy, H. W. (2006). *Game Cultures: Computer Games as New Media*. New York: Open University Press.

Flanagan, M., & Nissenbaum, H. (2007). *A game design methodology to incorporate social activist themes. CHI 2007 Proceedings: Politics & Activism* (pp. 181–190). San Jose, California, USA: Association of Computing Machinery.

Freitas, S. (2007). Learning in Immersive Worlds: A Review of Game-Based Learning. Retrieved Oct. 30, 2009, from http://www.jisc.ac.uk/media/documents/programmes/elearninginnovation/gamingreport_v3.pdf.Livingston, S., Dyer, J., & Swinson, D. (2005).

Galarneau, L. (2004). The eLearning edge: Leveraging interactive technologies in the design of engaging, effective learning experiences. *Proceedings of e-Fest 2004* (pp.1-10) Wellington, New Zealand.

Galarneau, L. (2005). Authentic learning experiences through play: Games, simulations and the construction of knowledge. *Proceedings of DiGRA 2005 Conference Changing Views – Worlds at Play.*

Gallagher, W. (2009). *Rapt: Attention and the Focused Life* (p. 19). New York: The Penguin Press.

Gladwell, M. (2008). *Outliers: The Story of Success.(86-89)* New York: Little, Brown and Company.

Gredler, M. (1992). The role of post-simulation activities. From *Designing and Evaluating Games and Simulations: A Process Approach (pp.1-15).*

Gregory, R. L. (1980). Perceptions as hypotheses. *Philosophical Transactions of the Royal Society of London*, 181–197. doi:10.1098/rstb.1980.0090

Hai-Jew, S. (2008). Building mental models with visuals for e-learning. *MERLOT: Still Blazing the Trail and Meeting New Challenges in the Digital Age*: Minneapolis, Minnesota, USA.

Hai-Jew, S. (2009). Exploring the immersive parasocial: Is it you or the thought of you? MERLOT Journal of Online Learning and Teaching, 5(3). Retrieved Oct. 9, 2009, from http://jolt.merlot.org/vol5no3/hai-jew_0909.htm.

Ip, A., & Naidu, S. (2001). Experienced (sic)-based pedagogical designs for elearning. *Education Technology XL, I*(5), 53–58.

Kenworthy, J. (2006). Simulations—Bridging from thwarted innovation to disruptive technology. *Developments in Business Simulation and Experiential Learning, 33*, 149–158.

Kirriemuir, J. (2005). Commercial games in the classroom. Games and Simulations, *Interact*. The Learning Technology Support Service, University of Bristol: Issue 31. 20 – 21.

Koster, R. (2005). *A Theory of Fun for Game Design.* Scottsdale: Paraglyph Press, Inc. 112 and 134.

Kreiger, H. (2006). Simulation-based learning content: How might simulation-based learning contribute to performance-based, meaningful employee learning? INN Faculty Research Conference 2006. 1 – 9.

Kruschke, J. K. (2003). Attention in learning. *Current Directions in Psychological Science, 12*(5), 171–175. doi:10.1111/1467-8721.01254

Levin, D. (2003). Preparing future education leaders through simulation-enhanced learning. Draft Only. 1 – 8.

Levinthal, D. A., & March, J. G. (1993). The myopia of learning. *Strategic Management Journal, 14*, 95–112. doi:10.1002/smj.4250141009

Li, Y., Patoglu, V., & O'Malley, M.K. (2009). Negative efficacy of fixed gain error reducing shared control for training in virtual environments. ACM Transactions on Applied Perception: *6*(1), 3:1 – 3:21.

Mandrin, P. A., & Preckel, D. (2009). Effect of similarity-based guided discovery learning on conceptual performance. *School Science and Mathematics, 109*(3). doi:10.1111/j.1949-8594.2009.tb17949.x

March, J. G., Sproull, L. S., & Tamuz, M. (1991). Learning from samples of one or fewer. *Organization Science, 2*(1), 1–13. doi:10.1287/orsc.2.1.1

McDaniel, M. A., & Schlager, M. S. (1990). Discovery learning and transfer of problem-solving skills. [JSTOR.]. *Cognition and Instruction, 7*(2), 129–159. doi:10.1207/s1532690xci0702_3

McMahon, A., Scott, D., & Browne, W. (2005). *An autonomous explore/exploit strategy. Gecco '05* (pp. 103–108). Washington, DC, USA: Association of Computing Machinery.

McHaney, R. (2009). Understanding Computer Simulation, Ventus Publishing ApS. Retrieved Oct. 15, 2009, from http://bookboon.com/us/student/it/understanding.

Might, R. J. (n.d.) Why do we build models and simulations? Fact Sheet #3. Innovative Management Concept, Inc. Retrieved Oct. 9, 2009, from http://www.imcva.com/simulation_3.htm.

Might, R. J. (n.d.). What are the most common mistakes made when building a simulation? Fact Sheet #6. Innovative Management Concept, Inc. Retrieved Oct. 9, 2009, from http://www.imcva.com/simulation/Fact%20Sheet%206%20What%20are%20most%20common%20mistakes%20-finalv2.pdf.

Mihal, S., Kirkley, S., Christenberry, T. C., & Vidali, A. (2003). *Continuous learning environments: Incorporating performance metrics into next generation simulation-based eLearning environments for military and law enforcement* (pp. 2–31). Institute for Operational Readiness and Continuous Education in Security.

Moher, T. (2009). *Putting interference to work in the design of a whole-class learning activity. IDC 2009* (pp. 115–122). Como, Italy: Association of Computing Machinery.

Nardi, B. A., & Zarmer, C. L. (1991). *Beyond models and metaphors: Visual formalisms in user interface design* (p.487) IEEE. 487.

Oppenheimer, M., O'Neill, B. C., & Webster, M. (2008). Negative learning. *Climatic Change, 89*, 155–172. doi:10.1007/s10584-008-9405-1

Prensky, M. (2002). The motivation of gameplay or, the REAL 21st century learning revolution. *Horizon, 10*(1), 1–14.

Raab, M. (2003). Games and eLearning: Attempt to identify reasons why games are popular and how they can be applied to make eLearning more popular. (pp. 1 – 6).

Radcliff, J.B. (2005). *Executive Viewpoint: Why soft-skills simulation makes a hard case for sales training.* CompeteNet Publications. 1 – 13.

Roth, W.-M. (2001). Gestures: Their role in teaching and learning. Review of Educational Research: 71(3), 365-392. American Educational Research Association. Retrieved Dec. 28, 2009, from http://www.jstor.org/stable/3516003.

Sanchez, A., & Smith, P. (2007). Emerging Technologies for Military Game-Based Training. Retrieved October 29, 2009, from http://portal.acm.org/citation.cfm?id=1404859.

Schönwald, I., Euler, D., Angehrn, A., & Seufert, S. (2006). EduChallenge Learning Scenarios: *Designing and evaluating learning scenarios with a team-based simulation on change management in higher education. SCIL Report, 8*, 1–39.

Seitz, A. R., Nanez, J. E., Holloway, S. R., Koyama, S., & Watanabe, T. (2005). Seeing what is not there shows the costs of perceptual learning. [JSTOR.]. *Proceedings of the National Academy of Sciences of the United States of America, 102*(25), 9080–9085. doi:10.1073/pnas.0501026102

Thiagarajan, S., & Stolovitch, H. D. (1978). *Instructional Simulation Games.* The Instructional Design Library. Englewood Cliffs: Educational Technology Publications. D.G. Langdon, Series Ed.

Thomas, R. (2001). *Interactivity & simulations in e-learning* (pp. 1-16) MultiVerse Publications. 1 – 16.

Thomas, R.C. & Milligan, C.D. (2004). *Putting teachers in the loop: Tools for creating and customizing simulations. Journal of Interactive Media in Education.* (Designing and Developing for the Disciplines, Special Issue): 15. n.p.

U.S. Congress. Office of Technology Assessment, Distributed Interactive Simulation of Combat, OTA-BP-ISS-151 (Washington, DC: U.S. Government Printing Office, Sept. 1995). Retrieved Oct. 27, 2009, from http://www.fas.org/ota/reports/9512.pdf.

Van Biljon, J., Kotzé, P., Renaud, K., McGee, M., & Seffah, A. (2004). The use of anti-patterns in human computer interaction: Wise or ill-advised? In the proceedings of the Annual Conference of the South African Institute of Computer Scientists and Information Technologists (SAICSIT 2004): 176 – 185.

Van Eck, R. (2007). Building artificially intelligent learning games. Chapter XIV. *Games and Simulations in Online learning: Research and Development Frameworks.* In D. Gibson, C. Aldrich, and M. Prensky, (Eds). Hershey, PA: Information Science Publishing. 284.

Weber, C., & Fayed, A. (2008). *On the value of technological knowledge in semiconductor manufacturing.* PICMET 2008 Proceedings: Cape Town, South Africa. Slide 2.

Wells, J. D., & Fuerst, W. L. (2000). *Domain-oriented interface metaphors: Designing Web interfaces for effective customer interaction.* IEEE. 1.

Williams, J. P., & Smith, J. H. (2007). *The Players' Realm: Studies on the Culture of Video Games and Gaming. Jefferson: McFarland & Company, Inc.* Publishers.

Withers, D. (2005). Authoring tools for educational simulations. Retrieved Oct. 2007, from http://www.sfu.ca/~dwithers/articles/publications/WithersEdSimReport.pdf. 1 – 57.

KEY TERMS AND DEFINITIONS

3D: Existing in three dimensions, known as the x, y and z axes

Agent: A software program that has been programmed to perform particular independent or autonomous actions

Artificial Intelligence: A computer simulation of human intelligence and analysis through programming

Artificial Life: The simulation of various types of (often-simple) life-forms that exist and evolve and interact in virtual ecologies

Conceptual Drift: The changing of an idea over time away from the original (accurate) understanding

Debriefing: A systematic way of analyzing learning after a simulation or immersive experience or interaction

Gameplay: The action, decision-making, thought and engagement during the playing of a virtual game that makes it fun or not

Goal-based Scenario: An immersive learning environment in which learners focus on problem-solving and achieving a particular objective

Immersion: The state of being deeply engaged in a virtual space with multi-sensory content

Negative Learning: Unintended and inaccurate learning that may be attained through a poorly designed simulation or immersive experience

Simulation: The imitation of a particular scenario, social interaction, situation, event, machine behavior, or other learning situation

Transference: The act of transferring one's sense of identity to an inanimate object (such as an avatar).

Appendix
Unintended Negative Learning with an Industrial Simulation

Roger W. McHaney
Kansas State University, USA

"Punch your time card and get off my floor!" The plant foreman's face blazed crimson as he used a string of expletives to roust a chastened assembly station attendant from a corner where he had been drinking from a soda can. "I don't care what the simulation shows, you can't goof around for the first two hours of your shift and expect to meet production!"

Manufacturing and service industries provide large commercial venues for computer simulation use. Often, models are developed initially as aids in decision-making or as part of early design processes. After system installation, some models are validated then transitioned into a second use as training tools. In many ways, simulations are ideal for training because they incorporate a visual component that 'brings a system to life' and they recreate the nuances of internal dynamics in a realistic fashion. While using models in this way can provide a safe, meaningful approach to learning, the intrinsic nature of computer simulation may result in unexpected outcomes, some in the form of negative learning.

For instance, a discrete event computer simulation was developed with Arena®, a modeling environment from Rockwell Automation. Initially, the simulation was used to design an automated guided vehicle system and determine vehicle fleet size to ensure assembly line parts could be supplied at the desired rate. Following system installation, the model was calibrated to match the real world system and then transitioned into a new role as a system operator training tool. Operators used the 3D animation capabilities of the model together with an interface created by programmers to vary parameters such as vehicle count, battery size, throughput rates, human staffing numbers, product mix and other features, then run the model and view the system in action.

Figure 1. Initial bias in steady state simulation

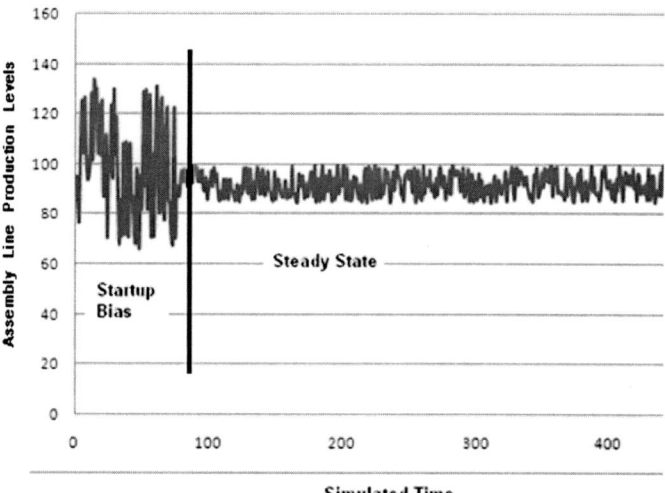

Using the model as a training tool was well-received by both staff members and management but at times was marginalized. Some called it a 'video game' and would occasionally push the model into unusual scenarios and laugh about the consequences. In many instances, the training provided useful insight for the participants and encouraged them to investigate the ramifications of poor decisions in a safe and risk-free way. However, problems related to negative learning emerged, in part due to characteristics of simulation that aren't always considered when a modeling tool is used for training.

Taking a step backward to understand the nature of computer simulation can help reveal a potential source of negative learning. Computer simulation can be broadly defined as: "Using a computer to imitate the operations of a real world process or facility according to appropriately developed assumptions taking the form of logical, statistical, or mathematical relationships which are developed and shaped into a model" (McHaney, 2009, p. 10).

On the surface, particularly when animated, a model appears to closely match reality. That similarity disappears when the mechanisms underlying simulation are more closely examined. For instance, analysts using simulation for decision making recognize model outputs represent a single observation. Simulations rely on distributions of random numbers to introduce realistic variance into operations. Like any experiment, in order to develop a result which can be confidently communicated, data from a sufficient number of runs must be collected then interpreted with statistics to estimate real world system characteristics.

Another feature differentiating simulation from the real world operation relates to startup bias. Often, when a simulation is started, it does not operate in a manner typical of its steady state. When an animated version of a simulation is used without accounting for startup bias, the users might inadvertently misunderstand the nature of various entities or objects. They may experience the training without recognizing gaps exist in their knowledge. Later when using the real world system, they might not realize their perceptions are inaccurate and unreliable. Figure 1 "Initial Bias in Steady State Simulation" represents how startup bias might result in the acquisition of inaccurate knowledge from a simulation. This would be particularly true in the startup bias area near the beginning of the simulated time frame.

Startup bias in simulation can be eliminated using different methods. First, a warm-up period can be used to push the model into a steady state after which the model will operate with more realistic characteristics. Many simulation software packages have the capability of resetting statistics to make this easier. Another approach is to initialize the model with realistic, steady state conditions by presetting levels of resource utilization and stocking the model with customers or other strategically placed entities. Sometimes this is called 'preloading' or 'priming' the model (McHaney, 2009, p. 122).

In the situation with the Arena® simulation, model startup bias resulted in negative learning. An assembly line station attendant had used the simulation to virtually conduct his job. His learning took place during the model's startup bias period and resulted in faulty perceptions including one that made him believe he had "extra time to spare" when his shift started. Of course, his supervisor with years of real world experience had no such misapprehension. As a result, the station attendant received unintended messages which left him with an illogical and inaccurate belief about the real world system's operation.

The eventual solution to the problem was to redesign the model's user interface to ensure it operated in a steady state mode prior to results to being viewed on the computer screen. The station attendant, of course, had to be reeducated to undo the negative learning.

After some time, the color in the supervisor's face returned to normal, and the system resumed operation as intended.

Appendix
Negative Learning and its Mitigation in Army Simulations

Brent A. Anders
Kansas State University, USA

The use of general computer-aided simulations as well as fully immersive simulations has been greatly explored and utilized by the U.S. Army. It is through this extensive use that that the military has been able to note the potential problem of negative learning. Various reviews and research reports continually look at the Army's use of simulations and negative learning effects (example: *Distributed Interactive Simulation of Combat,* September 1995, *A Training Technology Evaluation Tool*, 2005). The Army constantly reviews its training and simulations so as to find ways to modify and improve. A key component, which the Army is starting to fully realize, is that it isn't just a matter of making a "perfect" simulation, it is also a matter of using it correctly and with the right guidance/manager or subject matter expert (SME). "… where games [simulation] are inadequately used, selected without clear criteria or incorrectly embedded into practice there are indications that this may lead to negative learning experiences," (Freitas, 2007).

As a Sergeant First Class (SFC), with over 15 years of experience in the U.S. Army, I have personally experienced and witnessed several occasions where the use of an SME helped mitigate negative learning as well as where the lack of proper guidance caused negative learning to occur. This military based information is valuable in that many of its aspects and lessons learned can be applied to other domains.

One scenario that occurred roughly three years ago, involves the use of a fully immersive simulation. Several other soldiers and I were being trained on how to best conduct a security patrol within a vehicular convoy. We had real steering wheels, real (mock) mounted weapons and wore helmets that had built-in 360 degree monitors to give us a fully immersive environment. The training consisted of driving along a simulated road in a virtual Iraq that had several overpass bridges that we would drive under. We were directed to watch out for IEDs (Improvised Explosive Devices) and enemy combatants near bridges.

Figure 1. Virtual vehicle convoy simulation

Our SME/trainer began the scenario but was then called away and so a technical assistant continued on with the scenario. Within about 30 minutes we had gone through the scenario several times and were congratulating ourselves on how well we had done. At that moment the subject matter expert (SME) came in, quickly reviewed what we had done during the scenario and said we were going to do it again. Just before we began again the SME went to the gunners and moved them to the other side of room and had them sit down. In a loud voice he told the rest of the class that these soldier were now in Fort Leavenworth (Army prison), because in the previous scenario they had "accidently" killed three civilians. Each one of the civilian deaths could have been avoided and occurred because we were too focused on completing the mission and eliminating all enemy combatants. If the SME had been with us throughout the scenario he could have directed us to be more precise and selective. Initially at the end of our training, we had learned to simply destroy any enemy combatant and the surrounding area (negative learning). It was correct within the scenario and allowed us to succeed in the mission, but as we learned from the SME trainer, we failed in that we killed innocent bystanders which would cause second and third order effects that would be detrimental both militarily and politically.

In another example, while training for a deployment to Kosovo, my squad was being trained on Tactical Operations Center (TOC) procedures. We used computer simulations to practice various scenarios and how to react to them. One scenario learned dealt with riot control. Through the training we learned to interpret various sources of intelligence, send additional patrols to monitor and to notify local authorities and assist if absolutely needed. In training this was straightforward and all was learned efficiently and actions taken occurred quickly. Once we arrived "in country" and started to actually do these operations in "real life," I noticed that everything occurred much slower and was not as efficient. In reviewing and comparing the simulation to real life the big difference was the human interaction element. The Kosovo mission is a multinational endeavor that requires the U.S. military to work together with militaries from many other nations.

The computer simulations did not take the interactions with other militaries fully into account. Cultural difference, language barriers and emotions were beyond the scope of the simulations. The other militaries where there in Kosovo to assist us (U.S. military), not to simply take orders from us. I instructed my soldiers, and I as well, began to develop a more personal relationship with the soldiers from the other militaries. Actions to take during operations where still given, but orders were dispatched in a more

Figure 2. Virtual vehicle convoy simulation

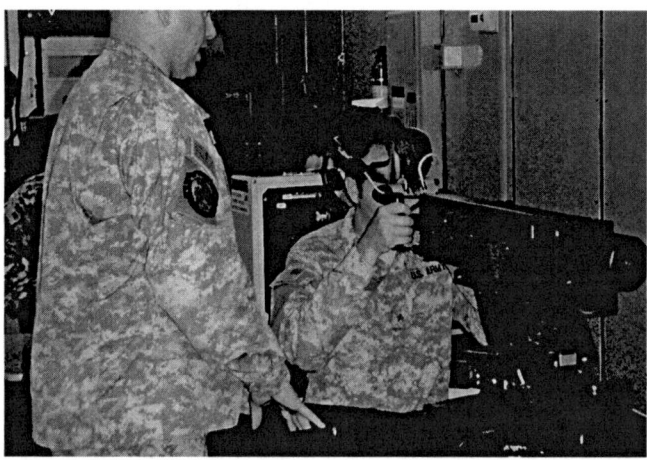

diplomatic and friendly way. This resulted in dramatic increases in efficiency and time to complete missions. Negative learning occurred because of the limits of the simulation. Since the importance of the interaction variable was not addressed in the simulation, neither my soldiers nor I noted it as important. Additional guidance during the simulation would have greatly improved the overall learning effect. This lesson learned has been addressed by the Army and is now being used in their training as well as within briefings of follow-on forces.

Simulations as training tools are a huge asset to training and education in general, but the possibility of negative learning will always exist. SMEs and clear guidance should always be utilized to achieve maximum results with any simulation. The more immersive the simulation the more accountable the user should be so as to see the full extent for all actions (second, third order effects). To further illustrate this point the U.S. Army has a game/simulation publicly available called "America's Army." It used to be that you couldn't shoot another U.S. soldier within the game (the simulation simply wouldn't register it), which of course could directly lead to negative learning (Sanchez et al., 2007). Current versions of the game now register fratricide hits and according to the game's Frequently Asked Questions section "...players who engage in fratricide or who violate their rules of engagement incur significant penalty points. At a certain threshold, these penalty points result in a player being removed from game play to a virtual version of the Army Disciplinary Barracks at Fort Leavenworth (www.americasarmy.com)." Negative learning can be mitigated but it takes diligence, accountability, observation and constant review in comparing "real life" to the simulated environment(s).

Compilation of References

A comparison of simulation-based and conventional training methods. (n.d.) Experience Builders LLC. 1 – 6.

A Training Technology Evaluation Tool. Retrieved Oct. 28, 2009, from https://www.benning.army.mil/arifb/Research/Report%20Summary/2005/A%20Training%20Technology%20Evaluation%20Tool.htm.

AAAS. (2004). *Invention and Impact: Building Excellence in Undergraduate Science, Technology, Engineering and Mathematics (STEM) Education.* Washington, DC: American Association for the Advancement of Science.

AACN - American Association of Colleges of Nurses. (2003). *The Role of the Clinical Nurse Leader.* Washington, DC: American Association of Colleges of Nursing.

Activeworlds, Inc. (n.d.). *Home page.* Retrieved January 24, 2010, from http://www.activeworlds.com/

Adamo-Villani, N., Doublestein, J., & Martin, Z. (2005). Sign language for K-8 mathematics by 3D interactive animation. *Journal of Educational Technology Systems, 33*(3), 243–259. doi:10.2190/KUB1-6M7X-NHY5-3BWG

Adamo-Villani, N., & Wilbur, R. (2008). Two Novel Technologies for Accessible Math and Science Education. *IEEE Multimedia – Special Issue on Accessibility,* October -December 2008, pp. 38-46.

Addison, A., & O'Hare, L. (2008). How can massive multi-user virtual environments and virtual role play enhance traditional teaching practice? *Proceedings from Researching Learning in Virtual Environments International Conference (reLIVE 08),* November 20-21. The Open University, UK. Retrieved from http://www.open.ac.uk/relive08/documents/ReLIVE08_conference_proceedings.pdf

Ahdell, R., & Andresen, G. (2001). *Games and simulations in workplace eLearning: How to align eLearning content with learner needs.* Master of Science Thesis, Norwegian University of Science and Technology. 1 - 158.

Akkary, P. L., Bell, E., Roberts, R. L., Dudrick, S. J., & Duffy, A. J. (2009). The role of haptic feedback in laparoscopic simulation training. *The Journal of Surgical Research, 156*(2), 312–318. doi:10.1016/j.jss.2009.04.018

Alani, H., Dasmahapatra, S., O'Hara, K., & Shadbolt, N. (2003). Intelligent information processing: Identifying communities of practice through ontology network analysis. *IEEE Intelligent Systems,* 18–25. doi:10.1109/MIS.2003.1193653

Albano, G., Iovane, G., Salerno, S., & Viglione, S. (n.d.) *Web based simulations for virtual scientific experiment: Methodology and tools.* 1st International EleGI Conference on Advanced Technology for Enhanced Learning. 1 – 9.

Aldrich, C. (2004). *Simulations and the future of learning.* San Francisco: Pfeiffer.

Aldrich, C. (2005). *Learning by doing.* San Francisco: Pfeiffer.

Alessi, S. M., & Trollip, S. R. (2001). *Multimedia for Learning: Methods and Development.* Boston: Allyn and Bacon.

Ally, M. (2004). Foundations of educational theory for online learning. In T. Anderson & F. Elloumi (Eds.), *Theory and practice of online learning* (pp. 3-31). Althabasca University: Canada. Retrieved January 24, 2010, from http://cde.athabascau.ca/online_book/pdf/TPOL_book.pdf

American Association for the Advancement of Science. (2004). *Invention and Impact: Building Excellence in Science, Technology, Engineering and Mathematics (STEM) Education.* Washington, DC: American Association for the Advancement of Science.

Ammar, M. B., Alimi, A. M., Neji, M., & Gouardères, G. (2004). Agent-based collaborative affective e-learning system. In *the proceedings of the First International Conference on Immersive Telecommunications* (n.p.). Bussolengo, Verona, Italy.

Anaraki, F. (2004). Developing an Effective and Efficient eLearning Platform. *International Journal of the Computer, the Internet and Management 12*(2), 57–63.

Anderson, L. W., & Krathwohl, D. R. (Eds.). (2001). *A taxonomy for learning, teaching, and assessing: A revision of Bloom's Taxonomy of Educational Objectives.* New York: Longman.

Andrejevic, M. (2007). *iSpy: Surveillance and Power in the Interactive Era.* Lawrence: University Press of Kansas.

Annetta, L., Murray, M., Laird, S., Bohr, S., & Park, J. (2006). Serious games: Incorporating video games in the classroom. *EDUCAUSE Quarterly Magazine, 29*(3), 16–22.

Antonacci, D. M., & Modress, N. (2008). Envisioning the educational possibilities of user-created virtual worlds. *AACE Journal, 16*(2), 115–126.

Antonacci, D., & Modaress, N. (2005). Second Life: The educational possibilities of a massively multiplayer virtual world (MMVW). *Proceedings from EDUCAUSE Southwest Regional Conference.* February 16: Austin, Texas. Retrieved from http://net.educause.edu/ir/library/pdf/WRC0541.pdf

Aoki, N., Ohta, S., & Masuda, H., Naito, Sawai, T., Nishida, K., Okada, T., Oishi, T.M. Iwasawa, Y., Toyomasu, K., Hira, K., & Fukui, T. (2004). Edutainment tools for initial education of type-1 diabetes mellitus: initial diabetes education with fun. *Studies in Health Technology and Informatics, 107*(Part 2), 855–859.

Arakji, R., & Lang, K. (2008). Avatar business value analysis: A methods of the evaluation of business value creation in virtual commerce. *Journal of Electronic Commerce Research, 9*(3), 207–218.

Ariely, D. (2008). *Predictably irrational: The hidden forces that shape our decisions.* New York: Harper Collins.

Arreguin, C. (2007). *Reports from the field:* Second Life *community convention 2007 education track summary.* New York: Global Kids, Inc. Retrieved from http://www.holymeatballs.org/pdfs/VirtualWorldsforLearningRoadmap_012008.pdf

Au, W. J. (2009, March 23). *For Some Combat Veterans, Second Life Used For PTSD Therapy "Working when nothing else has",* Ret. Lt. Col. Says. Message posted to http://nwn.blogs.com/nwn/2009/03/posttraumatic-stress.html

AuthorMapper. (2009). *AuthorMapper.* Retrieved September 18, 2009, from http://qa.authormapper.cmgsites.com/

Avatar Languages Blog. (n.d.). *Dogme 2.0: What "Teaching 2.0" can learn from Dogme ELT.* Retrieved January 24, 2010, from http://www.avatarlanguages.com/blog/dogme-elt-web20-dogme20/

Avatar Languages. (n.d.). *Home page.* Retrieved January 24, 2010, from http://www.avatarlanguages.com/home.php

Azevedo, R., Moos, D. C., Greene, J. A., Winters, F. I., & Cromley, J. G. (2008). Why is externally-facilitated regulated learning more effective than self-regulated learning with hypermedia? *Educational Technology Research and Development, 56*(1), 45–72. doi:10.1007/s11423-007-9067-0

Babich, A., Senk, D., & Mavrommatis, K. (2005). *Combination of lab experiments and online simulations in master course* (pp. 1–7). Tainan, Taiwan: Exploring Innovation in Education and Research.

Badger, C. (2008). *Recipe for Success with Enterprise Virtual Worlds.* Retrieved from http://www.forterrainc.com/images/stories/pdf/recipe_for_success_10509.pdf

Bajcsy, R., Encisco, R., Kamberova, G., & Nocera, L. (1998). 3D reconstruction of environments for virtual collaboration. *Proceedings of the 4th IEEE Workshop on Application of Computer Vision. IEEE.* 160 – 167.

Bakhtin, M. M. (1981). *The dialogic imagination* (Emerson, C., & Holquist, M., Trans.). Austin, TX: University of Texas Press.

Balkissoon, R., Blossfield, K., Salud, L., Ford, D., & Pugh, C. (2009). Lost in translation: Unfolding medical students' misconceptions of how to perform a clinical digital rectal examination. *American Journal of Surgery, 197,* 525–532. doi:10.1016/j.amjsurg.2008.11.025

Balogh, J., Michael C., & Giangola J. (2004). Voice User Interface Design: Minimizing Cognitive Load. *Addison Wesley Professional* 2004.

Bangham, J. A. Cox, S.J., Elliott, R. Glauert, J.R.W. Marshall, I., (UEA) Rankov, S., Wells, M. (2000). An Overview of ViSiCAST. *IEE Seminar on Speech and language processing for disabled and elderly people,* London, April 2000.

Barab, S., Thomas, M., Dodge, T., Carteaux, R., & Tuzun, H. (2005). Making learning fun: Quest Atlantis: A game without guns. *Educational Technology Research and Development, 1*(53), 86–107. doi:10.1007/BF02504859

Barab, S. A., Scott, B., Siyahhan, S., Goldstone, R., Ingram-Goble, A., Zuiker, S., & Warren, S. (2009). Transformational play as a curricular scaffold: Using videogames to support science education. *Journal of Science Education and Technology, 18,* 305–320. doi:10.1007/s10956-009-9171-5

Barack, L. (2009). Green libraries grow in SL: Eco-friendly Emerald City launches in Second Life. *School Library Journal, 55*(1), 12–13.

Baranowski, T., Baranowski, J., & Cullen, K. W. (2003). Squire's quest! Dietary outcome evaluation of a multimedia game. *American Journal of Preventive Medicine, 24*(1), 52–61. doi:10.1016/S0749-3797(02)00570-6

Bares, W. H., Zettlemoyer, L. S., & Lester, J. C. (1998). Habitable 3D learning environments for situated learning. In B. P. Goettl, H. M. Halff, C. L. Redfield, & V. J. Shute (Eds.), *Proceedings of the Fourth International Conference on Intelligent Tutoring Systems: Vol. 1452 Lecture Notes in Computer Science* (pp. 76-85). Berlin: Springer-Verlag.

Barfield, W. (2006). Intellectual property rights in virtual environments: Considering the rights of owners, programmers, and virtual avatars. *Akron Law Review, 39,* 649–700.

Bartfay, W. J., & Bartfay, E. (1994). Promoting health in schools through a board game. *Western Journal of Nursing Research, 16*(4), 438–446. doi:10.1177/019394599401600408

Bartle, R. A. (2006). Virtual Worldliness. In Balkin, J. M., & Noveck, B. S. (Eds.), *The State of Play: Law, Games and Virtual Worlds (34.).* New York: New York University.

Beach, R., Anson, C., Breuch, L., & Swiss, T. (2008). *Teaching writing using blogs, wikis, and other digital tools.* Norwood, MA: Christopher-Gordon.

Beach, R., & Doerr-Stevens, C. (in press). Learning to engage in dialogic argument through participation in online role-play . In Kadjer, S., & Young, C. (Eds.), *Technology and English education.* Greenwich, CT: Information Age Press.

Beach, R., & Doerr-Stevens, C. (2009). Learning argument practices through online role-play: Toward a rhetoric of significance and transformation. *Journal of adolescent and adult literacy*, March, *52* (6).

Beilharz, K. (2005). *Gesture-controlled interaction with aesthetic information sonification. In the proceedings of the Second Australasian Conference on Interactive Entertainment* (pp. 11 – 18). Sydney, Australia. ACM.

Bell, T. (1997). Virtual trade dress: A very real issue. *Maryland Law Review (Baltimore, Md.)*, *56*, 384–532.

Benford, S., Greenhalgh, C., Rodden, T., & Pycock, J. (2001). Collaborative virtual environments. *Communications of the ACM, 44*(7), 79–85. doi:10.1145/379300.379322

Benvenuti, L., Hennipman, E. J., Oppelaar, E. J., van der Veer, G. C., Cruijsberg, B., & Bakker, G. (2008). Experiencing Education with 3D Virtual Worlds. In Kinshuk, D. G. Sampson, J. M. Spector, P. Isaías, & D. Ifenthaler (Eds.), *Proceedings of the IADIS International Conference on Cognition and Exploratory Learning in the Digital Age* (pp. 295-300). IADIS: Freiburg, Germany.

Berge, Z. L. (2008). Multi-user virtual environments for education and training: A critical review of Second Life. *Educational Technology, 48*(3), 27–31.

Bierema, L. L., & Merriam, S. B. (2002). E-mentoring: Using computer mediated communication to enhance the mentoring process. *Innovative Higher Education, 26*(3), 211–227. doi:10.1023/A:1017921023103

Biggs, J. (1987). *Student approaches to learning and studying*. Hawthorne, Australia: ACER.

Biocca, F., & Levy, M. (1995). *Communication in the age of virtual reality*. Philadelphia, PA: Lawrence Erlbaum Associates.

Biocca, F. (1992). Will simulation sickness slow down the diffusion of virtual environment technology? *Presence (Cambridge, Mass.), 1*(3), 334–343.

Bishop, M. J., & Cates, W. M. (2001). Theoretical foundations for sound's use in multimedia instruction to enhance learning. *Educational Technology Research and Development, 49*(3), 5–22. doi:10.1007/BF02504912

Blanchard, E., & Frasson, C. (2006). *Easy creation of game-like virtual learning environments*. Paper presented at the Workshop on Teaching with Robots, Agents, and NLP, held in conjunction with the Eighth International Conference on Intelligent Tutoring Systems (ITS 2006), Jhongli, Taiwan, June 26-30. Retrieved July 30, 2009, from http://facweb.cs.depaul.edu/elulis/Blanchard.pdf

Blascovich, J., Loomis, J., Beall, A., Swinth, K., Hoyt, C., & Bailenson, J. (2002). Immersive virtual environment technology as a methodological tool for social psychology. *Psychological Inquiry, 13*(2), 103–124. doi:10.1207/S15327965PLI1302_01

Bliss, J., Askew, M., & Macrae, S. (1996). Effective teaching and learning: Scaffolding revisited. *Oxford Review of Education, 22*(1), 37–61. doi:10.1080/0305498960220103

Bloom, B. S. (Ed.). (1956). *Taxonomy of educational objectives: The classification of educational goals. Handbook 1: Cognitive domain*. New York: David McKay.

Boehle, S. (2005). Simulations: The next generation of e-learning. *Training (New York, N.Y.)*, 1–6.

Boekaerts, M. (1995). Self-regulated learning: Bridging the gap between metacognitive and metamotivation theories. *Educational Psychologist, 30*(4), 195–200. doi:10.1207/s15326985ep3004_4

Boekaerts, M., Pintrich, P. R., & Zeidner, M. (Eds.). (2000). *Handbook of self-regulation*. London: Academic.

Bogost, I. (2007). *Persuasive Games – the expressive power of videogames*. Cambridge, MA: MIT Press.

Bouras, C., Philopoulos, A., & Tsiatsos, T. (2001). E-Learning through Distributed Virtual Environments. *Journal of Network and Computer Applications, 24*(3), 175–199. doi:10.1006/jnca.2001.0131

Bouras, C., & Tsiatsos, T. (2006). Educational Virtual Environments: Design Rationale and Architecture. *Multimedia Tools and Applications*, *29*(2), 153–173. doi:10.1007/s11042-006-0005-7

Bouras, C., Fotakis, D., Kapoulas, V., Koubek, A., Mayer, H., & Rehatschek, H. (1999). Virtual European School-VES. In Proceedings *of the IEEE International Conference on Multimedia Computing and Systems* (pp.1055-1057), Florence, Italy, June 7 - 11, IEEE.

Bouras, C., Giannaka, E., & Tsiatsos, T. (2003). Virtual Collaboration Spaces: The EVE Community. In *Proceedings of the 2003 Symposium on Applications and the Internet* (pp. 48-55), Orlando, Florida, USA, January 27 - 31, IEEE.

Bradyn, J. A. (1985). A review of mobility aids and means of assessment. In Warren, D.H. & Strelow, E.R. (eds.), *Electronic spatial sensing for the blind*. Martinus Nijhoff, 13-27.

Brandsford, J., & Gawel, D. (2006). Thoughts on Second Life and learning. *Proceedings of the First Second Life Education Workshop, San Francisco, California.*

Bronack, S., Riedl, R., & Tashner, J. (2006). *Learning in the Zone: A social constructivist framework for distance education in a 3D virtual world. Interactive Learning Environments, 14*(3), 219–232. doi:10.1080/10494820600909157

Bronack, S., & Sanders, R. Cheney, A., Riedl, R., Tashner, J. & Matzen, N. (2008). Presence pedagogy: Teaching and learning in a 3D immersive world. *International Journal of Teaching and Learning in Higher Education.* Retrieved September 1, 2009 from http://www.isetl.org/ijtlhe/pdf/IJTLHE453.pdf

Bronack, S., Sanders, R., Cheney, A., Riedl, R., Tashner, J., & Matzen, N. (2008). Presence Pedagogy: Teaching and learning in a 3D virtual immersive world. *International Journal of Teaching and Learning in Higher Education, 20*(1), 59-69. Retrieved December 11, 2008, from http://www.isetl.org/ijtlhe/articleView.cfm?id=453

Bronstein, I. N., & Semendjajew, K. A. (1979). *Taschenbuch der Mathematik*. Verlag Harri Deutsch, Thun and Frankfurt am Main, reprint of the 20th edition.

Brooks, F. P., Jr. (1986). Walk Through- a Dynamic Graphics System for Simulating Virtual Buildings. *Proc. of 1986 Workshop on Interactive 3D Graphics*, (pp. 9-21).

Brown, A. L. (1992). Design experiments: Theoretical and methodological challenges in creating complex interventions in classroom settings. *Journal of the Learning Sciences, 2*(2), 141–178. doi:10.1207/s15327809jls0202_2

Brown, S. J., Lieberman, D. A., Germeny, B. A., Fan, Y. C., Wilson, D. M., & Pasta, D. J. (1997). Educational video game for juvenile diabetes: results of a controlled trial. *Medical Informatics, 22*(1), 77–89. doi:10.3109/14639239709089835

Bruner, J. (1966). *Toward a theory of instruction*. Cambridge, MA: Belknap Press of Harvard University Press.

Bruner, J. (1968). *Processes of cognitive growth: Infancy*. Worcester, MA: Clark University Press.

Bruner, J. S. (1961). The act of discovery. *Harvard Educational Review, 31*(1), 21–32.

Bruner, J. S. (1962/1979). *On knowing: Essays for the left hand*. Cambridge, MA: Belknap.

Bruner, J. S. (1986). *Actual minds, possible worlds*. Cambridge, MA: Harvard University Press.

Bruner, J. (1996). *The culture of education*. Cambridge: Harvard University Press.

Brush, T., & Saye, J. W. (2001). The use of embedded scaffolds with hypermedia-supported student-centered learning. *Journal of Educational Multimedia and Hypermedia, 10*(4), 333–356.

Bugeja, M. (2008). Second thoughts about second Life. *The Chronicle of Higher Education, 54*(3), C1.

Burdea, G., & Coiffet, P. (2003). *Virtual Reality Technology*. New York: John Wiley & Sons.

Burdea, G., & Coiffet, P. (2003). *Virtual reality technology* (2nd ed.). New York: John Wiley and Sons.

Burigat, S., & Chittaro, L. (2007). Navigation in 3D Virtual Environments: Effects of User Experience and Location-Pointing Navigation Aids. *International Journal of Human-Computer Studies*, *65*(11), 945–958. doi:10.1016/j.ijhcs.2007.07.003

Burmester, M., & Dufner, A. (2006). Designing the stimulation aspect of hedonic quality—An exploratory study . In Pivec, M. (Ed.), *Affective and Emotional Aspects of Human-Computer Interaction: Game-Based and Innovative Learning Approaches* (pp. 217–233). Amsterdam: Ios Press.

Byrne, M. (1996). *Water on tap: the use of virtual reality as an educational tool*. Unpublished doctoral dissertation, University of Washington, Seattle.

Cabanero-Johnson, C., & Berge, Z. (2009). Digital natives: back to the future of microworlds in a corporate learning organization. *The Learning Organization*, *16*(4), 290–297. doi:10.1108/09696470910960383

Cacioppo, J. T., Petty, R. E., Feinstein, J. A., & Jarvis, W. B. G. (1996). Dispositional differences in cognitive motivation: The life and times of individuals varying in need for cognition. *Psychological Bulletin*, *19*(2), 197–253. doi:10.1037/0033-2909.119.2.197

Cagiltay, K. (2006). Scaffolding strategies in electronic performance support systems: Types and challenges. *Innovations in Education and Teaching International*, *43*(1), 93–103. doi:10.1080/14703290500467673

Campbell, A. P. (2003). *Foreign language exchange in a virtual World: An intercultural task-based learning event* [Electronic version], submitted as partial documentation for an M.Ed. in e-Learning at the University of Sheffield, U.K. Retrieved January 24, 2010, from http://e-poche.net/files/flevw.html

Campbell, B., Collins, P., Hadaway, H., Hedley, N., & Stoermer, M. (2002). Web3D in ocean science learning environments: Virtual Big Beef Creek. In *Proceedings of the Seventh International Conference on 3D Web Technology (Web3D 2002)* (pp. 85-91). New York: Association for Computing Machinery.

Capocchi Ribeiro, M. A. (2002). An interactionist perspective to second/foreign language learning and teaching. *Opinion Paper*. (ERIC Document Reproduction Service No. ED 469392).

CARLA (Center for Advanced Research on Language Acquisition). Content-Based Language Teaching with Technology. (n.d.). *Content-Based Second Language Instruction: What is it?* Retrieved January 24, 2010, from http://www.carla.umn.edu/cobaltt/CBI.html

Carr, D. (2005). The rules of the game, the burden of narrative: Enter the matrix . In Gillis, S. (Ed.), *The matrix trilogy: Cyberpunk reloaded* (pp. 1–10). London: Wallflower Press.

Carr, D., Oliver, M., & Burn, A. (2008). Learning, teaching, and ambiguity in virtual worlds. *Proceedings from reLIVE 08: Proceedings of Researching Learning in Virtual Environments International Conference, 20-21 November 2008*. The Open University, UK. Retrieved from http://www.open.ac.uk/relive08/ documents/Re-LIVE08_conference_proceedings.pdf

Cashmore, P. (2006, May 30). *Second Life +Web 2.0= Virtual World Mashups*! Message posted to http://mashable.com/2006/05/30/second-life-web-20-virtual-world-mashups/

Castranova, E. (2005). *Synthetic worlds: The business and culture of online games*. Chicago: University Of Chicago Press.

Castronova, E. (2007). *Exodus to the Virtual World: How Online Fun is Changing Reality*. New York: Palgrave Macmillan.

CDC. (2008). *Virtual worlds – ehealth marketing*. Retrieved September 14, 2009 from http://www.cdc.gov/healthmarketing/ehm/virtual.html

Cervantes Institute. (2009). *Instituto Cervantes*. Retrieved September 22, 2009, from http://secondlife.cervantes.es/

Cessario, L. (1987). Utilization of board gaming for conceptual models of nursing. *The Journal of Nursing Education*, *26*(4), 167–169.

Chamberlain, J. P. Morford, & R. I. Mayberry (eds.), *Language acquisition by eye*,(pp. 165-190). Mahwah, NJ: Lawrence Erlbaum Associates.

Chan, K. K. P., & Lau, R. W. H. (2004). Distributed sound rendering for interactive virtual environments. *IEEE International Conference on Multimedia and Expo*, 1823-1826.

Chandler, P., & Sweller, J. (1999). Cognitive Load While Learning to Use a Computer Program. [University of New South Wales.]. *Applied Cognitive Psychology*, 1996.

Chang, W.-C., Wang, T.-H., Lin, F. H., & Yang, H.-C. (2009). Game-based learning with ubiquitous technologies. *IEEE Internet Computing*, *13*(4), 26–33. doi:10.1109/MIC.2009.81

Chapelle, C. A. (1998). Multimedia CALL: Lessons to be learned from research on instructed SLA. *Language Learning & Technology*, *2*(1), 22–34.

Chee, Y. S., & Lim, K. Y. T. (2009). Development, identity and game-based learning. In R.E. Ferdig (Ed.), *Handbook of research on effective electronic gaming in education* (pp. 808-825). Hershey, PA: Information Science Reference, IGI Global.

Chee, Y.S. (2007). Embodiment, embeddedness and experience: Game-based learning and the construction of identity. *Research and practice in technology enhanced learning, 2* (1), 3-30.

Chen, C. J., & Toh, S. C. (2005). A feasible instructional development model for virtual reality (VR)-based learning environments: Its efficacy in the novice car driver instruction of Malaysia. *Educational Technology Research and Development*, *53*(1), 111–123. doi:10.1007/BF02504861

Chen, C. J., Toh, S. C., & Wan, M. F. (2004). The theoretical framework for designing desktop virtual reality-based learning environments. *Journal of Interactive Learning Research*, *15*(2), 147–167.

Chen, C. J., & Wan, M. F. (2008). Guiding exploration through three-dimensional virtual environments: A cognitive load reduction approach. *Journal of Interactive Learning Research*, *19*(4), 579–596.

Chen, C. J. (2006). The design, development and evaluation of a virtual reality based learning environment. *Australasian Journal of Educational Technology, 22*(1), 39-63. Retrieved November 18, 2008, from http://www.ascilite.org.au/ajet/ajet22/chen.html

Chen, C. J., Toh, S. C., & Wan, M. F. (2003). Virtual reality: A potential technology for providing novel perspective to novice driver education in Malaysia. In N. Ansari, F. Deek, C.-Y. Lin, & H. Yu *(*Eds.), *Proceedings of the International Conference on Information Technology: Research and Education (ITRE 2003)* (pp. 184-188). Piscataway, NJ: Institute of Electrical and Electronics Engineers.

Chen, Y. (2006). A study of comparing the use of augmented reality and physical models in chemistry education. In Proceedings of the 2006 ACM international Conference on Virtual Reality Continuum and Its Applications (Hong Kong, China) (VRCIA'06, pp. 369-372). New York: ACM.

Chenin, A. (2007). A practical look at virtual property. *St. John's Law Review*, *80*, 1059–1090.

Chin, J., Diehl, V., & Norman, K. (1988). Development of an Instrument Measuring User Satisfaction of the Human-Computer Interface. *Proceedings of CHI*, 213-218.

Chittaro, L., & Ranon, R. (2007). Web3D technologies in learning, education and training: Motivations, issues, opportunities. *Computers & Education*, (49): 3–18. doi:10.1016/j.compedu.2005.06.002

Chittaro, L., & Ranon, R. (2002). New Directions for the Design of Virtual Reality Interfaces to E-Commerce Sites. In *Proceedings of the 5th International Conference on Advanced Visual Interfaces* (pp.308-315), Trento, Italy, May 22 - 24, ACM Press.

Christou, C. G., & Bulthoff, H. H. (1999). View dependence in scene recognition after active learning. *Memory & Cognition*, *27*(6), 996–1007.

Clark, K. (2002). *Inspired 3D Character Animation*. Portland, OR: Premier Press.

Clark-Carter, D., Heyes, A., & Howarth, C. (1986). The effect of non-visual preview upon the walking speed of visually impaired people. *Ergonomics*, *29*(12), 1575–1581. doi:10.1080/00140138608967270

Cobb, P. (2001). Supporting the environment of learning and teaching in social and institutional context. In Carver, S., & Klahr, D. (Eds.), *Cognition and instruction: 25 years of progress* (pp. 455–478). Mahwah, NJ: Lawrence Erlbaum Associates, Inc.

Cockburn, A., & McKenzie, B. (2002). Evaluating the Effectiveness of Spatial Memory in 2D and 3D Physical and Virtual Environments. In *CHI '02: Proceedings of the SIGCHI Conference on Human Factors in Computing Systems* (pp.203-210), Minneapolis, Minnesota, USA, April 20 - 25, ACM Press.

Collins, A., Brown, J. S., & Newman, S. E. (1989). Cognitive apprenticeship: Teaching the craft of reading, writing, and mathematics. In Resnick, L. B. (Ed.), *Knowing, learning, and instruction: Essays in honor of Robert Glaser* (pp. 453–494). Hillsdale, NJ: Lawrence Erlbaum.

Collins, A. (1992). Toward a design science of education. In Scanlon, E., & O' Shea, T. (Eds.), *New directions in educational technology* (pp. 15–22). New York: Springer-Verlag.

Collins, C. (2008). Looking to the future: Higher education in the metaverse. *EDUCAUSE Review*. Retrieved December 13th, 2009, from http://www.educause.edu/EDUCAUSE+Review/EDUCAUSEReviewMagazineVolume43/LookingtotheFutureHigherEducat/163164

Coluccia, E., & Louse, G. (2004). A UML-Based Software Engineering Methodology for Agent Factory. In *Proceedings of the 16th International Conference on Software Engineering and Knowledge Engineering*, Alberta, Canada.

Colwell, C., Petrie, H., Kornbrot, D., Hardwick, A., & Furner, S. (1998). Haptic virtual reality for blind computer users," in *Proceedings of the 3rd International ACM Conference on Assistive Technologies (ASSETS '98)*, (pp. 92–99), Marina del Rey, Calif, USA.

Consultants-E. (n.d.). *SLanguages*. Retrieved January 24, 2010, from http://www.slanguages.net/home.php

Coolican, H. (2004). *Research Methods and Statistics in Psychology*. Hodder Arnold.

Cooper, G. (2004). *Research into Cognitive Load Theory and Instructional Design at UNSW*. University of New South Wales. <http://www.google.com/scholar?hl=en&lr=&q=cache:BP2uyE_8R1EJ:www.uog.edu/coe/ed451/tHEORY/LoadTheory1.pdf+research+into+cognitive+load+theory+and+instructional+design+at+unsw>.

Cordier, F., Seo, H., & Magnenat-Thalmann, N. (2003). Made-To-Measure Technologies for an Online Clothing Store. *IEEE Computer Graphics and Applications*, *23*(1), 38–48. doi:10.1109/MCG.2003.1159612

Cowan, B., Shelley, M., Sabri, H., Kapralos, B., Hogue, A., Hogan, M., et al. (2008). Interprofessional care simulator for critical care education. *In Proceedings of the ACM FuturePlay 2008 International Conference on the Future of Game Design and Technology* (pp.260-261) Toronto, Ontario, Canada, November 3-5 2008.

Cowen, K. J., & Tesh, A. S. (2002). Effects of gaming on nursing students' knowledge of pediatric cardiovascular dysfunction. *The Journal of Nursing Education*, *41*(11), 507–509.

Crandall, W., Bentzen, B., Myers, L., & Mitchell, P. (1995). *Transit accessibility improvement through talking signs remote infrared signage, a demonstration and evaluation, Tech*. San Francisco, Calif, USA: Rep., The Smith-Kettlewell Eye Research Institute, Rehabilitation Engineering Research Center.

Crosier, J. K., Cobb, S. V. G., & Wilson, J. R. (2000). Experimental comparison of virtual reality with traditional teaching methods for teaching radioactivity. *Education and Information Technologies*, *5*(4), 329–343. doi:10.1023/A:1012009725532

Cross, J., O'Driscoll, T., & Trondsen, E. (2007, March 22). Another life: Virtual worlds as tools for learning. *eLearn Magazine*. Retrieved from http://www.elearnmag.org/subpage.cfm?section=articles&article=44-1

Cruz-Neira, C. (1998). Making virtual reality useful: Immersive interactive applications.? *J. Future Generation Computer Systems*, *14*, 147–156. doi:10.1016/S0167-739X(98)00017-X

Csikszentmihalyi, M. (2000). Das Flow-Erlebnis. Jenseits von Angst und Langeweile . In *Tun aufgehen. (The flow-experience. Beyond anxiety and boredom: merging into action.)*. Stuttgart: Klett.

Curtis, P. (1992). Mudding: Social Phenomena in Text-Based Virtual Realities. In *Proceedings of the Conference on Directions and Implications of Advanced Computing (sponsored by Computer Professionals for Social Responsibility)*. Berkeley,CA, April.

Dabbagh, N. (2003). Scaffolding: An important teacher competency in online learning. *TechTrends, 47*(2), 39–44. doi:10.1007/BF02763424

Dalgarno, B., Bennett, S., & Harper, B. (2010). The importance of active exploration, optical flow, and task alignment for spatial learning in desktop 3D environments. *Human-Computer Interaction*, *25*(1), 25–66. doi:10.1080/07370020903586670

Dalgarno, B., Bishop, A. G., Adlong, W., & Bedgood, D. R. Jr. (2009). Effectiveness of a virtual laboratory as a preparatory resource for distance education chemistry students. *Computers & Education*, *53*(3), 853–865. doi:10.1016/j.compedu.2009.05.005

Dalgarno, B., & Lee, M. J. W. (2010). What are the learning affordances of 3-D virtual environments? *British Journal of Educational Technology*, *40*(6), 10–32. doi:10.1111/j.1467-8535.2009.01038.x

Dalgarno, B., & Harper, B. (2004). User control and task authenticity for spatial learning in 3D environments. *Australasian Journal of Educational Technology, 20*(1), 1-17. Retrieved April 4, 2007, from http://www.ascilite.org.au/ajet/ajet20/dalgarno.html

Dalgarno, B., Bennett, S., & Harper, B. (2004). *The design, development and formative evaluation of a 3D virtual chemistry laboratory*. Paper presented at the International Conference on Computers in Education (ICCE 2004), Melbourne, Australia, November 30 - December 3.

Daly, C. (2010) Virtual worlds continue to make real-world gains. Retrieved on August 24, 2010 from http://technorati.com/technology/article/virtual-worlds-continue-to-make-real/

Darken, R., & Peterson, B. (2000). *Handbook of Virtual Environment Technology, Stanney, K.* Spatial Orientation, Wayfinding and Representation.

Darken, R. P., Cockayne, W. R., & Carmein, D. (1997). The Omni-Directional Treadmill: A Locomotion Device for Virtual Worlds. *Proc. of UIST'97,*(pp. 213-221).

Davis, E. A., & Miyake, N. (2004). Scaffolding [Special issue]. *Journal of the Learning Sciences*, *13*(3).

de Freitas, S. (2008). *Serious Virtual Worlds. A scoping study*. Bristol: SGI.

de Jong, T., & van Joolingen, W. R. (1998). Scientific discovery learning with computer simulations of conceptual domains. *Review of Educational Research*, *68*(2), 179–201.

De Luca, A., Mattone, R., & Giordano, P. R. (2007). Acceleration-level control of the CyberCarpet. *2007 IEEE International Conference on Robotics and Automation*, Roma, I,(pp. 2330-2335).

Dede, C. (1995). The Evolution of Constructivist Learning Environments: Immersion in Distributed, Virtual Worlds. *Educational Technology*, *35*(5), 46–52.

Dede, C., Salzman, M., Loftin, R. B., & Ash, K. (1997). *Using virtual reality technology to convey abstract scientific concepts. Learning the sciences of the 21st century: Research, design, and implementing advanced technology learning environments*. Hillsdale, NJ: Lawrence Erlbaum.

Dede, C., Clarke, J., Ketelhut, D. J., Nelson, B., & Bowman, C. (2005). *Fostering motivation, learning, and transfer in multi-user virtual environments*. Paper presented at the Annual Meeting of the American Educational Research Association Conference, Montréal, Canada, April 11-15.

deHaan, J., & Diamond, J. (2007). The experience of telepresence with a foreign language video game and video. In *the proceedings of the Sandbox Symposium 2007* (pp. 39 – 46). San Diego, CA: Association of Computing Machinery.

Desser, T. (2007). Simulation-Based Training: The Next Revolution in Radiology Education? *Journal of the American College of Radiology, 4*(11), 816–824. doi:10.1016/j.jacr.2007.07.013

DeWeerdt, S. (2009). A welcome disappearing act. *Columns: The University of Washington Alumni Magazine.* (pp. 20 – 21).

Dewey, J. (1997). *Experience and education.* New York: Simon and Schuster. (Original work published 1938)

Dickey, M. D. (2005). Three-dimensional virtual worlds and distance learning: Two case studies of Active Worlds as a medium for distance education. *British Journal of Educational Technology, 3*(36), 439–451. doi:10.1111/j.1467-8535.2005.00477.x

Dickey, M. (2003). 3D Virtual Worlds: An Emerging Technology for Traditional and Distance Learning. In *Proceedings of the Ohio Learning Network; The Convergence of Learning and Technology-Windows on the Future*, Easton, Ohio, USA, March 3 - 4.

Dieterle, E. (2009). Neomillennial learning styles and River City. *Children . Youth and Environments, 19*(1), 246–279.

Dodson, A. H., Moore, T., & Moon, G. V. (1999). A Navigation System for the Blind Pedestrian [Genoa, Italy.]. *GNSS, 99*, 513–518.

Doherty, P., & Rothfarb, R. (2006). Building an Interactive Science Museum in Second Life. In *Proceedings of the Second Life Education Workshop at the Second Life Community Convention* (pp. 19-24), San Francisco, California, USA, August 18 – 20.

Downs, R., & Stea, D. (1977). *Maps in Minds: Reflections on Cognitive Mapping.* New York: Harper and Row.

Downs, R. M., & Stea, D. (1997). Cognitive Maps and spatial behaviour: Process and Products. In R.M. Downs & D. Stea (Eds,), *Image and Environment* (pp. 8-26). Chicago: Aldine.

Dreher, C., Reiners, T., Dreher, N., & Dreher, H. (2009). Virtual worlds as a context suited for information systems education: Discussion of pedagogical experience and curriculum design with reference to Second Life. *Journal of Information Systems Education, 20*(2), 211-224. Retrieved November 7th, 2009, from ABI/INFORM Global. (Document ID: 1755224801).

Dünser, A., Steinbügel, K., Kaufmann, H., & Glück, J. (2006). Virtual and Augmented Reality as Spatial Ability Training Tools. In *Proceedings of the 7th ACM SIGCHI, Design Centred HCI*, (Vol. 158, pp. 125-132). ACM Press.

Duranske, B. (2008). *Virtual law.* Chicago: ABA Books.

Dyer, S., Martin, J., & Zulauf, J. (1995) *Motion Capture White Paper.*

Earnshaw, R. A., Gigante, M. A., & Jones, H. (Eds.). (1993). *Virtual Reality Systems.* Academic Press, 1993.

Edirisingha, P., Nie, M., Pluciennik, M., & Young, R. (2009). Socialisation for learning at a distance in a 3-D multi-user virtual environment. *British Journal of Educational Technology, 40*(3), 458 – 479. doi:10.1111/j.1467-853 5.2009.00962.x

Educause (2006). *SciFair: Game worlds for learning.* Retrieved September 23, 2009, from http://www.educause.edu/ir/library/pdf/ELI5010.pdf

Eduserv. (2008). *The Autumn 2008 Snapshot of UK Higher and Further Education Developments in Second Life.* Retrieved January 24, 2010, from http://www.eduserv.org.uk/foundation/sl/uksnapshot102008

Egbert, J., & Hanson-Smith, E. (Eds.). (1999). *CALL environments: Research, practice, and critical issues.* Alexandria, VA: TESOL.

Egbert, J., Chao, C. C., & Hanson-Smith, E. (1999). Computer-enhanced language learning environments: An overview . In Egbert, J., & Hanson-Smith, E. (Eds.), *CALL environments: Research, practice, and critical issues* (pp. 1–13). Alexandria, VA: TESOL.

Ekman, P., & Friesen, W. V. (1978). *Facial Action Coding System (Manual).* Palo Alto, CA: Consulting Psychologists Press.

El Ariss, O., Xu, D., Dandey, S., Vender, B., Mcclean, P., & Slator, B. (2010). A Systematic Capture and Replay Strategy for Testing Complex GUI☐based Java Applications. In *Proceedings of the 7th International Conference on Information Technology: Next Generations.*

Eliëns, A., Feldberg, F., Konijn, E., & Compter, E. (2007). VU @ Second Life: Creating a (Virtual) Community of Learners. *EUROMEDIA 2007.* Delft, Netherlands.

emlab. (n. d.). *Exploring the Nardoo.* Retrieved January 22, 2010, from http://emlab.uow.edu.au/products/nardoo.html

Employeefactor. (2009). *Generation z - The igeneration.* Retrieved August 23rd, 2010, from http://www.employeefactor.com/?p=275g

Engage Digital Media. (2009). *200+ youth-oriented worlds live or developing.* Retrieved November 9th, 2009, from http://www.virtualworldsmanagement.com/2009/youth-01-26-2009.html

English Village. (2007). English Village. Retrieved January 2, 2008, from http://slurl.com/secondlife/English+Village/207/193/101/

Ensher, E. A., Heun, C., & Blanchard, A. (2003). Online mentoring and computer-mediated communication: New directions in research. *Journal of Vocational Behavior, 63*(2), 264–288. doi:10.1016/S0001-8791(03)00044-7

Eppler, M. J., & Schmeil, A. (2009). Learning and knowledge sharing in virtual 3D environments: A classification of interaction patterns . In Bertagni, F., La Rosa, M., & Salvetti, F. (Eds.), *Learn how to learn.* Milan, Italy: FrancoAngeli.

Erpenbeck, J., & Sauter, W. (2007). *Kompetenzentwicklung im Netz. New Blended Learning mit Web 2.0. (Developing competence on the net. New Ways of Blended Learning with Web 2.0.).* Köln: Wolters Kluwer.

Ertan, S., Lee, C., Willets, A., Tan, H., & Pentland, A. (1998). A Wearable Haptic Navigation Guidance System. *2nd International Symposium on Wearable Computer* (pp. 164-165). Pittsburgh, PA

eSIGN at UEA (2003). Retrieved from http://www.visicast.cmp.uea.ac.uk/eSIGN/

Espinosa, M., & Ochaita, E. (1998). Using tactile maps to improve the practical spatial knowledge of adults who are blind. *Journal of Visual Impairment & Blindness, 92*(5), 338–345.

Esteves, M., Fonseca, B., Morgado, L., & Martins, P. (2009). Using Second Life for Problem Based Learning in Computer Science Programming. *Journal of Virtual Worlds Research, 2*(1), 3–25.

Federal Trade Commission. (2009). *Web sites warned to comply with Children's Online Privacy Law.* Retrieved November 13th, 2009, from http://www2.ftc.gov/opa/2000/07/coppacompli.shtm

Federation of American Scientists. (2006). *Summit on Educational Games – Harnessing the power of video games for learning.* Washington, DC: Federation of American Scientists.

Feingold, C. E., Calaluce, M., & Kallen, M. A. (2004). Computerized patient model and simulated clinical experiences: Evaluation with baccalaureate nursing students. *The Journal of Nursing Education, 43*(4), 156–163.

Feldon, D., & Kafai, Y. (2008). Mixed methods for mixed reality: Understanding users' avatar activities in virtual worlds. *Educational Technology, Research and Development, 56*(5/6), 575-593. Retrieved November 7, 2009, from Research Library. (Document ID: 1632036171).

Fraser, M., Glover, T., Vaghi, I., Benford, S., Greenhalgh, C., Hindmarsh, J., & Heath, C. (2000). Revealing the realities of collaborative virtual reality. *In Proceedings of the Third international Conference on Collaborative Virtual Environments* (San Francisco, California, United States) (pp.29-37). E. Churchill and M. Reddy, Eds. CVE '00. ACM, New York, NY.

Freksa, C. (1997). *Spatial and Temporal Structures in Cognitive Processes* (LNCS 1337, pp. 379–387).New York: Springer, Berlin, Heidelberg.

Freundschuh, S. M., & Egenhofer, M. J. (1997). Human conceptions of spaces: Implications for geographic information systems. *Transactions in GIS, 2*(4), 361–375.

Frey, K., & Frey-Eiling, A. (1992). *Allgemeine Didaktik. (General Didactics.)* Zürich, Switzerland: Verlag der Fachvereine an den schweizerischen Hochschulen und Techniken AG.

Fruchterman, J. (1995). Archenstone's orientation tools: Atlas Speaks and Strider. In Gill, J.M. & Petrie, H. (Eds.). *Orientation and Navigation Systems for Blind Persons,* Hatfield, UK. 1-2 February 1995. RNIB.

Fulcher, G. (2007a). *Virtual Medical Office for Bonwit-West: Clinical Procedures for Medical Assistants* (6th ed.). Philadelphia: Elsevier-Saunders.

Fulcher, G. (2007b). *Virtual Medical Office for Young: Kinn's The Administrative Medical Assistant* (6th ed.). Philadelphia: Elsevier-Saunders.

Fulcher, G. (2007b). *Virtual Medical Office for Young and Proctor: Kinn's The Medical Assistant* (10th ed.). Philadelphia: Elsevier-Saunders.

Gaggioli, A., Bassi, M., & Delle Fave, A. (2003). Quality of experience in virtual environments. In Riva, G., Davide, F., & Ijsselsteijn, W. A. (Eds.), *Being There: Concepts, Effects and Measurements of User Presence in Synthetic Environments* (pp. 121–135). Amsterdam: IOS Press.

Galas, C., & Ketelhut, D. J. (2006). River City, the MUVE. *Learning and Leading with Technology, 33*(7), 31–32.

Gao, F., Noh, J., & Koehler, M. (2008). "*Comparing Student Interactions in Second Life and Face-to-Face Role-playing Activities*". In K. McFerrin et al. (Eds.), Proceedings of Society for Information Technology and Teacher Education International Conference pp. 2033-2035. Chesapeake, VA: AACE.Gerald, S. & Antonacci, D. (2009). Virtual world learning spaces: developing a Second Life operating room simulation. *Educause Quarterly, 32*(1). Retrieved from http://www.educause.edu/EQ/EDUCAUSEQuarterlyMagazineVolum /VirtualWorldLearningSpacesDeve/163851

Gapp, K. P. (1995). An empirically validated model for computing spatial relations. In Wachsmuth, I., Rollinger, C.-R., & Brauer, W., editors, *KI-95: Advances in Artificial Intelligence. 19th Annual German Conference on Artificial Intelligence,*(pp. 245–256) New York: Springer.

Gee, J. P. (2003). *What video games can teach us about literacy and learning.* New York: Palgrave-Macmillan.

Gee, J. P. (2004). *Situated language in learning: A critique of traditional schooling.* New York: Routledge.

Gee, J. P. (2005). *Introduction to discourse analysis: Theory and Method.* Oxon: Routledge.

Gee, J. (2007). *Good video games and good learning: Collected essays.* New York: Peter Lang Publishing.

Gee, J. P. (2001). Identity as an analytic lens for research in education . In Secada, W. G. (Ed.), *Review of research in education, 25* (pp. 99–125). AERA.

Gee, J. (2007). *What video games have to teach us about learning and literacy.* (2003, Second Edition 2007).

Gee, J. P. (2009). Games, learning, and 21st century survival skills. *Journal of virtual worlds research, 2*(1), 3-9, Pedagogy, Education and Innovation in 3-D Virtual Worlds. Geertz, C. (1972/3). Deep Play:Notes on the Balinese Cockfight. *The Interpretation of Cultures* (pp. 412-53). New York: Basic Books.

Gelman, R., & Brenneman, K. (2004). Science learning pathways for young children. *Early Childhood Research Quarterly, 19*, 150–158. doi:10.1016/j.ecresq.2004.01.009

Genee, I., & De Vries, L. (2008, 3-6 September). Toward a typology of functions for the discourse move. Paper presented at 13th International Conference on Functional Grammar, University of Westminster, London.

Gibson, D., Aldrich, C., & Prensky, M. (2007). *Games and simulations in online learning*. Hershey, PA: Information Science Publishing.

Giddens, A. (1991). *Modernity and self-identity: Self and society in the late modern age*. Cambridge: Polity Press.

Gierke, C., & Müller, R. (2008). *Unternehmen in Second Life. Wie Sie Virtuelle Welten für Ihr reales Geschäft nutzen können. (Companies in Second Life. How to use virtual worlds for your real life business.)*. Offenbach, Germany: GABAL.

Giess, C., Evers, H., & Meinzer, H. (1998). Haptic volume rendering in different scenarios of surgical planning, in *Proceedings of the 3rd Phantom Users GroupWorkshop (PUG '98)*, (pp. 19–22).Cambridge, MA: MIT.

Goffman, E. (1956/1959/1973). *The presentation of self in everyday life*. Garden City, New York: Doubleday.

Golding, A. R., & Lesh, N. (1999). Indoor navigation using a diverse set of cheap, wearable sensors. *Third International Symposium on Wearable computers*, San Francisco, CA, 29-36.

Golledge, R. G., Klatzky, R. L., Loomis, J. M., Speigle, J., & Tietz, J. (1998). A geographical information system for a GPS based personal guidance system. *International Journal of Geographical Information Science, 12*(7), 727–749. doi:10.1080/136588198241635

Golledge, R., Klatzky, R., & Loomis, J. (1996). Cognitive mapping and wayfinding by adults without vision. In Portugali, J. (Ed.), *The construction of cognitive maps* (pp. 215–246). The Netherlands: Kluwer. doi:10.1007/978-0-585-33485-1_10

Gollub, R. (2007). *Second life and education*. ACM Crossroads, 14.1. Retrieved September 12, 2009, from http://www.acm.org/crossroads/xrds14-1/secondlife.html

Good, J., & Thackray, L. (2008, Sept 9–11). Spanning the boundaries. Poster presentation at *ALT-C 2008 conference introduction and abstracts* (pp. 140–141), 15th International Conference of the Association for Learning Technology. The University of Leeds, UK.

Goodyear, M. (2006). Mentoring: A learning collaboration. *EDUCAUSE Quarterly, 29*(4), 51-53. Retrieved December 3, 2007, from http://net.educause.edu/ir/library/pdf/eqm0647.pdf

Gorman, P., Lieser, J., Murray, W., Haluck, R., & Krummel, T. (1998). Assessment and validation of force feedback virtual reality based surgical simulator, in *Proceedings of the 3rd Phantom Users Group Workshop (PUG '98)* Cambridge, MA: MIT.

Götzenbrucker, G. (2001). *Soziale Netzwerke und Internet-Spielewelten. (Social networks and internet gaming worlds.)*. Wiesbaden, Germany: Westdeutscher Verlag.

Graham, C. R. in Bonk, C. J. & Graham, C. R. (Eds.). (2006). Blended Learning Systems: Definition, Current Trends, and Future Directions. *Handbook of blended learning: Global Perspectives, local designs*. San Francisco, CA: Pfeiffer Publishing. Retrieved from http://www.publicationshare.com/graham_intro.pdf

Gresalfi, M., Barab, S. A., Siyahhan, S., & Christensen, T. (2009). Virtual worlds, conceptual understanding, and me: Designing for consequential engagement. *Horizon, 17*(1), 21–34. doi:10.1108/10748120910936126

Gronstedt, A. (2007). Second Life produces real training results. *T + D Magazine*, August.

Gutierrez, M., Vexo, F., & Thalmann, D. (2004). The mobile animator: interactive character animation in collaborative virtual environment. *In Proceedings of Virtual Reality conference,* 125-284.

Gutwin, C., Benford, S., Dyck, J., Fraser, M., Vaghi, I., & Greenhalgh, C. (2004). Revealing delay in collaborative environments. *In Proceedings of the SIGCHI Conference on Human Factors in Computing Systems* (Vienna, Austria, April 24 - 29, 2004). CHI '04. ACM, New York, NY, 503-510.

Guzdial, M. (1994). Software-realized scaffolding to facilitate programming for science learning. *Interactive Learning Environments, 4*(1), 1–44. doi:10.1080/1049482940040101

Hai-Jew, S. (2008). Scaffolding discovery learning spaces. *MERLOT Journal of Online Learning and Teaching, 4*(4), 533-548. Retrieved May 8, 2009, from http://jolt.merlot.org/vol4no4/hai-jew_1208.pdf

Hai-Jew, S. (2009). Exploring the immersive parasocial: Is it *you* or the thought of you? *Journal of Online Learning and Teaching, 5*(2). MERLOT.

Halliday, M. A. K. (1985). *An introduction to functional grammar.* London: Edward Arnold.

Halloun, I. A., & Hestenes, D. (1985). The initial college state of college physics students. *American Journal of Physics, 53,* 1043–1055. doi:10.1119/1.14030

Handley, B. (2000). *Another path: Homeschooling Deaf and Hard of Hearing Children.* Retrieved from http://www.pacinfo.com/~handley/index.html

Hanna, D. E. (2003). *Building a leadership vision: Eleven strategic challenges for higher education. EDUCAUSE.* July/ August.

Hannafin, M. J., Land, S., & Oliver, K. (1999). Open learning environments: Foundations, methods, and models . In Reigeluth, C. M. (Ed.), *Instructional design theories and models: A new paradigm of instructional theory (Vol. 2,* pp. 115–140). London: Lawrence Erlbaum.

Hansen, M. M. (2008). Versatile, immersive, creative and dynamic virtual 3-D healthcare learning environments: A review of the literature. *Journal of Medical Internet Research, 10*(3). doi:10.2196/jmir.1051

Harkin, J. (2006). Get a (Second) Life. *Financial Times,* Published: November 17 2006 .

Harris, P. D. (2009). Immersive learning seeks a foothold. *Training & Development,* 40–45.

Harris, A. L., & Rea, A. (2009). Web 2.0 and virtual world technologies: A growing impact on IS education. *Journal of Information Systems Education, 20*(2), 137 – 144. Retrieved Nov. 22, 2009, from http://www.jise.appstate.edu/Issues/20/V20N2P137-abs.pdf.

Harris, H., Bailenson, J., Nielsen, A., & Yee, N. (2009). *Presence: Teleoperators & virtual environments.* Retrieved November 12, 2009, from http://vhil.stanford.edu/pubs/2009/harris-tracking.pdf

Harris, J. (2008). eMentoring—the future of online learner support. *International Journal of Excellence in e-Learning, 1*(2), 1-8.

Harvard University. (2007). *The River City Project.* Retrieved October 19, 2008, from http://muve.gse.harvard.edu/rivercityproject/

Haymes, T. (2008). The three-e strategy for overcoming resistance to technological change. *Educause Quarterly.* Retrieved from http://net.educause.edu/ir/library/pdf/EQM08411.pdf

Heeter, C. (1992). Being there: The subjective experience of presence. *Presence (Cambridge, Mass.), 1*(2), 262–271.

Hehl, W. (2008). *Trends in der Informationstechnologie. Von der Nanotechnologie zu virtuellen Welten. (Trends in information technology. From nanotechnology to virtual worlds.)* Zürich. Switzerland: vdf.

Heinrichs, L., Youngblood, P., Harter, P., & Dev, P. (2008). Simulation for team training and assessment: case studies of online training with virtual worlds. *World Journal of Surgery, 32,* 161–170. doi:10.1007/s00268-007-9354-2

Helal, A. S., Moore, S. E., & Ramachandran, B. (2001). Drishti: An integrated Navigation System for Visually Impaired and Disabled. *5th International Symposium on Wearable Computers.* Zurich, Switzerland.

Henderson, J., Fishwick, P., Fresh, E., & Futterknecht, F. (2008). An Immersive Learning Simulation Environment for Chinese Culture. In *Proceedings of Interservice/Industry Training, Simulation, and Education Conference (I/ITSEC)*, Orlando, Florida, USA, December 1 - 4.

Hengeveld, K., & Mackenzie, J. L. (2008). *Functional discourse grammar. A typologically-based theory of language structure.* Oxford, UK: Oxford University Press. doi:10.1093/acprof:oso/9780199278107.001.0001

Henry, J. M. (1997). Gaming: A teaching strategy to enhance adult learning. *Journal of Continuing Education in Nursing, 28*(5), 231–234.

Herrman, T., & Grabowski, J. (1994). *Sprechen – Psychologie der Sprachproduktion.* Berlin, Heidelberg: Spektrum Akademischer Verlag.

Hickey, D., Ingram-Goble, A., & Jameson, E. (2009). Designing Assessments and Assessing Designs in Virtual Educational Environments. *Journal of Science Education and Technology, 18,* 187–208. doi:10.1007/s10956-008-9143-1

Hirose, M., & Yokoyama, K. (1997). Synthesis and transmission of realistic sensation using virtual reality technology. *Transactions of the Society of Instrument and Control Engineers, 33*(7), 716–722.

Ho, M. L. C., Rappa, N. A., & Chee, Y. S. (2009). Designing and implementing virtual enactive role-play and structured argumentation: Promises and pitfalls. *Computer Assisted Language Learning, 22*(4), 323–350.

Ho, M. L. C. (2006). Introduction . In Ho, C., Teo, P., & Tay, M. Y. (Eds.), *Teaching the General Paper: Strategies that work* (pp. 1–4). Singapore: Pearson Longman.

Ho, M.L.C. (in press). Dealing with life and death issues: Engaging students through scenario-driven pedagogy. *Journal of the Imagination in English Language Teaching, 9.*

Hoffmeister, R. (2000). A piece of the puzzle: ASL and reading comprehension in deaf children . In Chamberlain, C., Morford, J. P., & Mayberry, R. I. (Eds.), *Language acquisition by eye* (pp. 143–164). Mahwah, NJ: Lawrence Erlbaum Associates.

Hogan, K., & Pressley, M. (Eds.). (1997). *Scaffolding student learning: Instructional approaches and issues.* Cambridge, MA: Brookline.

Hogan, M., Sabri, H., & Kapralos, B. (2007). Interactive community simulation environment for community health nursing. *In Proceedings of ACM FuturePlay 2007 International Conference on the Future of Game Design and Technology.* Toronto, Ontario, Canada, November 15-17.

Hollander, J., & Thomas, D. (2009). *Journal of planning education and research 29*(1), 108-113. Retrieved November 9th, 2009, from http://jpe.sagepub.com/cgi/content/abstract/29/1/108

Hollerbach, J. M., Xu, Y., Christensen, R., & Jacobsen, S. C. (2000). Design specifications for the second generation Sarcos Treadport locomotion interface. Haptics Symposium, *Proc. ASME Dynamic Systems and Control Division,* (*DSC-Vol. 69-2*, pp.1293-1298) Orlando, Nov. 5-10, 2000.

Horrigan, J. B. (2007, May 7). *A typology of information and communication technology users.* Pew Internet & American Life Project. p. ii. Retrieved from http://www.pewinternet.org/~/media//Files/Reports/2007/PIP_ICT_Typology.pdf.pdf

Howe, N., & Strauss, W. (1993). *13th Gen – Abort, retry, ignore, fail?* New York: Vintage Books.

Howe, N., & Strauss, W. (2000). *Millennials Rising: The Next Generation. New York: Vintage Books Institute of Medicine (2003). Health professions education – A bridge to quality.* Washington, DC: National Academy Press.

Hu, J. (2010) Educators save money switching to Open-Sim. *Hypergrid Business.* Retrieved August 24, 2010, from http://hypergridbusiness.com/2010/04/educators-save-money-switching-to-opensims/

Hudson-Smith, A. (2002). *30 Days in Active Worlds: Community, Design and Terrorism in a Virtual World. The Social Life of Avatars: Presence and Interaction in Shared Virtual Environments* (pp. 77–89). New York, New York, USA: Springer-Verlag.

Huizinga, J. (1955). *Homo ludens; a study of the play element in culture.* Boston: Beacon Press.

IBM. (n.d.). *Virtual World Guidelines.* Retrieved from http://domino.research.ibm.com/comm/ research_projects.nsf/pages/virtualworlds. IBMVirtualWorldGuidelines.html

Ieronutti, L., & Chittaro, L. (2007). Employing virtual humans for education and training in X3D/VRML worlds. *Computers & Education, 49*(1), 93–109. doi:10.1016/j.compedu.2005.06.007

Ijsselsteijn, W. A., de Ridder, H., Freeman, J., & Avons, S. E. (2000). Presence: Concept, determinants and measurements. *Proceedings of the Society for Photo-Instrumentation Engineers, 3959,* 520–529.

Ijsselsteijn, W., & Riva, G. (2003). Being there: The experience of presence in mediated environments . In Riva, G., Davide, F., & Ijsselsteijn, W. A. (Eds.), *Being There: Concepts, effects and measurements of user presence in synthetic environments* (pp. 3–16). Amsterdam: IOS Press.

Indiana University. (n.d.). *Quest Atlantis: Learning gains.* Retrieved January 24, 2010, from http://atlantis.crlt.indiana.edu/#66

Insko, B. E. (2003). Measuring presence: Subjective, behavioral and physiological methods. In G. Riva, F. Davide, & W. A. Ijsselsteijn (Eds.), *Being There: Concepts, effects and measurements of user presence in synthetic environments* (109-119).Amsterdam: IOS Press.

Interactive Multimedia Learning Laboratory. (1996). *Exploring the Nardoo* [CD-ROM]. Developed by the Interactive Multimedia Learning Laboratory, Faculty of Education, University of Wollongong in collaboration with the New South Wales Department of Land and Water Conservation. Wollongong, Australia: Interactive Multimedia Pty Ltd.

Iriberri, A. & Leroy, G. (2009). A life-cycle perspective on online community success. *ACM Computing Surveys, 41*(2), 11:1 – 11:29.

Irwin, C., & Berge, Z. (2006, March). Socialization in the online classroom. *e-Journal of Instructional Science and Technology, 9*(1). Retrieved from http://www.usq.edu.au/electpub/e-jist/docs/vol9_no1/papers/full_papers/irwin_berge.htm

ISO/IEC JTC1/SC29/WG11. Overview of the MPEG-4 Standard. Available at: http://www.chiariglione.org/mpeg/standards/mpeg-4/mpeg-4.htm

Ittelson, W. (1973). *Environment and Cognition. Environment perception and contemporary perceptual theory* (pp. 1–19). New York: Seminar Press.

Iwata, H., Yano, H., Fukushima, H., & Noma, H. (2005). CirculaFloor. *IEEE Computer Graphics and Applications, 25*(1), 64–67. doi:10.1109/MCG.2005.5

Iwata, H., & Yoshida, Y. (1999). Path Reproduction Tests Using a Torus Treadmill. *Presence (Cambridge, Mass.), 8*(6), 587–597. doi:10.1162/105474699566503

Iwata, H., & Fujji, T. (1996). Virtual Preambulator: A Novel Interface Device for Locomotion in Virtual Environment. *Proc. of IEEE VRAIS'96,*(pp. 60-65).

Iwata, H., Yano, H., & Tomioka, H. (2006). Powered Shoes, SIGGRAPH 2006 Conference DVD (2006).

Iwata, H., Yano, H., & Tomiyoshi, M. (2007). String walker. Paper presented at SIGGRAPH 2007.

Jackson, R. L., & Fagan, E. (2000). Collaboration and learning within immersive virtual reality . In *Proceedings of Collaborative Virtual Environments.* San Francisco: ACM.

Jacob, R. J. K., Girouard, A., Hirschfield, L. M., Horn, M. S., Shaer, O., Solovey, E. T., & Zigelbaum, J. (2008). Reality-based interaction: A framework for post-WIMP interfaces. *In the proceedings of the CHI 2008: ACM Special Interest Group in Computer Human Interface* (pp. 201 – 210). Florence, Italy.

Jacobson, M. J., & Azevedo, R. (Eds.). (2008). Scaffolded learning with hypermedia [Special issue]. *Educational Technology Research and Development, 56*(1). doi:10.1007/s11423-007-9066-1

Jacobson, D. (1999). On theorizing presence. Retrieved on 2 May, 2009, from http://www.brandeis.edu/pubs/jove/HTML/V6/presence.HTML

Jacobson, M. J., Kim, B., Lee, J., Lim, S. H., & Low, S. H. (2008). An intelligent agent augmented multi-user virtual environment for learning science inquiry: Preliminary research findings. Paper presented at the 2008 Annual Meeting of the American Education Research Association (AERA), New York, March 24-28.

Jacquet-Chiffelle, D-O. (2009). Virtual persons and identities. The future of identity in the Information Society (FIDIS) Summit event - Challenges and Opportunities.

Jang, S., & Lim, W. C. (2008). The effects of scaffolding types on the problem solving phase. In J. Luca & E. Weippl (Eds.), *Proceedings of World Conference on Educational Multimedia, Hypermedia, and Telecommunications 2008* (pp. 2402-2406). Chesapeake, VA: Association for the Advancement of Computers in Education.

Jansson, G., Fanger, J., Konig, H., & Billberger, K. (1998). Visually impaired persons' use of the phantom for information about texture and 3D form of virtual objects, in *Proceedings of the 3rd Phantom Users Group Workshop.* Cambridge, MA: MIT.

Jenkins, H., Clinton, K., Purushotma, R., Robinson, A. J., & Weigel, M. (2006). *Confronting the challenges of participatory culture: Media education for the 21st century.* Illinois, US: MacArthur Foundation.

joeeisner. (2009, May 13). *Bang for your online buck: Facebook vs. Second Life.* Message posted to https://forums.genesyslab.com/showthread.php?t=430

Johnson, L., Levine, A., & Smith, R. (2009). *The 2009 Horizon Report.* Austin, Texas: The New Media Consortium.

Johnson, L. F., & Levine, A. H. (2008). Virtual worlds: Inherently immersive, highly social learning spaces. *Theory into Practice, 47*(2), 161–170. doi:10.1080/00405840801992397

Johnson, K. (2008). *Lost Cause, an interactive film project. MM '08: ACM Multimedia* (pp. 569–578). Vancouver, British Columbia, Canada: Association of Computing Machinery.

Johnson, L. F., & Levine, A. H. (2008). Virtual worlds: Inherently immersive, highly social learning spaces. *Theory into Practice, 47*, 166–167. .doi:10.1080/00405840801992397

Johnston, O. &Thomas, F. (1995). *The Illusion of Life: Disney Animation.* Disney Editions; Rev Sub edition (October 5, 1995).

Jonassen, D. H. (1994). *Technology as cognitive tools: Learners as designers.* Retrieved June 3, 2005, from http://itech1.coe.uga.edu/itforum/paper1/paper1.html

Jonassen, D. H. (1997). *INSYS 527: Designing constructivist learning environments.* Retrieved September 21, 2009 from http://www.coe.missouri.edu/~jonassen/INSYS527.html

Jones, J. G., & Bronack, S. C. (2008). *Rethinking Cognition, Representations, and Processes in 3D Online Social Learning Environments. Digital Literacy: Tools and Methodologies for Information Society* (pp. 176–217). Hershey, PA: IGI Global.

Jones, J. G. (2004). 3D on-line distributed learning environments: An old concept with a new twist. In R. Ferdig & C. Crawford (Eds.), *Proceedings of the Society for Information Technology and Teacher Education International Conference.* (507-512). Atlanta, GA.

Jones, M.G., Minogue, J., Tretter, T.R., Negishi, A., & Taylor, R. (2005). *Haptic augmentation of science instruction: Does touch matter?* Wiley InterScience. DOI 10.1002/sce.20086.

Jonsson, E. (2002). *Inner Navigation: why we get lost and how we find our way* (pp. 27–126). New York: Scribner.

Junglas, I. A., Johnson, N. A., Steel, D. J., Abraham, D. C., & Loughlin, P. M. (2007). Identity formation, learning styles and trust in virtual worlds. *The DATA BASE for Advances in Informatin Systems, 38*(4), 90–96.

Juul, J. (2005). *Half-Real: video games between real rules and fictional worlds*. Cambridge, MA: MIT Press.

Kalning, K. (2007) *If Second Life isn't a game, what is it? MSNBC*. Retrieved from http://www.msnbc.msn.com/id/17538999/

Kamel-Boulos, M. N., Taylor, A. D., & Breton, A. (2005). A Synchronous Communication Experiment within an Online Distance Learning Program: A Case Study. *Telemedicine Journal and e-Health, 11*(5), 283–293.

Kane, Y. (2009). Online gaming-family edition. *Wall Street Journal Online Digital Network*. Retrieved on November 4th, 2009 from http://online.wsj.com/article/SB123802714524742875.html

Kato, P. M., & Beale, I. L. (2006). Factors affecting acceptability to young cancer patients of a psychoeducational video game about cancer. *Journal of Pediatric Oncology Nursing, 23*, 269–275. doi:10.1177/1043454206289780

Kavan, L., Collins, S., Zara, J., & O'Sullivan, C. (2007). Skinning with dual quaternions. *Proc. of the 2007 symposium on Interactive 3D graphics and games*, (pp. 39-46). Seattle, Washington.

Kay, L. (1980). Air sonar with acoustical display of spatial information. In Busnel, R. G., & Fish, J. F. (Eds.), *Animal Sonar System* (pp. 769–816). New York: Plenum Press.

Keegan, V. (2010). Virtual worlds: is this where real life is heading? The Observer. Retrieved August 24th, 2010, from http://www.guardian.co.uk/technology/2010/aug/22/discover-virtual-worlds-revolution

Kemmerling, M., & Schliepkorte, H. (1998). *An Orientation and Information System for Blind People based on RF-Speech-Beacons*. Helsinki: TIDE.

Kemp, J., Livingstone, D., & Bloomfield, P. (2009, May). SLOODLE: Connecting VLE tools with emergent teaching practice in Second Life. [Retrieved from Academic Search Premiere Database.]. *British Journal of Educational Technology, 40*(3), 551–555. doi:10.1111/j.1467-8535.2009.00938.x

Kemp, J., & Livingstone, D. (2006). Putting a Second Life Metaverse Skin on Learning Management Systems. In *Proceedings of the Second Life Education Workshop at the Second Life Community Convention* (pp.13-18), San Francisco, California, USA, August 18 – 20.

Kennedy, R. S., Lane, N. E., Berbaum, K. S., & Lilienthal, M. G. (1993). Simulator Sickness Questionnaire: An enhanced method for quantifying simulator sickness. *The International Journal of Aviation Psychology, 3*(3), 203–220. doi:10.1207/s15327108ijap0303_3

Kerres, M. (2001). *Multimediale und telemediale Lernumgebungen. Konzeption und Entwicklung. (Multi- and telemedia based learning environments. Conception and Development.)*. München, Germany: Oldenbourg.

Kerres, M., & de Witt, C. (2003). A didactical framework for the design of blended learning arrangements. *Journal of Educational Media, 28*, 101–114.

Ketelhut, D. J., Dede, C., Clarke, J., & Nelson, B. (2006). *A multi-user virtual environment for building higher order inquiry skills in science*. Paper presented at the American Educational Research Association, San Francisco, CA.

Kidz Connect. (2009). Retrieved August 1, 2009, from http://www.kidzconnect.org/

Kiili, K. (2005). Digital game-based learning: Towards an experiential gaming model. *The Internet and Higher Education, 8*(1), 13–24. doi:10.1016/j.iheduc.2004.12.001

Kim, P. (2006). Effects of 3D virtual reality of plate tectonics on fifth grade students' achievement and attitude toward science. *Interactive Learning Environments, 1*(14), 25–34. doi:10.1080/10494820600697687

Kirriemuir, J. (2009). *Early summer 2009 Virtual World Watch snapshot of virtual world activity in UK HE and FE*. Eduserv.org.uk. Retrieved from http://virtualworld-watch.net/ wordpress/wp-content/uploads/2009/06/snapshot-six.pdf

Kirschner, P. A., Sweller, J., & Clark, R. E. (2006). Why minimal guidance during instruction does not work: An analysis of the failure of constructivist, discovery, problem-based, experiential, and inquiry-based teaching. *Educational Psychologist, 41*(2), 75–86. doi:10.1207/s15326985ep4102_1

Kitchen, D., & McDougall, D. (1998). Collaborative Learning on the Internet. *Telemedicine Educational Technology Systems, 27*(3), 245–258.

Kitchin, R. M., Blades, M., & Golledge, R. G. (1997). Understanding spatial concepts at the geographic scale without the use of vision. *Progress in Human Geography, 21*(2), 225–242. doi:10.1191/030913297668904166

Kock, N. (2008). Collaboration and e-commerce in virtual worlds: The potential of Second Life and World of Warcraft. *International Journal of e-Collaboration, 4*(3), 1–13.

Koenraad, A. L. M. (2007). *3D and language education.* White paper on the rationale for the ViTAAL project. Retrieved January 24, 2010, from http://www.koenraad.info/vrall-2/3d-and-language-education-1/view

Koenraad, A. L. M. (2008). How can 3D virtual worlds contribute to language education? Focus on the language village format. *Proceedings of the 3rd International WorldCALL Conference (WorldCALL 2008)*. Retrieved October 30, 2009, from http://www.koenraad.info/vrall-2/how-can-3d-virtual-worlds-contribute-to-language-education/view

Kolb, D. A. (1984). *Experiential learning: Experience as the source of learning and development*. Upper Saddle River, NJ: Prentice Hall.

Korolov, M. (2010) OpenSim grows faster than Second Life. *Hypergrid Business*. Retrieved on August 24, 2010, from http://hypergridbusiness.com/2010/01/opensim-grows-faster-than-second -life/

Krashen, S. (1981). *Second language acquisition and second language learning*. Oxford, UK: Pergamon Press.

Krashen, S. (1987). *Principles and practice in second language acquisition*. New York: Prentice-Hall.

Krashen, S. (1988). *Second language acquisition and second language learning*. Upper Saddle River, NJ: Prentice-Hall International.

Krashen, S. D. (1982). *Principles and practices in second language acquisition*. New York: Prentice-Hall, Prentice Hall International.

Krashen, S. (1980). The input hypothesis . In Alatis, J. (Ed.), *Current issues in bilingual education* (pp. 165–180). Washington, DC: Georgetown University.

Krathwohl, D. R. (2002). A revision of Bloom's Taxonomy: An overview. *Theory into Practice, 41*(4), 212–218. doi:10.1207/s15430421tip4104_2

Kumar, A. (2008). *Mobile broadcasting with WiMAX: Principles, technology, and applications*. Boston: Focal Press.

Kumpulainen, K., & Wray, D. (2001). *Classroom interaction and social learning*. London: Routledge.

KZero. (2010). *Radar chart: Toys/games, fantasy and mirror worlds*. Retrieved August 24th, 2010, from http://www.kzero.co.uk/blog/?cat=107

Lab, L. (2009). *1 billion hours, 1 billion dollars served: Second Life celebrates major milestones for virtual worlds*. Retrieved November 1st, 2009, from http://lindenlab.com/pressroom/releases/22_09_09

Laffer, B. (2008). *Second life money: The status of financial industries in Second Life*. Retrieved November 13th, 2009, from http://www.slentre.com/second-life-money-the-state-of-financial-industries-in-second-life/

Lafsky, M. (2009). Can training in Second Life teach doctors to save real lives? *Discover Magazine*. July-August, 15.

Lagorio, C. (2007, January 7) The Ultimate Distance Learning. *The New York Times*. Retrieved from http://www.nytimes.com/2007/01/07/education/edlife/07innovation.html

Lahav, O., & Mioduser, D. (2003). A blind person's cognitive mapping of new spaces using a haptic virtual environment. *Journal of Research in Special Educational Needs*, *3*(3), 172–177. doi:10.1111/1471-3802.00012

Lahav, O. (2003). *Blind Persons' Cognitive Mapping of Unknown Spaces and acquisition of Orientation Skills, by Using Audio and Force-Feedback Virtual Environment*. Doctoral dissertation, Tel-Aviv University, Israel (Hebrew).

Lai, M., & Law, N. (2006). Peer scaffolding of knowledge building through collaborative groups with differential learning experiences. *Journal of Educational Computing Research*, *35*(2), 123–144. doi:10.2190/GW42-575W-Q301-1765

Laister, J., & Kober, S. (2002). Social Aspects of Collaborative Learning in Virtual Learning Environments. In *Proceedings of the Networked Learning Conference*, Sheffield, UK, March 26 - 28.

Lang, H. G., McKee, B. G., & Conner, K. (1993). Characteristics of effective teachers: a descriptive study of the perceptions of faculty and deaf college students. *American Annals of the Deaf*, *138*(3), 252–259.

Langley, G. B., & Sheppeard, H. (1985). The visual analogue scale: its use in pain measurement. *Rheumatology International*, *5*(4), 145–148. doi:10.1007/BF00541514

Languagelab.com. llc. (n.d.). LanguageLab. Retrieved June 2, 2009, from http://www.languagelab.com/en/

Laurillard, D. (1993). *Rethinking university teaching: A framework for the effective use of educational technology*. London: Routledge.

Laurillard, D. (2002). *Rethinking university teaching: A conversational framework for the effective use of learning technologies* (2nd ed.). London: RoutledgeFalmer. doi:10.4324/9780203304846

Lave, J., & Wenger, E. (1991). *Situated learning: Legitimate peripheral participation*. Cambridge, UK: Cambridge University Press.

Lave, J. (1991). Situating learning in communities of practice . In Resnick, L. B., Levine, J. M., & Teasley, S. D. (Eds.), *Perspectives on socially shared cognition* (pp. 63–82). Washington, DC: American Psychological Association. doi:10.1037/10096-003

Lee, M. (2009). How can 3D virtual worlds be used to support collaborative learning? An analysis of cases from the literature. *Journal of e-Learning and Knowledge Society*, *5*(1), 149 – 158.

Lehtiniemi, T. (2007). Measuring aggregate production in a virtual economy using log data. *Journal of Virtual Worlds Research*, *2*(3), 3–21.

Lemke, J. L. (1990). *Talking science: Language, learning and values*. Norwood: Ablex Publishing Company.

Lepper, M. R., Drake, M. F., & O'Donnell-Johnson, T. (1997). Scaffolding techniques of expert human tutors . In Hogan, K., & Pressley, M. (Eds.), *Scaffolding student learning: Instructional approaches and issues* (pp. 108–144). Cambridge, MA: Brookline.

Leutner, D. (1993). Guided discovery learning with computer-based simulation games: Effects of adaptive and non-adaptive instructional support. *Learning and Instruction*, *3*(2), 113–132. doi:10.1016/0959-4752(93)90011-N

Lewis, J. (1991). Psychometric Evaluation of an After-Scenario Questionnaire for Computer Usability Studies: the ASQ. *ACM SIGCHI Bulletin*, *23*(1), 78–81. doi:10.1145/122672.122692

Lewis, D. J., Saydak, S. J., Mierzwa, I. P., & Robinson, J. A. (1989). Gaming: A teaching strategy for adult learners. *Journal of Continuing Education in Nursing*, *20*(2), 80–84.

Lieberman, D. (1997). Interactive video games for health promotion: Effects on knowledge, self-efficacy, social support and health. In Gold, R.L. &Manning, T. (eds.) *Health Promotion and Interactive Technology*, (103–120). Norwell, NJ: Lawrence Erlbaum Associates.

Lin, Y. C. (2009). *Research on vocabulary acquisition of upper elementary school students in a collaborative virtual environment*. Unpublished master's thesis, National Dong Hwa University, Hualien, Taiwan.

Linden Research Inc. (n.d.). *Second Life*. Retrieved January 24, 2010, from http://secondlife.com/

Linden, A. (2009). *Second life lives behind a firewall*. Retrieved October 26, 2009, from https://blogs.secondlife.com/community/workinginworld/blog/2009/04/01/second-life-lives-behind-a-firewall

Lipman-Blumen, J., & Leavitt, H. J. (1999). *Hot groups: Seeding Them, Feeding Them, and Using Them to Ignite Your Organization*. Oxford, UK: Oxford University Press.

Livingstone, D. & J. Kemp (2006). Massively Multi-Learner: Recent Advances in 3D Social Environments. *Computing and Information Systems Journal 10*(2).

Locklee, B., Moore, M., & Burton, J. (2002). Measuring Success: Evaluation Strategies for Distance Education. *EDUCAUSE Quarterly*, *1*, 20–26.

Long, M. (1983). Native speaker/non-native speakers conversation and the negotiation of comprehensible input. *Applied Linguistics*, *4*(2), 126–141. doi:10.1093/applin/4.2.126

Long, M. (1985). Input and second language acquisition theory . In Gass, S., & Madden, C. (Eds.), *Input in second language acquisition* (pp. 177–393). Rowley, MA: Newbury House Publishers, Inc.

Long, M. (1996). The role of the linguistic environment in second language acquisition . In Ritchie, W., & Bhatia, T. (Eds.), *Handbook of second language acquisition* (pp. 413–468). San Diego, CA: Academic. doi:10.1016/B978-012589042-7/50015-3

Long, S., Aust, D., Abowd, G. D., & Atkeson, C. (1996). Cyberguide: Prototyping Context-aware Mobile Applications. In *CHI '96 Conference Companion*, pp.293-294.

Loomis, J. M., Golledge, R. G., & Klatzky, R. L. (2001). GPS-Based Navigation System for the Visually Impaired . In Barfield, W., & Caudell, T. (Eds.), *Fundamentals of Wearable Computers and Augmented Reality* (pp. 429–446). Mahwah, NJ: Lawrence Erbaum Associates.

Luria, A. R. (1976). *The cognitive development: Its cultural and social foundations*. Boston: Harvard University Press.

Lynch, K. (1960). *The Image of the City*. Cambridge, MA: MIT Press.

Mack, C. (n.d.). SmallWorlds grows bigger with hi5. *Inside social games; tracking innovation at the convergence of games and social platforms*. Retrieved November 12th, 2009, from http://www.insidesocialgames.com/2009/06/11/smallworlds-grows-bigger-with-hi5/

Madsen, K.A., Yen, Wlasiuk, S.L., Newman, T.B., & Lustig, R. (2007). Feasibility of a dance videogame to promote weight loss among overweight children and adolescents. *Archives of Pediatrics & Adolescent Medicine*, *161*(1), 105–107. doi:10.1001/archpedi.161.1.105-c

Makena Technologies, Inc. (2010). *There*. Retrieved January 24, 2010, from http://www.there.com/

Mangold, K. (2007). Educating a new generation: Teaching baby boomer faculty about millennial students. *Nurse Educator*, *32*(1), 21–23. doi:10.1097/00006223-200701000-00007

Martinez, M. (2003). High Attrition Rates in E-Learning: Challenges, Predictors, and Solutions. *The E-Learning Developers' . Journal*, *14*(1).

Massey, A. P., Montoya-Weiss, M. M., & O'Driscoll, T. M. (2005). Human Performance Technology and Knowledge Management: A Case Study. *Performance Improvement Quarterly*, *18*(2), 37–55.

Mathers, D. (2006). *Virtual clinical Excursions – for Black and Hawks Medical-Surgical Nursing: Clinical Management for Positive Outcomes* (7th ed.). Philadelphia: Elsevier-Saunders.

Mathsigner (2009). Retrieved from http://idealab.tech.purdue.edu/Mathsigner/Home.html

Matthews, V. (2008). Generation Z: New kids on the virtual block. *Personnel Today*. Retrieved November 12, 2009, from http://www.personneltoday.com/articles/2008/09/14/47303/generation-z-new-kids-on-the-virtual-block.html

Matzen, N., & Edmunds, J. (2007). Technology as a catalyst for change: The role of professional development. *Journal of Research on Technology in Education, 4*(39), 417–430.

Mayer, R. E. (2004). Should there be a three-strikes rule against pure discovery learning? The case for guided methods of instruction. *The American Psychologist, 59*(1), 14–19. doi:10.1037/0003-066X.59.1.14

McArdle & Bertolotto. (2010). (in press). *Assessing the Application of 3D Collaborative Technologies within an E-Learning Environment, Interactive Learning Environments*. Boca Raton . *FL:Taylor & Francis*.

McInnerney, J., & Roberts, T. (2004). Online Learning: Social Interaction and the Creation of a Sense of Community. *Journal of Educational Technology & Society, 7*(3), 73–81.

McKay, S. M., van Schie, J., & Headley, S. (2008). Embarking on an educational journey in Second Life. In K. McFerrin, R. Weber, R. Carlsen, & D. A. Willis (Eds.), *Proceedings of the Society for Information Technology and Teacher Education International Conference 2008* (pp. 1762-1766). Chesapeake, VA: Association for the Advancement of Computers in Education.

McLellan, H. (1996). Virtual realities . In Jonassen, D. (Ed.), *Handbook of research for educational communications and technology*. New York: Macmillan.

McLoughlin, C. (2002). Learner support in distance and networked learning environments: Ten dimensions for successful design. *Distance Education, 23*(2), 149–162. doi:10.1080/0158791022000009178

McLoughlin, C. (1999). Scaffolding: Applications to learning in technology supported environments. In B. Collis & R. Oliver (Eds.), *Proceedings of World Conference on Educational Multimedia, Hypermedia, and Telecommunications 1999* (pp. 1827-1832). Charlottesville, VA: Association for the Advancement of Computers in Education.

McLoughlin, C., & Lee, M. J. W. (2010). Personalised and self-regulated learning in the Web 2.0 era: International exemplars of innovative pedagogy using social software. *Australasian Journal of Educational Technology, 26*(1), 28-43. Retrieved August 26, 2010, from http://www.ascilite.org.au/ajet/ajet26/mcloughlin.pdf

McMahan, A. (2003). Immersion, engagement and presence: A method for analyzing 3D video games . In Wolf, M. J. P., & Perron, B. (Eds.), *The video game theory reader* (pp. 67–86). New York: Routledge.

McPherson, C., Glazebrook, C., Forster, D., James, C., & Smyth, A. (2006). A randomized, controlled trial of an interactive educational computer package for children with asthma. *Pediatrics, 117*(4), 1046–1054. doi:10.1542/peds.2005-0666

Mercer, N. (1995). *The guided construction of knowledge: Talk amongst teachers and learners*. Clevedon: Multilingual Matters.

Mertens, S. B., & Flowers, N. (2004). Research summary: Professional development for teachers. *National Middle School Association*. Retrieved from http://www.nmsa.org/ Research/ResearchSummaries/ Summary22/tabid/249/Default.aspx

Messinger, P., Stroulia, E., & Lyons, K. (2008). A Typology of Virtual Worlds: Historical Overview and Future Directions. *Journal of Virtual Worlds Research, 1*(1). Retrieved from http://journals.tdl.org/jvwr/article/view/291.

Michael, D., & Chen, S. (2006). *Serious games: Games that educate, train and inform*. Boston: Thomson Course Technology.

Michael, J. A., Richardson, D., Rovick, A., Modell, H., Bruce, D., & Horwitz, B. (1999). Undergraduate students' misconceptions about respiratory physiology. *Advances in Physiology Education, 22*(1), 127–135.

Millrood, R. P. (2002). Discourse for teaching purposes. In Research Methodology: Discourse in Teaching A Foreign Language. Tambov: Tambov State University Press.

Mills, C., & Dalgarno, B. (2007). A conceptual model for game-based intelligent tutoring systems. In R. Atkinson & C. McBeath (Eds.), *ICT: Providing choices for learners and learning. Proceedings of the 24th ASCILITE Conference* (pp. 692-702). Singapore: Nanyang Technological University. Retrieved January 19, 2010, from http://www. ascilite.org.au/conferences/singapore07/procs/mills.pdf

Miner, N., & Hofmann, J. (2009) It's [Not] The Technology Stupid. *American Society for Training and Development.* Retrieved from http://www.astd.org/lc/2009/0309_hofmann.html

Ministry of Education. (2004). *Framework for the new 2006 "A" Level curriculum.* Retrieved April 11, 2005, from http://www.moe.gov.sg/corporate/preu_01.htm

Minocha, S., & Tingle, R. (2008). Socialisation and Collaborative Learning of Distance learners in 3-D Virtual Worlds. *Proceedings from Researching Learning in Virtual Environments International Conference (reLIVE 08)*, November 20-21. The Open University, UK. Retrieved from http://www.open.ac.uk/relive08/documents/ReLIVE08_conference_proceedings.pdf

Minsky, M. (1980). Telepresence. *Omni*, June, 45-52.

Misconception (2009). *The American Heritage Dictionary of the English Language*, Fourth Edition. Boston: Houghton Mifflin Company.

Mitchell, M. (2009). *Complexity: A Guided Tour* (p. 15). Oxford, UK: Oxford University Press.

Mitchell, A., & Savill-Smith, C. (2004). *The use of computer and video games for learning: A review of the literature.* Retrieved January 13, 2010, from http://www. LSDA.org.uk.

Miyake, Y., Yohei, O., & Ernst, P. (2004). Two Types of Anticipation in Synchronization Tapping. *Acta Neurobiol, 64*, 415–426.

Mofobian, B. (2009). Bubbles mofobian: A triumph of the human spirit. *Scene in smallworlds.* Retrieved from http://www.smallworlds.com/

Moher, T. (2006). Embedded phenomena: Supporting science learning with classroom-sized distributed simulations. In *the proceedings of CHI 2006: Conference on Human Factors in Computing Systems* (pp. 691 – 700). Quebec, Canada.

Monahan, T., McArdle, G., & Bertolotto, M. (2008). Virtual Reality for Collaborative E-Learning. [Elsevier Science.]. *Journal of Computers and Education, 50*(4), 1339–1353. doi:10.1016/j.compedu.2006.12.008

Montello, D. R. (1993). Scale and multiple phychologies of space . In Frank, A., & Campari, I. (Eds.), *Spatial Information Theory: A theoretical basis for GIS* (pp. 312–321). New York: Springer.

Montoya, M., Massey, A., & Ketter, P. (moderator). (Recorded February 3, 2009). *Virtual Presence in Virtual Worlds. What it Means for Online Training* [webinar]. Retrieved from https://astdevents.webex.com/ec06051/eventcenter/recording/recordAction.do?siteurl=astdevents&theAction=archive

Moore, M. G., & Kearsley, G. (2005). *Distance Education: A Systems View* (2nd ed.). Belmont, CA: Wadsworth.

Morie, J. F. (2009, January 22). Re-Entry: Online virtual worlds as a healing space for veterans. *Proceedings of the Society for Photo-Instrumentation Engineers, 7238,* http://ict.usc.edu/files/publications/Morie-2009-2SPIE-FINAL.pdf.

Mowlds, F., Roche, B., & Mangina, E. (2005). ABITS: Learning More about Students through Intelligent Educational Software. *Campus-Wide Information Systems, 22*(3), 131–139. doi:10.1108/10650740510606126

MPK20. Sun's virtual workspace. Retrieved from http://research.sun.com/projects/mc/mpk20.html

Nadler, D. (2008). Exergaming: Cardiovascular fitness in immersive virtual environments. *Learning & Leading with Technology. International Society for Technology in Education*, 28 – 29.

Naef, M., Staadt, O., & Gross, M. (2002). Spatialized audio rendering for immersive virtual environments. In *the proceedings of the VRST '02: Virtual Reality Software and Technology* (pp. 65 - 72). Hong Kong.

National Research Council. (2000). *How people learn: Brain, mind, experience, and school*. Washington, DC: National Academy Press.

National Research Council. (2001). *Knowing what students know: The science and design of educational assessment*. Washington, DC: National Academy Press.

National Research Council. (2005). *How students learn: History, mathematics, and science in the classroom*. Washington, DC: National Academies Press.

National Research Council. (2009). *Computational Technology for Effective Care: Immediate Steps and Strategic Directions*. Washington, DC: National Academies Press.

Neal, L. (Interviewer) & Dublin, L. (Interviewee). Five Questions... for Lance Dublin. (2006). *eLearn Magazine* [Interview Transcript]. Retrieved from http://elearnmag.org/subpage.cfm?section=articles&article=41-1

Neuenhausen, B. (2004). *Bildung in der Digitale. Zur Bildungsrelevanz virtueller Welten. (Education in the digital. Concerning the relevance of virtual worlds for education.)*. Frankfurt am Main: Peter Lang.

New England Business Bulletin. (2009, May 22). *New Corporate training options include virtual worlds*. Retrieved from http://www.southcoasttoday.com/apps/pbcs.dll/article?AID=/20090522/NEBULLETIN/906010309

New Media Consortium. (2007). *Spring 2007 survey of educators in Second Life*. Retrieved November 13th, 2009, from http://www.nmc.org/pdf/2007-sl-survey-summary.pdf

New Media Consortium. (2008). *2008 NMC Educators in Second Life Survey*. Retrieved 2 May, 2009, from http://www.nmc.org/publications

New Media Consortium. (2009). *Immersive learning initiative*. Retrieved 2 January, 2009, from http://www.nmc.org/initiatives/immersive-learning

Nicole, K. (2008). SmallWorlds has virtual Flickr posters, YouTube tv, and more. *Mashable; the social media guide*. Retrieved November 12th, 2009, from http://mashable.com/2008/05/21/smallworld/

Nielsen, J. (1993). *Usability Engineering*. San Francisco: Morgan Kaufmann Publishers Inc. Redfern, S. & Naughton, N. (2002). Collaborative Virtual Environments to Support Communication and Community in Internet-Based Distance Education. *Journal of Information Technology Education*, *1*(3), 201–211.

Noma, H., & Miyasato, T. (1998). Design for Locomotion Interface in a Large Scale Virtual Environment. *ATLAS: ATR Locomotion Interface for Active Self Motion ASME-DSC*, *64*, 111–118.

O'Brien, L. (2005). The game advances in ultrarealistic simulation let soldiers experience the war in Iraq—before they go. *SF Weekly*. Retrieved from http://www.forterrainc.com/index.php/resources/white-papers-a-articles/70-asymmetric-warfare

O'Reilly, T. (2005). What is Web 2.0. *O'Reilly Network*. Retrieved January 24, 2010, http://oreilly.com/web2/archive/what-is-web-20.html

Oblinger, D. (2003). *Boomers & Gen-Xers, Millennials: Understanding the "New Students"*. EDUCAUSE Review. July/August.

Ojstersek, N., & Kerres, M. (2008). Lernen in Second Life betreuen. (Supervising learning in Second Life.). In Hohenstein, A., & Wilbers, K. (Eds.), *Handbuch E-Learning (Handbook E-Learning) (Kap. 4.31, 25. Erg.-Lfg Juli 2008)*. Köln, Germany: Verlag Deutscher Wirtschaftsdienst.

Oliver, M., & Carr, D. (2009). Learning in virtual worlds: Using communities of practice to explain how people learn from play. *British Journal of Educational Technology*, *40*(3), 445–457. doi:10.1111/j.1467-8535.2009.00948.x

Ormrod, J. E. (1995). *Educational psychology: Principles and applications*. Upper Saddle River, NJ: Prentice Hall.

Ozmen, H. (2004). Some student misconceptions in chemistry: A literature review of chemical bonding. *Journal of Science Education and Technology*, *13*(2), 147–159. doi:10.1023/B:JOST.0000031255.92943.6d

P.L. 105-304. (1998). *Digital Millennium Copyright Act*. Retrieved on November 12th, 2009, from http://www.copyright.gov/legislation/dmca.pdf

Padden, C., & Ramsey, C. (2000). American Sign Language and reading ability. In C.

Pakstas, A. (2009). MPEG-4 Facial Animation: The Standard, Implementation and Applications. Adobe Digital Editions. Prinz, P. (2002). Cross-linguistic perspectives on sign language and literacy development. In Schulmeister, R., & Reinitzer, H. (Eds.), *Progress in sign language research: In honor of Siegmund Prillwitz* (pp. 221–233). Hamburg: Signum.

Palfrey, J., & Gasser, U. (2008). *Born digital*. Philadelphia, PA: Basic Books.

Palincsar, A. S. (1986). The role of dialogue in providing scaffolded instruction. *Educational Psychologist*, *21*(1/2), 73–98. doi:10.1207/s15326985ep2101&2_5

Parry, M. (2009). Case Western Reserve U. Debuts Private Version of Second Life. *The Chronicle of Higher Education*. Retrieved from http://chronicle.com/wiredcampus/article/3758/case-western-debuts- private-version-of-second-life

Patel, V. L., Yoskowitz, N. A., Arocha, J. F., & Shortliffe, E. H. (2009). Cognitive and learning sciences in biomedical and health instructional design: A review with lessons for biomedical informatics educaiotn. *Journal of Biomedical Informatics*, *42*, 176–197. doi:10.1016/j.jbi.2008.12.002

Pätzold, H. (2007). E-Learning 3-D – welches Potenzial haben virtuelle 3-D-Umgebungen für das Lernen mit neuen Medien? (E-Learning 3-D – What is the potential of virtual 3-D-environments for learning with new media?) *Medienpädagogik*, Zeitschrift für Theorie und Praxis der Medienbildung (www.medienpaed.com/2007/paetzold0709.pdf)

Pausch, R., Crea, T., & Conway, M. (1992). A Literature Survey for Virtual Environments: Military Flight Simulator Visual Systems and Simulator Sickness. *Presence (Cambridge, Mass.)*, *1*(3), 344–363.

Payne, J., Keir, P., Elgoyhen, J., McLundie, M., Naef, M., Horner, M., & Anderson, P. (2008). Gameplay issues in the design of spatial 3D gestures for video games. In *the proceedings of CHI 2006: Special Interest Group in Computer Human Interface* (pp. 1217–1222). Montréal, Québec, Canada. Association of Computing Machinery.

Pea, R. D. (2004). The social and technological dimensions of scaffolding and related theoretical concepts for learning, education, and human activity. *Journal of the Learning Sciences*, *13*(3), 423–451. doi:10.1207/s15327809jls1303_6

Pearce, C. (2006, 25-27 October). *Seeing and Being Seen: Presence & Play in Online Virtual Worlds. Position Paper presented for Online, Offline & The Concept of Presence When Games and VR Collide, USC Institute for Creative Technologies*. Retrieved 12 April, 2009, from http://www.lcc.gatech.edu/~cpearce3/PearcePubs/PearcePosition.pdf

Pellerin, C. (2007). *U.S. Government presence grows in Second Life online world*. Retrieved September 14, 2009, from http://montevideo.usembassy.gov/usaweb/2007/07-234EN.shtml

Peterson, M. (2005). Learner interaction in an avatar-based virtual environment: A preliminary study. *PacCALL Journal*, *1*(1), 29–40.

Peterson, M. (2006a). Learner interaction management in an avatar and chat-based virtual world. *Computer Assisted Language Learning*, *19*(1), 79–103. doi:10.1080/09588220600804087

Peterson, M. (2004). MOO virtual worlds in CMC-based CALL: Defining an agenda for future research . In Jeong-Bae, S. (Ed.), *Computer-assisted language learning: Pedagogies and technologies* (pp. 39–59). Queensland, Australia: Asia-Pacific Association for Computer-Assisted Language Learning.

Peterson, M. (2006b). Network-based computer assisted language learning (CALL): Emergent research issues . In Yoshitomi, A., Umino, T., & Negishi, M. (Eds.), *Readings in second language pedagogy and second language acquisition* (pp. 247–262). Amsterdam: John Benjamins.

Peterson, M. (2008). Non-native speaker interaction management strategies in a network-based virtual environment. *Journal of Interactive Learning Research, 19* (1), 91-117. Abstract retrieved October 30, 2009, from http://www.editlib.org/p/21889

Petrie, H. (1995). User requirements for a GPS-based travel aid for blind people . In Gill, J. M., & Petrie, H. (Eds.), *Orientation and Navigation Systems for Blind Persons* (pp. 1–2). UK: February. RNIB.

Petschenka, A., Ojstersek, N., & Kerres, M. (2004). Lernaufgaben beim E-Learning. (Learning assignments for E-Learning.) . In Hohenstein, A., & Wilbers, K. (Eds.), *Handbuch E-Learning (Handbook E-Learning) (Kap. 4.19, 7. Erg.-Lfg. Januar 2004)*. Köln, Germany: Fachverlag Deutscher Wirtschaftsdienst.

Pew Research Center. (2007). *How Young People View Their Lives, Futures and Politics: A Portrait of Generation next*. Retrieved October 5, 2009, from http://people-press.org/report/300/a-portrait-of-generation-next

Peyton, J. K. (1999). Theory and research: Interaction via computers . In Egbert, J., & Hanson-Smith, E. (Eds.), *CALL environments: Research, practice and critical issues* (pp. 17–26). Alexandria, VA: TESOL.

Phillips, R. (1998). Models of learning appropriate to educational applications of information technology. In B. Black & N. Stanley (Eds.), *Teaching and learning in changing times. Proceedings of the Seventh Annual Teaching Learning Forum* (pp. 264-268). Perth: The University of Western Australia. Retrieved December 19, 2009, from http://lsn.curtin.edu.au/tlf/tlf1998/phillips.html

Piaget, J. (1973). *To understand is to invent: The future of education*. New York: Grossman.

Piaget, J. (1955). *The construction of reality in the child (Trans. M. Cook)*. Routledge and Kegan Paul.

Pica, T. (1985). The selective impact of classroom instruction on second language acquisition. *Applied Linguistics, 6*, 214–222. doi:10.1093/applin/6.3.214

Pica, T., Holliday, L., Lewis, N., & Morgenthaler, L. (1989). Comprehensible output as an outcome of linguistic demands on the learner. *Studies in Second Language Acquisition, 11*(1), 63–90. doi:10.1017/S027226310000783X

Pica, T. (1996). Second language learning through interaction: Multiple perspectives. *Working Papers in Educational Linguistics, 12*, 1-22.

Pilling-Cormick, J., & Garrison, D. R. (2007). Self-directed and self-regulated learning: Conceptual links. *Canadian Journal of University Continuing Education, 33*(2), 13–33.

Prensky, M. (2001). *Digital game-based learning*. New York: McGraw-Hill.

Prensky, M. (2006). *Don't bother me mom – I'm learning: How computer and video games are preparing your children for twenty-first century success – and how you can help*. New York: Paragon House.

Presenccia (2006). Presence: Research encompassing sensory enhancement,neuroscience, cerebral-computer interfaces and applications. *European Sixth Framework Program, Future and Emerging Technologies*. Retrieved on 1 May 2009 from http://www.presenccia.org/

Privantu, R. (2007). *Tips on developing an MMO economy, part I. DevMaster.net*. Retrieved on November 11th, 2009, from http://www.devmaster.net/articles/mmo-economy/part1.php

Project Wonderland. Toolkit for Building 3D Virtual Worlds. Retrieved from http://developers.sun.com/learning/javaoneonline/2008/pdf/TS-6125.pdf

Pulley, J. (2007). Serious games. *Health IT, 2*(2).

Puntambekar, S., & Hubscher, R. (2005). Tools for scaffolding students in a complex learning environment: What have we gained and what have we missed? *Educational Psychologist, 40*(1), 1–12. doi:10.1207/s15326985ep4001_1

Quality Education for Minorities Network. (1992). *Together we can make it work: A national agenda to provide quality education for minorities in mathematics, science, and engineering*. Washington, D.C.: QEM Network.

Quest Atlantis. (n.d.). *Learning gains*. Retrieved January 24, 2010, from http://atlantis.crlt.indiana.edu/#66

Raschke, M. (2007). *Im Computerspiel bin ich der Held'. Wie virtuelle Welten die Identitätsentwicklung von Jugendlichen beeinflussen. („In computer games I am the hero". How virtual worlds contribute to the development of adolescents' identities.)*. Hamburg, Germany: Diplomica Verlag.

Raubal, M., & Worboys, M. (1999). A formal model for the process of wayfinding in built environments. In Freksa, C. & Mark, D. M.(Eds.), *Spatial Information Theory (Proceedings of COSIT 99). Springer, Berlin,* (pp. 381–399).New York: Springer.

Reich College of Education – Appalachian State University. (2005). *Conceptual Framework*. Retrieved.

Retrieved November 7, 2009, from ABI/INFORM Global. (Document ID: 1755224811).

Reuters, E. (2007). *Rival grids threaten Linden's monopoly on SL Technology*. Retrieved on August 24, 2010 from http://secondlife.reuters.com/stories/2007/09/06/rival-grids-threaten-lindens-monopoly-on-sl-technology/

Reznek, M. A., Chantal, L. R., & Krummel, T. M. (2002). Evaluation of the Educational Effectiveness of a Virtual Reality Intravenous Insertion Simulator. *Academic Emergency Medicine, 9*(11), 1319–1325. doi:10.1111/j.1553-2712.2002.tb01594.x

Ricardo, S. (2004). Vygotsky & language acquisition. Retrieved January 24, 2010, from http://www.sk.com.br/sk-vygot.html

Riedl, R., Barrett, T., Rowe, J., Smith, R., & Vinson, W. (2001). Sequence Independent Structure in Distance Learning. In *Proceedings of the Conference on Computers and Learning*, Coventry, UK, April 2 - 4.

Rieser, J. J. (1989). Access to knowledge of spatial structure at novel points of observation . *Journal of Experimental Psychology. Learning, Memory, and Cognition, 15*(6), 1157–1165. doi:10.1037/0278-7393.15.6.1157

Rittmann, T. (2008). *MMORPGs als virtuelle Welten. Immersion und Repräsentation. (MMORPGs as virtual worlds. Immersion and representation.)*. Boizenburg, Germany: Werner Hülsbusch.

Roblyer, M. D., Edwards, J., & Havriluk, M. A. (1997). *Integrating educational technology into teaching*. Upper Saddle River, NJ: Merrill.

Romano, D. M., & Brna, P. (2000). ACTIVE World: Manipulating time and point of view to promote a sense of presence in a collaborative virtual environment for training in emergency situations. In *Proceedings of the Third International Workshop on Presence (PRESENCE 2000)*. Delft, The Netherlands: Delft University of Technology. Retrieved August 23, 2008, from http://www.temple.edu/ispr/prev_conferences/proceedings/98-99-2000/2000/Romano%20and%20Brna.pdf

Rosen, L. (2010). *Rewired; understanding the igeneration and the way they learn*. New York: Palgrave Macmillan.

Rosen, J. (2006, June 27). The people formerly known as the audience. *PressThink* [web log]. Retrieved October 10, 2007, from http://journalism.nyu.edu/pubzone/weblogs/pressthink/2006/06/27/ppl_frmr.html

Rovai, A. P. (2002). Developing an instrument to measure classroom community . *The Internet and Higher Education, 5,* 197–211. doi:10.1016/S1096-7516(02)00102-1

Rowe, J., McQuiggan, S., & Lester, J. (2007). Narrative presence in intelligent learning environments. *Working Notes of the 2007 AAAI Symposium on Intelligent Narrative Technologies* (pp.126-133). Washington, DC.

Ruben, D. (1999). Simulations, games, and experience-based learning: The quest for a new paradigm for teaching and learning. *Health Education Research . Theory into Practice, 30*(4), 498–505.

Ryan, M. (2008). 16 ways to use virtual worlds in your classroom: pedagogical applications of Second Life. *Proceedings from Researching Learning in Virtual Environments International Conference (reLIVE 08),* November 20-21. The Open University, UK. Retrieved from http://www.open.ac.uk/relive08/documents/ ReLIVE08_conference_proceedings.pdf

Sabelman, E. E., Burgar, C. G., Curtis, G. E., Goodrich, G., Jaffe, D. L., Mckinley, J. L., et al. (1994). Personal navigation and wayfinding for individuals with a range of disabilities, Project *report: Device development and evaluation.* http://guide.stanford.edu/Publications/dev3.html.

Sadowski, C. J., & Gülöz, S. (1996). Elaborative Processing mediates the relationship between need for cognition and academic performance. *The Journal of Psychology, 130*(3), 303–307. doi:10.1080/00223980.1996.9915011

Sadowski, W., & Stanney, K. (2002). Measuring and Managing Presence in Virtual Environments . In Stanney, K. (Ed.), *Handbook of virtual world environments technology* (pp. 791–806). Mahwah, New Jersey: Lawrence Erlbaum Associates.

Salmon, G. (2009, May). The future for (second) life and learning. *British Journal of Educational Technology, 40*(3), 526–538. doi:10.1111/j.1467-8535.2009.00967.x

San Chee, Y. (2001). Networked Virtual Environments for Collaborative Learning. *in Proceedings of ICCE/School-Net: the 9th International Conference on Computers in Education* (p. 311), Seoul, South Korea, November 11 - 14.

San Chee, Y., & Hooi, C. (2002). C-VISions: Socialized Learning through Collaborative, Virtual, Interactive Simulations. In *Proceedings of Computer Supported Collaborative Learning (CSCL)* (pp.687-696), Boulder, Colorado, USA, January 7 - 11.

Sánchez, J., & Sáenz, M. (2005). 3D sound interactive environments for problem solving. *ASSETS '05: The Seventh International ACM SIGACCESS Conference on Computers and Accessibility* (pp. 173 - 179). Baltimore, Maryland, USA.

Sandberg, J., & Wielinga, B. (1992). Situated cognition: A paradigm shift? *Journal of Artificial Intelligence in Education, 3*(2), 129–138.

Sanders, D., & Welk, D. S. (2005). Strategies to scaffold faculty facilitator learning: Applying Vygotsky's Zone of Proximal Development. *Nurse Educator, 30*(5), 203–207. doi:10.1097/00006223-200509000-00007

Sanders, R. L., & McKeown, L. (2007). Promoting reflection through action learning in a 3D virtual world. *International Journal of Social Science, 2*(1), 50-55. Retrieved November 8, 2009, from http://www.waset.ac.nz/journals/ijss/v2/v2-1-8.pdf

Sanders, R., Bronack, S., Riedl, R., Cheney, A., Matzen, N., Rhyne, S., et al. (2008, March). *The digital native best practice design project.* Presentation at the Teaching and Learning with Technology Conference, Raleigh, NC.

Sanne, M. B., Botden, I., & Jakimowicz, J. J. (2009). What is going on in augmented reality simulation in laparoscopic surgery? *Surgical Endoscopy, 23*(8), 1693–1700. doi:10.1007/s00464-008-0144-1

Savery, J., & Duffy, T. (1995). Problem based learning: An instructional model and its constructivist framework. *Educational Technology, 35*(5), 31–38.

Saye, J. W., & Brush, T. (2002). Scaffolding critical reasoning about history and social issues in multimedia-supported learning environments. *Educational Technology Research and Development, 50*(3), 77–96. doi:10.1007/BF02505026

Schachter, J. (1986). Three approaches to the study of input. *Language Learning, 36,* 211–225. doi:10.1111/j.1467-1770.1986.tb00379.x

Schachter, J. (1983). Nutritional needs of language learners . In Clarke, M., & Handscombe, J. (Eds.), *On TESOL '82* (pp. 175–189). Washington, DC: TESOL.

Schachter, J. (1984). A universal input condition . In Rutherford, W. (Ed.), *Universals and second language acquisition* (pp. 167–183). Amsterdam: John Benjamins.

Schiller, S. (2009). Practicing learner-centered teaching: Pedagogical design and assessment of a Second Life project. *Journal of Information Systems Education, 20*(3), 369-381. Retrieved November 7, 2009, from ABI/INFORM Global. (Document ID: 1870617241).

Schmeil, A., & Eppler, M. J. (2009). Knowledge sharing and collaborative learning in Second Life. *Journal of Universal Computer Science, 15*(3), 665–677.

Schmeil, A., & Eppler, M. J. (2008). Collaboration patterns for knowledge sharing and integration in Second Life: A classification of virtual 3D group interaction scripts. *Proceedings I-KNOW 08,* Graz, Austria.

Schmidt, F. A. (2006). *Parallel Realitäten. (Parallel realities.).* Sulgen, Switzerland: Niggli.

Schön, B., & O'Hare, G. M. P. (2008). Navigational Support Methodologies for 3D Virtual Worlds. In *Proceedings of the 21ˢᵗ Annual Conference on Computer Animation and Social Agents (CASA 2008),* Seoul . *Korea & World Affairs,* (September): 1–3.

Schön, B., O'Hare, G. M. P., Duffy, B., Martin, A., & Bradley, J. (2005). The AMPERE algorithm – Area-Based Masking with the PERformance Equation. *In Proceedings of FLAIRS 2005, AAAI,* Clearwater Beach, Florida, USA, May 15 - 17

Schrock, K. (No Date). Message posted to http://www. hotchalk.com/mydesk/index. php/editorial/44-online-professional-development/86- second-life-interactive-professional-development-pt-1

Schubert, T., Friedmann, F., & Regenbrecht, H. (1999). Embodied presence in virtual environments . In Paton, R., & Neilson, I. (Eds.), *Visual representations and interpretations* (pp. 269–278). London: Springer.

Schuemie, M., van der Straaten, P., Krijn, M., & van der Mast, C. (2001). Research on presence in virtual reality: A survey. *Cyber psychology and behavior, 4* (2). Retrieved June 2, 2007, from http://graphics.tudelft.nl/~vrphobia/surveypub.pdf.

Schulmeister (1996). *Grundlagen hypermedialer Lernsysteme. (Basic principles of hypermedial learning systems.)* München, Germany: Oldenbourg.

Schultheis, M., & Rizzo, A. (2001). The application of virtual reality technology for rehabilitation. *Rehabilitation Psychology, 46*(3), 296–311. doi:10.1037/0090-5550.46.3.296

Science Daily. (2008, October 31). *Researchers Find New Way of Measuring 'Reality' of Virtual Worlds.* Retrieved from http://www.sciencedaily.com/releases/2008/10/081029084038.htm

SciVal. (2009). *Unlock the promise of your research.* Retrieved December 31, 2009, from http://www.scival.com/

Second Life Blogs. 2009 end of year Second Life economy wrap up (including Q4 economy in detail. Retrieved August 24ᵗʰ, 2010, from http://blogs.secondlife.com/community/features/blog/2010/01/19/2009-end-of-year-second-life-economy-wrap-up-including-q4-economy-in-detail

Second Life. (2009). *Linden's Second Life.* Retrieved September 23, 2009, from http://www.secondlife.com

Secondlifegrid.net (2009) Retrieved on November 12ᵗʰ, 2009, from http://secondlifegrid.net/slfe/education-use-virtual-world

Selfe, C. L., & Hawisher, G. E. (2007). *Gaming lives in the twenty-first century – Literate connections. New Yor.* Palgrave Macmillan. doi:10.1057/9780230601765

Semwal, S. K., & Evans-Kamp, D. L. (2000). *Virtual environments for visually impaired*. Paper presented at the 2nd International Conference on Virtual worlds, Paris, France.

Serwatka, J. A. (2005). Improving Retention in Distance Learning Classes. *International Journal of Instructional Technology and Distance Learning, 2*(1), 59–64.

Shaffer, D. W. (2006). Epistemic frames for epistemic games. *Computers & Education, 46*, 223–224. doi:10.1016/j.compedu.2005.11.003

Shaffer, D. W. (2007). *How computer games help children learn*. New York: Palgrave Macmillan Ltd.

Shaffer, D., & Gee, J. (2006). *How computer games help children learn*. New York: Palgrave McMillan. doi:10.1057/9780230601994

Shaffer, D. W. (2006). *How computer games help children learn*. New York: Palgrave Macmillan. doi:10.1057/9780230601994

Sharma, P., & Hannafin, M. J. (2007). Scaffolding in technology-enhanced learning environments. *Interactive Learning Environments, 15*(1), 27–46. doi:10.1080/10494820600996972

Shen, J., & Eder, L. (2009). Intentions to use virtual worlds for education. *Journal of Information Systems Education, 20*(2), 225–233.

Sheridan, T. (1992). Musings on telepresence and virtual presence. *Presence (Cambridge, Mass.), 1*(1), 120–125.

Sherin, B., Reiser, B. J., & Edelson, D. (2004). Scaffolding analysis: Extending the scaffolding metaphor to learning artifacts. *Journal of the Learning Sciences, 13*(3), 387–421. doi:10.1207/s15327809jls1303_5

Shiau, T. F. (2009). *Readers Theater in the virtual classroom: A case study of three sixth-grade readers*. Unpublished master's thesis, National Dong Hwa University, Hualien, Taiwan.

Shields, R. (2003). *The Virtual*. London: Routledge.

Shih, Y. C. (2009). An innovative approach to task design and implementation in multimodal collaborative virtual environments. *The JALT CALL Journal, 5*(1), 61–73.

Shih, Y. C., & Yang, M. T. (2008). A collaborative virtual environment for situated language learning using VEC3D. [SSCI]. *Journal of Educational Technology & Society, 11*(1), 56–68.

Shih, Y. C. (2003). 3D virtual immersion English learning experiences: College student views of their needs and challenges. *Proceedings of APAMALL 2003 and ROCMELIA 2003* (pp. 385-394). Paper presented at The Seventh International Conference on Multimedia Language Education of ROCMELIA, National Chia Yi University, December 19-21.

Shih, Y. C. (2010). *VEC3D Home page*. Retrieved January 24, 2010, from http://faculty.ndhu.edu.tw/~vec3d/

Sibert, L., Templeman, J., Page, R., Barron, J., McCune, J., & Denbrook, P. (2004). *Initial Assessment of Human Performance Using the Gaiter Interaction Technique to Control Locomotion in Fully Immersive Virtual Environments. (Technical Report)*. Washington, D.C: Naval Research Laboratory.

Siegel, A. W., & White, S. H. (1975). The development of spatial representations of large-scale environments . In Rees, H. W. (Ed.), *Advances in child development and behavior (Vol. 10*, pp. 9–55). New York: Academic Press.

Signing Science. (2007). Retrieved from http://signsci.terc.edu/

Sim, O. (2009). *Grid list*. Retrieved November 13th, 2009, from http://opensimulator.org/wiki/Grid_List

Simons, P. R.-J. (1992). Constructive learning: The role of the learner . In Duffy, T. M., Lowyck, J., Jonassen, D. H., & Welsh, T. M. (Eds.), *Designing environments for constructive learning* (pp. 291–313). Berlin: Springer-Verlag.

Simons, J. A., Irwin, D. B., & Drinnien, B. A. (1987). Maslow's hierarchy of needs. *Psychology—The Search for Understanding*. New York: West Publishing Company. Retrieved Dec. 11, 2009, from http://honolulu.hawaii.edu/intranet/committees/FacDevCom/guidebk/teachtip/maslow.htm.

Sims, E. M. (2007). Reusable, lifelike virtual humans for mentoring and role-playing. *Computers & Education*, *49*(1), 75–92. doi:10.1016/j.compedu.2005.06.006

Sims, E. (2000). *SigningAvatars. Final Report for SBIR Phase II Project, U*. S. Department of Education.

SimTeach. (2007). *Institutions and organizations in SL*. Retrieved January 24, 2010, from http://www.simteach.com/wiki/index.php?title=Institutions_and_Organizations_in_SL

SimTeach. (2008a). *Second Life Education Wiki*. Retrieved January 24, 2010, from http://www.simteach.com/wiki/index.php?title=Second_Life_Education_Wiki

SimTeach. (2008b). *Top 20 Educational Locations in Second Life*. Retrieved January 24, 2010, from http://www.simteach.com/wiki/index.php?title=Top_20_Educational_Locations_in_Second_Life

Sinclair, B., & Ferguson, K. (2009). Integrating simulated teaching/learning strategies in undergraduate nursing education. *Int J Nurs Educ Scholarsh., 6* (1), Article 7.

Slater, M., Usoh, M., & Steed, A. (1995). Taking Steps: The Influence of a Walking Metaphor on Presence in Virtual Reality. *ACM Transactions on Computer-Human Interaction, 2*(3), 201–219. doi:10.1145/210079.210084

Slator, B. M. (1999) Intelligent Tutors in Virtual Worlds. In *Proceedings of the 8th International Conference on Intelligent Systems (ICIS-99)*. June 24-26. Denver, CO: 124-127.

Slator, B. M., & Chaput, H. (1996). Learning by Learning Roles: A Virtual Role-Playing Environment for Tutoring. In *Proceedings of the Third International Conference on Intelligent Tutoring Systems (ITS'96)*. Montréal: Springer-Verlag, June 12-14, (pp. 668-676). (Lecture Notes in Computer Science, edited by C. Frasson, G. Gauthier, A. Lesgold).

Slator, B. M., Chaput, H., Cosmano, R., Ben Dischinger, C. I., & Vender, B. (2006). A Multi-User Desktop Virtual Environment for Teaching Shop-Keeping to Children. *Virtual Reality Journal, 9*, pp. 49-56. Springer-Verlag. LambdaMOO version of Virtual Cell (thesis and/or other papers).

SLED. (Second Life Educators electronic mailing list), archived at http://tinyurl.com/y234ht

SLED/ Partridge, W. (2009b, April 6). Thinking worlds—immersive learning simulations via Shockwave.

SLED/Freese, W. (2009, March 13). Teaching Early Childhood Education.

SLED/Holt. D. (2009, February 23). Re: Playing Devil's Advocate: SL vs Virtual Worlds vs Better Learning: Second Life Educators electronic mailing list), archived at http://tinyurl.com/y234ht

SLED/Loon. R. (2009a, February 26). Re: Playing Devil's Advocate: SL vs Virtual Worlds vs Better Learning. Second Life Educators electronic mailing list), archived at http://tinyurl.com/y234ht

SLED/Loon. R. (2009b, March 17). *Re: the meandering thoughts of a girl who has gone to the dogs, darkside of the moon, and been a lion all before lunch. . . Second Life Educators electronic mailing list*), archived at http://tinyurl.com/y234ht

SLED/Partridge, W. (2009a, March 30). audiences in sl, was Re: Opinion—Text or voice?

SLED/Tadros. M. (2009, March 31). Re: Ouch – story from the UK Telegraph. Second Life Educators electronic mailing list), archived at http://tinyurl.com/y234ht

SmallWorlds. (2009). *Current known scams*. http://forum.smallworlds.com/showthread.php?t=1973

SmallWorlds. (2009). *Gold, tokens, and VIP memberships*. http://www.smallworlds.com/?target=/2009/08/05/help-and-support/

SmallWorlds. (2009). *Internet safety guidelines*. Retrieved November 13th, 2009, from http://www.smallworlds.com/?target=/newspaper/help-tips/

SMILE. (2007). Retrieved from http://www2.tech.purdue.edu/cgt/I3/SMILE/

Sorrows, M. E., & Hirtle, S. C. (1999). The nature of landmarks in real and electronic spaces. In Freksa, C. & Mark, D. M.,(Eds.) *Spatial Information Theory (Proceedings of COSIT 99)*,(pp. 37–50), New York: Springer.

Souza, I. A., Sanches, C. Jr, & Zuffo, M. K. (2009). A virtual reality simulator for training of needle biopsy of thyroid gland nodules. *Studies in Health Technology and Informatics, 142*, 352–357.

Spencer, J. A., & Jordan, R. K. (1999). Learner centred approaches in medical education. *BMJ (Clinical Research Ed.), 318*(7193), 1280–1283.

Spencer, B. S. (2006). Incorporating the Sense of Smell Into Patient and Haptic Surgical Simulators. *IEEE Transactions on Information Technology in Biomedicine, 10*(1). doi:10.1109/TITB.2005.856851

Sprengel, D. (1994). Learning can be fun with gaming. *The Journal of Nursing Education, 33*(4), 151–152.

Squire, K. D. (2008). *Videogame literacy: A literacy of expertise. Handbook of research on new literacies* (pp. 635–669). New York: Lawrence Erlbaum Associates.

Stackpole, B. (2008, January 6). Military broadens use of virtual reality. *Design News*. Retrieved from http://www.designnews.com/article/ 7775-Military_ Broadens_Use_of_ Virtual_Reality.php

Standen, P. J., Brown, D. J., & Cromby, J. J. (2001). The effective use of virtual environments in the education and rehabilitation of students with intellectual disabilities . *British Journal of Educational Technology, 32*(3), 289–299. doi:10.1111/1467-8535.00199

Stanney, K. M., Salvendy, G., Deisigner, J., DiZio, P., Ellis, S., & Ellison, E. (1998). Aftereffects and sense of presence in virtual environments: Formulation of a research and development agenda. Report sponsored by the Life Sciences Division at NASA Headquarters. *International Journal of Human-Computer Interaction, 10*(2), 135–187. doi:10.1207/s15327590ijhc1002_3

Stapleton, A. (2004). Serious games: Serious opportunities. *In Proceedings of the 2004 Australian Game Developers Conference*,1-6, Melbourne, Australia.

Steed, R. (2009). Instruction in cultural competency in a virtual 3D world. *Journal of Interactive Instruction Development, 21*(2), 19.

Stern, S. B. (1989). Creative teaching strategies. *Journal of Continuing Education in Nursing, 33*(4), 151–152.

Steuer, J. (1992). Defining virtual reality: Dimensions determining telepresence. *The Journal of Communication, 42*(2), 73–93. doi:10.1111/j.1460-2466.1992.tb00812.x

Stevens, H., & Pettey, C. (2008, May 15). Gartner Says 90 Per Cent of Corporate Virtual World Projects Fail Within 18 Months. *Gartner*. Retrieved from http://www.gartner.com/it/page.jsp?id=670507

Stone, C. A. (1998). The metaphor of scaffolding: Its utility for the field of learning disabilities. *Journal of Learning Disabilities, 31*(4), 344–364. doi:10.1177/002221949803100404

Strauss, W., & Howe, N. (1997). *The Fourth turning: An American prophecy*. New York: Broadway Books.

Strauss, W., & Howe, N. (1991). *Generations: The history of America's future*. New York: William Morrow and Company, Inc. 1.

Strong, M., & Prinz, P. (1997). A study of the relationship between ASL and English literacy. *Journal of Deaf Studies and Deaf Education, 2*, 37–46.

Strong, M., & Prinz, P. (2000). Is American Sign Language skill related to literacy? In Chamberlain, C., Morford, J., & Mayberry, R. (Eds.), *Language acquisition by eye* (pp. 131–141). Hillsdale, NJ: Lawrence Erlbaum Associates.

Strothotte, T., Fritz, S., Michel, R., Raab, A., Petrie, H., Johnson, V., et al. (1996). Development of Dialogue Systems for the Mobility Aid for Blind People: Initial Design and Usability Testing. *ASSETS '96*, Vancouver, British Columbia, Canada, 139-144.

Stytz, M. R., Garcia, B. W., Godsell-Stytz, G. M., & Banks, S. B. (1997). A distributed virtual environment prototype for emergency medical procedures training. *Studies in Health Technology and Informatics, 39*, 473–485.

Sullins, E. S., Hernandez, D., Fuller, C., & Tashiro, J. S. (1995). Predicting who will major in a science discipline: Expectancy-value theory as part of an ecological model for studying academic communities. *Journal of Research in Science Teaching, 32*(1), 99–119. doi:10.1002/tea.3660320109

Sun, P., & Cheng, H. (2007). The Design of Instructional Multimedia in ELearning: A Media Richness Theory-based Approach. *Computers & Education, 49*(3), 662–676. doi:10.1016/j.compedu.2005.11.016

Sun Microsystems, Inc. (n.d.). *Project Wonderland*. Retrieved January 24, 2010, from http://www.project-wonderland.com/

Swain, M., & Lapkin, S. (1995). Problems in output and the cognitive processes they generate: A step towards second language learning. *Applied Linguistics, 16*, 371–391. doi:10.1093/applin/16.3.371

Swain, M. (1995). Three functions of output in second language learning . In Cook, G., & Seidelhofer, B. (Eds.), *Principle and practice in applied Linguistics: Studies in honor of H.G. Widdowson* (pp. 125–144). Oxford, UK: Oxford University Press.

Swain, M. (1985). Communicative competence: Some roles of comprehensible input and comprehensible output in its development . In Gass, S., & Madden, C. (Eds.), *Input in second language acquisition* (pp. 235–256). New York: Newbury House.

Sweller, J., van Merriënboer, J. J. G., & Paas, F. G. W. C. (1998). Cognitive architecture and instructional design. *Educational Psychology Review, 10*(3), 251–296. doi:10.1023/A:1022193728205

Talab, R., & Botterbusch, H. (2009). Ethical and legal issues in teaching and learning in second life in a graduate online course . In Russell, D. (Ed.), *Collaborative virtual learning environments; processes and interactions*. Hershey, PA: IGI Global.

Tamsyn, B. (2009, January 27). Educators reach out to more students through the virtual world. *The Globe and Mail*. Retrieved February 1, 2009, from http://www.theglobeandmail.com/life/article655208.ece

Tan, B., Aziz, A. R., Chua, K., & The, K. C. (2001). Aerobic demands of the dance simulation game. *International Journal of Sports Medicine, 23*(2), 125–129. doi:10.1055/s-2002-20132

Tang, T. Y., & McCalla, G. (2009). A multidimensional paper recommender: experiment and evaluations. *IEEE Internet Computing, 13*(4), 34–41. doi:10.1109/MIC.2009.73

Tarone, E., & Liu, G. Q. (1995). Situational context, variation, and second language acquisition theory . In Cook, G., & Seidelhofer, B. (Eds.), *Principle and practice in applied linguistics: Studies in Honor of H.G. Widdowson* (pp. 107–124). Oxford, UK: Oxford University Press.

Tashiro, J. (2009). Ethical analysis of publisher and faculty roles in building and using electronic educational products. *Journal of Electronic Commerce in Organizations, 7*(1), 1–17.

Tashiro, J., & Dunlap, D. (2007). *2007. ACM digital Library 978-1-59593-943-2/07/0011.* The Impact of Realism on Learning Engagement in Educational Games. In Proceedings of FuturePlay.

Tashiro, J. T., Sullins, E. S., & Long, G. (2003c). *Virtual clinical excursions for nursing care of infants and children*. St. Louis, MO: Mosby.

Tashiro, J. T., Sullins, E. S., & Long, G. (2003d). *Virtual clinical excursions for fundamental concepts and skills for nursing*. St. Louis, MO: Mosby.

Tashiro, J. T., Sullins, E. S., Long, G., & Kelly, M. (2001a). *Virtual clinical excursions in medical-surgical nursing: assessment and management of clinical problems*. St. Louis, MO: Mosby.

Tashiro, J. T., Sullins, E. S., Long, G., & Kelly, M. (2001b). *Virtual clinical excursions for fundamentals in nursing*. St. Louis, MO: Mosby.

Tashiro, J. T., Sullins, E. S., Long, G., & Kelly, M. (2003a). *Virtual clinical excursions medical-surgical nursing: clinical management for positive outcomes*. St. Louis, MO: Mosby.

Tashiro, J. T., Sullins, E. S., Long, G., & Kelly, M. (2003b). *Virtual clinical excursions for basic nursing: essentials for practice*. St. Louis, MO: Mosby.

Tashiro, J., & Rowland, P. McD. (1997). What works: Empirical approaches to restructuring courses in biology and environmental sciences. In McNeal, A. & D'Avanzo, C. (Eds.) *Student-active science: Models of innovation in college science teaching,* 163-187. Orlando, Fl: Harcourt Brace and Company.

Techcrunch. Retrieved November 7th, 2009, from http://www.techcrunch.com/2009/07/02/does-anybody-still-use-second-life-and-if-so-how-much-is-it-worth-today/

TERC. (2007). Retrieved from http://www.terc.edu/

Ternier, S., Verbert, K., Parra, G., Vandeputte, B., Klerkx, J., & Duval, E. (2009). The Ariadne infrastructure for managing and storing metadata. *IEEE Internet Computing, 13*(4), 18–25. doi:10.1109/MIC.2009.90

The Information Resource Management (IRM) College of the National Defense University. (2009). The federal consortium for virtual worlds. Retrieved November 8th, 2009, from http://www.youtube.com/watch?v=wKh8-QyL1Bs&feature=player_embedded

The Straits Times. (2009). Virtual worlds used to teach real life to kids. 21 May.

Theil, S. (2008). Tune in tomorrow. *Newsweek*, August 18-25 issue.

Thomas, M. (2009). A review of Edward Castronova's *Exodus to the virtual world*. *British Journal of Educational Technology, 40*(3), 575–577. doi:10.1111/j.1467-8535.2009.00969_3.x

Thomas, L. P. (2008). There's still a future for virtual worlds. *Media Bullseye*. Retrieved from http://mediabullseye.com/mb/2008/05/theres-still-a-future-for-virt.html

Thompson, D., Baranowski, J., Cullen, K., & Baranowski, T. (2007). Development of a theory-based Internet program promoting maintenance of diet and physical activity change to 8 year old African American girls. *Computers & Education, 48*(3), 446–459. doi:10.1016/j.compedu.2005.02.005

Thornbury, S. (2000). A Dogma for EFL. *IATEFL Issues, 153*, 2. Retrieved January 24, 2010, from http://www.thornburyscott.com/assets/dogma.pdf

Thornbury, S. (2005). Dogme: *Dancing in the dark?* Folio, 9/2, 3-5. Retrieved January 24, 2010, from http://www.thornburyscott.com/assets/dancing%20in%20dark.pdf

Thousands protest, sign petitions over closing of Disney online game. (2009). Retrieved November 12th, 2009, from http://www.clickorlando.com/technology/15881453/detail.html

Tobler, W. (1976). The geometry of mental maps . In Golledge, R. G., & Rushton, G. (Eds.), *Spatial choice and spatial behavior* (pp. 69–82). Columbus, OH: Ohio State University Press.

Tolman, E. (1948). Cognitive maps in rats and men. *Psychological Review, 55*, 189–208. doi:10.1037/h0061626

Tomek, I. (2001). Knowledge management and collaborative virtual environments. *Journal of Universal Computer Science, 7*(6).

Topp, R., & Din, H. W.-S. (2005). Modular small-scale media: Achieving community curation through rural Alaska. In *the proceedings of the International Conference on Computer Graphics and Interactive Techniques*. Los Angeles, California, USA. ACM.

Toyoda, E., & Harrison, R. (2002). Categorization of text chat communication between learners and native speakers of Japanese. *Language Learning and Technology, 6*(1), 82-99. Retrieved January 24, 2010, from http://llt.msu.edu/vol6num1/pdf/toyoda.pdf

TSTC takes one small step for virtual worlds, one giant leap for virtual world education. (2009). *PRWeb*. Retrieved from http://www.prweb.com/releases/TSTC/virtual_education/prweb2419874.htm

Turkle, S. (1998). Identity in the age of the Internet: Living in the MUD. R. Holeton, Ed. *Composing Cyberspace: Identity, Community, and Knowledge in the Electronic Age*. Boston: McGraw Hill. 5 – 11.

Tversky, B. (1993). Cognitive Maps, Cognitive Collages, and Spatial Mental Models. In *Spatial Information Theory. A Theoretical Basis for GIS, COSIT'93*, (pp. 14–24).

Ungar, S., & Blades, M. M., & Spencer, S (1996). The construction of cognitive maps by children with visual impairments, In J. Portugali, (Ed) *The Construction of Cognitive Maps*, pp. 247–273,The Netherlands: Kluwer Academic Publishers.

University of Utrecht. (2009). *NIFLAR Project Home Page*. Retrieved January 24, 2010, from http://cms.let.uu.nl/niflar

Unnithan, U. V., Houser, W., & Fernhall, B. (2006). Evaluation of the energy cost of playing a dance simulation video game in overweight and non-overweight children and adolescents. *International Journal of Sports Medicine, 27*(10), 804–809. doi:10.1055/s-2005-872964

van Joolingen, W. R. (1999). Cognitive tools for discovery learning. *International Journal of Artificial Intelligence in Education, 10*(3/4), 385–397.

Varela, F., Thompson, E., & Rosch, E. (1991). *The embodied mind: Cognitive science and human experience*. Cambridge, MA: MIT Press.

Vargas, J. A. (2006, February 14). Virtual Reality Prepares Soldiers for Real War. *The Washington Post*. Retrieved from http://www.washingtonpost.com/wp-dyn/content/article /2006/02/13/AR2006021302437.html

Vass, E. (2002). *Friendship and Collaborative Creative Writing in the Primary Classroom. Journal of Computer Assisted Learning, 18(1)*. New York: Blackwell Science.

Vcom3D (2007). Retrieved from http://www.vcom3d.com/

VEC3D. (2010). *Home page*. Retrieved January 24, 2010, from http://faculty.ndhu.edu.tw/~vec3d/

Vickers, H. (2007). *SurReal quests: Enriched purposeful language learning in Second Life*. Retrieved January 24, 2010, from http://www.avatarlanguages.com/articles/surrealquests1_en.php

Virtual World News. (2009a, June 26). IBM Releases Virtual Collaboration for Lotus Sametime. Retrieved from http://www.virtualworldsnews.com/2009/06/ibm-releases-virtual-collaboration-for-lotus-sametime.html

Virtual World News. (2009b, February 27). *IBM Saves $320,000 With Second Life Meeting*. Retrieved from http://www.virtualworldsnews.com/2009/02/ibm-saves-320000-with- second-life-meeting.html

Vlahos, J. (2006). The smell of war. *Popular Science*, 8.

VRML. ISO 14772:1997. See also www.web3d.org/x3d/specifications.

VU University Amsterdam. (2007). *VU Second Life*. Retrieved May 28, 2008, from http://www.vu.nl/secondlife.

Vyas, D., & van der Veer, G. C. (2006). *Rich evaluations of entertainment experience: bridging the interpretational gap.* 13th European Conference on Cognitive Ergonomics, 2006, Switzerland. (pp. 137-144).

Vygotsky, L. S. (1962). *Thought and language.* Cambridge, MA: The MIT Press. doi:10.1037/11193-000

Vygotsky, L. S. (1978). *Mind in society: The development of higher psychological processes.* Cambridge, MA: Harvard University Press.

Vygotsky, L. (1986). *Thought and language.* Cambridge, MA: The MIT Press.

Wagner, C. (2008). Learning experience with virtual worlds. *Journal of Information Systems Education, 19*(3), 263 – 266. Retrieved Nov. 22, 2009, from http://www.jise.appstate.edu/Issues/19/V19N3P263-abs.pdf.

Wagner, C., & Ip, R. (2009). Action learning with Second Life - a pilot study. *Journal of information systems education, 20*(2), 249-258. Retrieved November 7th, 2009, from ABI/INFORM Global. (Document ID: 1755224831).

Wagner, D., & Barakonyi, I. (2003). Augmented reality Kanji learning. *In Proceedings of the 2nd IEEE/ACM international Symposium on Mixed and Augmented Reality* (October 07 - 10, 2003). Symposium on Mixed and Augmented Reality. IEEE Computer Society, Washington, DC, 335.

Walker, H., & Walker, L. (1990). *Readers Theatre in the elementary classroom: A take part teacher's guide. North Vancouver, B.C.* Canada: Take Part Productions Ltd.

Walther, B. K. (2005). Atomic actions—molecular experience: Theory of pervasive gaming. *ACM Computers in Entertainment, 3*(2), 1–13.

Wang, Y., & Braman, J. (2009). Extending the classroom through second life. *Journal of Information Systems Education: 20*(2), 235 – 247. Retrieved Nov. 22, 2009, from http://www.jise.appstate.edu/Issues/20/V20N2P235-abs.pdf.

Warburton, S. (2007). *Virtual spaces, second lives: what are the potential educational benefits of MUVEs?* Retrieved December 19, 2008, from http://www.slideshare.net/stevenw/virtualspaces-second-lives-what-are-the-potential-educational-benefits-of-muves-presentation

Warburton, S. (2009). Second Life in higher education: Assessing the potential for and the barriers to deploying virtual worlds in learning and teaching. *British Journal of Educational Technology: $0*(3), 414 – 426. **doi:10.**1111/j.1467-85 35.2009.009 52.x

Warren, D., & Strelow, E. (1985). *Electronic Spatial Sensing for the Blind.* Boston: Martinus Nijhoff.

Warren, S. (2006). Researching a MUVE for teaching writing: The Anytown experience. In C. Crawford et al. (Eds.), *Proceedings of Society for Information Technology and Teacher Education International Conference 2006* (pp. 759-764). Chesapeake, VA: AACE.

Warren, S., Stein, R. A., Dondlinger, M. J., & Barab, S. A. (2008). A look inside a MUVE design process: Blending instructional design and game principles to target writing skills. *Journal of Educational Computing Research, 40*(3). Baywood Publishing Company.

Warschauer, M. (1996). *Computer-mediated collaborative learning: Theory and practice* (Research Note 17). Honolulu: University of Hawaii, Second Language Teaching Curriculum Center.

Washburn, D. A., Jones, L. M., Vijaya Satya, R., Bowers, C. A., & Cortes, A. (2003). Olfactory use in virtual environment training. *Modelling and Simulation (Anaheim), 2*(3), 19–25.

Wauters, R. (2009). Does anybody still use Second Life? And if so, how much? TechCrunch. Retrieved August 25, 2010, from http://techcrunch.com/2009/07/02/does-anybody-still-use-second-life-and-if-so-how-much-is-it-worth-today/

Weast, T. (2008) *Questions in American Sign Language: A quantitative analysis of raised and lowered eyebrows.* Doctoral dissertation, University of Texas, Arlington.

WebProNews. (2009, March 16). Retrieved from http://www.webpronews.com/topnews /2009/03/16/second-life-still- alive-and-kicking

Weimer, M. (2002). *Learner-centered teaching: Five key changes to practice*. San Francisco, CA: Jossey-Bass.

Welk, D. S. (2002). Designing clinical examples to promote pattern recognition: Nursing education-based research and practical applications. *The Journal of Nursing Education, 41*(2), 53–60.

Wells, G. (1999). *Dialogic inquiry: Towards a sociocultural practice and theory of education*. Cambridge: Cambridge University Press. doi:10.1017/CBO9780511605895

Wenger, E., McDermott, R., & Snyder, W. M. (2002). *Cultivating communities of practice: A guide to managing knowledge*. Boston: Harvard Business School Press.

Wenger, E. (1998). Communities of practice: Learning as a social system. *Systems Thinker, 9*(5), 1 - 10. Retrieved Dec. 8, 2009, from http://www.open.ac.uk/ldc08/sites/www.open.ac.uk.ldc08/files/Learningasasocialsystem.pdf.

Werner, S., Krieg-Bruckner, B., Mallot, H. A., Schweizer, K., & Freksa, C. (1997). Spatial cognition: The role of landmark, route, and survey knowledge in human and robot navigation . In Jarke, M. (Ed.), *Informatik '97 GI Jahrestagung* (pp. 41–50). New York: Springer.

Werner, T. (2008a). *Travels with Tom*. Retrieved from http://www.slideshare.net/twerner/travels- with-tom-workplacerelated-places-in-second- life-presentation

Werner, T. (2008b, July 10). *Canadian border-guard training in Second Life*. Message posted to http://brandon-hall.com/tomwerner/?p=338

Werner, T. (2009, March 29). Using Second Life for workplace learning. *Brandon Hall Research Presentation*. Retrieved from http://www.slideshare.net/twerner/using- second-life-for- workplace-learning-032509?type=powerpoint

Wetherell, M. Taylor, S. & Yates, S. (2001). *Discourse theory and practice*. London: Sage.

What does it cost to use a virtual world learning environment? (2008, November). *T+D*, p. 88.

Wheeler, M. (2009). Developing the Media Zoo in Second Life. *British Journal of Educational Technology, 40*(3). New York: Blackwell Publishing.

White, D. (2008, September 9–11). From swords to hairstyles; bridging the divide between massively multilayer game design and Second Life. Paper presented at *ALT-C 2008 Conference Introduction and Abstracts* (pp. 16–17), 15th International Conference of the Association for Learning Technology, The University of Leeds, UK.

Whitepaper, A. (2008). *Introduction to virtual worlds*. Retrieved November 13th, 2009, from http://www.scribd.com/doc/5570819/Introduction-to-virtual-worlds

Wikidot. (2007). *Web 2.0/language learning: Second Life*. Retrieved January 24, 2010, from http://web20andlanguagelearning.wikidot.com/second-life

Wikipedia. (n.d.). *Whyville*. Retrieved December 12th, 2009, from http://en.wikipedia.org/wiki/whyville

Wikipedia. (n.d.). *SmallWorlds*. Retrieved December 12th, 2009, from http://en.wikipedia.org/wiki/Smallworlds

Wikipedia. (n.d.). *There*. Retrieved November 12th, 2009, from http://en.wikipedia.org/wiki/There

Wilbur, R. B. (1994). Eyeblinks and ASL phrase structure. *Sign Language Studies, 84*, 221–240.

Wilbur, R. B. (2000). The use of ASL to support the development of English and literacy. *Journal of Deaf Studies and Deaf Education, 5*, 81–104. doi:10.1093/deafed/5.1.81

Wild, M., & Kirkpatrick, D. (1996). Multimedia as cognitive tools: Students working with a performance support system. In C. McBeath & R. Atkinson (Eds.), *The learning superhighway: New world? New worries? Proceedings of the Third International Interactive Multimedia Symposium* (pp. 412-417). Perth: Promaco Conventions. Retrieved December 19, 2008, from http://www.ascilite.org.au/aset-archives/confs/iims/1996/ry/wild.html

Wilson, C. (2008). Avatars, Virtual Reality Technology, and the U.S. Military: Emerging Policy Issues. *CRS Report for Congress*. Retrieved from http://fas.org/sgp/crs/natsec/RS22857.pdf

Winn, W. (1993). A Conceptual Basis for Educational Applications of Virtual Reality. *HITLab Tech Report R-93-9*. Seattle, WA: University of Washington, Human Interface Technology Laboratory.

Winne, P. H. (1995). Inherent details in self-regulated learning. *Educational Psychologist*, *30*(4), 173–187. doi:10.1207/s15326985ep3004_2

Winnips, J. C. (2001). *Scaffolding-by-design: A model for WWW-based learner support*. Unpublished doctoral dissertation, University of Twente, Enschede, The Netherlands.

Winnips, K., & McLoughlin, C. (2000). Applications and categorization of software-based scaffolding. In J. Bourdeau & R. Heller (Eds.), *Proceedings of World Conference on Educational Multimedia, Hypermedia, and Telecommunications 2000* (pp. 1798-1799). Charlottesville, VA: Association for the Advancement of Computers in Education.

Winnips, K., & Mcloughlin, C. (2001). Six WWW based learner supports you can build. In C. Montgomerie & J. Viteli (Eds.), *Proceedings of World Conference on Educational Multimedia, Hypermedia, and Telecommunications 2001* (pp. 2062-2067). Charlottesville, VA: Association for the Advancement of Computers in Education.

Witmer, B., & Singer, M. (1998). Measuring presence in virtual environments: A presence questionnaire. *Presence (Cambridge, Mass.)*, *7*(3), 225–240. doi:10.1162/105474698565686

Witting, T. *(2007)*. Wie Computerspiele uns beeinflussen. Transferprozesse beim Bildschirmspiel im Erleben der User. (How computer games influence us. Processes of transfer in the context of computer and video games in the users' experience.) *München, Germany: kopaed.*

Wong, G. (2006). *Educators explore 'Second Life' Online*. CNN online, Technology section. Retrieved September 14, 2009 from http://www.cnn.com/2006/TECH/11/13/second.life.university/

Wood, D., Bruner, J. S., & Ross, G. (1976). The role of tutoring in problem solving. *Journal of Child Psychology and Psychiatry, and Allied Disciplines*, *17*(2), 89–100. doi:10.1111/j.1469-7610.1976.tb00381.x

Worldwide Advertising, T. M. P., & Communications, L. L. C. (2007, February 12). TMP Worldwide Brings Recruitment To Second Life [Press Release]. Retrieved from http://www.tmp.com/articles/press_00004.html

Yee, N. & Bailenson, J.N. (2007). The Proteus effect: Self transformations in virtual reality.

Young, J. R. (2002, March 22). 'Hybrid' Teaching Seeks to End the Divide Between Traditional and Online Instruction. [Retrieved from Academic Search Premier Database.]. *The Chronicle of Higher Education*, *48*(28), A33.

Young, M. F. (1993). Instructional design for situated learning. *Educational Technology Research and Development*, *41*(1), 43–58. doi:10.1007/BF02297091

Zimmer, G. (2004). Aufgabenorientierte Didaktik des E-Learning. (Task-oriented didactics in E-Learning.) . In Hohenstein, A., & Wilbers, K. (Eds.), *Handbuch E-Learning (Handbook E-Learning) (Kap. 4.15. 7. Erg.-Lfg. Januar 2004)*. Köln, Germany: Fachverlag Deutscher Wirtschaftsdienst.

Zimmerman, B. J., & Schunk, D. H. (Eds.). (1989). *Self-regulated learning and academic achievement: Theory, research, and practice*. New York: Springer-Verlag.

About the Contributors

Shalin Hai-Jew works as an instructional designer at Kansas State University (K-State); she teaches for WashingtonOnline (WAOL). She has taught at the university and college levels for many years and was tenured but left tenure to pursue instructional design work. She taught in the People's Republic of China from 1988 – 1990 and 1992 – 1994, the latter two years with the United Nations Volunteers Programme of the UNDP. She has Bachelor's degrees in English and psychology, and a Master's degree in Creative Writing from the University of Washington (where she was a Hugh Paradise Scholar); she has an Ed.D. (2005) in Educational Leadership with a focus on public administration from Seattle University, where she was a Morford Scholar. She reviews for several publications—Educause Quarterly and MERLOT's Journal of Online Learning and Teaching. She was born in Huntsville, Alabama, in the US.

* * *

Nicoletta Adamo-Villani is Associate Professor of Computer Graphics Technology at Purdue University. She has an MS in Architecture from University of Florence and she is a certified 3D modeler/animator for Autodesk. Adamo-Villani is an award-winning animator and creator of 2D/3D films that aired on national television. Her research interests focus on the application of 3D animation to deaf education, HCC (Human Computer Communication), and visualization.

Tanja Adamus is Research Assistant at the Chair of Educational Media and Knowledge Management, University Duisburg-Essen, Germany. Her research interests are in e-sports and virtual worlds.

Brent A. Anders is an Electronic Media Coordinator for the Office of Mediated Education at Kansas State University. His work includes: educational media consulting, videography (directing, capturing, editing and final production), live webcasting and web accessibility/usability. Mr. Anders has a Bachelor's degree in Psychology, human computer interaction focus, and a Master's degree in Education with an instructional technology focus. He also serves in the Army National Guard as a Sergeant First Class, senior instructor for several military courses (Army Basic Instructors Course and Basic Non-commissioned Officers Course). Mr. Anders has been in the education field for over 12 years dealing with military training, distance education, educational media, and higher education in general.

Penny Barker is a Business and Technology teacher in Ashe County, North Carolina. She utilizes and promotes the integration of 3D technologies into curriculum instruction. She holds a B.S. in Business from Gardner-Webb University and an M.A. in Instructional Technology from Appalachian State

University. Barker is an instructor with the STEM and ICT Instructional Worlds: The 3D Experience, National Science Foundation ITEST Project.

Laura Benvenuti graduated in mathematics. She is assistant professor at the Open Universiteit Nederland, the Dutch University for distance learning. Until 2006, she was lecturer at the Hogeschool Utrecht (University for Applied Science, Utrecht, the Netherlands), where she co-founded the Multimedia curriculum of the degree course "Digital Communication". At the Open Universiteit Nederland, she alternates face-to-face lectures, online classes, the development of innovative courses for distance learners, and research.

Zane L. Berge is Professor and former Director of the Training Systems Graduate Program at the University of Maryland System's UMBC campus. With 10 books and 300 articles, chapters and presentations, Dr. Berge is a prolific scholar in the related fields of distance education, computer-mediated communication, and elearning.

Michela Bertolotto received a BSc in 1993 and a PhD degree in Computer Science in 1998 from the University of Genova in Italy. Subsequently she worked at the National Center for Geographic Information and Analysis (NCGIA) and the Department of Spatial Information Science and Engineering of the University of Maine as a postdoctoral research associate. Since September 2000 she has been working in the School of Computer Science and Informatics at University College Dublin, where she currently holds a Senior Lecturer position. Her main research interests include spatio-temporal data modeling, mobile and web-based GIS, the development of progressive spatial data transmission techniques, the application of case-based reasoning techniques to GIS and Health and interactive e-learning interfaces.

Otto Borchert was born in Valley City, North Dakota, and raised in various locales throughout the tri-state area. He graduated with a Bachelor's in Computer Science with a minor in Psychology from North Dakota State University in 2001. He continued on to graduate work at NDSU with Dr. Brian M. Slator as his advisor and completed the Masters degree in 2008 resulting in the thesis "Computer Supported Collaborative Learning in an Online Multiplayer Game" He is currently a Ph.D. candidate and research technician at NDSU. His research interests include computer supported collaborative learning, immersive virtual environments for education, computer science education, networks and network security, and microcomputer graphics.

Hope R. Botterbusch is an adjunct graduate faculty member of Kansas State University in the College of Education, Educational Computing, Design, and Online Learning. She holds a BS in Education, a MSLS in Library and Information Science and has over 30 years experience in K-12, Community College and University classroom teaching, district curriculum supervisor, and coordinating university programs. She specializes in teacher training in the STEM disciplines, specifically formal and informal environmental science education. She received awards for her sponsored educational classroom materials and environmental outreach programs, is a published author of book chapters and journal articles on copyright issues in education, and teaching and learning in virtual worlds. She is past chair of the Intellectual Property Committee and IP Column Editor of TechTrends, of the Association for Educational Communications and Technology. She currently serves on the editorial board of new journal, the International Journal of Cyberethics.

Barney Dalgarno is an Associate Professor of Educational Technology in the School of Education at Charles Sturt University. His research interests include the educational affordances of 3D virtual learning environments, the application of constructivist theories to technology facilitated learning design, critical exploration of the impact of generational changes on learners, learning and learning technologies, and the use of functional brain imaging to explore interactivity and cognition. As well as being awarded a number of research and teaching grants, he has received national recognition through awards for innovative teaching and learning design using leading-edge technologies. He is an Editorial Board Member of the leading peer-reviewed publication Distance Learning (the official journal of the Open and Distance Learning Association of Australasia – ODLAA) well as being a former Executive Committee Member of the Australasian Society for the Advancement of Computers in Education (ASCILITE).

Judi L. Davidson Wolf has been training Federal government employees for more than 25 years, mostly in the areas of writing, editing, and graphic design. More recently, she has been teaching and coaching in-house trainers in using technology to deliver training. Currently pursuing master's degree studies in Instructional Systems Development at the University of Maryland, Baltimore County, she is a digital immigrant who is intrigued and fascinated by the potential of virtual worlds as a training venue. She has a bachelor's degree from Dartmouth College and currently lives in Columbia, Maryland, with her husband and two daughters.

Ben Dischinger was born and raised in Anoka, Minnesota. He graduated from North Dakota State University with a Bachelors degree in Computer Science and Mathematics with a minor in Physics. He is currently working towards a Masters degree in Computer Science in the area of immersive virtual environments. He is also a Software Engineer at Sun Microsystems working on hierarchical storage management solutions.

Miguel A. Garcia-Ruiz graduated in Computer Systems engineering and obtained his MSc in Computer Science from the University of Colima, Mexico. He received his PhD in Computer Science and Artificial Intelligence at the University of Sussex, UK. He took a virtual reality course at Salford University, UK, and a graphics techniques internship at the Madrid Polytechnic University, Spain. Miguel is a professor of Computer Science with the College of Telematics of the University of Colima. He has published various scientific papers in major journals, book chapters and two books, and directed a video documentary on virtual reality. His research interests include virtual reality and usability of multimodal human-computer interfaces. Currently, Miguel is a Visiting Professor at the University of Ontario Institute of Technology, Canada.

Kyle Hayward graduated from Purdue University with a BS degree in Computer Science in 2009 and is a graphics programmer for Human Head Studios, Inc. His background is in real-time rendering, including natural effects rendering, volume rendering, and reflections and refractions using non-pinhole cameras. His current research interests are in real-time facial and skeletal animation for sign language applications.

Caroline M. L. Ho is Assistant Professor with the English Language and Literature Academic Group, National Institute of Education, Nanyang Technological University, Singapore. Her research interests include new media and new literacies, discourse analysis of computer-mediated communication, and language pedagogy in the areas of argumentation and critical thinking. Her work has appeared in Journal of Applied Linguistics, Computer Assisted Language Learning, Computers and Education and Innovation in language teaching and learning among other publications. Her latest book (edited with K. Anderson and A. Leong) is Transforming Literacies and Language: Multimodality and Literacy in the New Media Age (in press, London: Continuum).

Guy Hokanson was born and raised in Fargo, North Dakota, and the surrounding lake country. He graduated from North Dakota State University in 2000 with a Bachelor's degree in Computer Science. He is currently a Research Technician for the Computer Science Department at North Dakota State University, and Programmer/Analyst for the NDSU Center for Science and Mathematics where he works on the development and implementation of a number of virtual learning environments. He is also in the Masters program at NDSU where his research interests include immersive virtual environments for education and expert tools for content creation.

Bill Kapralos is an Assistant Professor in the Game Development and Entrepreneurship Program at the University of Ontario Institute of Technology. His current research interests include: generation of real-time, multi-modal virtual environments, and videogames/serious games, acoustical modeling and spatial sound generation for virtual environments and videogames, and the perception of auditory events. He is currently involved in a number of serious games initiatives including those for training accountants, community health nurses, critical care providers, and orthopaedic surgeons. Bill chaired the ACM FuturePlay International Conference on the Future of Game Design and Technology in 2007 and 2008, and the ACM FuturePlay @GDC Canada 2009 conference. He is also chairing the ACM FuturePlay @ Vancouver Digital Week 2010 conference.

Michael Kerres is Professor of Education and holds the Chair of Educational Media and Knowledge Management at University Duisburg-Essen, Germany. His present main research interests include learning innovations in higher education, instructional design of learning environments, and usability research in e-learning.

Mark J.W. Lee holds Adjunct Senior Lecturer appointments with the School of Education at Charles Sturt University and with the Distance Education Hub (DE Hub) research centre at the University of New England, as well as concurrently serving as an Honorary Research Fellow with the Graduate School of Information Technology and Mathematical Sciences at the University of Ballarat. Before entering academia, he worked in a variety of teaching, instructional design, and managerial roles within the private vocational education and higher education sectors. Lee has published widely in the fields of educational technology, e-learning, and innovative pedagogy in higher education, with 50 refereed book chapters, journal articles, and conference papers to his name. He is the immediate past Chair of the New South Wales Chapter of the Institute of Electrical and Electronics Engineers (IEEE) Education Society, and previously served as a Director of the International Board of Standards for Training, Performance and Instruction (ibstpi), an Executive Committee Member of the Open and Distance Learning Association of Australasia (ODLAA), and a State Council Member of the Australian Institute of Training and Development (AITD). Lee is currently the Editor-in-Chief of Impact: Journal of Applied Research in Workplace E-learning, and sits on the editorial boards of several other international journals in the fields of educational technology and online learning.

Catherine M. J. Lithgow is a senior Instructional Designer with 12 years of experience in training, writing, editing, web design, training material design and the development of formal corporate training programs. Lithgow creates webpage and on-line tutorial content utilizing her skills in writing and technical authoring to develop electronic deliverables. Currently pursuing a Master's Degree in Instructional Systems Development at the University of Maryland, Baltimore County, she is highly motivated to maintain her status as a contributing member of the virtual learning community. Lithgow currently holds a Bachelors Degree in Psychology from the College of Wooster in Ohio, and lives in Silver Spring, Maryland, with her husband and two children.

Julie Marklin is an Instructional Technology Specialist in the Davie County, NC, school district. She has a BA in Elementary Education from UNC-Chapel Hill and a Master's Degree in Library and Information Science from UNC-Greensboro. In addition, she is National Board certified and holds a licensure endorsement in Instructional Technology. Marklin is an instructor for Stem and ICT Instructional Worlds: The 3D Experience at Clemson University.

Miguel Vargas Martin, PhD., PEng. is an Associate Professor at the University of Ontario Institute of Technology (UOIT) and Chief Technology Officer of Hoper, Inc., an Oshawa-based R&D company that offers innovative web tools. Before joining UOIT, he was a post-doctoral researcher at Alcatel Canada and Carleton University (Ottawa). He is a licensed Professional Engineer in Ontario and holds a Ph.D. in Computer Science, a Master's degree in Electrical Engineering, and a Bachelor of Computer Science. He has reported his work in over forty journals, book chapters, conference papers, technical reports, and pending patents, and so far has supervised almost 20 students at the graduate and undergraduate level. His current research interests include computer forensics, mitigation of denial-of-service attacks, security and human computer interaction, hidden communication channels, and web modeling and optimization.

Nita Matzen is an Assistant Professor of Library Science at Appalachian State University and the Principal Investigator of STEM and ICT Instructional Worlds: The 3D Experience (STEM-ICT 3D), a National Science Foundation ITEST Project. Dr. Matzen uses 3D virtual immersive technology in the graduate courses that she teaches and has been actively involved in the study of the pedagogy used in virtual environments including the development of an instructional framework known as Presence Pedagogy.

Gavin McArdle received a BSc degree in computer science in 2003 from the National University of Ireland, University College Dublin. During his final year, he studied issues surrounding the presentation of complex datasets using an interactive 2D interface. In 2008 Gavin completed his PhD degree in University College Dublin where he investigated the use of collaborative and virtual reality environments for learning, collaborating and socializing online. In June 2008 Gavin took up a postdoctoral researcher position with the Strategic Research Cluster in Advanced Geotechnologies (StratAG), investigating map and interface personalization by utilizing user preferences. Dr McArdle's research interests include e-learning, graphical user interfaces, personalisation techniques, location aware technologies, location-based services and user profiling.

Phillip McClean is a member of the Department of Plant Sciences at North Dakota State University. In addition, he is director of the NDSU Genomics and Bioinformatics program, and associate director of the NDSU Center for Agricultural Biotechnology. His primary teaching interests are in the areas of genetics and molecular genetics with an emphasis on plants. Dr. McClean was awarded the Excellence in Teaching, Early Career award in the College of Agriculture in 1994. In 1998, he was awarded the first Peltier Award for Innovative Teaching. This is a university-wide award. And in 2000, he was awarded the Excellence in Teaching, Senior Career for the College of Agriculture. Dr. McClean is also the principal investigator for the Virtual Cell Animation Project (http://vcell.ndsu.edu/animations). This project develops high quality animations in the field of molecular and cellular biology. Education research that investigates the best methods for presenting scientific information in animations is also a component of the VCell project. Dr. McClean is also co-designer for the VCell educational game. His primary responsibilities focus on scientific content.

Axel Nattland is Research Assistant at the Chair of Educational Media and Knowledge Management, University Duisburg-Essen, Germany. His research interests are: web 2.0, virtual learning environments, learning management systems, instructional design and virtual worlds.

Nadine Ojstersek is Research Assistant at the Chair of Educational Media and Knowledge Management, University Duisburg-Essen, Germany. Her research interests are: instructional design of learning environments, virtual worlds, learner support in distance and e-learning.

Roger W. McHaney is a University Distinguished Teaching Scholar and professor of management information systems. He currently serves as Interim Management Department Head. A K-State faculty member since 1995, McHaney teaches courses in enterprise systems, systems design and business computing. He also has been instrumental in the development of K-State distance learning programs and offers several courses via computer mediated technologies. His current areas of research include discrete event computer simulation, educational technology, Web 2.0 applications in business, and organizational computing. McHaney holds bachelors and masters degrees from Lake Superior State University and a doctorate in computer information systems and quantitative analysis from the Sam M. Walton College of Business at the University of Arkansas. McHaney has won numerous awards including the Coffman Chair for University Distinguished Teaching Scholars in 2006-7. During that time, he developed an award-winning, online video teaching exchange for K-State distance learning faculty and has since co-created ELATEwiki, an Electronic Learning and Teaching Exchange wiki. Additionally, McHaney has publications in journals, encyclopedias, books, and instructional venues.

Kanubhai K. Patel is an Assistant Professor at the Schools of ICT of Ahmedabad University, Ahmedabad, India. He was previously a faculty member at GLS ICA, Gujarat University, Ahmedabad. He is pursuing PhD degree from the Faculty of Technology at Dharmsinh Desai University, Nadiad. He received his MCA from Gujarat Vidyapith, Ahmedabad in June 1997. His research interests include assistive technology, spatial cognition, human-computer interaction and virtual learning environments. He has authored over nine publications, including a refereed journal paper and two book chapters. He has also authored a book – "Data Structures: Theory and Problems".

William Edward Roberts received his MA in Technology Education from Appalachian State University in Boone, North Carolina, in 2004 with a concentration in Junior College & Community College Teaching, with a minor in physics. Roberts earned his doctorate of education degree at North Carolina

State University Technology Education program with a minor in training and development from NC State University at Raleigh, North Carolina in May 2009. Dr. Roberts is the 3D Modeler/Programmer for Stem and ICT Instructional Worlds: The 3D Experience.

Bianca Schön received a BSc degree in computer science in 2002 from the University of Applied Sciences Darmstadt, Germany. In 2008 Bianca completed her PhD degree in University College Dublin where she investigated novel and intuitive techniques for offering navigational support in 3D desktop environments, employing a Multi-Agent System (MAS). After working as a technology consultant for Hewlett-Packard, Bianca took up a postdoctoral research position in July 2008, working in a collaborative project between UCD's School of Computer Science and Informatics and UCD's School of Architecture, Landscape and Civil Engineering, investigating the visualisation, analysis and manipulation of Light Detection and Ranging (LiDAR) data. This research has already resulted in a journal publication that has been rated among the top 5% most cited publications of 2009, and a patent application for an efficient LiDAR indexing technique. Bianca's research interests include human computer interaction, e-learning, spatial data storage and manipulation, location aware technologies and multi-agent systems.

Ya-Chun Shih was born in Taiwan on November 16, 1971. She received her M.A. and Ph.D. degrees in Curriculum and Instruction (Bilingual Education emphasis) from Pennsylvania State University in 1997 and 2000 respectively. In 2001, Dr. Shih joined the faculty of National Hualien University of Education, located near the world-famous Taroko Gorge, as Assistant Professor of English Language Teaching. In 2009, the University was renamed as National Dong Hwa University. She is currently Assistant Professor in the Department of English at National Dong Hwa University, Hualien, Taiwan and one of the computer-assisted language learning (CALL) practitioners. She has pursued a wide range of technology supported language learning issues, including serving as an instructor, instructional designer, researcher, journal reviewer, guest speaker, advisor and committee member on related issues. Under Dr. Shih's leadership, the VEC3D (3D Virtual English Classroom), an interdisciplinary research team of instructional designers and computer science experts, designed and developed a variety of innovative language learning platforms. The VEC3D innovation started with an inspired idea for contextual language learning. Dr. Shih and her research team are expanding beyond the traditional language learning environments and methods by incorporating technology into daily lessons and communicative activities. Her current research focuses on integrating virtual reality technologies and language learning in education. She has investigated the effect of virtual reality assisted language learning (VRALL) on students' achievement of English as a foreign language. She has also explored issues related to the use of 3D collaborative virtual environments (CVEs) within a social and cultural context. The central research issues for the VEC3D project include research on (non)verbal communication, developing communicative competence and cultural awareness. Her research has been heavily supported by a grant from the Taiwan National Science Council.

Brian M. Slator was raised in Minnesota and graduated with a Bachelors in Computer Science (with a second major in English), from the University of Wisconsin - La Crosse in 1983. He attended graduate school at New Mexico State University where he studied with Yorick Wilks and received a PhD in Computer Science in 1988. After serving six years as a research scientist at the Institute for the Learning Sciences at Northwestern University, he joined the Computer Science department at North

Dakota State University in 1996 where he is currently a professor and engaged in research dealing with learning in role-based simulations.

Rosemary Talab is Professor and Coordinator of the Educational Computing, Design, and Online Learning graduate program at Kansas State University, which offers a KSU Graduate School Certificate, two master's degree specialties, and a Ph.D. She has written two books on technology and copyright law, one currently in the second edition, and several book chapters. She has made over 60 presentations at the state, national, and international levels, including keynote addresses, and over 30 articles and research papers. She is on the editorial board of a new journal, the International Journal of Cyberethics. She was chair of the Intellectual Property Committee and IP Column Editor of TechTrends, of the Association for Educational Communications and Technology, for several years through 2008. She was the first Fulbright Scholar to the Higher Colleges of Technology in Abu Dhabi, the United Arab Emirates, in 2007.

Jayshiro Tashiro, PhD, BSN, RND is currently a Professor in the Faculty of Health Sciences at the University of Ontario Institute of Technology (UOIT). His research focuses on telehealth and disease management, the relationships between evidence-based learning and evidence-based practice in healthcare, and assessment of complex competencies within clinical simulations. Beginning in the mid-1990s, Tashiro led research teams in the development and evaluations of virtual clinical simulations that monitor users' choices during treatment of complex patients within the simulations. The principal focus of these monitoring systems has been clinical judgment, with the software conducting automated analysis of choices made by the user while working within a simulation. Funding related to virtual learning environments has been over $10 Million since 1990. At UOIT, Tashiro teaches In the Health Information Management Program and is currently building and evaluating simulation-rich courses that promote interprofessional collaborative patient-centred care. Tashiro also helped establish and now is part of the Management Team for the Health Education Technology Research Unit at UOIT.

Gerrit C. van der Veer graduated in Cognitive Psychology. His PhD was on the design of User Interfaces. Currently he is a full professor of Computer Science, teaching Human-Computer Interaction in the Dutch Open University, and Design in the University of Sassari, Italy. His research focuses on the application of new information and communication technology and multimedia to support human learning and distance education.

Bradley Vender was born and raised in Bismarck, North Dakota. He moved to Fargo to attend college at North Dakota State University (NDSU) and graduated from that institution with a Bachelor's in Computer Science in 1998 and a Masters in Computer Science in 2004. While studying at NDSU, he first encountered text based multi-user environment servers such as LPMud, MUSH and others before meeting Dr. Brian M. Slator and joining Dr. Slator's research projects. He is currently a research technician at NDSU where he has worked on the Virtual Cell and other environments as part of Dr. Slator's research group.

Sanjay K. Vij received his PhD degree from IIT, Bombay, in 1974. He is currently a Director in the Department of CE-IT-MCA, Sardar Vallabhbhai Patel Institute of Technology (SVIT), Vasad. His research interests include Text Mining, Knowledge Management, and NLP. He has authored over twenty publications, including over seven refereed journal papers and two book chapters. He is a registered PhD guide with Dharmsinh Desai University, Nadiad. He is Member Board of Studies at MS University, Baroda and Dharmsinh Desai University, Nadiad. He had been a panel of experts/advisor in GSLET and GPSC. He is reviewer in couple of peer reviewed journals. He has been Chairman of Computer Society of India, Vadodara Chapter.

Index

Symbols

2D 153, 159
3D 1, 3, 4, 5, 6, 7, 8, 13, 14, 15, 16, 21, 22,
    23, 24, 28, 30, 37, 38, 41, 307, 314, 325,
    328, 330
3D applications 173
3D characters 256, 259, 266
3D context 125
3D developing 49
3D digital imagery 224
3D environments 3, 126, 133, 198, 213
3D graphics 277
3D immersive environments 100
3D immersive spaces 95
3D immersive virtual environments 124, 125,
    130, 133, 134
3D learning spaces 96, 114
3D libraries 212, 214, 215, 217
3D maps 171
3D objects 56, 214, 219
3D programming 51
3-D rotational data 252
3D simulation 100
3D social network 274, 277, 281
3D spaces 213, 221
3D spatial gesture 213
3D Studio Max 48
3D Virtual Chemistry Laboratory 138, 140,
    153
3D Virtual English Classroom (VEC3D) 79,
    80, 85, 86, 87, 88, 89, 90, 92, 93
3D virtual environment 81, 85, 88, 124, 126,
    138, 167
3D virtual immersive learning environment
    124

3D virtual learning 138
3D virtual reality 83, 85
3D virtual spaces 96, 132, 215
3D virtual worlds 80, 87, 91, 123, 124, 126,
    127, 137, 176, 212
3D worlds 59

A

acceleration-based navigation 232
Active Words 85
Active Worlds 4, 5, 23, 45, 46, 48, 49, 51, 52,
    172, 188
adenosine diphosphate (ADP) 195, 196, 211
adenosine triphosphate (ATP) 195, 196, 211
ad-hoc methods 5
ad hoc virtual communities 219
advanced technologies 3
AETZone 124, 127, 137
Agent 328
American Association for the Advancement of
    Science (AAAS) 271, 299
American Sign Language (ASL) 249, 250,
    252, 253, 254, 256, 257, 258, 259, 260,
    261, 262, 263, 264, 265, 266
American Society for Training and Develop-
    ment (ASTD) 33
animated character 4
Animated Signing 266
Appalachian State University 123, 124, 125,
    126, 127, 135, 137
Application Programming Interface (API) 158,
    167
Artificial Intelligence 56, 165, 166, 168, 224,
    328
artificial intelligence robots 312

Artificial Life 328
ASL proficiency 250
Assay 211
assistive navigation technologies 231
Assistive Technology 266
Asterix 46, 48, 49
asynchronous communication 2, 3, 21
augmented environment 276
augmented reality simulators 276
Authentic Learning 167
autonomy 274
avatars 6, 50, 55, 57, 58, 60, 61, 62, 63, 64,
       66, 70, 72, 73, 95, 97, 99, 112, 145, 167,
       173, 174, 177, 179, 182, 183, 184, 186,
       187, 189, 190, 193, 213, 214, 218, 221,
       224

B

beneficence 274
bi-dimensional correlation coefficients (BCC)
       234, 238, 239, 248
biological ecosystems 309
Blackboard 27, 42
blindness 226, 248
blogs 79, 89, 94
Boundary Relation Heuristic (BRH) 236, 237
brain-computer interface (BCI) 227

C

Carolina Virtual Worlds Consortium (CVWC)
       125
Center for the Advancement of Distance Educa-
       tion (CADE) 279
Centers for Disease Control and Prevention
       (CDC) 283, 300
Children's Online Privacy Protection Act
       (COPPA) 175, 186
classroom atmosphere 63
classroom community 47, 51, 53
Classroom Community Scale (CCS) 45, 47, 51
Clemson University 124, 125, 126, 129
closed economic simulations 57
Closed Grid 42
cognitive domain 56
Cognitive Load 167, 169, 240, 243, 244, 248

cognitive map 227, 229, 232, 234, 236, 239,
       240
Collaborative Learning 167
Collaborative Learning Environments with
       Virtual Reality (CLEV-R) 1, 3, 5, 6, 7, 8,
       9, 10, 11, 12, 13, 14, 15, 21, 24
Collaborative Virtual Environment (CVE) 78,
       79, 81, 82, 83, 85, 86, 87, 88, 89, 90, 94,
       158, 159, 168, 169
collaborative virtual reality environments
       (CVREs) 282
Community of Practice 127, 128, 137
complex organism interactions 309
Computer Animation 258, 266
computer-assisted language learning (CALL)
       78, 79, 82, 83, 84, 85, 89, 90, 91, 92, 94
computer-based simulations 57
computer-generated imagery (CGI) 201
computer simulations 270, 274
Conceptual Drift 328
conceptual models 311
Constructivist Learning 233, 235, 248
Contextual Learning 167
Cosmo Player 209, 211
cross-media concepts 48
Crystal Island 98
CVE learning 79
C-Visions 4
cyberspace 218

D

data structures 215
Deaf Education 266, 267
Debriefing 319, 328
declarative knowledge 57, 62, 72, 77
degrees of freedom (DOF) 252, 259
depth-of-field 264
dialogic interaction 96, 99
Didactical Requirements 54, 55
digital artifacts 215, 221
Digital Communication 45, 46
Digital Natives Best Practices project 126
digital objects 213, 214, 218
digital personas 95
digital simulations 95
digital technologies 99

Discovery Learning 138, 168

E

e-commerce 3
educational goals 47
educational media 70
educational technologies 271, 272, 274
educational tools 52
e-learning 1, 2, 3, 4, 5, 8, 15, 16, 19, 21, 55, 69, 80
Electronic Travel Aids (ETAs) 232
Electron Transport Chain (ETC) 195, 196, 211
emergency department (ED) 280, 294
enactive role 95, 96, 100, 102, 103, 112, 113, 114, 117, 120
end-user license agreements (EULAs) 170, 180, 182, 183
English as a Foreign Language (EFL) 79, 82, 84, 85, 87, 93
English as a Second Language (ESL) 82, 85
Environmental space 228
ethical framework 273
EVE 4, 21, 22
evidence-based learning 269, 271, 272, 274, 278, 288, 290, 296, 298
Experiential Learning 168
Expert System 168

F

Facebook 26, 32, 39
face-to-face format 33
face-to-face instructions 69
face-to-face interaction 63
Facial Animation 253, 255, 260, 266
Facial Animation (FA) 255
Facial Animation Parameters (FAP) 255
Fading 147, 168
false identities 309
Federal Trade Commission (FTC) 175, 176
Figural space 228
fraudulent schemes 309

G

Gameplay 328
General Paper 96, 117

Generation Next 272
Generation Y 171, 272
geographical information systems (GIS) 228, 232, 244, 246, 247
Geographical space 228
Global Positioning Systems (GPS) 232, 245, 246
Goal-based Scenario 329
Google Sketch-Up 126, 127, 129, 130, 131, 132, 133, 134
graphical manipulation 61
Graphical User Interface (GUI) 6, 168
Guided Discovery 168

H

haptic device 275
Heads-Up Display (HUD) 149, 152, 153, 168
healthcare education 269, 272, 273, 274, 277, 278, 281, 283, 287, 296
health sciences education 271
high reliability organizations (HROs) 324
Hogeschool Utrecht 45, 46
Hospital Emergency Incident Command System (HEICS) 280
HTML 6
HTTP 199, 201, 208
human-embodied avatar 309
human intelligence 328
humanoid avatar form 312
Human Performance Technology (HPT) 33, 40
human relationship management 212, 214
HumanSim 280

I

iFACE 255, 256
iGeneration 171
imaginative play 96
immersion 1, 5, 23, 24, 97, 98, 224, 316, 317, 320, 329
immersive learning 218, 222
immersive learning environments 270
immersive spaces 307, 309, 310, 311, 314, 315, 322, 323, 324
immersive virtual environments 95, 115
immunological activity 211

information and communication technology (ICT) 123, 124, 125, 126, 128, 130, 134

information exchange and management 212, 214

Innovative Technology Experiences for Students and Teachers (ITEST) 123, 124, 134, 137

Inquiry-Based Learning 168

Inquiry-Based Learning Project 137

intellectual property theft 309

Intelligent Agent 168

Intelligent Tutoring System (ITS) 158, 161, 168

interactive 95, 96, 99, 100, 111, 112, 114, 116, 121

interactivity 312, 328

inter-language development 84

International Society for Technology in Education (ISTE) 33

interpreting contexts 96

Inverse Kinematics 251

INVITE 4, 5

J

Japan Association of Language Teachers (JALT) 89, 92

Japanese-language Education Worldwide Electronic Learning Space (JEWELS) 84

Java 37, 42

JavaMOO 194, 202, 203, 204, 205, 206, 207, 208, 209, 210

justice 274

K

Kenworthy model 321

keyframe animation 252, 253, 260

Kidz Connect 99, 117

knowledge managing 80

Knowledge Skills 101

KZero 171, 191

L

Lac Operon 211

LambdaMOO 198, 199, 201, 202, 203, 204, 205, 206, 207, 208, 209, 210, 211

LambdaMOO core database 211

Landmark-Route-Survey (LRS) 226, 228, 248

language teaching 79, 82, 83, 89

laparoscopic surgery 276, 304

laws of statistics 56

learning assignments 54, 55, 56, 57, 58, 59, 62, 63, 65, 67, 68, 69, 70, 72, 73

learning communities 125, 127, 136

learning environment 3, 6, 15, 16, 19

Learning Management Systems (LMSs) 2, 3, 4, 5, 38, 69, 167

learning risks 309, 314, 317, 324

Lecture Room 6, 7, 12

lecturers 45, 47, 48, 49, 50, 51, 52

Library 7, 8, 21

Lighthouse Learning Island 33, 34

Linden Labs 282, 283, 285

Linden Scripting Language (LSL) 71

linguistic resources 96, 115

LinkedIN 26

live digital data feeds 213

local area network (LAN) 283, 287, 288, 289, 290, 291, 292, 293, 294, 295, 297, 298

Locomotion Interface 246, 248

Longitudinal 219, 224

low rendering quality 258

LPMud 199, 211

M

Main Grid 179, 180, 186

Maslow's pyramid 218

mass information losses 309

Massively Multiuser Online Role Playing Games (MMORPGs) 68, 75, 172

Mathematics and Science Education Center (MSEC) 124

Mathsigner 255, 256, 259, 260, 261, 262, 266

media-supported learning environments 55

Meeting Rooms 7, 9

mental models 310, 311, 312, 319, 324, 326

Metaphor Theory 312

Metaplace 172

millennials 272, 273

MOBIC Travel Aid 232

Modular Synthetic Research Evaluation and Extrapolation Tool (mSTREET) 281
Moodle/Angel 42
MOOs 169
motion capture animation 252, 253
MPEG-4 255, 265, 266
multimodal communication 78, 87
multi-modal communications 125
multi-party 95, 96
multiplayer online role-playing games (MMORPGs) 124
multiple-choice tasks 56, 59
multi-scale environments 310
multi-sensory communications 213
Multi-User Dungeon (MUD) 198, 199, 203, 211
Multi-User Virtual Environments (MUVE) 25, 26, 27, 29, 30, 31, 37, 38, 42, 79, 81, 94, 146, 148, 163, 168, 169
Multiverse 172
myocardial infarction (MI) 294
MySpace 26

N

nanobot 277
NASA TLX 240, 241
National Research Council (NRC) 271
National Science Foundation 123, 124, 134, 137
National Technical Institute for the Deaf (NTID) 256
Native American gaming project 318
natural communication 81
Negative Learning 307, 314, 315, 317, 318, 319, 323, 329, 330, 332
Network Interaction in Foreign Language Acquisition and Research Project (NIAF-LAR Project) 80, 83, 88
Network Latency 306
New Media Consortium (NMC) 99, 118, 120
NOAA 29, 36
non-maleficence 274
non-manual animated signs 264
non-visual spatial learning (NSL) 228, 233, 234, 243

North Carolina Department of Environment and Natural Resources (NCDENR) 124
North Dakota State University (NDSU) 194, 195, 209

O

Oconee-Pickens Speedway 129, 131
Online Interactive Virtual Environment (OL-IVE) 37, 172
Online Learning 23, 24
online learning environments 124, 125
Open Grid 42
OpenSim 172, 173, 174, 190, 191
operating room (OR) 283
OSGrid 173, 174

P

parasocial relationships 309
pedagogical dimension 142, 144, 145
Perceived Virtual Presence (PVP) 33
Perpetual 224
Persistence 212, 215, 216, 219, 221, 224
Personal Digital Assistant (PDA) 152, 153, 154, 155, 156, 157, 158
personal identity compromises 309
personally identifiable information (PII) 323
photo-realistic imagery 310
Photosynthesis 195, 196, 211
Plenary debriefings 321
position-based navigation 232
presence 95, 96, 97, 98, 99, 100, 101, 103, 104, 105, 106, 107, 109, 110, 111, 112, 113, 114, 115, 117, 118, 119, 120, 240, 243, 245, 246, 247, 248
Presence Pedagogy framework 124
problem-based learning 169, 278, 293, 295
problem-solving 96, 114, 275
problem solving assignments 56, 63
psychomotor skills 275, 296

Q

Quest Atlantis 125, 134

R

Radio Frequency (RF) 232, 246

ReactionGrid 173
real-life environments 227
Real Life (RL) 26, 30, 31, 42
Real Money Trade (RMT) 172, 174
real-time voice communication 57
real world 54, 55, 63, 65, 67, 72, 73
reflexive learning 312
region connection calculus (RCC) 229
River City 125, 148, 149, 163
role play games 67
role playing 99, 312

S

Scaffolding 138, 141, 146, 150, 151, 161, 162, 163, 164, 165, 166, 167
SciCentr 125
science, technology, engineering, and mathematics (STEM) 123, 124, 125, 126, 127, 128, 129, 130, 134, 137, 249, 259
Second Language Acquisition (SLA) 78, 81, 82, 90, 91, 92, 93
Second Life 4, 5, 22, 23, 24, 25, 26, 27, 31, 32, 33, 35, 37, 38, 39, 40, 41, 42, 43, 46, 52, 53, 54, 55, 57, 59, 61, 62, 63, 64, 65, 66, 67, 68, 69, 70, 71, 72, 74, 75, 76, 78, 79, 80, 81, 83, 85, 87, 89, 90, 91, 92, 93, 94, 95, 96, 99, 100, 103, 113, 116, 118, 119, 120, 121, 170, 172, 173, 174, 179, 180, 181, 182, 183, 184, 185, 186, 187, 188, 189, 190, 191, 192, 193, 217, 222, 224, 274, 277, 279, 281, 282, 283, 284, 285, 289, 290, 301, 302, 303, 304, 306
Second Life URL (SLURL) 186
segmented avatar 251, 252
self-directed learning (SDL) 169
self-regulated learning (SRL) 169,
Serious Games 269, 274, 277, 306
Shared Content Object Reference Model (SCORM) 38, 43
share values 47
short message service (SMS) 152
signal data 313
signed animation 262, 264
signing avatars 249, 250, 256, 258, 259, 264, 265

Signing Science Dictionary (SSD) 256
Sign Language 252, 256, 266, 267
simulations 61, 62, 76, 307, 308, 309, 310, 311, 312, 313, 314, 315, 316, 320, 321, 322, 324, 325, 326, 327, 328, 329, 330, 331, 332, 333
Simulator Sickness Questionnaire (SSQ) 241, 242, 246, 248
Skype 26
SLanguages virtual conference 80
SLED 27, 28, 30, 31, 32, 37, 38, 41, 43, 187
SLOODLE 38, 40, 43
SmallWorlds 170, 172, 174, 176, 177, 178, 179, 181, 183, 184, 185, 186, 189, 191, 192
SMILE 256, 259, 260, 261, 262, 266
social activities 176
social constructivist perspective 82
social environments 5
social experiences 312
social institutions 82
social interaction 1, 2, 3, 5, 7, 8, 9, 10, 11, 14, 15, 23, 24, 329
social networking 26, 32, 34, 38, 171, 189, 219
social networking sites 322
social presence 57, 72, 73
social relationships 58, 63
Social Rooms 7
social skills 3
social tools 5, 15
Society for Intercultural Education, Training and Research 60
socio-cultural barriers 125
socio-spatial information 213
socio-technical systems 324
software environment 79
Space Station Leonis 99
Special Interest Group (SIG) 89
Split Attention Effect 169
STEM and ICT Instructional Worlds: The 3D Experience (STEM-ICT 3D) 123, 124, 126, 128, 130, 134
STEM-ICT 3D project 126, 134
strategic thinking 96
streaming live 6
subject matter experts (SMEs) 316, 317, 334

Successful Applications of Learning Technologies (SALT) 125
synchronous communication 4
synchronous learning 6, 7
synthetic animation 252, 253
synthetic worlds 213, 214, 224

T

target language 78, 81, 82, 85, 89
Teleplace 124, 126, 127, 128, 129, 133, 134, 137
Teleplace 3D immersive world 126
TERC 256, 266
terms of service (TOS) 170, 172, 180, 181, 182, 183, 185, 188
Terms of Use (TOU) 182
text 2, 4, 5, 6, 7, 9
text-based web-pages 2
Three-Dimensional Virtual Learning Environment (3DVLE) 146, 148, 152, 157, 159, 167, 168, 169
topological map 228, 230, 236
Transference 329
triangulate data 316
tutorial support 73
Twitter 26

U

Usability 8, 23, 24
User Interface 267
users 1, 2, 4, 5, 6, 7, 8, 11, 13, 16, 18, 19, 20, 21, 24, 171, 172, 173, 174, 176, 179, 181, 183, 184, 189, 190

V

Vcom3D 250, 256, 266
velocity-based navigation 232
video conferencing 6
video games 270, 273, 278, 289, 299, 300, 301, 302, 303
Virtual Big Beef Creek 146, 161
Virtual Cell 194, 195, 196, 197, 198, 199, 200, 201, 202, 203, 204, 206, 207, 208, 209, 210, 211

Virtual Chemistry Laboratory 138, 140, 149, 150, 151, 152, 153, 154, 155, 156, 157, 158, 160
virtual dialoguing 96, 97, 98, 100, 102, 110, 111, 112, 114, 115, 121
Virtual Emergency Room (VER) 280
virtual environments 78, 79, 87, 92, 93, 95, 96, 97, 100, 115, 116, 118, 119, 120, 121, 124, 125, 130, 133, 134, 136, 245, 246, 248, 309, 310, 312, 313, 326
Virtual European Schools (VES) 4, 21, 22
virtual experiences 213, 216, 221
virtual learning 308, 323
virtual learning environments (VLEs) 96, 139, 140, 142, 145, 146, 147, 148, 155, 156, 158, 159, 160, 168, 217, 226, 227, 228, 250, 259
Virtual Reality Assisted Language Learning (VRALL) 80, 85, 90, 94
virtual reality medical simulator 276
Virtual Reality Modeling Language (VRML) 169,
virtual reality simulation 275
virtual reality (VR) 1, 2, 3, 4, 6, 8, 15, 16, 17, 18, 19, 20, 21, 22, 23, 24, 223, 224, 226, 228, 231, 242, 243, 300, 301, 303, 306
virtual setting 45, 50
Virtual Singapura 146
virtual space 4, 6
virtual worlds (VWs) 25, 35, 45, 46, 47, 48, 49, 51, 52, 54, 55, 57, 58, 59, 60, 61, 63, 65, 66, 67, 68, 69, 70, 72, 73, 74, 75, 76, 77, 170, 171, 172, 173, 174, 180, 181, 182, 183, 184, 185, 186, 187, 188, 189, 190, 191, 192, 222, 224
ViSiCAST 256, 265
Vista space 228
Visual Analogue Scale (VAS) 47, 51
visual feedback 275
visually impaired people (VIP) 233
ViTAAL 80, 83, 91
voice chat 4, 9, 24
voice over IP (VoIP) 282
VRML 198, 209, 211
VRML 2.0 198, 211

VRML97 211
VR paradigm 3

W

Web 78, 79, 87, 88, 89, 90, 91, 94
Web 2.0 78, 79, 87, 88, 89, 90, 91, 94, 139,
    165
Web 3.0 139
Web 3D Consortium 211
web-based learning management systems 128
Web-cam 5, 6
Webkinz 171
Whyville 170, 172, 174, 175, 176, 181, 183,
    184, 185, 186, 189, 192
Wiki 80, 93
wireless network 275, 284
World of Warcraft (WOW) 30, 43, 124, 172,
    183

Worldwide Interoperability for Microwave Ac-
    cess (WiMAX) 284, 302
World Wide Web 194, 195, 201
World Wide Web Instructional Committee
    (WWWIC) 194, 195, 196, 197, 202

X

X3D 169, , 211
Xface 256
Xj3D 209, 211
XML 169, 231

Y

YouTube 26

Z

Zone of Proximal Development (ZPD) 82, 141,
    158, 165, 166, 169,

Breinigsville, PA USA
19 October 2010
247598BV00007B/1/P